To Robert —
With love,
Duke & Mary
Christmas 1976

1st Ed.
LeRoy
NeimanCover

THE WONDERFUL WORLD
OF PROFESSIONAL GOLF

MARK H. McCORMACK

THE WONDERFUL WORLD OF PROFESSIONAL GOLF

ATHENEUM   NEW YORK

1973

Copyright © 1973 by Mark H. McCormack
Library of Congress catalog card number 68-13716
ISBN 0-689-10550-9
Published simultaneously in Canada by McClelland and Stewart Ltd
Manufactured by Kingsport Press, Inc., Kingsport, Tennessee
Designed by Harry Ford
First Edition

TO THE GAME

For giving us heroics that are compelling
and minutiae that are absorbing

I would like to express my deep appreciation for the invaluable help in the conception and compilation of the material for this volume received from DOC GIFFIN, WALT BINGHAM, BOB SOMMERS *of the U.S. Golf Association,* LEONARD CRAWLEY *of Golf International,* MARK WILSON *of the London* Daily Express, GWIL BROWN, GEOFFREY COUSINS, SAM McKINLEY, BEN WRIGHT, RICHIE BENAUD, *and* ROBERT RAY.

CONTENTS

[1] *The Game Comes of Age* 3

[2] *A Galaxy of Stars—Jones, Snead,
    Hogan, Nicklaus, and Arnie's Army* 17

[3] *The U.S. Open—From Newport to
    Pebble Beach* 56

[4] *The British Open—Scotland Where
    It All Began* 148

[5] *The Masters—Bobby Jones Makes the
    Augusta Grass Grow Green* 180

[6] *The PGA—The Final Leg* 231

[7] *The U.S. Tour—Bing and Bob Join
    Disney and Firestone* 279

[8] *Special Events—TV Means Dollars* 323

[9] *The Courses—Putting Nature to Work* 360

*Appendix: Statistics covering tournament winners,
    leading money-winners, world
    stroke average leaders, and more* 381

Index

ILLUSTRATIONS

---

*Color**   Following page 52

Ben Hogan
    Sheedy & Long
Trevino sweats it out
    Walter Iooss, Jr.
Gene Sarazen
    James Drake
A classic Arnold Palmer
    Walter Iooss, Jr.
Ken Venturi winning the 1964 U.S. Open at Congressional Country Club, Washington, D.C.
    Walter Iooss, Jr.
Britisher Tony Jacklin
    Walter Iooss, Jr.
A pensive Nicklaus
    Walter Iooss, Jr.
Young John Miller
    Eric Schweikardt
The power of Jack Nicklaus
    Walter Iooss, Jr.
A happy Trevino
    Walter Iooss, Jr.
Tom Weiskopf being congratulated by Charles Coody
    Eric Schweikardt
A young Palmer
    Richard Meek

Following page 372

The Royal and Ancient Golf Club of St. Andrews, St. Andrews, Scotland
    Gerry Cranham
The infamous Rae's Creek (12th hole), Augusta National, Augusta, Georgia
    Marvin Newman

* *These photographs appear courtesy of* Sports Illustrated © *Time, Inc.*

The 13th hole at Dune's Golf and Beach Club, Myrtle Beach, South Carolina
Jay Leviton

The 18th hole at Pebble Beach Golf Links, Pebble Beach, California
Marvin Newman

The 11th hole at the Merion Golf Club, Ardmore, Pennsylvania
Walter Iooss, Jr.

Cypress Point and Spyglass Hill, Pebble Beach, California
Marvin Newman

"The Church Pews," Oakmont Country Club, Oakmont, Pennsylvania
John G. Zimmerman

Hazeltine National Golf Club, Chaska, Michigan
Walter Iooss, Jr.

The 6th hole at the Seminole Country Club, Palm Beach, Florida
Marvin Newman

The 7th hole at Pebble Beach Golf Links, Pebble Beach, California
Fred Lyon

The 1st hole at the Merion Golf Club, Ardmore, Pennsylvania
James Drake

Muirfield Golf Links, East Lothian, Scotland
Alan Clifton

Black and White

Tom Morris	2
1913 Boston headline	20
Harry Vardon	20
Wide World Photos	
Bobby Jones parade, New York, 1930	23
Wide World Photos	
Bobby Jones, 1926	24
Wide World Photos	
Bobby Jones, 1930	25
Wide World Photos	
Walter Hagen, 1925	26
Wide World Photos	
Francis Quimet with famous caddie Eddie Lowery	32
USGA	
A jubilant Sam Snead, 1937	33
Wide World Photos	
Tommy Armour and Gene Sarazen	35
Associated Press	
Byron Nelson, 1945	37
UPI-Acme	

Hogan shortly after accident   38
International News Photo–UPI

Sam Snead   42
The Greenbriar

Snead at White Sulphur Springs, 1950   43
International News Photo–UPI

Snead wins 1938 Canadian Open   44
Pictures, Inc.–*Life*

Snead lines up putt   45
USGA

Palmer wins 1954 Amateur   48
USGA

John J. McDermott   61
USGA

Sam Parks, Jr., wins 1935 Open   76
Wide World Photos

Lawson Little wins 1940 Open at Canterbury   79
Wide World Photos

Lloyd Mangrum   81
Wide World Photos

Hogan in 1950 Open at Merion   89
USGA

"Dark Horse" Jack Fleck wins 1955 Open at Olympic   99
USGA

Hogan lines up putt during 1960 Open   106
Life, Ralph Crane

Palmer comes from 7 strokes off to win 1960 Open   107
Wide World Photos

Gene Littler   112
USGA

Tommy Jacobs holes a 60-foot putt to tie Open record with a round of 64   120
Associated Press

Gary Player's donation   124
USGA

Player during 1965 Open   124
USGA

1966 Open at Olympic   126
USGA

"Super Mex" Lee Trevino   139
Wide World Photos

Trevino on way to victory in 1971 Open   140
USGA

Orville Moody fights off hay fever at 1972 Open   143
USGA

Nicklaus wins another   146
USGA

South Africa's Bobby Locke   161
Wide World Photos

Peter Thomson   162
Wide World Photos

The late Tony Lema in London   168
Sound Stills, Ltd.

Palmer in trouble, 1966 British Open at Muirfield   171
H. W. Neale

Player on way to victory in 1968 British Open   173
H. W. Neale

Bobby Jones at Augusta   181
Sports Illustrated

Byron Nelson   190
Wide World Photos

Hogan struggling on last day of 1952 Masters   195
Life, Robert Kelly

Billy Joe Patton makes run during 1955 Masters   200
Life, Leonard McCombe

Jackie Burke   201
Life, Leonard McCombe

Palmer blowing lead on 18th hole, 1961 Masters   215
Life, George Silk

Palmer on way to a win at 1964 Masters   216
Life, Wayne Wilson

*Nicklaus after sinking birdie putt on 2nd hole, 3rd round, 1955
Masters*   219
Associated Press

Player at 1961 Masters   220
Life, George Silk

Nicklaus successfully defends Masters crown in 1966   225
Life, Flip Schulke

Jones and Hogan   229
Wide World Photos

Byron Nelson   242
Wide World Photos

Ben Hogan, 1948   245
USGA

Trevino chats with gallery   267
UPI

Casper and Boros   268
Wide World Photos

Arnie and "Ike"   281
Joseph C. Duval

Palmer with Nixon 282
Arnold Palmer

Palmer and Agnew at Bay Hill 283
Associated Press

An early Billy Casper 309
USGA

Tony Lema celebrates his 31st birthday, 1965 311
Associated Press

The Palmer swing 320
USGA

The Palmer swing 320
USGA

The Palmer swing 321
USGA

The Palmer swing 321
USGA

Tony Jacklin drives across the Thames 324
Sport & General Press Agency, Ltd.

Palmer and "friend" 324
Arnold Palmer

Snead and Hogan at 1953 Open at Oakmont 340
Wide World Photos

Nicklaus at the Piccadilly 349
Central Press Photos

Early Ben Hogan 357
Fort Worth *Star-Telegram*

Later Hogan 358
USGA

Memorable moments at Merion 371
Associated Press

THE WONDERFUL WORLD
OF PROFESSIONAL GOLF

⌈ 1 ⌉

THE GAME COMES OF AGE

THIS IS A BOOK about how things change—and how they remain the same. It is certainly a history and a reference work, and it is conceivably something of a social treatise, though this last the reader may have to glean on his own.

The photograph on the facing page is old Tom Morris, golfing champion of another era. I have an original engraving of the photograph, given me by a friend, and long cherished. It is stained across the top as if, while framed, it had been hung against a wall that leaked, the moisture gathering against the cardboard on the back and then imprinting itself in a seeping wave upon the original. This somewhat mars the aesthetic quality of the sky, but nothing detracts from the photographer's portrayal of his subject. Old Tom Morris is there; his stance wide, his grip too open by the standards of today, his head held awkwardly to give fullest perspective to the look of champions. His white beard is full, his suit as worthy, rugged, and unpressed as a Scottish moor.

I doubt that Tom Morris got much out of his picture. We would change all that today. A four-time British Open winner, well, let's see. The suit is an excellent move; Tom was no dummy. A big thing can be done there with Harris tweed; get them to fashion some patterns just for golf, you know, sell Harris full use of the name for ten years—Morris Tweed. Shoes? Yes. The Morris full-fashion shoe, so elegant you could wear it to church. The worn-looking grip on the golf club? Absolutely. The Morris Grip. Give your clubs the rich, deep-brown look of leather; from craftsmen's hands for the hands of craftsmen. In simulated leather with artificial sweat stains. The ball? Of course. The Morris Marvel for pros ("You gutta get home from wherever it percha's") and the Morris Lie for popular use. (Old Tom felt this name had an unfortunate double meaning but was quickly won over when it was explained to him that the catch-phrase possibilities for ad campaigns were considerable—From this lie I will fly, etc.) The League of St. Andrews Travel Agents is clamoring for a major tie-in. The Scottish government's bureau of recreation has been sold on the notion that with the construction of more courses—the towns of Carnoustie and Muirfield already are requesting subsidies to back their own eighteens—the country's entire economy could be stabilized by links tourism (commonly known as OLWF—Our Links With the Future. Critics dub it OLWFul, but they are few and unheeded). Ostensibly because of his concern over such matters, the Prime Minister would golf with Tom Morris frequently, an event never missed by the front pages of the *Observer*. Industrialists would be intrigued, the wage spiral being well in hand, production capability high, but sales low. Demands need creating and who better to do it than our Tom, Scotland's favorite the world around? His name would be merchandised throughout the British Isles. Automobiles are the coming thing. The champion would get into the car business. His industrialist friends would see to that. Even here he might lend his name. But with grace and modesty, as ever. We would call the car the Morris Minor.

Enough? Certainly, and all the above is fun and feathers. Mostly. But the gap is bridgeable—Tom Morris to today. It is noteworthy that professional golf, probably more so than any other sport, stitches together the decades of our century. Pro golf was born in a time of elitism, it grew in an era of sweet reason, and has boomed in a generation of personal expression. Its heroes have fitted their times: from Tom Morris to Bobby Jones to Arnold Palmer. Morris was a worthy plebeian, a workingman. Jones was a classicist in what has come to be called the Golden Age of Sport. And Palmer was the bold attacker in a time as yet unnamed. One brought attention, one brought adulation, and one brought the cult of personality. Each was totally apt.

Essentially, this book is about the third of these time periods, the last quarter-century. After the first British Open in 1861—Tom Morris was the winner at Prestwick—there was simply the sport of golf. From the viewpoint of the fan, there was little distinction to be made between the amateur and professional games. The sport's greatest name, Bobby Jones, was an amateur. His fabled Grand Slam included two amateur tournaments. Certain professionals were international celebrities, their prestige thoroughly established, but professional golf had not yet marched into the arena of big-time spectator sport. The modern era of professional golf, indeed the true history of pro golf as we know it, begins in 1946.

This book is a chronicle of the quarter-century in which professional golf took advantage of the changing attitudes toward sport in the United States and emerged, like football, baseball, and basketball, as a huge entertainment with all but limitless financial backing. The golf pro has followed the path from servant—when Arnold Palmer was a boy, pros weren't expected to set foot in clubhouses—to friend of presidents, hero of kings, idol of millions, and sometimes worth millions, too. Here is the story of the years in which professional golf grew to be the most representative of all international sports. Its rules are virtually the same around the world. Its players compete around the world. The tour format is growing continent by continent, following the lead of the United States, as sponsors realize that golf and its clean-cut country club image constitute a fine vehicle with which to call quality products to the attention of potential buyers. I am confident that within a few years there will exist what amounts to a world golf tour—a series of lucrative, prestigious events in which the best 60 or so pros will play. Golfers are already world celebrities. The prize money is available. The result is inevitable.

A few statistics establish the dimensions of the change this quarter-century has seen in professional golf:

- In 1946 the total purse money on the U.S. tour was $411,533. In 1972 it was $7,747,149.
- For winning the Masters Championship in 1946, Herman Keiser received $2,500. For winning the Masters Championship in 1972, Jack Nicklaus received ten times as much.
- In 1946 the most remunerative golf tournament in the world was the $45,000 All American at Tam O'Shanter. The next biggest offered a total purse of $15,000. In 1972 the biggest was the Pacific Masters Championship at Sohbu Country Club in Chiba Prefecture, Japan. The purse was $300,000. The winner, Gay Brewer, received $65,000. Most top pros passed the event up.
- The leading money winner for the year 1946 was Ben Hogan, with $42,500. Jack Nicklaus won $320,542 in 1972.
- The lifetime winnings of Sam Snead are estimated at $720,000 —estimated because prior to 1942 nobody bothered to keep very accurate records about such things. Snead is sixty years old, has been a touring professional for 35 years, has won three Masters, three PGA Championships, and one British Open. Jerry Heard is twenty-five years old and has been a touring professional for only four years. He is a promising young golfer, but no more than that. He has won $310,000. It took Sam Snead 21 years to reach that figure.
- When Lloyd Mangrum won the 1946 U.S. Open at Canterbury there were 5,573 four-day tickets sold. The total paid attendance was 14,638. When Jack Nicklaus won the 1972 U.S. Open at Pebble Beach the USGA restricted the ticket sale to 80,000 for the four days.

There is little mystery about why all this came to pass. It would be nice to think that the big names of the Sixties—Arnold Palmer, Gary Player, Jack Nicklaus—had some unique quality of character that Bobby Jones or Walter Hagen or Sam Snead or Ben Hogan or Byron Nelson lacked. This is not the case. The blunt fact is that when the lights went on again all over the world, as the old World War II song went, they went out in the United States. The Big Blackout came. Living rooms from coast to coast went dark as Uncle Miltie ushered in a new way of life. Television was the ingredient that was to make postwar pro golf different from the game in any other era. There would have been growth in the pro tour without TV, to be sure, but Arnold Palmer never could have attained the folk-hero dimensions he did without his television exposure. Palmer was made for the medium, and it for him. He is one of the most photogenic athletes who ever lived. Editors at *Sports Illustrated*, which estimates it has taken 10,000 pictures of him in the last 15 years, say that no athlete in the history of the magazine photographs with such excitement. Palmer expresses his emotions in a fashion that film can capture. The flight of a golf ball may not make for scintillating sport TV—television has never been particularly at ease with its golf coverage—but the expressionistic qualities of Palmer made, and still make, excellent TV. Because of him, and especially his dramatic wins in the 1960 Masters and U.S. Open, golf became a spectator sport of the masses. Frank Beard has said he owes 25 cents of every dollar he has made to Arnold Palmer, and he well may be right. For years the touring pros have called Palmer "The King," as in, "What did The King shoot today?" It is not necessarily a term of affection or praise, and is not a reference to his shotmaking ability. But it decidedly is a measure of his role in moving the game into the position it has attained in the early Seventies.

The basic elements of what happened to pro golf in the postwar years reflect a theme that runs through much of U.S. sport. Social factors—more leisure time, a deterioration of the work ethic, the availability of increased disposable income, and plain, unvarnished escapism, first from the tensions of the Cold War, then from the depressing qualities of the Vietnam war— almost necessitated a surge in sporting interests. These things, when combined with television, turned professional football and basketball into successful enterprises and caused degrees of expansion in other sports that no one had anticipated. Yet I believe that on a national basis—and surely on a world basis—no sport benefited as much as professional golf. Perhaps the reason is that golf, alone among all major professional sports, has both a spectator and participant element. In addition, the participant can, one time a round, or one day a year, execute a shot with precisely as much mastery as Jack Nicklaus or Arnold Palmer can bring to it. Thus he knows exactly what Nicklaus or Palmer is achieving with a given seven-iron approach, say. On rare occasions he hits his seven-iron every bit as well. Consequently, Palmer and his fans are truly embarked on a common cause. They have a complete affinity of experience.

No other sport offers anything comparable. This is the only explanation I can give for the fact that men of power and prestige are so fascinated by the very presence of golf's most famous figures, and are so inclined to use these personalities to further, when applicable, their economic enterprises. I represent some of the world's best athletes in many fields: Jean-Claude Killy, Jackie Stewart, Rod Laver, John Havlicek, Brooks Robinson, Dick Butkus, Bill Shoemaker, Pele, and many others. But none of them have had the income opportunities or associations that have accrued to the three best-known golfers I have worked on behalf of: Palmer, Gary Player, and, until recently, Jack Nicklaus.

The extent of the commercialization of golfers and the esteem in which they are held is an interesting phenomenon, and will be the subject matter of the rest of this chapter. It is not, in the strictest sense, a proper area of attention for a history of professional golf, but I think it is the framework for all that follows. It is only by understanding these matters that a history of professional golf takes on perspective. Traditionalists will be pleased to know that this is the only chapter dealing with such things. The rest of the book is concerned with what is the lifeblood of any sport: the competitive achievements of its athletes. But now, for a moment, let us consider what has happened to the professional golfer, what kind of place in society's sun he has won for himself. One thing is certain. With his cashmere sweater, alligator shoes, ever-bronze complexion, and studied ease of manner, he is out of the shade of the pro shop. He can eat in the clubhouse now.

ITEM: Prince Bertil of Sweden, who is sixty-two years old, asks if he can caddy for Arnold Palmer during an exhibition match in Stockholm in 1972. Palmer says of course. The Prince makes an able and attentive caddy. All Sweden is entranced.

ITEM: President Nixon is making his 1972 acceptance speech to the Republican Convention in Miami. Watching on a television set, one sees Henry Kissinger and Pat Nixon. Seated between them is Arnold Palmer.

ITEM: The King of Morocco wants Palmer to play in a tournament there. He offers to send an Air Maroc jet to Latrobe, and to pay a $25,000 appearance fee if Arnold will come. A schedule conflict makes it necessary to decline.

ITEM: The doorbell rings at Latrobe. Standing there are Ike and Mamie Eisenhower. The former President has completed an oil landscape that he wants to give to his good friend Arnie as a birthday present.

ITEM: The Duke of Windsor says that if he could be any man in the world other than himself, he would like to be Arnold Palmer.

ITEM: The U.S. has a problem. A certain military dictator in the Far East is refusing to see the U.S. Ambassador. Perhaps, the State Department suggests, Palmer could arrange to play a goodwill golf exhibition in the country. The dictator, a golf fanatic, would certainly want to play his own personal 18 holes with Palmer. And if he did, he could hardly avoid asking the U.S. Ambassador to join the foursome, and . . .

*   *   *

In short, what has happened in the last 15 years is that pro golf has gone VIP. And its stars have become VIPs at a level other athletes have been unable to attain. Prime Minister Heath goes to see Tony Jacklin play in the British Open at St. Andrews. Princess Margaret does the same at Muirfield. Jacklin, the son of a truck driver, lives on a country estate, drives a Rolls Royce, has an audience with the Queen, is a personality of stature throughout the British Isles—yet he is only twenty-eight years old and has much to learn about the game he plays. Gary Player is the most celebrated personality in South Africa. He has firmly prodded the government of his country on the subject of interracial sport and the government has listened, an astonishing accomplishment. And Arnold Palmer? At the end of 1969 he was proclaimed the Athlete of the Decade. Today he moves in the highest circles of United States politics and commerce.

I cannot fully account for the transformation of star golfer into VIP, I can only report it. Take Palmer. He is a good friend, and a man I have represented since 1959. He had already won his first Masters at that point. He was thirty years old, no child prodigy. He had the usual business accouterments of pro golf success at the time. He had a contract agreeing to let Heinz ketchup use his name—for $500 a year. He was getting free golf balls as long as he would play that brand (Wilson) and free shirts (Munsingwear) if he would wear them, with small bonus payments for every tournament he won with the balls and every time the shirt's symbol showed up on television. It was the old, old days, ones that seem a century ago. Today Palmer wears shirts made by his own company (sales of his clothing now gross more than $500,000,000 annually around the world). He uses golf balls made by his own company, and golf clubs, too. And he uses any ketchup he feels like. He owns or has a controlling interest in many corporations. He is a millionaire many times over. The list of his franchise operations is long, and familiar. A meaningful point about his financial success is that he has not attained the bulk of his wealth in the manner most athletes do—by wise investment of their capital in other areas. He has earned it on the strength of his own ability and name.

How valuable is this name and this presence? The answer to that question reveals much of what has transpired in the last decade of professional golf. What has happened to Palmer has happened, to a lesser degree, to every top professional in the sport. Jack Nicklaus, who in celebrity terms labored under the shadow of Palmer for so long, is just beginning to establish himself as a VIP-star. Gary Player has been one for a long time. Lee Trevino, because of his unique personality, can generate outside income at a rate that transcends his achievements on a golf course—though let me hastily add that these achievements are formidable, too. These men are attaining levels of hero worship that were once granted to movie stars—Clark Gable, Cary Grant, Humphrey Bogart. Indeed, this particular trend—the athlete emerging as super-celebrity—is occurring throughout sport. Consider Killy, Stewart, and Laver. And I am not sure that this is a bad thing at all. The disciplines of the athlete set worthwhile standards for emulation in a world that seems unsure of many of its moral goals.

What does being a celebrity of this stature mean? Here are a few examples from early 1972 concerning Palmer. United Airlines decides to renew its five-year contract with Palmer. United will pay a lot of money over the next five years to have Palmer in its friendly skies. The Pennsylvania Natural Gas Association decides that nobody can speak for the state—and natural gas—better than the famous resident of Latrobe. Would Palmer, for a handsome fee, do some commercials for the association? Of course. Meanwhile—it is still the same month—the *Ladies Home Journal* signs a long-term contract with Arnold. For a hefty fee, the *Journal* gets to have Arnold as its golf expert, and articles appear in the magazine under his byline. My guess is that this is the least of his value to the *Journal*. More to the point was the day he joined some top *Journal* executives for lunch at the Brussels restaurant in New York. The *Journal* had invited a few people—the chairman of Nabisco, the president of Bristol-Myers, and a group of high-echelon advertising agency representatives. You can believe that the people who were invited came. They wanted to meet Arnold Palmer. And they were impressed that the *Journal* could produce Arnold Palmer. And they hung on every word for an hour after lunch as Arnold Palmer answered their questions, chatted about life on the tour and gave them a feeling of being on the inside of their favorite sport. I left that lunch, as I often do such gatherings, somehow startled at the audience Palmer can command—and convinced the *Journal* most certainly got its money's worth.

That very morning, Palmer and I had been talking with the executives of another magazine, *Newsweek*. Palmer has been under contract to *Newsweek* for eight years. Like the *Journal*, *Newsweek* makes limited use of Palmer in the magazine, but considers him to be of great promotional value. On this morning he was photographed with his hands holding a rolled-up *Newsweek* as if it was a golf club; part of a major advertising campaign with Palmer. We also discussed the schedule for what we call VIP golf days. This is an idea that I first worked out with *Time* magazine in 1961. It was possible to see, that early, the fascination on the part of the corporate executive with the star golfer, something that has increased manyfold since then. *Time* wanted to entertain—and dazzle—a number of its Japanese advertisers. The Japanese, delayed for 100 years in their discovery of golf, are rushing pell mell to catch up. (I startled myself awake one night recently with the thought that the richest golf tour in the world ten years from now may well be in Japan.) Since *Time*'s advertisers were golfers, I suggested we bring Palmer and Player to Japan to play golf with *Time*'s guests. The idea was a great success, and customer golf, or entertainment golf, or VIP golf—whatever you want to call it—has become a significant part of a golf star's income.

When you pay a golfer $12,500 a day—Palmer's fee for such an outing—and at the same time throw him in close social association with a small group of top executives from a U.S. Steel or a Chase Manhattan Bank or a Ford or Allied Chemical, you are hardly presenting him with an unrewarding day. The company presumably benefits, too. (It was a slightly different thing, but a major American railroad once paid Jack Nicklaus a staggering fee to play a private round of golf with the president of a Japanese steel company. It seems there were two railroads the steel company might have used to get coal from West Virginia to a seaport, and since the steel company president was a golfer, somebody figured. . . .)

The fact that Palmer is on such terms with the heads of corporations sometimes has an awesome affect on subordinates, whose understandable aim is to please. Once early in Palmer's association with Lincoln-Mercury I got a panicky phone call at my home late at night. "You don't know me, Mr. McCormack, I'm from Lincoln-Mercury," the caller said. "I'm taking care of the cars for Bermuda and I want to know where the photography is, because I want the cars in the right place." Palmer was having his sportswear line photographed for advertisements in Bermuda, and one of the peripheral benefits Lincoln-Mercury was to get in its contract with Arnold was to have its automobiles lurking around in the background whenever he had advertising pictures taken. "Well, the photography is to take place tomorrow, do you know that?" I asked. "Oh yes," he said. "We are flying the cars down. We have to get a green one and a red one, because that is what they need. The only place we can get a green Cougar is Schenectady, N.Y. We are there right now, and then we pick up the red one in North Carolina and go right to Bermuda in the morning. But where do we go?"

I told him that all sounded very nice and I would call him back. But I am thinking, wow! this is costing some money. So I call the man who handles Palmer's sportswear business, ask where the photography is being done and tell him the story. "My God," he says. "They called me up the other day and said they heard we were shooting and what color cars did we want. I was in a hurry and I said, 'Hell, I don't care. Red and green.' It was the first two colors I could think of." So Lincoln-Mercury was flying all over the East Coast to get red and green cars.

If you watch Palmer long enough with corporate executives you begin to appreciate why he gets along so well with them. Right or wrong, like it or not, a lot of high-level American business is conducted on the fairways and in the grill rooms of country clubs. The atmosphere is at once congenial, exclusive, and fraternal. There is a universal challenge: the game. It puts everyone on common ground, and humbles all. The man it humbles least is a welcome and worthy inspiration in such circles. I wonder what value can be put on the phrase: "As Arnold Palmer explained it to me just the other day. . . ." That is the currency of VIP golf. Palmer understands this. He maintains his role as star. Yet as he sits there in his cashmere with a company president and a chairman of the board, he knows he has his private jet waiting for him, just as they do. He is very much part of their world, and almost regally aware of it. I like to think of Palmer at the moment in March of 1970 when he stood on the first tee at Bay Hill. He was perfectly at ease. Why not? He owned the course, and he had brought together the rest of the foursome: Vice President Agnew, the Chairman of the Board of NBC, and the President of NBC. Those three had a lot to say to each other, but when Arnold spoke I am sure all listened closely.

I don't want to leave this subject, or this chapter, without reflection on a different kind of superstar, another of my clients and good friends, Gary Player. Palmer's lifestyle is almost a cliché, so familiar is it to Americans. A Republican, a conservative, a believer in law and order, a dollar's pay for a dollar's work, well-groomed hair, and the verities of life, Palmer reminds us of all the good and true things we had before it was "Bye Bye Miss American Pie." He lives as he believes. Latrobe is still his home; he has never owned one anywhere else. He is of the country, rural strong, both flint and steel, consumed with but one passion—victory. Jack Nicklaus, a generation later, is similar in many ways. He, too, is a cool, controlled personality. He sees himself as on the level of Palmer, although most do not. I am sure it was Jack's desire to get out from under the possibility of playing his second-fiddle role to archrival Palmer that led him to terminate his business arrangement with me in 1972. (I had convinced Jack to turn pro in 1961, and had served as his representative since.) In recent years, as Jack's confidence about himself has grown, he has overcome a certain perversity of spirit that had limited his rapport with galleries. With any measure of sound management, he too will end up a millionaire many times over. Since golf never before has seen a player of his caliber, Jack much merits the stature he is sure to attain.

But Gary Player. Ah. He is somewhat different. His will to win rivals Palmer's. His dedication may exceed Arnold's. He is gutty and outspoken and often right. (Player's recent verdict on what would happen to a lot of the U.S. tour's $100,000 winners if they had to play the game around the world the way the champions do: "They could hardly bust a grape.") He is as much a figure of prestige in his country as Palmer is in his. He has had the fortitude to play tournaments in America while under threat of death, and the resolution to arrange and play an exhibition tour in South Africa with the U.S. tour's best black golfer, Lee Elder, thus causing a momentous wrench in some of the deepest apartheid attitudes of that country.

Gary, in many ways, is a freer spirit than Palmer or Nicklaus. He is decidedly less predictable, more of a throwback to what we thought famous athletes used to be before they all began to prepare themselves—with very good reason—for the great Board of Directors' meeting in the sky. It would not be proper to assess where golf has come today without stopping for a vignette or two about a man like Gary Player.

Gary is small—5′8″. This is a drawback when you are trying to be the best at a game that has come to depend to a certain degree on strength. So he has countered this with the most impressive physical and psychic armor that modern golf has known. This is necessary, Player says, if he is to beat the big guys. Since he beats the big guys with regularity, he cannot be ignored when he begins to talk to you about, say, wheat germ. Player is the total convert. The interesting aspect of this is that he is a total convert to whatever he happens to believe at the very moment. And he is also a missionary. This means that with all the good will in the world he will attempt to convert *you* to his mission of the moment.

Throughout everything Player does is this element of charming inconsistency. For a time years ago he believed in fingertip pushups. Then somebody told him that they would cause him to get musclebound, so he gave them up. He later switched to weight lifting, only to decide that this was shaping the wrong parts of his body. He wanted to strengthen his legs; he felt, correctly, that this is where Nicklaus gets the strength in his golf swing—Jack's thighs are the size of Gary's waist. So Gary started running —frontward and backward—as part of his fitness program. It nearly reached the point that to have a business talk with Gary I could find myself trotting down a hotel hallway backward, which isn't easy. For a while Gary would eat nothing but dark bread, and would lecture me on its virtues. Then he developed a health problem and was told by his doctor that dark bread was bad for him, that he should eat white bread. So he did a complete reversal. He always had advocated a lot of health foods—honey, bananas, raisins, nuts, fresh fruit—and applauded the merits of fresh garlic, which he eats by the clove.

Player's sense of the impromptu pervades much of what he does. He is extremely difficult to schedule, because what he wants to do next week depends on what he has done this week. What he really wants to do, he usually thinks, is spend all of his time at home in South Africa. He is a devoted family man. But this is difficult because he also really wants—he thinks— to prove that he, Gary Player, is the best world-class golfer who ever lived. Considering some of his achievements on a worldwide basis, this desire was not absurd—though Nicklaus has moved pretty far ahead of everybody in the last 18 months. So Gary wants to play and he doesn't want to play. If he wins the Masters he wants to fly straight home. If he loses he wants to stay in the U.S. and win the next week just to show them he can. Which is fine if you are nothing but a touring pro. Unfortunately, Gary cannot do his VIP days and exhibitions and fashion photography and all such on his off days between U.S. tournaments if he is back home in South Africa having just won the U.S. Open Championship or some such thing. So we work out alternate schedules—"if" schedules—and then hope Gary will at least adhere to some of the ifs.

These matters would be less important if Player lived a more modest personal life. In these matters, Palmer is a joy. But again, Gary lives with flair. Like Arnold, he hates the notion of borrowing money for any purpose. Which presents some problems. Player has a major investment in a large timber farm in South Africa. He loves this rugged country, and his farm is very good for him. As neighboring pieces of land became available, he bought them. "Don't you think it's a good idea to buy land adjoining your land?" he asked one of my South African people who manage his finances. "Well, Napoleon did," the fellow told Gary. Then Gary got interested in race horses, and pretty soon the farm had to have a track and stables. His first horses seemed to him a good buy—the price was right—and Gary had asked couldn't he afford them? Four of them cost $20,000, delivered to South Africa. What was I going to say? If I said no, he would ask me what had he been working for all these years? If I said yes, I knew the horses had to cost another $200,000 in improvements, etc., on the farm, which pretty much has proved to be the case. My South African representative had the best advice. He said at the time we ought to shoot the four horses the minute they are unloaded at Cape Town. He was right.

Player has a lake on his farm, and a few years ago Jack Nicklaus was coming for a visit. Jack and Gary are good friends and Gary knew how much Jack liked to fish. So he had the lake stocked with trout. But he put in too many and there was not enough feed for them so they started eating each other. At one point Gary was kidding that by the time Jack arrived there was going to be just one giant trout left in that lake. He had to buy trout food, and have it shipped in all the way from Norway. I think Jack fished about two hours when he finally got there, and it probably cost Gary about $2,500 an hour.

It is important in assessing all this to realize how similar Player's position in South Africa is to Palmer's in the United States. The golf-corporation-commercialization ties are exactly the same. So Gary has a contract with the South African Marine Shipping Corporation (which also agrees to ship his horses for nothing), South African Airways, Coca-Cola, and Ford of South Africa. He has a successful golf course architecture company that is building clubs in South Africa and Rhodesia, one of them near Victoria Falls, and has recently entered into a major association with a new luxury recreation development in Spain called La Manga, which is hosting the Spanish Open for five years commencing in 1973. In addition, there were some lesser South African endorsements—a very useful post-hole digger, the Edblow mattress company, and Jungle Oats cereal, to name a couple.

All golfers have their problems with equipment endorsements. In part the problems are beautiful ones—endorsement contracts for clubs and balls are extremely rewarding over a period of years. But there is the nagging difficulty that if you endorse something you are at least implying that you use it. Now a golfer who has an aspirin contract—Trevino does—is not going to get in too much trouble if he is seen popping a Bufferin. But the same is not true of golf clubs and balls. There is even a spy system used on the tour to verify what ball a pro is playing in a tournament. The Titleist is a ball many golfers like, but if they are under contract to another company they must order their Titleists under phony names, or Titleist, which pays nobody to play its ball, will joyfully spread the word (the balls have to be ordered, not just bought in a pro shop, because the tournament balls used by pros meet specifications for consistency and performance that presumably exceed those of the balls sold the average golfer).

The difficulty is that confidence plays a larger role in golf than in most other sports. The golfer must have faith in his equipment. The first thing he does when he misses a five-iron shot is look down at his five iron to see how it happened to betray him. Is something wrong with *it?* The ball hooked. Was something wrong with the ball? As a consequence, the romance between equipment manufacturers and the players who endorse their products is always an uneasy one.

Gary Player was involved in the most interesting case of this in recent times, and the story bears repeating here because of the additional insights it affords into the commercialization aspects of pro golf. Player's initial equipment contract of consequence was signed in 1961 with the First Flight company. The president of First Flight was a man named Jack Harkins, a flamboyant personality well known on the golf tour for his antic behavior. He enjoyed, for example, trying to pay dinner checks with a $1,000 bill he always carried. Jack thought the consternation of the waitresses hugely amusing. Gary got on well enough with First Flight, but a few years later, shortly before his First Flight contract was due to expire, we got a call from the Shakespeare Company, primarily a manufacturer of fiberglass fishing rods. Shakespeare wanted to make a major impact on the golf club market with fiberglass shafts. The company felt that to do this properly it had to have the endorsement of one of the Big Three—Palmer, Player, or Nicklaus. By now Palmer had his own club manufacturing company and Nicklaus had signed an excellent long-term contract with Mac-Gregor, so Player was Shakespeare's only hope.

We were interested—the offer was a big one—and Gary began using the glass shafts in practice rounds and in the Bahamas. After several weeks he decided he could play with the glass, and we drew up a contract with Henry Shakespeare, who was the founder of the company and something of a character in his own right. We agreed to meet with Shakespeare in Dallas, but because Jack Harkins had always treated us fairly, we felt it only proper to have Jack come in and state any final case he had for Gary remaining with First Flight. What followed was one of the funniest scenes I have ever witnessed in my business career.

Jack Harkins had brought along some First Flight clubs, and a handful of Shakespeare clubs. We had some clubs in the room, too. Jack was claiming that fiberglass was not a strong enough material for a pro's golf club (an assessment that eventually proved to be correct), because there was excessive torque in the shaft. All of a sudden he stood up and said in his boisterous way, "These clubs have so much torque you can twist the heads right off them." Harkins was a very strong man, and he picked up one of the Shakespeare clubs, took the grip in his left hand and the head in his right and sure enough, he twisted the head until it just about fell off the shaft. Well, that was more than Henry Shakespeare could bear. Henry jumped up and said, "You can take First Flight irons and you can bend them right over your knee like nothing," and he picked up one of Harkins's irons and bent it into an L just like he said. So Jack twisted off another head, just to show how effortlessly he could do it, and Henry bent another iron, and pretty soon the argument was down to who could break the other guy's golf clubs using the least possible effort, and there were ruined golf clubs everywhere. As far as we were concerned Henry won the argument—with his money, not his clubs—and Player signed with Shakespeare.

But it was not too long before we realized Gary had a serious problem. Shakespeare had poured tremendous capital into its golf club project, but the shafts simply were not suitable for tournament play. Finally they bothered Player so much that he had some steel shafts painted black to look like the fiberglass shafts and he used those, there not being any eager FTC men around looking at such things in those days. But Shakespeare insisted, because the integrity of their product was at stake, that Gary go back to the real thing. He did, and he won the 1965 U.S. Open at Bellerive using fiberglass shafts. To this day, Player considers that to be his greatest golfing achievement—simply because he won with the glass shafts. We felt the Open win in some measure gave Henry Shakespeare a fair return on what he had invested in Gary, and not too long after that we agreed with Shakespeare on an early termination of the contract. Today, the fiberglass shaft is rarely seen.

And so it goes. Everywhere. The U.S. Masters is a sellout in January. The British Open is on television six hours a day. A Japanese bank sees a net profit in hosting a $300,000 event. One of my representatives is arranging a major pro tournament in Morocco and has to flee for his life down a beach to avoid being shot in an abortive palace coup. (We were on the wrong side of that one. Our contact was the general who reportedly led the coup. But our man survived—the general didn't—and soon we were again arranging an event in Morocco for King Hassan.) In England they name a rose for Tony Jacklin. In Belgium one of the world's most esteemed candy makers, Godiva, wants to make an Arnold Palmer chocolate golf ball. Gary Player plans a VIP day with Ralston Purina—part of the payoff being a year's supply of horse feed.

Viewed from this perspective, the whole thing may seem like something of a horse race, a candy ball, a rose by any other name. But pro golf is so much else today. It is magnificent sport, unsullied by scandal, free of the deadly excesses of chauvinism, uncrippled by growth pains. Its financial rewards are great, but its players have not demeaned themselves in the pursuit of them. (Would that could be said of many other sports.) Through good management, and good luck, pro golf has kept the one characteristic that is central to its history: class. It offers us, and always has, the highest sort of sporting drama—man against himself. Professional golf's achievements are on the record. What follows is where it came from, and how it got to where it is today.

[2]

A GALAXY OF STARS— JONES, SNEAD, HOGAN, NICKLAUS, AND ARNIE'S ARMY

I N T H E hundred years and more since professional tournament golf
began, there has evolved a pattern of stars. That there should be stars
—and superstars too—is inescapable in a game that is so individual and
competitive. Golf is basically an affair of one person and his equipment, and
this is true of every level of the game. The superstar, such as Arnold Palmer
or Jack Nicklaus, faced with hitting and holding the last green at the end
of a championship, or with holing a tiddler to clinch that championship, is
just as alone with his problems as the high-handicap player measuring his
nerve and skill against a tiny putt at the end of a country club competition.
This is what sets golf apart from any other game; it is also what sets the
stars and the superstars apart from their fellow professionals. The superstars are the ones who best come to terms with the challenge, who do it
over a longer period, in different conditions of climate and terrain, in
competition with all manner of challengers, and now, in modern conditions,
under pressures of publicity and scrutiny and the rigors of travel in the jet
age.

The first star to enter the golfing public's view was Young Tom Morris
a century ago. He was the first great player with whom golfers as a group,
and the wider public too, identified. He was the first of the stars because
of the quality and the character of his play. He won four open champion-

ships in a row, the first when he was only seventeen, and although the competition then was almost laughable in comparison with modern conditions, he was so far ahead of his contemporaries that he won one of his championships by 12 strokes over 36 holes. What might have been said of his score of 149 was what Bobby Jones said of Nicklaus's score when he won the Masters by 9 strokes nearly a century later: he was playing "an entirely different game."

Young Tom was, therefore, a player apart from his peers, a superstar by the standards of a century ago, and to some degree he also satisfied one of the conditions which present-day superstars must satisfy, that they are not just lords of their own domain. Young Tom took his talents out of Scotland and won a professional tournament at Hoylake, the first important professional tournament held in England. He was, by all accounts, a forceful player, never more formidable than when seemingly in the toils, and a brave, resourceful putter—it might almost be a pen portrait of Palmer. (Morris died when only twenty-four, on Christmas Day, of what his admirers claimed to be a broken heart because of the death of his young wife and their baby.)

The next to blaze in the professional golfing firmament was not one star but a constellation of three—the Triumvirate of Harry Vardon, James Braid, and John Henry Taylor. They must be included in any galaxy of the stars because they were durable, they dominated the game even more absolutely than their modern counterparts in the Sixties—Palmer, Gary Player, and Nicklaus—they were equally formidable in stroke play and match play, and two of them, Vardon and Taylor, established their mastery in the unfamiliar conditions of American golf just as surely as did Walter Hagen, Gene Sarazen, and Bobby Jones in Britain in the decade after World War I and the Big Three a generation later.

Vardon won six open championships when that was the only competition of true significance in the world. The U.S. Open Championship was virtually a parochial affair until the Twenties, when the success in Britain of Hagen first, then Jones and Sarazen, raised its status until it is now rated the hardest of all championships to win. Braid won five opens and so did Taylor, and there was a period of 21 years from 1894 until 1914 when only five other players interrupted the Triumvirate's monopoly.

They were equally effective in match play, which was the original form of golf and some would argue still the best, and the match over four greens in which Braid was joined with Sandy Herd, one of the open championship winning interlopers, against Vardon and Taylor rated as much attention in the public prints of 1905 as the World Match Play Championship at Wentworth, England, does today. They were national figures, without benefit of TV or radio and with only their great skill and contrasting temperaments to feed an assiduous and awakening press.

They had much of golfing greatness in them. Vardon was so much a public figure, although he was a person of quiet demeanor and serene temperament, that he was given the credit of inventing the Vardon grip. He popularized it, certainly, but the overlapping grip was invented by an amateur of renown, J. E. Laidlay, and it was used by Taylor before the public detected Vardon's huge hands wrapped around the club in a way not then generally familiar.

The Triumvirate was, too, the stuff of legend. It used to be said of Vardon—and people believed it—that if he played 36 holes in a day the only hazards he was likely to meet in his second round were the divot marks he had made in the first, so accurate and consistent was his driving. Of Taylor it used to be said, to emphasize the accuracy of *his* play, that on one course where there were several blind holes, the only hazards he encountered were the guide poles at those holes. All very engaging and highly unlikely, but evidence that they were heroes and stars, and that the public adored them. Oddly, Braid, the most stoic and yet most heroic of them all, was the source of least legend, but even he was touched a little by genius when he gave his son Harry the middle name of Muirfield because he was born about the time his father won his first open championship there in 1901.

James Braid in his playing days was regarded with awe rather than affection, for he was monumentally calm even in the direst crisis, rather as Nicklaus is today, and never given to extravagant gestures, not even when unintentionally provoked by a lady whom he had been persuaded to partner in a mixed foursome. He was, namely for his powers of recovery from evil places, very much as Palmer is today, but the lady had put the ball into the heart of a gorse bush, and although Braid demolished the bush the ball hardly moved. "Oh, Mr. Braid," she gushed, "I'm so glad to see that you too can miss a shot."

It is a pity that American golfers never saw this great man, but they did see Vardon and Taylor, who finished first and second in the American Open Championship at Wheaton, Illinois, in 1900, so they were equally good on either side of the Atlantic and in disparate conditions of turf and climate. And Vardon, of course, with Ted Ray, was beaten by Francis Ouimet in the playoff for the championship at Brookline 13 years later, the playoff whose shots rang 'round the world of golf and ushered in a new chapter in the game.

The Triumvirate was perhaps fortunate that World War I came when it did. They were then in their forties, just as full of honors as Bobby Jones was when he retired when only twenty-eight, and although Hogan was to show nearly 40 years later that a man of that age could still win so prestigious a championship as the British Open, their best golf was probably behind them. They were thus able to leave the firmament for other, newer, even more brilliant stars. There were three of these in the Twenties, all Americans, all endowed with every quality of the superstar, masters of

THE BOSTON TRAVELER
AND EVENING HERALD
****

BOSTON, SATURDAY, SEPTEMBER 20, 1913.   12 PAGES.   ONE CE

FINAL EXTRA

UG PUTS TO DEATH OUTH END

Flames and Husband to Injuries After Rescued

LLS OF HEARING THE BACKYARD

FRANCIS OUIMET, BOSTON AMATEUR WINS OPEN GOLF TITLE ON PLAY O

After the Greatest Battle in the History of American Golf

Woodland Club's Youthful Star in Card of 72; Vardon Second 77; Ray Third on 78

A RECORD GALLERY OF 10,000 FOLLOWS PLA

HOW THE BETTING RULED ON

FRANCIS OUIMET IN CENTRE, VARDON ON HIS RIGHT AND RAY ON HIS LEFT.

ALLEGED SLAYER TO FACE TRIAL

All the Golf Experts Give Ouimet Highest Praise for His Superb Game

HOTEL MAN SHOT BY IRATE HUSBAND

1913 Boston headline

Harry Vardon

stroke play, masters of match play, masters of themselves, the darlings of the crowd, equally at home and equally capable in the chill of a British spring and in the humid heat of an American summer, great players, great if diverse personalities, the true architects of modern American golf. They were, of course, Hagen and Sarazen from the professionals and Jones, the nonpareil amateur.

Before Jones fulfilled his youthful promise, Walter Hagen had pre-empted the status later to be achieved by less than a handful of players. He was the first man to satisfy completely all the conditions of being *facile princeps*. He won everything there was to win in both America and Britain not once but, usually, several times. He survived disaster, as in his first essay at the British Open in 1920, and came back to triumph. He won the American Open Championship twice, the first time in 1914, and he won his fourth and last British Open Championship 15 years later; and even four years after that he was still a threat in the early rounds at St. Andrews, though the Old Course was hardly the kind of links where his genius flourished. So he was durable. He was a terrific match player. He won the American PGA Championship at match play five times in seven years in the Twenties, four times in a row, and was beaten by Sarazen in one final in that remarkable seven-year hitch. It was one of the greatest of all golfing achievements, and let no man think he was a big fish in a small pond. The men he beat in the final were Jim Barnes (twice), Bill Mehlhorn, Leo Diegel, and Joe Turnesa, all sturdy campaigners, who, if they could have played their golf in the last ten years, would have occupied high places in the dollar-earnings ratings.

Hagen was much more than a great player, with an unequaled talent for winning when it mattered most. He was the first compelling personality in professional golf, the man who gave the profession a new standing by abolishing the distinctions that sent the professional into clubhouses by the service entrance. He looked the part of the successful entrepreneur, his clothes were the envy of his imitators, and his *obiter dicta* passed into the folklore of the game. He was affectionately, and admiringly, dubbed "Sir Walter," and all the world knew who "the Haig" was just as surely as all the world today knows who Arnie is. And all this before the small screen brought the world's great performers into every living room and therefore into the life and understanding of people who cannot, as Herbert Warren Wind has put it in another context, tell a midiron from a midwife.

It may be argued, of course, that Hagen won his open championships in Britain against much less intense competition than Palmer, Player, Nicklaus, and Trevino faced in the Sixties and Seventies. That is true, but he did win four times in eight years, and some of the players he had to beat were justly famous in their day—George Duncan and Abe Mitchell of Britain, Barnes, Jock Hutchison, and Macdonald Smith from the United States, and, in his fourth and final victory, the full might of an American

Bobby Jones parade, New York, 1930

Bobby Jones, 1926

Bobby Jones, 1930

Ryder Cup team as well as the best of Britain.

Hagen, like Jones, was spared one adjustment that Americans now make, of their own choice, when they play in Britain—the change from the 1.68 ball to the 1.62 size. When Hagen was winning his four championships in Britain and when Jones was winning his three opens and one amateur, Americans and Britons were using the same kind of ball. It was not until the beginning of 1931 that the United States increased the size of the ball. It may be argued that Hagen and Jones would not have been the force with the big ball that they were with the small one, but they would probably have effected the transition just as smoothly, if reluctantly, as the Triumvirate changed from the gutty to the rubber-core. Genius will out.

Hagen was indisputably a genius. He must have been to have hit so many bad shots while winning so much and so often. Maybe that was one of his great attractions, as it is Palmer's. He made golf look difficult, and because most golfers find the game difficult they were able to identify with Hagen just as they identify with Palmer although accepting the gulf that exists between their own play and that of the masters. Watching Hagen was therefore exciting in the same way that watching Palmer is exciting. Every once in a while there was the prodigiously bad shot, usually followed by the incredibly bold and accurate recovery. And when Hagen got to the green, he putted with clinical accuracy. No wonder he was the terror of his contemporaries. He could charge through a field like an avenging flame

Walter Hagen, 1925

when the spirit moved him. And everywhere, at all times, the personal magnetism was superabundant. It was once said of him that he made tying his shoelaces look more exciting than the other man's hole in one, just as many people would rather watch Palmer hitch up his pants in mid-fairway than contemplate a Billy Casper hitting a perfect shot.

No one can seriously doubt that the man who said "I don't want to be a millionaire: I just want to live like one" would in fact have made millions if he had lived at the right time. He was just too late to be a force in the Masters, which was the kind of tournament he would have adorned and possibly dominated ten years earlier, but he was a master for all that. So was his great rival, contemporary, teammate, and friend, Gene Sarazen. He also satisfied the conditions of being a superstar. He won his first U.S. Open in 1922, his second ten years later, and tied for first in 1940. He won the British Open Championship once and was desperately near winning both before and after his record-breaking success in 1932 at Princes, Sandwich. He won the Masters, and in the process played possibly the most spectacularly successful single stroke ever accomplished—the four wood into the cup at the 15th hole in the final round for a double-eagle 2. He won the PGA at match play in the year he won the U.S. Open for the first time and again the following year. So he won everything, one of only four men who have triumphed in what has come to be accepted as the Grand Slam of professional golf—the U.S. and British Opens, the Masters, and the PGA. The four are illustrious indeed—Sarazen, Ben Hogan, Gary Player, and Jack Nicklaus—and it takes nothing at all from Sarazen's record, but rather adds to it, that he won the PGA at match play and not over 72 holes of stroke play.

Sarazen kept his game longer than almost any other first-class professional. In 1958, when he was fifty-six, he completed four rounds in the British Open Championship at St. Anne's in 288, admittedly 10 strokes worse than the winner but only one stroke more than the aggregate that won Bobby Locke the third of his four opens on the same course six years earlier. He was therefore durable, holding on to his swing and also his competitive instinct just as firmly as he gripped the club with his interlocking fingers and planted his sturdy underpinnings. He was the best "little man" of his time, since surpassed only by Gary Player, who has also shown the fallacy of the old adage that "a good big man will always beat a good little man."

Sarazen made contributions to the professional game, indeed to golf generally, other than his great record and enduring combativeness. He claims to have invented—he certainly popularized—the sand wedge, which more than any other technological development helped the pros to reduce scores and raise standards. He was an inveterate tinkerer with his clubs, like Palmer, and came up with the reminder grip, which was shaped and thickened under the left hand. He even invented the "over-40 finger" grip for putting in which the right index finger is stretched down the right side of the shaft. It was all part of his genius for publicity, and for inspired thinking about the game which he adorned as a player for nearly 40 years.

The unsurpassed adornment of the game in the same era that Hagen and Sarazen were the superstars of the professional world was, of course, Bobby Jones, the amateur, who possessed the plus factor to a degree unequaled by anyone except, possibly, Nicklaus in our own day. He was the only amateur of modern times who could take on the professionals at their own game, on either side of the Atlantic, and beat them time after time. His grand slam—victory in the amateur and open championships of both the United States and Britain in the course of one year, the *annus mirabilis* 1930—will almost certainly now never be equaled. Nor will his influence on the game in its wider aspects. To the end of his life, long after he had ceased because of illness to be able to play on courses which he used to bestride like a Colossus, his thinking and judgments were a profound influence for good.

Jones devised the Masters tournament and made and developed the Augusta National course, which themselves would be monument enough for any man. But before then he had been the most famous athlete in the world, admired not only for his supreme talents but regarded with such universal affection that when he paid a flying visit to St. Andrews in 1936 for a game on the Old Course on his way to the Olympic Games at Berlin, thousands of onlookers flocked to see him play. And how well he did play, too, although he had been out of the competitive orbit for half a dozen years. He played the first nine holes in 32, and although he took 40 to come home, he had given proof of his enduring talent. He had, of course, a special relationship with St. Andrews. It was there that he grew up as a tournament player. In the 1921 Open Championship there when still only nineteen but already bearing the stamp of greatness, he picked up his ball in pique after a sustained period of sorry play. He realized the enormity of his offense, to himself as well as to his followers, and never thereafter displayed other than the most impeccable demeanor. He got his reward at St. Andrews, for there he won two of his championships, one of his three British Opens and the solitary "Amateur," which he said was the hardest of all to win. No wonder that in 1958, when he captained the American Eisenhower Trophy team there, St. Andrews made him a freeman of the burgh and there was hardly a dry eye in the hall at the end of the ceremony as he made his way down the aisle in the electric trolley his illness forced him to use to the sound of "Will ye no' come back again?"

Only someone very special could win such affection for his contribution to golf, an affection not withheld by the professionals whose prestige and performance he challenged so successfully for eight marvelous years between 1923, when he broke through in the U.S. Open Championship at Inwood, and 1930, when he retired wreathed in laurels. It is idle to speculate how Jones would have fared in today's fiercely competitive arena. His swing was perhaps a bit too complicated to repeat as surely as did Hogan's, but if it was complicated, it was lovely to look at. It might have been said of him as was said of a great English sportsman in another discipline that he was "elegance, all elegance, fit to play before the King in his parlour."

The complaint has been made that when Jones retired in 1930 he sold his name and talents and movie exhibitions for large sums of money and therefore became, automatically, a professional, although he was lauded to the end of his days as the great amateur. Jones was a sensitive man, with an uncanny perception of the difference between right and wrong. True, he did capitalize his enormous golfing talents but he never became a professional in the accepted sense. He never played for money, he never taught for money. He became a *nonamateur* in a commercial sense but he remained an amateur in the larger sense for all his long life. And it is a measure of his greatness that when he died in 1971, millions mourned who had never seen him play, never heard him speak in that rumbling Southern drawl, never had the opportunity of admiring his exemplary behavior on the links. Somehow, he communicated his essential qualities to the golfing world just as surely as does Palmer with all the aids of modern communications media.

With the retirement of Jones, the aging of Hagen, and the onset of economic adversity on both sides of the Atlantic, professional golf entered a period from which only one new star emerged, Henry Cotton, an English public-school boy who had the great good fortune to come to full stature at the right moment. He won two British Open Championships in the Thirties, the first at Sandwich with a brand of golf not hitherto produced by anyone in Britain, the second at Carnoustie against the full strength of an American Ryder Cup side.

Cotton satisfied all the requirements of a professional star of the first magnitude except one—he played in the United States but never with the success he won in Europe. He won three British Open Championships, the last in 1948 at Muirfield with an aggregate of 284, only 2 strokes more than Nicklaus would win with nearly 20 years later and on a course not significantly changed in the interval. He was a great match-player when he set his mind to it, which was usually when he had small personal liking for his opponent. And because he ended a long period of American domination of the British Open Championship, he was a national hero in his own country. Cotton was not, however, a popular hero in the fullest sense. He was less charismatic than most of the great players mentioned earlier. He inspired admiration but not affection. He walked the links stone-faced like Buster Keaton and seemed at times to be the embodiment of strength through misery. He was not outgoing, certainly not while he was playing, and it's doubtful whether even Lee Trevino could have made him crack his concentration enough to bare a wintry smile.

But Cotton was a great player and, in his own way, an innovator. He was the first of the stars to manufacture his own brilliance. He had much natural talent, but he schooled himself by unremitting practice to develop a method as near foolproof as he could devise. Before Hogan had consolidated his repeater swing, before Gary Player had made a fetish of physical fitness, Cotton had subjected himself to a grim discipline. He dieted to conquer a weak stomach. He drilled his body, especially his hands, until he was master of every muscle. He practiced harder than anyone before or after has ever practiced, except the one-track-minded Player. He spent so many hours crouched over his putter head that his body became permanently tilted to the right. He commanded success, whatever the cynic might say to the contrary, and he deserved it. What is more, he retained his command over a lengthy period, interrupted by six years of war, when the only golf he played was in exhibition matches for charity when he was part of the Royal Air Force. He was a star in his own right, but he was also a link between the Golden Age of the Twenties and the period after World War II when professional golf exploded into the excitement and entertainment of a worldwide spectator sport. As a twenty-year-old he played with distinction in Jones's 1927 Open Championship at St. Andrews. Thirty years later, at the same site, he scored 287 for four rounds, only 2 strokes more than Jones's then record aggregate, and finished tenth. Not many professionals could have fared so well at fifty. By then he was something of a legend in British golf but never the immensely popular figure that, say, Tony Jacklin was to become. Yet he did for British professionals what Hagen had done for Americans—he elevated the profession to heights until then unknown. His life style was spectacular. He drove Mercedes sports cars at a time when not one British professional in twenty had a car of any kind. He built a handsome house at Ashridge, Buckinghamshire, where he was for some time professional, and called it Shangri-la. He toured the music halls with a golfing act and made a great success as an entertainer despite his façade of austerity. He made money, lots of it by the standards of the Thirties and Forties. He was honored by his country by being appointed a Member of the Order of the British Empire. He wore a left-hand glove and the glove industry boomed. If only this golfing paragon had been able to play as well in the United States as he did in Britain, he might have qualified to be a superstar.

One of Cotton's near-contemporaries who did take on the might of America on its own turf and lined his plus-four pockets in the process was the first of the stars who was neither American nor British. South African Bobby Locke had a supreme competitive talent and the most unlikely method of any of the great modern players. He was, like Jones, a boy wonder, and it was because he shared Jones's precocity that he shared, too, the affectionate diminutive appellation to which his own given names of Arthur D'Arcy provided no true warrant. He satisfied fully all the criteria of star status except one—he won four British Open Championships but never the U.S. Open. He came close, desperately close, more than once. He tied for third in 1947 when Lloyd Mangrum won, and four years later only a superlative final round of 67 by Ben Hogan relegated him to third place after he had led at the halfway stage and tied for the lead with Jimmy Demaret with one round to play. Still, he did beat all the best Americans more than once, including Hogan in his own state of Texas in the Houston Open in 1947. He won the Canadian Open, the Tam O'Shanter twice, and the Goodall Round Robin twice, once from a field that included Byron Nelson and Sam Snead, to say nothing of two winners of the U.S. Open Championship, Mangrum and Cary Middlecoff. He did not fare well in his attempts to win the Masters, possibly because he was not quite long enough for the Augusta National, which rewards length from the tee. But he could win in any company, largely because his temperament was as smooth as his swing, though a good deal less complicated, and he had the best educated putter in the whole world of golf.

Locke is a fascinating study. When he was a young man he was all fire and celerity, lean as a lathe and vibrant with eagerness. As a stripling amateur of only eighteen, he finished ninth in the British Open Championship at Hoylake in 1936, 7 shots behind the winner but only 3 behind such a gifted campaigner as Gene Sarazen. Twenty-two years and four victories later he was still a formidable competitor, oddly enough sharing the same aggregate of 288 with the same Sarazen. And even up to 1972, his now portly figure was still perambulating the links of Muirfield in the Open Championship, bringing no threat to the Trevinos, Nicklauses, and Jacklins but a rare dignity to the golfing scene.

Locke's enduring success was the more remarkable because, like Ben Hogan, he suffered a serious motor car accident when he was still in the full flush of manly vigor. Although he did not make such a spectacularly successful comeback as did Hogan, he retained enough of his old skills to remain a figure of consequence.

Locke was one of the first golfers to establish a drill, which he performed precisely and unvaryingly before every shot. Long before Lee Trevino quartered the green looking at a putt from every angle, Locke had established a similar routine, which included a minute inspection of the hole, as though he expected a toad to be in waiting to head his dying putt out of the cup. Two practice swings (like Casper) of the putter head, a step forward, and a smooth delivery, with the putter head taken back well inside the line of travel. You felt that if your life depended on a putt's being holed, you would summon Bobby Locke to the task—and you would live. He was not a great shotmaker, though he made some wonderful shots, and he was never a good driver, being content for most of his competitive life to use his brassie, even his spoon, and keep the ball in play. He completely disbelieved the mathematical precept that the shortest distance between two points is a straight line. He hit every shot—except his putts—with a marked

Francis Quimet with famous caddy Eddie Lowry

A jubilant Sam Snead, 1937

draw. Small wonder that when he took his swing to the United States for the first time, it was regarded as too comical for belief. Besides, he was told, his left hand was weak. "I take the checks with my right hand," was Locke's retort, and his right hand got plenty of practice at that agreeable exercise.

Locke's durability, like Sarazen's and Cotton's, was endorsement of Vardon's dictum that "It takes longer to kill the golf in a man than to breed it." Some great players either lacked that capacity to produce their best over a prolonged period or were strictly products of their own environment. Tommy Armour, for example, won the Open Championship of the United States, Britain, and Canada, but his tour at the top was brief. Dr. Cary Middlecoff was a great force in American golf for ten years in the late Forties and Fifties, winning two U.S. Opens and the Masters, but he was unable to export his expertise. Julius Boros was and is durable, for he won his first U.S. Open as long ago as 1952 and 16 years later won the PGA by one stroke over Palmer and Bob Charles. But he made only rare excursions to Britain and these were not successful, although he was much admired there as elsewhere for the briskness and seeming nonchalance of his approach to what for most competitors is a desperately anxious business. He flourished in the Age of Hogan, and he was still flourishing in the Age of Palmer and Nicklaus. Of only one other professional can that be said— and he must be examined later in more detail—Samuel Jackson Snead.

First, consider a man who was supreme in his day, who established standards of achievement no one had previously reached, a man who should have been a superstar even in a period when the incomparable Hogan was reaching the height of his unexampled powers. Byron Nelson was possibly unlucky in that he burst upon the astonished world of professional golf at the wrong time, only a year or two before the outbreak of war, in which he was unable, for medical reasons, to serve as did so many of his contemporary rivals. He won his only American Open Championship in 1939 but he twice won the PGA at match play and was three times beaten in the final. He won the Masters twice, once during the war after a playoff with Hogan, and for three years in a row won more money than anyone else. But for all his notable record, the fires of competitiveness burned low in Nelson and he virtually retired from the fray just at the time when golf began to be a worldwide spectator sport. His game was still good enough to let him win the French Open Championship in 1955, and he competed more than once in the British Open, but without great distinction. He was the superstar *manqué*, the man who had everything except the determination to drive himself to the limit of his physical and mental resources over a long enough period. No one in his day hit more perfect golf shots, played more perfect rounds, not even his archrival Hogan. For half a dozen years he drove himself hard, possibly too hard, and a bad back and a weak stomach were handicaps he had to shrug off or nurse. It was hardly sur-

Tommy Armour and Gene Sarazen

prising that he cried "Hold, enough" when still in his early thirties, preferring to become an elder statesman and television pundit rather than a gladiator in the arena.

Two of Nelson's exact contemporaries—they were born in the same year, 1912—were made of sterner stuff. One, Ben Hogan, became the first superstar of the new era that began with the release of war tensions and inhibitions in the late Forties; the other, Sam Snead, played on to become probably the most durable great player who ever put spike to turf.

Hogan is part of golfing history. No one disputes his place there. If it were possible to proclaim one man as the greatest golfer who ever lived, he would assuredly be a candidate. No less an authority than Gary Player, who does not distribute praise readily, proclaimed as late as 1972 that Hogan was the supreme master golfer because he knew exactly what to do and how to do it, and did it when it mattered most. He did it, too, over a long period, in both Britain and the United States, in stroke play and match play, against the best players of his own age and against the best players of a later generation.

Take first his durability measured only by time. The Age of Hogan began, technically, in 1948 when he won the first of his four U.S. Open Championships, but as long ago as 1940 he had won the U.S. Vardon Trophy for having the best stroke average over a series of tournaments. So he was formidable then, so formidable that in the same year he was only 3 strokes behind Little and Sarazen when they tied for the U.S. Open. Next year he was third after having been fourth in the Masters, and, before he went off to the war for three years, he tied for the Masters with Nelson, losing the playoff with 70 to 69. He was therefore knocking hard on the door, and he was knocking even harder when golfing hostilities were renewed in 1946. He was second in the Masters that year, one stroke behind the now forgotten Herman Keiser, and one stroke behind the three who tied for the Open. He took three putts on the last green in each tournament or he would have tied for both—a double lapse which would have embittered a lesser man but which for Hogan was just another spur to his essential combativeness and tenacity. So, far from being downcast, he was more determined than ever, and promptly and handsomely won the PGA at Portland to record his first major success. Twenty-one years later, then fifty-five years old, he was capable of scoring 66 in the third round of the Masters. The years were many, but the shots were few.

If the Sixties were the period of the Big Three, the early Fifties were the period of the Big One. Hogan was supreme—first as a player because of his performances, but after his accident and his miraculous recovery of both body and spirit, because of his personality as well. He was the man who came back, who snatched life out of death, who drilled his mind and body until he was a better golfer than he had been in full health. No movie or TV writer would have dared to contrive such a tale of triumph, disaster,

Byron Nelson, 1945

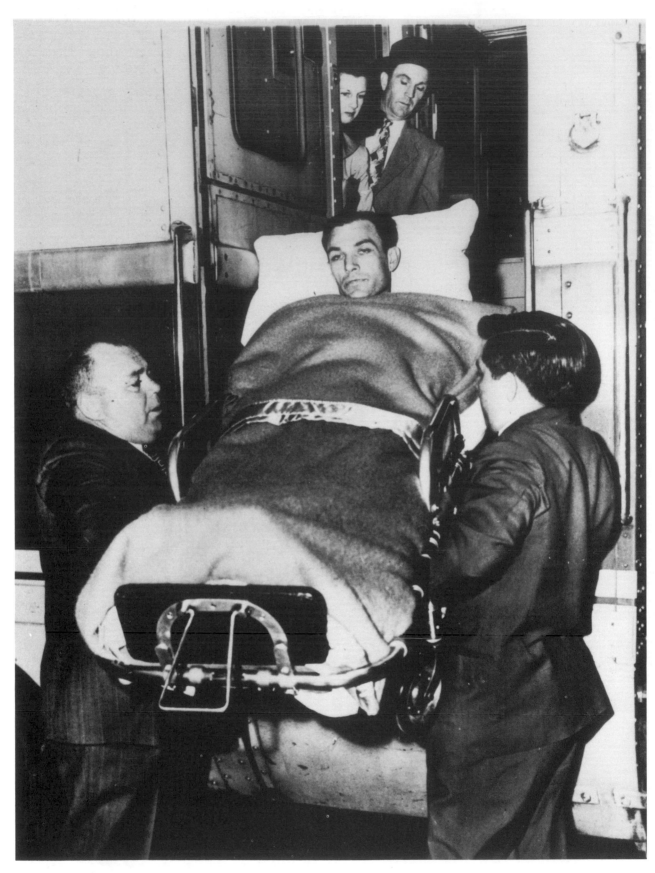

Hogan shortly after accident

and still greater triumph as Hogan lived. But there was only one Hogan. In the space of six years between 1948 and 1953, one of which was spent in hospital beds and then in the long, slow process of recuperation and recovery, he won no fewer than eight major championships—four U.S. Opens, two Masters, the PGA, and, possibly the sweetest of all his successes, the British Open. Three of them he won in the one year—the Masters, U.S. Open, and British Open—something no one else has done. So Hogan achieved what we may call the Little Slam, and it's not all that little. He did it, too, after having had for him a lean year in 1952, when he did not win a major championship. He was to blaze brighter than ever in 1953 and he might have been excused if after capturing the British Open at Carnoustie in his first and only attempt he had retired to Fort Worth as full of honors and acclaim as was Jones in 1930. But now he displayed his plus factor—a competitive urge unequaled in his day and matched in more modern times only by the Big Three and Lee Trevino.

He had one more ambition, to become the first man to win the U.S. Open five times, and twice he came desperately close to realizing it. True, he failed rather dismally, for him, in his defense of the title in 1954, although he tied for sixth place, but it was a different story the following year at Olympic, San Francisco. He was seated in the clubhouse with the title virtually in his pocket when the unknown Jack Fleck came from nowhere with two birdies in the last four holes to tie. Hogan failed to win the playoff just as surprisingly, to the eye of the dedicated fan, as Palmer failed to beat Casper in the playoff on the same course 11 years later. There was no playoff in 1956, though there might have been if Hogan, who used to be one of the best holers-out in the business, had not missed a little putt on the 71st green. That missed putt left him one stroke behind the winner, Cary Middlecoff, and that was really the end of Hogan's chapter in the U.S. Open, although he continued to enrich it with his presence for a good few years afterward. He had done more than enough to prove to the world, and to himself, that he was the greatest player of his time—perhaps of all time.

It is a sobering, even rueful, thought that Hogan might have continued to win championships, including that elusive fifth open, if he had enjoyed the conditions that players today accept as the natural order of things. In Hogan's day, and indeed right up to 1964, the last day of the U.S. Open was a climactic test of physical endurance as well as nerve and intrinsic talent. Thirty-six holes were played on the final day, and only the cream of the crop could keep their swings going and their nerves at concert pitch for all of a long day in high midsummer heat. For Hogan, whose gait was always stiff-legged and stumpy after his accident in 1949, two rounds in a day must have been an ordeal beyond what his fellows had to suffer. If he had enjoyed the luxury of one round a day, as now prevails in both the U.S. Open and the British Open, he might have kept on winning championships until he was fifty or older, although by then his mastery of every club did not extend to his putter. His mastery of himself was absolute. He had always been a thinking, dedicated golfer, one who slaved at practice until he had schooled his swing, but it was after his accident, when for more than six months he did not handle a golf club, that he drilled his mind and spirit to a new discipline.

So well did he succeed that less than a year after his mangled body had been extracted from his wrecked car, he contrived to play four rounds in the Los Angeles Open in 280 strokes. It would have been the perfect storybook ending if he had won the tournament, but Snead came with a late burst of birdies to tie, and when the playoff was postponed for a week because of bad weather, it was a tired Hogan (he had played another tournament in the interval) who lost by four strokes.

Hogan was the most uncompromising of champions. When he won his third U.S. Open at Oakland Hills in 1951, retaining the title he had won after a playoff with Mangrum and George Fazio in the year he came back, he refused to make the customary sweetness-and-light acceptance speech. "I am glad," he said sternly, "that I brought this course, this monster, to its knees." He may not have loved a challenge but he accepted one when he had to, and one of the great challenges he chose to accept was to play in the British Open Championship in 1953 when he had won both the Masters and his fourth U.S. Open. Sarazen is usually given the credit for having persuaded, some would say needled, Hogan into proving himself in British conditions. He had virtually nothing to gain by playing, for his position and prestige were secure for all time anyway. But probably he realized that there was a plain duty to try to do what other great Americans had done—Hagen, Sarazen, Jones, Snead in 1946—and what some great Americans, such as his once archrival Nelson, had failed to do. So to Carnoustie he went, and from the first he meant business.

Here was an alien land, alien weather, and a course that in its own fashion was something of a monster, too. He gave himself every chance. Not for him the flying visit such as Tony Lema was to make 11 years later and Trevino in 1971, when they flew in almost as the starter was clearing his throat and won the championship within the space of less than a week. Hogan arrived ten days before the championship, and such was the magic of his name and the nature of his preparations that his every movement, his every practice stroke—he played three balls at each hole in every practice round—was charted in the newspapers and reported to an expectant if, at first, skeptical British public. He did what he set out to do, he won as he did at Oakland Hills, improving his score with each round. He finished with a record 68 to beat by 4 strokes four fine players who tied for second place —the amateur Frank Stranahan, Dai Rees, Peter Thomson (who was to go on to win no fewer than five British Opens), and the Argentinean Tony Cerda.

It was shrewdly said of Hogan's last round that he looked capable of scoring a 64 if that had been needed, but possibly the most significant moment of his victory came when he was playing the last hole—superbly, as one might have expected. No fewer than four former winners of the championship were playing their last few holes about the same time, and all of them halted their play to watch the little man in gray with the white cap, the face set grimly, stiff-legging his path along the last fairway to reach his enormous drive. And that was at the end of a long, chilly day, at the end of 36 holes on a course of more than 7,000 yards, when Hogan was fighting the onset of flu as well as the challenge of a great course and great players snapping at his heels. He was the authentic hero.

Hogan possibly drew some benefit from having come back from his accident. He had been heroic in adversity, and all the world loves a hero, but he had not in his person any of the obvious graces and élan that, say, set Arnold Palmer apart from his fellows and were responsible for the recruitment of Arnie's Army. Hogan, on and off the golf course, had the qualities of the Duke of Wellington and Stonewall Jackson on the field of battle —stern, uncompromising, full of cold valor, his own most severe judge and critic. He cared nothing for easy plaudits, though in his later years he clearly warmed to the hurrahs of the crowd as he fashioned his 66 at Augusta when young lions less than half his age were taking 10 strokes more. He set a standard, of performance, of behavior, of combativeness, of cold resolution that golf is unlikely ever to see again.

It was the lack of this last quality of cold resolution that was perhaps the only flaw in his great rival and contemporary, Sam Snead. Snead had almost everything that a superstar should have. He had a swing so flawless as to be the envy of everyone, and to remain the envy of everyone until he was in his sixties. He could hit the ball a country mile, and hit it straight, and golfers everywhere love to see the big hit. He could hit long irons that enchanted the connoisseur. Maybe he putted at times "like an auld sweetie wife," as the Scots caddy might have put it, but that just endeared him to people who could not putt either. He swiftly earned the sobriquet "Slammin' Sam," and later, when he was picking up pots of gold every other week, he was called "the affluent hill-billy" because he was a country boy who won fame and more than one fortune with his golf. His ingenuous, off-the-cuff comments proclaimed an innocence, real or assumed, that was endearing. His straw hats became as familiar as Hogan's white cap, and he could be roughly rude in a manner that would have been an affront from anyone else. So he had a sort of homespun charisma about him that earned him a grudging affection, while always there was unstinted admiration for his superb, athletic swing, which combined grace and power as had not been seen since Jones.

Snead is perhaps the greatest of all might-have-beens in golf. There have been several superb golfers who were labeled "the greatest who

Sam Snead

Snead at White Sulphur Springs, 1950

Snead wins 1938 Canadian Open

Snead lines up putt

never won an Open"—Macdonald Smith in the United States, Abe Mitchell and Dai Rees in Britain—but Snead is clearly the supreme example even though he did win one British Open. He blew the 1939 U.S. Open by taking an 8 at the 558-yard 18th hole at Spring Mill, Philadelphia, when a 5 would have won and a 6 put him in a tie with Nelson, Craig Wood, and Denny Shute. Two years earlier, when only twenty-five, he had played Oakland Hills in the Open in 283 only to see Ralph Guldahl break the record aggregate with 281 for the first of his two successive victories. So Snead was unlucky once, and culpable once, and there was a third time when he might have won, should indeed have won—in 1947. What is more, he deserved to win, for his finish in the championship proper was as heroic as his failure at Spring Mill was abysmal. He had to get a birdie at the 419-yard 18th to tie Lew Worsham, and knew what he had to do. And he got it, with a 20-foot putt. If virtue were rewarded in life and not, as is claimed by W. S. Gilbert, "only in theatrical performances," Snead would have won the playoff and joined the immortals by right of conquest in the one championship that measures the mighty. But he failed by a stroke, and what a miserable stroke, too—a 30-inch putt on the last green.

So Snead never won the U.S. Open Championship, and for years people have been saying he never will. They are right, of course, doubly right because he is now in his sixties, and you don't win major championships at that age. Or do you? As recently as 1972 Snead finished a bare four strokes behind Gary Player when the South African won his second PGA Championship at the same Oakland Hills where Sam had nearly won the 1937 U.S. Open, finishing with a fourth round of 69. The total performance, one of the most remarkable in the lifetime of this wholly remarkable man, was at least on a par with Hogan's 66 in the Masters at age fifty-five, and it proved yet again that it takes an uncommonly long time to breed the golf out of the right kind of man.

Even one victory in the U.S. Open would have been enough, for Snead has won everything else—two PGA Championships at match play, one British Open Championship, at St. Andrews in 1946, and three Masters, most notably his first in 1949 when he finished with two 67s without putting particularly well. He has played with distinction in Ryder Cup matches and even captained the American side, without distinction, in 1969. He claimed that his greatest day in golf was when he won the British Open at St. Andrews. In the end he won easily, by four strokes from Bobby Locke and his old buddy and traveling companion, Johnny Bulla, with whom he and Dai Rees were joint leaders after three rounds. But Snead nearly jettisoned his chance of winning "the big one" when he took 40 for the first nine holes of his final round. It was then he showed the same fighting qualities he was to show when he tied with Worsham the following year in the U.S. Open. He came home in 34 against a searing St. Andrews wind, and that was the mark of a champion. But he could never quite do it in the harder, more intense competition of his own country.

Snead and Hogan were the last of their generation, the last of the stars who shone a little too early, before the arrival of television and the intensive promotion of tournament golf. That development coincided with the arrival, almost simultaneously, of three players who became the super-stars of the Sixties, who were tailor-made for television although cut from three different patterns—Arnold Palmer, Gary Player, and Jack Nicklaus.

But before they come under scrutiny, it would be less than just to ignore two men who have on occasion challenged and mastered the Big Three and who, in their own highly individual ways, have made a significant contribution to golf at all levels. They are Peter Thomson of Australia and Billy Casper of the United States, two players of quality who fall just short of being superstars. Oddly, they have one thing in common that makes them eminently watchable—they play quickly, with minimum fuss, and with methods that seem so simple that even the humblest hacker feels he can learn from them. He can never hope to match Nicklaus's awesome power, or Palmer's thrusting irons, or Player's "mighty atom" action. But Casper swings quickly and freely as though golf were the simplest operation, and Peter Thomson always looks to have so much in reserve that he will probably be as good at sixty as Snead is. But each has a fatal flaw when measured with the superstars.

Thomson has won five British Open Championships, one of them from a field that included the Big Three and Tony Lema, that wonderful stylist who might have become an all-time great if he had not died in an air crash when he was at the height of his considerable powers. And Thomson was twice second in other British Opens, so he nearly equaled Vardon's record of six wins compiled in a different era and against lesser competition. But Thomson never made a serious impact in the United States. He seemed to sense that his game was better suited to British than American conditions, although he had no fear of even the best Americans, as he showed not only in the British Open but also by beating Palmer in the Piccadilly World Match Play Championship, though he could never clinch that championship itself. Perhaps he did not have enough length for American conditions, perhaps he was the best judge of his own capabilities. He was personable enough to have captured the public fancy if he had been able to add an American title to his five British honors, to say nothing of the host of other tournaments he won all round the world outside the United States.

Billy Casper, by contrast, could not win outside of America. He won two American Opens, in 1959 when he was regarded as a roly-poly golfer who could putt, and in 1966 when, slimmed down, he could play all the shots and still putt. Possibly that second victory would have been more impressive if the feeling had not persisted that it was Palmer who lost rather than Casper who won. Palmer had victory in his grasp and then

Palmer wins 1954 Amateur

threw away a winning lead, no fewer than 7 strokes in the last nine holes, and lost the playoff comprehensively enough. What is not often enough remembered is that Casper's tying total was 278 on the same Olympic course where Hogan and Jack Fleck had tied with 287 11 years earlier.

Casper is not only consistently good, he is durable. He won his only Masters (so far) in 1970, and he must always come into the reckoning in any tournament. He had his chance of joining the ranks of those who have won both the U.S. Open and the British Open, but the one year when he seemed to have the latter won (1968 at Carnoustie), he took 78 in his last round when a 74 would have given him victory over Gary Player by one stroke. Of the first 20 players in that championship, only one had a worse last round than Casper, but since he was Tony Jacklin perhaps not too much should be made of that. Still, Casper showed in that championship, as he has demonstrated more than once, that he lacks something of drive, of flair for the biggest occasion. He seems to be content to play his game, admittedly superb, without making a positive attempt to lift it to satisfy a special need. Maybe it is the result of being a method golfer, doing the same thing all the time in the same way. It works beautifully day in, day out, and so disciplined is Casper's mind and swing that he has been one of the greatest money-winners of all time. But he plays golf like an accountant, everything neat and tidy—and, it often seems, without imagination.

There is no lack of imagination, no lack of flair or drive or the ability to lift their game, about the Big Three and the man who has joined them at the summit, Lee Trevino. All four have everything. The only difference between Trevino and the Big Three is that he has not had it very long. But that is not to say he won't outlast all of them, even though he has a swing that is a calculated lurch and almost an affront to aesthetic values. Anyone who can in the space of five years come from nowhere to win two U.S. Opens and two British Opens is by achievement alone a superstar. But the way Trevino won all of his major titles set him apart. In winning his first U.S. Open, he broke par in every round and equaled the record low aggregate set up by Nicklaus the year before. He won his second U.S. Open after a head-to-head playoff with Nicklaus, 68 to 71. His first British Open victory at Birkdale in 1971 was spectacular beyond belief. On greens that everyone criticized, he putted like an angel, an avenging angel perhaps, for he had been roughly handled on the same course in the Ryder Cup match a couple of years earlier by a mere boy, Bernard Gallacher. Trevino had the championship firmly in his grasp with only two holes to play and then, under the eyes of thousands on the course and millions watching on TV, he took a horrid 7 at the 17th. Was he to be another Snead, as it were, in reverse? Trevino had the answer: two perfect shots and two perfect putts at the last, and he finished like a lion. He did precisely the same at Muirfield in 1972 after two days of battling with Tony Jacklin, for they were paired for the final two rounds. He holed two chip shots, he holed a bunker shot on the first bounce when he seemed doomed to perdition, and then, reprieved, played the testing last hole better than anyone had played it the whole week.

Trevino has everything—the golf, the ability to win, the flair for the big occasion, the capacity to play outrageously successful shots when they are most needed, and a personality so outgoing and engaging that he, an American, was voted by the British public Sportsman of the Year. He is articulate in front of the TV microphones, but even when he is not communicating directly he radiates energy, gaiety, and a wholesome, almost cavalier, approach to the habitually grim business of big-money and championship golf that is vastly endearing. He is the antithesis of Hogan in every way and yet he might become another Hogan on the score of achievement. He lacks nothing at all in competitive instinct. In 1971, he won three major championships, the U.S. and British Opens and the Canadian Open, in the space of four weeks, which postulates a willingness to drive himself to the brink.

It is a willingness not entirely shared by the only British golfer since Henry Cotton to join the ranks of the truly great players. Tony Jacklin has almost everything that a superstar should have, although, like Trevino, he has not had it very long. He has won the British Open and the U.S. Open, the first British player for fifty years to beat America's best on their own terms and turf. He has been fifth once and third twice in recent British Opens. He is capable of the most spectacular play and the most spectacular strokes. He holed in one under the eyes of the TV cameras when winning his first major tournament, the British Dunlop Masters, in 1967, and he holed a full pitch at the ninth at St. Andrews in 1970, one of Nicklaus's years, to reach the turn in an improbable 29 strokes, 7 under par. No doubt such strokes are lucky, but some players seem to have the knack of producing them, and Jacklin is one of them. He has the further knack common to some champions of being able to play his bad shots when they will hurt him least. If he has a flaw, it is one bred in him by the age and circumstances in which he has flourished. No British golfer ever made so much money in so short a time, and Jacklin has sought to live a life of compromise between fulfilling his obligations as a gladiator in the arena and as a family man seeking to build and live a normal life. As a result, he has sacrificed something of the compelling urge to win, to prove himself to himself and the world, that energizes the three men who have dominated professional golf in the modern, big-money, jet-age, TV-influenced era.

Palmer, Player, and Nicklaus are a modern phenomenon of sport. They are known and admired all over the world. Arnie's Army has its regiments in every country where he has played, and he seems to have played everywhere except some of the coral atolls in the Pacific. Nicklaus is accepted as being in the same bracket as Hogan and Jones as one who might be classed the greatest player of all time. Player is so influential through his golf that he has almost changed the policy of the government of South Africa, his native country, on the question of multiracial sport.

Palmer was the first to arrive, beating Player by one year as a professional winner although he had won the U.S. Amateur Championship at match play as long ago as 1954. In 1958 he won his first Masters and then won in alternate years until 1964, and in the years when he didn't win he was third, equal second twice, and fourth, a truly astonishing record. His record in the U.S. Open Championship is equally remarkable, though nothing like that conclusive success. He won in 1960, after a fantastic final round in which he scored 65, making up 7 strokes on the leader. It was the first of his famous "charges." He has not won since. Three times he has tied for first, and each time he lost. He tied with Nicklaus in 1962 at Oakmont, with Boros and Jacky Cupit at Brookline the following year, and, most bitterly of all, with Casper at San Francisco in 1966. In 1960 he was within a stroke of completing the same Little Slam as Hogan achieved in 1953. He followed his victories in the Masters and the U.S. Open by going to St. Andrews for the Centenary British Open. It was his first visit to Britain, although British golfers had seen him on TV and were familiar with his play and his personality. He was the favorite, not only on form but in affection, and he failed by a single putt to justify both hopes and expectations. Kel Nagle, the placid, quietly cheerful Australian golfer, did 278, a record aggregate for the Old Course, and Palmer was 279. He played so well, and took his defeat so well, that he immediately secured his place in the admiration of the British public.

Palmer made no mistake the following year at Birkdale or the year after that at Troon. He won both times, the first by the smallest of margins from the smallest of the top British professionals, Dai Rees, but only after calling a penalty on himself for a violation only he could have known about. That was in character, for although Palmer was then and still is the supreme professional, he plays in the Corinthian spirit of the true amateur. His victory at Troon was something altogether different. The course was in poor shape (apart from the greens) after a dry spring and early summer. The fairways were hard and lumpy, kicking the ball every which way, but Palmer mastered it from the start and set up a record aggregate of 276 to win by no fewer than 6 strokes from the man who had nosed in front of him two years earlier. He was partnered with Nagle on the final day, and they were followed by the whole West of Scotland and protected, it seemed, by the entire Ayrshire county police force. There never was such a triumphal procession as the march up the last fairway. When first Nagle holed a huge putt for a birdie 3 and Palmer followed him in from 12 feet, also for a 3, there was such a roar of appreciation as might have rocked the granite bulk of Ailsa Craig out in the Firth of Clyde.

Palmer has not won the British Open since 1962 and has not even been very close, but he has only to appear on a British tee or on British TV to have the fans clamoring for more.

Palmer is the classic example of the right man being in the right place at the right time. It was not only his superlative scoring that set him apart. It was the kind of golf he played and the kind of person he was. He lived dangerously on the course. Like Hagen, he was capable of producing atrocious shots, and then of following them with heroic recoveries. He was the most exciting golfer of his time because his play was full of daring, from tee to green. The powerful swing with the idiosyncratic high finish, as though he were always fighting a hook, defied imitation but it made him unmistakable as far as the eye could see. The long irons, torn from the turf, were thrilling, and no one ever putted with more audacity and to such telling purpose. It was more fun to watch Palmer scoring in the high 70s than to watch a pedestrian performer breaking 70. And all the time, on the course and off it, on the small screen in close-up or at a distance, there was this vibrant, immensely likable person. Arnie has all the advantages of splendid athletic build, conventional good looks, and a rich speaking voice with an international accent agreeable to every kind of listener. He is articulate, invariably talking common sense but never in a commonplace way, and he has the capacity to make fun of himself. Like Hagen before him and like Cotton in Britain, he has a highly individual life style. He has his own jet, which he flies himself, something no professional golfer had done before. He has sold his name to all manner of enterprises and became the first millionaire golfer, as much from his prowess as a player as from his shrewd business instincts. But so far as the public can detect, he has never been in the least spoiled by his success. He talks with crowds and keeps his virtue, he walks with kings (or their republican equivalent) and keeps the common touch. He is Arnie to everyone, from presidents to caddies, and always will be.

Of his two great contemporaries, Gary Player and Jack Nicklaus, Player is by far the more complicated character. He is almost too intense for the good of his public image, a condition that probably stems from his early days as a competitor. He was only twenty when he won his first major tournament in Britain, having made an unsuccessful trial trip the year before. He was roughly handled by the critics and by his fellow professionals, who condemned his grip, his swing, and his excessive single-mindedness. He could pitch and putt but that was all, they said. The sensitive youth was hurt and resentful but, though he does not laugh easily, he had the last laugh. He went on to become one of the greatest players of all time. Player's record is unsurpassed, not even by Nicklaus, if you count his victories in the open championships of his native South Africa and Australia as well as his successes in the wider competitive fields in the United States and Britain. He has twice won the British Open, in 1959 at Muirfield when only twenty-three and again at Carnoustie in 1968 after an eye-to-eye duel on the final day with Nicklaus. He won the U.S. Open in 1965, the first foreign

Ben Hogan (recent)

Trevino sweats it out

Gene Sarazen

A classic Arnold Palmer

Ken Venturi winning the 1964 U.S. Open at Congressional Country Club, Washington, D.C.

Britisher Tony Jacklin

A pensive Nicklaus

Young John Miller

The power of Jack Nicklaus

A happy Trevino

Tom Weiskopf being congratulated by Charles Coody

A young Palmer

player to do so since the bulky English professional, Ted Ray, won in 1920. He won the Masters in 1961, with a little help from Palmer, who had a 4 to win and took 6, and he tied with Palmer and Finsterwald the following year, in one important playoff Palmer did win. That year Gary went on to win the PGA Championship, and ten years later, in 1972, he won again, with a display of controlled, confident golf that brought him home in a late run when he was the only one of the leaders to keep his head and his swing in the final stretch.

Player has been equally formidable in match play, to prove that he is armed at every point. He has four times won the Piccadilly World Match Play Championship at England's Wentworth, out of eight tournaments, twice beating Nicklaus over 36 holes in head-to-head competition. In one of his winning years, he beat Tony Lema after having been no fewer than 7 holes down with 17 to play, one of the most astonishing recoveries in the history of match-play golf. And all this achievement from one with no obvious advantages at all. He has none of the physical attributes of Palmer and Nicklaus, and for years he fought a battle to overcome shortcomings of physique. He drilled his body even more assiduously than he drilled his mind and spirit. He did pushups to strengthen his hands and forearms, and he jogged and ran to strengthen his legs. He practiced constantly. If he did make something of a parade of his diligence, at least the results proved the virtue of his discipline. He enlisted any help, natural or supernatural, that might shave a stroke from his score. It was sometimes a little hard to take, as when he claimed Divine guidance in the year he won the Masters. But his sincerity was so apparent, his dedication so absolute, that those who came to scoff remained to praise.

Player is, of all the great modern professionals, the greatest of all commuters. He jets back to his farm in South Africa, his family, and his friends between tournaments, and thinks nothing of flying halfway around the world and stepping on to a championship first tee with apparent lack of regard for time lags and the like. Sometimes he has made life hard for himself; sometimes it has been made hard for him because he is a South African and the South African government pursues racial policies that arouse hostility thousands of miles from home. Thus Player has competed in the United States and Britain under the threat of assassination or, at the very least, open hostility. But it is a measure of the little man's character that he has not only survived but even flourished in such an atmosphere. One man, even one so secure in his fame as Player, could hardly do more to influence his government's thinking on racism in sport. He is the smallest of the Big Three, but in some ways the biggest. And he has done it all on his own, with fewer aids than either Palmer or Nicklaus, for more than a dozen years. He is a superstar by any measurement—achievement, durability, versatility, character. He may not be adored as Palmer is, or viewed with awe like Nicklaus, but he is admired and respected equally with Hogan, and no one can say more than that.

The last of the superstars of modern golf, Jack Nicklaus, is by some reckoning the greatest of them all, possibly the greatest of all time. He satisfies all the criteria. He has won more major championships than anyone else. He began early and has kept it up ever since. Jack was a Walker Cup player at Muirfield when only nineteen and U.S. Amateur Champion for the first time a few months later. He was still an amateur, and only twenty, when he finished second to Palmer in the U.S. Open, and not many weeks later he played four rounds of Merion in the Eisenhower Trophy in 66, 67, 68, and 68 to finish no fewer than 13 strokes ahead of the next man. In a matter of months he had served notice on the world that here was a young man who could play matches, who could play the medal game on the most severe courses, and who could do it in a way that not even Jones had been able to do at his age. From then on it was a procession of triumphs. A second U.S. Amateur title won in 1961 gave Nicklaus a perfect passport to professionalism, and right away he won the big one, the U.S. Open, after a playoff with Palmer, who was so much a folk hero by then that for anyone to beat him, especially a pudgy ex-amateur still wet behind his professional ears, was a sin against the light. And that state of affairs endured for years, with Nicklaus winning only grudging acclaim despite his run of successes. He failed dismally on his first attempt to win the British Open in 1962 at Troon, and Palmer's fans felt that Arnie's playoff defeat had been avenged, for Palmer won handsomely and Nicklaus was nowhere. Jack even took a 10 at one hole, and his detractors gloated. But next year he won the first of his three Masters titles, and the PGA Championship for the first time, and by now he was the man to beat whenever he stepped onto the first tee. The parade continued—the British Open at Muirfield in 1966, when the rough was so thick and the fairways so narrow that some wit said he would rather have the hay concession than win the championship, and a second British Open at St. Andrews in 1970, though that was one that nearly got away, because Doug Sanders three-putted the Tom Morris green when two putts would have given him the championship. Nicklaus, who was such a good match-player as an amateur, showed that he had not lost his talent for man-to-man combat when he won the Piccadilly World Match Play in 1970 from the new star, Trevino, despite having been roughly handled twice in the final of this event by Player.

Nicklaus was not, like Palmer, an instant favorite when he began to win championships. He was fat, he took an unconscionable time to play, he was too serious. Sure, he hit the ball miles and miles and so was thrilling to watch, but he never registered dismay like Palmer or frowned massively like Player when things went wrong. Though without a single bad habit or ungracious action, he was considered too contained, too much a master of his emotions, without, it seemed, a single endearing trait. But gradually, as he learned more about himself, he changed. He slimmed down to more athletic proportions without sacrificing anything of his stupendous power. He wore more modern clothes, let his hair grow a little but not too much, and acquired something of the ease of manner that Palmer has always possessed. His speaking voice is not immediately attractive, and voice is important in establishing an image in these days of universal TV and the instant interview. But in private conversation he is wholly charming, modest but essentially honest with himself. If Nicklaus says he is playing well, he is playing well. If he says he is playing badly, then his game is indeed sour. Palmer, on the other hand, is always playing badly—according to Palmer; and Player, by contrast, is always playing well—according to Player. Nicklaus has no illusions. Golf is a difficult game that has to be worked at. When he is working well, he is playing well, and his record suggests that he works uncommonly well most of the time.

Nicklaus will never quite supplant Palmer in the affections of the gallery, although his simple candor—as when he calmly said he was going for the Grand Slam in 1972—has struck a responsive chord among the golfing faithful. There was a vast amount of sympathy for him when he arrived at Muirfield in 1972, having already won the Masters and the U.S. Open, to a course where he had played in the Walker Cup match as a beefy boy, where he had won the championship in 1966 by skillful management of his game and himself on a course specially prepared to tame the tigers. He failed to win the third leg of the modern "impregnable quadrilateral" but he failed so gloriously that he was as much the hero of the hour as Trevino, who won, or Jacklin, who finished third, bearing all the hopes of the home crowd. Nicklaus played a last round of 66, but he took his comparative failure with such grace and dignity, fighting to the last putt with infinite courage and not so much as a twitch of dismay, that he must have established himself securely in the heart of everyone who watched at close range on the course or on remote television screens.

And so, golfers who have played their own game and watched the play of the stars in the last quarter of a century need have no regrets that they did not live in what used to be called the Golden Age of Golf, the Twenties, when Hagen, Sarazen, and Jones were giving a new dimension to the tournament game. True, in those days, before crowd control became a necessity, it was possible to tread on the heels of your favorite, perhaps even to hear a word from the great man's lips. You could see the whites of his eyes, the flush of anger or shame as he missed a little putt, and you could preen yourself and become a clubhouse bore as you began, "I was there when . . ." We are all there now, by courtesy of television, and we can see more from the comfort of our armchair than even the most avid and eager watcher could see in the Twenties. There is more to see, too, more great shots from more great players, more stars and superstars, setting a standard with which, as Jones said of Nicklaus when he won the Masters in 1965, even he was not familiar. That Masters, it is surely no accident, was won by Nicklaus from the two men who, with him, have been the makers, the masters, the superstars of modern professional golf, Arnold Palmer and Gary Player—truly the Big Three.

[3]

THE U.S. OPEN—FROM NEWPORT TO PEBBLE BEACH

***

GOLFERS, like most humans, are driven by different urges. For some, it is the lure of the money they can win week after week on the pro tour; for others, it is the glamour, the ego satisfaction, the chance to strut before the admiring galleries.

For the very best of players, however, the chance at immortality overshadows the prize of the moment—the chance to have their names remembered as the Vardons and Taylors, the Joneses and Hagens, the Hogans and Sneads, the Palmers and Nicklauses are remembered. The one sure way to win that immortality is to win a major tournament.

In the early years of golf, before World War I, the British Open was the ultimate goal. In the 1920s the emphasis shifted to the United States Open, and today it is still the most important of them all.

The qualities that go into prestige are somewhat elusive, but they can be roughly defined. Certainly it is not prize money, or else the most important tournament of all time would have been the Dow Jones Open, played in 1970. It offered $300,000, but ask yourself who won. If you remember it was Bobby Nichols, you're rare. The chances are much better that Tony Jacklin will be remembered as the winner of the 1970 Open.

For a tournament to last, a solid organization must be behind it. Look at the oldest golf tournaments in existence in the United States, and then look at the organizations behind them. The oldest, of course, is the Open, which began in 1895 and is run by the ruling body of golf in the United

States—the United States Golf Association. The Western Open began in 1899 and is run by the Western Golf Association. The PGA began in 1916, and behind it is the Professional Golfers Association of America. The Masters is the youngest of the principal tournaments, and its rise to such prominence was rather amazing. But it was originated in part by Bobby Jones, and no name is more closely linked with American golf than his; it has been played since its beginning in 1934 at the same location, the Augusta National Golf Club, one of the finest courses in the country, and it has had a continuing organization behind it, directed by Clifford Roberts.

These organizations are dedicated to their tournaments as golf competitions, not as a means of raising funds, although it would be foolish to say they don't make money. In the early Seventies both the PGA and the USGA were being paid over $300,000 for their television rights alone.

Now look at the courses they play. In the early years the Open went wherever there was a golf course. Since the Masters became so prominent in the early Fifties, there is a continuing discussion of whether it is better to hold a tournament on the same course every year, as the Masters does, or to move around, as the Open and PGA do. Both methods have their points. Play the tournament on the same course and you can find the weak spots and improve it, as the Masters Committee does. Move it around and you lose this benefit, but then you can bring the tournament to different parts of the country and play it at the nation's great courses, as the USGA does with the Open. The normal tour tournament is played at the same course each year, but the course is not especially groomed for the tournament. The club may allow the grass in the rough to grow for a week, but it will be reluctant to pull the rough lines in and tighten the course because of complaints from members who themselves like to play.

The Open is moved about the country, the East one year, the Midwest another, the Southwest, the Far West, wherever there is a golf course of merit whose members would be willing to give up a lot of their golf course and their club for a year or so. While the USGA may have made some mistakes in course selection over the years, the choices generally have been outstanding. The first postwar Open was played at Canterbury Golf Club near Cleveland, a fine course. It's been played at Merion, Oakmont, Oakland Hills, Oak Hill, Medinah, Baltusrol, Olympic, Southern Hills, Winged Foot, and, in 1972, Pebble Beach, possibly the finest golf course in the world. (It's also been played at Hazeltine, Bellerive, Congressional, and Champions, courses that just don't have the character of those others.)

While it has been played at the great courses, there are some great courses where it has *not* been played. It's regretful that the Open has never been to Pinehurst, where Donald Ross, one of the finest golf course architects of them all, created that wonderful Number 2 course. But Pinehurst's location has drawbacks. It is in a thinly populated area of North Carolina, and one thing any major tournament needs is a large population center, for spectators, for advertising revenue, and for the volunteer workers who sell tickets and program advertising, marshal the galleries, organize facilities for the press, serve on the transportation committee that drives players back and forth between the golf course and their hotels, and even drive them, as they did at Merion and Pebble Beach, between the golf course and the practice range.

1895–1908

It was not always so, of course. The Open, in fact, was born as an afterthought to the principal order of the day—the Amateur Championship. The first Open was played in 1895 as a sideshow to the Amateur. The USGA had been formed only the previous December so that an amateur championship could be played under circumstances that were acceptable to old Charles Blair Macdonald, who had lost two previous "national amateur championships." His first complaint was that a championship could not rightly be settled by stroke play, the format of the first tournament. Another "amateur championship" was held later in the year, this time at match play, and once more Macdonald lost. Now he complained that one club—in this case, St. Andrews in Yonkers, New York—could not properly conduct a national tournament. There must be a national organization to conduct championships.

Thus was the USGA born, and the following October, 32 players met at the Newport Golf Club in Rhode Island to settle the championship of the land. On October 3, Macdonald finally won the Amateur and peace came over the land.

The Newport Golf Club had a nine-hole course, and the next day, professionals were invited to play for the Open championship. Ten pros and one amateur played four times around the nine holes, and when it was over Horace Rawlins had shot 173 for 36 holes to win by 2 strokes over Willie Dunn. Rawlins was a twenty-one-year-old Englishman who was serving as an assistant at Newport, and he did not shoot any nine holes under 41. It should be remembered, though, that this was the day of the gutta-percha ball, the ground was awfully rough compared to golf courses as we know them today, and the competition was not all that keen. The game had been introduced into this country only seven years before. The best players of that time were of British origin. Dunn, the runner-up to Rawlins, was a Scottish professional who came to North America to design some courses, decided the land had promise, and stayed. He laid out the original course at Shinnecock Hills, on the sand dunes of Long Island's south shore where the second Open was played. Jim Foulis, another Scot, won, and in the process shot a 74 in the second round, a record that would stand until Willie Anderson shot 73 at Baltusrol in winning the 1903 championship. By then the rubber-core ball had come into wide use, and scores from the "gutty" period were doomed. Also, in 1898 the Open had been extended to 72 holes in two days.

British-born players would continue to dominate the Open through those early years; Willie Anderson won four times, three years in succession from 1903 through 1905; Harry Vardon came over to play a series of exhibitions in 1900, stopped off in Chicago with J. H. Taylor, a member of the Triumvirate, and the two finished first and second. Laurie Auchterlonie won, and so did Fred Herd and Joe Lloyd, Willie and Alex Smith, of that great family of Carnoustie golfers, and Alex Ross and Fred McLeod.

1909

By 1909, though, homebreds were beginning to show some muscle. Tom McNamara, who was then representing the Wollaston Golf Club near Boston, shot 69 in the second round after an opening 73 and led the field after the first day with a 36-hole score of 142. Now it looked as if a homebred might win, but McNamara faded on the second day with 75, 77—152, and the title went to George Sargent, another Englishman, who had played with remarkable steadiness, shooting 75, 72, 72, 72—291. This was a new 72-hole record, one that would stand until 1916, and it beat McNamara by 4 strokes. McNamara had been the first native American to threaten to win the British championship.

1910

The next year saw the dawning of a truly remarkable and yet tragic career. Johnny McDermott, a native Philadelphian who had learned the game in the caddy yards, was a cocky youngster who thought he could beat everybody, and the truth was he just about could. He was eighteen years old in 1910 when he entered the Open at the Philadelphia Cricket Club. He was in a very tough field: Willie Anderson was still playing, Alex Ross, Alex and Macdonald Smith, George Sargent, McNamara, Jock Hutchison, Fred McLeod, and Gil Nicholls were considered the class of the game.

McDermott played two very steady 74s the first day and found himself tied with Nicholls and Tom Anderson, 2 strokes behind Alex Smith, who shot two 73s. The next morning McDermott added 75, and there he was in the lead, an eighteen-year-old American leading that band of crusty Britishers with but one round to play in the national Open Championship. Unfortunately for McDermott, it wasn't over yet. Alex Smith came through with 73 in the final round, and his younger brother Macdonald came roaring in with 71, and when McDermott shot 75, they were all three tied for the Open Championship.

Mac Smith next day shot 77 and finished third, but it was not yet McDermott's year, for Alex Smith shot 71 against his 75 and won his second Open. He had beaten brother Willie by 7 strokes in 1906 at Onwentsia Club in Lake Forest, Illinois. Willie, in turn, had won in 1899, setting a record that still stands. He shot 315 at the Baltimore Country Club and won by 11 strokes over George Low, Val Fitzjohn, and Bertie Way.

1911–1913

McDermott was not discouraged by that loss. He took a job at the Atlantic City Country Club, practiced with diligence until he became the finest mashie player of his day. In 1911 he was among 79 entrants at the Chicago Golf Club in Wheaton, Illinois, and after the first round he looked as if he might just as well have stayed home. He shot 81 and was 7 strokes behind Alex Ross, but bounced back to just 4 strokes behind at 153. A 75 the next morning put McDermott in a strong position, for Ross was collapsing. A closing 79 forced McDermott into a three-way tie with George Sargent and Mike Brady, both of whom shot 75 in that final round.

All three were off form for the playoff the following day, and McDermott won with an 80 against 82 by Brady and 85 by Sargent. This was a really significant day for American professionals; it was the end of domination by British golfers, a fact that was not really appreciated until two years later at The Country Club in Brookline, Massachusetts. When McDermott won in 1911 and again at the Country Club of Buffalo in 1912, he beat those British players who had come over to America to live; no one had yet beaten those strong British players who remained at home and who played among themselves. They were, without question, the finest golfers of their era, and at that time the only golf title really worth holding was the British Open. Occasionally they would come over to play exhibitions, as

John J. McDermott

Vardon and Taylor had in 1900, but they were never here during the Open. Then in 1913 Vardon and Ted Ray came to play another exhibition series, and, incidentally, a few tournaments, among them the Open. This was quite an occasion, for the American players felt they were being challenged; at least McDermott, after a tournament at Shawnee on Delaware, Pennsylvania, leaped onto a chair and told the world that those British weren't going to take "our cup" away. He was a bit offensive about it, and word of his behavior reached the USGA. For a time it seemed possible that McDermott would not be permitted to defend his championship, but eventually he was admitted into the field.

At the same time, another entry withdrawal was being considered, but this one was voluntary. Francis Ouimet was a twenty-year-old Boston amateur, a member of the Woodland Country Club, and he lived in Brookline near The Country Club and had caddied there. He had become interested in golf very early, and he and his brothers had carved some rough holes in their backyard. Francis had grown up to be a rather accomplished player, and had been a semifinalist in the Amateur. When Robert C. Watson, President of the USGA, heard that Francis did not intend to play in the Open, he took him aside and convinced him he should enter.

It is difficult to believe that he had any thoughts of winning, for Vardon and Ray were here, and so were McDermott, Mac Smith and Alex Smith, McNamara, Sargent, and a young Rochester professional who had come to Brookline to help McDermott beat the British. It was Walter Hagen's introduction to national competition.

By 1913 the Open had grown so that 36-hole qualifying rounds were needed to cut the field to workable size. Then the field turned to the real competition, two days of 36 holes each over a difficult par 71 layout with the ground softened by rain. At the end of the first day, Vardon was tied for the lead with Wilfrid Reid, another Englishman, at 147. Ouimet, meanwhile, shot 151 and, with half the championship over, was just 4 strokes behind the leaders, tied with young Hagen.

Rain began falling shortly after midnight and continued through the next day. It was British weather, and yet it was the young American who played best. Another 74 on the morning of the final day and Ouimet picked up 4 strokes on Vardon and 11 on Reid. Ray, meanwhile, tied at 225 with Vardon and Ouimet. By now the course was sodden and it was becoming more difficult to play by the minute. Ray, off first among the three leaders in the afternoon, staggered around in 79, giving him 304 for the 72 holes, fully 10 strokes above McDermott's winning score of the previous year. Vardon was next, and he, too, shot 79 and 304. Ouimet then had problems of his own. He went out in 43, and followed that by making a 5 on the short 10th hole. To catch Vardon and Ray, he would have to play the remaining eight holes in one under level 4s. At the 17th, though, he had just two tough par 4s left, and still needed a birdie. The 17th is a

360-yard, par-4 hole that doglegs left around a deep bunker. Francis hit his drive safely onto the fairway, and then hit the green with a jigger, a shallow faced iron with the loft of a four-iron. He was 20 feet past the hole, and he was faced with a slippery downhill, sidehill putt. No time for timidity here; either this putt went down, or he would have to birdie the 18th, a longer par 4. Francis stroked the ball for the hole; it began to slide downhill, took the break, and then smacked solidly against the back of the hole. Then it dropped. A birdie 3! The gallery went wild, and even the placid Jerry Travers, who had beaten Francis in the semifinals of the Amateur, leaped with delight.

Now for a par 4 at the 18th, or, better yet, another birdie. Ouimet's drive was adequate, but his approach hit against the slope that rises from the race track that encircles the fairway and stopped short. His chip left his mud-spattered ball 5 feet short. Calmly, Ouimet strolled up to the putt, and stroked it firmly into the hole. It was impossible, but Ouimet had tied Vardon and Ray, and he would meet them the following day in an 18-hole playoff.

They finished the first nine all square at 38 strokes apiece. On the first hole of the second nine Ouimet went ahead when both Vardon and Ray three-putted this 140-yard par 3. Francis made his par there, held them off with another par 4 at the 11th, and then added to his lead with still another par at the 12th. The Englishmen both made 5s, and Ouimet now led them by 2 strokes with six holes to play.

On the 15th, Ray made 6 on this par 4, after apparently being saved when his drive, heading into rough, plunked against a spectator's derby hat and bounded onto the fairway. By now Ray was 4 strokes behind Ouimet and he was through. It was between Vardon, the seasoned Briton who by 1913 had won the British Open five times, and twenty-year-old Francis Ouimet, the Massachusetts amateur champion. Of the two, the inexperienced Ouimet seemed the calmer; he had recovered very nicely from two very bad shots, while Vardon had begun hooking his irons, something he never did. And then on the 16th hole Vardon lit a cigarette; he had never before been known to smoke on the golf course.

They halved the 16th in pars, then on to the 17th, where Vardon tried to cut the corner of the dogleg and carry the bunker. If the gamble worked he would have a simple little pitch to the green and a chance at a desperately needed birdie. Again Vardon hooked, and his ball dipped into the bunker. He had no chance to go for the green, and so he had to play back to the fairway, and carded a 5. Now Ouimet had a chance to pick up another stroke on Vardon if he could nurse the ball down in two putts, and he could use a 2-stroke edge with one hole to play. He stroked the ball smoothly and it began to run downhill toward the hole, closer and closer, until finally it tumbled in. He had birdied the 17th again, and now as he walked to that 18th tee he had a 3-stroke bulge. Only a miracle could keep him from winning now. There was no miracle. Ouimet played the extra round in 72 to beat Vardon by 5 strokes, Ray by 6. It was a marvelous day for American golf for many reasons, but perhaps the most important was this: for the first time a serious challenge from the British had been turned back. While it is true that McDermott had been the first American-born player to win the Open two years before, the field he had beaten contained no visiting players of consequence. But the field Ouimet had beaten contained two of the greatest English golfers of the age. They could be beaten. Never again would the British come to the United States with such confidence; nor would they have reason to be confident for 50 years.

1914

The news of Ouimet's victory sped across the country, and was read by some budding young golfers. It was read in Chicago by Chick Evans, and in Atlanta by eleven-year-old Bobby Jones. Both of them were to give us some glorious moments in the Open. Before their time, though, Walter Hagen made his impact. Hagen had finished fourth in his first attempt at Brookline the year before, just behind Ouimet, Vardon, and Ray, and he might have tied them had he not pressed in playing his second shot to the 14th green during the final round. He topped the shot, made a 7 on the hole, and dropped behind. He was never behind at Midlothian the next year. His opening 68 led Ouimet by a stroke, and then he followed with 74, 75, and 73, for 290. In those days the amateurs were every bit as good as the pros, and Chick Evans was perhaps the best amateur of the day. He made contact with the ball at least as well as anyone else, and although he was a little shaky with his putter, the rest of his game made up for it. Evans had not been particularly impressive in the first two rounds, shooting a 76 and a 74, but on the morning of the second day he played Midlothian in 71, and in the afternoon he was doing better. He came to the final green needing an eagle 2 to tie Hagen. He hit a nice drive and then a fine pitch to the green. The ball hit, rolled a little, . . . and hit the cup. It stayed out; Hagen had won, and the career of the most flamboyant personality in golf history had been launched.

1915

Jerry Travers was the second amateur to win the Open. He had won the Amateur championship four times, defeating Ouimet in the semifinals in

1913, and at Baltusrol in 1915 he played the last six holes in one under par to beat the luckless McNamara by a stroke.

1916

The year 1916 belonged to Chick Evans as no year had belonged to any amateur golfer before. Evans was twenty-six years of age, and he had been trying to win a national title for seven bitter years. His primary goal was the Amateur championship, but every time he had it within reach, something happened. He reached the semifinals in 1909, 1910, and 1911 and was beaten by players not in his class. He went to the final in 1912, had a three-hole lead on Travers, but lost, 7 and 6. But in 1916 Evans was at the peak of his game. He carried only seven clubs, but the shots were ringing from them with power and direction, and for once the putts were falling. The Open was first in 1916, played at Minikahda, in Minneapolis. Evans opened with a 70, 69, and clearly a new scoring record was probable, for no man had begun the Open quite like this. Chick was not up to that caliber of golf on the second day, but his 74, 73 was good enough to hold off Jock Hutchison, who came roaring out of the pack with 72, 68. Evans's four-round 286 beat the old scoring record by 4 strokes and set a new one that would stand for 20 years. The Open concluded on June 30; in September, Evans realized his life's ambition—winning the Amateur championship. He was the first player to hold both American titles in the same year.

1919

With the coming of World War I, major golf competitions were suspended, and the Open was discontinued until 1919. Hagen by then was acknowledged to be the finest professional golfer in the land, but he came down to the last six holes at Brae Burn trailing Mike Brady and needing to play those six holes in one-under 4s. He was one under playing the 18th, and if he could birdie he could win outright. A stone wall runs along the Brae Burn boundary behind the 18th, and anyone going for the green risks overclubbing and going out of bounds. Hagen was not known for timidity, and so he lashed a midiron shot to within 8 feet of the hole. As he walked toward the green, Hagen had Brady called from the clubhouse to watch him hole the putt and win the Open. Brady was somewhat stunned, but he came out anyhow. Hagen's putt ran straight for the hole, caught the edge, dipped in for an instant, and then sat on the edge. It would be a playoff the next day, one that will be remembered for a long time. Hagen lost his ball on the 17th hole and Brady found it embedded in mud. Hagen asked for a free lift, because the ball was so deep he felt someone must have stepped on it. The officials would not give it to him. Hagen thought for a moment and then asked permission to identify the ball, which he was entitled to do. He lifted it, examined it carefully, announced that it was indeed his ball, and then placed it back where it had been. By this time, though, the hole had oozed closed and Hagen had a playable lie. He recovered smartly, and saved a stroke. He won the playoff, 77 to 78.

Prize money in the Open had been increasing steadily ever since it began. While Horace Rawlins had been awarded $150 and a $50 gold medal for winning the first Open, Hagen won $500. Prize money in 1919 was up to $1,745, and money was awarded to the 11th and 12th place finishers.

1920

British golf was not the same once the war ended, and even the British were aware of it. Still, when Vardon and Ray came back to America in 1920, they were among the favorites at Inverness Club in Toledo, Ohio. Ray was still a powerful hitter even with his curiously light driver, and he slugged his way around the course in 295. He was not given much chance to win, though, for Vardon was still out, and he had to play the last seven holes in just two under 5s to win. The weather, though, had been threatening, and suddenly the wind began blowing at gale force. Vardon was fifty years old by then, and while he still had the fluid, graceful swing of his earlier years, the wind was just too much. Shot after shot began to slip away, and he finally staggered off the course with 296. He had played the last seven in even 5s and lost by a stroke.

1921

A new era was about to begin in American golf. Bobby Jones was just eighteen in 1920, and he played in his first Open at Inverness, shot 299, and tied for eighth. The next year he was back, and while Jim Barnes won by 9 strokes at the Columbia Country Club near Washington, Jones climbed to fifth. Barnes shot 289 and beat Hagen and Fred McLeod, who had 298. Jones shot 303.

1922

One more drama had to come before Jones took over the Open completely. Gene Sarazen, a twenty-year-old ex-caddy from Harrison, New York, recovered from a wobbly first nine in the third round and won by one stroke over Jones at the Skokie Country Club in Glencoe, Illinois. Sarazen was 3 strokes behind John Black after two rounds, 142 to 145, and then made six 5s on the first nine and shot 40. He made a strong finish in the third round, however, and saved a 75 with three straight birdies on the closing holes. On the final hole of the final round, Sarazen got down in two putts for a birdie and 288. The others couldn't match it. Black and Jones tied for second at 289.

Meanwhile in England an event had taken place that was to change the complexion of golf throughout the world. Walter Hagen had won the British Open a few weeks earlier at Sandwich, and when he did, the United States Open became the most important championship in the world. Now it would become a struggle for the British to win their own championship.

1923

Before he would win the British Open, Jones finally broke through in the United States. Ever since he was fourteen, in 1916, Jones was expected to do great things, but his career until then had been full of frustration. While it is true Jones had been losing to players of uncommon ability, he was still losing . . . and Jones wanted to win.

He came to Inwood, on Long Island, New York, in 1923 still without a national title after seven years of trying, finally in control of a burning temper that caused him more trouble than any of his opponents. Jones had been graduated from Georgia Tech with a degree in mechanical engineering, and then went to Harvard Law School, where he had little time for golf. In early summer he came home to Atlanta to begin preparation for the

Open, but was so terrible that Stewart Maiden, his only teacher, decided it might be best if he went to Inwood with Jones. Inwood is a rather narrow course, and it will not tolerate wildness. Jones was wild in his practice rounds and had a hard time breaking 80. Once the tournament began, his game came together and he shot 71 in the morning round of the first day, one stroke under par and one stroke behind Jock Hutchison, who played a 70, the best round of the tournament. A second-round 73 for Jones was again one stroke above Hutchison, and so when the first day ended, Bob was just 2 strokes behind the leader and one stroke ahead of Bobby Cruickshank.

Jones had one of the shocks of his life in the third round the next morning. He shot 76, and instead of losing ground, he led the championship by 3 strokes, as Hutchison shot 82 and Cruickshank 78. After 54 holes Jones had 220, Cruickshank 223, and Hutchison 224. With three holes to play in the final round, Jones was in the lead. Now, though, the strain began to tell. He hit his second shot out of bounds on the 16th and holed a 6-foot putt to save a 5. He missed his approach to the 17th and made another 5. Then the 18th, a 425-yard par 4, long and narrow, bordered by wiry rough and with a pond guarding the front. The wind was in Bob's face, and he drilled a drive into the teeth of the breeze. Ordinarily he could reach that green with a long iron, but today he took a spoon to avoid pressing. The ball came off the club face nicely, headed for the left side of the green, but then it began to turn to the left. He missed the green and the ball settled behind a chain fence near the 12th tee. After the chain was removed, Jones dunked his third shot into a pot bunker, and finally staggered off the green with a 6. Now Cruickshank could catch him with a par and a birdie on the last two holes. He made his par at the 17th, and then played a magnificent midiron 6 feet from the flag on the 18th and holed the putt. He had tied Jones at 294 with a closing 73 against Bob's 76, forcing a playoff.

The playoff was in question to the last hole. Through the first 17 holes they had halved only three, and as they stood on the 18th tee they were once more even. Now everything rode on that final hole. Cruickshank was up first and hooked his drive low and left into the rough. Jones hit his drive along the right side, and it came to rest on bare dirt at the edge of the rough. Cruickshank could only play a safety shot short of the lagoon, thus giving Jones an opening, if he could take advantage of it. Hardly hesitating, Jones whipped a midiron from his bag and played the shot that changed the course of golf in America, a low, boring shot that screamed toward the green and rolled 6 feet from the hole. Jones had won the Open, and from that moment until his retirement after the 1930 season, Jones dominated world golf.

1924

Jones was the favorite at Oakland Hills Country Club near Detroit the following year, and he started well enough, shooting 74, 73—147 to share the lead after two rounds, but he had a poor finish, 75, 78, and the title went to Cyril Walker, who played a remarkably steady four rounds. Walker was a small man, almost as small as Fred McLeod, who weighed 108 pounds when he won in 1908. He was an Englishman who represented the Englewood, New Jersey, Golf Club. Walker shot three 74s and a 75 for 297 and beat Jones by 3 strokes.

1925

Jones was back again the next year and lost once more, but he put up a tough fight, moving up from 36th place to 10th to 4th and then tied for first, forcing the first double-round playoff in Open history. The 1925 Open will stand up to any Open for an exciting finish. With 9 holes to play, eight men had a chance to win, and over the next eight only one of them fell aside—Mike Brady. With one hole to play, seven men could win. Leo Diegel, the first to reach the 18th, made 8. John Farrell made 4 and 292; Ouimet matched it; Sarazen made 4 and 293; Hagen went for a birdie and 291, and instead, made 5 and 293, and then along came Jones. On in 2, down in 2, for 291. Only Willie Macfarlane could catch him now. His pitch went to the back slope of the green, 40 feet from the hole. He barely nudged the ball down that slippery grade, and it finally stopped a foot from the hole. He did not have an easy shot left, though, for the ball had settled in a ball pit. Willie used a midiron rather than risk having the ball squirt off line, and he knocked it in.

Macfarlane was playing better than Jones in the early stages of the first playoff round, and Jones saved himself only by holing a pitch on the 14th. They finished the round tied at 75, and then had to play another 18 holes. Jones went 4 strokes ahead on the first nine, but Macfarlane made two 2s early in the second nine and caught Jones on the 15th when Bobby pressed trying to reach this 555-yard hole in two for a crushing birdie, and instead made bogey 6 to Willie's par 5. That was the difference. Jones shot 73, Macfarlane 72.

1926

Jones's career was to run only five years longer, and he made an absolute shambles of the competition in the next five Opens, winning three of them and losing a playoff in another. He won the British Open for the first time in 1926, and then added the U.S. Open later, the first time anyone had ever done it.

The U.S. Open was played at Scioto, like Oakland Hills a Donald Ross course, and the championship took on some of the features it has today. It was extended to three days, one 18-hole round on each of the first two days, and then the classic double round the last day, and 16 sectional qualifying rounds were needed to reduce the field from the original entry of 694. Professional golf was given another boost when the prize money was increased to $2,145, and eight places were added to the prize list, raising it to 20. First prize was still $500, but more players were getting a share of the money.

Jones, of course, was not taking any of it away from the professionals, but this was of small consolation; he was still beating them. Bill Mehlhorn was off fast with 68 in the first round, but Jones was close behind at 70. Then Bob's game shattered in the second round the next day and he shot 79, including a penalty shot when his ball moved as he was about to putt. Jones apparently was having a nervous problem, and on the morning of the final day he went to a doctor to get something to settle his stomach. Another good round of 71 in the morning left him still 3 strokes behind Joe Turnesa. At the end of nine holes Turnesa was 4 strokes up; he was still 4 up with seven to play, but Jones picked up 2 strokes on the 12th with a birdie against a bogey, and then 3 more. After 17 holes he was a stroke ahead of Turnesa. Joe then made a marvelous birdie at the 18th, and Jones needed a birdie of his own to win. He simply crushed a drive, every bit of 300 yards, and he had only a mashie-iron left, the equivalent of a seven iron, to a 480-yard, par-5 hole. His approach was 20 feet past the hole, and he got down in two putts for a birdie of his own and a one-stroke victory. Jones had played the last 12 holes in two 3s and ten 4s. His final round was a 73 and his 72-hole score was 293.

1927

The one poor Open of Jones's reign came in 1927 at the Oakmont Country Club near Pittsburgh. Tommy Armour, a Scot who had recently become a professional, holed a 10-foot birdie putt on the final green to tie Harry Cooper, who had three-putted earlier at 301. Armour then won the playoff, 76, 79.

1928

Jones was back again in 1928, but this was an Open that should have been won by Roland Hancock, an obscure player from Wilmington, North Carolina. Hancock was leading with only a couple of holes to play, and then made two 6s on the closing holes to let Jones and Johnny Farrell slip by him. The Championship was played at Olympia Fields, a mammoth complex near Chicago, and Jones seemed on his way to his third Open with rounds of 73, 71, and 73 in the first three rounds. His last round was a nightmare: a 77 that opened the door for Farrell to make up 5 strokes. They tied at 294, a stroke ahead of the luckless Hancock, and then went on to the playoff, which had been extended to 36 holes. Farrell took a 3-stroke lead in the morning round, 70, 73, and then held off Jones in the afternoon with a 73 against Bob's 71: 143 to 144.

1929

That was the last time Jones lost an Open. In 1929 he overcame a pair of 7s in the final round, holed a 12-foot putt on the last green to tie Al Espinosa, and then beat him in a laughable playoff at Winged Foot. Jones, understandably embarrassed by his two 7s the previous day, played two solid rounds in the playoff, a 72 in the morning and a 69 in the afternoon for 141, and beat Espinosa by 23 strokes! Espinosa played like a weekend amateur, shooting a ghastly 84 in the morning, and then improving only slightly in the afternoon to 80. It was an incredible showing for an accomplished professional, but Jones did those things to everyone.

1930

There has never been a year in golf like 1930. This was the year of the grand slam, when Jones won the Amateur and Open championships of both the United States and Great Britain. It is unlikely that it will ever happen again because, principally, the attractions of professional golf today are so alluring that no promising young player is likely to remain an amateur with so much money to be made as a professional. In 1930 the money was not all that great, and so good amateurs tended to remain good amateurs; the pros were coming up from the caddy ranks, not from the college campuses, where Jones came from.

Jones had gone to Britain early in the year to play in the Walker Cup Match, shortly after winning the Southeastern Open at Augusta, beating Horton Smith by 13 strokes. He won his singles and his foursomes, and then won his first British Amateur. If it could be possible, his game seemed better than ever, and he won his third British Open at Hoylake. Now it was on to Minneapolis and Interlachen for the U.S. Open in early June.

The pressure on Jones was intense, but he was off quite well with 71 and 73 on the first two days for 144, 2 strokes behind young Horton Smith. Cooper was even with Jones and Mac Smith was a stroke behind at 145. During the second round Jones hit what has come to be known as the water-lily shot. The 9th hole at Interlachen is a relatively short par 5 with a pond in front of a rise to a plateaued green 30 yards beyond the water. Jones had hit a good enough drive, and just as he was at the top of his backswing of his second shot, two little girls bolted from the gallery. Jones flinched, but he couldn't hold back. He topped his spoon shot badly and it seemed certain the ball would sink into the lake. Instead the ball skipped across the water, much as a flat stone will skip when it is thrown properly, and reached dry land beyond. (Some spectators believed the ball hit a water lily and bounced across, but Jones was never convinced.) From there Jones pitched on and holed his putt for a birdie; a lucky birdie, it's true, but still a birdie 4.

He seemed ready to blow the championship apart in the third round with a great 68. He played the first nine in 33, and after 16 holes he was 6 under par. He couldn't keep it up; he bogeyed the last two holes, but even then he had a 5-stroke lead with one round to play. Surely he would win with ease. In the afternoon Jones played the out nine in 38, and made three pars to start home. Perhaps the thought of what he was about to accomplish hit him there, for he began to play loose golf. Two over par on the 13th, a par 3, and then two birdies on the next three to recover the lost strokes. Then he heeled his tee shot on the 262-yard 17th into a dried-up water hazard. Jones didn't even look for the ball; he sat down on his bag and asked for a ruling. The dried-out swamp was declared a water hazard, Jones dropped another ball, pitched on, two putts and a 5. The 18th is a 402-yard par 4. Jones split the fairway with his drive and dropped his approach 40 feet from the cup. He holed it; and he made Mac Smith's assignment next to impossible.

Smith had picked up 4 strokes on Jones, but with that birdie he needed a 2 on the last hole to catch him. Because of the ruling that Jones had requested, the 18th tee was badly tied up, and when Smith reached it, six pairs of golfers were waiting to play that last hole. Then a strange thing happened. By silent agreement they all stepped aside to allow old Mac to go through. Of course he didn't make it, and his final-round 70 left him 2 strokes behind Jones at 289. Jones finished with 75 for 287, his lowest winning score and just one stroke off the Open record.

This was Jones's last Open; later in the year he won the Amateur and completed the Grand Slam, a different version from the one we know today, but one that may never be done again. With that, Jones retired from serious competition.

1931

With the passing of Jones and the beginning of the Depression, golf went into a period of decline. Golf courses were closing. More important, it was a period when golf was searching for a new leader, for this game, as all others, thrives on the outstanding performer, the equivalent of the Tilden or the Gonzales, the Ruth or the Robinson. In 1931 golf had Hagen and Sarazen, but Hagen hadn't won an Open since Jones came onto the scene, and Sarazen hadn't won in nine years. At Inverness, Billy Burke shot 292 and watched as George Von Elm birdied the last hole to tie him. Playoffs then were over 36 holes. Burke played them in 73, 76—149, and again Von Elm birdied the last hole to tie. On to another 36 holes. They were even with five holes to play, and then Burke picked up a stroke. He finished with 77, 71—148, and Von Elm couldn't make his birdie on the 18th. He finished with 76, 73—149. It took 144 holes of golf to determine a successor to Jones—as champion, not as monarch.

1932

Sarazen finally won his second Open in 1932 at Fresh Meadow on Long Island, New York, playing his last 28 holes in 100 strokes. He was 7 strokes behind after eight holes of the morning round on that final day, sticking to a plan that seemed wholly uncharacteristic of him. Sarazen was best when he was bold, but he had determined to play this Open cautiously.

As he stood on the 9th tee he looked back at what caution had done for him—a 74, a 76, and now a par 3 for 38. Forget it—he would play his own game. He played his iron right at the flagstick and holed his putt for a birdie 2, then raced around the second nine in 32, giving him 70 for the third round. In the afternoon he shot 66, setting the Open's 18-hole record and matching the 72-hole score set in 1916 by Chick Evans. It was the last one Sarazen would win.

1933

The professionals in 1933 had still not shaken off the threat of the amateurs, and John Goodman, a short, blond young man from Omaha, became the last amateur to win. It should have been among the easiest of victories, for Goodman started off with 65, 76, 70, and after three rounds was 6 strokes ahead of the field. He began his last round 4, 3, and 2, three under par, and suddenly, strangely, changed tactics. Where he had been rifling his shot at the flag, he began playing conservatively, and the strokes began slipping away. Goodman shot 76 on that final round, and Ralph Guldahl might have caught him had his approach to the 18th hit the green instead of tumbling into a bunker. Guldahl needed a par 4 to tie, and instead made a 5. Goodman won with 287.

1934

Guldahl would be back in a few years, but first Olin Dutra, a man wracked with dysentery, won at Merion, holing a slippery 15-foot birdie putt on the 15th hole and breaking the heart of Gene Sarazen, who stood watching helplessly as Dutra finished bogey, bogey to beat him by a stroke. Earlier in the day Sarazen had taken 7 strokes on the treacherous little 11th, a 370-yard par 4 with a creek cutting across the fairway and flowing placidly alongside the green. Bobby Cruickshank had driven into a divot on this same hole, tried to dig it out, and the shot came up short. Bobby saw it drop between the banks, and then rocket out of the creek bed and come down on the green. He had been saved by a rock. When he saw his ball rise from the depths, he flung his niblick high and, as he cried "Thank you, Lord," the club came crashing down on his head. His playing partner that day was Wiffy Cox, another of that band of great players who could never win a national championship. Cox's chances were ruined when his shot to the 12th hole, a dogleg-right par 4, rolled slightly over and onto a man's coat. The man became excited, snatched up the jacket, and as he did the ball was flung out of bounds.

Still the main story of this Open was Dutra, a tall man from Monterey, California, of Spanish ancestry. He played the first two rounds in 76, 74, and as the final day began he was 8 strokes and 17 men behind. He passed them all with 71, 73 on the final day, and his record of making up 8 strokes has never been beaten, although Arnold Palmer would equal it in 1960.

1935

It was Sam Parks's year in 1935, the man still remembered as the most obscure of dark horses, but the only man capable of holing a putt on the marble-like greens at Oakmont. His score of 299 was 11 over par, and he did not match par 72 in any one round. Twice he shot 73, and he finished with 76. None of the leaders, however, could better 75, and so golf won a legend that year. Ever since, the question is always asked on the eve of the Open, "Will we have another Sam Parks?"

1936

In 1916 Chick Evans shot 286 to win the Open at Minikahda using just seven clubs. Sixteen years later Gene Sarazen matched it at Fresh Meadow, and in 1936 it would be beaten by Tony Manero, a short, dapper man who played the last round at Baltusrol's Upper Course in a daze, shot 67, and broke the record by 4 strokes with 282. He also shattered Harry Cooper, another of those tragic figures of American golf who always seemed to come close and yet not win anything really big. Cooper had already beaten the record by 2 strokes with 284 when Manero came down that final fairway being coaxed by Sarazen. Cooper would threaten a few more times, but he was never able to win.

Sam Parks, Jr., wins 1935 Open

1937–1938

Ralph Guldahl was a tall, handsome man who liked to keep his long, wavy brown hair in place, and it was a rather ludicrous sight to see him facing a slippery 40-footer and comb his hair before he stroked the putt. But Ralph Guldahl could play golf. Since McDermott in 1911 and 1912, only three golfers have won the Open in consecutive years, and Guldahl was one of them. Jones and Hogan were the others.

By 1937 the United States was climbing out of the Depression, and prize money for the Open had been increased to $6,000, a hike of $1,000 over the previous year. First prize remained at $1,000.

This was the first Open for Sam Snead, who had come out of the Virginia hills early in the year and began winning almost immediately. When he played four rounds at Oakland Hills in 283, it looked as if he might win the biggest tournament of them all, since he was only one stroke above the new record set by Manero the year before. But Guldahl played the last round in 69 and broke Manero's record with 281. The next year he came back to win with ease at Cherry Hills in Denver, once more finishing with 69, to beat Dick Metz by 6 strokes. Guldahl shot 284.

Snead's loss in 1937 was not considered tragic at the time. He was just twenty-six, and he had a swing that would last as long as he lived, a big, fluid, graceful swing that was as natural to Sam as breathing. Sam Snead was a stylist, much like Macdonald Smith. Their similarities ran much deeper, which was unfortunate for Sam. Smith had tied for the Open championship as a twenty-year-old in 1910 and lost to his brother Alex. No one took that loss too seriously, for Mac had so many years left. But like Sam, that big year never came, and even though Mac played some great golf, he couldn't win the Open. Neither could Snead.

1939

Perhaps the most tragic moment in all the Opens took place at the Spring Mill Course of the Philadelphia Country Club in 1939 when Snead needed only a par 5 on the final hole to win. Spectators were swarming over the fairway when Snead reached the tee, and he had to wait nervously while a lane was cleared wide enough to play through. He hooked his drive, barely got his brassie second airborne, pushing it into a bunker some 100 yards short of the green, and then played a perfectly terrible shot that didn't get out of the sand. His fourth barely cleared the lip of the bunker, he was on in five, putted to within 3 feet of the hole, and then left his second putt 6 inches short. He made 8.

Byron Nelson won that Open in a double playoff with Craig Wood. Wood had come to the final hole needing a birdie 4 to tie, and, unlike Snead, had done what he had to do: cracking two big woods to the green, then getting down in two putts. Denny Shute also had tied at 284, but he had been eliminated in the first playoff round when he shot 76. Wood looked as if he might win after one round, but Nelson holed a birdie putt on the 18th green to match Wood's 68. They went out again, and Nelson actually won it on the 4th when he holed a full one-iron shot. He had 70 in that second round against 73 by Wood.

1940

Lawson Little won at Canterbury, defeating Gene Sarazen in a playoff 18 years after Sarazen had won his first Open. Three players actually shot 287 at Canterbury in 1940, but Porky Oliver was disqualified. He had seen a storm developing while he was having lunch between rounds the final day and had teed off ahead of schedule. In one of the most unpopular decisions it ever made, the USGA ruled Oliver out of the playoff.

1941

Wood won at the Colonial Country Club in Fort Worth in one of the more ironic Opens. His back was so painful that he considered withdrawing before play began. Once he started he was nearly invincible, shooting 73, 71, 70, 70—284 and winning by 3 strokes over Denny Shute.

1942

With the onset of World War II, an era had come to an end. The country was well on its way out of the Depression, and some really great

Lawson Little wins 1940 Open at Canterbury

players were beginning to develop—Snead, Nelson, Horton Smith, Jimmy Demaret, Lloyd Mangrum, and that Texan, Hogan, who finally made the cut in 1939, finishing 62nd, climbed to fifth in 1940, and to third in 1941. He had finally won a tournament in 1940, the North and South at Pinehurst, and in 1942 he won the wartime substitute for the Open, called the Hale America National Open, but no one has ever really recognized that tournament as the national championship.

1943–1945

For the last few years there had been little doubt that Hogan was the best player on the tour, but until he broke through in the North and South, he had not won a tournament of any description, and he still hadn't won a major championship when he was called into the service in 1943. As kids caddying at Glen Gardens Country Club in Fort Worth, Hogan and Nelson had been firm friends. They had remained friends through their early years on the tour, but eventually their once-friendly rivalry turned bitter, partly because of the enthusiasm of their supporters. Nelson had arrived at the peak of his game earlier than Hogan, and when Ben was in the Air Force, Nelson was winning golf tournaments, lots and lots of them, and compiling a scoring average that seems utterly unreal—69.67 in 1944, and 68.33 in 1945, when he won 19 tournaments, 11 in succession. Nelson had been rejected for military service because of hemophilia, and he and Jug McSpaden had "owned" the pro tour. When the war ended in 1945, Nelson decided he had had enough competition. He had a nervous stomach to begin with, and high-tension tournament golf was doing nothing to help it.

1946

Still, Nelson would play in the 1946 Open at Canterbury, the first postwar Open, and the rival camps—Hogan's and Nelson's—anticipated a battle between their two men for the national championship. Neither was entirely happy with the result: they both had a chance to win, and both failed miserably in the last few holes. Nelson lost a stroke through a penalty in the third round when his caddy squirmed through the huge crowd, lost his balance, and stepped on Nelson's ball. Still he could win by

Lloyd Mangrum

2 strokes if he played the last three holes in even par. Instead, he three-putted the 17th, a par 3, and made 6 on the par-4 18th hole.

He was paired with Lloyd Mangrum, an ex-soldier who was twice wounded during the Battle of the Bulge, near Bastogne, Belgium, in December of 1944. Even after an experience like that, a golf tournament could be unsettling. He had been a stroke behind Nelson with those three holes to play, and while Byron was utterly falling to pieces, losing 3 strokes to par, Mangrum was picking up only the one stroke he needed to tie Nelson and Vic Ghezzi, who was already in with 284. When Hogan came to those last three holes, it looked as if his backers would have their day. He needed only three pars to win, and, barring that, he surely could tie Nelson and the others. Hogan lost a stroke quickly, and when he came to the 18th he needed a par 4 to tie, a birdie 3 to win. He three-putted. Once more he had finished behind Nelson in a major championship.

Nelson was not to win, though. Mangrum went 4 strokes ahead in the first playoff round, but lost all his lead, and at the end they were tied once more at 72. With six holes remaining in the second playoff, Mangrum was 3 strokes behind Ghezzi and two behind Nelson, and then birdied three of the last six and won with 72 against 73s by the others.

There would be no more confrontations between Nelson and Hogan. Porky Oliver defeated Nelson, one up, in the semifinals of the PGA Championship in August that Hogan won. Nelson played in no more Opens, and so he was not in the field when Hogan finally broke through in 1948.

1947

In 1947 Open prize money went into five figures for the first time. The USGA put up $10,000, and the winner, Lew Worsham, received $2,000, a heady amount for those times. Something of greater significance happened at the St. Louis Country Club that June. A television camera was set up in the back of a truck behind the 18th green—just one camera feeding a local station, which in turn fed 600 television sets in St. Louis, a lot of them in saloons, but that one camera was the beginning of modern professional golf. That one camera would transform the $10,000 prize money into the $200,000 purses that are so common in the 1970s.

It has often been said of Snead that the reason he did not win the Open is because he could not putt. Of course, Snead certainly *can* putt; you can't win as much as he has won without being able to putt some. When he came to the final hole of the 1947 Open, he needed a birdie 3 to tie Worsham, who was already in with 282 after taking bogeys on the 15th, 16th, and

17th. Snead powered a drive estimated at perhaps 300 yards, then lofted an iron, over the hump to the blind green, about 16 feet from the hole. With Worsham standing in the gallery, Snead holed the putt. Tommy Armour called it one of the very great putts of golf.

The next afternoon Worsham and Snead played off for the title, and they came to that same green tied. Both had played 3 and were almost the same distance from the hole. Snead stepped up to putt, but then Worsham called for a measurement. Snead was half an inch farther from the hole than Worsham, 30½ inches away, and so he putted first. The delay seemed to break Snead's concentration; he missed the short putt. Worsham made his and won.

1948

While Worsham may have been the national champion, by the late 1940s everyone knew that Ben Hogan was really the best golfer in the world. Four times he had been leading money-winner and three times he'd won the Vardon Trophy for the lowest scoring average. He'd won the Los Angeles Open, the North and South, the Western Open, the Texas Open, and in 1948 he won the PGA Championship for a second time. And yet he'd never won the National Open. He'd won the wartime substitute in 1942, but in the real Open he'd had nothing but frustration. He was beginning to seem like another, smaller version of Snead, except for one thing: Hogan had the determination that Snead seemed to lack. The years of failure tempered him differently; instead of becoming discouraged, he became determined. His hours on the practice tee have become part of golf legend; he drove himself, drove himself, drove himself, and after his disappointment at St. Louis, once more rebuilt his swing. Finally it all came together in the 1948 Open in Los Angeles.

The Open that year was played at the Riviera Country Club, to Hogan familiar and friendly ground. It was the site of the Los Angeles Open quite often, which Hogan had won three times, including 1947 and 1948. He had been so successful at Riviera that his friend Jimmy Demaret had named it Hogan's Alley. At 7,020 yards, it was the longest golf course ever used for the Open, and even though Hogan, 35 at the time, weighed but 135 pounds, he was not intimidated by its length. Hogan could hit the ball as far as anyone. He had such massive forearms, he reminded some of Popeye.

The first four holes at Riviera measure, respectively, 513, 466, 415, and 245 yards. The 1st is a par 5, the 4th a par 3, and the other two are par 4s. Hogan began the 1948 Open birdie, birdie, par, birdie. Two more birdies and a bogey demolished the first nine in 31 strokes. He cooled on the second nine, shooting an even par 36, with two birdies and two bogeys, and finished with 67.

When he had won in 1947, Lew Worsham had very little reputation. He had been an assistant pro at Congressional near Washington, and just before the Open had signed a contract as head pro at Oakmont. His contract permitted him to play only in a limited number of tournaments, and so when the 1948 championship began, he wasn't given much chance because he had been away from competition. Still, in that first round he was the only man in the field able to keep up with Hogan, and he did it with a much neater round than Hogan's, hardly missing a green, while Ben had to scramble on his second nine. Snead was 2 strokes behind when the round ended, and the next day he shot another 69, saving himself from another disastrous hole that could have been like the 18th at Spring Hill. The 11th hole is a 569-yard par 5. Snead hooked his tee shot badly into the trees. From there he had to punch a low shot under the branches, and it came to rest behind a refreshment stand. Snead was given a free lift, but he was still blocked by trees. He played a big, sweeping hook around the trees and across a wide barranca to within pitching distance of the green, and then dropped his fourth shot within 6 feet of the hole. He made it and saved a par.

It was fairly obvious by then that the Open's scoring record might be broken. Snead's 138 was the lowest 36-hole score ever shot in the Open (Evans's 139 in 1916 was best until then), but he was only a stroke ahead of Hogan, who had 72. The next morning Hogan went ahead by 2 strokes, with 68 and a 54-hole score of 207. Demaret was next at 209, and he was off the tee first in the afternoon. A birdie on the 8th saved him a 36 on the first nine—one over par. He started for home birdie, birdie, birdie—four birdies on five holes—and was 5 feet from another on the 13th, a 440-yard par 4. His putt slid by, just as Hogan was holing a birdie putt on the 10th, a little par 4 of 315 yards. Demaret broke the Open's 72-hole record with 278, but he could not keep up with Hogan. Ben had made the nine-hole turn in 33, and his birdie on 10 had dropped him 3 below par. He slipped once coming home, making a bogey on the 15th, and finished with 276, breaking the 72-hole record by 5 strokes. Jim Turnesa also broke the old 72-hole record with 280, but poor Sam Snead couldn't stand the possibility of winning; after that marvelous start, he foundered on the last day, shot 73 and 72, and finished fifth with 283.

Hogan finally had broken through, and who knew what he might accomplish. He stayed out on the tour the rest of the year, and won six more tournaments—the Motor City, Reading, Western, Denver, Reno, and Glendale Opens—and then began 1949 by winning the Crosby, then a 54-hole tournament, and Long Beach Open, and finishing second to Demaret at Phoenix, losing in a playoff. With that, Ben decided to take a rest. He was exhausted, and before he left for his new home in Fort Worth he told a friend that he wanted to die an old man, not a young one.

Hogan and his wife Valerie packed their Cadillac and began to drive home. The night was black and a ghostly ground fog covered West Texas. As they neared the small town of Van Horn, Hogan was creeping along, barely able to see the road ahead. Suddenly from out of the mist two lights bore down on the Hogan car; they belonged to a Greyhound bus, and there was no way to avoid a crash. Hogan flung himself across Valerie, trying to save her from the impact. In this one selfless action Hogan saved his life; when the bus slammed into Hogan's car, the steering column was driven through the driver's seat. The car was a wreck, and Hogan was little more than that. He suffered a double fracture of the pelvis, a broken rib, a broken collarbone, and two other injuries that would haunt him the remainder of his competitive career—a broken left ankle and some damage to his left knee. He was alive, all right, but some serious questions were raised that he would ever walk again. A month after the accident Hogan's condition became quite serious. Blood clots began to form and doctors performed a two-hour abdominal operation tying off the principal blood vessels in his legs. His life was saved once more, but now serious competitive golf was out of the question.

1949

Golf once more was without that one dominating personality or impassioned rivalry that so attracts the attention of the sports fan. There was still Snead, and a young dentist, Cary Middlecoff, who had been named to the 1947 Walker Cup Team but had declined because he thought he would play professional golf. The Open in 1949 was played at the No. 3 course of the Medinah Country Club near Chicago, and Middlecoff was in the field. He had shot 291 at Riviera the year before, 15 strokes worse than Hogan, and when he opened with 75 in the first round it looked as if he might do worse than in 1948. He recovered smartly with 67 in the second round and then was only a stroke behind Al Brosch, who had opened with 70, 71. On the last day of the Open, Middlecoff was paired with Clayton Heafner, a big, burly man who lived in North Carolina. Heafner was one of those fringe players, never quite good enough to win a national championship, but strong enough to threaten. He had played the first two rounds in 73 and 71, and when he made another 71 on the morning of the third day he was 3 strokes behind Middlecoff. Cary shot 69 and finally pushed himself into the lead.

Middlecoff was just 26. He had been on the tour only two years, and so he was understandably a little nervous when the final round began. Strokes began to slip away, and after nine holes he had been caught by Heafner. Middlecoff had played the first nine in 39 and Heafner in 36. Now they started back together, Heafner taking the lead when Middlecoff three-putted the 11th, then giving it back at the 12th where he lost 2 strokes to par. A 20-footer that dropped on the 13th pulled him even. Middlecoff went ahead to stay with a par on the 15th, but Heafner threw a fright into him with a solid iron 6 feet from the hole on the 18th. He missed and Middlecoff had the lead at 286. Only Snead could catch him now, and Sam needed 33 on the second nine to do it. With four holes to play he needed just four pars. Sam made his figures on 15 and 16, then he missed the green of the par-3 17th by inches. Sam tried to putt from the heavy grass and rolled the ball past the hole by 6 feet, and then missed coming back. Now he needed a birdie on the 18th, but had to settle for a one-putt par. Middlecoff had won and Sam was frustrated once more.

By this time Hogan was out of bed after 58 days on his back, and playing golf—not tournament golf, but a few holes now and then. His strength was coming back, and he was regaining most of the 20 pounds he had lost when he was bedridden. He played his first tournament the following January, and in perhaps the most amazing comeback in sports, tied Sam Snead for the Los Angeles Open. Snead won in a playoff, but the whole world knew that Hogan was back. He played in the Crosby but finished out of the money, and then went to Phoenix, where he had last played before the accident. They had renamed the tournament the Ben Hogan Open, and Hogan played. He finished 20th; Demaret won once more, just as he had the last time Hogan played. He played in the Masters, his first really big tournament, and finished fourth to Demaret, which was certainly encouraging, and then he went to Greenbrier, Snead's home, for a tournament over the Old White course. If there was any doubt that Ben Hogan could play golf once more, it was shattered there. He shot 64, 64, 65, 66—259 and won the tournament by 10 strokes; Snead had 269. Just for laughs, Hogan also played in the Celebrities tournament at the Army Navy Country Club in Arlington, across the river from Washington, and shot 99 for 27 holes. His last 72-hole tournament before the Open was the Colonial National Invitation, and he finished third to Snead.

1950

The 1950 Open was played at the Merion Golf Club on Philadelphia's Main Line. With Pebble Beach, it ranks as one of the two finest golf courses in the country; it is short, only slightly more than 6,500 yards, with narrow fairways, small, firm greens, and deep bunkers, and three of the hardest finishing holes in golf—two long par 4s, and a long par 3.

In retrospect, it was an ideal Hogan course because it has to be played with intelligence, and no one ever played the game more thoughtfully than Hogan. The question in everyone's mind was not Hogan's ability to play the game, rather it was his ability to walk 36 holes in one day, the day of the double round on Saturday. Gene Sarazen watched Hogan warming up one day and declared that he would pick Hogan to win without hesitation, "if they were going to play without walking—just hitting shots."

Thursday, the first day of the Open, was a lovely, soft spring day, sunny and warm, an ideal day for golf. Hogan was off miserably; five 5s on the first nine and 39 out. The greens were like marble; they had been shaved, sanded, and rolled, and only the most precisely hit shots would stop quickly. Downhill putts were almost impossible. Hogan never soled his club behind a downhill putt. Once he faced a 20-footer, and he knew if he soled his club the ball would move. He stepped up cautiously, careful not to touch the putter blade to the ground, and the ball rolled 4 feet toward the hole. Hogan glanced up quickly at a USGA official nearby. "It's all right," the official said, "you didn't address the ball."

His game quieted down on the second nine, and Hogan finished with 33 and a 72. He was 8 strokes off the lead, for earlier that day Lee Mackey, an unemployed young professional from Birmingham, Alabama, had set the Open scoring record with 64. Obviously the course could be played. (When Mackey stepped from the 18th green after shooting the lowest one-round score in the history of the Open, he had just one question to ask of the USGA: "What do you think will make the cut?" He shot 81 the next day and finished the 72 holes with 297, tied for 25th place.)

Hogan ranked 18th after the opening round, and then climbed to fifth with 69 in the second. His 36-hole score was 141, and only Dutch Harrison (139), Johnny Bulla (140), Jim Ferrier (140), and Julius Boros (140) were ahead of him. Boros was playing in his first Open as a professional.

Lloyd Mangrum shot ahead after the morning round on Saturday with 69 for 211. Hogan had another 72 and was tied at 213 with Middlecoff, his playing partner, and Johnny Palmer. Hogan was obviously weary when the final round began. Before he went onto the course each day he had to wrap his aching legs in yards of elastic tape, and at night he had to soak in a hot tub to ease the pain. He had no time to soak his aching legs now, though. All he could do was have a quick lunch and get back onto the course.

Middlecoff soon eliminated himself from contention. He was shooting 79, including a 6 on the 16th, where his second shot went into the quarry, and that would be no good at Merion this day. George Fazio, who had won the Canadian Open in 1946, started the round at 216, 5 strokes behind

Mangrum, but he played the last round in even par 70, giving him 287 for the 72 holes. The longer that 287 stayed on the scoreboard, the better it looked. Then Mangrum staggered in with 76 to tie, and Harrison limped off the 18th with a 76 of his own. This was one stroke too many, for Dutch finished at 288.

Hogan, pushing himself, reached the 12th tee one over par and leading by 3 strokes. He made his normal swing with the driver . . . and something happened to his legs. They locked and he nearly fell. Harry Radix, a man from Chicago who promoted golf tournaments, was there, and Hogan limped over to him. "Let me hang on you for a while," Hogan said. He moved his foot very slowly, and his legs felt as if they had turned to stone. "My God, Harry," Hogan said, "I don't think I can finish."

Up ahead Middlecoff was looking back, wondering what was happening. Hogan began walking again, reached his ball, and then hit his approach to the back of the canted green. He three-putted, and now one stroke of that precious lead was gone. Pars on 13 and 14 kept him ahead, and then on the short doglegged 15th Hogan played a lovely pitch 8 feet below the hole, perfect position for a go at a birdie that surely would cinch the title, and if not the birdie, then a sure par. Hogan three-putted—his second putt was inside 2 feet and he left it short, and his lead was down to one stroke. He made par on the 16th, the quarry hole, and then pulled his tee shot to the 200-yard 17th into a bunker. He came out weakly and failed to get down with his first putt. His lead was gone, and now he faced that terribly difficult 18th needing a par 4 to tie.

The 18th at Merion is one of the great finishing holes in golf, 458 yards across a stone quarry that had been abandoned before the golf course was built in 1912. It calls for a big uphill drive across the stone face of the quarry, and it must carry 200 yards to reach the fairway. From the top of the hill the fairway runs relatively level, but then begins a gentle drop where the very longest drives could reach before rising to the level of the big green. Hogan played the drive perfectly, just over the crest of the hill, sitting on a level patch that gave him the best shot to the green. It was not an easy shot, however; the gallery was closing in and Hogan had only a narrow lane through the spectators. The hole was cut on the right side of the green behind a bunker, and Hogan thought of cutting a four-wood shot close to the hole, but instead he played more conservatively, a one-iron he hoped would put him on the front of the green. It was one of the classic shots in golf, boring into the ultramarine sky and braking to a stop on the front of the green. While the thousands of spectators ringing the fairway and green screamed in approval, Hogan was downcast. He had a long putt, perhaps 40 feet, which he thought would break to the right; instead it broke left, and he still had a perilous 4-footer left. He thought he had blown the Open; he walked up to that treacherous putt, and, in a most un-Hogan manner, simply set the putter down behind the ball and hit it. The ball

Hogan in 1950 Open at Merion

went right into the center of the hole. Later he was to say he could not have cared less if the ball fell in or stayed out.

"I was so discouraged. If you can't hold a three-stroke lead through six holes, you ought to be someplace else."

Hogan's was not the only drama taking place that bright and sunny day. Joe Kirkwood, Jr., was making a serious run for the Open and he might have beaten the other three if it had not been for a spectator. Joe, Jr., is the son of the old trick-shot artist who had barnstormed the world with Hagen and Sarazen. He was not really in the Hogan-Mangrum class as a golfer, but he was popular. He was blond and handsome, and he played the starring role in some movies based on the comic strip character, Joe Palooka. Kirkwood had won the Philadelphia Open in 1949 and he was playing extremely well at Merion. His first three rounds were 71, 74, 74— 219, but after 15 holes of the final round he needed just three pars for 67 and 286.

A newspaper story that morning had casually identified Kirkwood as the son of the old trick-shot artist, but had mistakenly said that Kirkwood, Sr., had died in an automobile accident some months earlier. Neither Kirkwood nor his playing partners had seen the botched-up account, but a spectator had, and in those days the galleries walked along with the players on the fairway. The fan approached Joe after he had played the 15th hole and said how sorry he was to learn of Joe, Sr.'s, death in that automobile accident. Kirkwood was shaken; as far as he knew his father was alive and well, waiting to hear what happened at Merion. Now he had some reason to believe his father had died the night before. He lost all concentration, naturally, and played the next three holes in bogeys, then rushed to a telephone. He was relieved to learn that Joe, Sr., indeed was all right, but the mistaken newspaper report may have cost him the Open.

It was a day for all kinds of recriminations. Mangrum sat in the locker room, his hat pushed back on his head, and laughed bitterly about his collapse. "I was always a strong finisher; that was my game. But the way I played today . . . it was embarrassing." Hogan went back to his hotel, unwrapped the bandages from his legs, and soaked for hours in a hot tub. He had to or else he would develop severe leg cramps.

A gallery of 12,000 swarmed over Merion the next day to see if Hogan could complete the comeback. They did not have long to wait, for something had happened to Hogan overnight. No longer was he playing the course defensively; he was flying his shots at the flag and going for the birdies. "You know," he said to Joe Dey on the 4th tee, "this is the first time I've felt I could attack this course." His game was immaculate, and by the end of 15 holes he was a stroke ahead of Mangrum and 4 ahead of Fazio. The 16th was the critical hole of the playoff. It is a 440-yard par 4 with the fairway sloping downward from the tee, and the green is set behind the quarry, high above the drive zone. The quarry itself is wild and unkempt, full of rocks and underbrush, and only a narrow path leads through it to the green high above, flanked by mounds on either side. Mangrum had been in tall rough off the tee, and rather than risk a shot that might fall into the quarry, he played safe and then lofted a pitch 18 feet from the hole. As he was about to putt, a bug sat down on his golf ball. In 1950 the rules of the game did not permit cleaning the ball on the green; whenever a player marked his ball he very gingerly lifted it between two fingers, and just as gingerly replaced it. Impetuously Mangrum set his putter behind the ball to mark its position, lifted it to his lips and blew the bug off. Hogan winced; he realized that with all those USGA officials watching, Mangrum would be penalized. Nothing was said then, and Mangrum holed that long putt. Everyone thought he had saved his par 4, and the gallery was astonished to see the caddy who carried the scoring standard erase the one-over-par figure and replace it with 3 over par. The officials approached Mangrum and told him he would be penalized 2 strokes for lifting his ball when it was in play. Mangrum was startled. He said later he did not know the rule, and added that it was the first time he had ever been penalized. "I lifted my ball to blow off an insect. What would I have done if it had been a snake?" Nobody knew, and a moment later nobody cared, for on the 17th Hogan rolled in a putt of at least 50 feet, up the slope that leads from the lower level, and right into the cup. Now he was 4 strokes ahead with only the 18th to play. The adrenalin was flowing like a flood now. A big drive down the heart of the fairway, and instead of the one-iron he used the day before, a five-iron to the green. He had a big putt left, but what difference did it make? He left it 12 feet short of the hole, and then after Mangrum and Fazio had holed out, he ran it in for his par 4. Hogan had played the extra round in 69; Mangrum had 73 and Fazio 75. The Age of Hogan had arrived, and for the next six years it was Hogan against the field. He was favored to win every tournament he entered, just as Jones had been 20 to 30 years before, just as Palmer would be in the 60s, and Nicklaus in the 70s.

1951

Hogan may have played better golf later in his career, but he won no more dramatic tournament than this. He came back in 1951 and played the brutally difficult Oakland Hills course in 287 and won again, but he was expected to win that year. Oakland Hills by 1951 needed modernizing. It was a Donald Ross creation and basically sound in design, but the members felt it was not quite strong enough for the Open. And so they called in

Robert Trent Jones to toughen it. The result was one of the most controversial Open courses in history. The fairways were pinched in the drive zone by bunkers and rough, and the players had to find their way through them rather than over them. Actually the course was so severe it eliminated some skill from the game, rather than added skill to it. One of the strengths of Hogan's game is the ability to hit the side of the fairway that opens the green to the approach. At Oakland Hills the drive zone was too narrow; all he could hope to do was thread his drive between the bunkers. His 76—6 over par—in his first round left him 5 strokes behind Snead and worried.

A 73 in the second round and Hogan was still 5 strokes off the lead, but by then Snead had done the usual, shot 78 and fallen back to 149, the same as Hogan. Bobby Locke was in front at this point with 73, 71—144, and Hogan was tied with ten others and behind 15 more. It was not a comfortable spot, and Hogan knew it. "It would take two sub-par rounds for me," he said, "and even then it might not be good enough."

He gave it a try, though. Out in 32, he lost a stroke to par on the 14th, missing a 4-foot putt, and then butchered the 15th, a dogleg-left par 4 with a deep bunker in the middle of the fairway at the turn. Hogan hooked his drive into woods to the left, only moved it a short distance with his second, still in the rough, hit his next into a bunker, and took a 6. He had labored through 13 holes to get 3 under par, and then lost it all on two holes. It was not over yet: he finished par, bogey, par for 71. He had gone into the 14th hole 3 under par, and came off the 18th one over. You don't lose 4 strokes to par in five holes and win in this league. Locke, still out in his third round when Hogan began his fourth, would finish sharing the 54-hole lead at 218 with Jimmy Demaret; Julius Boros and Paul Runyan were next at 219, followed by Hogan at 220, along with Dave Douglas and Clayton Heafner.

Ben was still very much in contention. Two quick pars, and then a slip on the 3rd where he missed a putt for a par. Three more par 4s, and then a soft pitch to the 7th 2 feet from the hole. The crowd roared and Hogan smiled. "Wait 'til I make it," he said softly . . . and then he holed it. Even par now, and he finished the first nine in 35. On the 10th he hit what he called his best shot of the tournament, a blazing two-iron that covered the flag all the way and braked itself 5 feet from the hole. Another birdie and another roar from the huge crowd that swelled with every hole. Two more pars, and then a lovely iron from 15 feet from the hole on the 13th, a par 3. Hogan holed it and was then 2 under par. He slipped on the 14th when his approach rolled over the green, and then he faced that terrifying 15th once more. No driver this time; instead a three-wood that came down safely short of the bunkers at the turn of the dogleg, and then another three-wood onto the green 5 feet from the hole. His putt rolled right into the cup, and Hogan was 2 under par once more.

Ben was playing an inspired round of golf, the kind of golf that happens only on those rare instances when a great player is at the peak of his game on a great occasion. A big drive on the 16th, a marvelously conceived par 4 of 405 yards with a second shot that must carry a willow-lined lake, and then an iron that floated down feather-soft 7 feet from the hole. His putt skimmed by, and he made his 4. Then a par 3 on the blind uphill 17th, and Hogan stood on the 18th tee needing a par 4 for 68, the only subpar score of the championship thus far, and probably his third-straight victory in the Open. He split the fairway with his drive, clearing those bunkers calculated to swallow the long drives, and then his approach skidded to a stop 15 feet from the hole. He was mobbed; fans swarmed over the course, and Hogan had to struggle through the crowd to reach the green. Douglas putted out first and gave center stage to Hogan. He squatted behind the hole to line up his putt, then looked at it from behind the ball. Finally he set the putter down behind the ball, waited those long seconds as he normally did, and stroked the ball. It died on the left side, and tumbled in. A 67, a 287, and victory! Clayton Heafner came in later with 69, but he finished two strokes behind Hogan at 289. They were the only players in the field able to break par in one round.

Hogan has called his triumph at Merion the greatest tournament he ever played, but he calls that final 67 the finest single round he ever played in competition. His progress through the championship should shed some light on his character. He was the only man in the field who bettered his score each day—76, 73, 71, 67—287. When it was over he said those lines that have become so well-known—"I'm glad I brought this course, this monster, to its knees."

Hogan had now won three Opens, and only two players had won four —Willie Anderson in the very early years of American golf, and Bobby Jones. Could Hogan match them?

1952

The 1952 Open was scheduled for the Northwood Club in Dallas, and that is Hogan territory. When he played the first two rounds in 69, 69 he was considered a certainty to win once more. Hogan would be forty in two months, when that 1952 Open began, an age considered almost senility for an athlete. Certainly the forties did not figure to be the peak years of a games player's life, especially when the weather turned hot and humid. Saturday was hot; the temperature would reach 94 during mid-afternoon, and Hogan evidently felt the effects. He played the morning round in 74, and when Julius Boros came in with 68, he led Hogan by 2 strokes. It was a strange kind of 68—one that easily could have been 75. Boros was constantly in trouble, hitting approaches into bunkers, but he was one of the finest wedge players of the age, and he constantly found a way to get down in 2 strokes. He used only 11 putts on the second nine, and in his closing 71 he had used but 29 putts.

Boros, the son of immigrant Hungarian parents, grew up in Bridgeport, Connecticut, had been an accountant, and at the same time a rather good amateur golfer. Approaching thirty, he decided to quit business and play golf for a living. He finished ninth at Merion in his first Open, and then climbed into a tie for fourth at Oakland Hills. Clearly he could play the great courses, the kind that called for excellence in tee-to-green play, much the same as Hogan. He had recently lost his wife, the former Ann (Buttons) Cosgrove, in childbirth, and so his victory was considered fitting. He won big—281 to the 285 turned in by Porky Oliver. Oliver played the last two rounds with Hogan and beat him out for second place by holing a 50-foot putt on the last green. Hogan had 286.

Hogan was disappointed. For the first time since 1947 he had not won either the Open or the Masters (barring 1949 when he was inactive). There was even some thought that he was through. Hogan decided he needed a long rest. He took off ten months, worked on his game, and in 1953 would have the greatest year in major competitions any golfer has had since Jones in 1930. In April he won the Masters with a record score of 274; in June he won the Open by six strokes; in July he won the British Open and set a course record at Carnoustie in the last round.

1953

The 1953 Open was at Oakmont where Sam Parks had won in 1935, and where Tommy Armour had won in 1927. The entry had grown so that a new scheme of qualifying was being tried out. Those who had qualified in sectional rounds and a number of players exempt from sectional eliminations were required to play two more rounds at the championship site—one round at Oakmont, the other at the Pittsburgh Field Club nearby. Only Boros was exempt from the on-the-site qualifying. Hogan had no trouble getting into the field, and once the Open began he had no trouble with it, either. He shot 67 in the first round and led by 3 strokes over George Fazio, Walter Burkemo, and Frank Souchak, an Oakmont member and older brother of Mike Souchak. A 72 in the second round cut Hogan's lead to 2 strokes over Fazio, who shot 71, and Snead, who followed his opening 72 with a 69 in the second round. Snead picked up another stroke on Hogan with 72 in the third round, when Hogan was shooting 73, and then lurked only a stroke behind with 18 more holes coming up that afternoon. Snead was understandably nervous. He was forty-one years old by then, and this might be the last chance he would ever have to win the Open. It turned out to be no chance at all. Once more Sam squandered his opportunity, turned in a shoddy 76, and finished with 289.

There was simply no stopping Hogan this year. Par at Oakmont was 71, and after 15 holes he was 2 over. He made par at the 16th, a strong par 3, and then aimed his drive on the 17th to hit the left rough. The 17th is a little par 4, less than 300 yards in length, but uphill all the way. The green is long and narrow, and although it can be reached by a powerful drive, the ground falls away to the right. Hogan wanted his tee shot in that left rough to give him a good angle at the pin. The shot didn't come off quite right. It flew slightly right of Hogan's intended spot . . . and rolled onto the green. Even his bad shots turned out good this day. Two putts for a birdie 3, and then another birdie 3 on the murderously hard 18th, a 468-yard par 4, and Hogan was in with 283. He had won by 6 strokes and he was the first player to lead every round since Jim Barnes back in 1921.

He had won the Open four times, as many as Anderson, as many as Jones. Unlike Jones, though, Hogan wanted to continue. His schedule had been cut back some years before, it's true, but Hogan was not going to retire completely. He would continue to play in the Open and the Masters, and a few other tournaments important to him—the Colonial National Invitational, the Seminole Pro-Am, the Crosby. Above all, he would play in the Open, for Hogan was and is a proud man. He was not content to match Jones, he wanted to win more—at least five. The end of the Hogan era didn't seem in sight that June afternoon.

1954

Hogan was of course favored the next spring at Baltusrol in the New Jersey suburbs of New York, but he finished in a tie for sixth, his chances ruined by a miserable 76 in the third round. Gene Littler, who had won the Amateur championship the previous September, led at 36 holes with 70, 69—139, and he, too, shot 76 in the third round. Meanwhile Ed Furgol was making a bid. Furgol was thirty-seven years old, grew up in Utica, New York, and had been crippled in a childhood playground accident. His left arm was permanently bent because of a severe elbow injury in the accident, and it was a few inches shorter than the right. He hit every shot with his right hand, confounding the theorists, but he hit them long and straight. His first three rounds were 71, 70, 71, and as he stood on the 18th tee he needed a par 5 for 284, a score that could win. He hooked his tee shot into the pines that act as a barrier between the 18th hole of the Lower Course and the 18th of the Upper Course, where the '36 Open was held, and as he stood in the woods, Furgol remembered some talk going around the locker room. Hogan had been in those same woods earlier in the tournament, and he had asked USGA officials if it would be permissible to play to the Upper Course. He was told it was all right. Recalling the story, Furgol pitched out, and then lofted a shot onto the green. He was down in two for his par 5. Moments earlier Dick Mayer had come to the 18th needing a par 5 for 284 and had pushed his drive to the right under a low growing evergreen. It was unplayable and Mayer made a 7. A little later Gene Littler needed pars on the final four holes to tie. He saved his par on the 15th with a fading iron shot from a depression near a tree, and then lost a stroke on the 210-yard 16th. He made 5 on the 610-yard 17th, and then put his third shot in a bunker on the 18th. He came out well, about 8 feet from the hole, but missed the putt. Furgol had won.

1955

Furgol was, of course, an unexpected winner, but he had been on the pro tour since 1945, winning some money occasionally. His name was at least familiar to golf fans. But Jack Fleck? How in the world could he ever win the Open, especially at a golf course like Olympic where the 1955 championship was played? No; Olympic was custom-made for Hogan; short at 6,700 yards, its narrow fairways bordered by thick and clumpy rough of Italian rye grass imported some 30 years earlier. The blades of this grass are almost half an inch wide, and in some areas, admittedly well off the target zone, it was a foot deep. From this there was no escape with anything less than a medium to short iron. The greens were small and fast.

Hogan, however, was playing rather indifferently when the Open began. He shot 73 and 72 in the first two rounds, and really was lucky to be in good position when the final day began. Tommy Bolt had led the first round with 67, 3 strokes better than anyone else, but he had thrown away this great opportunity with a miserable 77 the next day. Sam Snead did the opposite: 79 in the first round, 69 in the second. Meanwhile, Fleck opened with a 76, and then came back with 69, and when the final day began he was tied with Hogan and Boros at 145, a stroke behind Bolt and Harvie Ward, the amateur. A solid 72 in the morning and Hogan led at 54 holes with 217; Boros and Snead were a stroke behind at 218, followed by Bolt and Bob Rosburg at 219, and Fleck and Ward at 220.

Hogan was off an hour ahead of Fleck and three holes ahead of Snead. Once more it looked as if Snead might have a chance, and in those days there was nothing more thrilling than a confrontation between Snead and Hogan. Hogan had beaten Snead by 6 strokes in the 1953 Open; Snead had beaten Hogan in a playoff for the 1954 Masters, and here they were in a tense duel once more. Snead fell 3 strokes behind by playing the first two holes in 5 and 5 while Hogan was going 4 and 4. Ben turned in 35, Sam in 37, but then Snead began to play some superb shots: an eight-iron 9 feet past the hole on 12; a four-iron that almost went in for an ace on 13 and rolled 5 feet past; a five-iron 7 feet from the hole on 14. Great as his iron play was, he made none of those putts, and it must have taken some of the heart from Sam. He bogeyed 16 and 17 and was out of it.

Hogan, meanwhile, was conceding nothing to Sam in shotmaking. He lost a stroke to Snead when his tee shot went over the par 3 13th, and then the controlled fade he labored so hard to perfect drifted too much to the right and settled in the rough on the 14th. From there Hogan hit a perfectly beautiful golf shot. The rough at that point was 5 inches deep, the kind where you normally use a medium iron for escape. Hogan took a four wood, cut it through the grass and onto the green 20 feet from the hole. He holed it for a birdie, then finished with three standard pars, a 70, and 287. It was all over . . . or so everyone thought. Hogan had apparently won his fifth Open. Didn't Gene Sarazen tell the listening and watching audience on television? Didn't Hogan himself donate the ball he used on that final hole to the USGA? Wasn't Jack Fleck the only man still on the course with a mathematical chance to tie, and didn't he need 67 to do it?

Fleck by then was through the 11th, 2 under par. He had to clip another stroke from par to match Hogan, and for a relatively untested operator of two municipal courses in Davenport, Iowa, that seemed a bit much. His prospects became even more discouraging when he dropped a stroke on the 14th. Now with four hard holes coming up he needed two birdies. He made one right away, dropping his tee shot on the 15th 5 feet from the cup and holing the putt. A par 5 at the 16th after missing the green with his third, and then he hit two solid woods to the back of the 17th, a long par 4 of 461 yards, uphill all the way. His 40-footer just missed the hole.

Hogan was sitting at his locker quietly accepting congratulations from the press and the other players when reports of Fleck's progress began coming through. He had driven into the rough at the 18th. He had played a seven iron onto the green about 7 feet from the hole. A roar and then, "The kid's sunk it," someone said. Hogan looked around at the group. "I was wishing he'd make either a 2 or a 5. I was wishing it was over—all over."

The next day the era of Hogan came to a close the way it had begun— with Ben Hogan hooking into the left rough. Through five holes Fleck played without a mistake and he was a stroke ahead. Then he ran into trouble at the 6th, hitting into a bunker and coming out 25 feet from the hole. He sank it. Hogan holed a 50-footer on the 8th, and Fleck matched it from 8 feet. Fleck holed another from 25 feet on the 9th, and still another from 20 feet on the 10th. Hogan was staggered; he was playing reasonably well, even par, and he was 3 strokes behind with eight holes to play. He chipped 2 strokes off Fleck's lead with a birdie on the 14th and a par on the 17th where Fleck went one over. Then they stood on the 18th tee with Hogan needing the birdie this time.

Hogan was up first, and as he swung into the ball, his foot slipped on the sandy tee. The ball careened wildly into the deep, deep rough. It was all over; there was simply no way to reach the green from there—in fact it took him three swats just to reach the fairway. Hogan played his fifth shot to the back of the green, discouraged and disheartened. Then you could almost see him pull himself together. Hopelessly beaten, Hogan stood up to that last putt and stroked it right into the hole. Never mind that Fleck would have to five-putt to give him a chance; Hogan was never more a champion than he was in playing that stroke.

Fleck made his par 4 and joined the Sam Parkses and Tony Maneros among the really dark-horse winners of the Open. As for Hogan, he left some doubt that he would play in the Open any more.

"I don't think I can go through that again," he said, "and that's not discouraging talk. It's that damned preparation. From now on, I'm a pleasure golfer."

1956

Of course he was not. He continued in the Open, and in fact came close to tying the next year, along with Boros and Ted Kroll. The Open in 1956 belonged to Cary Middlecoff, and as it happened in 1949, it was a case of Middlecoff putting his score on the board early, and then waiting nervously while the others made a run at it.

Meantime, the Open had undergone some changes during the Age of Hogan. When Ben won his first championship in 1948, the purse was $10,000 and his share was $2,000. When Fleck won in 1955, prize money had more than doubled to $25,480, including bonus money for the playoff. Something else more ominous had happened, too. When Hogan won his first in 1948, the field included 171 players. In 1949 it was cut to 162, and in 1959 it would drop to 150. The reason? Slow play. Each year a round of golf seemed to take longer, until five hours for 18 holes was not uncommon.

"Dark horse" Jack Fleck wins 1955 Open at Olympic

In 1956 the field still included 162 players, and as far as Demaret and Middlecoff were concerned, it should have been just 161. They would have been happy if Henry Cotton had not entered. Cotton, the great English golfer who first won the British Open in 1934, hit his second shot on the 17th hole into a bunker in the first round. He came out, putted once and missed, and then reached across the hole to tap the ball in. What happened next is open to interpretation. Either he lost his balance and jammed the putter into the green to regain it—his version—or else he reached across to tap the ball into the hole and stubbed it—the possibility proposed by Demaret and Middlecoff. Anyhow, Cotton was brought before the USGA committee and questioned about the incident. In a case like this, what do you do but take a man's word? No penalty, but it was pretty heady stuff in the press tent, where one of the boys recalled that old seafaring slogan, "Britannia *waives* the rules."

This could have been the most unusual day in the annals of the Open. In addition to the Cotton incident:

•   Walker Inman did not hear his name called and was late reporting to the first tee, although he had been at the course for some time and was practice-putting when he should have been driving.

•   Doug Ford hit a ball in the general direction of a creek, took one look, decided it was in the water, and dropped another ball. A spectator saw the original ball, told Ford, who picked up the ball he had dropped and played the original ball in violation of the rules.

•   Jack Burke signed a scorecard that gave him a 4 on a hole where he actually made 5. (Gil Cavanaugh did the same in the second round.)

Every one of them was eligible for disqualification, but in a mood of generosity, the USGA gave them all a 2-stroke penalty and sent them back onto the golf course. (The consequences of this day would be felt a year later in the Women's Open at Winged Foot when Jackie Pung would have her championship taken away from her because she signed a wrong scorecard, even though it was clear to everyone that she actually shot the lowest score. After that day at Oak Hill the USGA had decided to be more strict with rules violators.)

Middlecoff played four very steady rounds. He opened with 71, and then added three rounds of 70. He finished early and waited while Hogan, Boros, and finally Kroll had a run at it. With two holes to play Hogan was tied with Middlecoff, but his chances ended on the 17th. The hole is normally a par 5 for members, but in the Open it played as a 468-yard par 4. Hogan's second shot, an iron, rolled over the back edge. He chipped past the cup about 30 inches, and then set himself up for the par putt. He seemed ready to hit . . . and then he stepped away from the ball. There are times when you know in your soul that you cannot make even the shortest putt, and it seemed Hogan knew it then. He set himself up once more, and the ball never once looked as if it might go in. It started right and broke right. A 5, and now he needed a birdie on the 18th. His drive went into the right rough and he cut a four-wood out beautifully to the lower left corner of the green, 30 feet from the hole. He gave the putt a good chance, but missed. He was a stroke off at 282. Boros next. He needed two birdies on the last five holes to tie. He hit five of the last six greens and made one birdie—on the 14th—and twice had putts stop on the very lip of the hole. The most frustrating of all was on the 18th, where he hit a marvelous drive down the right side, and then a low, boring three-iron that came to a stop 17 feet from the cup. Taking no more time than if it were a friendly Saturday Nassau, Boros stroked the ball at the hole. It actually hit the inside of the cup and spun out. Boros dropped the putter from his hand, staggered a little, smiling all the while, and then tapped his next putt in for a 282 that matched Hogan's. Next came Kroll. He wanted only four pars to win with 280—just 3, 4, 4, 4. Instead he finished 4, 7, 5, 4. He hooked his drive on the 16th hole under a low-growing spruce and tried to play the shot out while kneeling. He needed 2 strokes to knock the ball loose, and by then it was all over. He finished with 285, 4 strokes behind Middlecoff.

Oak Hill was another Donald Ross creation, and perhaps that had nothing to do with it, but it is interesting to note that of the first 11 finishers in that 1956 Open, nine won either the Open, British Open, PGA, or Masters during their careers—Middlecoff, Hogan, Boros, Furgol, Peter Thomson, Arnold Palmer, Ken Venturi, Doug Ford, and Jerry Barber. Only Kroll and Wesley Ellis won none of the prestige tournaments, but Kroll did win that "world" championship at Tam O'Shanter, and at that time it was the highest-paying tournament in golf.

1957

The career of Middlecoff was brief, but it was brilliant. Few men have been able to play quite so well, although his prominence ended so suddenly it is almost possible to say it ended on a Sunday afternoon in 1957 at the Inverness Club in Toledo, Ohio, the day he lost a playoff for the Open to Dick Mayer. When he was on his game, Middlecoff was practically unbeatable. He was the longest straight driver of his day, and his irons were crisp and pure. And he was capable of magnificent streaks of putting; if he holed one putt from 30 feet, he might hole a dozen. They still talk of the putt he made on the 13th at Augusta when he won the 1955 Masters. It must have been 75 or 80 feet.

Middlecoff's greatest drawback, and at the same time his greatest strength, was his emotions. He seemed to be a mass of dangling, exposed nerve ends, and he fidgeted endlessly over what appeared to be the simplest of shots. But when those dangling nerve ends were under control, Middlecoff was capable of anything, including one of the greatest finishes in Open history. Middlecoff had played the first two rounds in 71, 75—146, and he was 8 strokes behind Billy Joe Patton, the amateur, and Mayer, who shared the 36-hole lead at 138, a record score. Patton fell from contention with 76, 76—152 the last day, and the Open developed into a three-man race among Middlecoff, Mayer, and Demaret, who was having his last fling.

Demaret opened with 68 on a day when play was delayed over an hour during a wild rainstorm with winds gusting over 60 miles per hour. He dropped behind with 73 in the second round, but then with a 70 on the morning of the final day he took the lead by a stroke over Mayer, 211 to 212, with 18 holes to play. Middlecoff, meanwhile, had worked himself back into contention with 68 in the morning. He was lurking at 214, and he was doing everything right. Demaret was off first in the afternoon, and after 14 holes was 4 over par, and headed for 285, which surely would be too high. Somehow he collected himself for the final push and finished birdie, par, birdie, and par for 283. With that he went into the clubhouse and stood watching the 18th green from an upstairs window.

Next came Mayer. When Demaret holed out, Dick was two holes behind. He needed pars on the 17th and 18th to tie, a birdie and a par to go ahead. He made his par on the 17th, a 451-yard par 4 with a severely tilted green, and then played a three wood from the 18th tee. The 18th at Inverness is a 330-yard par 4 with bunkers flanking the fairway and a huge cavern of a bunker set across the front of the plateaued green. Mayer had played the three wood to keep the tee shot in play, and then hit a marvelous wedge that carried just 9 or 10 feet past the hole. His putt was perfect, taking a small break and tumbling into the hole. Demaret saw the putt drop, and his eyes turned a little misty. "The boy certainly made a wonderful, wonderful putt," he said.

Middlecoff came roaring down the final few holes. He was still playing with the same sureness as in the morning. He was out in 34—even par—and he needed another 34 on the home nine to match Mayer. He was on the 13th when Mayer finished, and he needed those two birdies on the last six holes. He missed from 20 feet on the 13th, and then had to scramble for pars on the 14th and 15th. He made one birdie with a good-sized putt on the 16th, and then made another par on the 17th. Now it was all riding on the 18th; he could not win now, all he could do was tie. Cary ignored the fairway bunkers and hit an enormous drive estimated at 290 yards and played a soft wedge about 10 feet to the right of the hole. It was a wicked-looking putt that had to break almost a foot. He looked at it from the front, the back, and both sides, stood up to it, then backed off and looked at it again. Finally he hit it. The ball seemed to be too far right, but it broke right into the hole. He had tied. Middlecoff had played the last 36 holes in 68, 68—136 and had tied the record set 25 years before by Gene Sarazen when he won at Fresh Meadow in 1932.

The playoff the next day was strictly no contest. It was as if Middlecoff had wired himself to play 72 holes, and when those 72 holes were over he had nothing left. He was pathetic in the playoff. At the end of nine holes Mayer was 3 strokes ahead even though he was a stroke over par. Middlecoff played the second nine in 41, and Mayer shot 37 and won by seven strokes—72, 79. Curiously, they both went into a decline after this. Middlecoff had trouble with his back and Mayer never again reached the heights he had scaled at Inverness. He tied for 23rd the next year when the Open was played at the Southern Hills Country Club in Tulsa in the searing heat of an Oklahoma spring.

1958

That was Tommy Bolt's Open; it was almost Gary Player's. Bolt missed the cut at Inverness, but in his native Oklahoma he was never out of first place. He shot 71 in the first round to tie Boros and Dick Metz. Another 71 gave him the lead at 36 holes with 142, and his 211 for 54 holes put him 3 strokes ahead of Gene Littler. And then a funny thing happened. With 18 holes to play, Bolt decided to change drivers because he had missed so many fairways. It was estimated he had wasted ten shots just getting back to the fairway from the roughs he had hit. Lloyd Mangrum talked him out of it at lunch, and so Bolt shot 72 in the afternoon and won by 4 strokes over Player, who was making his first start in the U.S. Open. Bolt claimed he had changed, that he had tamed his temper and sweetened his disposition, that he was no longer the club-throwing champion of the pro tour, and that he had found a new peace of mind. "I just decided golf wasn't worth breaking a blood vessel over," he said, "so I relaxed. I'm a different man." He carried a card that he often read. The card said, "God grant me the serenity to accept the things I cannot change, the courage to change things I can, and the wisdom to know the difference."

One week later Tommy Bolt stepped off a plane in New York on his way to the Pepsi Cola Open and allegedly threw a punch at one of the tournament's officials. So much for serenity.

Temper or not, though, you had to say of Tommy Bolt that he was perhaps the purest striker of the ball in the game at that time. There is no knowing what he might have accomplished if it had not been for his disposition. But he faded after that and never won another tournament of consequence.

1959

When Bolt won the Open, his prize money amounted to $8,000; the total purse was up to $35,000, and the tournament was becoming a television staple. When it came to Winged Foot in the Westchester suburbs of New York in 1959, prize money was up to $50,000 and first prize was worth $12,000, which was more than the total in 1948 when Hogan won his first Open. It wasn't the richest tournament on the schedule. The Masters was worth $76,000 and the PGA was offering $51,000, but it was keeping up with the competition.

Winged Foot was the scene of one of the most amazing exhibitions of putting ever seen in a golf competition. Billy Casper won by one stroke over Bob Rosburg, and he used just 114 putts for 72 holes. Consider that two putts per green for 72 holes comes to 144, and you can see that Casper was 30 strokes under par on the greens. Since he was 30 under on the greens and his score was 2 over, he must have been 32 over par on his tee-to-green play. Oh well, they still pay off on total score. Tommy Bolt, for instance, had used 100 putts for 54 holes. Casper used 28 putts in the first round, 30 in the second, 27 in the third, and 29 in the fourth, when he one-putted the first five greens—all of them to save pars.

It was a week of terribly bad weather, with lightning, high winds, and heavy rain. It came down hard on Saturday, traditionally the day of the double round, and for the first time since the Open began the final round had to be postponed until Sunday.

Hogan was back and looked for a while as if he would walk off with the title when he played the first nine in 32 the first day. He had missed the 1957 Open because of an attack of pleurisy the morning of the first day, and even though he was permitted a delay of an hour he had to withdraw. The next year he injured his wrist and finished 10th, only once dipping as low as 71. His 32 was about all he did at Winged Foot. He slipped to 37 on the second nine, then played two 71s and a dismal 76 on the last day, wrapped in a long-sleeved woolen shirt, a sweater, and rain pants to keep out the chill. Even though he was not all that sharp, he was still in the chase until that last round. He had a score of 211 for 54 holes, and only Casper was ahead of him, at 208. Rosburg and Arnold Palmer were next at 212, followed at 213 by Mike Souchak and Claude Harmon, the pro at Winged Foot. But there was no way to stop the kind of putting Casper was capable of that week. Rosburg pulled even at the 12th hole, but he made 5 on the 13th, a par 3, and could never recover.

1960

By 1959 it was becoming quite evident that golf was about to enter another age. The Age of Hogan was over, no doubt of that, and at that time Arnold Palmer was the greatest attraction in the game. Palmer had won the National Amateur in 1954 and almost immediately turned pro. He won his first tournament in 1956—the Insurance City Open in Hartford—and a month later won his second, the Eastern Open in Baltimore.

In 1958 he won his first Masters and twice he had good finishes in the Open: seventh in 1956, fifth in 1959. Then in April of 1960 Palmer won the Masters for a second time with a birdie, birdie finish, and there was no doubt that he was the best player in the game. He was strong and durable, and he had streaks where he might hole anything (and he usually believes he can).

Golf in the postwar era can be divided into three periods: the Age of Hogan, the Age of Palmer, and the Age of Nicklaus. For one glorious moment in 1960, all three came together at the Cherry Hills Country Club in Denver. It was the last dying gasp of Hogan, the first glimmer of the marvelous potential of Nicklaus, and the brightest moment in the era of Palmer. He would never win another Open, but Palmer won this one like no one ever has.

At 7,004 yards, Cherry Hills seemed like it would be a very good test for the modern pro, but in that mile-high atmosphere the ball travels great distances, and it soon became apparent that the golf course could be had. Hogan's record 276 seemed certain to be beaten, and when the 150 players started off it looked as if Mike Souchak would be the man to do it. Souchak played the first nine in 31 with a streak of chipping and putting that recalled Casper a year earlier. He needed only 11 putts on the out nine, and when he came back in 37 he needed only 13 more. He had 24 putts for the round of 68, and right away the first nine of Cherry Hills was exposed— it was weak. Henry Ransom, suffering with hay fever, was 4 under par through 14 holes, but lost strokes at 15 and 17 to finish with 69, tied with Jerry Barber, who missed 11 fairways and somehow wrung another 69 from the course.

Meanwhile, Palmer, the favorite, the man who went into the Open with such confidence and with such gallery support, was playing Cherry

Hogan lines up putt during 1960 Open

Palmer comes from 7 strokes off to win 1960 Open

Hills in 72. True that was only a stroke above par, but it was not a very stimulating round, and a lot of people were ahead of him, including Jack Fleck and Don Cherry, the voice in the Mr. Clean commercials. Hogan was back there with him, and old Sam Snead, still at it, shot 75. Still, Sam was 10 strokes better than Tommy Bolt, whose temper that day reached heights never before scaled. Tom drove out of bounds on 11 and then dunked a shot into the water hazard on the 12th, a par 3, and took 5. He had played the first nine in 35, and so a potentially good score was flying by. His round reached its explosive end at the 18th, a par 4 across a wide and beckoning lake. Tommy teed up a ball and drove it into the water. He teed up another ball and drove it into the water. He teed up another ball and belted one across the lake onto the fairway. Tommy Bolt is one of the sweetest swingers of a golf club who ever lived. After his third ball had reached land, he drew back his club once more, and still using the Vardon grip and with his right elbow in perfect position, snug against his right side, he flung the offending club after those first two balls. He was absolutely majestic. He finished with 85, and actually turned in his score, but later he withdrew.

That lake is stocked with fish, and as Doug Sanders stood on the tee he needed only his 4 to tie Souchak. As he was about to swing a big fish leaped clear of the water and came down again with a loud splash. Unnerved, Sanders sent his first ball after the fish and made 6. "I thought somebody was unloading a truckload of empty beer cans," he moaned.

The scoring became hotter the next day. Souchak was out in 33, back in 34 for 67, and a halfway total of 135. He was 3 strokes ahead of Sanders, who had followed his 70 with the 68 he might have had the day before, and 5 ahead of Dow Finsterwald, Jerry Barber, and the surprising Fleck. Souchak had set a new 36-hole record of 135, 3 strokes below Snead's old record of 138, which had stood since Riviera in 1948. The cutoff also was a new low, 147, a stroke better than Riviera.

Souchak was not so sharp the morning of the final day, but even so he stood on the 18th tee even par and needed the 4 for a 71 and 206, a rather healthy prospect, for he would probably lead the Open by 4 strokes with 18 holes to play. Just as he was about to hit his tee shot, a movie camera began to whirr. It had been smuggled onto the course by a spectator. Souchak drove into the water, made 6, and instead of 206 he had 208, and instead of leading by 4 he led by 2. With 18 holes remaining on a hot afternoon, the standings looked like this:

SOUCHAK	67, 68, 73—208
BOROS	73, 69, 68—210
FINSTERWALD	71, 69, 70—210
BARBER	69, 71, 70—210
NICKLAUS	71, 71, 69—211

HOGAN	75, 67, 69—211
FLECK	70, 70, 72—212
CHERRY	70, 71, 71—212
POTT	75, 68, 69—212
PLAYER	70, 72, 71—213
HARRISON	74, 70, 70—214
CASPER	71, 70, 73—214
SNEAD	72, 69, 73—214
SHAVE	72, 71, 71—214

Palmer was another stroke behind this group at 215 after rounds of 72, 71, 72 and clearly was going nowhere—or so it seemed. If Souchak didn't run away with it, golf fans were in for one of the wildest scrambles in the history of the Open. Well, Souchak didn't run away with it—far from it. At one point, ten players had a chance, but in the end it resolved into a contest among three—the three best players of the postwar era— Hogan, Palmer, and Nicklaus. And it was Palmer who came through with the most explosive round of golf ever seen in the Open.

As the final round began Palmer was 7 strokes behind, and even his most dedicated followers were not giving him a chance to make up those strokes. He was also behind 14 other players, and you just don't pass that many in one round of the National Open.

The first hole at Cherry Hills is just 346 yards long, and in that thin mountain air the ball travels a long way. Palmer drove the green and got down in two putts from 20 feet. Birdie. He chipped in on the 2nd hole from 35 feet for another birdie. He was just short of the 3rd off the tee and chipped within a foot of the hole for still another birdie. A wedge 18 feet from the hole on the 4th, and then he holed the putt for his fourth straight birdie. He drove the rough on the 5th and made par. On the 174-yard 6th his seven-iron was 25 feet from the cup and he holed it, and then capped it with a wedge 6 feet from the hole on the 7th and made that one. Six birdies in seven holes, and now Arnold Palmer was right in the middle of the battle. He was out in 30 and on his way to a 65, the lowest score ever shot in the last round by the eventual champion. But at the end of nine holes it was not quite over. Kroll started his final round at about the time Palmer finished nine, and he almost matched Arnold, making five birdies on the first seven, and Fleck birdied five of the first six.

Hogan and Nicklaus were playing together and Jack was out in 32, helped by an eagle 3 on the 5th hole. He bogeyed the 10th, made a par on the 11th, and then came to the 12th, a 212-yard par 3. Nicklaus hit a two iron 20 feet past the hole, and Hogan hit a three wood inside him. They both holed their birdie putts, and at that moment twenty-year-old Jack Nicklaus led the Open. He was 5 under par for the 66 holes and not at all in awe of the prospect of becoming Open champion. Then he three-putted the 13th and he was tied with Boros, Fleck, and Palmer, just a stroke ahead of Hogan. Nicklaus three-putted the 14th from 40 feet, missing his second from 7 feet, and then he was out of even a share of the lead.

Hogan, meanwhile, was coming on. He hit his tee shot to the 196-yard 15th 20 feet from the hole and ran it in for a birdie. It was his first sizable putt of the day and it dropped him to 4 under par. He was then tied with Palmer and Fleck, for Boros had fallen behind with a bogey on the 14th. Hogan now had three holes to play, and that fifth Open title was clearly within his reach. He hit the green on the 16th 12 feet from the hole, and once more a birdie putt failed to drop. Hogan had played magnificently so far. He had hit 34 greens that day—every one he played—but he had made only one long putt. His approach putting was awful, and he was a bit discouraged because nothing would fall for him. He had two holes left and he had to do something soon.

The 17th is a 548-yard par 5 with an island green set some 20 feet into the lake that also acts as the water hazard on the 18th. Hogan hit a drive and then a three iron that came down about 20 yards short of the water. He shook his head in disgust. He understood he was tied with five others for the lead while in truth it was just he, Palmer, and Fleck, and Fleck was about to lose it all. The pin on the 17th was cut very close to the front of the green, just beyond the water. Hogan felt he had to go for the birdie here to shake off some of those four challengers. The ball was sitting up about a sixteenth of an inch in a very good lie. Hogan laid back his wedge and hit what looked like a perfect shot, dead on line, and if it would just clear the front edge of the green it would be very close to the hole.

It didn't quite make it; the ball hit a foot or so short, smacked into the bank of the hazard, and rolled back into the water. Hogan took off his shoe and sock, and thousands of fans gathered around the green cheered when he stepped into the water to play out and try to save his par. He didn't. Hogan made 6, and then, disheartened, hit a shot into that lake from the 18th tee, finished with 73, and instead of winning a fifth Open, finished in a tie for ninth place. Later he thought about that 17th once more. "When will I ever learn not to go for a birdie in a situation like that?" he asked.

Palmer, meanwhile, was behind Hogan, playing very steady golf—nothing brilliant like his magnificent beginning, but he wasn't losing any strokes to par either. He had birdied the par-5 11th after reaching the green in 2, and when he came to the 18th he needed a par 4 for 280. He hit a useful drive, and then an iron that stopped just off the edge of the green. A few minutes earlier Nicklaus had come to the 18th needing a birdie for 280. His second shot was short and his chip was 6 feet away. Nicklaus wasn't aware of how close he was to winning the Open, and so he putted rather quickly for him, and missed. Instead of 280 he finished with 282. Palmer did not make that mistake. He chipped to within 4 feet, and then holed the putt. When the ball fell into the hole, Arnold whipped off his sun visor and flung it toward the screaming crowd.

He had come from 7 strokes off the lead and he had passed 14 other players in one stirring round. A lot of the Palmer legend was born that day, and it seemed as if he could go on forever.

1961

Palmer was favored in every tournament he entered, and as 1961 began he deserved to be. He won at San Diego, Phoenix, and Baton Rouge, tied for first in the Seminole Pro-Am, won the Texas Open, and lost a playoff to Doug Ford in the 500 Festival. Sometimes he lost in a classic manner. He could have won the Masters for a third time, but he hit his approach on the 18th into a bunker, exploded across the green, made 6 on the hole, and lost by a stroke to Gary Player.

He was by far the betting choice when the Open came back to Oakland Hills ten years after Hogan's great finishing round. Something had happened to Oakland Hills in those ten years; it simply wasn't the severe test it had been in 1951. It was tough enough, make no mistake, but it yielded low rounds much more easily. For instance, in the first round a young man named Bobby Brue shot 69. Only Hogan and Clayton Heafner had been able to break 70 in 1951. Then in the second round eight players broke 70; two of them had 67s, matching Hogan's closing score. Bob Rosburg was one of the 67 shooters (Bob Harris was the other), and Rosburg shared the lead after 36 holes with Doug Sanders at 137.

Palmer was not making a very spirited defense of his title. He seemed stale and apparently had difficulty keeping his mind on the game at hand. His first two rounds were 74 and 75, no better than he needed to make the 36-hole cut. Such was the mood of the times, though, that no one counted Palmer out of contention even though he was trailing by 10 strokes. Amend that. One person *did* count him out—Palmer himself. As he sat among a knot of writers in the upstairs locker room, someone mentioned that Arnold had two rounds left to make up those 10 strokes, and didn't he make up 7 in one round the year before? "Yes," agreed Palmer, "but last year I thought I could do it; I don't think I can this year."

Palmer did not make up the 10 strokes, although he played two rounds of 70 the next day and finished in a tie for 14th place with Hogan and Dave Douglas, a veteran player who had been paired with Hogan the last two rounds at Oakland Hills in 1951. It was the first time since 1940 that Hogan had finished outside the first ten when he had played.

A 71 in the morning round gave Sanders a 54-hole score of 210, but

Gene Littler

the field was tightly bunched. In all, 13 players were under 215 going into that final round. Gene Littler had opened with 73, then 68, and added a 72 in the morning round of the final day. He came to the last hole needing a par 4 for 280 and a score no one could touch. He dropped his second shot into the left green-side bunker and made a bogey 5. By now Sanders was the only challenger with a chance, and he needed a birdie on the last hole to tie. Sanders tried to cut the corner of the left-to-right dogleg with his drive, but the ball did not clear the woods. It dropped among some trees and in rough, but Sanders played a superb recovery to the very edge of the green. Now if he could chip it in he would tie and force a playoff. The chip barely missed the cup. Sanders finished with 282 and shared second place with Bob Goalby, a new player on the tour. Mike Souchak shot 284 and shared fourth place with Nicklaus.

Littler, the new champion, was another enigma. He had a classic swing, one that was envied by almost every other player, and there were some fans who would as soon watch Littler on the practice tee as anyone else in the heat of competition. It was smooth and fluid, as graceful a motion as had come along since Sam Snead. To watch him take the club away from the ball is to understand the meaning of the term "one-piece swing." He was an adequate putter; no, make that a good putter, and his temperament seemed ideal. He was calm, perhaps placid is a better word, and he never seemed upset. Certainly he could play. He had won the Amateur in 1953 and the next year in his first Open as a pro, he very nearly caught Ed Furgol at Baltusrol, finishing one stroke behind him. But something was missing. He just didn't win as everyone felt he should. Perhaps it was his temperament; perhaps he was too calm. Too placid. Too lazy? He didn't have that inner fire, that determination, that ambition, if you will.

1962

Littler evidently thought what he lacked was length off the tee, and so in 1962 he tried to lengthen his drives. It didn't work, and even though he led the first round in the Open with 69, mainly the result of a chip-in eagle 3 on the 9th, he never was a contender after that.

The Open in 1962 was played at the Oakmont Country Club, right in the heart of Palmer country. Arnold had grown up in Latrobe, about 40 miles east of Pittsburgh, and he was, of course, the hero of all of western Pennsylvania. It seemed as if everyone in the western part of the state wanted to see Arnold win the Open, and they came in record numbers. The total for the three days was 62,300, well above the 47,975 who had attended the 1961 Open at Oakland Hills, and prize money by then was up to $73,800.

The effects of Palmer's presence in the game were beginning to make themselves felt that June. The change in galleries had been coming on steadily, but it was here that the change had its first real impact. Golf galleries through the years had been made up of golfers, largely people who played the game and who wanted to see the great players perform, perhaps along the way pick up a tip that might help their own games. They understood the special tensions of the players since they had them themselves, and they understood the etiquette of the game. While they could not help having their own favorites, they rooted them on almost silently and they were polite to the other players. If the player they wanted to lose hit a good shot, they applauded, and in most cases they meant it, for they understood the meaning of a good shot. The earlier galleries were, in short, polite, mannerly, and refined. At Oakmont they were rude, loud, and offensive. Until 1962 yelling "miss it" when a golfer was trying to hole a putt was unheard of. You heard it at Oakmont. Most of the remarks were directed against Nicklaus. They cheered when he hit into a bunker, they coaxed his ball into rough, and if they could have found a way to throw his clubs onto the Pennsylvania Turnpike, they probably would have.

Nicklaus had won the Amateur for a second time the previous September, and he had turned pro shortly after that. He was in his first full season as a professional, and while he had not sent many tour regulars home cringing in fear, he had consistently won money, even in his first tournament, the Los Angeles Open. In Pittsburgh that June, though, he was the villain. Everyone was a villain if he stood in Palmer's path.

Arnold opened with 71 and was 2 strokes behind Littler after the first round and one ahead of Nicklaus. Jack had started with three straight birdies, but after nine holes he was one over par. Oakmont was taking back every stroke it gave away. It was on this day that Phil Rodgers became entangled with a tree on the 17th hole. This is the 295-yard par 4 that Hogan drove accidentally in 1953. Rodgers hooked his tee shot into the left rough where a number of small evergreens had been planted since the 1953 Open to prevent players from driving into the rough to open the green to the pitch. Rodgers' tee shot lodged in one of those trees well above ground. He chopped at it several times before knocking it loose from the tree and made 8—four over par—and finished the round with 74.

Inspired by his cheering fans, Palmer shot 68 in the second round and moved into a tie for the lead with Bob Rosburg once more at 139. Over 24,000 fans streamed through the gates on Saturday, the greatest single-day crowd ever in the Open. Arnold had a chance to blow it apart when the challengers were shooting high scores. Rosburg shot 74 in the morning, Nicklaus 72, but Palmer was having trouble of his own and limped in with 73. He couldn't get his ball into the hole; the man who thought he could hole anything had needed 38 putts in that morning round, and three times missed from 2 feet. He had made an eagle 2 on the 17th, driving the green and coaxing in a 10-foot putt, but then he had missed from 2 feet on the home green. He went into that final round tied for the lead with Bobby Nichols at 212. Rodgers was a stroke behind at 213 and Nicklaus had 214.

Palmer went to work. Through eight holes he was one under par and had passed Nichols, playing ahead of him. Nicklaus by then was 3 strokes behind and just hanging on. The 9th hole at Oakmont is a short par 5 of 485 yards uphill and back to the clubhouse, where a milling and cocky throng was waiting for him. Arnold hit a big drive and then a fairway wood hole-high but a few yards off the right side of the green 20 yards from the hole. He had the simplest kind of shot, a little chip from a reasonably level lie over some grass and onto the green. He had nothing between him and the green but rough, and if he didn't make his birdie 4, surely he would make par 5.

With the Open clearly in hand, Palmer stubbed the chip. He moved it only a few yards and didn't get it to the green. Another chip and two putts, and Arnold had made a bogey 6 where he figured to make a birdie 4. Instead of a 4-stroke lead over Nicklaus, it was down to 2, and a moment later when Jack holed a birdie putt on the 11th it was down to one stroke.

The decisive hole in the 1962 Open was the 13th, perhaps the most forgettable hole on the course. It is a little par 3 of about 160 yards with the green set at the base of a slight, tree-covered hill. After the slip on the 9th, Palmer had made his figures the next three holes and he still had a one-stroke edge on Nicklaus. Both Rodgers and Nichols had played themselves out of contention, and now it was a question of whether Palmer could hold off the young challenger. Palmer's tee shot missed the green to the right and settled in a bunker. He made a bogey 4, and they were tied. Nicklaus was up ahead, and since dropping that 14-foot birdie on the 11th, he made nothing but pars, two of them by holing missable putts of 3 feet on the 16th and 4 feet on the 17th. Jack played two fine shots to the 18th and had a 15-foot birdie chance. The putt glided by the hole.

Palmer had two more chances to win the Open. He placed his drive to the 17th just in front of the opening to the green and then left his little pitch 12 feet short of the hole, cut to the right rear. He missed that one, and then missed another 12-footer on the 18th. Palmer and Nicklaus had tied at 283, the same score Hogan had shot in 1953. There would be a playoff the next day.

On Sunday another huge crowd turned out, about 10,000, to watch Palmer and Nicklaus. Predictably it was a heavily pro-Palmer gallery and certainly among the most ill-behaved ever. They had little to cheer them. Palmer bogeyed the first hole and he never caught up. At the end of six he was 4 strokes behind, and he was still behind coming to the 9th, the hole that had cost him so dearly the day before, then birdied the 11th, an uphill par 4. The 12th is a good par 5 of 598 yards. Arnold was almost on in 2 with a couple of really ponderous woods. When he made his 4 there he was only a stroke behind. Then came that 13th again and once more it was to cost Palmer a stroke. His tee shot caught the right edge of the green and stayed on, but Arnold took three putts from 40 feet. Now he was 2 strokes behind again, and he could not catch up. Nicklaus parred all the way to the 18th. There he drove into the left rough and when Palmer's second shot missed the green to the right, Nicklaus pitched out short of a huge fairway bunker, then played a nine-iron onto the green. Palmer gave it a good try. From the rough short of the green he played a marvelous chip that just missed the flagstick and rolled well past. That was the end; Nicklaus had won with 71 in the playoff against Palmer's 74. Nicklaus, who had won the National Amateur the previous September, had won the Open in his first year as a professional. And Palmer had lost. Surely, though, there would be other Opens for Palmer, for at 32 he was at the peak of his career.

1963

The 1963 Open was played at The Country Club, in Brookline, Massachusetts, where 50 years earlier Francis Ouimet had met and beaten Vardon and Ray in that legendary playoff. This had to be the only conceivable reason for holding the Open at this golf course.

To begin with, the golf course is truly out of date. It was much the same as when Ouimet won in 1913. The Country Club has three nines, and when it was the site of the 1957 Amateur, holes from all three were used to make a strong 18. The same thing was done for the Open. The 11th, for instance, was a combination of two holes from different nines. (It was very probably the best hole on the course.) But the 12th was a calamity, a big par 4 that called for a second shot to be played with a long iron to a green set high over the crest of an escarpment pocked with bunkers. The green was set so far back that a flagstick nearly double the normal height of 8 feet was necessary to mark the hole.

Not only was the design out of date, the course had lain under a sheet of ice for weeks during a bitter New England winter, and the spring had been very dry. The condition of the course was well below the normal standards, and then just before the tournament began some vandals etched obscenities in at least one green. No, it was not an ideal location, even though Francis Ouimet was there reliving those moments of 50 years before.

Besides the spotty condition of the golf course, the weather was hardly made for controlled golf shots. The wind blew for three days, swirling down among the wooded fairways, and the flight of a golf ball was unpredictable. Nicklaus was expected to make a strong defense of his championship, but he shot 76 in the first round, 77 in the second, and missed the cut. The championship came down to a battle among four players, Julius Boros, Palmer, Jacky Cupit, and Tony Lema—and it was not decided until the final holes.

Palmer, Cupit, and Dow Finsterwald shared the 36-hole lead at 142, a stroke ahead of Dean Refram and Walter Burkemo. Boros was 3 strokes behind at 145, and he seemed through when he shot 76 on the morning of the final day. But no one was playing well in that gusty wind. As the final 18 holes began, Cupit was leading with 218, 5 over par.

Boros was out early and began playing remarkably steady golf for the circumstances. When he reached the 17th tee he was 3 over par and headed for a score of 295, and nobody had won the Open with a score that high since Sam Parks in 1935. Boros birdied the 16th, a par 3, and followed with another birdie on the 17th. Par on the 18th gave him 293, and the way the scoring was going, he might have a chance. He ordered a beer and sat down to wait. Only three players had a chance to catch him, and the outcome was settled in one incredible moment. Cupit was playing to the 15th, Palmer to the 16th, and Lema to the 17th all at once. Lema had played his tee shot a trifle strong on the 17th and he had to avoid a big tree set against the right side of the 17th green. His approach was over the green, and he made 5 and followed with another bogey on the 18th. Cupit was a stroke ahead of Palmer as he played the 15th, and he missed the green with his approach. His ball was sitting in rough to the right front, and Palmer was safely on the 16th. As Cupit stood up to chip, Palmer rolled in a birdie putt to tie, and Cupit had to step away until the roar of Palmer's gallery died down. Then he calmly chipped into the hole for a birdie of his own to lead once more. Then Palmer three-putted the 17th as Cupit got down in 2 from 18 feet on the 16th, and now Cupit was 2 strokes ahead with two holes to play. Surely he would win, for there really is not much to making two pars on 17 and 18.

Cupit played a three-wood from the 17th tee trying to avoid going through the fairway, which bends to the left. Instead he pulled the shot into the bunker where 50 years before Harry Vardon had lost his chance to tie Ouimet in the playoff. Cupit's lie was good enough and possibly he could have reached the green, but he hit slightly behind the ball and was about 30 yards short. Still, a 5 was a reasonable expectation. Cupit tried to pitch close to the upper level of the green, but his shot was too strong and it rolled over the back. From there he chipped 4 feet past the hole and missed. He had made 6. Just then Palmer was putting on the 18th, and he thought he had no chance until a big 6 went up on the scoreboard for Cupit. Palmer made his par 4 there and Arnold, too, had 293. Now Cupit needed a birdie 3 on the 18th to win. He played a good drive, then a six-iron onto the green about 15 feet from the hole, clearly within birdie range. His putt was true, but it broke a little quickly and slid beneath the hole. A par 4 and 293. Now three players were tied and there would be another three-man playoff the next day, just as it was 50 years earlier.

For a while it looked as if Cupit might win the playoff by default. All the golf balls had been stolen from Boros's locker. The modern pro does not buy golf balls from the display case in your friendly corner pro shop. The balls he uses are specially tested for uniformity of compression. They're not "hot" balls, they're just more uniform than the ordinary pack of three you buy from the display case. Luckily, he had three new balls in his bag, which, he said, was more than he would need. Next, Palmer came tearing through the locker room obviously not well. He had been suffering from an intestinal disorder and had not slept very much the previous night. Cupit was only nervous.

Boros was forty-three years old in 1963, and only one player that age had won the Open. Ted Ray was forty-three in 1920. Boros, though, was a remarkable player and his record in the Open was hard to believe. He had played in 12 Opens beginning in 1950, won one, finished second once, third twice, fourth twice, fifth once, and ninth once. He had been fifth or better in seven of 12, ninth or better in eight of 12. He had missed the cut in 1961 when he had had a painful shoulder, and he had missed filing his entry in 1962.

Never a great putter, Boros usually did well on courses that demanded solid tee-to-green play, and he had a shot that was ideal for an Open course with its tall rough close against the greens. It was a little lob pitch played with a sand wedge. It came out of the grass with little or no spin and just ran at the hole. Boros missed the first green to the right and simply played that little lob up to the hole and made his 4. Nobody made a move until the 4th, where Boros threw a soft pitch onto the green and holed for a birdie. He was never caught. Cupit stayed close, but he shot 73 against a 70 by Boros, his only subpar round of the tournament. Palmer's chances died on the 11th, where he hooked his drive into the woods to the left and found the ball inside a rotted tree stump. He tried to play out and wasted a couple of shots, finally took 7, and finished with 76.

It was a frustrating tournament for Arnold. For the third time in four years he had the best 72-hole score in the tournament proper, and yet he had won only one Open. Would he ever win again?

1964

He looked as if he might in 1964, but the man who could come from behind utterly wilted on the last day and dropped from second to a tie for fifth. His final two rounds were 12 strokes higher than his first two; 149, 137. The Open in 1964 was played at the Congressional Country Club in the Maryland suburbs of Washington. It was a long course, at 7,053 yards the longest ever for the Open, and until the week of the tournament it had vicious rough, wiry and clumpy bluegrass, tall and thick. The members had been tortured by it for a year waiting for the Open, and when the season began the automatic sprinklers had been turned on almost constantly, for the Eastern seaboard was parched by a lingering drought. The week before the tournament began the rough was still healthy but on Sunday it began to weaken, on Monday it began to wilt, and by Thursday it had just lain over and died. There was simply no rough, and shots that went off line were not penalized as severely as they would have been earlier.

Still, Congressional was no pushover, even though it was far from one of the better Open courses. In the first round only Palmer could better the par of 70, an artificially low figure since two holes that were called par 5s for members were called par 4s for the Open. Palmer shot 68 and he was in the lead by 2 strokes over big, blond Bill Collins, who had learned to play golf just 40 miles away in Baltimore. Palmer followed with 69, giving him a record-equaling 36-hole score of 137, but even with that he lost the lead. Tommy Jacobs holed a 60-foot putt on the home green for a 64 that matched Lee Mackey's record set in 1950. Jacobs led with 206.

In 1964 Ken Venturi was washed up. He had been the bright young star of the pro tour in the late 1950s, nearly winning the Masters as an amateur in 1956, and again as a professional in 1960, but he shot 80 in the final round of the 1956 tournament, and Palmer made a birdie, birdie finish in 1960 to beat him. Now Palmer was playing the best golf of his career and Venturi was barely hanging on the tour. He had to depend on sponsor exemptions to get into the regular tour tournaments, and his swing, once a graceful, fluid motion, had become flat and jerky. Still, he was easily remembered from happier days as he duck-walked down the fairway in his gray trousers, white shirt, and white cap.

Venturi had played steadily through Thursday and Friday, shooting 70 in the first round and 72 in the second, but he was 6 strokes behind Jacobs, 5 behind Palmer with the grueling double round coming up. On the morning of the final day something happened to Venturi. He still was not swinging as he once did, but the shots were ringing from his clubs as they did in the late 1950s, splitting the fairways and covering the flagstick. He dropped his approach on the 1st hole 10 feet from the hole, and his putt sat on the lip of the cup for what seemed like a full minute before it fell. Another birdie from 15 feet on the 4th, still another on the 6th, and then he holed a 25-footer on the 8th. As he strolled down the fairway of the 9th hole, a terribly conceived par 5 of 600 yards, he was told a scoreboard was nearby if he wanted to look at it, for by then he had passed both

Tommy Jacobs holes a 60-foot putt to tie Open record with a round of 64

Palmer and Jacobs. "No," he said. "I can't change what's up there and I can't control what the other guys are doing. One shot at a time, that's all that interests me."

That next shot was a deft pitch across a chasm and onto the green 10 feet above the hole. When that touchy, curling putt dropped, Venturi had played the first nine in 30 strokes, equaling still another Open record. Venturi picked up another stroke on the second nine, and when he reached the 17th tee he was 6 under par. The heat in Washington was becoming unbearable. The sun was searing, and the temperature was climbing to 100 degrees. The humidity was high and Venturi was feeling the effects. He was shaking when he gripped his putter on the 17th. He made a bogey 5 there, and another on the 18th, and lost the chance to match Jacobs's 64. Still, he had a 66, but when he went into the massive clubhouse for lunch, there was some question that he would be able to continue. A doctor was called. He prescribed some tea and a rest during the luncheon break, and so Venturi stretched out on a locker-room bench. He was determined to continue, for by then it was a two-man race, just Venturi and Jacobs, with Jacobs ahead, 206 to 208. Palmer had not made a birdie in 18 holes and had slipped to 75 in the morning and 212 for 54 holes.

The doctor followed Venturi around in the afternoon carrying an ice pack, which he refilled at refreshment stands, and occasionally he would hold it against the back of Venturi's neck. It seemed that at any moment Ken would simply have to give up, but his shots never wavered; they were as true as they had been six years earlier, and he kept piling up his pars. Meanwhile, Jacobs, not Venturi, was collapsing. While Venturi was going around in a steady 70, Jacobs was shooting 76, and going from 2 strokes ahead to 4 strokes behind. By the time he reached the 17th, Venturi knew he had won if only he could keep going. He got by the 17th, and there before him lay the 18th hole, a fine par 4 down a gentle slope to a green set on a finger of land jutting into a lake. The ground along the length of the fairway sloped upward on the right, and as he stood on the tee Venturi saw a great mass of spectators along the right side. It seemed as if every one of the 20,000 fans was there to see him finish, for this was a magnificent moment in Open history. When Joe Dey, who was refereeing, along with Hord Hardin, a USGA Vice President, suggested that Venturi might like to hold his chin up as he walked to the final green, he said, "I'm going to march down that 18th fairway with my head so high they won't recognize me."

And he did. He played a good enough drive, not long, but not risking the tangled rough on the left, and then played short of the green and to the right, guarding against the chance of calamity. His ball rolled into a little pot bunker, but he had many strokes in hand by then and he could afford to waste a stroke. From the bunker he came out 10 feet from the hole, and then holed the putt. He let his putter drop, held his hands out from his side, palms up, looked upward, mouth agape, and cried, "My God, I've won the Open!"

Not only did he win, but he broke Congressional's par by 2 strokes with 278, the first score under 280 since 1948, and he finished 4 strokes ahead of Jacobs. It was his first victory in four years and it gave him substantial hope that he would rise to the top once more. Later that season he finished fifth in the PGA Championship and won at Hartford and the American Golf Classic in Akron. But never again. He was stricken by an unusual circulatory ailment and lost some feeling in his hands. A golfer with restricted feeling cannot hope to play championship golf. His career as a tournament player was through, tragically over just when it seemed to be beginning once more. He had fought and scratched his way back to the top and now he was headed back down once more.

1965

When the Open moved to St. Louis in 1965, Venturi, the defending champion, was given no chance to repeat. Perhaps he was bitter inside, but he did not let it show. Seated before his locker in the Bellerive clubhouse, Venturi's head hung low. A man stopped and said how disappointed Venturi must be, especially after last year. Venturi looked up. "At least there was a last year," he said quietly.

Bellerive Country Club, the site of the 1965 Open, was another unfortunate choice. It was a Robert Trent Jones design, terribly long and with huge greens. It was just 9 yards short of 7,200 yards, and on some greens it seemed as if you could barely see from one side to the other. The Open was reduced to a contest of who can get down in 2 most often. Some shots that looked as if they were shanked wound up on greens—not close to the holes, but on the green.

By 1965 something had happened to the Open. Prize money was up to $124,000 in the Championship proper and another $7,800 in sectional qualifying, which was good, but instead of that double round on Saturday, the tournament had been extended to four days, 18 holes a day. The day that seemed to be the single most exciting day in American sport was gone; now they played the Open just like they played the Tucson or Pensacola or Quad Cities Open. True, some, perhaps most, players like it this way, but when the USGA changed the format of the Open, the tournament lost something. It was no longer unique. Why was it changed? The only possible reason was to accommodate television and incidentally collect more money in rights fees. The Open had been shown only on Saturday; now it could be on the air on both Saturday and Sunday. Of course the USGA gave some feeble excuses like the threat of bad weather causing a postponement, when in the entire history of the championship going back to 1895 a round had been postponed only in 1959 because of the heavy rain.

With conditions like this—a champion who could not possibly repeat, and quite probably would not make the cut, a golf course that promised nothing more than a putting contest, and a format like every other tournament on the pro tour—is it any wonder it was a dull Open? Nothing exciting happened until the last few holes, and the most exciting development of all came at the very end when the prizes were awarded. But it was also dull for other reasons: Arnold Palmer shot 76, 76—152 and missed the cut, Jack Nicklaus shot 78, 72—150 and missed being in contention. Venturi took 40 putts in his first round and stumbled in with 81. A 79 the next day and mercifully it was over. It was embarrassing for everyone to see Venturi play, and it must have been embarrassing for him.

Kel Nagle, a forty-four-year-old Australian, took the first-round lead with 68, and then Gary Player moved a stroke ahead of him after 36 holes with 140 on two rounds of 70. Nagle had 141, tied with Mason Rudolph. Player lengthened his lead to 2 strokes over Nagle with 71 in the third round, and he had the championship in hand with three holes to play in the last round, for Nagle had made 6 on the par-4 15th. The 16th hole is a big par 3 of 218 yards with a mammoth green and a big bunker in front of it. Player's tee shot fell into the bunker. He played a fine recovery 15 feet from the hole, rolled his first putt 3 feet past, and then his second hit the rim of the cup and refused to drop. Just at that moment Nagle holed a birdie putt on the 17th, a 606-yard par 5. This was a swing of 3 strokes in one hole, and it left both of them tied. Nagle parred the 18th to finish at 282, and Player made his pars on the last two to match Nagle's score. Once more there would be a playoff, this time between two foreigners. A foreign player had not won the Open since Ted Ray in 1920, but there would be a foreign champion this year. It was Player. Nagle had difficulty with his control, and by the time they had played five holes he had hit two spectators. His composure was shattered, and at the end of eight holes he was 5 strokes behind. Player won handily, 71 to 74.

In 1962 Player had said that if he ever won the Open he would not take the prize money. He meant it. At the presentation ceremony he donated $5,000 of his $25,000 first prize to cancer research, and the other $20,000 to the USGA to help promote junior golf. It was a marvelously thoughtful gesture. Gary hadn't even considered the possibility that he might have to pay a tax on the donation. (He did not.)

Gary Player's donation

Player during 1965 Open

1966

The Open in 1966 returned to the Olympic Club, just down the coast from the Golden Gate Bridge and just a few hundred yards from the Pacific Ocean. It had been the site of the Hogan-Fleck confrontation in 1955, and it was to be the scene of another playoff this year. The golf course itself was changed very little from 11 years before. The course was still of modest length, just 6,700 yards, and the 17th hole had been shortened a bit; you could reach the green with an iron second instead of a wood. The rough was not nearly so severe, and overall the course was in marvelous condition, moistened as it is by mist from the sea. The greens still were terribly small, and the narrow fairways weaved among the pine, eucalyptus, and cypress trees. It still had but a single fairway bunker on the left side of the 6th, which brings up a story.

Since finishing 14th in 1961, Ben Hogan had not played in an Open; he had withdrawn after filing an entry in 1962 because of an attack of bursitis, and had never entered again. Most speculation claimed he was too proud to subject himself, a four-time Open champion, to the uncertainties of 36-hole sectional qualifying. In any event, he did not enter. Then in 1966 the USGA took an unusual step. It invited Hogan to play in the Open as an added starter, the 151st man, citing the 1955 Open when he almost won a fifth championship. Hogan accepted, and played well enough to win an exemption for the following year at Baltusrol.

Before the tournament began, Hogan was playing a practice round with Bruce Devlin and acting as a guide, for Devlin had not played the course before. When they reached the 6th tee, Hogan pointed to the trap. "That's the only fairway bunker on the course," Hogan said. "Is it in play, Ben?" Devlin asked. Hogan shook his head slightly and said, "No. You just hit to the right of it." That says something profound about Hogan.

It should be mentioned that while Hogan, the loser in 1955, was invited back, Fleck, the champion, had to win a place through sectional qualifying. He did. He played nowhere nearly as well as he had in 1955 or 1960, and missed the 36-hole cut. Player, the defending champion, almost joined him, for he shot 78 in the opening round, 72 in the second, and made it by one stroke. Al Mengert, who had lost in the final of the 1952 National Amateur, but was now a pro in the Pacific Northwest, led the opening round with 67, a stroke ahead of Gene Littler and Don Massengale. Palmer, meanwhile, had a 71 and was tied with Nicklaus, a stroke ahead of Hogan. The next day Mengert suffered the fate of many a first-round wonder, shot 77 and disappeared. The second day of the Open belonged to Arnold Palmer

1966 Open at Olympic

and to Rives McBee, a twenty-seven-year-old Texan who simply could not miss a putt. Only four players broke 70 that dull and overcast day, and McBee brought in a 64, equaling the Open record set first in 1950 and matched in 1964. McBee hit 14 greens, which is not impressive in itself, but his putting was: two putts from 20 feet, two more from 15, one from 12, one from 10, two more from 8 feet, and three missable 4-footers.

Marvelous as this round was, it was very nearly matched by Palmer, who stormed around in 66. Arnold was off early and played a very methodical and strong round. He did not miss a green until the 17th, and he was in the rough only once. Were it not for two putts from 5 feet that failed to drop on the 17th and 18th, he would have tied McBee. Palmer was in with 137, and as the afternoon wore on, only Bill Casper was keeping up. Casper had played the first round in 69—his was the only sub-70 round other than Mengert's—and then he shot 68 on Friday to tie with Palmer. Arnold, who was staying with some friends, asked a visitor what was happening at Olympic. When he was told that, with one exception, the scores were running high, he said, "I'll bet the exception is Casper."

Palmer and Casper were paired together the next day, and by the end of nine holes it looked as if it would be no contest. Arnold played the first nine in 34 and Casper shot 37. Arnold was 3 strokes ahead, but he began to have trouble on the in nine, losing a stroke here, another there, and finishing with 70. Casper, meanwhile, had hit only 11 greens—he was in the rough seven times and in traps three—and even though Palmer played a little loosely on the second nine, he could not make up any strokes. He finished with 73. Palmer led going into that last day with 207 against 210 by Casper and 211 by Nicklaus, who had won his second consecutive Masters tournament in April. By then it certainly looked like Arnold's Open, except . . . Palmer had injured his back in New Orleans earlier in the year, and at Olympic he had shown a tendency to tire late in the round. Arnold had always been a hooker, but he began to hit his tee shots straight in 1966, and then as the Open approached, he began to apply the slightest bit of a fade, for most of the holes at Olympic had a left-to-right break. It worked wonderfully until he began to tire, and then on the second nine that Saturday, some tee shots began to veer off more sharply. Now it wasn't a fade; it was a slice.

By the end of nine holes on Sunday, it really didn't seem important what his tee shots did the rest of the round. The first five holes at Olympic are probably the hardest on the course, and Palmer played them in 2 under par. He reached the turn in 32, and by then he was 7 strokes ahead of Casper, who was paired with him once more. Arnold had the Open in his pocket . . . but somehow the pocket developed a hole.

The record score for the Open was 276 set by Hogan 18 years earlier in 1948. Par in, and Palmer could break that record by 2 strokes with 274. Winning seemed a certainty now, and the record a practical goal. Casper was forgotten. What happened next is still hard to believe. Palmer attacked the record and invited disaster while Casper played on with stoic determination.

Palmer hooked his approach on the 10th to the edge of the green and took 3 to get down. Casper made a par 4. Palmer's lead was down to 6. Both made their par 4s on the 11th, and they matched birdie 3s on the 12th. The 13th is a 191-yard par 3; Palmer hit a four-iron and missed the green to the left. He made a bogey 4, and Casper parred. Down to a 5-stroke lead, but more to the point, Palmer now needed a birdie to beat Hogan's record. He didn't get it on the 14th, and then he went for the pin on the 15th, a little 150-yard one-shotter to an elevated green. Casper had hit a seven iron 35 feet from the hole, and Palmer mishit his seven iron and the ball went into a bunker. He came out 15 feet from the hole and missed his putt. Casper, meanwhile, holed his 35-footer and picked up 2 strokes on Palmer. Arnold had now lost 4 shots of his 7-stroke lead in six holes.

Standing on the 16th tee, Palmer suddenly remembered that he had not won the Open just yet and he had better forget Hogan and start thinking about Casper. He also remembered that his most reliable tee shot is that old draw which he had not been playing, and that the 16th hole was the perfect spot for it. The 16th is a 604-yard par 5 that bends to the left around a stand of tall trees and matty rough; it is the only hole on the course that breaks just that way, and Palmer decided he had better play the shot he could rely on, for the pressure was building to a terrible pitch. The spectators were beginning to believe they might see the greatest turn-around in Open history, and surely the thought had occurred to both Palmer and Casper. Billy, somewhat unsure of himself early in the round, by now was playing with confidence.

Palmer tried to play his reliable draw, but what came off the club was a sharp hook that careered into the trees, hit a branch, and dropped straight down barely 150 yards from the tee. Casper, meanwhile, had played nicely into the center of the fairway. Arnold now had to make a choice: either he would play safely out, make sure he got to the fairway, and then still need two shots to reach the green, or he could gamble that he could hit a shot far enough to make the green with his next. He gambled. He played a three iron, but the ball did not get airborne, it was snuffed out by the rough. Next he chopped out with a nine iron, and hit his fourth shot, a three wood, into a green-side bunker. Casper played his third onto the green 15 feet from the hole. Palmer came out nicely 4 feet from the hole and could save a bogey with a good putt. Before he could try, Casper rolled in his putt for a birdie 4. Even though Palmer then made his 6, he had lost 2 more strokes and with two holes to play, he was now only one shot up. He lost even that stroke on the 17th. He missed the green and made 5, Casper made a par 4, and they were tied. Casper had made up 5 strokes in three holes, 7 strokes in eight holes. When Palmer hooked his tee shot on the

18th it seemed possible that Casper might make up still another stroke and win right there, because Palmer needed a miraculous shot to reach the green from that heavy grass; somehow he chopped it out and onto the green 30 feet above the hole. It was a shot that called for great strength. Arnold got down in two from 30 feet and Casper made his 4 from 14 feet to set up the playoff the next day.

What had just taken place was very difficult to believe even by those who saw it. The impression everyone took away that night was that Palmer had had the championship in hand, only to let it slip away. That was true enough, but what was largely overlooked, as it had been 11 years before, was the marvelous play of the man who came from behind—Fleck in 1955, Casper in 1966. Casper had played the second nine in 32 while Palmer was shooting 39. Casper had calmly played his own game, never giving up, and every time Palmer slipped, Billy was there to grab away a stroke, sometimes two. He shot 68 in that round, and Palmer had 71.

The playoff the next day was almost like a dream, as though you were seeing again what you had lived through the day before. Palmer was off the mark fast once more, playing the first nine in 33 against a scrambling 35 by Casper, who made a 5 on the 9th, three-putting for the first time. But once more Arnold could not hold the strokes he had in hand. He lost them both on the 11th, a 430-yard par 4, where he took 3 from the edge while Casper was holing a 25-foot birdie putt. Casper went ahead for the first time in the Open by holing a 30-foot putt on the 13th, added another stroke on the 14th, and went 3 ahead on the 15th when Palmer bogeyed them both. It was over. He even gained a stroke when he three-putted the 16th for a bogey 6, for Palmer was making 7. The final margin was 4 strokes, 69 to 73; Palmer once more had been beaten by that second nine. After an outgoing 33, he played the home nine in 40. Casper, meanwhile, came back in 34. The last two times Palmer played the second nine he had 79 shots—Casper played it in 66.

When Casper had won the Open at Winged Foot, he did it almost exclusively with his putting. While he did not three-putt a green during the four days of the championship proper at Olympic, and one-putted 25, he was not that much better than Palmer on the greens. Arnold had three-putted only twice and had one-putted 25 greens also.

It was a tragic loss for Palmer, who by then had not won a major title since the 1964 Masters, and it was his third loss in a playoff for the Open. It was also the second time an Open at Olympic would be remembered more for who lost than for who won, and once again Hogan's record was safe—for the time being.

1967

It had been five years since Nicklaus defeated Palmer in that playoff at Oakmont, and even though he had won the Masters twice, the PGA, and the British Open in the intervening years, he had not been a significant force in the Open again. He finished third at Olympic in 1966, it's true, but it was a rather poor third, 7 strokes behind Casper and Palmer. When that fateful last nine began, he was 9 strokes behind Palmer, and when Arnold was shooting 39 and losing 7 strokes to Casper, he lost only 2 to Jack.

Now it was 1967, and the Open was back to Baltusrol after 13 years. Baltusrol was another big course, 7,015 yards, and it had the longest hole in Open history. The 17th measured 623 yards and there was simply no way to reach it in two, for the green was protected by bunkers and raised well above fairway level. Despite the overall length of the course, there was a pervading feeling among the players that it could be had, that scoring could be very low, and that Hogan's record conceivably could fall here. The condition of the course was a major factor in that hunch, for Baltusrol was immaculate. Its fairways were cut close and the ball sat up nicely. Its greens were true, and even though they were full of subtle little rolls, the ball went where it was hit.

Marty Fleckman was a young amateur from Texas, and in the first round he played like a sound pro. Fleckman shot 67, and when he looked behind him he saw eight players at 69, among them Palmer, Casper, Player, and Deane Beman, who had recently turned pro after a distinguished amateur career. Beman, incidentally, opened the championship by holing a full four wood on the first hole for an eagle 2. (Beman was the shortest hitter on the tour, but in four rounds he made two birdies, an eagle, and a par on this 465-yard hole, which he could not reach with an iron.) Nicklaus, meanwhile, shot 71 in the first round and was 4 strokes behind. Fleckman slipped to 73 in the second round, and Palmer took over the lead at 137 following 69. Nicklaus had saved his par on the 4th hole, a one-shooter across a lake, after a horrid pull hook, and then went on a scoring rampage. He shot 67, his best score ever in the Open, and was a stroke behind Palmer with two rounds to play.

The two leaders, Palmer and Nicklaus, were paired together on Saturday, and naturally enough, they took most of the huge gallery with them. The gallery had to be disappointed because, after 16 holes, neither one had made a birdie. While Palmer and Nicklaus were playing their insignificant golf, Casper was making up ground. With four holes to play, he was 4 strokes in front, and Nicklaus and Palmer had also been passed by Fleckman and Beman. Then something strange happened. Casper, the man who had made up 7 strokes on Palmer in nine holes a year before, went sour, bogeyed the 15th, 16th, and 17th holes, and finished with 71. Nicklaus and Palmer were jarred by their ghastly putting on the 16th, Nicklaus birdied the last two holes, both par 5s, and Palmer finished par, birdie. Arnold had struggled around in 73 and Jack had been one stroke better. By then, though, Fleckman had taken the lead once more with a third-round 69 and a 54-hole total of 209. Nicklaus, Palmer, and Casper were a stroke behind at 210, and they would be paired together in the final round, next to last off the tee, just ahead of Fleckman and Casper.

Nicklaus was simply unbeatable, despite a lapse on the second where he made a bogey 5. He was hitting everything right at the flag, an eight iron to 12 feet on the third, three iron 4 feet on the fourth, another long iron 15 feet from the fifth. He holed all three putts—three birdies in a row— and took the lead, for Fleckman had lost strokes on the first two holes and Casper was not doing much better. Now the Open was between Nicklaus and Palmer. Arnold was just a stroke behind playing the 7th, a 470-yard par 4 that bends to the right. After a good enough drive, Palmer drilled a magnificent one iron that bore straight at the flag and dug into the green 8 feet from the hole. It was a shot to remember, and right there you could see the old confidence coming back into Arnold. Nicklaus then played another superb shot, a three iron 22 feet from the hole. Jack putted first and holed it for a birdie 3; Arnold's putt missed by an inch, and now Jack was 2 strokes ahead. Jack picked up 2 more strokes on the 385-yard 8th, where Palmer pushed his drive to the right behind a tree and had to waste a shot getting back to the fairway. Jack, meanwhile, played a soft wedge 4 feet from the cup and holed his fifth birdie putt in six holes. He played the next four holes in three pars and a bogey, and then began a series of marvelous pitches—a wedge to 4 feet on 13; a seven iron to 5 feet on the 14th, for two more birdies. Pars on the 15th, 16th, and 17th, and Nicklaus headed for the home hole 4 strokes ahead of Palmer, who had finally made a birdie of his own on the 17th.

The 18th at Baltusrol is a 542-yard par 5 from an elevated tee down a sloping fairway. At the base of the slope a creek cuts across the fairway, and then the ground rises to the green set behind a series of bunkers. A birdie here would better Hogan's record, but Nicklaus determined to play safe and not risk taking the 7 that cost Dick Mayer a chance at the 1954 Open, and had almost cost Ed Furgol the championship. Jack played a one-iron from the tee, but he pushed it into the right rough near a television cable. He was permitted a free drop to get away from the cable, and the ball landed on bare dirt. Jack played a second safe shot, an eight iron he wanted to keep short of the creek, but he hit behind the ball and moved it only about 50 yards. Now he had a full one iron to the green. He hit it flush and the ball braked to a stop 20 feet from the hole. He had certainly won the Open and he had two putts to match Hogan's record of 276. His putt ran right into the hole and instead of matching it, he had snapped the old record with his 275. Jack's final round was 65, one of the great finishes in Open history, matching the 64 that Arnold shot in 1960. Arnold had a record of his own. He had finished with 279 and at that time became the only man in Open history to better 280 twice. Strangely, he didn't win either time.

While Nicklaus was making his triumphal march through Baltusrol, a few fans sneaked away momentarily to take a look at a young Texan who had played three steady rounds of 72, 70, and 71 and was showing no signs of wilting in the pressure of the final round. It was their first glimpse of Lee Trevino, and they left trying to forget the horrible sight of his backswing lest their own game be ruined. Trevino finished fifth at Baltusrol, won $6,000, and stayed on the tour the rest of the year and won $30,000. His swing, awkward though it seemed, was as sound as any on the tour, and in one respect at least it was better. Trevino stood up to the ball facing left of the target, and then swung right. He took the club back in a flat plane and sort of lurched at the ball, finally finishing with his hands in anything but the classic high position. But in that crucial 3 feet of the swing, the point just before and just after impact, his club was heading right for the target, and his extension through the ball was probably the longest since Hogan. But would he ever win a major tournament? Doubtful, especially after he shot 80 in the last round of the Masters early in 1968 after being in contention, and then came to the 17th hole of the Houston Champions leading Roberto de Vicenzo by a stroke and played two bad irons and lost.

1968

Because he had finished fifth at Baltusrol, Trevino was exempt from qualifying for the 1968 Open, which had returned to Oak Hill in Rochester where Cary Middlecoff had won in 1956. Once more the course was much the same as it had been, but it seemed to be playing easier than 12 years before. Bert Yancey confirmed it with a 67 in the opening round. Only two other players broke 70 that day—Charles Coody and Lee Trevino. Yancey came back with a 68 and a 36-hole score of 137. Trevino picked up a stroke on Yancey with another 69 in the third round against Bert's 70, and they left the first tee together on Sunday, Yancey, the tall, erect, dignified former West Point cadet with the classic swing and the obsession to win a major tournament, and Trevino, a laughing, short, pot-bellied Mexican, former gunnery sergeant in the Marines, with a swing that English writer Leonard Crawley named an "agricultural method."

They both bogeyed the 1st hole, and Trevino scraped out a one-putt par on the 2nd to match Yancey. Suddenly on the 3rd hole the Open was all tied up. Trevino hit his first green, Yancey missed his, and then after a fine chip, he missed a 5-foot putt.

Up ahead, Nicklaus had gone into that final round trailing Yancey by 7 strokes, but while Yancey was losing 2 strokes to par on the first three holes, Jack was making birdies on the 3rd and 4th, and with 14 holes to play he was just 3 strokes behind the leaders. Jack had two more birdie chances on the 7th and 8th, but he missed, and right there lost the Open. If he could have put some more pressure on Trevino and Yancey, he might have been able to shake them up. But he didn't and soon Trevino straightened himself out, and ran off with the championship. Right then, though he was still locked in a battle with Yancey, Trevino scraped out another one-putt par on the 4th, and on the 5th he went ahead for the first time when Yancey caught a bunker, came out 3 feet from the hole, and once more missed a short putt. For the first time Yancey was out of the lead. Bert bounced back with a birdie on the 6th to pull even once more, but it did not last, for he drove into the rough off the 7th tee and hit bunkers on the 8th and 9th. He made the turn in 38 against 36 for Trevino.

Trevino widened his lead with a par 4 on the 10th, where Yancey hooked into the woods and missed still another short putt, then Lee holed a 35-foot birdie putt on the 11th and followed with another birdie on the 12th. It was all over. Yancey three-putted the 13th, shot 76 and finished with 281, 2 strokes behind Nicklaus, who shot a closing 67 for 279. Every crucial shot Trevino hit after that turned out perfect. He was short of the long par-4 17th, chipped 12 feet past, and holed it for his par; drove into the rough on the 18th, chopped his second just a little closer to the green, still in the rough, and then played a wonderful wedge 4 feet from the hole for another par. His final round was 69, and he had matched Nicklaus's one-year-old Open record of 275. Hogan's 276 had stood for 19 years, and then it was broken twice within two years. Trevino had become the first player in the Open's long history to play all four rounds in the 60s. His 18-hole scores were 69, 68, 69, 69.

1969

Still Trevino was an enigma. He had won the Open, it's true, and had matched the record, but there had been fluke winners before, and when he missed the cut in 1969 the doubts about his game were strengthened. The 1969 Open was played at the Champions Golf Club in Houston, not a very good course as Open sites go, and Trevino's game matched it. He did one thing right that week—he picked the winner, Orville Moody, an ex–Army sergeant with a moon face, sad eyes, a cross-handed putting method, and for one week, at least, a very sound game.

Moody had spent 14 years in the Army and he had become friendly with Trevino during that period, but when the field gathered at Champions on a hot and humid day in June, it is safe to say that hardly anyone else in Houston had ever heard of Moody. He had won such things as the Korean PGA and Korean Open, but this was a different league here. Moody was thirty-five in 1969 and in only his first full year on the tour. He left the Army briefly in 1962 to take a fling at the pro tour and played in the Open at Oakmont. He missed the cut and couldn't find anyone willing to sponsor him in golf, and so it was back to the Army. By 1969, though, he had found backers, and here he was in Houston along with all the Palmers and Nicklauses, and Players and Caspers.

Moody shot 71 in the opening round and he was 5 strokes behind Bob Murphy, the ex-Amateur champion, who opened with 66. Par was broken by seven players that day, and Murphy had only a slender one-stroke lead over Miller Barber, a tour regular who wore prescription sunglasses, a baseball-type cap pulled low over his eyes, a pot belly, and a swing that made Trevino's look a bit more like Sam Snead's. Barber took the club back as though he were driving railroad spike, but, like Trevino, he was solid through the ball. Right behind Barber came Al Geiberger, a reed-thin Californian who had won the PGA in 1966, and Deane Beman, who played one of the remarkable rounds of the Open. A short hitter, Beman on this day used fairway woods on seven par-4 holes and one par 3. He was better with his woods than almost anybody else with their irons, for he shot 68. The next day Beman shot 69 and took the 36-hole lead at 137, a stroke ahead of Murphy and Barber. Moody, meanwhile, added a 70 to his opening 71, and stood at 141 with Nicklaus, Tony Jacklin, and young John Miller, a tall blond from San Francisco who had finished ninth as an amateur in 1966. Trevino, meanwhile, shot 74, 75—149, and missed the 36-hole cut by a stroke.

The next day Beman shot 73, Geiberger 72, and when Barber came in with 68 he held a 3-stroke lead over Moody, who had matched Barber's 68. Barber had 206, Moody 209, and Barber was confident. "They have to catch me," he told Chris Schenkel, the television announcer, "I don't have to catch them." Lots of people caught Barber. He shot 78 in that final round and dropped into a tie for sixth. The final day of that 1969 Open was as hectic as any since the tournament began in 1895. At one time on the second nine, eight players were within 2 strokes of one another, and one of them was Palmer. Arnold played the first two rounds in 70, 73 for 143, and then shot 69 in the third round with nine 3s—half the holes. He made six birdies, but he also made five bogeys. What opportunities the man had thrown away in this championship! He threw away one more in the final round. He was just 2 over par playing the 15th and hooked his drive into the sandy rough. He was blocked from the green by low-growing tree branches, but he played a beautifully conceived low hook that ran onto the green 40 feet from the hole. With a chance to stay in contention, Arnold three-putted, and that was the end of him.

Meanwhile, Moody went ahead to stay on the 12th. He and Barber were even, and they both pushed their tee shots on this 213-yard par 3 into the woods to the right of the green, avoiding a lake that crowds against the left side. Moody pitched on close to the hole and made his 3, but Barber dumped his second in a trap and made 5. Two more men had shots at tying Moody. Geiberger had just birdied the 15th to get down to one over par, and then three-putted the 16th while Palmer was playing the 15th. Al struggled to save his par on the 17th, holing a good 10-foot putt, and he needed a birdie on the 18th to catch Moody. His 20-footer curled away from the hole in the last few inches. He finished at 282.

Next came Bob Rosburg, who had done nothing in the Open since 1959, when he finished second. Rosburg came to the 18th needing a par 4 for 281. He snap hooked his drive and it hit a tree, dropping into a bad lie barely 200 yards from the tee. Somehow, he played a marvelous recovery with a wood and reached the right green-side bunker. From there he played an exceptional recovery just 3 feet from the hole, and then, with hardly a look at the line, he stepped up to the putt and jabbed at the ball. The putt missed.

Now Moody needed only pars on the 17th and 18th to win. He was just over the green on the 17th, and from 30 feet chipped close and made the putt. He flailed at his drive on the 18th, then played an eight iron 14 feet from the hole, left his first putt a foot short, and then somehow got it in for 281 and the championship.

Later, before the prize ceremony, Moody was summoned into the clubhouse to answer a telephone call from President Nixon. The President congratulated Moody and said it wasn't often that a man spends 14 years in the Army and then comes out to win the U.S. Open.

"No, sir," said Moody. "It's the first time."

1970

With Moody the victory was not really decided until late in the final round. When the Open moved to Hazeltine National Golf Club near Minneapolis in 1970, the outcome was decided almost from the very first hole. This is a 456-yard par 4 that doglegs sharply to the left. At dawn on opening day a gusty 40-mile-an-hour wind was sweeping across the plains, ripping tents and bending trees, and it even partially uprooted a huge scoreboard anchored in the ground by 6-by-6 pilings. Frothy waves were lapping against the shores of Lake Hazeltine, and the wind blew foam onto the tenth green, once covering Gene Littler's ball. With a wind of this velocity blowing from behind, it is next to impossible to stop a ball on the green, but somehow Tony Jacklin held the first green with his approach, made a birdie 3, and right there the 1970 Open was about over. Jacklin shot 71 on that first day, the only player to break par 72, and he was 2 strokes ahead of Julius Boros, Chi Chi Rodriguez, and Mason Rudolph. Jacklin's round was anything but steady. He had six birdies, three bogeys, and one double bogey. The carnage this day was incredible. Jack Nicklaus shot 43 on the first nine and played the second nine well enough to shoot 81. Palmer had 79, and Gary Player 80.

From that round on, Jacklin did nothing but add to his lead. A second-round 70 for 141 gave him a 3-stroke lead, and he increased it to 4 at the end of 54 holes following another 70 for 211. His final margin was 7 strokes over Dave Hill. Jacklin shot 281, Hill 288, even par. Jacklin looked as if he might lose his lead on the first nine during the final round when he went over par on both the par-5 7th and the par-3 8th holes, but his 25-foot putt on the 9th hole, struck much too hard, hit dead center of the cup, jumped about a foot, sat on the edge of the cup for an instant, and then tumbled into the hole for a birdie 3. From then on he could not be caught, and he finished with another 25-foot birdie on the 18th.

Hill criticized the course severely, and in extremely poor taste. While Hazeltine will not go down as one of the fine courses of Open history, it did not deserve what Hill said about it. For instance:

"If I had to play this course every day, I'd find me another game."

"What does it lack?" he was asked.

"Eighty acres of corn and a few cows. They ruined a good farm when they built this course."

"What would you recommend?"

"Plow it up and start all over again. The man who designed this course had the blueprints upside down."

1971

The same criticisms were not expressed when the Open moved to Merion once more in 1971, for this is one of the classic courses of American golf, perhaps the best in the country, and if not, then second only to Pebble Beach. And when great championships are played on great courses, it is only to be expected that great players win.

By 1971, Nicklaus's place as the finest golfer of them all was firmly established. He had already won three Masters tournaments, two U.S. Opens, two PGA Championships, and two British Opens. That is nine major tournaments, and if you count his two national Amateur championships, it comes to 11. He was expected to win the Open at Merion for a number of reasons. For one, he had already won the PGA, which was played at the PGA National Golf Club in Palm Beach in February, and he had finished second in the Masters in April. For another, he played four simply superb rounds over Merion in the 1960 World Amateur Team Championship, shooting 269 for 72 holes, 10 years after Hogan, Mangrum, and Fazio had tied for first place in the Open at 287. (The comparison is not really fair, for Merion in 1960 was set up to accommodate relatively unskilled amateurs who represented such countries as India, Iceland, China, and Norway, not the field for the National Open.)

To be sure, the normal complement of 150 players was in Philadelphia —the Palmers and Caspers and Players, the Bemans and Weiskopfs, and even some amateurs like Jim Simons, a young man from Butler, Pennsylvania, and Wake Forest College, plus Lanny Wadkins, the National Amateur Champion. Tony Jacklin was there too, defending his championship, and even Dave Hill, strangely quiet.

Lee Trevino was there, too, attracting his share of supporters, as well he should. He had played in 19 tournaments, and had finished among the ten leaders 11 times. He won twice, was second twice, and was third in three more. Since late April he had finished seven tournaments and had been out of the first five only once. Nicklaus arrived at Merion a week early to study the course, but Trevino did not arrive until tournament week. He played ten holes on Monday, and called Merion "a nice little course. It's strictly driving. If you keep the ball down the middle you gotta burn it up." Two days later he was saying something else. "This is the hardest course I've ever seen. I don't see how anybody can bust par." With that, Trevino said all there is to say about Merion.

Trevino and Nicklaus played well through the first round, with Jack shooting 69 and Lee 70. Labron Harris was the first-round leader (somebody like that always seems to lead the first round) with 67, a stroke ahead of Bob Goalby, Wadkins, and Doug Sanders. Palmer had shot 73 in the first round, but he started the second by holing his nine-iron approach on the first hole for an eagle 2, and the tempo of the Open quickened; Arnold lost those 2 strokes quickly with bogeys on the 2nd and 3rd, but he got them back and finished with 68, back in the battle. Nicklaus and Trevino were up ahead of Palmer, and each was to run into disaster. Trevino's bad hole came at the 6th, a 420-yard straight-away par 4. He drove into the right rough, was still in the grass after his second, pitched his third over, flubbed a chip, then took two putts for 7, a triple bogey.

Nicklaus picked a more picturesque and historic spot: the 11th, where Jones had completed the Grand Slam in 1930, and where Sarazen threw away the Open in 1934. Jack's performance was much closer to Sarazen than to Jones. Nicklaus hit a one iron from the tee into the right rough. He yanked an eight iron across the fairway into the left rough and among the trees. From there he pitched short of the green, then over; next, a bold chip well past the hole and one putt. Easy 6. Both Nicklaus and Trevino shot 72s that day. The lead was taken over by Bob Erickson, a forty-five-year-old club pro who had recently lost his job, and Jim Colbert, one of the young pros. They each had 138, and they were a stroke ahead of Jerry McGee, another relatively young pro. Jacklin missed the cut, the third straight champion to do it.

On Saturday, young Jim Simons took over the lead with a solid 65 that missed matching the single-round record by one stroke. Also on Saturday, Lee Trevino shot 69 and thrust himself into the picture as a solid contender for the first time. After 16 holes that day, Simons was 6 under par after holing a 15-foot birdie putt, and he needed only two pars for 64. On 17, a long par 3 of 200 yards, he pushed his two iron into a green-side bunker and made 4, then finished with a par on the 18th for his 65. Nicklaus, meanwhile, was playing Merion in 68, and when the round was finished, the standings looked like this:

SIMONS	207
NICKLAUS	209
NICHOLS	210
TREVINO	211
COLBERT	211
ERICKSON	211

Everyone at Merion on Sunday really expected Simons to wilt, and he started off as if he might. From the first tee he drove into the right rough. His approach settled on the left fringe, and he putted 5 feet from the hole—real choking distance. He rolled it right in. No, he would not wilt. By the end of nine holes, though, Simons's lead had been trimmed to 1 stroke over Nicklaus, 2 over Trevino and Nichols. Simons lost his lead with a bogey 5 on the 10th, and then Trevino caught them both with a birdie 3 on the 12th. Another birdie on the 14th and Trevino had the lead for the first time. He made pars on the next three holes, but then missed the 18th green to the right and needed 3 more to get down for a bogey 5 and even par 280 with his fourth-round 69.

Nicklaus had to sink successive 6-footers to save pars on the 15th, 16th, and 17th holes, and then he hit a superb four iron just 15 feet from

"Super Mex" Lee Trevino

Trevino on way to victory in 1971 Open

the hole on the 18th, clearly a birdie chance. Jack hit a good putt, but it slid by the right side of the hole by 2 inches, and he finished with a 280 that matched Trevino.

The playoff the next day lasted only about three holes. Trevino bogeyed the 1st, and then Nicklaus hit his second shot on the 2nd hole into a bunker. Trevino was in the right rough 50 yards short of the green in 2, and played a lovely pitch 12 feet from the hole. Nicklaus dug his feet into the sand, swung smoothly, and left the ball in the trap. He made 6, and they were tied again. The 3rd hole is a 180-yard par 3. Trevino up first, hit into the left green-side bunker. Jack followed him. Now, Trevino is one of the best bunker players in the game, and came out 3 feet from the hole. Incredibly, Nicklaus left another shot in a bunker and made 5. He was then 2 strokes behind after three holes, and even though he would cut the margin to one stroke occasionally, he could never catch up. He reached probably the height of his frustration on the 10th, a little more than a flick wedge to the green. He hit it fat and the ball didn't get there. Another 5.

The description of the 10th may not really be fair to Nicklaus—nor to Trevino—for they both played marvelously well after the 3rd hole. It was simply one superb shot after another, with Lee almost holing his approach on the 8th, and then Jack playing his tee shot within 2 feet of the cup on the 9th. It all climaxed on the 15th. Trevino played his approach onto the green 25 feet from the hole, and then Nicklaus put his ball 8 feet away. Trevino putted first and holed it. Nicklaus holed it on top of him. But it was all over for Jack. He was still 2 strokes behind with two to play, and then he hit his tee shot on the 17th into a bunker. Trevino had won his second Open, all the time laughing and joking, and telling the world that Jack Nicklaus is the greatest golfer ever—and saying with his eyes, "But I can beat him."

1972

Trevino's chances of beating Nicklaus in the 1972 Open were considered very slight, simply because he was still in a hospital bed early in Open week recovering from a mild case of bronchial pneumonia. He arrived late Tuesday and played only one practice round before the championship began on Thursday.

It seems incredible that the Open had never been played at Pebble Beach before 1972, for here is one of the great golf courses. It is also probably the most scenically spectacular course in the world, routed as it is along the headlands above the Pacific Ocean on California's Monterey Peninsula.

Each year two rounds of the Bing Crosby Pro-Am are played at Pebble Beach, and the players felt they knew the course. They didn't, for Pebble Beach in June is a different proposition from Pebble Beach in January. The wind is coming from a different direction, and the holes that played short in the Crosby played long in the Open. In addition, the grass had been pampered through two years of preparation, and the course had never had so much cover. Normally the fairways are a bit bare and the ball will run great distances. Not in the Open; you got what you carried and little more. The USGA had also made some strategic changes, principally adding a few bunkers, including one on the left side of the 10th fairway that eliminated a shortcut and forced tee shots to the center or right side, flirting with a sheer drop of 40 or 50 feet to the beach below.

Once more, when the championship began Jack Nicklaus was considered unbeatable, particularly now that Trevino certainly would not be much of a factor. Jack had won the Masters in April, and had never been out of first place in four rounds. He had been trying for two years to win all four major tournaments in one season—Masters, Open, British Open, and PGA—and all four were being played in 1972 on courses he liked. The Masters was, of course, at Augusta National, the Open at Pebble Beach, where he had won the Crosby in January, the British Open at Muirfield, where he had won in 1966, and the PGA at Oakland Hills, where he had finished fourth in the 1961 Open as an amateur.

Jack opened with a steady two-birdie, one-bogey 71 on Thursday, and when he looked around he was in the company of five others, including Orville Moody, Old Sarge, who wore a surgical mask between shots to filter pollen that irritated his hay fever condition. Gary Player was among four players at 72, Trevino shot an encouraging 74, and Arnold Palmer was way back there at 77. Pebble Beach was turning out to be a very tough course. Of the 150 starters, 48 players, nearly one third of the field, did not break 80. At Pebble Beach you had to make your birdies early, for the course surely would claim strokes from you on the second nine. For instance, through four rounds Homero Blancas was 19 strokes higher on the second nine than on the first. In the first two rounds he made 11 birdies, but his total score was 144—even par.

Nicklaus shot 73 in the second round, and, instead of losing ground, he was still tied for first place, again with five others, including Bruce Crampton, who finished second to him at Augusta. Trevino, weak though he was, somehow shot 72, and was just 2 strokes off the lead with 36 holes to play. It was during the second round that Palmer suddenly came to life. Faced with the possibility of missing the cut, Arnold shot 68 in a round that included six birdies. Palmer was playing some of his best shots in years, and he was consistently near the hole with his approaches. His

Orville Moody fights off hay fever at 1972 Open

putting, though, was still a little shaky; he missed makable birdie putts on the 5th, 6th, and 7th, and then a 2-foot putt on the 8th that cost him a par. With that one round Palmer was now in the thick of it, just a stroke behind the leaders with 145.

Nicklaus moved in front in the third round with an even par round of 72 and a 54-hole score of 216, again even par, but he was still being dogged by Trevino, who simply would not wilt. Lee shot 71, thus improving his score each day. He made five birdies in that round, four of them on the second nine. Palmer was dogging Nicklaus with almost as much determination as Trevino, and he even caught Jack momentarily with a par 3 on the 5th. Nicklaus moved ahead once more when Palmer made a bogey 5 on the 8th, and Jack was not caught the rest of that round. And so when the last round began, Nicklaus was ahead at 216; Trevino, Crampton, and Kermit Zarley were tied for second at 217, followed by Palmer and John Miller at 218.

Sunday was a brutal day. The wind came up strong and gusty, and the Pacific was frothy. Small-craft warnings were hoisted along the coast, and a regatta scheduled off shore from Pebble Beach had to be canceled. Unfortunately, by the time the high winds began, the USGA had already set the pins, anticipating quiet weather, and Pebble Beach was almost too hard to play. Nicklaus went to bed the night before, believing a round of par or better would be needed for him to win, but when he saw the wind he realized that no one would break par this day.

He and Trevino were last off the tee, and Lee's weakened condition finally overcame his spirit. He and Nicklaus matched par 4s on the first hole, and then Trevino drove into the left rough on the second, a 507-yard par 5. Nicklaus, meanwhile, hit the fairway and then played a two iron onto the green, giving himself a sure shot at a birdie. Trevino's second stayed in the rough short of the ravine that slashes across the fairway before the green. His third went over and into the woods, and he needed 4 strokes to get on. He made 6. When Nicklaus made his birdie he led Trevino by 3 strokes.

Jack then played some strange golf. He bogeyed the 4th, a little 325-yard par 4, three-putting, bogeyed the 5th, scraped out a par on the 6th after playing into two bunkers, and then somehow scraped out a birdie on the 7th, the little 120-yard par 3 from an elevated tee to a small green set on a promontory that juts into the ocean. To give some idea of the wind, both Nicklaus and Trevino hit seven irons on that hole. Jack turned slightly on his shot, but it held the line long enough to catch the left side of the green. From there he rolled in a 22-foot putt for a much-needed birdie. From then on Jack's only threat came from Palmer and from himself. Playing ahead of Nicklaus, Palmer fell 3 strokes behind when Jack birdied the 2nd. He made up all three on the next three holes, and so when both men had played five holes, they were even. This is misleading, however, for Palmer was two holes ahead, and he had already bogeyed the 6th before Nicklaus had played the 5th and 7th, and so they were never even on the scoreboard.

Nicklaus reached the 10th tee in par 36, and now we were heading into the most dramatic moments of the Open, the 10th through the 12th holes, where it was almost lost. As Jack reached the top of his backswing on the 10th tee, a strong gust whipped in from the sea, and it seemed to flip Jack's driver as he began the downswing. Whatever happened, the ball soared well to the right and plummeted down the cliff onto the soft sandy beach. He was within ground designated as a lateral hazard, and so he dropped another ball at the top of the cliff, taking a one-stroke penalty. From there he played a two iron, which was not enough club. The hazard takes a turn into the fairway just before the green, and once more Nicklaus was in the hazard. He played his shot from there, however, and made a 6. Two shots of his lead were gone, and Palmer was closing in. Arnold had made a 5 on the 10th, but then he played the 11th, 12th, and 13th holes in pars. Nicklaus got past the 11th with another par 4, and then he came to the 12th, a 205-yard par 3 with trees on the right and a sharp drop behind into matty and wiry rough. The Open was settled right here.

At this time Palmer was playing the 14th, a par 5 of 555 yards that doglegs right. He hit two adequate shots up the fairway, and then a soft pitch to the green about 8 or 10 feet from the hole. Nicklaus, meanwhile, was playing a three-iron to the 12th green. The shot came off too hot; it hit the green and bounded over the back and down into that coarse, clumpy grass. Jack dug at it and moved it only halfway up the incline. He hit it again and sent it 8 feet past the hole.

Here, now, is the scene: Palmer is hunched over an 8-footer for a birdie on the 14th and Nicklaus is over another 8-footer for a bogey on 12. If Palmer makes his putt and Nicklaus misses, Arnold will lead the Open. If they both hole they will be tied.

They both stroked their putts at almost the same instant. Jack's putt rolled true, right into the hole. He had saved a 4. Arnold's putt just grazed the left edge of the hole, and it did not drop. A 5. Nicklaus was still ahead by a stroke, and some of the heart seemed to go out of Palmer. His face screwed up in anguish and he sagged slightly. He followed by driving the rough on both the 15th and 16th, making bogeys on both, and when Nicklaus survived a poor drive on the 13th, playing a crisp nine-iron approach from a dirt road to save par, and followed by holing a 12-foot birdie putt on 15, Arnold was 4 strokes off the lead. That is how he finished.

From then on, it was simply a triumphant march for Nicklaus. He made a routine par 4 on the 16th, and then played a superb one iron to the 17th, hitting the base of the flag on the first bounce. The ball settled within 6 inches of the hole for another birdie. He played the 18th cautiously, almost creeping up on the hole, and took three putts for a bogey 6. He finished

Nicklaus wins another

3 strokes ahead with 290. Crampton had held on to finish second with 293, and Palmer had 294. In the record book, Jack's last round will always read simply 74, but it must have been the finest 74 ever shot under the circumstances. Only Mason Rudolph did better, somehow shooting 70, but Mase had already shot 80 and 86 in the previous two rounds, and so he was awfully loose. Trevino shot 78 in that last round and finished in a tie for fourth at 295.

With that victory, Nicklaus had matched the record of Bobby Jones, with 13 victories in major competition. It was the third Open for Nicklaus. Only Jones, Hogan, and old Willie Anderson had won four, and when the big red sun dipped into the Pacific that night, Jack was only thirty-two, and there was hardly any doubt that he would win more Opens.

Golf, though, is an unpredictable game. What about Sam Snead? Didn't everyone think he would win more than one Open, and didn't he fail to win any? And what of Ralph Guldahl? Didn't he win two in a row, and then fall into a slump that could not be explained or analyzed, and never win another? And more recently, what of Ben Hogan? Did he not have his finest year in 1953, winning the Open, the British Open, and the Masters, and did he not fail to win ever again? And then what of Palmer? Who would have considered that when he played so well at Augusta in 1964, hitting shots as he had never hit them, he had won his last major tournament? Who would have thought?

⌐4⌐

THE BRITISH OPEN—
SCOTLAND WHERE IT
ALL BEGAN

M OST OF the important happenings in British golf have had small beginnings, and the British Open Championship, now one of the world's four major tournaments, is no exception. It started in a modest way when what had been a purely Scottish game was taking the first steps toward becoming a worldwide pastime. The introduction in 1848 of the solid gutta-percha ball (replacing the expensive, unreliable feather-stuffed ball) was a key factor, since golf became both easier and cheaper—and therefore more widely popular. Soon after, a few particularly skillful players began to be well known as rivals in money matches. In 1853, one of these, Tom Morris of St. Andrews, went to the newly formed Prestwick Golf Club, on the West Coast of Scotland, as professional. His wage was 15 shillings a week. His duties included those which would now be carried out by a greenskeeper.

Tom Morris had already attracted attention by playing a number of fiercely close matches with his great rival from Musselburgh (near Edinburgh), Willie Park. The knowledge that their professional was one of the two best players in the country encouraged the Prestwick members to invite eight leading players to compete in a 36-hole competition called "A General Golf Tournament for Scotland," with a Challenge Belt going to the winner. The inaugural event was played at Prestwick on October 17, 1860, and as expected, Park and Morris fought it out to the finish, with Park winning with a total of 174 for 36 holes, (three rounds of the Prestwick links, which then numbered only 12 holes). Morris was second with 176, and Andrew Strath of St. Andrews third with 180. None of the three profited financially because the only prize was the Belt, which the winner could keep for one year. Twelve months later the tournament was repeated, with the additional condition that it should henceforth be "open to the world." Thus, the Open acquired its title and Tom Morris, who turned the tables on Park with a winning total of 163 to 166, became the true first "Open Champion." He successfully defended his title in 1862.

In the fourth Championship (1863), prize money was offered for the first time, but only for the second, third, and fourth places, worth about $25, $15, and $10 respectively. Park regained the Belt, but Morris won the big money. Morris cashed in again in 1864, winning the Belt for the third time and also pocketing the new first prize of about $30. Andrew Strath, who won the Belt in 1865, was the only player to interrupt the Park-Morris monopoly during the first eight years. But in 1868 a new star appeared who was destined to be the greatest golfer the game had yet seen. Young Tommy Morris he was called, to distinguish him from his bearded father, and at seventeen, having first beaten all the best professionals in a tournament at Montrose, he went to Prestwick and won the Championship with a remarkable total of 157, beating the previous record by 5 strokes. Next year the prodigy shot 154, and in 1870 he managed an almost unbelievable 149 to win by 12 strokes.

The length of the Prestwick course in those days was only 5,500 yards for 18 holes. But when one considers the limited distance attainable with the gutta-percha ball, the imperfect, unmatched wooden clubs, the rough nature of the terrain from tee to green, and the crude condition of the putting surfaces themselves, Young Tommy's 1870 average of 74½ strokes per round can be seen as one of the greatest achievements in the history of golf. By winning the Open three times in succession, Young Tom gained permanent possession of the Belt, and it is now one of the prized trophies of the Royal and Ancient clubhouse at St. Andrews.

For the organizers of the Championship, the immediate problem was how to continue without a trophy, and 1871 went by without a tournament while new arrangements were discussed. But fortunately, the event had established itself so that both the Royal and Ancient Golf Club and the Honourable Company of Edinburgh Golfers (who then played at Musselburgh) were easily persuaded to join with the Prestwick club in providing a Challenge Cup (perpetual this time) to be competed for at Prestwick, St. Andrews, and Musselburgh in rotation. So in the autumn of 1872 the leading professionals gathered again at Prestwick to compete for the famous vase which today's winner holds aloft as he is saluted by thousands of spectators. Those who applauded Young Tommy Morris when he was handed the new trophy in 1872 could be counted in tens, but the occasion was historic. The genius of St. Andrews had won for the fourth time in succession—a record which has stood to the present day and may well stand for ever. Tommy Morris was only twenty-one when he reached this peak of his fortunes, and what other heights he might have scaled will never be known. Three years later he was dead.

The Championship, now fairly launched, began to attract larger fields, including not a few amateurs, some equal to the best professionals in skill. But no amateur was able to win until 1890. John Ball, Jr.'s victory in that year startled everyone. It was true that Ball had won the past two Amateur Championships, but his winning at Prestwick was a double blow. For the first time, the Open had been won by an amateur; for the first time, the Open had been won by an Englishman. Scottish golf *and* the professionals had been humbled at once.

The 1890 Championship marked the end of one era and the beginning of another. The old school of crude, rough-and-ready professionals had faded before the advance of new men who were raising the general standard of skill and bringing more polish into the game. In 1892, when the Championship was extended to its present format of 72 holes, another gifted amateur, Harold Hilton, of Hoylake, was the winner. Still another amateur, J. E. Laidlay, nearly won in the following year, finishing second to Willie Auchterlonie of St. Andrews. Auchterlonie, who many years afterward became honorary professional to the Royal and Ancient Golf Club, occupies an unenviable niche in the gallery of champions because he was the last Scot entered from a Scottish club to win the title. Many Scots were migrating to England and other countries to be professionals at new clubs, lured by terms which, while not munificent, were considerably better than those prevailing in their own country.

In addition, the spread of golf was producing a new strain of English-born professionals; the first to make his mark was John Henry Taylor, who won the 1894 Championship with 5 strokes to spare. The Scottish monopoly, already damaged by the amateur victories of Ball and Hilton, was now demolished by the first of the great English professionals.

That 1894 Championship was held on the Royal St. George's links at Sandwich—another indication of the bigger part now being played by Englishmen. In 1893 the Royal St. George's and Royal Liverpool clubs joined the three Scottish promoting clubs in a consortium; and a five-year cycle was started, the Championship to be held in rotation at Prestwick, Sandwich, St. Andrews, Muirfield, and Hoylake. The shift to Sandwich, which required the Scottish competitors to make a long journey, might have helped Taylor's chances, but he proved 12 months later that he was equally at home in Scotland by retaining the title at St. Andrews.

In 1896, however, Taylor was defeated by one who was to outstrip him in the race for lasting fame—Harry Vardon. Vardon began as a gardener but soon followed his brother Tom into professional golf. In the 1896 Championship at Muirfield, the new home of the Honourable Company, Vardon tied with Taylor and then beat him in the playoff by 4 strokes.

The battle was joined. Harold Hilton won the Championship for the second time on his home course, Hoylake, but Vardon regained the crown in 1898, retained it in 1899, and then lost it to Taylor in 1900. Early in that year, Vardon had made his famous American tour. The trip was exhausting, and although he finished second to Taylor in the Open, the gap between them was 8 strokes. Vardon was to recover his form later, but in 1901 he and Taylor had to give way to a tall, lean Scot named James Braid, destined to join the other two in the celebrated Great Triumvirate. Braid was a contemporary of Vardon and Taylor, in fact a few months their senior, but he had come late to professional golf after several years as a successful amateur. He made up for lost time. His victory over Vardon by 3 strokes at Muirfield in 1901 marked the start of a decade in which he won the Open five times, was runner-up three times, and was match-play champion three times.

The year 1902 marked the first use in the Championship of an invention which was to totally change the game—the Haskell rubber-core ball. Although it was already known in America, the ball was met with suspicion and skepticism by the British professionals. Among the doubters was Alexander (Sandy) Herd, a crafty little Scot from St. Andrews. But after a practice round with John Ball, who was playing the Haskell ball, Herd changed his mind, bought a supply of the new balls, and proceeded to win the Open with them. The "guttie" was routed, just as the "featherie" had been fifty years earlier, and golf was set for its biggest expansion. A sign of golf's widening popularity was the 1907 victory of a Frenchman (Arnaud Massey), the first win by a foreigner. But British golf was still dominant, and the rivalry between "the three" of Taylor, Vardon, and Braid continued to the start of World War I. In that idyllic summer of 1914, on Prestwick's links, the final tussle for supremacy was played out, with Vardon winning the title for the sixth time, and edging one win ahead of his two rivals. Among them, they had won 16 Opens in 21 years.

The Championship was suspended during the war years, but peace saw the arrival of a new generation and a new overseas menace.

It all started with Jock Hutchison, St. Andrews–born but a naturalized American. Hutchison won the 1921 Championship on the Old Course, where he had learned the game. Of course, the result could be claimed a semi-Scottish victory, and there was the added fact that an English amateur, Roger Wethered, had tied with Hutchison, only to lose in a 36-hole playoff.

That was the first of 13 years during which golfers from the United States scored 12 victories in the Open, the foremost being Walter Hagen and Bobby Jones, who won seven times between them. Hagen scored the first of his four wins in 1922 at Sandwich, but it was the narrowest of victories. The American had been prematurely hailed as the winner while

George Duncan was still out on the course making a tremendous run. Starting the last round 4 strokes behind Hagen, Duncan came to the 18th hole needing only a 4 to tie, but missed the decisive putt by a whisker. He had gone around in 69 to beat the course record by 3 strokes but the Cup, for the first time, was in the hands of an American-born golfer.

Hagen nearly won again in 1923, being nipped by one stroke at Troon by Arthur Havers, who thus checked for a year the American march. But Hagen was back in the saddle in 1924, and after winning for a third time in 1928, he wound up his record in great style at Muirfield in 1929, winning by 6 strokes from Johnny Farrell, with a third American, Leo Diegel, in third place.

The story of Jones in the Open Championship is a part of the whole Jones saga of seven glorious years during which the great Georgian amateur won 13 national titles on both sides of the Atlantic. He had a desperately close battle in 1926 and another in 1930, when he won at Hoylake to complete the second leg of his Grand Slam. But in 1927 at St. Andrews, he was at his masterful best. An opening round of 68 put him 4 strokes in front of everyone, and his aggregate of 285 was 6 strokes lower than his own record for the Championship, and 11 strokes better than the St. Andrews record for 72 holes.

Bobby's 1926 win was notable, of course, for the shot he played from sand at the 17th hole in the final round, a shot commemorated by a plaque at the spot and a glass case in the Royal Lytham and St. Anne's clubhouse containing the mashie iron he used. Jones, who was having putting troubles, had trailed his playing partner, Al Watrous, for most of the last day. He finally drew even at the 15th hole, but pulled his tee shot on the 17th into a nest of bunkers about 170 yards from the green, with trees and bushes on the line of his intended shot. Jones watched Watrous's iron shot land safely on the green. Then to everyone's surprise, instead of playing safely short, Jones went for the green with his mashie iron. The ball had to be hit as cleanly as possible in order to get both the necessary distance *and* the trajectory required to clear the intervening scrub. The stroke was played with absolute perfection. The ball landed on the green, a startled Watrous took three putts, to fall behind, and Jones went on to win the Open for the first time.

There was plenty of drama, too, in Jones's third win in 1930. For the first two rounds everything seemed to favor the young American, who earlier in the season had won the British Amateur at St. Andrews. At Hoylake, Jones led by one stroke after 36 holes, but Archie Compston had a record-breaking third round of 68 to take the lead by a stroke. When Compston reacted with a shattering fourth round of 82, Jones, a later starter, seemed very well placed when his second shot was almost on the green at the par-5 8th. When he walked off the green with a 7 on his card, this alarming prodigality with precious strokes left the situation critical. But

Jones's ability to stay calm, when inwardly he must have been seething, saved him. He got his 4 at the 9th and covered the long road home in 37 to win by 2 from Macdonald Smith and Leo Diegel. Jones retired at the end of 1930, but the American steamroller went on. Tommy Armour (Scottish-born) won in 1931, Gene Sarazen in 1932, and Denny Shute in 1933.

Those who saw the 1934 event at Sandwich will never forget the scenes which followed a famous victory by Henry Cotton, a Briton. Twelve months earlier there had been an all American playoff (Shute beating Craig Wood), and now there was a young British golfer of twenty-seven ending ten years of American domination. Cotton had a 66 in the first qualifying round on the Royal St. George's links, and in the first two rounds of the Championship proper he had 67 and 65 to establish a winning lead. With a third-round 72 he was 10 strokes ahead with 18 holes to go. An attack of stomach cramps made the outward half a nightmare, but he recovered sufficiently to score 79 and win by 5 strokes.

This great performance seemed to have a paralyzing effect on American golf, but in fact a lot of the power had gone from the invading forces. Jones had retired, Hagen was no longer a contender, and several others who had been prominent were past their peak. So this new tale of British victories continued until World War II, with Alfred Perry, Alfred Padgham, Cotton, Reg Whitcombe, and Dick Burton winning in that order. Cotton's second victory in 1937, gained on the great Carnoustie links, is generally considered to be the finest of his three wins because of the brilliant final round of 71 played in terrible weather. After Burton's victory in 1939, the Open Championship was suspended for five years as war broke out.

1946

With the growth of the American tour in prewar years, the prestige of the British Open declined. Negligible purses and a sponsor unequipped to stage a large, modern tournament handicapped the Championship, which had an increasingly hard time attracting the best players from abroad. The U.S. pros could stay home and make more money.

But with the end of World War II, there was considerable excitement when the Royal and Ancient decided to hold the Open again at its own course. More than 200 players entered, many from overseas, including Sam Snead, Lawson, and Johnny Bulla of the U.S.A., Bobby Locke of South Africa, and Norman Von Nida of Australia. Britain had heard of Snead and Little before the war. Snead was supposedly the greatest prospect since Jones. And Little? Well, he had made the Little Slam by winning both the

U.S. and British Amateur Championships for two straight years, then turned professional and won the U.S. Open. Bulla, a monumental figure of a man, an airline pilot turned professional golfer, was new on the scene, but Locke had been appearing in Britain for years. He, too, was an airman with a long record of flying in the Middle East behind him. Von Nida had a considerable reputation Down Under.

Snead began as a hot favorite and won by a substantial margin of 4 strokes from Locke and Bulla, who tied at 294. Cotton played a pair of magnificent 70s in the first two rounds and led Snead by a stroke, but, with the wind going into the northwest on the last day—when 36 holes were played—the greens became fast, a condition which never suited Cotton. He began to putt defensively and faded with rounds of 76 and 79.

Snead began the last round poorly with three 5s but had a priceless stroke of luck at the long 5th. His second shot sliced into the nearly impenetrable rough. There he found not only his ball but enough clearance to swing his club. In the circumstances, he played a poor stroke, which just reached the edge of the green. But he holed the putt from 50 feet for a birdie 4 and thereafter played his own imposing game, completing the second half downwind in 35. He also had another extraordinary piece of luck. American professionals at the time were in the habit of roughing up the faces of their iron clubs and, hearing that one of his pitching clubs was likely to be queried by members of the PGA, he had sought permission to use it from a member of the Championship Committee. The old fellow, delighted at the opportunity of talking to Snead, passed it without a murmur. Snead was the only player who could stop the ball downwind on those lightning-fast greens in the last nine holes, and 35 home after 40 out made him a clear winner. A year later Lawson Little, listening at Hoylake to a eulogy on Snead at St. Andrews, commented drily, "He also had the club." But it seemed fitting that this tremendous player had won the British Open.

1947

A fine golfer, Fred Daly of Northern Ireland, won a thrilling Championship at Hoylake from Reginald Horne of Hendon and Frank Stranahan, an American amateur, who tied at 294 for second place, a stroke behind Daly.

Daly at the time may have been considered a lucky winner, but his subsequent performances in the Open, the Match Play Championship, which he won twice, and in Ryder Cup matches proved him to be a great competitor. Some golfers are good winners, others good losers. Fred Daly was both.

He had a poor third round of 78 with three gratuitous putts at the 13th, leaving him tied for the lead with Cotton, Arthur Lees, and Von Nida with a round to go. Stranahan, in some ways the hero of the Championship, was one further back.

Daly was lucky with the weather, since he was out early in the afternoon of the last day before it began to blow. He was also lucky at the short 13th, where he completely missed his tee shot and shanked his second 15 yards from the hole. But he sent the putt down for a 3 that restored his confidence. He played the next three desperate holes in 4 each, but at the 17th he took three shots to reach the green, where this painstaking, immaculate putter took three more. Horne with a fine 71 had already established a target of 294, and Daly, after his tragic 6, was left with a 4 to tie and a 3 to beat Horne. After a superb second to the home hole, Daly holed out from 12 feet for his 3 and took the lead.

Meanwhile, Stranahan, out almost last, was playing great golf in the high wind that grew to gale force. He hit two magnificent shots to the 17th, but for once this mechanical man took three putts, leaving him with a 2 to tie. His second shot on the final hole, the finest ever played in a last, desperate throw, hit the flag and fell one inch from the cup. He had played the most heroic back nine ever played in such conditions over Hoylake, but Fred Daly had won.

1948

Henry Cotton won his third Championship at Muirfield in 1948 by five clear shots from Fred Daly, the holder, who though never at his brilliant best defended gallantly. Cotton had spent the early part of the year in the Argentine and America, and the sunshine and stiff competition with the big ball had tuned him up to his best game. He had done well in tournaments before the Championship and, asked by a friend about his chances in the Open, had said, "If I can beat the big Argentinean, Roberto de Vicenzo, I think I can win." This proved an accurate forecast since de Vicenzo, without a word of English and thus unable to talk to his caddy, tied Von Nida for third place at 290. Alfred Padgham, the 1936 winner, was runner-up.

Apart from de Vicenzo, the field was not a good one, and after a brilliant second round of 66 (watched by King George VI, himself a fair golfer), Cotton was secure.

1949

For the next decade, with weak fields due to the absence of the American pros, the Championship was dominated by two great golfers from the Commonwealth: Bobby Locke of South Africa and Peter Thomson of Australia. They won eight of the next ten Championships (four each), with Thomson winning a fifth in 1965. Only Max Faulkner, in 1951, and Ben Hogan, in 1953, could break the Locke–Thomson hold on the British Open.

They were two most interesting players—Locke, completely unorthodox, his whole game dependent on a beautiful rhythm acquired at the age of twelve from watching Cyril Tolley when that great player had visited South Africa; and Thomson, strictly orthodox, an excellent athlete, easy to watch since, unlike Locke, he played at a fine, brisk pace.

Temperamentally, too, they seemed poles apart, though they had one thing in common: each kept himself to himself and was difficult to know. Both made fortunes and wisely kept them. And it is still conceivable that Thomson may yet win a sixth championship to equal Vardon's record. Both have been tremendous competitors, but whereas Locke, so unorthodox in all but rhythm, found the big ball and American conditions entirely to his liking, Thomson, the classical stylist and more naturally gifted of the two, never really made his mark in the United States. His many admirers said, rightly or wrongly, that he did not like America or Americans, but it is significant that only once in his long run of successes in the Open has he won against a top-class field with Americans—at Royal Birkdale in 1965.

It was in 1949 at Royal St. Georges that Bobby Locke won the first of his four British Open Championships, after a tie with Harry Bradshaw, an unorthodox but brilliant Irish golfer. Bradshaw found his ball resting in the base of a broken beer bottle at the 5th in the second round and attempted to play it, risking his eyesight from splintered glass. It undoubtedly cost him a stroke and the Championship. At the 72nd hole, Locke made the bravest little pitch from behind the bunker on to a downward slope, and then sunk an equally brave putt of 3 feet to get into the playoff. In perfect weather conditions, Locke played two superb rounds of 67 and 68, and poor Bradshaw was crushed.

1950

At Troon, Locke defended his title successfully, setting a new record of 279 to win by two strokes over Roberto de Vicenzo.

Locke opened with a majestic 69, but in his second round at the short 4th hole he hooked his tee shot, and from 20 yards proceeded painfully to get down in 6. His subsequent play showed his courage as he finished in 72.

De Vicenzo was hopelessly bunkered from the tee at the famous short 8th, known as the "Postage Stamp." He took one look at his ball under the lip, deemed it unplayable, and returned to the tee. His second shot hit the flag and stayed one inch from the hole. At the time the Royal and Ancient was experimenting with the rules, as many were moaning about the inequities of being allowed to "deem unplayable" at the cost of distance only. One may imagine that it was Roberto's "Postage Stamp" at Troon in 1950 that made the Rules Committee think again.

1951

Before the end of the Locke era, other exciting things were to happen. Breaking the England-Scotland tradition, the Championship committee decided to hold the British Open at Royal Portrush in Northern Ireland, a fine course laid out in glorious golfing country with dunes and sandhills of unrivaled scenic splendor.

The Championship was won by a strong and stylish player, Max Faulkner, who had learned much of his game from Henry Cotton. Blessed with superb physique, he was a beautiful swinger. And, too, he reminded oldtimers of the late Archie Compston with his extravagant boasts about the mincemeat he was going to make of his adversaries. These boasts hid a highly strung temperament, but Faulkner arrived at Portrush with a new sylphlike, feather-weight putter, with which he declared he would never miss a sinkable putt again. He missed very few at Portrush, where he became the last British player to win the Championship for 18 years.

Locke, who finished sixth, for once showed his fallibility; in the prevailing wind "Calamity Corner," the famous short 14th, disturbed his usually imperturbable composure.

1952

Locke won for the third time at Royal Lytham and St. Anne's in 1952 by a single stroke from the rising Peter Thomson. Locke had become an appallingly slow player, and after two rounds, Norman Von Nida of Australia lodged a complaint to the Championship Committee about Locke's play. In those days this Committee was not yet fully confident of its authority to govern, and the Chairman appeared diffident about warning Locke that "he must hurry or accept the consequences." Locke accepted the resulting admonition in dignified silence and played more slowly than ever next day. He thereby demonstrated that the greatest golfers will play at their own pace, just as Tommy Armour, the first great slow player, had done years before, and Cary Middlecoff and Jack Nicklaus have done in recent years. Locke was to win for the fourth and last time in 1957 but the intervening years belonged first to Ben Hogan, and then to Peter Thomson.

1953

Ben Hogan's very presence at Carnoustie made the 1953 Championship one of the most important for years. His 1953 triumphs in the U.S. Open and the Masters had gained him his preeminent position in the world of golf, but he still had not played in the British Open. For some this gap made his otherwise splendid achievements seem incomplete.

Hogan could not have chosen a better moment to accept the challenge. The Open was being held at Carnoustie, the most severe test of all the great seaside courses in Britain. Tommy Armour in 1931 and Henry Cotton in 1937 had won there previously, and perhaps it was these two names that prompted Hogan to enter. From the day of his entry, record crowds and a great tournament were assured.

Hogan apart, the field was not a great one though there were a dozen or more capable of winning, such as Locke, the holder; Peter Thomson; the Argentines, Cerda and de Vicenzo; and the American amateur, Frank Stranahan.

With no artificial watering facilities, the course was in poor shape, following a long dry spell. The fairways of this public course were hard and scarred with thousands of divot marks, and the greens were coarse and slow. The greens improved during the week after some welcome rain, but Hogan never really mastered them.

In those days the entire field was required to play in the qualifying rounds on the Monday and Tuesday before the Championship proper began. Special trains and buses brought thousands of spectators, and a vast crowd watched Hogan tee off on the Burnside course. The stewards lost all control as a wild scene developed. Hogan remained calm in the scramble and started with a 3, while his partner, Bill Branch, was almost trampled under foot. Hogan's qualifying aggregate of 70, 75—145 was 9 below the cut of 154, but 9 behind Locke's leading total of 65, 71—136.

Stranahan stole the limelight in the first round of the Championship itself next day with a fine 70. Eric Brown of Scotland was next with 71, with Bobby Locke, Peter Thomson, Dai Rees, and Roberto de Vicenzo at 72. Hogan, followed by a vast army, was in with 73 after having been caught in a freakish July hailstorm at the 6th. His long game was almost perfect but he was consistently short with his approach putts, leaving himself some uncomfortable holing out on many holes. At the 16th after a marvelous bunker shot he was 2 inches short from 8 feet. Though he chipped to 3 feet at the 17th, he again missed the putt. Finally at the 18th, after hitting the pin with his third, he failed to touch the hole with his first putt.

On the following morning, with Rees going great guns ahead and Stranahan drawing cheers from his supporters, Hogan went off in the still atmosphere as if intent on setting the course afire. Those who saw the first five holes declared they ought to have been five 3s. You had to see the amazing accuracy of Ben's iron play to appreciate the full stature of this astounding golfer.

But he missed his 4 from short range at the long and desperate 6th for the first and only time in the Championship, and thereafter his misery on the greens began all over again.

What was so nearly 32 to the turn became 36, and he reeled off par after par coming home with not a break in sight on the greens. When he stepped almost wearily from the last green with a 71, he had once again taken 34 putts. Locke, for the second time, had taken only 28.

Rees and Brown were now in the lead at 142, with de Vincenzo at 143, and Hogan, Thomson, and Stranahan at 144. Locke was 145 in company with Faulkner; and Cerda, who in the third round was to be the first man ever to break 70 over this great course in an open Championship, made a progressive move with 71 for 146.

In his third round Hogan, followed by a large crowd, drilled his way to the turn in 35 shots, then started for home with a 3 at the 10th. He three-putted the 12th, but came back with a glorious 2 at the 13th, and when he got his 3 at the 16th for the first time in the Championship, he was 4 under par and threatening the course record.

After missing his long iron to the 17th, he was bunkered in front of the green; an indifferent explosion and he was left with a 25-foot putt. He took three, and that frightful 6 spoiled the morning for thousands. Still, there he was sharing the lead now at 214 with his score (73, 71, 70) coming down all the time, warming up in preparation for his final thrust. Like Hagen, he appeared to have the indefinable quality of bringing himself to his supreme peak when his need was most urgent and the pressure greatest. But unlike the erratic Haig, Hogan was the nearest thing Britain had seen to the perfect golfing machine.

The fortunes of the main contenders ebbed and flowed dramatically throughout the long final day. Stranahan, who had lost ground with a 73 in the morning, was first home and came surging back with a glorious 69, to set a target of 286, which would require a 71 from Hogan to tie.

Before Hogan's finish, Rees and Thomson also managed 286s. But Hogan was better. He went off with four perfectly played 4s and then at the 5th, with the pressure rising, got the break that must have convinced him he was going to win. His tee shot finished in a poor lie on the fairway. His second to the green appeared perfect but the ball spun back onto the grassy bank of a bunker. Grimacing (for once) when he saw the lie, he studied the position with care. Finally, his mind made up, he sent his caddy to the pin and, chipping with a straight-faced club, rattled the ball into the hole.

At the last hole, he hit one of his finest second to 4 feet, although his putt finished inches short. 73, 71, 70, 68! Bernard Darwin wagged his head when it all was over, observing quietly, "One was quite certain he could have played a 64, for Hogan gave you the distinct impression that he was capable of getting whatever score was needed to win." It was Hogan's only appearance in the British Open.

1954

The Championship went to Royal Birkdale for the first time in 1954, and with Hogan failing to defend, Peter Thomson scored the first of his three consecutive victories (which eventually became five in all). Without Hogan, the American entry was once again very poor.

After the usual scramble for the lead at the end of two rounds, it appeared that the winner would be found from among Locke, Thomson, Syd Scott, who had had a brilliant second round of 67, and Dai Rees. Scott, a sound and consistent golfer if not a very powerful one, finished early with a well-played last round of 72 for a total of 284. Later Rees, often poised to win the Open and unlucky never to have won, arrived at the home hole needing only a 4 to beat Scott. His strong second bounced hard and ran through the green, and after taking three more to get down, he was left tied with Scott. Thomson reached the turn in 35 on his last round. After a good 10-foot birdie putt at 14, he arrived at the 18th needing a 5 to beat Scott and Rees. Although bunkered after his second, he had no difficulty in getting his 5. Locke could have tied with a 3, but the task was beyond him.

South Africa's Bobby Locke

1955

Although Thomson's victory at St. Andrews in 1955 was over a weak field, he played like a champion throughout the tournament: after opening rounds of 71 and 68, he led Locke by 4, and the old champion was never able to close the gap. John Fallon, with the lowest score of the tournament (a 67 on the second round), finished second, 2 back of Thomson.

1956

Thomson won again at Hoylake in 1956 and became the first man to win the championship three years in a row since it had been held over 72 holes. He played throughout with great confidence, and it was unfortunate that his victory was again tarnished by the absence of a strong American entry, for his golf was magnificent. On the other hand, many of those participating in the Canada Cup the week before at Wentworth, notably Roberto de Vicenzo, Antonio Cerda, Al Balding, Gary Player, Bruce Crampton, Flory Van Donck, and the rising generation from the Far East, were there to make the field a true international one. Thomson won by three clear shots from Van Donck, with two future Open champions, de Vicenzo and Gary Player, four and five shots further back. Of Van Donck, many will agree that he was a world-class performer for at least a decade, but an unlucky one. At the time the rules of golf permitted the flagstick to remain in the hole throughout the putting stroke if the player so wished. Van Donck was one of quite a number of professionals who considered that the flag in the hole assisted the striker. But during this Championship, he hit the flagstick five times and the ball failed to drop on every occasion. Had he not been obsessed with this theory, he might have holed at least three or four of the five putts and come very close to winning.

1957

At St. Andrews in 1957 the American entry was again a poor one.

Cary Middlecoff, a former Open champion of the United States and winner of the Masters, came over, perhaps hoping to add a third title to his

Peter Thomson

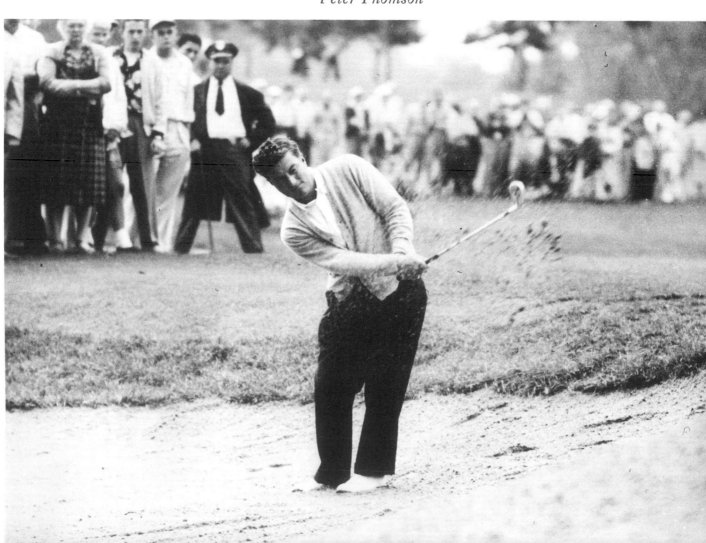

fine record. But he had no real experience in British seaside golf, and neither he nor the other significant American entrant, Frank Stranahan, was ever really in the running.

In a state of semiretirement, Locke had grown fat. He had been playing poorly before the Championship, and was given little chance to win. But from the start, he was in the midst of the struggle with Thomson and Eric Brown, a fierce and determined Scot.

The story of this championship can be wrapped up in a few sentences. Brown delighted his countrymen with a brilliant first round of 67, and slowly faded, gradually leaving Locke and Thomson to fight it out. With 36 holes to go, Locke led by a stroke. A perfectly planned and executed third-round 68 increased his lead to 3. Both he and Thomson played fine 70s in the last round, and Locke had won his fourth and greatest Open.

There was some clamor over an incident on the 72nd hole. Locke's second shot finished within 3 feet of the hole, and he had three putts to win. But when he replaced his ball after marking, he clearly did *not* replace it on the exact spot where it originally lay—although he was not nearer the hole. But the committee ruled that he had won by three strokes.

1958

Peter Thomson won for the fourth time at Royal Lytham and St. Anne's in 1958 after a tie with David Thomas of Wales in the new record total of 278. One stroke behind came Eric Brown and Christy O'Connor, two distinguished Ryder Cup players.

Scoring was particularly good in the all-important third round—Thomson 67, Thomas 69, Van Donck 67, Cotton 69, and Eric Brown 65, despite a 6 on the 72nd hole.

Though he had his problems in the last round, Thomson played magnificently with his three-round total of 205 setting a tremendous pace. Thomas, a wonderful driver, fairway wood, and long-iron player, hung on, but his weakness around the green caught up with him in the 36-hole playoff as Thomson won by 4 strokes. Two veterans, Henry Cotton and Gene Sarazen, played remarkably well, 284 and 288 respectively, Sarazen at the age of fifty-six having led the qualifying rounds with 138. It was sad to reflect that he was the only first-class representative of American golf.

1959

Back at Muirfield the following year, Gary Player, the great South African, won for the first time. It is no disparagement of him to say that he won from one of the worst fields in postwar years in a Championship that remained up for grabs until the last nine holes. Suddenly the large crowds seemed to sense that Player was going to win, and they swarmed around him about the turn. When he finished with a 68, he was awarded an ovation. Van Donck of Belgium played well, but once again was disappointed. He tied for second place with Fred Bullock, an Englishman who had never before and never since played a notable part in the Championship.

For the first time in years, an amateur, Reid Jack, a Scot, was in contention with nine holes to play, and two others, Michael Bonallack and Guy Wolstenholme, were not many shots behind the winner.

1960

Since 1933, the British Open had been on a pronounced decline—a slide interrupted only twice by the one-time visits (and wins) of Snead and Hogan. But with the Centenary Open of 1960 at St. Andrews, this slide was permanently halted, the turnaround accomplished by one man—Arnold Palmer. Fresh from victories in the Masters and U.S. Open, and talking of a Grand Slam (the first time *that* term had been used for 30 years), Palmer singlehandedly brought about the renaissance of the British Open. Ironically, he did not even win this first time out.

But he came so close. The Championship was won by Kel Nagle of Australia, in 278, a single stroke ahead of Palmer, and a record over the Old Course. Nagle had visited the British Isles twice since the war and had also been playing the American tour—all without leaving any particular impression other than that of an agreeable companion and a no more than fairly competent professional golfer. But quite suddenly, at the age of forty, he blossomed into a world-class player, winning the British Open at St. Andrews, the Canadian Open a few years later, and tying with Player for the U.S. Open in 1965.

Nagle began brilliantly with rounds of 67 and 69, and after three rounds was leading de Vicenzo by 2 shots. Palmer and Syd Scott were

4 shots back. At the outset of the final eighteen, a violent storm broke, forcing play to be abandoned for the afternoon.

In brilliant sunshine the next day, Nagle, de Vicenzo, and Palmer each reached the turn in 34, as Bernard Hunt, an early starter, was finishing with a record 66 for 282. But the pace of the leaders was so hot that Hunt's total never seemed likely to stand up.

Palmer, playing grand golf in front of Nagle, had threes at the 13th and 18th and finished in 68 for 279, but Nagle, holing a 10-footer of vital importance at the 17th, left himself with a 5 to win.

1961

Arnold Palmer returned to win at Royal Birkdale in 1961 by a single stroke from Dai Rees, who suffered so many disappointments in the British Open. Palmer showed all the characteristics that have made him a world-famous figure. The weather was appalling, the arrangements nearly as bad, but he neither grumbled nor groused. His golf was magnificent all through, and he proved once again that a great American player can also be the master of foul English weather. His judgment and control in the wind were wonderful. He also showed the extraordinary variations of his temperament: the indomitable cavalier ready to take all manner of risks, as at the 16th in the first round, when he preferred to play a recovery shot through a small gap in a bush rather than play safe, and was justified with a birdie. And, in the very next round, the calm philosopher was able to forget the disaster of a penalty stroke in a bunker, one which he called against himself.

1962

John Henry Taylor said that the easiest way to win a Championship was to win it very easily, and this is exactly what Arnold Palmer did at Troon in 1962. Throughout, he played like an emperor, winning by 6 strokes from Kel Nagle of Australia in the record score of 276, with rounds of 71, 69, 67, 69. After remodeling, the Troon links (with Carnoustie and Muirfield) had become one of the three most severe tests of golf in the British Isles.

Palmer won the championship at the 485-yard, par-5 11th hole. The fairway at the 11th is very narrow and fast. The tee shot must carry 230 yards over scrubby country and should be faded. Choosing a one iron, Palmer was in perfect position on every round. The second shot for ordinary mortals was a three or four wood if the player was prepared to go for the tiny green surrounded by gorse, knee-high bunkers, and the railway at the back. But Palmer cracked it up each time with one of his big irons and marched on for the kill. He scored 4, 3, 5, and 4 at this "killer hole," so it was not surprising that with six holes to play in the last round, he was leading the field by 10 shots.

Kel Nagle finished second, and neither Gary Player nor Jack Nicklaus made the cut for the two final rounds. Palmer, on the other hand, in three attempts at the British Open, had finished second, first, and first. His victory was the most popular in Scotland since those of Bobby Jones.

1963

Arnold Palmer's grand performances in the three previous championships did much to enhance the rising prestige of the Open, and by 1963 there was a capital field at Royal Lytham. This included Palmer, Player, Nicklaus, Nagle, Thomson, Phil Rodgers, and Bob Charles of New Zealand.

Charles, a left-hander, had surprised everyone by turning professional after the Eisenhower Trophy at Merion in 1960. He was generally considered too short off the tee for professional golf, but by sheer application, he managed to gain enough distance to hold his own. It also helped that he had one of the finest short games in the world and the temperament of an iron horse. He came right to the top at Royal Lytham.

With Palmer out of contention for the first time in three years, the championship was dominated by foreign players. Charles played a wonderful third round of 66 in which he required only 26 putts, and it was this round that put him in contention and ultimately won him the title after a tie with Rodgers, an amusing character from the United States.

There was an exciting finish since Charles's finish of 71 had left Rodgers a 69 to tie, which he duly accomplished. Charles won the 36-hole playoff with considerable ease, but many thought that Nicklaus, playing behind them in the fourth round, was unlucky not to be involved in the tie. He hit a fine second to the 17th which bounced hard and finished over the green, leaving him a hanging downhill-lie shot impossible to get close to the hole. A 5 there. Under the impression that he had a 4 to win and a 5 to tie (an impression encouraged by the then faulty British score reporting on the course), Nicklaus played safely to get his 5, only to learn that he was not in a three-way playoff after all.

1964

Tony Lema, arriving at St. Andrews fresh from a victory in the Cleveland Open, was too tired from the long flight to play more than a nine-hole practice round before the start of the 1964 British Open. He had never seen a seaside links of any kind, much less the Old Course, where the hidden pot bunkers, invisible to the player on the tee, make a knowledge of the layout so critical. As if the lack of practice wasn't enough, he was greeted on the first day of the Championship with typical British Open weather—a 50-mph wind. But Lema went unruffled, and playing from strength to strength, he captured the only major title he would win, as he died just two years later in a plane crash.

Lema in 1964 was at the peak of his game, the hottest golfer in the world. Always a beautiful swinger, he had recently adopted an Arnold Palmer putter and had been using it to beat Palmer and everyone else on the U.S. tour. His first round of 73 in the gale baffled the locals of St. Andrews, who could not make up their minds whether to admire his skill or to damn his eyes for rank impertinence to their historic links. But still he was 2 strokes behind the leaders, Jean Garaialde of France and Christy O'Connor of Ireland. Lema had been most ably assisted throughout this round (during which he was seeing nine of the holes for the first time) by "Tip" Anderson, a local caddy, and a great favorite among leading American golfers.

With plenty of wind on the second day, Lema shot a remarkable 68, displaying perfect control and putting. He was now 2 strokes ahead of Harry Weetman, who played in fine style for 71, and 3 in front of O'Conner and Bruce Devlin.

By now it was realized that Lema had both the game and the temperament to win the championship. Though he started poorly in his third round, he contrived to reach the turn in 36. As he was playing the 12th, he got news of a brilliant front nine of 32 by Jack Nicklaus. But having started home with two 3s, Lema remained inspired, and with three more 3s he was home in 32, for a third round of 68.

Nicklaus returned an astounding card of 66, one of the best rounds ever played under pressure over the Old Course, but Lema was now too far ahead. Though some felt he was likely to tumble in the last round, he again played with the utmost authority for 70. Despite another grand perform-

The late Tony Lema in London

ance by Nicklaus, who wound up with a 68, Lema was a clear winner by 5 strokes.

1965

After a disappointing showing in the British Open at St. Andrews in 1964, Peter Thomson bounced back to take the title for the fifth time at Royal Birkdale 1965. It was his greatest triumph, for it was gained, for the first time, against the might of a full-scale American entry. On this account it was the sweetest win of all for him, for he had never troubled to conceal his disapproval of Americans, their golf courses, and their way of life. His hostility was reciprocated in full measure.

Formerly a nearly flawless tee-to-green player, Thomson had developed a nagging hook in his effort to hit up with the Palmers and Nicklauses of the new era. At Birkdale he won with his scrambling.

Lema, the defender, was off like a greyhound, setting a blistering pace with an opening round of 68. Thomson's 74 left him in the pack, 6 shots back. Biding his time patiently, he came back with a 68 of his own to close on Lema, who struggled for 72.

This was the last occasion in which the final 36 holes of the British Open were played on the last day, and Thomson and Lema were paired together at the end of the field. Only Bernard Hunt's 70 improved on Thomson's third round of 72. Lema took 75, and the Australian was where he wanted to be—in the lead and marching firmly toward the title with his busy walk. It was his last win in the British Open, but his record had been astounding: five wins, three seconds, and in the top ten 17 out of 20 years.

1966

The British Open at Muirfield in 1966 may have been the first of the modern championships. Prize money was 20 percent higher than ever before, provisions were made for large galleries, and on-the-course scoreboards were improved. But more important was Jack Nicklaus's win by one stroke over Doug Sanders and David Thomas of Wales, a win that finally came after so many narrow misses.

Before the tournament the committee had decided that Muirfield, at

6,800-odd yards, was barely long enough for the modern golfer. Rather than building new tees, they narrowed the fairways and let the rough grow —and grow. Nicklaus had played in the 1959 Walker Cup Match at Muirfield, but fond memories of the course he had known then were erased by the course he saw in 1966—yards and yards of waist-high grass waving like wheat in the persistent wind. Nicklaus declared that he hardly recognized the place, and set out forthwith to formulate an entirely new plan of attack—one with accuracy rather than length at a premium. The Nicklaus strategy was to use irons off most of the tees, to play safe, and above all, to keep the ball in play.

As so often happens in the Open, British players went off well in the first two rounds, with Jimmy Hitchcock joining Nicklaus in the lead at the end of the first. Close behind were Doug Sanders, Harold Henning, and Kel Nagle.

The next day Nicklaus established himself as leader by one stroke over Peter Butler, the Midland professional, who returned a miraculous 65—the lowest round of the championship. Rodgers, who for several years played extremely well in Britain, astonished everybody on the third day by going to the turn in 40 strokes, and then, seemingly out of it, closing with an incredible 30.

When Nicklaus went out for his third round, there was a stiff westerly wind blowing, and the course was emphatically more difficult than the one Butler and Rodgers had found. Playing with great care, he reached the turn in even par to remain 5 under, giving him a commanding lead. Butler, his nearest rival, had fallen 4 strokes behind, and Rodgers 7. Nicklaus continued serenely with four well-played pars. But then, for some unaccountable reason, he started to drop strokes, misjudging distance now and again. When he nearly missed his par 5 at the 17th, where a golfer of his caliber has no difficulty in reaching the green in two, his confidence was clearly shaken. He then missed his par 4 at the 18th when he pushed his second into the long bunker to the right of the home green, and all of this added up to an indifferent 75. So now, at the end of 54 holes, Rodgers was the leader with 210. Nicklaus was 2 behind him, Sanders 3, and Palmer and Thomas 4.

On the final Saturday, the wind was still in the west, and though blustery, it was subsiding. Five were in contention, with Rodgers and Nicklaus out last, Palmer and Sanders just in front of them, and Thomas and Henning one further ahead. When Rodgers bogeyed the 1st hole, Nicklaus tied for the lead with a birdie. He reached the turn in a superb 33 after two more birdies and six pars, and with another par at the narrow 10th, he was comfortably out in front again—3 strokes ahead of Rodgers and 4 ahead of Thomas and Sanders. Palmer, who had plowed his way down the rough to a 7 at the 10th, was now out of it. At the 11th, a short par 4, Nicklaus played a fine second. Looking for another birdie, he jerked

Palmer in trouble, 1966 British Open at Muirfield

his putt and then missed the 15-inch tap-in. This seemed to put him out of his stride, and for the next half-hour or so, he played loosely. Suddenly he had lost his entire lead.

It was at this moment that he learned that Thomas had finished with a 69 for 283 and that Sanders, playing the 18th, was also heading for 283. Nicklaus had a great struggle to get his par 4 at the 15th, after a weak approach and a rather jittery 4-foot putt. Though he hit a good tee shot to the 198-yard 16th, he was 30 feet short. But his first putt stopped just inches short, and this stroke, his first really good putt since the 10th hole, restored his confidence. At the par-5 17th, his three iron from the tee and five-iron second were perfection. He two-putted from 18 feet for the birdie. He now had a 4 to win at the 429-yard 18th. He hit two glorious shots into the wind, a one iron and a five iron, and with two putts from no distance, the Championship was over.

1967

Somehow Roberto de Vicenzo, whose style, majesty, and deportment on the golf course had been the envy of all who had watched him, had seemed to lack something needed to break through to his rightful place among the great champions of the game. By 1967, at age forty-four, he had won 38 national opens, but never one of the four major championships that counted most. Despite a swing unmatched by even Jones himself, his best previous finishes in the British Open were one second and five thirds. The winner's cup seemed beyond his grasp. For years he had been threatening "this is my last time."

But finally, at Hoylake, his time came. Old men who had been seeing him come so close for years stood speechless with tears in their eyes as the gentle, bronzed de Vicenzo strode down the last fairway in the July afternoon, certain of victory, victory at last.

Over Hoylake, which might have been designed for him, de Vicenzo had begun the last round 2 strokes ahead of Player, 3 ahead of Nicklaus, and 4 ahead of Clive Clark and Bruce Devlin. General opinion favored Player and Nicklaus.

Both Nicklaus and Player began the fourth round uncertainly, but de Vicenzo, with his par figures, showed that he could be dangerous. He reached the turn in 36, but Nicklaus in front of him had gained a stroke, to draw even with Player. By the 14th, however, de Vicenzo was 10 under par for the tournament, 4 strokes ahead of Nicklaus, with Player virtually out of it.

With great courage, Nicklaus stormed the last four holes with 4, 4, 4, and 3 to finish in 69. He left Roberto knowing exactly what he had to do, and de Vicenzo did it without a vestige of uncertainty or wavering. He had three putts for the championship from a few feet, and he had won it at last.

1968

Gary Player, who had not won a major title in three years, emerged from his mild slump by winning his second British Open at Carnoustie, a course which many consider to be the most difficult in Britain. He won it in a head-to-head duel over the last day with Jack Nicklaus, whose diffident putting stroke probably cost him the tournament.

Bob Charles of New Zealand, the tall left-hander, tied with Nicklaus in second place. Billy Casper, one of the most consistent players, finished in fourth place, and his final round of 78 was a result of going all out, and going all out does not always come off.

Nicklaus's opening left him struggling from the start. He followed with a 69, to become with Casper (68) only the third and fourth players

Player on way to victory in 1968 British Open

to break 70 in three British Opens at Carnoustie. Player, working steadily, came to the last day's struggle with Nicklaus always near the lead.

1969

Tony Jacklin became the first British golfer to win the British Open in 18 years when he broke through at St. Anne's in 1969. It had been a long drought for English fans since Max Faulkner's victory in 1951. Jacklin's win was no fluke. He had been playing often and well on the American tour (a win at Jacksonville in 1968), and he went on to win the 1970 U.S. Open, the first British golfer ever to hold both the U.S. and British titles at the same time.

Jacklin had shown an aptitude for games since boyhood, finally settling on golf rather than soccer. Prompted by Bill Shankland, an English teaching pro, he decided to attempt the American circuit. There he polished his game, concentrating especially on advice given him by his two best American friends, Bert Yancey and Tom Weiskopf—reducing his swing speed. Jacklin's natural inclination since his caddy days had been to swing the club like lightning, but he had been learning to swing smoothly. In addition to a fine all-around game, Jacklin seemed to be able to play his best in the big events, and especially reserving his most consistent efforts for the British Open.

At Royal Lytham and St. Anne's in 1969, this consistency paid off. Jacklin was off with a roar, beginning the Championship with a birdie 2 and finishing with a 68. Bob Charles, however, was out in front with a 66.

Charles again played fine golf for 69 next day, and with two rounds to go led the field at 135. Christy O'Connor, with 65, jumped into second place at 136, and Jacklin with 70 was at 138. In the third round, Charles, who ranks with the great putters, was for once out of touch on the greens. His 75, coupled with Jacklin's 70, jumped Jacklin into a 2-shot lead with a round to go. Nicklaus, with a 68, had closed to within 3 of Jacklin, but could get no closer in the last eighteen.

Jacklin and Charles were paired in the last round, Charles's bogey 4 on the 1st hole and Jacklin's birdies on the 3rd and 4th left Tony 4 ahead of de Vicenzo and 5 ahead of Charles at the turn.

Short of disaster, it now looked as though he would win. His game was not quite immaculate, but he saved himself several times with superb bunker shots around the green, each time getting down in one putt.

He stood on the last tee, 2 shots ahead of Charles and 3 ahead of Thomson and de Vicenzo. The tee shot at this hole is a very narrow one and demands a big carry over a bunker that creeps in from the left side of the fairway. On the right is impenetrable scrub and gorse. He swung his club beautifully, and without looking where the ball had gone picked up his tee. He knew the drive was a good one. He played a perfect second, and with two putts a British golfer had won again. Bob Charles with a fourth round of 72 finished second and Thomson and de Vicenzo tied for third.

1970

It is possible that of all Jack Nicklaus's major triumphs the one that gave him greatest satisfaction was the British Open at St. Andrews in 1970. Without a "big four" victory since 1967, with many saying he had lost his desire and would never be the player he was, Nicklaus wanted to win very badly, especially because of the venue—the historic Old Course. He was never quite at his best, and was closely hounded all the way by the courageous Doug Sanders, but in the end he had courage of his own that pulled him through.

It was the 99th British Open. The press called it the greatest; it was certainly the most exciting. There was a record entry of 468 players. Eighty thousand spectators went through the main turnstiles, with perhaps another 5,000 through the Aberdonian Gates down by the sea. The weather played a devastating part throughout the championship but in the end Nicklaus, unquestionably the best golfer in the field, won on the very last green of the playoff with Sanders.

Play was delayed for two hours by fog in the first round, but early in the afternoon there was not a breath of wind. With this rare Scottish weather, and with the Old Course in perfect condition, scoring was very low. Neil Coles quickly broke the course record with 65, Tommy Horton followed with 66; Harold Henning, Maurice Bembridge, and John Richardson had 67s apiece, and among the dime-a-dozen 68s were Nicklaus, Trevino, Palmer, and Peter Thomson.

Defending champion Tony Jacklin was still to come. By tea time he had reached the turn in an incredible 29, having holed his pitch at the 9th for an eagle 2. He started for home, 3, 3, 4, and 4, and now 8 under par was set to break all records. But ominous clouds that had been gathering all day began to break open with rain as Jacklin got his par 4 on the 13th. He hit a perfect tee shot to the 14th; but, drenched to the skin in the alarming storm, he hit his hurried second into a gorse bush. At that point, with the greens flooded all over the course, play was suspended for the day. Jacklin resumed with a drop from his gorse bush at 7:30 the next morning and took 6. The double bogey seemed to take his inspiration away and what could have been a 61, 62, 63, or 64 became a disappointing 67.

He went on in the second day's mixture of cloud, sunshine, and westerly wind to post a 70. At the halfway stage, the scoreboard showed Trevino in the lead, after a second round of 68, at 136; Nicklaus and Jacklin at 137; Coles, Clark Sanders, and Richardson at 139; and Palmer and O'Connor at 140.

The wind was harder on the third day and scoring was higher. Trevino and Jacklin paired together, and last out, took 70 and 73 respectively. This left Trevino at 208, Jacklin at 210—bracketed with Sanders (71) and Nicklaus (73). Young Peter Oosterhuis, who had only recently turned professional, played remarkably well and was a stroke further behind at 211. Both Trevino and Jacklin began to fade in the last round in the now boisterous wind, and it was evident that the championship would be fought out between Nicklaus and Sanders.

Nicklaus, two holes ahead of Jacklin, was hitting the ball magnificently but three-putted five times, including the last green out of the "Valley of Sin," for a 73. He seemed lost when Sanders, from an almost impossible in-the-road bunker at the 17th, pitched stone-dead to save par, and came to the 18th needing only a par to win. But Sanders's pitched second seemed a little thin, and his ball finished about 40 feet above the hole. His approach putt was on the cautious side, leaving him with a putt of a full yard. He hesitated over the putt, stepped away, and then missed it.

The general opinion was that Nicklaus would crush him in the next day's playoff, but Sanders, though painfully slow, stuck to his game, a game well suited to British conditions. After being four strokes behind at the end of 13 holes, he birdied the long 14th, and then the 15th as well, when he ran down a putt of 12 feet. Nicklaus dropped another shot to a par 4 at the 16th, and the 17th was halved. So Nicklaus's lead was down to one as they came to the par-4 home hole.

Removing his top sweater to free his swing, Nicklaus hit an almost unbelievable drive that rolled *over* the green and into the rough on the grass bank beyond the hole. It left him with a very awkward downhill chip back to the flag. Sanders, meanwhile, hit a superb second from 40 yards out, finishing 4 feet from the flag. Nicklaus chipped cautiously to 7 feet, and after an agony of suspense holed his next. He had achieved a life-long ambition to win a British Open at St. Andrews.

1971

In the long history of the game of golf there has never been anyone quite like Lee Trevino. At the end of an exhausting three weeks, he arrived at Birkdale having won the U.S. Open at Merion after a playoff with Jack Nicklaus, and the Canadian Open after a playoff with Art Wall. Little more than 12 hours after getting off the plane, he was out practicing and telling everyone that, yes, he could win three national opens in a row. He could indeed.

Trevino shared the lead with three others at the end of the first round, the most dangerous being Tony Jacklin, who again began with three birdies in a row, bringing back memories of St. Andrews and Lytham. Nicklaus, who had started a strong favorite (since he had been practicing at Birkdale during the week of the Canadian Open), seemed certain to take the lead when, with two holes to play, he needed only two 4s for a 67. But he took 6s at both, and his 67 became a 71. This disaster seemed to affect him for the rest of the Championship.

At the halfway stage, Trevino and Jacklin were still in the lead at 139, but Jacklin had been forced to scramble for his 70. Liang Huan Lu, a Formosan known to the galleries as "Mr. Lu," was at 140 after a pair of 70s. The unusually hot weather and fast greens, reminding him of familiar Far East conditions, were working to his advantage.

With a round to go Trevino (69) was at 208, a shot ahead of Jacklin (70) and Mr. Lu (69) at 209. Player (71), but not playing well, and Defoy (68) were at 212, followed by Oosterhuis (66), Hayes (70), and de Vicenzo (72) at 213, and Nicklaus (72) at 214. The three leaders birdied the 1st hole in the final round. Mr. Lu alone birdied the 2nd, where Jacklin with a disastrous 6 faded from contention.

From then on, the Championship suddenly came alive. Those who had given up the struggle of following through the sun-baked dunes saw something they could scarcely believe. Three after three appeared on the scoreboards by Trevino's name until there were five of them in a row, including one at the dreaded long 6th. Check and countercheck confirmed that Trevino, far from wilting under the strain of his nonstop schedule, was off on an irresistible run of 31 strokes to the turn. No one could stay with him. Jacklin, out in 38, had dropped 7 shots in those scorching nine holes and only Mr. Lu, 35, could keep Trevino's heels in sight. The Championship seemed over.

But one of the charms of Royal Birkdale as a spectator course, the impenetrable scrub among the mountainous sandhills, is one of its horrors for the players, and the scrub can change a situation in stroke play in a matter of minutes. It happened when Trevino came a-cropper at the 17th; Mr. Lu closed the gap to a single shot. Trevino's mistake was due to neither nerves nor weariness. His drive through the gap seemed perfect, but was in fact hit too well, and when the expected fade did not come, he was in dire trouble. But in the face of a terrible collapse, Trevino birdied the home hole with complete authority as though nothing had happened. The Championship was over.

Thus he became only the fourth man in history to win both the British and U.S. Open Championships in the same summer: Bobby Jones in 1930, Gene Sarazen in 1932, and Ben Hogan in 1953 were the others.

1972

Had Jack Nicklaus somehow contrived to win the Open at Muirfield and thus achieved the third leg on his run at the Grand Slam, his final round would have cast him forever as something slightly larger than miraculous. Unfortunately for Jack's Slam plans, it was Lee Trevino who produced the miracles. During the tournament Trevino saved at least four to six shots by holing out three chip shots and a bunker shot. He withstood Jack's dramatic challenge on the final day, recovered to save a tournament he appeared to have thrown away, and went on to become the first Open champion since Palmer in 1962 to successfully defend the title.

Even the usually ferocious Scottish weather seemed to be holding its breath in anticipation of Nicklaus's bid to add the British Open title to the U.S. Masters and U.S. Open championships he had captured earlier in the year. Except for a brisk breeze and light rain on the first day, the tournament unfolded with a benign blue sky, a bright sun, and temperatures in the 70s. Perhaps the unusually calm weather upset Jack's game plans. Expecting very tough and exacting scoring conditions, Nicklaus prepared to play cautiously, just as he had in 1966, and played his seven practice rounds accordingly, leaving his driver in his bag unless it seemed absolutely safe to use it. It was not until the final round that he abandoned caution for boldness.

The first-round lead was taken by twenty-two-year-old Peter Tupling, an English pro, with a score of 68. Jacklin, with 69, was second, Nicklaus, at 70, tied for third with Americans Dave Marr and Frank Beard and Britain's Craig DeFoy. Trevino was right behind at 71.

Tupling, who did not even regard himself as a challenger, dropped back in subsequent rounds, and the halfway lead was held by Trevino and Jacklin, who were at 141 a stroke ahead of Nicklaus and six others. Conditions seemed ideal for scoring but only John Miller of the U.S., who scored a double eagle on his way to a 66, was able to wrench a really good score from the course.

The breakthrough for everyone, it seemed, except Jack, came on the third day. Seven players shot in the 60s, with Trevino's 66 leading the way. Lee's 5-under-par round was fashioned with shocking suddenness over the last five holes. He sank birdie putts of 20 feet at both the 14th and 15th holes, holed out a bunker shot to birdie the 16th, two-putted for a birdie at the par-5 17th, and holed a 30-foot chip shot from behind the 18th green for his concluding birdie. A witness to this surge was his playing partner, Jacklin, who scored 2 under par over the same five holes but saw his two-shot lead dissolve into a one-shot deficit. After three rounds Trevino was at 207, Jacklin at 208, Doug Sanders of the U.S. at 211, husky Brian Barnes of Great Britain at 212, and Nicklaus at an even par 213.

The next day Jack began to play boldly and it became his turn to make birdies. After scrambling for par at the first hole, he birdied holes 2 and 3 with short putts, then added birdies on the 5th, 9th, 10th, and 11th. Suddenly there he was in front, holding a one-shot lead. This lasted until Trevino birdied the 11th and Jacklin the 14th. Finally the outcome turned on bad luck for Nicklaus at the 16th and good luck for Trevino at the 17th. Jack's four iron to the 16th green struck the putting surface but bounded off it and into heavy rough below on the left. He chipped well, but missed his putt of 5 feet, for a bogey that put him a shot back of the leaders, Trevino and Jacklin, once again paired together two groups back. Nicklaus then finished with pars for the 17th and 18th.

Meanwhile, at the 17th, Trevino came perilously close to fumbling away his chance. On this hole Jacklin hit two long shots just short of the green. Trevino, bothered by a pair of photographers running across the fairway ahead, first backed away from his tee shot, then pulled it into a deep bunker. He could only explode out. His third shot was hooked into heavy rough, still well short of the green. His fourth shot, somewhat carelessly hit, rolled over the green and up an embankment behind it. A bogey seemed a certainty now, a double bogey distinctly possible. Obviously disgusted, Trevino hit his chip quickly and then watched in amazement as it dropped into the cup for a par. Stunned, Jacklin thereupon three-putted from inside 20 feet for the bogey that had at first seemed destined for Trevino. Lee parred the final hole, two-putting from 10 feet. Tony bunkered his approach shot and bogeyed the hole. His bogey, bogey finish left him two shots back of Trevino and one behind Nicklaus, who, like Palmer in 1960, saw his Grand Slam attempt thwarted by the margin of a single stroke.

⌈ 5 ⌉

THE MASTERS–BOBBY JONES MAKES THE AUGUSTA GRASS GROW GREEN

EVERYONE has his own first sign of spring—onion grass in the garden, a pretty girl in a cotton dress, exhibition baseball games in Florida—but for some the first sign comes early, sometimes just after the first of the year. It is usually in the form of a bulletin, decorated with an outline of the United States, with a flag protruding from the southeast part of it, just about where Georgia is. Written over all this is Augusta National Golf Club. This first bulletin is a reminder that the Masters is coming, and if the Masters is coming, then surely so is spring.

If you have been to Augusta in April, if you have sat beneath the huge magnolia trees on the veranda of the clubhouse or strolled through the tall pine forests and breathed the sweet scents of dogwood and azaleas, then you know that there is no golf tournament in the world quite as special as the Masters. You cannot make a move around the clubhouse area without encountering some sort of tradition. There is a dinner for the amateurs on Monday night and one for Masters champions the next, hosted by the current champion. Wednesday afternoon all participants take part in a special nine-hole tournament on the club's par-3 course—and the winner receives a china tea set. On Thursday the tournament begins with two octogenerians teeing off first. Jock Hutchison and Fred McLeod once played the full eighteen, but now they limit their efforts to nine or less. On opening day,

Bobby Jones at Augusta

amateurs are always paired with past champions. Steuben Glass trophies are awarded for such achievements as low round of the day and eagles. The press is given a momento of the tournament. But the most famous Masters tradition of all, certainly the most cherished and desired, is the awarding of the green jacket to the winner. On Sunday, minutes after the final putt, officials of the club, headed by Clifford Roberts, assemble on the practice putting green, along with the new champion, the old champion, the low amateur and that player or players who have contributed to the excitement, usually someone who has finished second. In that setting, with the spring light fading, the old champion helps the new one slip into his jacket, and no matter how many golf tournaments you have seen or covered, it is a moment that stirs the emotions.

It could be argued that the Masters began the moment Bobby Jones sank his final putt at the 11th hole at Merion to beat Gene Homans 9 and 7, win the U.S. Amateur for the fifth time, and wrap up his Grand Slam. (For trivia fans, it was actually Homans who stroked the last putt, missed, and congratulated Jones.) With the completion of the Slam, Jones retired from competitive golf, although he remained very much involved in the game. He designed a set of Jones-model clubs which Spaulding produced and, together with his close friend, newspaperman O. B. Keeler, made two series of short, instructional golf films at Warner Brothers and, again with Keeler, did a weekly half-hour radio show. He continued to play golf, but only in friendly foursomes at his home course, the East Lake Club in Atlanta.

Jones had let it be known that he was interested in one other golfing venture, the building of a championship golf course somewhere in his native southland, a course that would conform to his own high standards. Enter Clifford Roberts, a tall, thin Wall Street investment banker who had long been going to Augusta as a winter vacationer. Jones's wife had lived in Augusta, and, in addition, both Jones and Roberts were mutual friends of Walton H. Marshall of the Vanderbilt Hotel in New York and the Bon Air Vanderbilt in Augusta.

Roberts knew of Jones's desire to build a course, and so late in 1930 he paid him a visit in Atlanta with the idea of organizing and building a club near Augusta. Both Roberts and Jones had a number of friends among the permanent and winter guests who could be counted on to form a nucleus of club members. The rest of the members would come from around the country—a truly national club, as the name Augusta National implies—a retreat where, as Jones once wrote, "men of means might play with kindred spirits."

Jones was receptive to the idea immediately. He realized Augusta would be perfect for what he had in mind, for while it was not too far from Atlanta, its courses were always in much better condition in winter than those of Atlanta. And so, one chilly December morning in 1930, Clifford

Roberts and Alfred Bourne, a member of the Singer Sewing Machine family, took Jones to a 365-acre tract of land that was up for sale at Depression prices. The land had been an old indigo plantation known as Fruitlands. In 1857 a Belgian nobleman named Baron Prosper Jules Alphonse Berckmans bought the plantation and turned it into a nursery, planting magnolia seeds along the driveway that led to his manor house. Those trees still stand today, forming an archway at the entrance to the clubhouse. The Baron also planted many of the azalea, camelia, and dogwood that dot the course.

Jones was intrigued immediately. As he later wrote: "I stood at the top of the hill (on what is now the veranda) before that fine old house and looked at the wide stretch of land rolling down the slope before me. It was cleared land, for the most part, and you could take in the vista all the way down to Rae's Creek. I knew instantly it was the kind of terrain I had always hoped to find. I had been told, of course, about the marvelous trees and plants, but I was still unprepared for the great bonus of beauty Fruitlands offered. Frankly, I was overwhelmed by the exciting possibilities of a golf course set in the midst of such a nursery."

Fielding Wallace, an Augusta textile manufacturer, was assigned to buy the property, while Jones and Roberts chose Dr. Alister MacKenzie, one of the world's leading golf architects, to design the course. Jones and MacKenzie worked well together. Jones was the adviser, MacKenzie the architect. Both were great admirers of the Old Course at St. Andrews, and for a while there was a rumor that the two wished to re-create every hole from St. Andrews. But, as Jones pointed out, this would have meant altering everything. It is true that they hoped to incorporate certain features of St. Andrews, simulating seaside conditions to the extent that the turf and terrain would allow.

Jones and MacKenzie also agreed that the course should offer the greatest enjoyment for the greatest number of players. As Jones said: "Our overall aim at the Augusta National was to provide a golf course of considerable natural beauty, relatively easy for the average golfer to play, and at the same time testing for the expert player striving to better par figures. We hoped to make bogeys easy if frankly sought, pars readily obtainable by standard good play, and birdies, except on the par fives, dearly bought."

Which is how it turned out. If you are a 90s shooter at your home club, chances are you will shoot rather close to your average score at Augusta (if you are fortunate enough ever to play there. It requires not only knowing, but playing with, a member). The fairways are wide, the greens large, there are few traps, and the overall length of the course—6,250 yards to 6,980, depending on the tee markers—is not overwhelming. The subtle hazards of the course, such as the undulating fairways, often affect the professional more than the club player.

Construction on the course was begun in the spring of 1931 and was completed in the fall of 1932. In the meantime, the club had been formed with about 100 charter members, each of whom paid an initiation fee of $350 and annual dues of $60. A clubhouse had been built in Southern plantation style with the original Berckmans manor house at the center. Ed Dudley was chosen as the club's first professional. Play on the course began in the fall of '32. The only sad note was that Alister MacKenzie died shortly after the course was completed. "The Augusta National represented my finest opportunity and finest achievement," he had said.

It was sometime during the second year of the club's existence that the idea for the Masters was born. Some of the club members, proud of their course and wishing to show it off, thought it might be possible to hold the U.S. Open there. But the Open was, and still is, a June event, and after many conversations with the USGA, it was agreed that the project was not feasible since the course in June would not be playable.

Clifford Roberts suggested that the club hold its own tournament in the spring, one that would show off the course and at the same time give the local golf fans a chance to see the game's best players. Roberts convinced Jones that the tournament could be distinguished from others on the pro circuit by casting Jones as host and having him invite leading players and his friends. That invitational quality still remains, although in reality it was altered greatly after the first year. Jones received so much static about who was invited and who was not that a qualification system was set up, the qualifying players then being "invited" to compete.

At first Jones declined to play in the tournament, but Roberts convinced him that it would be impolite to invite so many golfing friends to Augusta and not play himself. It was also the persuasive Roberts who coined the name "Masters" for the tournament. Jones at first rejected it on the grounds that it was too presumptuous, but the name stuck.

That first Masters began on March 22, 1934. "Eyes of Golfdom on Southern Course" was the *New York Times* headline. Maybe so, but the *Times* golf writer, William D. Richardson, was not there, choosing instead to do a story on regional qualifying for the U.S. Open. "Runyan established as co-favorite with Jones at 6–1 as ex-champion stages a comeback," the headnote continued. The *Times* referred to the tournaments as the Masters Invitational.

Not once did Jones regard his appearance in that first Masters as a comeback, and there is no doubt that even if he had won, he would have remained retired, appearing only in the Masters each year. He was paired that first day with Runyan himself, and the two teed off at 10:30, drawing most of the gallery with them.

For Jones, that first Masters was not the pleasant experience it might have been. He had hoped that the competition would be relaxed, that he would feel more or less the way he did during practice rounds with the pros, rounds he truly enjoyed. He told himself he would not let himself get upset, as indeed he used to feel when competing. Oddly, however, he came to realize that the very course he had helped create was the worst sort of place for a golfer to make a once-a-year public appearance. Hitting drives and irons were no problem, but the delicate touch needed to chip and putt, especially on Augusta's huge, lightning-fast greens, was hard to reacquire.

As Jones stepped to the first tee he discovered the initial signs of tension. Because he always developed a callus on the side of the middle finger of his right hand, he kept it wrapped in tape. As he stood there wrapping the finger, he noticed that his hands were trembling slightly. He was also aware of a churning in his stomach, a familiar sensation he always felt when beginning competition. This ended for Jones any idea that this first Masters would be merely a social outing for him.

The front nine that first year was what is now the back nine, so that a round began over the extremely difficult 10th, 11th, and 12th holes. Jones parred them all, even though he was not satisfied with some of his putts —"Again I felt the jerk. I think I knew then what was coming," he wrote later. He birdied the 4th, now the par-5 13th, but that was it. At the 5th (14th), a movie camera started whirring as he addressed his tee shot. He stepped back, then to the ball again, but his concentration was broken. He pushed his drive far to the right and, as he wrote, "I realized, too, that whatever part I might have in the Masters Tournament from then on would not be as a serious contender."

But the press did not give up on him. When he finished with a 76 for that first round, the *New York Times* headline was: "Unsteady Putting Drops Jones to Tie for 35th, Six Shots Behind Golf Leaders." No mention of Horton Smith or Jimmy Hines, who were those leaders. Jones shot a 74 the next day, which earned this *Times* headline: "Jones Trails by 8 at Half-way Mark in Augusta Golf Tourney." Smith, who was the leader after 36, finally made the 54-hole headline: "Smith's 212 leads Jones by 10." Jones had shot a respectable 72, but Smith had a 70.

The final headline was: "Augusta Golf Tourney Won by Horton Smith as Jones Finishes 13th." It was no runaway for Smith. Craig Wood seemingly had a tie in his grasp, but Smith sank a 17-foot putt on the 17th (8th) for a birdie and parred the 18th for a one-stroke lead. Jones, with a second straight 72, finished at 294.

And so the first Masters was over. "I hope everyone enjoyed himself," said Bobby Jones, "and I hope you'll all be back next year."

They did come back the following year and they have returned every year since, save for the brief period during World War II. There are many who argue that the Masters has become the best tournament of the year. Certainly it is the most special and, with remarkable frequency, the most exciting.

Because the Masters began only a few years before the first rumbles of World War II, the highlights of all 35 tournaments since that first one are presented here. Generally they are brief, but five of them—1954, 1956, 1960, 1961, and 1965—significant because of the player who won or the manner in which the title was won, are covered in detail.

1935

When Craig Wood birdied the 18th hole to finish at 282, a cheer went up that could be heard back at the 15th, where Gene Sarazen and Walter Hagen were approaching their drives in the fairway. "Well, Gene," said Hagen, "it sounds as if it's all over." Indeed, Wood, leading by 3 strokes over Sarazen, was on the veranda of the clubhouse, with his wife, accepting congratulations. To tie, Sarazen would need three birdies in the last four holes.

It has often been written what Gene Sarazen did that cold, windy afternoon. He took out his four wood and swung away toward the distant green guarded by the pond in front. The ball landed on the fringe of the green, bounced twice, and rolled into the cup for a double-eagle 2. It took Gene a few moments to understand what he had done; he had made, in effect, all three birdies in a single shot. Three pars put him on the veranda with Craig Wood, dead even.

Poor Wood never recovered. "He looked," said one reporter, "like a man who had won a sweepstakes and then had lost the ticket on the way to the payoff window." Sarazen won the 36-hole playoff with an even par 144 to Wood's 149. The victory made him the first golfer ever to have won the U.S. Open, the PGA, the British Open, and the Masters—the modern Grand Slam—though not in one year, of course.

1936

This will be remembered as the worst-weather Masters. Heavy rains canceled Thursday's opening round. On Friday it was windy and freezing. Saturday was not bad, but on Sunday, with 36 holes scheduled, another downpour forced a postponement until Monday. The footbridge at Rae's Creek was under water, as were several greens. Monday was really no better. The heavy rains started at noon, and when the field went out for the final eighteen, they ran into the tail end of a hurricane. The greens were lakes. Horton Smith, the first Masters champion, had to chip the ball toward the hole on the 10th green because of the water in between. Even so, he managed to shoot a brilliant 68, 72 that final day to pick up 7 strokes on Harry Cooper and win the third Masters by a single shot.

1937

There was no reason to believe that Ralph Guldahl would not be the winner when he stepped to the 12th tee on Sunday. He had a 4-stroke lead over the young Texan, Byron Nelson, who had opened with a brilliant 66 but had shown signs of nerves with a shaky 75 on Saturday. Guldahl surveyed the 12th green—whose shape approximates a Band-Aid laid out left to right—and decided to go for the pin on the right, also the narrowest part of the green. The shot was short, hitting the top of the bank beyond Rae's Creek and rolling back into the water. Double-bogey 5. At the 13th, Guldahl drove well, but hit his second shot into the ditch guarding that green. Bogey 6. He had played the two holes in 11.

Playing behind him—these were the days when the leaders did not necessarily go off last—Nelson hit the same sort of shot at the 12th that Guldahl had, but Byron's cleared the bank by a foot, the ball rolling close to the flag. Birdie 2. On the 13th, Nelson hit a magnificent second shot 8 feet from the pin and then sank the putt for an eagle 3. He had played the two holes in 5 strokes, thus picking up 6 shots on Ralph Guldahl, good for the 2-stroke lead that he held until the end. Several years ago Masters officials put up a plaque at the 13th green to commemorate Nelson's dramatic surge.

1938

It was another bad-weather year and the tournament did not begin until Saturday, with a double round on Sunday. Considering the number of dramatic finishes that had already taken place in the four-year history of the tournament, this one was pale. Henry Picard, a tall, soft-spoken pro from New England, led by a stroke after three rounds and had the advantage of teeing off last on Monday. When his closest pursuers crumbled early as he was shooting a brilliant 32 on the front nine, all Henry had to do on the back nine was stay alive. He barely did, shooting a 38 to win over Guldahl and Cooper by 2 strokes. Two youngsters who failed to make the top 24 in the tournament were Sam Snead, playing in his second Masters—Sam had finished 18th the year before—and a young Texan, Ben Hogan.

1939

After two straight second-place finishes, Ralph Guldahl, the big, slow-moving Norwegian, finally became a winner by conquering the back nine that had destroyed him against Nelson two years before. But in 1939 this was a different Guldahl. He was now a two-time U.S. Open winner, edging Sam Snead at Oakland Hills in 1937 and Dick Metz at Cherry Hills the following year, only the fourth player in history to win back-to-back Opens. Now it was Snead with whom he was contending again. As Guldahl finished the 9th hole, Snead was a few yards away, winding up the 18th with a 68 and a total of 280, a new tournament record. That meant Ralph had to play the back nine in 34 to tie, 33 to win. He started well, getting a birdie 3 at the tough 10th and parring the 11th. Now to the two holes that ruined his chances in 1937. At the 12th Guldahl cleared the creek and wound up 6 feet from the pin. He missed the putt but had an easy par. At the 13th he hit a magnificent second shot over the ditch, the ball coming to rest 6 feet from the hole. This time he made the putt for an eagle 3 and a stroke lead over Snead. Even par the rest of the way gave him the victory at 279, a score no one was to better for 14 years.

1940

It was a year of record rounds at Augusta. On opening day, a colorful young Texan—this was the era when Texans were beginning to dominate the tour—named Jimmy Demaret shot an entirely forgettable 37 on the front nine, then went birdie, birdie, par, birdie, par, birdie, birdie, birdie, par, for a 30. Demaret used only 12 putts on the nine holes. Even so, his record nine was not the big news of the day. Another Texan, Lloyd Mangrum, put together nine birdies, eight pars, and a bogey for a 64, a score which has never been bettered and was equaled only by Jack Nicklaus in 1965.

Mangrum and Demaret dueled for the rest of the week, and although neither was to break 70 again, Demaret used steady rounds of 72, 70, and 71 to pull ahead and win by 4 strokes. Earlier in the week, playing with Bobby Jones in a practice round, the fast-talking Demaret had said: "You've won so many tournaments, Bob, you must know the right thing to say when they give you the trophy. How about lending me one of your speeches? I may just need it before the week is out." And indeed he did.

1941

Although Craig Wood had won some 16 tournaments during his career, he had become better known for losing. He had lost each of the three major championships of the day—the Open, PGA and British Open—either in a playoff or during the last round and he had twice seen the Masters title taken from him at the last gasp. And indeed there were moments in 1941 when it seemed as if Wood was going to add another Masters to the list. After a sensational opening 66 gave him a 5-stroke edge on the field, Wood had held that lead going into the final round. But after nine holes, having shot a 38 to Byron Nelson's 33, it was all gone. Nelson, at the top of his game, had obviously caught everybody's favorite loser.

But Wood, playing several holes ahead, birdied the 13th hole. Nelson bogeyed the 12th and, trying to get the stroke back, bogeyed the 13th as well. When Wood birdied the 15th and 16th, he had his championship, and no one could call him a loser anymore.

1942

The war was on. Camp Gordon in Augusta had become headquarters for the Fourth Motorized Division, U.S. Army. Among the gallery, service men outnumbered civilians two to one. Only 42 of the 88 players invited were able to make it to Augusta, yielding the smallest field in the tournament's history. But the important players were there—Nelson, Hogan, Demaret, Snead.

After 36 holes, Nelson, with a 68, 67, had a thin one-stroke lead over Sam Byrd, the former baseball player, but, against his more formidable

Byron Nelson

opponents, 5 over Demaret, 8 over Hogan, and an even dozen over Snead. Home free, apparently. But while Nelson was finishing 72, 73, Hogan came blazing back with 67, 70, tying for the lead when he hit his approach shot on the 18th hole 3 feet from the pin.

The playoff was a classic. With Jones and Clifford Roberts trooping along as official scorers, Nelson started with the worst drive of his career, way off to the right near a concession stand. When he took a double-bogey 6, Hogan led by 2. At the end of the 5th hole, Hogan had picked up another stroke to lead by 3. Every year in Augusta during the Masters, newspapermen and golf enthusiasts still talk about the remarkable stretch of golf Nelson played during the next eight holes. Hogan played the 6th through the 13th in even par, and lost 6 shots to Nelson. With birdies at the 6th, 11th, 12th, and 13th and an eagle at the 8th, Byron took a 3-stroke lead. Hogan narrowed the margin to one, but that was it. Nelson, with a double bogey on the 1st hole and a bogey on the last, had still managed a 69 for his second Masters title.

1946

After an absence of three years, the masters were back in Augusta, the old champions like Horton Smith, Craig Wood, Henry Picard, and Ralph Guldahl; the current kings, Hogan, Nelson, Snead, and Demaret; and a few promising youngsters such as Cary Middlecoff and Frank Stranahan. Few followers of the game noticed a Navy veteran named Herman Keiser. But Keiser put together three rounds of 69, 68, 71 to take a 5-stroke lead over Hogan into the final day.

Still, a 5-stroke lead over Hogan was not as safe as it seemed. By nine holes, the margin was down to 3. Hogan, playing behind Keiser, made a birdie at the 12th and another at the 13th to reduce it to one. When Keiser, trying for a birdie at the 18th that he felt was necessary, three-putted instead for a bogey, Hogan was even. All he needed was three pars for a tie.

He got the first two, then hit a fine approach at the 18th just 12 feet from the hole. Waiting in the clubhouse, Keiser prayed against a tie. "Let him win it or lose it now," he said. Hogan putted and wheeled away in disgust. "The moment I hit it I knew it was going to miss," he said later. When he turned back he saw to his amazement that the ball had rolled 2½ feet past the cup. Hogan putted again and when that putt also missed, Herman Keiser had become a dark-horse winner of the first postwar Masters.

1947

Jimmy Demaret won his second Masters championship with four straight rounds under par—69, 71, 70, 71. He was tied for the lead with Nelson after 18 holes and with Middlecoff after 36. After 54 he had it to himself, prompting him to show up the next day, Easter Sunday, in canary yellow shirt and slacks. "If you're going to be in the limelight, you might as well dress for it," he quipped. And so he was, finishing 2 strokes ahead of Nelson and Stranahan.

1948

Claude Harmon was a teaching pro, spending his winters at Seminole in Florida, his summers at Winged Foot in Mamaroneck, New York. It was usually in early April that he moved his family north, and he regarded the one-week stopover in Augusta as a vacation, a chance to see the boys, swap a few stories, and play some friendly golf. He had no illusions about winning. Teaching pros don't step out of the pro shops and mix it up with the Hogans and Sneads.

His first-round 70 was pleasant enough, and he matched that the next day, but it was only when he turned in a third-round 69 that most people around the course began to take him seriously. It gave him a 2-stroke edge over Chick Harbert, 5 over Middlecoff, and 9 over Hogan, whose third-round 77 had put him far back. A huge crowd turned out Sunday to see if the tournament could produce its first home-state champion—Harmon was born in Savannah—and it did, despite some worrisome moments. A lucky bounce on the par-3 6th hole paved the way for three straight birdies, and Harmon finished with a 70 and 279 total, matching Guldahl's record and giving him the title by 5 shots over Middlecoff.

1949

What has been called the Era of Hogan-Snead began with the 1949 tournament, although Ben was at home in bed recovering from the automobile accident that nearly killed him. During the next six years, Hogan and Snead were to win five times. Snead began it.

For 36 holes there was little inkling that this was to be Sam's year. He started 73, 75 and found himself an uncomfortable 5 shots behind Herman Keiser and Lloyd Mangrum. Snead had come into the tournament as the tour's leading money winner, helped in part by a new putter called "the Velvet Touch" and a new stiff-wristed putting stroke. Snead, because of several well-publicized failures, had earned the reputation as a golfer who could power his drives further and more accurately than anyone else, then blow a 2-foot putt. "It's all in your mind, Sam," Walter Hagen once told him. "You're the only person who doesn't think you're a good putter."

In the third round, Sam started sinking some putts and his 67 put him just one stroke behind Johnny Palmer, and even with Mangrum. In the last round Palmer carded a respectable 72, Mangrum a very good 70, but Snead was too much. He went out in 33, and when he came to the 18th tee, he had a 2-stroke lead. Then he gave the crowd one last moment of doubt, slicing his drive into the woods on the right. A double-bogey 6 would throw him into a tie with Johnny Bulla, who had closed fast with a 69. Instead, Snead was able to hit a seven-iron through the trees and up onto the green, whereupon he sank an 18-foot putt for another 67. As he picked his ball from the cup he said: "Now whoever started that rumor that I couldn't putt?"

1950

Jimmy Demaret had finished his final round, and a look at the scoreboard made him reasonably certain of second place. Jim Ferrier, the Australian, was leading, and needed only a 38 on the back nine to bring himself home a winner. The others were out of it. Hogan, making a strong effort in his first appearance after the accident, had been 2 strokes ahead of Demaret going into the final day and only 2 shots off the lead, but, perhaps weary, he had shot 76. Snead was also out of it, 4 strokes behind Demaret. Nelson was tied with Hogan. So Jimmy sat on the veranda to await Ferrier, who had gone out in 34.

All went well—three pars on the tough 10th, 11th, and 12th—until Ferrier came to the 13th. For this tournament at least, the 13th was Demaret's hole, for he had played it in birdie, eagle, eagle, birdie—6 strokes under par. The other holes he had played in one over. Now Ferrier hit his drive out of play on the left and it cost him a bogey 6. He still had the lead, but he was shaken. He could par only one of the last five holes, finishing with a horrendous 41, 2 shots behind a surprised Demaret. The victory made Jimmy the first three-time winner of the Masters.

1951

After nine tries, Ben Hogan finally won the Masters, as everyone knew he must. After three rounds, he was one stroke behind Snead and Skee Riegel. "I can't depend on them fading," Ben said. "I've got to go after them." Snead did fade, in fact disappear, taking an 8 on the 11th hole and finishing with an 80. But Riegel, playing early, turned in a tidy 71 for 282. Hogan needed a 69 to win.

A 33 on the front nine helped, and a birdie at the 13th put him 4 under for the round. He came to the 18th needing only a bogey to win. With no stomach for a long downhill putt that could lead to anything, Hogan deliberately played just short of the sloping green in 2, then pitched his third short within 4 feet of the cup. The putt got him home in 68: 14 pars and four birdies. "If I never win another tournament, I'll be satisfied," said Hogan after Bobby Jones had helped him into his Masters green jacket. But, of course, there would be more to come.

1952

Again it was Sam Snead. After three rounds he had shaken loose from everyone in the field except, why, Ben Hogan, of course! Snead had started with a rather extraordinary 70 the first day, despite a 6 on the first hole and another 6 at 13. After his second-round 67 it looked as if he might run away from everyone, Hogan included, especially when Hogan, 3 shots back, fired a 74 in the third round. But Snead faltered badly, shooting a 77, so that the two golfing stars began the last day dead even. That 77, incidentally, remains the highest single round ever shot by a winner.

Snead's last round turned on one hole, the 12th. Playing about an hour ahead of Hogan, Sam hit his tee shot into Rae's Creek. Dropping a new ball, he managed to leave it in a depression from which he barely got it over the creek, the ball hanging precariously in the thick grass. Lying 3, Snead seemed on his way to a sure 6, but from an awkward stance, left foot well high of the right, he bounced a shot onto the green that rolled smack into

Hogan struggling on last day of 1952 Masters

the cup. Disaster had been turned into a routine bogey. From there, Sam went on to shoot a pretty par 72, and when Hogan shot an uncharacteristic 79, Snead was home free. Said Sam, watching Ben struggle up the last fairway: "I guess Hogan is human after all."

1953

But perhaps Sam Snead spoke too soon when he called Ben Hogan human. In 1953, little Ben was something else. He won the Masters with ease, the U.S. Open at Oakmont, and, a couple of weeks later, the British Open at Carnoustie. In those days the PGA followed the British Open immediately and Ben, weary, did not compete.

No surgeon ever prepared for an operation as carefully as Hogan prepared for the major tournaments in 1953. After the 1952 U.S. Open, Hogan had retired from the tour, but he showed up at Augusta two weeks early. He played 11 practice rounds, spent the final day putting, and announced he was ready.

Rounds of 70 and 69 gave him the halfway lead by a shot. Archrival Snead was 6 strokes back. On Saturday, Hogan ran away from everyone with a 6-under 66 and when he added a 69 on Sunday, he had finished in 274, 5 strokes better than the tournament record, 5 strokes ahead of Porky Oliver, and a whopping 18 strokes better than Snead. "That's the best I've ever played for 72 holes," Hogan said. "I hope I can come back next year and play the same caliber of golf."

"If you do," said Byron Nelson, who had played with him on Sunday, "you'll be playing here all by yourself."

1954

One day, months before the 1954 Masters was to begin, Clifford Roberts was going over the list of amateurs to be invited; he asked Bobby Jones if perhaps they should not include the alternates to the Walker Cup team. Jones, naturally partial to amateurs, agreed. And so it was that an invitation was sent to William J. Patton in Morganton, North Carolina, thirty-one, Wake Forest graduate, Navy veteran, lumber salesman, weekend golfer, and a long, but often erratic hitter. As anyone would, Patton quickly accepted. If nothing else, this would impress his friends at the Mamosa Golf Club.

Patton hardly had any serious thoughts about winning. What with Ben Hogan and Sam Snead in the field, how could he? Snead had won in 1949 and 1952, Hogan in 1951 and 1953. More, Hogan was coming off the greatest year any golfer ever had since Jones's Grand Slam in 1930. The year before Ben had won the Masters, U.S. Open, and British Open, and he had established a new scoring record at Augusta, 274. And yet before the tournament was over, Billy Joe Patton was to turn the Augusta National inside out and have a definite effect on the play of both these great pros.

Anyone who believes in omens might have been interested in the annual driving contest held the day before the tournament began. Billy Joe, his rimless glasses shining in the sun, hit his first drive with the gusto of a man trying for a home run in the office softball game. The ball landed 338 yards away. With that Patton quit, even though he was entitled to two more tries. "Why should I?" he asked. "I'll never match that one and I might swing and miss." No one else matched it either.

The sun was gone on Thursday, replaced by thunder, lightning, and heavy rains. It was just the start of bad weather that was to produce the highest winning score in the history of the Masters. To boot, the pins were placed in difficult positions the first day. "They ought to give each twosome a seeing-eye dog to help them find the holes," Hogan said. He had a 72, 2 strokes better than Snead but 2 worse than Dutch Harrison. Also 2 worse than that amateur who had won the driving contest, Billy Joe Patton. "Relax," Billy Joe told the press after his round. "I may shoot 80 tomorrow."

Galleries became charmed by the amateur, who laughed at his mistakes and talked with them between shots. The next day he was in the woods as often as he was on the fairways and he even spent some time in the water, but when his round was over, his 74 did not look bad. Co-leader Harrison had shot a 79, Hogan and Snead 73s. Billy Joe had the lead to himself.

Saturday should have been the day when Billy Joe was finally put away for keeps and so it seemed. While he was shooting a 75 to go 3 over par for the tournament, Hogan was producing the first sub-70 round, a 69 to go 2 under, 5 shots better than Patton. Snead, with a 70, was 3 behind.

On Sunday a huge gallery went off with Snead around noon to see if he could make up the 3 strokes on Hogan. As he approached the 7th green he was one over par, and when he missed a short putt there, much of the crowd abandoned him in favor of Hogan, who was teeing off on the nearby 3rd hole. But as everyone moved up the 3rd fairway, prepared to watch the game's greatest player protect his now more than comfortable lead, there came a roar from the 6th hole. Sitting in the clubhouse more than a quarter mile away, Bobby Jones heard the noise and accurately assessed it. "Billy Joe must have done something," he said.

And how! Using a five iron on the par-3 hole, Patton hit "an arrow in the sky." The ball hit the front edge of the green, bounced, and hit the pin a foot above the ground. Then it fell and remained wedged between the pin and the side of the cup. Before touching the pin, Billy Joe consulted Joe Dey, then executive director of the USGA. Dey warned Patton to be careful. If he removed the pin and the ball came out, he would have to play it. Billy Joe jiggled the pin and the ball fell for a hole in one.

Some players who make a hole in one follow it up with a string of bogeys, but Patton tacked on birdies at the 8th and 9th to make the turn in 32. He was now ahead of Snead, who had taken 37 and even with Hogan, who was on his way to a 37.

When Patton reached the par-5 13th he had fallen a stroke behind, having bogeyed the 12th and, anxious to get it back, he gambled for the green with a four wood. The ball fell short, landing in the ditch before the green. Billy Joe sat down, took off his shoes and socks, rolled up his pants and went in after it, but when he saw just how much water he was in, he changed his mind and took a penalty drop. Still in bare feet, he played a poor pitch short, another on, and took two putts for a 7. His fans were discouraged, but Patton was not. "Hey, everyone smile again," he said. "It's really not that bad."

So now Hogan was leading Billy Joe by 3 strokes as he played the 11th—only he did not know it. Convinced he would need birdies to win, Hogan abandoned his cautious tactics and went for the pin. The ball hooked into the water on the left and Hogan had a double bogey himself. Later he confessed that "if I'd known what had happened to Patton I'd have played it safe."

Hogan's disaster put Snead back into contention. After turning in 37, he produced a 35 for a 72, still one over for the tournament. Hogan's 6 at the 11th made him one over, too. And Billy Joe wasn't quite through yet. Having told his fans to smile, he helped them along by getting a birdie at 14. This tied him with Hogan and Snead at one over par, although perhaps he was not yet aware of Hogan's trouble at the 11th. But even if he was, he probably would have played the 15th no differently. Taking out a wood, he tried to carry the pond in front of the green and failed. And so he took a bogey, after which three pars put him in at 290, one behind Snead. Hogan, after the 11th, played five straight pars to stay even with Sam, then hit his approach shot on the 17th 5 feet from the flag. But when he missed the putt and could do no better than par the 18th, he finished even with his old rival, thus giving the Masters its first playoff since Ben himself had tied and later lost to Byron Nelson in 1942. And poor Billy Joe had missed by a stroke.

As so often in the past, the 13th hole was pivotal. The two were even to there, Hogan having made 12 straight pars, Snead two bogeys and two birdies, one of them a 65-foot chip shot at the 10th hole. At the 13th, Snead got off a booming drive that enabled him to reach the green with an iron. Hogan could not afford the gamble. "I knew the hole was cut at the front end of the green," he said. "I would have had to use a wood and thought I could not stop the ball, that it would run to the back or even off." So Hogan played short and tried to pitch close, but a soft lie hampered him and he left the ball just short of the green. He got down in 2, but so did Snead—a birdie—and Sam had a one-stroke lead.

Still one behind at 16, Hogan hit his tee shot about 20 feet from the pin and then did a very uncharacteristic thing. He three-putted, thus handing Snead the title. Later he said that he had been so intent on the line, he forgot to hit the ball. His putter struck both the ball and the ground and the ball stopped well short of the hole, from where he missed. On the 18th, still 2 back, Hogan sent his approach 18 feet away while Snead caught the trap on the right, but Ben missed his birdie try while Sam came out 5 feet from the flag. With a stroke to burn, Snead carefully two-putted to win by one. Thus Sam Snead took the lead over Ben Hogan, three Masters jackets to two, and although one would hardly have predicted it then, it was the last time either would win a major championship. The 1954 Masters was their last dance.

1955

We go directly to the 13th hole, second day, to pick up Cary Middlecoff. After a routine 72 the first day, Cary has birdied five holes on the front nine and just now hit his second shot on the 13th onto the green. But the ball is on the back right edge of the green and the pin is to the left and front, 75 feet away. We know it is 75 because Middlecoff, a very slow, deliberate golfer, has paced and repaced, fidgeted, adjusted, inspected, and scrutinized for what seems like hours. Jones, in his golf cart, is watching.

Finally Cary strokes his putt, a sort of mini-drive, and the ball rolls across plains, valleys, mountains, curves slightly, slows, and amazingly disappears from sight. An eagle 3. Middlecoff finishes with a 65. When a man sinks a putt like that, things are obviously going his way, and Middlecoff had little trouble the last two days. Hogan was just 4 strokes back after 36, but Middlecoff actually gained 3 more on the final 36 to win by 7. Snead was third, a stroke behind Ben.

A look at the top 24 in the Masters record book for 1955 reveals one name of interest. Shooting 76, 76, 72, 69—293 to tie for 10th was a rookie pro named Arnold Palmer.

1956

The sky was lead gray and a light drizzle was falling at the start of the tournament. A record 42 amateurs were in the field, and two of the best, Billy Joe Patton and Ken Venturi, were paired. Billy Joe had won the hearts of the Augusta galleries two years before with his brave, if reckless, play in the final round. Venturi, less known, had finished a very creditable 16th that same year and now, after a year's absence, he was back.

Not that either amateur was expected to win. After all, there was Cary Middlecoff, the defending champion, to say nothing of Ben Hogan and Sam Snead. Ben had nearly become the first player ever to win five U.S. Opens when, the previous June, he had tied for first and then lost in a playoff with a little-known pro, Jack Fleck. Sam Snead was still Sam Snead and he had looked good in practice. In addition, there were such

Billy Joe Patton makes run during 1955 Masters

Jackie Burke

young professionals as Gene Littler, Dow Finsterwald, and Jackie Burke, Jr., and a middle guard of Julius Boros, Doug Ford, and Bob Rosburg. Finally, those who like longshots might have chosen the former amateur champion who had turned pro the year before, Arnold Palmer.

Still, Patton and Venturi had a fair-sized gallery when they teed off early in the afternoon, thanks mainly to Patton and his penchant for daring, colorful play. And indeed the gallery was rewarded when both amateurs started with birdies, Venturi holing a putt from 15 feet, Patton from 10. Patton missed his birdie on the par-5 2nd hole, but Venturi made his with a 5-foot putt, and suddenly you could sense in the gallery the realization that maybe it was not so much Billy Joe as this other fellow, Venturi, they should be watching. Patton made a nice birdie putt on the 3rd, but so did Venturi from 12 feet away. And on the 4th he nearly hit his drive into the hole, the ball stopping a foot away. Still another birdie and 4 under after four holes. Five straight pars let him turn in 32, with Billy Joe on his heels at 34.

On the 10th hole Venturi hooked his drive so close to the trees on the left that he had no approach shot to the green and thus took his first bogey of the day. It looked then as if an old Masters story would be repeated. Young amateur goes out in 32, comes in with 43 for a 75. Shoots 85 the next day. But Venturi would have none of that. He parred the difficult 11th and 12th holes, then hit a four-wood approach shot over the ditch on the 13th and onto the green. When he sank a 16-foot putt for an eagle and, moments later, Billy Joe sank a 15-footer for his own eagle, the noise around the green was one of the loudest in the history of the tournament.

Four more pars and one birdie—a deuce on the 16th after a four-iron shot left him just 7 feet away—put Venturi in the clubhouse with a breathtaking 66. Billy Joe was in with a 70. Only twice before had a player started the Masters with a score as low as 66—Byron Nelson in 1937 and Craig Wood four years later. Both had won. Venturi's 66 gave him a one-shot lead over Middlecoff, 2 over Shelley Mayfield and Tommy Bolt, and 3 over Hogan. In other words, a brilliant round but hardly a commanding lead.

Still, the talk around Augusta that night was: just who is this Ken Venturi? Well, he was a tall, slender, dark-haired young man of twenty-four who grew up around San Francisco and whose parents were both avid golfers. In fact his father had just recently quit his job to run the golf shop at a San Francisco municipal course. The Venturis started their son playing at nine, and throughout high school and San Jose State College, the sport dominated Ken's life. He won three city golf titles and one state championship. While he was in college, Ed Lowry, a car dealer in San Francisco and a member of the executive committee of the USGA, became interested in him and offered him a job, thereby assuring him of time and money to compete in amateur events. Venturi became a member of the 1952 Americas

Cup team and the 1953 Walker Cup team, the latter qualifying him for the 1954 Masters.

Late in 1954 Venturi was drafted and sent first to Fort Ord in California, then to Austria where, among other things, he picked up the putter he was using in the Masters. "Some fellow had thrown it away," explained Ken. "I had it reshafted later in England." When Venturi got out of the Army in late 1955, it was obvious something had gone wrong with his swing, so Ed Lowery summoned Byron Nelson, who had worked a great deal with Ken several years before. The two had played a round together in 1952; Venturi had shot a 66, but Nelson, unimpressed, had said to him on the 18th green: "Meet me here at nine tomorrow morning. There are six or seven things about your swing that need adjustment."

The two had become close friends, so close that Venturi was to name Nelson as godfather of his first son. Now, with Venturi's swing rusty after a year in the Army, the two met in Palm Springs for a tune-up. "When Byron saw me swing he nearly fell out of his golf cart," Venturi said later. Nelson removed a loop in Ken's swing and adjusted his stance. Venturi then went out and finished fifth at Phoenix and upset Harvey Ward, another Lowery protégé, for the San Francisco City championship. Technically, he was not eligible for the Masters, but because he had finished in the top 24 two years before and had been unable to play in 1955, the Masters champions, as was their prerogative, voted him in.

On Friday a stiff breeze raked the course until late in the afternoon, making it more difficult. Whereas five players had managed to break 70 the day before, only one could do it Friday, but amazingly, that one was Ken Venturi. Hogan had a 78, Snead a 76. The wind was so strong Bob Rosburg used a four iron at the 12th. Just as he swung, the wind died, so that the ball cleared Rae's Creek, the green, the bank behind the green, and the fence behind the bank, his ball ending up on the property of the Augusta Country Club. Hitting again with the wind blowing, Rosburg stuck by his decision and landed his four-iron shot 10 feet from the pin.

Venturi, with Bobby Jones following him in a golf cart, played the first seven holes in par, then eagled the par-5 8th hole when he chipped with a six iron into the cup. Turning in 34, he bogeyed the 11th and 12th holes, but got the strokes back with birdies on the 13th and 15th, in each case going for the green with his second shot. He came to the 18th hole needing only a par for a 70, but instead he thrilled the huge gallery around the green by sinking a 23-foot putt for a birdie and a 69. That is the sort of finish people in Augusta love to see. Venturi's 36-hole total of 135 tied the record held by Henry Picard (who was 67, 68, then 76, 75 for fourth place in 1935) and it gave him a 4-stroke lead over Middlecoff. Three strokes behind Cary were Tommy Bolt, Doug Ford, and Pete Cooper. One further back and 8 behind Venturi was Burke, although no one was really noticing at the time.

A few old pros weren't about to concede the young amateur anything. "Yeah, he's done all right for 36 holes," said Lloyd Mangrum. "That's halfway." Said Middlecoff: "He's unproven in big medal-play tournaments, but I believe he'll hold up."

Venturi did hold up on Saturday, maintaining his 4-stroke lead, although it was not as easy as it sounds. In fact, for a few moments in the third round he fell out of the lead. Again a wicked wind swept the course and scores soared—only three players matched par 72. Venturi went out in 40, bogeying the 1st, 4th, 7th, and 9th holes, while Middlecoff, playing some 20 minutes behind him, was shooting a 35. This was what the old pros had been expecting, the collapse of the amateur.

But on the back nine it was the pro who collapsed, or nearly. Venturi bogeyed the 11th and 17th, but in between he birdied three straight, the 13th, 14th, and 15th, to finish with 35 and a 75 for the day, a good score under the circumstances. As for Middlecoff, a par at the 18th would have given him a fine 73 for the day—35, 38—and put him just 2 strokes behind Venturi, prime position. But Cary's approach fell in the trap to the right. He blasted out to 6 feet, still a chance for the par, but then not only missed the putt, but missed a 2-footer coming back. Just like that his 73 was a 75 and Venturi had the same 4-stroke lead he woke up with that morning. More than that, he had 7 strokes over the third-place man, Doug Ford, and 8 over Burke and Mangrum, who were tied for fourth. The pros were running out of holes.

It had been a tradition of the Masters in recent years to have Byron Nelson play the final round with the tournament leader, but because of the closeness between Nelson and Venturi, Masters officials decided that tradition, in this case, should be abandoned. Instead Venturi was paired with Sam Snead who, because of his taciturnity, is not the easiest player to have as a partner. Just ahead of them were Burke and Mike Souchak, while in the next twosome were Middlecoff and Doug Ford. Middlecoff started with two straight birdies, but after nine holes he had lost 4 strokes to par for a 38. Venturi also had a 38, bogeying the 7th and 9th, so that his 4-stroke lead was still intact starting the back nine. Observers moving back and forth between the two did not notice that Jackie Burke, with a birdie at the 2nd and eight pars, had shot a 35 and was "only" 5 shots behind.

On the back nine it seemed that Venturi could make nothing but bogeys—at the 10th, 11th, 12th, and almost the 13th too, where his drive landed in the woods. Middlecoff had played the same stretch in one over, so that Venturi's lead was down to 2, while Burke, playing them in even par, was also only 2 back. Both Burke and Venturi bogeyed the 14th, while Middlecoff parred it; and when Venturi also bogeyed the 15th, he had lost his lead. But only technically. Middlecoff was even then in the process of handing the championship back to Venturi by double-bogeying the 17th. His approach went beyond the green, his chip was weak, and he took three putts. It was his third double bogey of the round, and he was through.

Venturi learned of Middlecoff's misfortune as he teed off on the 16th. He had a 2-stroke lead again, he thought. What he didn't fully appreciate was that Burke was only one stroke back, teeing off at the 17th. But Burke knew. His playing partner had just told him: "Man, play some golf and you can win this one," Mike Souchak said. "They're shooting double bogeys out here." Burke drove well on the 17th, then hit his approach 15 feet from the pin. He thought he had left his putt short but, as he said later, "That wind just absolutely took the ball in." He was tied for the lead.

Burke parred the 18th, as Venturi, having parred the 16th, was tackling the 17th. His drive was good, but his iron to the green was too firm, the ball rolling down an embankment behind the green. He chipped back short, 12 feet from the cup, and when he missed the putt, he was behind.

It was not until he was on the 18th tee that he realized the position he was in. "Somebody told me Jackie had birdied 17 and that I need a birdie at 18 to win," Ken said later. "I wasn't even watching for him. I was running away from Cary and it seems that I ran into the door on the way out, doesn't it?"

Venturi gave himself a chance on the 18th, hitting his second shot 15 feet from the pin, but when he missed, he had lost the Masters he had all but wrapped up two hours earlier. Jack Burke, Jr., son of a professional golfer, Texan, thirty-three, a pro for 15 years, was the surprise winner. He had managed a neat 71 for 289 while Venturi had skied to 80—42 on the back nine—for 290. Middlecoff, with a 77, was third at 291. But while everyone was pleased for Burke, an extremely popular pro, the 1956 Masters would be remembered because of Ken Venturi, the amateur who *almost* won it.

1957

Something new was introduced into the Masters, as indeed it is almost every year—a new bunker here, a mogul there, scoreboards, concessions stands, ticket regulations. One of the things that makes the Masters such an outstanding tournament is its ability to blend tradition with change. "If we don't do something right the first time," Clifford Roberts has said, "we keep fiddling around until we do."

The change this year was something known as the cut, a rule that is commonplace in golf today. Because the field had grown to what was considered an unwieldy 102, it was decided to cut all but the low 40 golfers, plus ties, after 36 holes.

The rule caused a furor. Ben Hogan missed the cut by a stroke, shooting 151. Middlecoff was at 152 and was so angry he left town without staying around for the annual champions' dinner. Horton Smith, who had played in every single round of the Masters, said, "It's like being invited to dinner and then being asked to leave before dessert is served."

More pertinent was the question whether the cut deprived someone, say Hogan, of the chance to make a brilliant comeback. Snead led at 140 after 36, meaning Hogan would have been 11 shots back. When Snead added a 74 in the third round, the furor grew. A 67 by Hogan would have cut the margin to 4 and surely Ben was capable of a 67. Hadn't Jackie Burke gained 9 shots on Ken Venturi on the last round the year before?

It took Doug Ford to get Masters officials off the hook. With a closing 66, including a birdie 3 on the 18th from out of the bunker, Ford won the tournament by 3 shots over Snead, finishing at 283. Hogan would have needed a 67, 68 to catch Snead, a possibility, but he would have had to have shot a pair of 66s to match Ford and that was too much to credit even the great Hogan with.

1958

Arnold Palmer owed his first Masters Championship to his knowledge of the rules of golf and his ability to stay cool under pressure. After three rounds he was tied for the lead with Sam Snead, a young star against an old king, a perfect dramatic setting. But others were involved too—notably Ken Venturi. Venturi, paired with Palmer, was 3 strokes behind as the day began, and after ten holes he had cut the margin to one. Meanwhile old Sam had taken a double-bogey 6 at the first hole and was on his way to a 79.

At the 12th hole, both Palmer and Venturi hit irons beyond the green and onto the bank behind it. Venturi's ball trickled back down to the edge of the green, from where he made an easy par, but Palmer's ball imbedded itself in soft ground. He could hardly hit it and wound up with a 5, presumably falling a stroke behind Venturi.

But Arnold wasn't through. It had rained heavily the night before, so much that the rules committee invoked a wet-weather rule, allowing balls imbedded in wet ground to be lifted, cleaned, and dropped without penalty. After consulting with an official at the 12th, Palmer played a provisional ball, with which he made a 3. The official ruling would take a while, so both players teed off on the 13th. Palmer boomed a magnificent second shot

18 feet from the cup, and as he approached the green he got word—unofficial but authoritative—that his 3 would stand. As if to celebrate, Palmer made his eagle putt. With that Venturi fell back, three-putting the 14th and 15th holes. There were still a few anxious moments for Palmer—Ford and Fred Hawkins had birdie putts on the 18th to tie—but when they missed, he had his first Masters victory. The Age of Palmer had begun.

1959

Everyone was watching Arnold Palmer on the last round in his bid to become the first man ever to win the Masters two straight years. And a strong bid it was. With 71, 70, 71, he was tied with Stan Leonard, a Canadian, who was showing signs of cracking. Palmer reached the 12th hole at even par and in the lead. But this time the 12th did him in. His tee shot landed smack in the middle of Rae's Creek and he wound up with a triple-bogey 6. Fighting back, Palmer birdied the 13th and 15th, but a bogey for the 17th gave him a 74 for 286. Even so, it was the low score and there did not appear to be anybody on the course who was going to beat it.

Certainly there was no reason to suspect that lightning was about to strike Art Wall. Slender, quiet Art Wall had never broken 70 in the Masters. His 73, 74 beginning had gotten him past the cut by 2 strokes. He began the last day tied for 13th, 6 strokes behind Palmer. As Palmer bogeyed the 17th, Wall was playing the 13th and was only one under par for his round.

Enter lightning. Wall sank a 15-foot putt for a birdie at the 13th, a 20-footer at the 14th for another. On the 15th he almost made an eagle, but got a third birdie. After a par for the 16th, he birdied the 17th with a 15-foot putt. Now a mere par on the final hole would beat Palmer. Wall hit his approach 12 feet below the cup and made that one, too, for his fifth birdie in the last six holes and a glorious 66. It was just as well he made that last birdie, too, because Cary Middlecoff, with an eagle for the 15th and three pars, finished one stroke back.

1960

If the Age of Palmer was born in 1958, it reached full maturity in 1960. It was not so much that Palmer won both the Masters and the

U.S. Open that year, it was how he won them, coming out of the pack at the final turn and barreling past the leaders. Two words gained new meaning in 1960—army and charge. Army was Palmer's gallery at any given tournament—Arnie's Army—that whooping, encouraging, stampeding sea of people who came to watch their man perform heroics and were more often than not satisfied. And what Palmer did was charge. As in cavalry. Four shots back and five to play. Easy. During this period in Palmer's career he was quoted as saying, "I feel anytime I have to make a birdie, I can," and it seemed he was right.

Palmer was the favorite at Augusta in 1960. He had won four tournaments during the winter, including three in a row, and was the leading money-winner with $26,000. He had arrived at the course a week early to prepare, but cold, rainy weather had reduced his practice rounds to four. Even this seemed to work for Palmer, however, for the course, soggy from the rains, would work to the advantage of the long hitters, of which Palmer was certainly a leading example. Some others, such as Sam Snead and Mike Souchak, also figured to benefit from the slow course. Among the other pros thought to have a chance were Billy Casper, the U.S. Open champion, Julius Boros, Dow Finsterwald, Gary Player, the young South African, Ken Venturi, and, of course, Ben Hogan and Sam Snead. There was also a fine field of amateurs, Billy Joe Patton and Charlie Coe, and two young ones, twenty-year-old Jack Nicklaus, the U.S. champion, and twenty-one-year-old Deane Beman, who had won the British Amateur. On the day before the tournament began, the traditional driving contest was scratched in favor of a new par-three competition on a pretty little course behind the members' cabins. Sam Snead proved he had more than power by winning with a 23.

There were two remarkable rounds that first day. A huge crowd joined Palmer as he teed off just after noon, and he quickly gave them what they had come for. He birdied the 1st, with a six-iron shot to the pin, then birdied the 2nd, getting home in 2. A bogey at the 5th slowed him only momentarily. At the par-5 8th hole, he knocked a sand wedge out of a bunker and into the cup for an eagle. Minutes later, he had made the turn in 33. Three more birdies and one bogey on the back nine gave him a 34 and 67 for the round, a 2-stroke lead over Finsterwald and three others, but more important, a 4- to 6-stroke advantage over such other potentially dangerous rivals as Casper, Boros, Hogan, Snead, and Venturi.

Ah, Venturi! That was the day's second remarkable round. Just a 73 in your scorecard, but what a 73! As Palmer was winding up his round, Venturi was making the turn in 31, 5 under par. A record round, perhaps. Then came the kind of disaster that had struck Ken four years before. He three-putted the 11th for a bogey, then took a double-bogey 5 at the 12th when his tee shot landed on the green, but rolled over and into an indentation in the soft ground that had been made by another ball. Venturi asked for a lift but was denied. Shaken, he three-putted the 14th and 15th greens, and also bogeyed the 17th and 18th holes for an incoming 42 and a 73 total. Venturi was grim as he left the last green, but not ready to give up. "It's still a long tournament," he said. He was right.

A curious event happened on Friday, one that was to affect the tournament greatly. As Dow Finsterwald and Billy Casper finished the 1st hole, Finsterwald dropped his ball on the green and prepared to stroke it with his putter. "Don't do it," yelled Casper. "It will cost you two strokes." Finsterwald knew about the rule prohibiting practice putts on the PGA tour, but did not think it applied at Augusta. But, as Casper pointed out, the rule was clearly printed on the back of the scorecard. Finsterwald then recalled that on the 5th green the day before, he had done the same thing, stroking the ball off the green with his putter. He reported this immediately to an official at the 1st green, who advised him to play on while the rules committee decided what the penalty should be. There was a good chance he could have been disqualified, for if he were given a belated 2-stroke penalty, turning his 69 into a 71, then he would have been guilty of signing an incorrect scorecard. Remarkably, under this strain, Dow shot a second-round 70. Scoreboards around the course showed him at 139, the tournament leader, since Palmer had come in with a 73. But Finsterwald knew better. He definitely wasn't in the lead and maybe he wasn't even in the tournament. At last the rules committee decided to let him off with the 2-stroke penalty only, feeling that the circumstances were unusual, namely the penalty assessed the day after the breach of rules.

So Palmer was still in the lead, even though he was hobbled by an angry blister. Finsterwald was one back, along with Claude Harmon, Walter Burkemo, and Ben Hogan, who had reminded everyone he was still alive with a 68, the day's low round. One stroke behind them was, among others, Venturi, who had demonstrated admirable resiliency with a 69.

Saturday merely set the stage for Sunday's dramatics. Palmer struggled around in par 72, even though "I putted like Joe Schmoe." Twice he three-putted and once missed a 4-footer after a fine approach. Even so, he held the lead at 212, but bunched together one stroke behind him were the best players in the tournament—Hogan, Casper, Boros, Finsterwald, and the dogged Venturi. It meant, in effect, that Palmer would have to match the best round any one of them had if he were to win.

Rather quickly on Sunday, Hogan, Boros, and Casper played themselves out of contention, making bogeys and heading for rounds in the mid 70s. Venturi and Finsterwald were paired together, playing about an hour ahead of Palmer, and the two of them put on a dogfight that was not resolved until the final hole. Venturi birdied the 2nd, 3rd, and 6th, to lead the tournament. Finsterwald had to struggle for his pars at first, but rallied with birdies at the 8th and 9th to make the turn at 34. Venturi was at 33.

Palmer opened with a birdie at the 1st hole and later birdied the 8th, but in between were bogeys for the 3rd and 5th, giving him 36 for the nine.

When Venturi bogeyed the 11th, his approach catching the water, Finsterwald was even with him, Palmer one stroke back. Dow bogeyed the 12th but birdied the 14th to draw even again. Palmer, rolling off a steady stream of pars, remained a stroke behind. They stayed that way until the 18th, when Finsterwald's second shot, a two iron, caught the trap on the right. He came out well, leaving himself only 8 feet away, but he missed the putt. Venturi made his par for a 70, giving him a 283 for the tournament, 5 under par. Finsterwald was at 284. As the two left the green, Palmer was playing the 13th. He was 4 under par for the tournament and needed one birdie to tie, two to win. With both the 13th and 15th ahead of him, the task did not seem at all impossible. Venturi retired to the clubhouse TV to watch.

At the par-5 13th hole, Palmer whipped out his three wood and went for the green—his gallery would not have stood for anything less. He made it, but the ball rolled across and into a bunker behind. When he could not come out close, he had to settle for a par. Again at the 15th he tried for the green in two. He cleared the pond, but the hill was far to the right near the scoreboard. It took ten minutes to clear the gallery and the debris. When he finally chipped the ball, it stopped 15 feet short of the cup. Angry, he flipped his club at Ironman, his caddy, who gave him a stony stare. "That look Ironman gave me is the same sort my father used to," Arnold said later. "I decided I'd better calm down."

He did, but he also missed the putt. Par, but no birdie. Now there were only three holes left, none of them easy-birdie holes. At the 16th he hit a four iron short, about 35 feet from the flag. Putting uphill, he decided to leave the flagstick in. He rammed the putt and the ball banged into the stick, glancing off by a foot or so. Had he removed the flag the ball might have dropped, or, as Billy Casper, his playing partner, said: "If you ever had missed that stick you would have had a heck of a putt from the sand."

Two holes left. On the 17th tee Arnold hit a strong drive followed by an eight iron, but the ball stopped abruptly on the green, perhaps 27 feet from the cup. Watching on TV, Ken Venturi had every reason to feel optimistic. Twice Palmer addressed his putt and twice he backed off, distracted by people behind the green. When he finally stroked his putt, the ball went right at the cup, but slowly. It hesitated at the lip, then dropped, Palmer leaping wildly in the air as it did so. He had his birdie and now needed only a par to tie Venturi.

As he said later, that tie was his first concern. He kept his drive away from the woods on the right and gave himself a clear shot, a six iron, to the flag. It was this shot that won the Masters for him. "I thought it might go in," he said later. The ball hit 2 feet to the right of the flag, almost kicked into it and stopped no more than 6 feet away. There wasn't much to the putt. "I just tried to remember what my old friend George Low says," said Palmer. " 'Keep your head down and stay still.' " Palmer played the putt slightly to the left and it broke properly. For a brief second it seemed as if Palmer did not realize what that meant. He picked the ball out of the cup and started off the green as casually as you would on any Sunday afternoon. Then, all of a sudden he was jumping up and down, his face a gigantic smile.

Poor Ken Venturi. For the second time he had lost a Masters he had apparently won. "This gray coat I have on looked mighty green until Palmer sank that putt on 17," he said. Even Palmer felt bad, or at least a little. "I wanted to win more than anything, Ken," he said, "but I'm truly sorry it had to be this way." And although no one could suspect it at the time, it was the last time Ken Venturi would ever come close to winning the Masters.

1961

Although he had been playing in the Masters since 1957, Gary Player had yet to be a major factor in the tournament. In 1959, two closing rounds of 71 had put him in a tie for eighth, and the following year he had been just 3 strokes behind Arnold Palmer as the last round began, but there had been a covey of notable golfers in between—Ken Venturi, Billy Casper, Dow Finsterwald, Julius Boros, and even Ben Hogan—so that Player could hardly be rated a strong contender. A 74 in that final round gave him a tie for sixth.

But 1961 promised to be different. Player came to Augusta as the tour's money leader, having won two tournaments during the winter. Palmer, winner of both the Masters and the U.S. Open the year before, was the acknowledged king of golf, but Player had demonstrated at least once that he was not awed by him. In Pensacola several weeks earlier, the two had been paired in the final round. Neither could win the tournament but they were nearly tied for the money lead. Palmer shot a 71, but Gary threw a cool 65 back at him to take over first place. So while Palmer was the obvious favorite to win the Masters, Player was rated a very strong challenger.

To no one's great surprise, Palmer started fast, shooting a 68 to lead the tournament. It was a gray, drizzly day and the greens were soft, allowing golfers to hit their approach shots right at the flags without fear. Palmer shared the lead with Bob Rosburg, whose 68 was achieved thanks to a chip shot for a birdie on the 5th hole and a record 100-foot putt on the 14th. One stroke behind Palmer and Rosburg was Player, in with a 69. And so the duel had begun, one that would last until Monday evening and provide one of the most dramatic and incredible endings of any Masters in history.

But on Thursday evening it was not entirely clear that the tournament would become a two-man battle. After all, there was Rosburg wedged in there. And what about the twenty-one-year-old amateur, Jack Nicklaus, who had shot a 70? Byron Nelson had awakened the echoes with a fine 71, which put him in a group with Paul Harney, Doug Ford, and Johnny Pott. And there was Venturi at 72, along with Casper, Gene Littler, Tommy Bolt, and the amateur Charlie Coe, among others. Anyone acquainted with the Masters knew that Venturi was capable of closing a 4-stroke gap in less than nine holes.

On Friday, however, the focus sharpened. Rosburg, starting early on a beautiful, windless day, began to submerge with a 73, so that when Player teed off, with Palmer due to follow by half an hour, they were running one-two. Player got even immediately by birdying the 1st hole, and it was seesaw the rest of the afternoon. Palmer birdied the 2nd, Player the 9th. Palmer also birdied the 9th. On the back nine Player birdied the 13th, 15th, and 18th holes, Palmer the 13th and 16th. Each of these birdies was followed instantly by an explosion of cheers, so that there developed a game within a game, Player's ever-growing gallery letting Palmer's already huge gallery know that Gary had just made a birdie. For instance there was a moment toward the end of Friday when Palmer was lining up a 25-foot birdie putt on the 16th green. Suddenly there was a thunderous cheer from up at the 18th green. Player was there and it was obvious to everyone —Palmer, too, he later admitted—that Gary had made a birdie 3. Without the slightest indication that he had heard the noise, Palmer rolled in his long putt for a birdie 2 and then *his* gallery had a little message for Player's.

When both rounds were over, the two had reversed their scores of Thursday—Player 68, Palmer 69—so that they were co-leaders of the tournament at 137. The next best score was Rosburg's 141. The Masters had become a two-man battle.

It was during Friday's round that Player hit what he was later to call his best shot of the tournament, a wedge on the par-3 4th hole. He had gone one under with his birdie at the 1st hole, but now at the 4th, his four-wood tee shot drifted dangerously close to a trap at the left of the green. The ball ended up in some high grass and sand (an accumulation from previous golfers' sand shots) about 75 feet from the pin. "I didn't know whether to chip or explode from the lie," Player explained. "I finally decided to explode and play for a bogey." The shot wound up no more than 5 inches from the pin for a tap-in par.

The next day Palmer was the first to start and he immediately birdied the first two holes. It shook up Player. "There I am out on the putting green," Player said, "and I look at the scoreboard and see that Arnold's started 3, 4. I'm shocked, frightened stiff. Suddenly he's two shots ahead of me."

If Player was truly frightened stiff, he hardly showed it. After a big drive, he hit an eight iron 12 feet from the flag and sank the putt. When he birdied the 2nd, he was back even with Palmer. In fact, ahead, because Palmer was beginning to have problems. At the 4th hole he hit into the bunker and took a bogey. He also bogeyed the 5th and 7th holes and needed a birdie 4 at the 8th to make the turn in even par 36. Meanwhile Player, with two more birdies, reached the 9th tee 4 under for the round and 4 strokes ahead of Palmer.

Player's drive at the 9th sailed far left, well into the pine trees that separate the 9th and 1st fairways. He then was faced with a choice: punch the ball back onto the 9th fairway, a certain bogey, or gamble for the green by hitting a four wood out toward the 1st fairway and slicing the ball back toward the green. "I was hitting the ball well," he said later, "so I decided to attack." Player's shot came off perfectly, the ball taking off toward the clubhouse, then slicing and landing squarely on the green, where it rolled just off the back edge. From there he chipped close and got his par.

On the back nine Player's lead fluctuated between 5 strokes and 2. On the 11th he was short with his approach. Bogey. He three-putted the 12th. Another bogey. On the 13th he hit into the woods. A third straight bogey. Palmer also bogeyed the 13th when he hit into the ditch. Player rallied with birdies at the 15th and 16th, giving him a 69 and a 4-stroke lead over Palmer, who had an uncomfortable 73. "You have days like that," he said. "It started on the 4th hole and after that I never pulled the right club out of my bag. The course never played easier than it did today and I don't ever remember playing it worse."

Palmer's 73 had allowed a couple of other golfers to edge into the picture. Harney with a 68 and Coe, the amateur, with a 69 were only 2 strokes behind as everyone prepared for Sunday's play. Except that there was to be no Sunday's play. After half the final round had been completed, Augusta was deluged by a rainstorm that made further golf impossible. And so Gary Player had to sweat out his 4-stroke lead for an extra 24 hours.

Player started out on Monday as if he intended to win the tournament by a record margin, birdying the first two holes, just as he had the round before. "That was a key to winning," he said later. "I birdied the first two holes six times. It puts you in the right frame of mind to play the rest of the round."

Player turned in 34, and even though Palmer, playing about an hour behind, was making enough birdies to shoot a 33, Player still had a comfortable lead starting down the 10th. But a bogey there cut the margin to

2, and then came the 13th, about which "I'll have nightmares the rest of my life."

Gary hit his drive away from the woods on the left, so far away the ball went deep into pine trees on the right side of the hole just at the point where it doglegs left toward the green. Because the pines are scattered, he had a chance to play a shot out to the 14th fairway, from where he could reach the 13th green for his par 5. But executing the shot to the 14th meant clearing the huge gallery, and if you have ever been at what is called Amen Corner during the final round, you know there is little room to breathe, let alone move. The marshalls tried and Gary pleaded, but there were just too many people. "I should have sat down and waited," he said later. "Even if it had taken an hour, I should have waited. If it had been an earlier round I might have, but my 4-stroke lead was being cut and I was too excited and worried about the delay to think clearly."

Finally Player tried a two iron to get back on the 13th fairway, but the ball hooked sharply across the fairway and into the ditch on the left. That cost him a penalty stroke. Then came a three iron to the back edge of the green and, shaken, three putts to get down. The double-bogey 7 wiped out his lead.

Nor were his troubles over. Player bogeyed the 15th to fall a stroke behind Palmer and had to scramble desperately to get his pars for the 17th and 18th. On the final hole he hit a four iron into the trap on the right, but managed to get up and down in two for the par. Playing the hole in 4—and in that fashion—turned out to be not only meaningful but ironic.

When Player came off the last green he seemed on the verge of tears. He was certain he had just tossed away the Masters title, for he could see on the scoreboard that Palmer, playing the 15th, was leading by a stroke, and the 15th often means a birdie. Gary and his wife Vivienne then retired to the clubhouse apartment of Clifford Roberts to watch Palmer finish.

Those watching Palmer closely during those final holes might have detected a sign of what was to come. Scoreboard observers could see nothing but a succession of pars going up, but they involved some shaky shots. Several times he missed relatively easy birdie putts on the back nine. Charlie Coe, his amateur playing partner, who, incidentally, was alone in third place just a couple of shots behind Palmer, was frequently outdriving him, and Coe is not a long hitter. It was clear Palmer was tired, even tense.

And yet, as he teed off at the 18th, it seemed as if Arnie had weathered it all. He still had a stroke lead, so that par would win, bogey would tie. His drive was straight and reasonably long, and he used a seven iron— Player had needed a 4—to get home. But the approach faded right into the same trap Player had been in earlier. More, the ball landed in a slight depression. Using a sand wedge, Palmer hit a dreadful shot. The ball flew out of the sand, across the green, through the spectators and down a slope

Palmer blowing lead on 18th hole, 1961 Masters

Palmer on way to a win at 1964 Masters

toward a TV tower. He now had to get down in two merely to tie Player.

To give him time to relax, Charlie Coe putted out, perhaps not entirely appreciating his own position. Had Coe made his putt for a birdie, he would have tied Player. As it was, he missed, to finish a stroke back.

Palmer played his fourth shot back onto the green, the ball stopping some 15 feet from the pin. After inspecting the green from all sides and in eerie silence, Palmer stroked his putt and winced as the ball went by the cup on the left. Inside Roberts's apartment, Gary Player watched in disbelief. He had won the Masters after all, even if he had been forced to spend an agonizing hour contemplating how he had lost it.

1962

When Sunday came, it seemed as if the only question remaining would be whether or not Arnold Palmer would break Ben Hogan's record score of 274. Palmer, with rounds of 70, 66, and 69, needed only a 68 to do this. His lead over Dow Finsterwald was 2 strokes, hardly overwhelming, but the way Palmer was playing, it seemed unlikely he could be caught. Gary Player was 4 behind.

But then Palmer began playing like a Sunday duffer. Bogey followed bogey, and by the time he reached the 16th tee, he was 5 over par for the round and 2 shots behind Finsterwald and Player, who were in at 280. Palmer's shot off the 16th tee was slightly off the green, so he had to chip the ball. It was a marvelous stroke. The ball rolled dead into the cup, and Palmer had one shot back. He followed with a birdie at the 17th, and a par at the 18th threw the Masters into its first three-way tie.

On Monday Palmer again looked beaten. He was 3 strokes down to Gary Player at the turn, but when he holed a long birdie putt on the 10th green, the game, as he said, was on. He birdied the 12th, 13th, and 14th holes to go from 3 strokes down to 4 up. His 68 was 3 better than Player, 9 better than Finsterwald, thus making Arnold a three-time winner along with Jimmy Demaret and Sam Snead.

1963

Jack Nicklaus, at twenty-three, became the youngest of all Masters winners, but it wasn't easy. Despite a second-round 66 that gave him the lead, he found himself in a dogfight midway through the final round. When he bogeyed the 12th hole, he was 2 strokes behind Sam Snead, one behind Gary Player, both of whom were several holes ahead of him. Tony Lema and Julius Boros were just a stroke behind.

Then Snead charitably bogeyed the 16th and 18th and Player the 17th and 18th, while Nicklaus was picking up a birdie at the 13th. When Jack hit his 16th tee shot some 12 feet from the flag and made the putt, Snead and Player were beaten. But it was not quite over. Lema, playing in his first Masters, holed a long birdie putt on the 18th green, doing a memorable victory dance as the ball rolled in. Now Nicklaus needed a par to win. A drive, iron, and first putt left him a tricky 3 feet from the hole, but he stroked the ball home to take the title.

1964

Arnold Palmer had placed the green jacket on the shoulders of Jack Nicklaus the year before. Now it was Jack's turn to do the same for Arnold.

Of Palmer's four Masters titles, this was the easiest. As Bruce Devlin said midway through the tournament, "It looks as if we're all playing to see who will come in second." Arnold opened with a 69 and followed it with 68 and 69, to hold a 5-stroke lead over Devlin, 6 over Dave Marr, and a whopping 9 over Jack Nicklaus.

Nor was there any real suspense on Sunday. Oh, there was a moment when Marr reduced the lead to 3, but by the time Palmer reached the 18th tee, his lead was 6. His playing partner, Marr, needed a birdie to tie Nicklaus for second, and Arnold considerately asked him if there was anything he could do to help. "Yeah," cracked Marr, "shoot 12." And that's about what it would have taken to throw away the title. Instead, Palmer delighted the crowd and TV audience by ramming home a 25-footer for a birdie, thus moving one up on Sam Snead and Jimmy Demaret in the green jacket club.

1965

By now it was clear that the Masters was being dominated by Arnold Palmer, Jack Nicklaus, and Gary Player much in the fashion that Ben Hogan and Sam Snead had dominated it during the early Fifties. It had been Palmer in 1960, Player the next, Palmer again, then Nicklaus, and finally Palmer in 1964. During that period Palmer also had a tie for second, as did Nicklaus, and Player had lost a playoff. Certainly, the stage seemed set for a classic battle among the three at Augusta, and that is exactly what the galleries got—up to a point.

Round one, Thursday, went to Player. Weather forecasts had called for rain, and perhaps this is why Masters officials had moved the tee markers up and decided on relatively easy pin placements. Instead, the day was hot, dry, and windless, the best opening day oldtimers could recall. And the pros responded by turning the Augusta National into a local pitch-and-putt. In all, 33 golfers were under par. "The Scoreboard Dripped Blood," the Augusta paper was to scream the next morning, red being the color that denotes subpar scores at the Masters. When Player got set to tee off in the early afternoon, a glance at the scoreboard at the 18th told him that Tommy Aaron had already spun around in 67, that Dan Sikes and Tony Lema were on the way to doing the same thing, and, worse yet, so was Nicklaus. Besides there were seemingly dozens more headed in that direction—Frank Beard, Doug Sanders, Wes Ellis, Tommy Bolt, Ray Floyd, and George Bayer. The Masters was a birdie festival.

But Gary Player is not one to rattle easily. That week he had been

Nicklaus after sinking birdie putt on 2nd hole, 3rd round, 1955 Masters

Player at 1961 Masters

reading Norman Vincent Peale's *Power of Positive Thinking*, he had a new putter which he had bought in Japan for $50, and, as he was willing to tell the world, "I'm playing so well I can't believe it." As if to demonstrate, Gary hit his approach at the 1st hole 4 feet from the pin. Birdie. On the par-5 2nd, he hit a four wood to the green and two-putted. Birdie. On the 3rd he sank a 20-foot putt. Birdie. Three under after three holes. Player added a birdie on the 8th to make the turn in 32.

It was the 10th hole that cemented the round. He hit what he later called a "banawner" into the trees on his tee shot, then hooked a four iron short of the green and chipped 15 feet past the cup. Bogey? Not on this day. Gary made the putt to save his par, after which he made three more birdies, two of them on the par 5s, to turn in a brilliant 65, giving him a 2-stroke lead.

Later Player talked about his new weight-lifting program, which he felt had helped his game. "It's amazing what you can do with your body," he said. "I predict that within five years most players will be doing some sort of exercise along these lines. Jack and Arnie kid me a lot about my muscle building, but let me tell you, they wouldn't if they shrunk to 5 feet 7 and had to stand on a tee with me. Then we'd see who'd outhit who."

Of the players 2 strokes back, the one that naturally worried Gary the most was Nicklaus. In fact, when the subject of Hogan's record 271 was brought up and the possibility of someone breaking it, Player said: "There is no such thing as a par 5 on this course for Jack. He can reach any green in two. Not only that, he has great touch. I predict that if the weather is good, Jack will break the tournament record."

There had been nothing especially sensational about Jack's 67, and that in itself was frightening. In seven practice rounds leading up to the Masters he had not once shot over 70. For this he gave credit to a Dr. Scholl's foot pad and an old amateur friend. Jack had had a sore right hip and back, and it was finally discovered that his right hip was a half-inch lower than the left. The foot pad seemed to cure the problem.

Deane Beman, the old amateur friend, contributed an important tip. Nicklaus had been working in preparation for the Masters. On the Saturday before the tournament began, he and Beman were playing a practice round when Jack asked him where he was aiming when he addressed the ball.

"Your feet are square to the target," Beman told him, "but your shoulders and hips are aimed to the right of it. This is something you never did before." Beman explained that this was forcing Jack to make such a big body turn that his swing was no longer compact.

Jack shot a 70 in that practice round, flew back to Columbus for two days of practice, then returned to Augusta and shot a 67 on Tuesday that had him euphoric. His game, he felt, was falling into place just at the right time. His opening-round 67 did nothing to dispel the notion, even if he was 2 strokes behind Player.

Palmer was definitely unhappy with his 70, a good score some years, but not this one. Twice he three-putted from 20 feet. "It was ridiculous," said Arnold. His wife Winnie agreed. "The big difference between Jack and Arnie right now is confidence," she said. "It does not occur to Jack that he can miss a putt. It is when you get older that you realize you can miss one."

Confidence or not, round two, Friday, belonged to Arnie. When the players arrived at the course in the morning, they found some changes had been made, namely, tee markers moved back, pin positions toughened. A bulletin, issued in the names of Bobby Jones and Clifford Roberts, announced that "Officials will follow our established procedures with respect to pin positions and tee markers. We anticipate and hope for more low scoring today." To boot, there was a considerable breeze in the air. The Augusta National was a different animal on Friday.

For instance, Ray Floyd went from 69 to 83 and missed the cut. Beard followed his 68 with a 77. Some others: Aaron 67, 74; Bolt 69, 78; Lema 67, 73. More meaningfully, Player posted a 73, Nicklaus a 71, tying them for the lead at 138. And right there with them was Arnold Palmer, thanks to a brilliant 68, the only sub-70 round of the day. Among the top 14 finishers, only Palmer improved his first-round score on Friday.

Perhaps Arnold had been miffed at being left off the leader board Friday morning. Is that any way to treat the tournament's only four-time champion? Palmer immediately set things right by birdying the first three holes, chipping in on the 3rd. With that his Army exploded, and cries of "Go, Arnie" echoed through the pines. Two more birdies at the 13th and 15th offset a bogey, and Palmer cruised home with his 68, thus putting him even with his friendly rivals.

Rounds one and two may have belonged to Player and Palmer, in that order, but round three belonged to Nicklaus—and to history. Of the three players, Jack was the first to tee off. He began innocently enough with a par, hitting an approach putt from 50 feet to 6 inches. It was the 2nd hole, he said later, that made him think that perhaps it would be his day. His drive strayed far to the right, into the pines between the 2nd and 3rd fairways. He was concerned as he approached his ball, but then his face broke into a grin as he saw that he had an open avenue to the fairway. He hit a three iron some 110 yards short of the green, a wedge to 25 feet, and sank the putt for a birdie. He was off and running.

He parred the 3rd, birdied the 4th, then went birdie, birdie, birdie. The birdie on the 7th did much to upset Palmer. He was about to hit a short pitch to the 2nd when he heard the Nicklaus gallery roar. He already knew Jack had moved 3 strokes ahead and the roar meant 4. "I started pressing," he said later. "It was the turning point."

Nicklaus finished the front nine in 31. At every tee and green he received a tremendous ovation—"I hope it doesn't wake him up," said his wife Barbara—a marked contrast from two years before when a Nicklaus bogey posted on the scoreboard had been greeted with cheers. Jack parred the difficult 10th, 11th, and 12th, failing to sink a 5-foot putt on the 12th for a birdie. But he got birdies at both par 5s—the 13th and 15th—each time reaching the green in 2, and when he made an 8-footer on the 16th for still another birdie, he was 8 under for the round and had a chance to break Lloyd Mangrum's record of 64. On the 17th he left himself 70 feet from the pin and considered himself lucky to get down in 2 for the par.

Now let Jack describe the 18th. "I stepped up to the tee," he wrote later, "and thought, 'Well, let's not hit it to the left. Let's go all the way,' and I faded the drive around the trees on the right. It was the longest tee shot I have ever hit on this uphill hole—about 320 yards. I took out a pitching wedge, but as I got set to swing, a little single-engine plane came flying low, right down the line of the fairway. So I backed off the shot. When I got over the ball again the silence was eerie. It was so quiet that you might have thought every one of the 15,000 people around the green had gone home. I was a little too anxious with the shot, and pulled it to the left side of the green. The ball hit and rolled back about 25 feet to the left of the cup. I was not really too disappointed, just happy to be on the green and putting for a 3. It was a tough putt, rolling with the grain of the grass for the first half and against it the last half. I played it very carefully. I left it short, which was disappointing, but there was nothing disappointing about my 64."

Jack's round, in effect, ended the 1965 Masters on Saturday evening. Said Player: "To shoot 69 on this course and lose five shots is incredible." And Palmer, with a 72: "I guess I'll be looking at Jack's back all day tomorrow." As for Nicklaus himself, he rated five drives he hit during the round as bad and later enforced that statement by repairing to the practice tee, where he tore at the ball as a gallery of 1,000 watched. But when pressed, he admitted that the 64 was as fine a round as he had ever had.

Sunday's round was routine. In case anyone thought he might come back to earth with a crash and maybe lose his 5-stroke lead to Player, Jack birdied the 1st hole to set the thinking straight. All in all, he rated the round "the most enjoyable of his life" although he did not completely relax until he got past the 12th, where, as he said, "You can shoot anything." Instead, he birdied it with a 25-foot putt. He finished with a 69, good for 271, which broke Ben Hogan's 12-year-old record of 274 by 3 shots.

It was left to Bobby Jones to best sum up Nicklaus's performance. First he congratulated Palmer and Player, who tied for second at 280, a score that would have won all but five previous Masters. "Palmer and Player played superbly," said the old master. "As for Nicklaus, he plays a game with which I am not familiar."

1966

After his performance the year before, there were those who were convinced that Jack Nicklaus would be impossible to beat at Augusta for the next 20 years or so, and when he opened his defense with a ho-hum 68 and a 3-stroke lead, almost everyone agreed. It hardly seemed to matter at the time, but Tommy Jacobs was 7 strokes behind, Gay Brewer 6. But on Friday Jack came back to the field in a hurry with an ugly 76. The final 36 holes were a slugfest involving Nicklaus, Jacobs, Arnold Palmer, Doug Sanders, and Brewer. Brewer arrived at the 18th green needing two putts to give him the lead—and, as it turned out, victory—but he was 60 feet away. His first putt rolled 7 feet by the cup and he missed coming back. Nicklaus appeared to have won at the 17th when his approach landed 3 feet from the pin, but his putt broke sharply and missed. On the 18th green he had a long putt similar to Brewer's, and this one looked as if it was in, but at the last second it wavered slightly, stopping inches away. And so the Masters had its second three-way tie, Brewer, Nicklaus, and Jacobs.

Like so many playoffs, this one was anticlimactic. Jacobs hung gamely with Nicklaus for 14 holes, trailing by 2. At the 15th he was comfortably on in 2, a possible eagle, while Jack needed a 15-footer for his birdie. A Jacobs make plus a Nicklaus miss would tie it, but instead it was the other way around. And so for the first time in the history of the tournament, a Masters champion had successfully defended his title, thus posing officials with a problem. "Cliff and I have discussed this situation," Bobby Jones said at the victory ceremony. "We have decided you will just have to put the green jacket on yourself."

1967

By this time it seemed as if the Masters was the exclusive property of Jack Nicklaus, Arnold Palmer, and, to a lesser extent, Gary Player. In the past nine years, only Art Wall, in 1959, had broken the tight circle formed by the Big Three. When everyone teed off Thursday, the only question was which one of the three would win it this time. How could anyone foretell that the Masters was about to enter a five-year period when none of them would win, when in fact the tournament would be dominated by the ordinary touring pro?

Nicklaus successfully defends Masters crown in 1966

Bert Yancey began his strange romance with the Masters by opening with a 67, good for a 3-stroke lead. Midway through Sunday's round, Yancey still had a share of the lead, tied with Gay Brewer, Bobby Nichols, and Julius Boros. Jack Nicklaus, amazingly, was no longer in the tournament, having shot 72, 79 to miss the cut. Then Brewer birdied the 13th, 14th, and 15th to pull away to victory, thus picking up the green jacket he had nearly won the year before.

1968

This year provided one of the wildest, free-for-all final rounds in the history of the Masters. Sunday morning, Gary Player led at 6 under par, but one stroke back were Bob Goalby, Bruce Devlin, Frank Beard, and Don January, while a stroke behind them were Roberto de Vicenzo, Ray Floyd, and Miller Barber. An early clue as to what was about to happen was provided by Art Wall, who played early and returned a 67. Shortly after, Mason Rudolph breezed home in 66. Later, Bert Yancey scored a 65 for a 279 total, good enough to win in all but three years. But not this one.

The leader, Player, was on the practice green when he learned that he was not only no longer the leader, but 2 strokes behind. Old de Vicenzo, celebrating his birthday, had hit his second shot into the cup at the 1st hole for an eagle and had followed that with birdies on the 2nd and 3rd—4 under for three holes. Disheartened perhaps, Gary was to shoot a 72, which on this day was closer to 82.

Late in the afternoon all those contenders who were merely 2 or 3 under for their rounds were out of it, leaving only Goalby and Roberto. Goalby hit an iron to the 15th green—his second shot—and sank the putt for an eagle, just as television cameras showed de Vicenzo making a birdie at the 17th to take a one-stroke lead. He now needed only a par on the 18th for a record-tying 64, but a bogey put him in at 65 and 277. Goalby's drive off the 18th tee hit a tree on the right, but he managed a par anyway, holing a tough 4-foot putt. And so, apparently, the Masters had another playoff.

But no. Sadly, it was discovered that there was an error on Roberto de Vicenzo's scorecard, which had been kept by Tommy Aaron. Aaron had put down a 4 for Roberto on the 17th hole. He had affixed 65 to the total, which was correct, but the sum of the figures was 66. In the excitement of the moment, de Vicenzo had signed his card without checking carefully enough and although officials, including a much disturbed Bobby Jones, searched for a way out, they finally were forced to abide by the rules of golf and change de Vicenzo's score to 66 and 278, thus making Bob Goalby the winner. It was a wretched moment for all concerned, even Bob Goalby, who was to suffer for some time after as the man who somehow took Roberto's victory away.

1969

For a two-time Open champion, Billy Casper had never made much of an impression on the Masters, but an opening 66 followed by two conservative 71s put him at 8 under par on Sunday morning, the leader. George Archer, the 6'6" cowpoke from California, was a stroke behind, but such had been the caliber of Casper's golf that he looked as if he would be hard to catch.

Instead, Billy made four bogeys on the front nine to turn in 40, opening the door for Archer as well as a flood of others—George Knudson, Tom Weiskopf, and Charles Coody. Coody seemed in command and indeed had the lead at the 16th tee, but he finished bogey, bogey, bogey to destroy his chances. Every time someone had a chance, he seemed to do something wrong. It was finally Archer who took control, doing something wrong— the order of the day—but compensating. Trying for the 15th green in 2, he hit into the pond, but after a penalty drop, he chipped on and sank a tough putt for his par, thus maintaining a one-stroke lead. Anyone who could have made a birdie on the final three holes—Casper, Knudson, or Weiskopf—would have tied him, but no one did and Archer won the Masters nobody else seemed to want.

1970

Late Sunday afternoon, four men battled through Amen Corner—the 11th, 12th, and 13th holes. Bert Yancey and Gene Littler, paired together, were 8 under par. Directly behind them were Billy Casper at 7 and Gary Player at 6. Roars were met by counter-roars as all four men gave their fans something to cheer about. Player birdied the difficult 12th. Littler, up ahead, birdied the 13th to take the lead, Yancey missing a short birdie putt. Casper and Player both birdied the 13th to draw close to Littler. Yancey again just missed a birdie putt of 3 feet on the 14th to tie for the lead. Littler birdied the 15th, but bogeyed the 16th as Casper and Player were birdying the 15th. Seesaw all the way.

As they came to the 18th, Casper, Littler, and Player were tied for the lead, with Yancey a stroke back. Littler was on in 2, but missed his birdie putt. Yancey, shaving his approach close for the birdie he needed, landed in a trap and bogeyed. Now Casper and Player. Casper's approach was a good one, giving him a putt of perhaps 10 feet. Player, trying to match it, hit into the same trap Yancey had been in. He blasted out, but could not drop his putt, thus finishing a stroke out. Casper's putt was so close he started into a victory jig—something you rarely see Billy do—but the ball stayed out. Casper and Littler, two old friends from the San Diego area, had tied.

The next day was anticlimactic. Littler was well off his game, Casper on his, and Billy at last won a green jacket, 69 to 74.

1971

Clearly Jack Nicklaus was headed for his fourth Masters title. Tied with Charles Coody on Sunday morning, he began birdie, birdie, and for those few moments had a 2-stroke lead. But then came bogeys, and when the two finished nine holes, playing a twosome apart, they were still tied.

By this time, however, the gallery was aware that something was going on up ahead, and many of them hustled to find out what. They found a slim, blond-haired young man marching down the 11th fairway as if he owned the joint. A rookie pro, John Miller, 4 strokes back at the start of the day, had turned in 33 and was now only 2 back. When he daringly hit his approach directly at the pin on the 11th and made a birdie, he was one back. And then, having hit into a trap on the 12th, he blasted into the cup. He was tied for the lead.

Still another birdie on the 14th gave him the lead, a 2-stroke lead as a matter of fact, since both Nicklaus and Coody had bogeyed. Miller was 6 under for the day, with a birdie chance at the 15th coming up. He went for the green as any brash twenty-four-year-old would, winding up safe, but far right. It took him 3 to get down—a par. When he hit into the trap at the 16th and bogeyed just as Coody was making a birdie at the 15th, his lead was suddenly gone. And when Coody also birdied the 16th, the hole that had done him in two years before, Miller's magnificent try was over. Coody parred the final two holes to beat both Miller and Nicklaus, who had failed to birdie a single hole after the 6th, by 2 strokes.

Jones and Hogan

1972

Most golf tournaments build toward a Sunday climax, but this was an exception; most of the excitement occurred in the first round. For instance, there was the specter of Charlie Coody making a hole in one on the 6th, putting him 4 under par, an extraordinary start for the defending champion. But on the next hole, Charlie dumped his second shot into a bunker, and, when it took him four swings to get out, he had come crashing back to earth, there to stay for the rest of the week.

Sam Snead, age fifty-nine, shot a 69 the first day, which put him in third place, one stroke ahead of Arnold Palmer. The leader? Jack Nicklaus, with a 68, a score which thanks to a strain of grass called *poa annua* was not to be bettered throughout the tournament. The *poa annua* on the greens caused them to be bumpy and untrue, so that even short putts became a nightmare.

Only Nicklaus was able to better par for four rounds in what was, essentially, a dull tournament. No one ever seriously challenged Jack as he led from start to finish. So many times in the past the tension has been almost unbearable as the leaders have gone through Amen Corner—the 11th, 12th, and 13th—on Sunday afternoon. This time there was none, as Nicklaus held a 5-stroke lead. He won by a comfortable 3, thus giving him his fourth Masters title, tying him with his friendly rival, Palmer.

[6]

THE PGA—THE FINAL LEG

OF THE GAME'S four major tournaments, the PGA Championship has fallen last on the annual schedule more often than not since a Philadelphia department store scion put up its first cash kitty—$2,580— just before World War I. This position has been almost symbolic of its stature among this premium quartet of tournaments through the years since the Professional Golfers Association of America held its first Championship in 1916.

The tournament probably will continue to anchor these "Big Four" on the schedule—and this is not all bad. Think of the attention and prestige it might have attracted in 1972 if Lee Trevino had not holed a chip shot on the 71st hole of the British Open. Jack Nicklaus could have been teeing off on August 3 at one of America's great courses—Oakland Hills—with three legs up on the never-attained Professional Grand Slam of Golf—the two Opens, Masters, and PGA in a single season. The PGA already had its first ticket sellout in history before Trevino beat Nicklaus at Muirfield, and defections were heavy among the news media planning to be in Detroit after the sports story of the year went out the window in July in Scotland.

But even given the boost of being part of the wondrous Grand Slam, and granting the efforts that today's PGA officials are putting forth to make a true classic of their championship, the tournament seems destined to remain at best a distant fourth in the eyes of the golfing public. The upgrading of the caliber of its courses and the strengthening of its fields— overall, the PGA Championship now has the strongest of them all—are not likely to be enough to overcome the ground lost through the years.

For one thing, the PGA title carries little of importance to the leading foreign players. Unlike the U.S. Open or Masters, which have worldwide prestige painted all over the titles, a victory in our PGA Championship has little more value of any kind to a non-American pro than a win in one of our run-of-the-mill tour events. In 1972, Tony Jacklin decided to remain in Europe for the Swiss Open rather than return to America for the PGA at Oakland Hills. Explained Tony: "I don't think that the USPGA Championship is that important for me to win. Certainly I would like to win it as it is one of the Big Four, but of these Big Four, it is the least prestigious as far as I am concerned. As a foreign player, I can make little other than the first-prize money out of it if I win it. Although Gary Player has won it, he has played in very few PGA Championships."

The "late start" of the PGA certainly hampered its position. The British Open was 56 years old and the U.S. Open had been played 21 times before Rodman Wanamaker suggested to a handful of Eastern professionals over lunch and beverages at New York City's Taplow Club on January 16, 1916, that it was high time that America's pros formed a national organization comparable to the PGA of Great Britain rather than operate through a scattering of regional groups then in existence.

Wanamaker, son of the founder of the famous department stores in Philadelphia and New York bearing the family name, offered that prize money and one of the world's largest trophy cups to provide another enticement to membership in this new PGA of America. Eighty-two charter members founded the organization that April, and 145 more had joined by the time the first annual meeting was held in Minneapolis June 26 to 28. An Executive Committee was formed, with 19 of its 24 members from the East and Midwest. This was understandable, since early golf in this country was concentrated geographically in the northeastern quarter of the nation. Only six of the 25 PGA Championships prior to World War II were played west of the Mississippi or south of the Mason-Dixon Line. This Eastern domination of the organization has been one of the trouble spots that has beset the PGA from time to time throughout its history, particularly regarding the location of national headquarters and many of its activities in Florida.

In accord with Wanamaker's conditions, the PGA Championship was patterned after Britain's News of the World tournament—36-hole eliminations at match play—rather than the 72-hole medal, or stroke, play format of the U.S. and British Opens. It was a "closed" tournament, in which only PGA members, qualifying through their sections (originally, seven), could compete. This very format mitigated against the chances of this newcomer tournament approaching the stature of the Opens. Amateur golf held sway in the early years of the game in America just as in Great Britain. The U.S. Amateur was the prime championship, and the U.S. Golf Association was quickly established as the prestigious governing and watchdog body of the game, a position it still occupies despite the overwhelming dominance of the modern professional game. The early American professionals, almost all of them immigrants from the British Isles, were looked upon as they were in their native land as little more than hired help, rather than professionals in the true sense of the word today. Thus, a tournament in which the leading amateurs of the time and even certain of the better playing pros could not compete had little hope of attaining the prestige of the Open; by that time the Open was considered the national golf championship of America.

Nevertheless the PGA Championship has not wallowed in obscurity. A matter of timing prevented it from achieving early acclaim in the 1920s. From 1921 through 1927, it was totally dominated by Hagen and Sarazen, the professional dynamos of that time. Hagen was almost invincible during that period, winning the arduous tournament five times and, in capturing four straight titles from 1924 through 1927, winning 22 straight 36-hole matches. But amateur golf spawned its all-time superstar at almost the same time—Bobby Jones. The heroic feats of Jones in winning 13 Open and Amateur championships in the United States and Britain between 1923 and 1930 and climaxing it with the original Grand Slam that final year captured the fancy of golfers and sports fans everywhere.

During that so-called Golden Era of Sports, the PGA was expanding rapidly with the growth of interest in the game, but experiencing growing pains in the process. At the end of the 1920s, the PGA officers began struggling with the manifold problems confronting the association in its attempt to put the fast-growing tournament tour into some sort of a businesslike operation within the organization. As the PGA membership grew, the percentage of tournament professionals decreased within that membership, and it became evident that the PGA was really a single organization trying to operate two quite different businesses—one, encompassing a majority of its members, in which the game is taught, merchandised, and organized on the local level for small groups of members or customers; the other, with its small but star-studded cast, in which tournament golf is offered to a national public as a sports entertainment of ever-increasing popularity and income.

Tournament business was developing as the nation came out of the Depression doldrums, and the inevitable rifts began to appear. The playing pros feel that they and people responsible to them should be running the tournament show, not club professionals, who are in a different line of work and don't know the tournament business. On the other hand, the home pros feel that the PGA nurtured the tour through its formative years, and that the tour and its players should not take all the riches and not share them with the parent organization for the benefit of programs that have done much to enhance the game and the lot of the club professional.

What has this conflict to do with the PGA Championship itself?

For one thing, because it has been almost a running battle through the years, the PGA executives and officers have devoted a disproportionate amount of their time to tour tournament affairs and, as a result, probably not enough time to their Championship. While many changes for the better have come in very recent years, for instance, in the selections of the Championship courses and the better utilization of the field personnel who operate the tour tournament program in place of inexperienced PGA brass from the ranks of the club professionals, they still have not adopted many of the procedures and ideas employed by the USGA at the Open and Augusta National officials at the Masters that result in operations clearly superior to those at most of the PGA Championships.

It wasn't until a few years ago that the field competing for the PGA Championship became the strongest of the four major tournaments. Until the late 1960s, the PGA muddled along with constantly changing rules of eligibility and qualification for the Championship that, particularly in the Fifties and Sixties, produced an oversized field cluttered with home pros with virtually no chance of winning or even challenging and one that, at the same time, excluded quite a few of the touring pros who had that chance. The PGA stuck to its members-only requirement for participation in the Championship until the late Fifties and, because it takes approximately five years for a new tour pro to become eligible for membership, this kept many players of real ability out of the tournament in their early seasons. In 1957, when he had won three tour tournaments earlier in the season and went on to finish fifth on the PGA money list, Arnold Palmer could not play in the PGA Championship because he was not yet eligible for PGA membership. All of this reflected the small thinking and refusal of the club professionals in general to give any ground in their disputes with the tournament players, even though these changes made good sense in the improvement of their own Championship.

Finally, the Championship tournament became somewhat of a pawn in the most critical battle in the 1960s, one which primarily involved the importance of television in the overall tournament picture.

As TV became more and more interested in golf in that decade—contrary to earlier opinions of many in golf that the game didn't fit that medium—large sums of money were available. The players felt that the TV rights belonged to them and that the revenue so generated should go to them, via the tournament purses and their Tournament Bureau fund, which was untouchable by the parent PGA for other association purposes. PGA executives felt that a portion of the TV revenues should go into its general fund for the mutual benefit of all of the members.

In the middle of this was the PGA Championship. Along with the Masters, U.S. Open, and such unique tournaments on the regular tour as the Tournament of Champions and the Bing Crosby and Bob Hope events, with their "celebrity" formats, it was among the most salable products to television. The PGA national officers had always made a separate deal in selling the Championship to the networks. Now, with the chance to sell a "package" of the regular tour events, the players wanted the rights to the Championship to sweeten their share of the pot Marty Carmichael, the PGA's television representative, was trying to get. The PGA brass refused to yield on this point and persisted in demands for a piece of the action from the TV revenues generated by the regular tour. The players boiled.

This was now 1966 and the players made their first serious demands for autonomy on the eve of the PGA Championship at Firestone in Akron, although not directly threatening any action that might affect the play of that tournament. After meetings there during the week, things calmed down—briefly. When trouble inevitably was stirred up again in 1967, the players decided to use the Championship as a wedge. Through their representatives, they told the PGA two weeks before the tournament at Columbine in Denver that, unless an agreement satisfactory to them was reached, they would boycott the Championship. The PGA tried to brazen it out, stating that the Championship would be played, if only with a field comprised of loyalists from among the home pro ranks. No dice, said the people putting on the tournament in Denver. Law suit threats were brandished, both sides backed off, and the tournament was played.

Although the feud quickly heated up once more, the 1968 Championship at Pecan Valley was not brought into the fight, but, little more than a month after it was played, the pot boiled over. Put off once too often, the leaders of the players' revolt made the move the PGA brass didn't expect. In late August, they announced the formation of a new organization, the American Professional Golfers, and proceeded with the business of setting up a tournament operation and courting tournament sponsors to arrange a schedule for 1969. Legal action to demolish the new group failed, and virtually all of the regular tour sponsors open to negotiate 1969 contracts signed with the APG during the next three months. ABC told the PGA it would cancel its fat contract to televise the 1969 PGA Championship at the NCR Country Club in Dayton if the stars weren't going to play, and the sponsoring Dayton Chamber of Commerce said that if the PGA couldn't guarantee the presence of the top players the next summer, they would cancel. Max Elbin, PGA president, stuck to his guns until he went out of office in November, but his successor, Leo Fraser, convinced that a compromise had to be reached, softened the PGA's hard line, made concessions sought by the players that created the present Tournament Players Division and its virtually autonomous operation, and brought the tournament players back into the fold.

The Early Years

This history focuses on the era of the game since the mid-1940s, when its phenomenal growth began. But the first 30 years contributed considerably to the history of the PGA Championship.

A handful of pros dominated the early PGAs, starting with a native of Cornwall, England, named James M. Barnes. Appropriately, the first Championship was played not many miles from the Taplow Club—at the Siwanoy Country Club in the New York City suburb of Bronxville, October 10 to 14, 1916. Only 31 pros teed off in quest of the first title. Barnes and Jock Hutchison, the Scotsman from St. Andrews, reached the finals as expected from their showings (Hutchison second and Barnes third) in the U.S. Open that year. Barnes had little difficulty, going 35 holes in just one of the 36-hole matches, but Hutchison went the full distance before beating Hagen, then just twenty-three years old, by a 2-up score. The Championship match was a seesawing affair in which Barnes took the final lead at the 33rd hole and won, 1 up.

When the PGA Championship was resumed again in 1919 after World War I, Barnes repeated at Engineers Country Club at Roslyn on Long Island, moving rather easily through his early opponents and sinking Fred McLeod, the 1908 U.S. Open champion, in the finals. Barnes, 2 down after 28 holes, won the next five holes and scored a 6-and-5 triumph. Hutchison won at Flossmoor in Chicago in 1920 after Clarence Hackney had ousted Barnes in the second round. Jock's final victim was J. Douglas Edgar, whose star flashed briefly in winning the 1919 Canadian Open with a then-remarkable 278 score and in carrying Hutchison to the last hole after trailing by 4 through 28 holes. Ironically, Jock had failed to qualify that year but got into the field as an alternate.

Barnes was at the top of his game when the PGA returned to New York and the Inwood Country Club on Long Island in 1921. He had won the U.S. Open by 9 strokes earlier that season. He avenged the 1920 loss to Hackney in the first round and demolished McLeod, Bobby Cruickshank, and Emmett French to reach the finals again. This time his opponent was Hagen, who had been just as convincing in his earlier matches. Walter's golf was too much for Barnes. With a 69 in the morning round and an outgoing 33 in the afternoon, he took a 4-up lead and finished it at the 34th, 3 and 2, to become the first American-born PGA champion.

The tournament then became almost the exclusive province of the colorful professional from Rochester, New York, and Gene Sarazen, who, at age nineteen, had made his first mark on the tournament in 1921 by reaching the quarter-finals with an 8-and-7 defeat of Hutchison. Barnes remained a factor for several more years, but never won again, primarily because he couldn't beat either of the other two. In fact, Sarazen recalls in his book, *Thirty Years of Championship Golf*, that, spurred by a cutting remark by Barnes during a 1921 tour tournament in New Orleans that he couldn't excuse or forget, he won every PGA match he played against the Englishman after that.

In any event, Gene completed his U.S. Open–PGA sweep of 1922 at Oakmont Country Club, near Pittsburgh. (Only Ben Hogan, in 1948, has won both tournaments in the same year.) Sarazen, less than a year on the job at another Pittsburgh club, was still quite familiar with the treachery of Oakmont and showed it in cutting down Tom Mahan, Willie Ogg, and Frank Sprogell, the latter 9 and 7, in the first three matches. A round had been added to the 1922 championship to accommodate an expansion of the field to 64 players. Gene again defeated Hutchison, but this time by just 2 and 1 in the quarter-finals, and took out Cruickshank, 3 and 2, in the semi-finals. French, with whom he had roomed all week except on the eve of the finals, was the title opponent, and Emmett couldn't cope with Sarazen's excellence on the greens that day. Gene one-putted 13 times enroute to his 4-and-3 victory.

The 1923 championship was perhaps the most memorable in those early years. It was the first to go extra holes, but, more importantly, it pitted Hagen and Sarazen in the finals for the only time. Hagen had skipped the 1922 tournament because of other playing commitments, but was back the next year at Pelham Golf Club in New York. Sarazen's play had tailed off earlier that season, but he advanced easily through the first three matches, grimly took out Barnes, who was the pro at Pelham, with a birdie on the 36th hole, and defeated Cruickshank for the second year in a row in the semifinals. Meanwhile, Hagen had breezed through the lower bracket, drubbing George McLean in the semis, 12 and 11.

Hagen and Sarazen weren't exactly buddies at the time. They had each won one of two specially arranged 72-hole exhibition matches during the preceding year. Both were eager for the title that would earn them No. 1 acclaim for that season. Nothing was decisive in the morning, and they went to lunch even, neither having been more than one down at any time. Gene put together an outgoing 35 in the afternoon to go 3 up. Hagen fought back, winning the 29th and 34th, and evened the match sensationally at the long 35th, making a par after knocking his brassie second shot out of bounds, while an unnerved Sarazen three-putted. With Hagen's ball lying directly in his line, the stymie rule eliminated Sarazen's chance to make a 5-foot birdie putt at the 36th that would have won the match and championship.

Extra holes and a half at 37. With Hagen's next drive in perfect position, Sarazen tried to carry the trees in the dogleg at Pelham's 2-hole. He hooked the shot too much. The ball hit wood but dropped rather than ricocheting beyond the nearby out-of-bounds stakes. (Sarazen recalls that Hagen apparently was half-convinced that the ball had gone out of bounds and was tossed back in play by Sarazen supporters among the Italian families who lived on the edge of the course there.) With an opening, Sarazen played one of the finest shots of his career—don't forget the double eagle at Augusta—digging the ball out of a heavy lie clear of the trees and watching it bound onto the green and roll to a stop 2 feet from the pin. This time it was Walter who was unnerved. He dropped his short pitch shot into a trap and missed his game attempt to hole out from the sand. Sarazen holed for his second straight PGA Championship.

The PGA changed the format slightly again in 1924, reducing the starting field to 32, but adding a 36-hole qualifier at the site to set up the match play. That made no difference to Hagen, who began his record-setting, four-year reign with a hard-won victory over Barnes, 2 up, after Sarazen had gone out in the second round to a little-known pro named Larry Nabholtz at French Lick Springs, the only time the championship has ever been played in Indiana. Barnes had to go three extra holes in his first match, but otherwise the two men moved easily into the finals. Long Jim fought back from a 4-down situation after eighteen, narrowed the gap to 2 at the turn, to one at the 29th, and battled Hagen to the final green before bowing out.

A tournament pro from Texas, Wild Bill Melhorn, was Hagen's unsuccessful challenger in 1925 at Olympia Fields near Chicago as Sarazen was eliminated in the first round by Jack Burke, Sr., and Barnes was not in the starting field. Walter himself had his hands full most of that September week, going three extra holes against Al Watrous, four against Leo Diegel, and beating Harry Cooper on the 35th hole, 3 and 1, in the semifinals. In the finals, though, he eagled the 515-yard 1st hole at Olympia Fields and never trailed Melhorn. He won, 6 and 5, retaining the Wanamaker Trophy, which sometime afterward he managed to leave in a taxi. It turned up two years later, still packaged, in the basement of a sporting goods company.

Leo Diegel made his first determined bid for the PGA title in 1926. While Diegel was winning his matches by steadily decreasing margins, Hagen was moving easily through the upper bracket. Leo must have known it wasn't to be his day in the finals at Salisbury Golf Links at Westbury on Long Island. After watching a 35-foot putt by Hagen hang on the lip interminably, then drop, Leo missed his for a half on one of the morning holes. On the first hole in the afternoon, Diegel's approach rolled under who else but Hagen's car and into a deep rut. He tried to play it, took three swings to get it out, and lost the hole. The match ended, 4 and 3.

Hagen knocked out Joe Turnesa in the first round in 1926. The following year, Turnesa was in the opposite bracket and fared much better in that atmosphere. He reached the finals at Cedar Crest Country Club in Dallas, the PGA's first venture into any part of the South, scoring a 7 and 6 victory over John Golden while Hagen was squeezing past Al Espinosa, 1 up. Turnesa led Walter through most of the first 28 holes of the finals, but Hagen evened the match at the 29th and went ahead to stay at the 31st.

Just as Sarazen had done before Hagen's streak began, Diegel captured two consecutive PGA Championships. He was tremendous at Five Farms in Baltimore in 1928, ending Hagen's string of 22 straight match victories in the tournament with a 2 and 1 win in the quarter-finals and then trouncing Sarazen in the semifinals, 9 and 8. Al Espinosa, who had knocked out Horton Smith, 6 and 5, in the other semifinal, was no match for Diegel in the finals and went down, 6 and 5. Diegel's December victory in the first PGA Championship in California in 1929 was much the same. Again, he defeated Sarazen and Hagen, in that order, to reach the finals, then bumped off Johnny Farrell, the U.S. Open champion of the previous year, 6 and 4.

In 1930, Tommy Armour, another of the name players of the era but a pro for only six years, nailed the PGA title to go with his 1927 U.S. Open championship. The last British-born player to win the PGA, Armour won tough quarter-final and semifinal matches and then played Sarazen in a match at Fresh Meadow, another Long Island club, that Diegel, refereeing it, described as "the greatest golf match I ever saw." Sarazen had been the pro there since 1925 and knew every inch of the course, but Armour hung in tenaciously, even though Gene was inside him on most of the greens. Sarazen led by one after nine holes, but Tommy was on top by the same score at the break. After 27 holes the match was even. A brilliant recovery by Armour squared things after 35, and Tommy holed a 14-footer (says the PGA record book; Sarazen says 35) for the victory.

Sarazen, who had been just twenty when he won his first PGA Championship, was the next to last obstacle cleared by another twenty-year-old on his way to the 1931 title. Tom Creavy, a pro from Tuckahoe, New York, playing in his first national tournament, knocked out Sarazen in the semifinals, 5 and 3, and astonished the galleries at Rhode Island's Wannamoisett Country Club by edging Denny Shute in the finals, 2 and 1.

Interestingly, the unknown youngster made another run at the title in 1932 at St. Paul's Keller Golf Course, winning his first three matches and going 38 holes before bowing to Frank Walsh in the semifinals. Meanwhile, Olin Dutra, the Californian who had won the medal with 140, was riding herd on the upper bracket and polished off Walsh, 4 and 3, in the finals.

Sarazen won his second U.S. Open in 1932 (along with the British Open), and then went on to duplicate his victory sequence of a decade earlier by winning the 1933 PGA Championship as well. Ten years after his victory over Hagen at Pelham, Gene captured his third PGA crown at Blue Mound in Milwaukee. By all accounts a man who was irritated easily, Sarazen had not appreciated remarks by Armour that he, Hagen, and Sarazen were over the hill. After all, Gene was only thirty-one and he proved Armour wrong by winning his first four matches at Blue Mound by 4 and 3 scores and whipping Willie Goggin in the finals, 5 and 4.

The PGA had its second overtime match in 1934 at the Park Club of Buffalo, where Paul Runyan, a small man with a deft touch on and around the greens, won his first of two PGA titles. At Buffalo, Runyan bumped off three "name" players in a row—Johnny Farrell, Vic Ghezzi, and Dick

Metz—and added Gene Kunes in the semifinals to move into the title match against Craig Wood, for whom he had worked. It was a David-and-Goliath match, since Wood was one of the big hitters of the time, but Runyan's finesse carried the match into extra holes and Paul won with a fine bunker shot and an 8-foot putt at the 38th.

Yet another change in regulations was made in 1935 and it may have started the match-play format downhill. The PGA decided to push the field back up to 64, but play the early matches over 18 holes. A lesser player with a hot hand has a much better chance in a shorter match, and this proved out quite often during the remaining 22 match-play championships.

In fact, it happened right off the bat. Johnny Revolta, a relatively obscure twenty-four-year-old, ousted Hagen in the first round in 1935 at Twin Hills in Oklahoma City, although Revolta didn't follow the frequent pattern and lose himself the next time out. He went on through the upper bracket, although facing only one player of note, Jimmy Hines, until he reached the finals and Armour. Against Tommy, he birdied the 1st hole, shot 70 in the morning for a 4-up lead, and won easily, 5 and 4.

Shute, nosed out in his first bid for the Championship in 1931, captured the titles in 1936 and 1937. Four times in the earlier 20 years, players had put championships back to back—Barnes, Sarazen, Hagen, and Diegel—but nobody among all of the great players who have come along has been able to do this since then.

Shute's first championship was won at Pinehurst, where he eliminated Horton Smith and Melhorn before taking the final match over Jimmy Thomson, 4 and 3. Jug McSpaden, who won a flock of tour tournaments during his career but never landed a major championship, came closest in 1937 at the Pittsburgh Field Club, and if his nerves were unstrung after that week in Pittsburgh in May, no wonder. He went 20 holes in his second match; caught and defeated a young Sam Snead, 3 and 2, in the next round; went 39 holes before defeating Henry Picard in the quarter-finals; and nipped Ky Laffoon on the final green in the semifinals. Shute didn't have a much easier time in the upper bracket. In the Championship match, McSpaden missed a short birdie putt for a win on the 36th hole and lost on the first extra hole.

If the disastrous finish in the 1939 U.S. Open is Sam Snead's worst memory of that Championship, surely his defeat in 1938 has an equally dark place in his recollections of the PGA Championship. Snead had little trouble getting to the finals that year at Shawnee, the eastern Pennsylvania resort, but in doing so faced no players of note. Paul Runyan, on the other hand, had knocked out the likes of Lloyd Mangrum, Picard, Horton Smith, and Tony Manero, the 1936 Open champion. This obviously primed Runyan for an unexpected slaughter. He shot a morning 67 to take a 5-up lead, widened the gap to 7 up after 27, won the 28th, and halved the 29th for his 8 and 7 victory, the most decisive in the history of the PGA's match-play finals. Snead's days were yet to come.

So were those of Byron Nelson. At Pomonok Country Club in Flushing, New York, Nelson blasted into the 1939 finals with a 10 and 9 victory over Emerick Kocsis in the quarters and a 9 and 8 win over Dutch Harrison, the medalist, in the semis. Picard edged Dick Metz in the other semifinal match, 1 up. His putter won him the Championship against Nelson. A shot away from defeat, Henry holed a 25-footer for a half at the 34th to stay alive, a birdie putt at the 36th to square the match, and another birdie putt for the Championship at the 37th.

Nelson's turn came at Hershey, Pennsylvania, the next year at the expense of Snead in an exciting finish. Nelson reached the finals with a 1-up triumph over Ralph Guldahl, who was not to add the PGA to his Open and Masters successes, while Snead was taking out McSpaden, 5 and 4. In the title match, Snead took a 1-up lead at the 32nd, but Byron won the 34th and 35th to score a 1-up victory.

Lord Byron came closer than anybody has come since to a repeat victory in the PGA in 1941. Both he and Vic Ghezzi had several close calls before reaching the finals at Denver's Cherry Hills, Nelson in two early matches against obscure players and against Ben Hogan and Sarazen, while Ghezzi's were against Jack Grout, the man who taught the game to Jack Nicklaus, and Mangrum. The Championship match went the same way. Ghezzi fought back from a 3-down position on the final nine and holed a shaky 3-footer on the 38th to win the title.

Snead delayed his enlistment into the Navy in May of 1942 just long enough to play in the PGA at Seaview Country Club at Atlantic City, New Jersey, where the field had again been reduced to 32. Sam wanted one last crack at a major championship before donning a uniform. Jim Turnesa was a corporal in the Army by then, and most of the gallery was from nearby Fort Dix and rooting for him. He responded by eliminating, in order, Dutch Harrison, Jug McSpaden, Ben Hogan, and Byron Nelson. No mean feat. Snead had taken out Sam Byrd, Willie Goggin, Ed Dudley (then the PGA president), and Jimmy Demaret. Despite a hostile gallery, which Snead charges in his book, *The Education of a Golfer*, twice kicked Turnesa's ball out of trouble in the woods, Sam fought back from a three-hole deficit after 27 holes and birdied the 35th for a 2 and 1 victory, his first of three PGA Championships.

Just as he dominated golf in general during the late Thirties and early Forties, Nelson continued to command the PGA Championships during those years. Because of hemophilia, Byron was exempt from military service, and the government encouraged golf, with war bonds the prize money, as a morale booster.

After skipping 1943 in the heart of the war, the PGA resumed its Championship in 1944 at Manito Golf and Country Club in Spokane, Washington. In the six previous PGAs, Nelson's record was: quarter-

Byron Nelson

finalist in 1937 and 1938, runner-up in 1939, winner in 1940, runner-up in 1941, and semifinalist in 1942. At Manito, he breezed through the upper bracket, his closest victory 4 and 3 over Goggin. But, in the finals, he lost a tough battle against Hoosier Bob Hamilton, 1 up.

Byron's greatest year—when Snead and Hogan were both out of the service and back in action—was 1945, when he won a phenomenal 18 tournaments on the PGA schedule. The PGA Championship was one of them and the ninth in a record string of 11 straight victories. It was played at Morraine Country Club in Dayton, Ohio, and Nelson had few problems, beyond a painful back, after topping a Mike Turnesa birdie with an eagle on the 35th hole of their quarter-final match and winning, 1 up. Sam Byrd was the final victim, 4 and 3. Byron was 37 under par for his 204 holes in the Championship.

1946

If a player ever figured to win a tournament, Ben Hogan was that man in the PGA at Portland (Oregon) Golf Club. (He and Snead were never to meet in a single PGA Championship match.)

Hogan had been out of the Army and back on the tour only a year when the Championship began. In that period, he had won 14 tournaments, finished second eight times, third six times, and fourth on four other occasions, including the 1946 U.S. Open, in which a missed short putt on the final green kept him out of a three-way playoff. One of the seconds was in the 1946 Masters, in which he three-putted the final green to lose to Herman Keiser by a shot.

Ben drew relatively obscure opponents in the early rounds, then caught Jimmy Demaret in the semifinals. He routed jaunty Jimmy, 10 and 9. Meanwhile, Ed (Porky) Oliver was battling his way through the likes of Dick Metz, Chandler Harper, Nelson (a 3 and 2 loser in his final PGA match), and Jug McSpaden, whom he bounced, 6 and 5, in the other semifinal match.

Against Hogan, Oliver moved to a 3-up lead in the morning round with a 70. Ben had done little on the greens in shooting 73. After lunch, Hogan found his putting touch. He worked a 30 out of the front nine to go one up, holing putts from 17 feet at the 21st and from 12 feet at the 22nd and 23rd. He closed the match—6 and 4—with a conceded birdie on the 32nd when he rifled an approach 3 feet from the pin.

1947

The organizers at Plum Hollow in Detroit had an attendance plan for the PGA Championship: Schedule the semifinals on Monday and the finals on Tuesday. The big weekend crowds are certain anyway, and the name players in those last three matches will draw big galleries on Monday and Tuesday.

So who did they have in the semifinals and finals when the tournament was played? Art Bell, Vic Ghezzi, Chick Harbert, and Jim Ferrier. No slouches, but not players with crowd appeal such as Hogan, Demaret, McSpaden, and Bobby Locke, who were eliminated in the first round. Snead was ousted in the second round by Sarazen, who, in turn, lost to Ky Laffoon the next day when Mangrum also bit the dust.

That Championship first spelled out many of the problems of the match-play format, sort of the beginning of the end.

Ferrier, a naturalized U.S. citizen from Australia who was still playing occasionally on the tour in the early Seventies, emerged from among the final four survivors of the slaughter to win the title with a 6 and 5 victory over Harbert, but only a phenomenal finish saved him from a first-day exit with Hogan and the others. One down going to the 18th, lanky Jim holed a 60-foot chip for a winning eagle and birdied the first extra hole to beat Willie Goggin.

Although he was 27 under par for the 203 holes he played, Ferrier had fairly close matches in all except the semifinals, in which he blasted Bell, 10 and 9. Although rather wild against Harbert in the title match, Ferrier was deadly with his short game and was 5 under par when he closed the door, 2 and 1. Jim had been a bit distrustful of the pro-Harbert galleries and hired two special policemen for $100 to walk ahead and keep an eye on his ball.

1948

"I'm glad you won, Ben. If I had been the winner, I wouldn't go much farther, but you can win this tournament."

As reported in *The Professional Golfer* magazine, these were the words of Jock Hutchison, Jr., the young son of the 1920 PGA Champion,

Ben Hogan, 1948

as he shook hands with Hogan after carrying the great Texan five extra holes before losing to a birdie in the first round at Norwood Hills Country Club in St. Louis. Prophetic. Hogan did win that tournament, defeating Mike Turnesa soundly in the finals, 7 and 6.

But, Ben had other scares during the long week. In the second round on the afternoon after the Hutchison match, he was 2 down with three to play against Johnny Palmer and birdied all three for a 1-up win. Twenty-six years after his first PGA victory, Gene Sarazen rallied from a 3-down situation at lunchtime against Hogan in the first 36-hole match and just missed a long birdie putt at the 36th that could have sent that match into overtime.

Ben went 35 holes in each of the next two matches, beating both Harbert and Demaret, 2 and 1. He killed Turnesa on Norwood Hills' back nine in the finals. One up after nine, Hogan spurted to 4 up on the back nine, time and again displaying long-iron skill on a course scattered with bunkers in fairways that often forced layup tee shots. Turnesa matched Ben on the front nine in the afternoon, but Hogan ended the duel quickly on the back nine by winning the 10th, 11th, and 12th.

Hogan was a grim and determined man all week and, as the PGA's magazine reporter said, "Hogan's methodical, businesslike manner of beating his opponents did little to capture the gallery's fancy." Nor did his promise never to play in a seven-day tournament again.

That vow, whether completely serious or not at the time, also proved prophetic. Hogan's near-fatal highway crash occurred the following spring, and he never again played in the PGA while it was a match-play event. To understand what this, on top of Nelson's early retirement, meant to the PGA in its efforts to "sell" the championship in subsequent years, consider the plight of a sponsor in the 1970s if he knew from the start that he would not have Palmer and Nicklaus in his tournament. It was a mortal blow.

1949

When Sam Snead won his first PGA Championship at Atlantic City in 1942, he did it despite the most hostile gallery he ever faced—the Army buddies of his final opponent, Jim Turnesa.

Things were dead opposite when he won his second PGA title. The 1949 Championship was held at the Hermitage in Richmond, Virginia, not far from Sam's birthplace at Hot Springs. The place was jammed all week with Snead partisans, rooting their man to victory. In most of the matches, he needed all the help he could get.

After taking out young Jack Burke, 3 and 2, Sam had his hands full against Henry Ransom, eventually winning, 3 and 1. Dave Douglas was even tougher. Sam was 3 down with six to play in the first 36-hole match. He won on the last hole. Against Demaret in the quarter-finals, he was at the top of his game. He was six under par when he ended the match at the 33rd.

Jim Ferrier was hotter the next day. With a 67, the Australian took a 2-up lead after the first 18 and added another hole to his advantage at the 20th. But Snead holed a 90-yard wedge shot for an eagle deuce at the 21st and this turned the match around. He drew even with Ferrier at the 24th and finished him off with birdies at the 31st and 33rd and a half at the 34th.

Johnny Palmer, who had given Hogan such a battle in 1948, was the other finalist. Palmer had escaped Mike Turnesa in a 20-hole, first-round match and bumped off Lew Worsham and Mangrum, among others, to reach the title round. He held Snead even for 21 holes. Then Sam deuced the 22nd, won three holes to Johnny's one over the next nine, and halved his way to a 3 and 2 triumph.

1950

Lloyd Mangrum said it for all of the victims as only Mangrum could put it in that tough baritone voice of his: "Good Godamighty, what a putter."

Mangrum was talking in the locker room, then halfway to a 1-up defeat at the hands of the eventual champion, Chandler Harper, a thirty-six-year-old Virginian who had been on and off the pro tour since 1934. Even though the prematurely balding Harper had finally won his first tour title at Tucson earlier that year, nobody had considered him a threat over the 7,032 yards of the fine Scioto Country Club course in Columbus, Ohio, because of the relative lack of power in his game.

Chandler coped with Scioto with his putter, just as Mangrum said. After taking his opening match, 4 and 3, over Fred Annon, Harper went to the wire with each of his next four opponents—1 up in 18 over Dick Metz, 2 and 1 in 36 over Bob Toski, with both players well under par at the finish, 1 up over Mangrum with a birdie on the last hole and 2 and 1 over Jimmy Demaret.

The final match was almost anticlimactic. Harper's opponent was Henry Williams, Jr., a Championship pairing that didn't exactly captivate the golf world. And, it appeared that the two men had pretty much played themselves out in getting to the finals. With a morning wind making conditions difficult, they struggled. Williams bogeyed the first three holes to Harper's pars, falling behind to stay. Chandler shot 75 and Williams 79 in the morning, and the mild-mannered Virginian went on to a 4 and 3 victory.

1951

Despite his barrelful of tour titles, his two PGA Championships, and his British Open victory in 1946 at St. Andrews, some skeptics still had reservations in the summer of 1951 about Sam Snead's greatness, citing primarily his failures to win the U.S. Open and Masters over the period back to 1937.

While the Open title has never come his way, Snead later won twice at Augusta National. But, before that, he took the opportunity to silence those critics in the PGA Championship that year with a convincing series of victories that led to the title at one of the country's most fearsome courses—Oakmont Country Club near Pittsburgh.

It wasn't merely that Sam battled through four tough early matches and then crushed his opponents in the semifinals and finals to become just the third man in history to hold three PGA Championships. It was more that he was an astonishing 21 under par for the 166 holes he played on the rugged course, although Oakmont's lightning-fast greens weren't as treacherous as usual because of heavy rainfall in the area in the weeks before the tournament. In winning the Open there two years later, Ben Hogan was just 5 under par with his 72-hole 283.

Snead needed all his shots to get through the early matches in 1951 at Oakmont. Fred Haas, playing in his first PGA, carried Sam to the final hole of the opening match, and Marty Furgol forced their second-round match to 21 holes before bowing to a Snead birdie. Things weren't that much easier in the first two 36-hole matches as he took out Mangrum, 3 and 2, and Jack Burke, 2 and 1.

Walter Burkemo was having just as tough a time. The stocky Michigan pro, who had gone five extra holes in his home section just to get a ticket to Oakmont, went overtime in two of his first four matches. It took him 20 holes to eliminate Toby Lyons in the first round and 19 holes to dump Chick Harbert in the second round. He beat Dick Shoemaker in the third round, 2 and 1, and Reggie Myles, just 1 up, to reach the lower-bracket semifinals. It was all Snead the last two days. Sam trounced the surprising Charley Bassler, 9 and 8, in the semis, while Burkemo was fighting for his life against the veteran Ellsworth Vines, the one-time tennis star. Vines had Walter dormie after 34 holes, but Burkemo fought back to square the match on the 36th green and win it on the 37th.

With Snead in the finals, 10,000 fans turned out Sunday and saw Sam at his finest. Before Burkemo could catch his breath, he was 5 down, as Snead, playing at a 4-under-par clip, won five of the first six holes. He eagled the 1st hole and won the others with two birdies and three pars, holing a pitch shot for one of the birdies from off the upper bank at the par-4 5th. The margin went to 6 before the game Burkemo began to whittle it away. By the end of the morning round, Sam's lead was down to 3. What hopes Walter might have generated from that rally dissolved quickly after lunch. Snead holed a 6-foot birdie putt at the 1st hole, a 25-footer at the 2nd, and won the 3rd to get back to 6 up. Nine holes later, it was over, 7 and 6, a margin exceeded in the tournament's history only by Sam's 8 and 7 loss to Paul Runyan 13 years earlier.

Snead's victory at Oakmont brought to an end another period in the history of the match-play PGA Championship. It was the last time that one of the giants of the time won it, although the pairing of Doug Ford and Cary Middlecoff in 1955 was an attractive matching of opposites when both were leading players on the tour and eventually won 54 titles between them in tournament golf. Jack Burke, the 1956 winner, also enjoyed a fine career. But, in truth, the middle Fifties was really a transition period when tournament golf seemed to be "on hold," waiting for Palmer, Player, Nicklaus, and Trevino to come along. The courses during that six-year period were undistinguished.

1952

Three times over a quarter century, one of the Turnesa brothers reached the finals of a PGA Championship—and failed, as much because of the opponent they had to face as anything.

Joe Turnesa went for the title in 1927 and became the victim by only a 1-up score as Walter Hagen won his fourth straight PGA crown. Fifteen years later, Army Corporal Jim Turnesa bowed to Sam Snead in the finals, 2 and 1. Then, in 1948, Mike Turnesa ran into a Ben Hogan buzzsaw and lost, 7 and 6.

Jim got another crack at the championship in 1952 at Big Spring in Louisville, Kentucky, and didn't let it get away. The field was thinned of most of its name players fairly early, with Cary Middlecoff the only top star still alive for the quarter-finals. Ted Kroll took him out in 38 holes, then Turnesa, who had scored early victories over Bob Toski, Chandler

Harper, Roberto de Vicenzo, and Clarence Doser, knocked out Kroll, 2 and 1, to gain the finals.

In the lower bracket, Chick Harbert had moved fairly easily through the early rounds, then defeated Fred Haas, 2 and 1, in the quarter-finals, and Bob Hamilton, the 1944 winner, 1 up.

Chick worked out a 3-up lead in the morning round, but the long-hitting Michigan pro turned wild off the tee in the afternoon, and Turnesa chipped away at the margin despite some brilliant recoveries by Harbert. Jim squared the match with a birdie at the 32nd hole. Both men birdied the next two holes and reached the 36th still even. But Harbert had run out of luck. Chick, who had hit only three fairways in the afternoon round but was one under par at the time, drove his ball under a low-branched evergreen. He was barely able to knock the ball into play, reached the green with his third shot, but missed from 25 feet as Turnesa parred routinely for the title.

1953

Walter Burkemo won only one stroke-play tournament during his career on the pro tour, but, in the early Fifties, was considered one of the game's best match players. He lost to Snead in the 1951 PGA finals and reached the quarter-finals in 1952. In 1953, Walter went all the way at Birmingham Country Club in suburban Detroit, encouraged by hometown fans and members from his nearby club, Franklin Hills.

Burkemo's presence in the finals had to save the gate, since his opponent was unheralded Felice Torza, a club professional from St. Charles, Illinois. Torza gave Burkemo a good fight before bowing, 2 and 1.

Most of the fireworks came early in the tournament, as six former champions, including Sam Snead and Gene Sarazen, went out in the first two rounds. Torza accounted for Sarazen himself, then ousted Jim Turnesa, the defending champion, in the second round. His other victims were of lesser note—Wally Ulrich in 38 holes, Jimmy Clark in 36, and Jack Isaacs in 39.

Burkemo experienced little difficulty in eliminating Lou Barbaro, Mike Turnesa, and Pete Cooper in the early rounds. But Dave Douglas, who had knocked out Snead, won the 34th and 35th holes against Burkemo to draw within one of Walter. But, at the 36th, Burkemo fired a four-wood second shot within 30 inches of the cup on the par-5 hole to clinch the win with a conceded eagle. He nipped Claude Harmon, 1 up, in the semifinals.

1954

Two men familiar with PGA Championship matches wound up playing each other for the 1954 title at St. Paul's municipal Keller Golf Course, scene of the tour's regular Minnesota stop for many years.

In one corner—Walter Burkemo, with a 1–1 record in the finals and the defending champion. In the other corner—Chick Harbert, 0–2, the victim of Jim Ferrier in 1947 and Jim Turnesa in 1952.

It was Harbert's turn in 1954, although he had to do some fancy scrambling in that final match after losing three of the first four holes. He played the remaining 29 holes in 8 under par, never taking a bogey and one-putting 14 greens, many of them because of outstanding wedge play. At the lunch break, Chick held a 1-up lead. Then, on the first two holes of the afternoon round, he wedged within a foot of the cups for conceded birdies. Birdies at the 28th and 32nd holes and a half at the 33rd closed out Burkemo's bid to become the first repeat champion since Denny Shute in 1936 and '37.

Except for his 5-and-3 opening win over Mike Krak, Harbert weathered a series of tight matches in getting to the final round. He scored 3-and-1 victories over John O'Donnell and Porky Oliver and 1-up squeakers against Jerry Barber and Tommy Bolt, whom Chick had talked out of quitting during his preceding match with Sam Snead that he eventually won in 39 holes. Burkemo's toughest matches, were against Claude Harmon, 2 and 1, and Cary Middlecoff in the semifinals, 1 up.

1955

Doug Ford qualified for his first PGA Championship just in time—to win it.

That alone was unusual. Tom Creavy (1931) is the only other man to have won the PGA the first time out. Also unusual was Ford's march from medalist in the 36-hole qualifier for the match play to the title. Only Walter Hagen, Olin Dutra, and Byron Nelson had accomplished that.

Ford's short game was always his strong suit in tournament golf and he displayed it to the nth degree that week at Meadowbrook, another of the many courses in the Detroit area that hosted major championships through the years. It certainly contributed heavily to his final 4-and-3 victory over a tiring Cary Middlecoff, who had lost an extra-hole quarter-final match in 1952 and by a hole in the 1954 semifinals. Cary never won the PGA.

After 2-and-1 victories over George Fazio and Ted Kroll in the 18-hole matches, the fast-playing Ford rolled rather easily to the finals, playing so strongly that he finished the tournament 39 under par for 194 holes. The methodical, deliberate Middlecoff bumped off perennial contender Walter Burkemo, 2 and 1, in the first round and scored easy wins over Bill Nary, Mike Pavella, and Tommy Bolt around a 40-hole thriller against Jack Burke, who at one point had a five-hole lead.

Middlecoff's 67 in the morning round was only good for a one-hole lead on Ford in the finals. Doug finally went ahead to stay when Cary bogeyed the 26th hole. Birdies at the 29th and 30th opened the gap, and after trading wins at the next two holes, Ford ended it with a par as Middlecoff failed to save one from a trap.

Note one other oddity at Meadowbrook: Chick Harbert was the pro there and also the defending PGA champion. He lost to Johnny Palmer in the second round.

1956

Jack Burke received little credit for his victory in the Masters earlier in 1956, most people considering it the tournament Ken Venturi lost. However, there was no such derision of Burke's accomplishments in winning the PGA Championship that year at Blue Hill near Boston. The handsome Texan not only played excellently and putted spectacularly, but also was the first man to have to wade through seven matches to gain the title, the PGA having doubled the field that year to 128 starters in match play and eliminated the 36-hole, on-site qualifier.

Burke, who had blown a 5-up lead in losing a 40-hole quarter-final match in the 1955 PGA, staged several comebacks of his own—his advance through five 18-hole matches in 1956 against Leon Pounders, Bill Collins, Fred Haas (20 holes), Charles Harper, and Fred Hawkins; his semifinal match with Ed Furgol in particular; and the Championship match against Ted Kroll.

The Furgol match was almost a reverse of Burke's 1955 setback. Jack trailed Furgol by five holes at one point, but rallied to win in 39. Kroll led by three holes early in the Tuesday title match, yet Jack mustered a 3-and-2 triumph. Ted had passed tough tests in eliminating Sam Snead and Jim Turnesa before routing Bill Johnston, 10 and 8, in the other semifinal. Johnston had such little faith in his chances in the tournament that he hadn't reserved his room beyond Friday's opening round.

Besides Burke, only Sam Snead (1949) and Jack Nicklaus (1963) have won the Masters and PGA in the same year.

1957

They laid match play to rest in 1957 at Miami Valley Golf Club in Dayton, Ohio, but Lionel Hebert, a trumpeter of note, was not playing blues that day. He was celebrating, not that the match-play PGA Championship was dead but that he had just won that title.

The younger of the golfing Heberts from Louisiana's Cajun country outlasted the grimly determined Dow Finsterwald in the finals, 2 and 1. It was the seventh straight match in which Hebert won on the 17th green at Miami Valley. His first match went to the last hole and a 2-up victory over Max Evans. A sequence of tight matches followed: 3 and 1 over Marty Furgol and Charley Farlow, 2 and 1 over Mike Souchak and Claude Harmon, 3 and 1 over that great match player, Walter Burkemo, in the 36-hole semifinal, and the win over Finsterwald.

Finsterwald had just as many close shaves enroute to the title round. His best victory was a 2-and-1 defeat of Sam Snead in the fourth round.

Appropriately, the meeting of Hebert and Finsterwald was just as tight. The two were even after the morning round, and Hebert didn't get permanent possession of the lead until he sank a 15-footer at the 31st hole. The two matched birdies on the next two holes, but, for all intents and purposes, the battle was over when Dow put his approach in a ditch hazard at the 34th and Lionel went two up with his par. The final PGA Championship match ended when both parred the 35th.

In the final six years of match play, the format, not readily adaptable to the confines of TV, had rapidly lost favor because of the usual early elimination of the top stars. As a result, great clubs were reluctant to host the tournament.

The advent of the stroke-play format had no great immediate effect on the PGA Championship, other than the desired increase in attendance, compatibility for television, and reduction in the grueling nature of extended match play.

1958

Although he had won four tournaments during his first four years on the pro tour, Dow Finsterwald had much more often finished second during that time. He was thought of as "the perennial bridesmaid," the steady player who wins few titles but lots of money. Even in his first PGA in 1957, he had finished second to Lionel Hebert.

Then, the PGA made its big switch—from match to stroke play—and Finsterwald got his major title, coming from behind on the final day at Llanerch Country Club in suburban Philadelphia to score a 2-stroke victory. He finished with 276 on the 6,710-yard, par-70 course with a closing 67, just as he had started that Thursday.

The first 67 gave Dow a one-stroke lead over Jay Hebert, and only five others players at 69 were under par. Finsterwald and Hebert leveled at 139 Friday, but right behind them at 140 were Sam Snead, Bill Casper, and Julius Boros. Snead, a three-time champion, and Casper, playing in his first PGA, as, incidentally, was Arnold Palmer, shot 67s to launch their bids.

Snead did it again Saturday, but had to overcome three-putting on three greens and seven trips into the rough in the process. Sam's 207 gave him a one-shot lead on Casper and 2 on Finsterwald, who had matched par. Nobody else was a factor Sunday.

In fact, Dow had the tournament well in hand after 12 holes. Casper was matching birdies with bogeys ahead, and Finsterwald was winning a duel with Snead in the final threesome. Sam drew first blood with a birdie at the 2nd and both birdied the 3rd. Then, Dow caught Snead with birdies at the 4th, 5th, and 7th, and went in front when Sam bogeyed the 8th and 9th, missing short putts.

Casper slipped into second place on the back nine when Sam three-putted the 12th for a bogey and the 13th for a double bogey, but could not catch Finsterwald, who added a one-over-par 36 to his outgoing 31.

1959

The 1959 PGA Championship, played at Minneapolis Golf Club, was both won and lost. Bob Rosburg, who had been close but not winning for almost two years on the tour, truly won the PGA title with a blistering 66 finish on a windy Sunday afternoon in Minnesota. Jerry Barber, who had led or shared the lead through three rounds, lost the title on the last two holes.

The forty-three-year-old Barber had broken from a nine-player leadership of 69-shooters in the first round to take a 2-shot advantage the second day when he fired a 65 for 134. Mike Souchak was at 136 and nobody else was within 4 strokes of Barber. At the point, Rosburg trailed by nine shots.

Jerry faltered the third day, but held the lead by a stroke after holing a 35-foot birdie putt on the 18th green. Doug Sanders, with middle rounds of 66, 68, moved into second place and Rosburg still trailed by 6. Nine holes later, he was even with Barber and ahead of Sanders. He had birdied the 2nd, 3rd, 4th, 8th, and 9th for an outgoing 30, while Jerry and Doug were shooting 36s. Bob was unable to maintain the hot pace on the back nine. Playing well ahead of Barber and Sanders, he bogeyed the 15th, missing a short par putt, turned in his 66, and retired away from the TV sets in the clubhouse to await the finish. Jerry gained the upper hand again when he sank a 15-foot birdie putt at the 15th. He parred the 16th and needed only two more on two of the easier par-4 holes on the 6,850-yard course for a victory. Instead, Barber trapped approaches on both holes and failed to hole either par putt.

It wasn't until 1960 that the first of the present-day greats—Arnold Palmer—played a prominent role, and the pattern of different first-time winners each year, which began in 1952, continued without interruption until 1971. It was a parade of first-time champions, the good but not the great, that carried over from 1952 in match play through 20 tournaments until Nicklaus won his second stroke-play championship in 1971.

Palmer himself did much to elevate the stature of the PGA when he "invented" the Professional Grand Slam in 1960 after he had won the Masters and U.S. Open and was heading for the British Open. Kel Nagle intervened at St. Andrews, so the emphasis swung to an American Slam, to Akron, Ohio, to Firestone Country Club, and to the 1960 PGA Championship. Eight subsequent stroke-play PGAs had major bearings in one way or another on the careers of Palmer, Nicklaus, and Player, so they are dealt with more extensively on the following pages.

1960

If his spirit had been drained by his narrow defeat by Nagle in the British Open, Palmer showed no signs of it when he opened his third bid for a PGA Championship at Firestone, which had undergone major surgery under the knife of Robert Trent Jones, who converted it from a routine course to a truly championship layout with very few flaws. (Those who enjoy chiding Trent Jones, the country's most famous golf course architect today, tell him he did his best jobs rebuilding somebody else's courses.) Since then, Firestone, through the impetus and enthusiasm of the executives of the rubber industry giant, has been the most-used course in the country for major tournament golf.

Palmer was off and running that August, firing one of the four subpar scores of the opening round and taking a one-stroke lead on the field with his 67. Although he lost the lead to Jay Hebert's 139 the second day—Jay shot 67 himself, another of only 13 subpar rounds posted during the tournament on the 7,165-yard course—Arnold remained in a strong position at 141 despite a 74. He was still in good shape through 15 holes of the third round, but then disaster struck at Firestone's most celebrated and controversial hole—the 625-yard 16th. He was trapped off the tee and faded his wood second beyond the tree line separating the 16th and 17th holes. He spotted an opening and, in typical fashion, went for the green, but the ball ticked one of the tree limbs and dropped into the ditch hazard short of the pond that guards the green. The penalty stroke, a pitch, and three putts later, he had an eight. It led him to a 75, which dropped him too far back to challenge with his closing 70 on a day when a 69 by Wes Ellis was the lowest score.

With the favored Palmer no longer too dangerous that third day on a course where birdies don't abound, the championship evolved into a battle among four men—Hebert and Doug Sanders of the young set and two PGA champions of earlier decades—Sam Snead, 48, and Jim Ferrier, 45. Sanders, at 210, led the other three by a stroke going into the final round.

Hebert, whose younger brother Lionel had won the 1957 PGA, forged ahead of the other three by a shot on the front nine Sunday with a par 35. From there in, the exciting struggle seesawed. Ferrier, who had been relatively inactive and hadn't won a tournament in eight years, got on top at the 11th, which he birdied about the same time as Hebert was taking a 6 at the par-4 10th. But, after bogeys at the 14th and 15th, Jim had dropped a stroke behind the other three contenders.

Snead, playing with Ferrier just ahead of Hebert and Sanders, got the only birdie among the four at the 16th when he wedged across the water within a foot of the cup. The tables turned at the 17th, where Snead missed the green and bogeyed while Ferrier was holing a 2-foot birdie putt. Moments later, Hebert sank an 8-footer there to take the lead as Sanders parred.

By the time he was playing to the green on the tough 465-yard finishing hole, Jay knew what he had to do. Ferrier had parred, Snead had bogeyed. A par would beat Jim's 282 and would win the championship, provided Sanders didn't birdie that last hole. Doug made Hebert's job easier when he trapped his approach. Jay put his three-iron shot 25 feet from the pin and two-putted for the title. For the first and only time, two brothers owned PGA Championships.

1961

More often than not when a golfer blows a solid chance to win a major title on the closing holes, he doesn't get another chance—and, when he does, he usually fails again.

Jerry Barber had lost the 1959 PGA Championship by bogeying the last two holes. He got another chance, albeit a slim one, in the stretch of the PGA Championship two years later at Chicago's Olympia Fields. That time, he was not to be denied. He staged one of the most amazing putting exhibitions in history on the last three holes to squeak into a tie, and then won the title in a playoff against Don January the next day.

The early rounds had gone this way: Art Wall took the first-round lead with a 3-under-par 67 on the 6,722-yard Olympia Fields course. The second round was washed out. Barber took the halfway lead with 69, 67—136, 2 in front of January's 72, 66—138. With the last two rounds scheduled for Sunday, play started at dawn. January shot 67 for 205 to take the 54-hole lead by 2 over Barber and 5 over everybody else.

Don appeared to have the title in hand after 69 holes. He led Barber by 4 strokes. But Jerry put his putting touch to work. He birdied from 20 feet at the 16th, ran in a 40-footer for a par at the 17th, and tied January at 277 when he sank a birdie putt from 52 feet (his estimate) on the final green.

Jerry also trailed through much of the Monday playoff, the first for the stroke-play championship, but again fought back and, in a well-played duel, nipped January, 67 to 68. Like Barber, though, January's day was to come.

1962

South African Gary Player had made his mark on American golf by 1962, on the strength of his play in the U.S. Open (second to Tommy Bolt in 1958), in the Masters with his victory the previous year, and on the tour as 1961's leading money-winner. But, his record in the PGA Championship until then had been a virtual void. Player, Palmer, Nicklaus, and a few others hurried back from the British Open to play in the 44th PGA at Aronimink Golf Club in Philadelphia's Main Line suburbs. Gary had played in the PGA only in 1961 and tied for 29th at Olympia Fields.

The "Big Three" came into being as a catch phrase in 1962. Player had lost to Palmer in the Masters playoff and had finished sixth at Oakmont before Nicklaus beat Palmer in the U.S. Open playoff. Arnold had just won the British Open for a second time.

One of the three figured to win the PGA and it turned out to be Player, the first foreign citizen since Tommy Armour in 1930 to do it. (Ferrier was a naturalized American when he won in 1947.) Nicklaus made a belated rush—69, 67—to finish third at Aronimink, while Palmer, trying again to be the first man since Hogan in 1953 to win three of the major titles in a single season, was the center of all attention, but he could manage only four lukewarm rounds and tied for 17th.

Gary's victory at Aronimink was surprising. He was quite depressed after missing the 54-hole cut at Troon, a course he openly disliked. After he arrived in Philadelphia, he told an acquaintance he was fed up with the traveling and was thinking about chucking it all and returning to South Africa to stay. But the verdant setting of Aronimink worked wonders on him. As he related in his book, *Grand Slam Golf*, "A fantastic change came over me. Here was a marvelous course, green and ripe, with lush fairways, dazzling white bunkers, holding greens, lovely trees everywhere. All my life I have loved trees—and there are no trees at Troon. The whole setting was so peaceful and sympathetic to me, after the brutalities of Troon, that I felt happy and relaxed and invigorated."

Player concluded during his practice rounds that, although Aronimink measured 7,045 yards, the positioning of the fairway bunkers was such that four-wood tee shots with a draw on them would keep him out of the big traps on the right and short of those just a bit farther out on the left. It was solid strategy, although not too evident the first day when big John Barnum led with 66, five others broke the par of 70, and Gary shot 72.

The South African made his move in Friday's round, firing a fine 67 to move into a second-place tie with George Bayer and Cary Middlecoff at 138, just a shot behind Doug Ford. By Saturday evening, Player was in a commanding position. His 69 for 208 led Bayer and Bob McCallister by two strokes, Ford (who had shot 73) by three, and Bob Goalby by four.

As it turned out, all of the excitement of the final round was packed into the last threesome. The challenge came from Goalby, who was paired with Gary. They traded birdies through much of the early going and Player led by 3 after 13 holes. Then, Bob ran in a 20-foot birdie putt at the 14th and made another birdie at the par-5 16th to pull within a stroke of the lead. Both parred the 17th, but Goalby put his approach inside Gary's at the 18th. Player missed from 30 feet but left himself only a short putt. Goalby's bid for a tie failed. Gary, deadly sober and ashen-faced, knocked in the putt and seemed almost drained of emotion and strength as he hesitantly picked the ball out of the hole, a totally different scene than the usual jubilant behavior of a man who has just won a tournament. But Player, a very emotional man, was at that moment realizing that 15 rugged months without victory had come to an end and that he had a new lease on the life of his brilliant golf career. "I paused to give thanks to God for making it possible," he later revealed.

1963

If Gary Player was in a "down" mood just before he won the 1962 PGA Championship, Jack Nicklaus was in even lower spirits when he arrived in the 100-degree weather of Texas for the 1963 championship at the Dallas Athletic Club Golf Club. In his own mind, at least, he had just blown the British Open at Royal Lytham with three bogeys on the last four holes.

Again, it would be hard for anybody to figure that Nicklaus would proceed to win at Dallas with that on his mind and in the face of the drastic change of conditions he and the others who had come from Britain had encountered. But this is what makes the difference between the good and the great in the game.

The heat was so intense in Dallas that week that Jack and most of the players spent just about all of their off-course time in their air-conditioned rooms and the restaurants. At times the thermometer reached 110 degrees. Surprisingly, the 7,046-yard DAC course remained in top condition, although the greens were a shade soft because of the necessary constant watering.

As so often happens in the major championships, a little-known player grabbed the early headlines. At Dallas it was Dick Hart, a club professional and occasional tour player from Hinsdale, Illinois. Dick did it in rather sensational fashion, shooting a 5-under-par 66 that included a hole in one at the 16th. Asked during the subsequent press conference if his wife was with him, Dick revealed that the birth of their second child was imminent and that she was at home. "If she'd been out on the course today, she'd probably have had the baby at the 16th green," cracked Jim Trinkle of the Fort Worth *Star-Telegram*. Nicklaus was among five players tied for second at 69 that first day, but he lost another stroke to the lead on Friday when the twenty-seven-year-old Hart added a 72 to preserve his

3-shot margin over Julius Boros, Tony Lema, and Shelley Mayfield. Nobody shot better than 69 that torrid day.

The situation changed drastically on Saturday. Bruce Crampton produced a 65 to surge into the lead at 208, coming from 5 strokes off the pace after 36. Hart lost 11 strokes to Crampton, dropping out of contention with a 76. Dow Finsterwald, coming up with a 66 himself, moved into second place at 210, and a 69 by Nicklaus put him third at 211.

A three-way fight for the title developed on the back nine Sunday among Nicklaus, Crampton, and Dave Ragan, who birdied four of the first seven holes. Jack caught Crampton with a typical Nicklaus birdie—a drive, a one iron, and two putts on the 543-yard 12th hole. Ragan had also birdied the hole, but bogeyed the 13th, and in his position a hole ahead of the other two, he was tied with them. From there in, it was not so much a strong finishing kick by Nicklaus as failures by Crampton and Ragan. While Jack was making five pars and a 30-foot birdie putt at the 15th after a wild drive and fine recovery, Dave was taking two bogeys along with a birdie and three pars, while Crampton was also bogeying two holes and failing to score a birdie.

The 2-stroke lead Nicklaus had on the 18th tee turned out to be important. With a creek crossing the fairway some 290 yards out, he played safe with a three iron but hooked it into the rough. With that extra cushion, he wisely chipped out short of the water on the 420-yard hole, spun a nine-iron shot back to within 4 feet of the cup, and dropped the putt for a 2-stroke victory. Even though the win made him only the fourth man (Player has since become the fifth) to have won all three major U.S. titles, Jack didn't want any part of the Wanamaker Trophy that afternoon. The huge cup had been sitting out in the sun all afternoon and he wasn't about to lay his hands on it.

The other members of the "Big Three" were never in contention at Dallas, Player tying for eighth and Palmer for 40th.

1964

Bobby Nichols left Arnold Palmer and Jack Nicklaus in particular and the golf world in general shaking their collective heads after the four days of the 1964 PGA Championship at Columbus Country Club in Ohio.

Granted that at 6,851 yards and without water hazards Columbus Country Club, even with its narrowed fairways and heightened rough, was one of the easier courses used for the Championship in modern years. However, when a player like Palmer shoots four rounds in the 60s, something that had never been done before in a major tournament, he has to feel that he ought to have won the championship. Or, when a player like Nicklaus, though trailing by 6, fires a closing and record-tying 64, he has to figure he had a good shot at the leader and the title.

Really they never had a chance, because Bobby Nichols never ran out of miracles. In what was, without a doubt, the most unbelievable performance ever in the Championship, Nichols dug himself out of trouble again and again all week with remarkable pitches and putts and breezed to a 3-shot victory over Palmer and Nicklaus with a 271 that remains, by a full 5 strokes, the PGA Championship record. Player was never a factor, shooting 283 at Columbus.

The Nichols saga that week in mid-July began in Kentucky the Sunday before the Championship. While attending a party at Owl Creek Country Club near his Louisville home, Bobby found a used putter in a barrel in the pro shop that he liked. The price tag: $5. He bought it, and seven days later everybody was convinced that it was a magic wand.

Bobby used it in the first round. Result: Eight birdies and a championship record 64. Among his birdies were four putts from outside 10 feet. He putted only 13 times on the back nine. Yet Nichols had little cause for comfort, considering the players in closest pursuit—Nicklaus and Mike Souchak at 67, Palmer, Bill Casper, Bob Charles, and Don January, among others, at 68. The gap narrowed the second day as Bobby slipped to a one-over-par 71. Palmer advanced within a stroke with his second 68, while Ken Venturi, the U.S. Open champion who was enjoying the biggest year of his career, and Bo Wininger moved in at 137, Venturi on the strength of a 65.

The $5 blade and some amazing recovery shots converted a potential 80 into a 69 for Bobby in the third round as, at 204, he clung to his one-stroke lead over Palmer. A few of the miracles: No. 1, rough off the tee, trapped at the green, sank a 10-foot par putt; No. 2, trapped again at the green, sank a 20-foot par putt; No. 8, hit a tree off the tee, played down the adjacent 4th fairway, wedged to a foot; No. 12, trees off the tee, trapped his recovery, holed a long par putt; No. 15, under one tree and hit another with his first two shots, sliced a six iron onto the green and dropped a 25-footer for his par; No. 16, drove into ground under repair, hit a six iron 18 inches from the cup; and, finally and most astonishingly, No. 17, virtually shanked a two-iron tee shot some 70 yards off line and deep in the woods, lofted a wedge over the trees, the ball hitting the pin and dying within inches of the hole.

Arnold must have felt good in his position, figuring that Nichols had used up a year's supply of good luck and that his most dangerous threats—Nicklaus, Casper, Venturi, and, from the past, Ben Hogan—were 5 strokes behind him at 210. Only Mason Rudolph and Tom Nieporte were in between—at 207. Palmer undoubtedly felt even better when his outgoing 34 in the final round pulled him even with Nichols, who had watched a hooked tee shot, seemingly headed out of bounds, strike a tree and bounce back into play on the 2nd hole and gone on to a nine of 35. Rudolph had also caught up with a 32, and Nicklaus was on the move. His 32 left him 3 shots behind.

But Bobby's fortunes remained bright. At the 526-yard 10th, he hit the green with his second shot and rolled in a 35-foot eagle putt and was never headed after that, although some thrills remained. He put a four-iron shot on the green from heavy rough and holed a 15-footer for a birdie at the 15th, saved par with a 12-footer at the 16th, and wrapped it all up when he sank from a measured 51 feet at the 17th. Birdies at the 18th by Palmer and Nicklaus, Arnold from out of the trees with his third shot, merely reduced Bobby's winning margin to 3.

In becoming the first wire-to-wire winner in the Championship, Bobby took only 119 putts, 15 fewer than Nicklaus took in capturing the title the year before at Dallas.

Bobby's feats affected everybody. Hogan, who played in a few PGAs at stroke play during the 1960s, was paired with Nichols that last day. Recalled Bobby later: "I'd played maybe eight or nine rounds with Ben Hogan and I'd never seen him smile or even come close to it. He never said anything during that last round when I was making those impossible shots. But when I holed that long putt, there was Ben with a great big smile on his face. He looked at me, shook his head, and then had to smile again."

1965

The PGA moved from the backyard of Jack Nicklaus in 1964 to Arnold Palmer's neighborhood in 1965, and again the hometown boy failed to live up to the role. In fact, the first tournament at the six-year-old Laurel Valley Golf Club, nine miles from Palmer's front porch in Latrobe, was a virtual disaster for Arnold, and the trouble started even before he reached the 1st tee in the opening round.

Palmer had been a part of Laurel Valley, one of architect Dick Wilson's finest products, since its inception. Set up as an exclusive men's club— women golfers are tolerated during the slow times, the weekends, but not in the main part of the clubhouse—Laurel Valley was patterned in many ways after Augusta National. The members are wealthy, and few live in the lovely Ligonier Valley, where it was built on property that was originally a part of the vast holdings of the Mellon family. Palmer, who was the golfing pride of western Pennsylvania long before he gained national acclaim and fame, was the club's tournament professional from its opening year of 1959 and had much to do with getting the Championship there when, a year or so earlier, the PGA had suddenly found it couldn't play the tournament as scheduled in California. Paul Erath, long prominent in sectional and national PGA affairs, was both the resident professional and course superintendent at Laurel Valley. His ideas about golf courses were somewhat at variance with those of Palmer and others more familiar with tournament golf, and this led to a conflict early in the week of the Championship.

Arnold was not in the best frame of mind when he came home from Philadelphia the previous Friday night. After barely making the cut in the Philadelphia Classic, Arnold had withdrawn under a verbal agreement made with the tournament sponsors at the time he reluctantly agreed to play in that tournament. He was subjected to some criticism for doing so. Then, when he went out to Laurel Valley to prepare for the PGA, he discovered that Erath was quite unhappy that, over his objections, a huge fir tree had just been hauled in and planted at the right front of the tee of the par-5 3rd hole. The idea was to prevent players from firing shots into what would be a gallery area to "cut" the right-swinging dogleg. Arnold had recommended this change many months earlier. While neither man publicly assailed the other, it was clearly a disconcerting situation for a man about to try to win a major title in front of his friends and neighbors.

A heavy fog delayed the start of play Thursday but the PGA got the field around by starting the big group off both the 1st and 10th tees in two shifts, a frequent practice on the tour then and a standard one today. (That experience no doubt helped convince the PGA to reduce the size of its starting field two years later.) However, from what happened to him that Thursday, Palmer would have just as soon not seen the fog lift.

On the 1st hole he put his approach to the left near a temporary wooden bridge over a ditch. While waiting for a ruling on what relief he might have, if any, Arnold absent-mindedly watched zealous marshals, Palmer fans all, tear the railing off the bridge to clear his flight path. He played the shot to the green and made par, only to learn five holes later that the marshals' action had cost him a 2-stroke penalty. Despite that, he shot 72, but, when he drew another 2-stroke penalty at the 11th hole the next day for inadvertently grounding his club in a hazard, Arnold went on to a 75. So much for Arnold in that tournament.

Player fared no better, though without the public attention, eventually winding up with Palmer at 294, 14 shots off the winning score. Nicklaus, however, played steady golf for three rounds while Tommy Aaron was holding the lead. Aaron, the man of many challenges but few victories on the pro tour, started fast, just as he had done so many times earlier in the season. His 66 gave him a one-stroke lead over Gardner Dickinson and Mason Rudolph, and the tall Georgian widened his margin to 2 shots on Friday with a 71 for 137. Nicklaus and lightly regarded Dave Marr posted 139s, and Bill Casper came in at 140.

A one-under-par 70 over Laurel's 7,090 yards enabled Marr to catch Aaron on Saturday at 209, but most experts thought more of the chances of Nicklaus and Casper at 211, or even Dickinson at 210. Marr, the handsome, witty cousin of Jack Burke, fooled them, heeding the advice on a note Burke had slipped under his motel room door: "Fairways and greens, Cuz."

Aaron double-bogeyed the 1st hole and faded out of the picture, but, as expected, Casper overhauled Marr on the front nine. Then, Dave birdied the next two holes, the 11th while playing partner Nicklaus was bogeying the par-5 hole. With a relatively easy victory apparently within his grasp, Marr missed a par putt of little more than a foot at the 16th, cutting his lead to just one over Casper and 2 over Nicklaus. The situation was unchanged when Dave and Jack, the last players on the course, reached the tee on the very difficult 18th, having both made brilliant pars at the 17th, Nicklaus with an 18-foot chip from the fringe and Marr with an 8-foot putt.

Ahead, Casper bogeyed the 18th as Nicklaus was driving beautifully to set up his shot across a pond to an elevated and severely sloping green and Marr was hooking into the rough. Dave played a safe seven-iron shot short of the water, a wise move that proved even wiser when Jack's five-iron approach went over the back edge of the green. Dave dropped his nine-iron third shot just 3 feet from the hole and sank the putt for a 2-stroke victory over Nicklaus and Casper.

Only a friend of Palmer, as Dave was, could get away with the crack he made at the presentation ceremonies after the Laurel officials made Arnold a full-fledged member of the club: "I'm happy to see you fine people here at Laurel Valley make Arnold a member now that he is playing like one." Dave knew full well that Palmer had many fine tournaments and victories ahead of him. But, although he has become a fine golf telecaster for ABC, Dave's playing career went downhill after the 1965 PGA. He did not win a tournament in the next seven years.

1966

Officials at Firestone Country Club once proposed that the PGA base its Championship permanently at their course. If a vote on the suggestion had been taken among the players, I'm sure Al Geiberger would have tried to stuff the ballot box with yeses. The slender Californian came to love the tough, 7,165-yard course in the mid-1960s. He won the American Golf Classic at Firestone in 1965 and followed up the next summer by winning the PGA Championship there, going away. His closing 72 and his final, even-par total of 280 gave him a 4-stroke victory . . . and a peanut-butter contract.

Al had taken to carrying his own sandwiches, usually peanut butter, with him on the course because he got hungry and couldn't get to the concession stands. The snacks sustained him as he and Sam Snead, then fifty-four, shot 68s for the first-round lead. A 71 Friday was enough to give Snead the lead at 139 by a stroke over Geiberger and Don January.

Geiberger quickly moved in front Saturday, but Snead remained close until he inadvertently struck his ball twice during a putting stroke on the 10th green. Later, he took a double bogey at the dangerous 16th and his bid was over. Geiberger proceeded to shoot 68 and open a 4-stroke lead over Dudley Wysong. Player, Palmer, and Nicklaus were all in the field, but too far back to threaten Geiberger. In the final round, he took bogeys on three of the first four holes, but a birdie from 20 feet at the 5th stopped the slide and he breezed home the winner.

It was a big day for Geiberger, but a sad one for pro golf. Tony Lema died in a light-plane crash that evening on his way from Firestone to a Monday event in Illinois.

1967

That the PGA Championship was played at all at Columbine Country Club in the Denver suburb of Littleton was an achievement of note. It was scheduled there for 1966, but that was before the South Platte River went wild in 1965 and virtually destroyed seven of the holes. Denver traded years with Akron's Firestone. Then, Columbine got caught in the middle of the fight between the players and the parent PGA body and almost lost the touring-pro section of the field. Even after that was settled, the area was pelted by a hailstorm, and hasty repairs just got the greens back into shape in time for the Championship.

So, play got underway, to the great relief of tournament officials, who had $300,000 in revenues already in the till. The course, though not distinguished, was in fine shape by then. It measured 7,437 yards, but that figure is deceptive until you allow for the thin air at mile-high Denver.

Dave Hill showed it was deceiving when he opened with a course-record 66 and Tommy Aaron broke the record by a stroke the next day to take the second-round lead at 135. Yet another player was in front after 54 holes—Dan Sikes, on the strength of 69, 70, 70—209. Actually, Nicklaus and Palmer were very much in the picture at Columbine at this point, Jack with 67, 75, 69—211, and Arnold with 70, 71, 72—213. Don January, who had lost the heartbreaker to Jerry Barber in 1961, was also at 213 (71, 72, 70) and Don Massengale was virtually ignored at 215 (70, 75, 70).

Who would have thought that, with all the players ahead of and with them, January and Massengale would wind up in a first-place tie? Massengale came in early with a 66 for his 281 and, as Sikes, Nicklaus, and the others faltered, January moved past them with four birdies between the 12th and 17th holes and parred the 18th to match Don's 281.

January broke open the Monday playoff with a 30-foot birdie at the 10th and another after wedging to 3 feet at the 15th. His 69 won the Championship by 2 strokes.

1968

You would have thought that one unbearably hot July in Texas—the 1963 Championship—would have been enough to convince PGA executives. But, back they came in 1968 to San Antonio and to a five-year-old course called Pecan Valley Country Club. For the record, it must be noted that the 1968 Championship was awarded to Pecan Valley while the late Warren Cantrell was president of the PGA and working for the Pecan Valley developer, Jimmy Burke.

Although the players spent the week swallowing salt tablets and gulping a new thirst quencher called Gatorade, the tournament itself turned into a good one that saw Palmer come closer than he ever has to winning his first PGA Championship and Julius Boros add further to his stature as one of the finest, long-term players of the fifties and sixties. Boros and Palmer had others to contend with at San Antonio, but not Nicklaus, who shot 71, 79 and just missed the 36-hole cut, nor Player, who remembered Dallas and deposited his 1968 entry blank in the wastebasket.

A creek that snaked through nine holes of the course and lush Bermuda rough made the 7,096 yards of Pecan Valley tough, although Marty Fleckman, avoiding his driver on all except five holes, attacked it the first day with a 4-under-par 66, the lowest score of the week. Only four other players broke par, though—Frank Beard with a 68 and Mason Rudolph, Lee Trevino, and Don Bies, a player who seems to shoot his best rounds in important events, with 69s.

Palmer, who had opened with a 71, moved up to fourth place Friday with a 69 round that had "moments of ecstasy and stark raving terror." It included four birdies, a bogey, a double bogey, and pars out of traps on the first two holes. Arnold, Trevino, Miller Barber, Johnny Pott, and George

Trevino chats with gallery

Casper and Boros

Archer trailed Fleckman and Beard by 2 strokes, Marty dropping back into the tie at 138 when he made one of 31 double bogeys scored during the first two rounds on the controversial 18th hole, where the final drama of the tournament was to be witnessed two days later. Doug Sanders was at 139, and Boros ambled under a floppy hat and umbrella through two 71s to 142.

The top positions barely changed the third day. Fleckman, Beard, Palmer, Trevino, and Barber all shot 72s, and the latter three were joined at 212 by Boros and Bob Charles, who scored par 70s. Julius was running at the lead until he double-bogeyed the 14th and bogeyed the 15th. The leader boards remained jammed with contenders Sunday, as nobody could move away with a run of birdies. At the turn, Boros, Palmer, Charles, and Fleckman were on top with one-over-par scores of 246. Then, Boros broke the jam with his putter, holing 15-footers for birdies at the 11th and 16th. Despite a bogey at the 14th, he led by 2 strokes over Palmer, Fleckman, and Charles going to the testy 17th. He bogeyed it.

That brought it down to the final hole. For two days, the tee blocks were set at the 18th so that the creek that bisected the fairway was about 240 yards from the tee and about 220 from the green. It crossed at an angle, virtually forcing layup tee shots. That left the players with long-iron second shots to an elevated, blind green. Only 17 birdies were made in 336 cracks at it. For the last two rounds the PGA officials moved the markers back some 30 feet so that the pros could use their drivers, if they dared risk a well-hit ball dribbling into the water. And the long second shot remained.

Only two birdies had been scored there Saturday and Sunday when Palmer, 2 over par and playing just ahead of Boros, hooked his tee shot into the heavy rough. He was still deep in the grass after taking a free drop because an overhead TV cable interfered with his backswing. But Arnold knew that his only chance to reach the green was with his three wood, and he figured he had to have a birdie to even tie Julius. He slashed the ball out of the rough and, with its overspin, it bounded up onto the green, over the hogback, hit the pin and stopped 8 feet above the hole—one of the finest of many excellent pressure shots during the Palmer career. He stroked a putt that he thought he had made until the grainy Bermuda carried it just past the cup.

Boros was watching this from the other side of the creek, knowing he couldn't reach the green with his second shot. He didn't. But, with little wasted time and motion, Julius flipped a running chip shot over the hump about 3 feet from the hole and sank for the victory. He became, at forty-eight, the oldest champion in PGA history.

1969

The turbulent times in America caught up to the PGA Championship when it was played at the NCR Country Club at Dayton, Ohio, in 1969, and the disturbances might have prevented Gary Player from becoming, three years later, the first man to hold three PGA titles since Sam Snead won his third in 1951.

In the weeks before the Championship, civil rights activists placed a series of demands before the Dayton Chamber of Commerce, the tournament sponsor, threatening to "bring Dayton to its knees in embarrassment" if they weren't met. After quiet picketing through the week, the zealots among them began sporadic harassment of the players, choosing Gary as their main target because of his prominence and the racial policies of his native South Africa, which, ironically, he opposes.

It began Saturday, after Player had started the third round in second place, just a stroke behind Raymond Floyd. First, somebody pitched a program onto the tee as he addressed his shot at the 4th hole. Then, after a shout interrupted Jack Nicklaus, his playing partner, on the 9th green, a man pitched a cup of ice at Gary's face as they moved to the 10th tee. Two different men charged out of the gallery toward the two players while they were at the 10th green. Both agitators were intercepted. At the 13th green, a young woman rolled a plastic ball at Gary's feet. By then, 11 demonstrators had been arrested on the course and there were no further incidents. Gary somehow managed a 71 under those conditions. (Jack, who was worried about his wife and son in the gallery, triple-bogeyed the 18th for 74 and fell out of contention.)

With all of this preying on his mind, as a cordon of uniformed police kept him and the other contenders close company all afternoon, Player made a terrific run at Floyd on Sunday, producing a 70 that closed Ray's 5-stroke lead after 54 holes to a single shot at the finish.

High praise by many of the pros for the 6,910-yard South course, a Dick Wilson layout without a tournament reputation that was half of a 36-hole complex built by the National Cash Register Company for its 15,000 employees, was justified in Thursday's opening round of the Championship by a monumental logjam at the top of the standings. Nine men— Larry Ziegler, Charles Coody, Bunky Henry, Larry Mowry, Johnny Pott, Tom Shaw, Bob Lunn, Al Geiberger, and Floyd—crowded first place with 69s. But, as the reporters and headline writers around the country tried to figure out how to handle that, Arnold Palmer solved the problem in a negative fashion.

Arnold's ailing hip, which had bothered him off and on since the 1966 New Orleans Open, acted up that first day. He bogeyed the first four holes and really aggravated the injury when he put everything he had into a one-iron shot to reach the green in two at the 548-yard sixth hole. He turned in 40, went to 42 on the back nine. The 82 was the worst round he ever shot in a major championship. He delayed until the next morning his final decision to withdraw from the tournament. This was the big story that day.

Floyd, a freewheeling and somewhat unpredictable bachelor, took over everything Friday. Overnight rains had softened the course, and par was manhandled. Don Bies (there's that man again) set the course record with 64, and Player fired a 65, but bulky Raymond grabbed the lead with 66 for 135, even though he was boiling inside about the slow-playing pattern of Jim Ferrier, the fifty-four-year-old former PGA champion who was his only playing partner because Herman Keiser had withdrawn after 18 holes. Still seething afterward, Ray blasted Ferrier during his press conference for even playing in the Championship. "He shouldn't be out here. . . . Everybody knew he was going to miss the cut by 10 strokes," Floyd complained. (Actually, Jim missed by only 4). After a conference with officials, Raymond apologized for the remarks. But he didn't have to apologize for his golf. After a bogey at the 3rd hole, he ran off four birdies and an eagle on the next seven and went on to his one-stroke lead over Player, 2 over Henry, and 3 over Nicklaus, Bies, and Orville Moody, the reigning Open champion.

While Player and Nicklaus were facing the Saturday ordeal, Floyd was quietly fashioning a 5-stroke lead with a 67 for 202. He played a nearly flawless round, no doubt the finest of his career in a major event. He had no bogeys, saving par once from 20 feet, and finished sensationally with his fourth birdie of the day at the 18th, where he lofted an eight-iron shot from a fairway trap that stopped 6 inches from the hole. Five strokes back in second place were Player, Henry, and Bert Greene.

Floyd's game was obviously off on Sunday. He began playing defense and soon he had Player and Greene nipping at his heels. Gary, his playing partner, was his immediate concern. After nine holes, Player had chipped 2 strokes off Floyd's lead. Ahead, Greene had birdied the 10th to close within a shot, but that was to be his last gasp. Bogeys at both remaining par 3s led him to a 71 and 278.

The back nine became a Floyd–Player duel in the guarded arena. Ray holed a downhill 25-footer at the 10th, but Gary matched the birdie at the 12th and gained a stroke when Floyd was trapped at the par-3 13th and bogeyed. The 16th decided it. After trapping his approach at the 451-yard hole, Player made a typical excellent bunker shot. However, Floyd rolled in a sidehill 40-footer for a birdie and doubled his margin when Gary missed his par putt. Player's last bid was a birdie at the 17th and he still had life until a 40-foot birdie putt failed on the final hole after Ray had missed the green. His bogey for 74 and 276 beat Gary by a stroke.

With that, the Big Three were shut out of major titles in 1969. Starting in 1958 with Palmer's Masters victory, he, Nicklaus, or Player had won at least one of the four major titles every year since then.

With Jack Nicklaus becoming such a dominant figure in golf in the early Seventies, a tendency developed to underplay the Big Three image that had enveloped the Sixties. Perhaps the ascendency of Lee Trevino was responsible to a considerable degree. Arnold Palmer remained immensely popular and constantly sought after by every tournament sponsor, but he was no longer being considered automatically one of the pretournament favorites every time he teed up. Although Gary Player won U.S. tournaments in each of the first three years of the Seventies and several hundred thousand dollars in his relatively brief visits during that period, not to mention his continued brilliant international record, he was astonished to find that, in some quarters, Americans were even questioning his "right" to be still considered a member of the Big Three. Now, consider the impact of these three great players in the first three PGA Championships of the 1970s.

1970

Arnold Palmer's fourth and most recent strong bid for the elusive PGA Championship was frustrated by a man who did things that Arnold used to do when he was winning major titles a decade earlier. While he didn't produce a continuing series of miracles in the fashion of Bobby Nichols at Columbus in 1964, Dave Stockton came up with brilliant clutch shots at critical points to capture the 1970 Championship at prestigious Southern Hills Country Club in Tulsa, Oklahoma. Several of these came in the final round when the Californian was head to head against Palmer with only Arnold to beat for the title.

Southern Hills, an outstanding course spanning 6,962 yards of gently rolling terrain at the edge of Tulsa, had taken its toll of the others in the strong field. It proved just as demanding a test for a full house of pros as it had in five previous USGA Championships, including the Open in 1958 and the Amateur in 1965.

On the surface, nothing out of the ordinary happened in the first round, except that the standings didn't have the usual man at the top who didn't belong there. Jack Nicklaus and Johnny Miller led with 2-under-par 68s, and Charles Coody and Larry Hinson came in with the only 69s.

Palmer was at 70 after a birdie, a bogey, and 16 pars. Stockton matched par, too, but in a quite different manner. For instance, in a two-hole stretch, he hit the pin with a fast-moving downhill pitch shot, then sank another pitch-and-run shot for a birdie.

The subpar red numerals disappeared from leader boards Friday in windy, 104-degree weather. It was a nerve-wracking day as play jammed up early at the tough 2nd hole, causing five-hour rounds. When the ordeal ended, Stockton and Hinson shared the lead at 140. Dave, in a confident mood thanks to his father and a book on positive thinking, mustered his second 70 despite a double bogey and two bogeys on the back nine. His four birdie putts were all at least 12 feet long. It was the 10th straight round of 71 or better for Stockton, whose father, a former golf professional, had worked with him on his game a few weeks earlier on tour. Hinson had bogeyed the first three holes but still managed a 71.

Palmer had an excellent opportunity to lead. He was 2 under par after 11 holes, but pulled his approach to the 12th green into a water hazard and took a double bogey. He lost two more strokes coming in and finished at 142 with Gary Player, Bill Casper, and Dick Lotz. Mike Hill, Hale Irwin, and Mason Rudolph scored 141s, but Nicklaus and Miller faded badly, Jack to 144 and Johnny to 145.

Ray Floyd, the defending champion, took a real run at first place Saturday, firing a course-record 65 (with a bogey on the last hole) to post a 209. But Stockton also solved Southern Hills that day with seven birdies and three bogeys for 66. He putted just 28 times, as he moved into a 3-stroke lead over Floyd with 206. Palmer was third at 211, putting together a 69 although requiring 32 putts to do it. This set up the Stockton-Palmer pairing for Sunday's final round. (Nicklaus and Player were too far back, although Jack closed strongly with a 66 for 283. Gary scored 286.)

Floyd's hopes to be the first back-to-back PGA winner since Denny Shute in 1936 and '37 died on the front nine. His 39 knocked him out. Bob Murphy, who had won the 1965 Amateur at Southern Hills, finished an hour or so ahead of Stockton and Palmer with a 66 and 281, but the round was really almost a play by play account of the fortunes and misfortunes of Dave and Arnold. The front-nine theatrics came from Stockton as Palmer clicked off nine straight pars. Dave three-putted the 3rd but holed a 25-footer at the 6th. Still five ahead of Arnold. Then, at the 7th, his wedge approach from 120 yards spun into the cup for an eagle deuce, but he promptly gave back those two strokes by double-bogeying the par-3 8th. Stockton's drive on the next hole caught a fairway trap on the right side. The pin was right, and he had tree limbs in his line. He fired a six-iron shot that nicked a few leaves but carried the green and stopped 2 feet from the pin. He birdied and led by 6 at the turn.

Dave hooked badly into some trees at the 10th, but found a way to get a four-iron shot onto the elevated green and saved his par. Arnold got his first and only birdie at the 11th. Both parred the 12th, but Dave ran into trouble at the 13th, a converted par 5. He drove out of the fairway and pulled his second shot into the water to the left front of the green. Meanwhile, Arnold put his approach within birdie range on the green. Here was his opening—a probable swing of at least 2 strokes, possibly 3. But Stockton made his shot of the tournament at that point. He wedged a foot from the hole to save a bogey and, when Arnold missed the birdie putt, Dave lost only a stroke of his lead. The two traded bogeys on the next two holes and Stockton had 4 strokes in hand with three to play. Home free? Not really. He matched Palmer's par at the long 16th, but with one putt after visiting the trees and a trap. He plugged his approach at the 17th beneath the lip of a trap and just got it out of the sand with his third shot. He bogeyed to lose one shot and also bogeyed the 18th, winning the championship by 2 strokes over Palmer and Murphy with his 72 and 279.

1971

It all seemed out of place—until the tournament began. The PGA Championship in Florida in February, indeed! Don't those people at Palm Beach Gardens know that the Masters really opens the major golf season in April? Don't they know that people go to South Florida in the wintertime, pay high prices, and fill the hotels and motels so they can swim and fish and watch horse races and idly sun themselves or even play golf, but do not watch golf tournaments?

Well, as a matter of fact, the executives of the PGA did realize most of this, but went ahead anyway, partly because they thought it might work but much more importantly because they had to. One of the conditions of the settlement of a legal hassle the PGA had gone through in the mid-Sixties with John D. MacArthur, its influential and wealthy landlord at Palm Beach Gardens, was that the PGA Championship must be played at his PGA National Golf Club there—and the PGA had deferred scheduling of the championship there about as long as it could.

While the PGA did encounter some attendance and manpower problems in February of 1971 at Palm Beach Gardens, the Championship was a resounding success from an artistic standpoint, primarily because of Jack Nicklaus and the excellent 7,096-yard East course of PGA National, a championship layout that was marred only slightly for the tournament by somewhat heavy greens that had been deliberately overfertilized to protect against a frost that never came.

Nicklaus, who admittedly liked his chances for a pro Grand Slam that year because of the four courses on the schedule, prepared for the PGA according to his usual pattern, playing just three early-season tournaments out West and spending the rest of the time during those first two months of 1971 relaxing and working privately on his game at home at Lost Tree Village, just a few miles away.

Those who thought Jack's tournament record indicated, from its paucity of victories in Florida, that his chances weren't too good at Palm Beach Gardens forgot that he had scored his only pro victory in the state on that very PGA National course when he was partnered with Arnold Palmer in the second National Team Championship in 1966. Nicklaus quickly reminded them of that when he jumped out in front in the first round and was never headed. Besides the victory, with 69, 69, 70, 73—281, Jack accomplished several other things for the records:

- First player in history to win all four major championships twice each.
- First player to win the PGA Championship twice at stroke play.
- First previous PGA champion to win again since Sam Snead in 1951.

Things got a little sticky for Jack on the final couple of holes of the Championship Sunday before he completed his 2-stroke victory, but he probably won the tournament the first day with what he called "a good, bad, beautiful, terrible round" of 69. Consider that he missed six greens, drove out of nine fairways, and caught four traps. He three-putted twice for bogeys, but otherwise, using a revised putting stroke he had just picked up from an observation by his old friend, Deane Beman, he one-putted eight of the last ten greens, from 13 feet at the 16th, 6 feet at the 17th, and 9 feet at the 18th. He had worked a good score out of a bad playing round and was on his way.

At that point, he had a one-shot lead on Bobby Mitchell, Bob Goalby, and Bob Charles. Most of the name players—Player, Casper, Boros, Jacklin, Trevino, Devlin, and Snead—were in a crowd at 71, but Arnold Palmer, coming off a victory two weeks earlier at Palm Springs, had putting miseries, including a missed tap-in, took 75, and never got back into contention.

On Friday, Nicklaus posted another 69, this time a solid one on a course that had finally been wetted down by the area's first rain in months that began toward the end of the Thursday round. Except for two early bogeys, Jack had his game pretty much in hand as he widened his margin to 2 strokes over Miller Barber, who made only one bogey in shooting 72, 68—140. Gibby Gilbert was next at 141, while of the other eventual contenders, Casper and Player had 73s for 144 and Tommy Bolt a 74 for 146.

Nicklaus started slowly in the third round. After eight holes, he was one over par for the round, 5 under for the tournament. Gilbert had closed to a single shot. Then Jack exploded. He birdied the 9th from 25 feet and, after bogeying the 10th, birdied the next four holes, the 11th from 40 feet and the 14th from 20 feet. He lost a stroke at the last hole to finish with a 70 and a 4-stroke lead over Player. Gary, calling it "the type of round that could have been 64 as easy as could be," shot 68, making five birdies and missing six other times from inside 15 feet. Gilbert wound up with a 72 for 213, while Casper, Barber, and Bolt carried 215s to the final round.

Jack's sizable lead dwindled fast as he missed greens and bogeyed three of the first five holes. He birdied the 6th and turned in 38, as did Player, while Bolt, the fifty-two-year-old senior, and Casper moved up with 34s. With nine holes to go, Nicklaus led Bolt and Casper by 3, Player by 4, and everybody else was out of it.

Bolt kept his charge going with a birdie at the 10th and was within a shot of the top when Jack bogeyed the par-3 11th. But Tommy had run out of birdies and eventually finished third with a 69 and 284. Jack two-putted the par-5 12th for a birdie, but Player advanced by making birdies at that hole and the 13th. However, Gary got a terrible break at the 15th when his tee shot landed on a macadam cart path and bounded out of bounds. The double bogey there ruined him.

While all of this was going on, Casper, a twosome ahead, was holding his own. He was still 3 under par after 16 holes, then birdied the par-5 17th. As Bill played the 18th, Nicklaus was scrambling for a par at the 16th. With a 2-stroke lead, Jack played safely off the 17th tee with a three wood. Moments later, Casper dropped a 25-foot birdie putt at the 18th for 68 and 283. Because of the shorter tee shot, Nicklaus could not reach the 17th green in two, played short of the traps with a one iron, pitched to 5 feet, and made the birdie putt he wanted so desperately so that he could win with a bogey at the demanding 18th, a hole with two bodies of water between the tee and green 421 yards away. He had missed that green in each of the first three rounds, taking one bogey and twice one-putting it for pars. With the 2-shot cushion, Jack played a one iron off the tee, a two iron onto the fringe of the green, chipped to 3 feet, and sank the putt.

1972

Despite his almost-constant global traveling, Gary Player is really a homebody. When his golf schedule keeps him in America or other countries of the world for any extended period, he longs for his home and family in

South Africa. He'll skip important or rich tournaments to get home. On frequent occasions, he passed up the PGA Championship for this reason. But, much as he missed his wife and children, Gary gave no thoughts to passing up the 1972 PGA Championship, primarily because of its venue—the outstanding Oakland Hills Country Club course in the Detroit suburb of Birmingham.

Gary had played the 7,054-yard course in two previous tournaments and liked it. He had tied for ninth after a 75 start when the club hosted its fourth U.S. Open in 1961, and he was third behind Bobby Nichols and Arnold Palmer in the Carling World Open there in 1964. His 281 score in the Carling would have won two of the four Opens and tied him for first in the other two. In 1972, his 281 did win a title—Gary's second PGA Championship—in one of the tournament's more exciting finishes.

Player had taken the lead with a third-round 67, liked the position and his chances, but emphasized in the press room: "This tournament doesn't start until the 10th hole tomorrow." The unfolding of the final round under gray and dripping skies proved him correct. But first let's set it up:

If there was a flaw in the overall excellent organization at Oakland Hills, it was in the scoring system, as is usually the case for some reason at PGA Championships. Leader boards are frequently scarce and incomplete, unlike the thorough systems that always prevail at the Open and Masters. In any event, the first round at Oakland Hills produced its usual share of fast-starting lesser lights in the field, whose names never got onto the leader boards until after they had finished and had been posted in prime positions on the scoreboards. Brian (Bud) Allin, a slightly built Vietnam veteran who had won the Greensboro Open in 1971, had first place to himself until dusk, when he was joined at 68 by Stan Thirsk, a Kansas City area club pro who occasionally plays on the winter tour.

Among the 69s were three men who were to remain in contention into the final stretch Sunday—Jerry Heard, Jim Jamieson, and Ray Floyd. Arnold Palmer also was in that group, but a second-round 75 was to do permanent damage to his 15th vain try for a PGA Championship. Player opened with 71, Jack Nicklaus with 72, and Lee Trevino with 73.

Heard, who was playing with Palmer in front of the biggest gallery of the sellout crowd, stole Arnold's thunder Friday. Jerry shot 69 for 139, so those fans inadvertently had been watching the tournament leader. Floyd and Hale Irwin had par 140s; Jamieson, Gay Brewer, and Bob Smith 141s; Player (another 71), Tommy Aaron, Dan Sikes, and Lanny Wadkins 142s. Like Palmer, Nicklaus shot 75 Friday and put himself too far back on such a difficult course, even when he went out in 31 Saturday morning. Jack finished at 287.

Although he bogeyed the 9th and 18th Saturday, Player charged in front on the strength of his putting stroke. Among his five birdies were four putts in the 25-foot range on Oakland Hills' large, undulating greens.

Bill Casper also shot 67 Saturday, making only one bogey in one of his best rounds of the year. He stood second at 210. With the likes of Heard, Brewer, and Phil Rodgers at 211, Doug Sanders and Aaron at 212, and Jamieson at 213, no wonder Player anticipated that the marbles would be riding on the final nine holes of the championship Sunday.

At first, it seemed Gary wouldn't be among those with a chance to collect the biggest share of those marbles. He started bogey, birdie, bogey, bogey, and the game was on. At various times on the front nine, Casper, Heard, Jamieson, Brewer, Rodgers, and Floyd led or shared first place. Gary was playing steady par golf now, and the contenders began to thin out. Rodgers, Doug Sanders, Heard, Floyd, Brewer, and Casper fell back. But not Jamieson. The chunky young man from Illinois, who had won the Western Open just six weeks earlier, matched a Player birdie at the 11th with one of his own at the 12th. Then, he discovered himself with a 2-stroke lead when Gary missed short par putts at the 14th and 15th holes.

The fearsome 16th was the decisive hole. Jamieson, playing ahead of Gary, approached short and missed an 8-foot par putt and had also bogeyed the par-3 17th before Player reached the 16th. The hole measures 408 yards and doglegs sharply to the right around a wide lake that elbows up to the green. Gary's tee shot went far enough right that he wound up 150 yards from the pin but behind a large willow tree. Rather than try to fade a shot around it, he elected to go with a nine iron despite the distance to be certain he cleared the tree. The shot came off perfectly and the ball skidded to a stop 4 feet from the cup. Birdie.

With Jamieson in the process of making yet another bogey at the 18th, Gary had a pretty secure hold on matters, particularly when he holed a testing par putt after overshooting the 17th green. He needed only a bogey to win on the 18th, which, during the first two rounds with the markers back, couldn't even be reached in two by the biggest hitters. The tee blocks had been moved forward Saturday and Sunday. Gary played two perfect shots to the big green and just missed a birdie putt. With his 72, he had a 2-stroke victory over Jamieson and Aaron and his sixth major title (two PGAs and British Opens, U.S. Open, and Masters).

With the $45,000 that went with the title, he could easily afford the $250 he had spent on overseas phone calls that morning to relieve his homesickness by talking to his wife, his children, and his seventy-three-year-old father, who had asked Gary to win the Championship for him. Gary was very much the dutiful son.

[7]

THE U.S. TOUR—BING AND BOB JOIN DISNEY AND FIRESTONE

WHEN YOU SEE today's incredibly prosperous professional golf tour as it jets back and forth across the country, or flickers brightly as it does so frequently across millions of television screens, it is astonishing to reflect that the pro tour is a child of the Depression. To be sure, it had its first very casual and haphazard beginnings in the 1920s, that first so-called Golden Age of Sport. But the highly structured, tightly organized, multimillion-dollar movable feast we know today was first welded together in the Thirties, the Gloomy Age for practically everything. Perhaps this is sporting confirmation of the Darwinian Law of Survival. To have formed, to have survived, to have thrived, at a time when life was a daily struggle to avoid bankruptcy, must mean that professional tournament golf has served a very large need for a very large number of people, that the pro tour has been and certainly is a very fit and healthy animal.

As constituted in 1972, the professional golf tour consists of 64 tournaments, most of which are held over a four-day, 72-hole format. Each tournament is coordinated by the PGA (offices in Palm Beach Gardens, Florida, and New York City), but it is those sponsors out there in the country who really put up the money. Because these sponsors are so often heavily backed show biz personalities including singers Glen Campbell, Bing Crosby, Andy Williams, and Dean Martin, comedians Bob Hope, Jackie Gleason, and Danny Thomas, or major U.S. industries such as Eastern Airlines, the Florida Citrus Growers Association, National Airlines, Monsanto Chemical, Kemper Insurance, Firestone Tire & Rubber Company, Liggett and Myers Tobacco, Kaiser Aluminum, Walt Disney World, United Airlines, United States Industries, and IVB, not to mention a number of big-city chambers of commerce, total prize money available to the touring pros in 1972 reached an astounding $7.5 million. It could go to $8 million in '73.

Of the five dozen–plus events scheduled each year, approximately 45 are major league events. The others are known as "satellites" and form a sort of minor league tour for the large number of golfers, most of them unknown, who for one reason or another have not qualified for the major event being held the same week.

For a touring pro, having to qualify for a tournament can be an experience tantamount to undergoing the Spanish Inquisition. To be exempt from qualifying, therefore, is a state of blessedness for which a great many golfers would happily trade their souls, or at least the wife and kids. There are various ways to avoid the terrors of qualifying. Among them: Any player who wins the PGA Championship automatically qualifies for life to play in any regular tour event. Any player who wins a tour event, or a major championship for that matter, automatically qualifies to play in any tour event for the succeeding 12-month period. Any player who finishes among the leading 60 money-winners at the end of the year automatically qualifies to play throughout the following year. And finally, any player who makes the 36-hole cut at a tournament automatically qualifies to be an entrant for the next week's event. These various exemptions usually fill all but the ten or so of the starting places available each week. The poor player who hasn't received one must now compete in one of golf's toughest tests, the 18-hole pretournament qualifying round. It takes place on the Monday of the week the main event is being held. In it, some 100 to 300 contestants, are competing for those ten still-vacant spots. It can be a weekly nightmare for some players who travel the tour for weeks at a time without actually playing in anything but the Monday prequalifying. There are probably a large number of young players who seldom survive these prequalifying rounds who could, if somehow a magic wand were waved over their heads and thus exempt them, suddenly win a great deal of money. It's just that the Monday chore drives them nuts. Conversely, there are also a number of players so geared to winning one of these precious spots in the 18-hole round that they can't seem to survive 36 or 72 holes of competition after they have made it.

Though each tournament limits its field to about 150 starters, there are about 250 performers in this traveling circus who can be termed regulars. Unlike professionals in baseball, basketball, football, and ice hockey, the members of the pro tour must pay their own way. Taken all together, entry fees, caddies' fees, travel, and living expenses average out to about $400 a week, or about $18,000 a year for the player who sticks it out week

Arnie and "Ike"

Palmer with Nixon

Palmer and Agnew at Bay Hill

in, week out and doesn't try to live like King Farouk. Only 105 players
made enough in prize money alone during 1971 to cover this amount. The
leading 60 money-winners earned over $40,000 each in prize money; 25 of
them made in excess of $75,000; and the top three, Nicklaus, Trevino, and
Palmer, took in over $200,000 each in prize money. Nicklaus won a record
high of $320,542!

Prize money, however, is not the whole income story for the touring
pro. A golfer who has had any competitive luck at all, on the tour as a pro
or in his pretour days as an amateur, can usually count on affiliations with
an equipment manufacture, resort, or golf club, clothing endorsements,
and whatnot, to net a minimum of $5,000 to $10,000 for the rank-and-filer,
on up to hundreds of thousands of dollars for such top stars as Palmer,
Player, Nicklaus, and Trevino. To compete for these stakes, outdoors,
usually in fine weather and free of opponents intent on cutting him down
with a hockey stick, flying spikes, or a body-rocking block, surely makes it
worth the effort for even the luckless tourist who must undergo that Monday nightmare.

Prior to the Twenties, pro golf had its fixtures, if nothing that could
be called a touring circuit. The first of these was the United States Golf
Association's Championship, the U.S. Open, first played in 1895. The
Western Open joined the list in 1899, and later came the Metropolitan
Open in New York, the North and South Open at Pinehurst, North Carolina, and in 1916 the PGA Championship. The PGA was the only one of
these whose format called for head-to-head elimination match play. The
others were held at stroke play, as on today's tours. In addition, there were
a number of other small events, but these were of regional rather than national importance.

In those days tournaments were fine stuff for building a reputation,
but once you had earned one—like Walter Hagen and Long Jim Barnes—
exhibitions and honest-to-goodness club jobs provided the real money. Thus
the professionals of golf spent their summers in the North and their winters
in California or the South. The stars of that era, Hagen and Barnes, Jock
Hutchison, Tommy McNamara, Alex Smith, et al., would often find themselves all together down in Florida and they'd get up an informal little
tournament. An embryonic tour had formed.

"There was only one prize and it went to the winner," Barnes has recalled. "Often it was just a huge, wedding-size cake put up by one of the
resort hotels."

But although there might have been only a cake at stake, the crowds
turned out to watch these players, and so it began to occur to various resort
promoters and savvy young chamber of commerce executives that for a
couple of thousand dollars in prize money it might be possible to finance
the kind of tournament that would create datelines and therefore attract interest in newspapers coast to coast. By late winter of 1921, three tourna-

ments were held in Florida and paid a total of $8,545 in prize money. Texas got the word by 1922, and so the Texas Open started its long and always fascinating history on the Brackenridge Park public course in San Antonio, paying what was then reckoned as a pretty fabulous purse of $5,000. (Strangely enough, 23 years later, the Texas Open was still offering the same $5,000 purse.)

Tournaments began turning up on the West Coast, in Sacramento and in San Diego, and then the first of a long line of Los Angeles Opens, which continues vigorously into the present day, was played in 1926. During the mid-Twenties a rather intriguing idea, a professional golf league, came into being in Florida. Its roster included a large number of outstanding players, including seven U.S. Open champions. Two-man teams, representing various Florida cities and resort developments, competed against each other on a home-and-home basis. Walter Hagen and Joe Kirkwood played for the Pasadena Estates; Jim Barnes and Freddie McLeod for Temple Terrace, in Tampa; Gene Sarazen and Leo Diegel for Hollywood; Cyril Walker and Eddie Loos for Winter Haven; Johnny Farrell and Bobby Cruickshank for Tampa; Tommy Kerrigan and Dow George for Orlando; and Wild Bill Mehlhorn and Tommy Armour for Miami. It is fascinating to conjecture how such a league might have flourished and developed under suitable conditions, but the end of the Florida real estate boom meant the end of the league as well. A number of tournaments that had sprung up during the booming Twenties also melted away. Obviously the circuit concept of professional golf had reached a critical stage. If it was to survive, it would have to be on a controlled, organized basis rather than on the week-to-week whims of real estate and resort promoters.

Two things happened in that first Depression year of 1930 to serve this purpose. The St. Paul Junior Chamber of Commerce raised $10,000 in order to put on a tournament to follow the U.S. Open, which was played at nearby Hopkins, and so the summer division of the tournament circuit came into being. Next, the PGA hired a Chicago sports writer, Francis Powers, to serve as full-time tournament manager, and the tour, as a hardcore, organized entity, was born. Powers' task seemed enormous, but it was pretty clear cut what he needed to do: line up sponsors who would not be here today and gone tomorrow, and be an advance man who would promote and publicize the tour by the time the players came to town. All this must have proved just too Herculean a chore even for someone so staunchly named. In a short time Powers was replaced by one of golf's most indefatigable and imaginative promotors and publicists, Robert Harlow.

For many years Bob Harlow, formerly a newspaper man, had been Walter Hagen's business manager. In that role he had been exceptionally astute at channeling The Haig's flamboyant personality and almost magical skills as a golfer into an abundant flow of dollars and publicity. Harlow not only organized the rigorous series of exhibition matches that Hagen played year after year, all over the U.S. and all around the world, but also transformed them into a goldmine of publicity as well. As the PGA tournament manager, Harlow worked out how-to-do-it books for tournament sponsors, past performance charts on the players, and ready-made releases on the players and the tournaments for the press. It took a genius like Harlow to pull it off. The mid-Thirties, for reasons that went beyond the economic state of the nation, was not an easy time in which to trumpet the glories of the pro tour. Most of the heroes of the Golden Age—Jones, Hagen, Barnes, Sarazen, Armour—had either retired or were playing very little competitive tournament golf. Aside from Jimmy Thomson, whose chief thing was that he could hit a golf ball a mile, exciting personalities were not present in abundance. Its stars were Horton Smith, the Masters Champion of 1934 and '36, gifted with imposing good looks and a deluxe putting touch, but little charisma; Ralph Guhldahl, the archetype of dull consistency; Henry Picard, a tall, quiet Yankee from Massachusetts; Byron Nelson, who had not yet hit his period of greatness; blond Craig Wood, whose strong suit was erratic brilliance; Dick Metz, Denny Shute, Johnny Revolta, Jug McSpaden, Harry Cooper, Ray Mangrum, Jimmy Hines, Ky Laffoon, and Ed Dudley. These were fine golfers all, some of them very distinguished performers, but among this lot there could be found very little of the kind of drama, excitement, and color that would cause a press agent to do joyful handstands.

What the tour of the mid-Thirties did have going for it, however, was a high degree of technical efficiency. This was the era of the big scoring breakthrough. Suddenly scores in the 60s became commonplace, scores in the 70s were considered disasters, a justifiable cause for tantrums and club-throwing. The chief reason for this was that the clubs, the balls, and the courses they were used on had been dramatically improved. New developments in agronomy provided fairways and greens that were lush and healthy. New mowing equipment made it possible to trim the fairways and greens so that they were more consistently clean and smooth.

So far as equipment was concerned, a major assist was made by the substitution of steel for wood in the club shaft. This innovation was legalized for use in the U.S. by the U.S. Golf Association in 1924, by the Royal and Ancient for the rest of the world in 1930, just about the time it had reached its final stages of development. The wooden shafts tended to bend and twist if the club was swung too hard and the clubhead thus wrenched off line. To make sure he kept the ball in play, a golfer, therefore, had to concentrate on a smooth, rhythmic swing and be quite satisfied with a drive that sailed out no more than 225 yards. With the advent of steel, the twisting of the shaft and clubhead during the swing was greatly reduced and a golfer could lash at the ball with confidence. In addition, the use of steel shafts made it possible for manufacturers to produce evenly matched sets in which every club in the bag, from driver to pitching wedge, would produce the same balance, whippiness, and feel. Up until 1937, when the rules specified that a player could carry no more than 14 clubs, golf became an armament race. It was not unusual for some players, or rather their caddies, to carry up to 30 clubs, one for every conceivable situation.

Perhaps the most useful of all these innovative clubs was the sand wedge, the club used to explode a ball from a trap. This implement had a heavy, rounded flange across its sole which, when swung into the sand beneath a golf ball, would not knife straight down as did the more conventional, sharp-edged irons. It would tend to bounce back up instead and toss the ball toward the cup on a pillow of sand. Once the use of the sand blaster had been mastered, most skilled professionals fancied their chances at getting down in two strokes from a sand trap much more highly than they did trying to accomplish the same feat out of high grass.

Then, of course, there was the ball. Through the use of hypodermic devices it was possible to increase the internal compression of a golf ball far beyond anything that had been previously achieved. When badly struck by a duffer, a high-compression golf ball sounds and feels like a steel ball bearing; but when smashed cleanly by an efficient professional, it becomes a ballistic missile. The result was that, swinging steel-shafted clubs at this hopped-up, lively ball, a slugger like Jimmy Thomson could consistently send his drives hurtling 280 yards. Practically every pro on the tour, with the exception of tiny Paul Runyan, who had to work wonders with his long irons and fairway woods, was capable of zeroing in on almost any par-4 hole an architect might devise with nothing more than a drive and a middle or short iron. Even long par 5s suddenly came within range of two well-struck shots. Golf was no longer a game in which pars would suffice. You needed birdies to win and lots of them.

This pressure to make birdies quite logically placed a great deal of emphasis on the art of holing putts. It was no good hitting the ball stiff to the flagstick if you consistently blew the 10-footers. So, players suddenly were spending as much time on the practice putting green as out on the course or on the practice tee. The tourists became highly efficient at tapping ball into hole. In the Thirties perhaps the best of all was Horton Smith. He would spend hours on the practice green, not working on the line, but on developing a sound, smooth stroke. Smith's theory was that you hung on to the putter with your left hand, but you really hit the ball with your right hand. This was where the touch and feel for distance came from. In his later years Smith, who eventually served as the head professional at the Country Club of Detroit, was responsible for curing the putting jitters of many touring pros of the Fifties and Sixties.

Despite the absence of glamorous personalities, the new low scoring was exciting and the tour was getting solidly on its feet. The leading money winner could count on about $7,000, not bad reimbursement from a tournament calendar that seldom went over 12 to 15 events. A reasonably good year would net over $5,000, and just so-so results would probably yield something around $2,500. This was good money for those Depression years, and the pros would add to it by the salary and other fringe income they earned at their home clubs, plus bonuses paid them by equipment manufacturers. When the economy of the country began to show a little life in 1936, the players on the tour and those administering it could look to the future with more than a little optimism.

What happened to put the tour over the top as a major business enterprise was the arrival on the scene in 1937 of two of golf's unique characters: Sam Snead, straight from the hills of Virginia, and Fred Corcoran, a promotional genius from the staid environs of Boston.

Corcoran got there first, stepping smack into the middle of the kind of administrative dogfight that has periodically marked the tour's history. In 1936 the chairman of the PGA tournament committee was the great putter, Horton Smith, a man of strong purpose and rigid character. Smith's responsibility was to represent the interests of the players. Harlow, of course, was the tournament manager at that time. Harlow and Smith were very close friends. This made their work on the tour relatively simple, but it also created a belief among many of the touring pros that their tour was being operated for the benefit of the few, that the supporting artists had very little to say about how it was conducted. Adding to the general tone of suspicion concerning how Harlow was doing his job was the fact that Harlow was a man who wore a great many golf caps. He was Walter Hagen's business manager. He was also the promoter who organized exhibition tours for Hagen, Smith, Johnny Farrell, Joe Kirkwood, Paul Runyan, and Ed Dudley. He was a golf writer who authored a syndicated column that appeared in newspapers throughout the land. Harlow spread himself pretty thin, and a possible conflict of interest was involved here.

So in 1936 George Jacobus, head pro at the Ridgewood Country Club in New Jersey, but more significantly President of the PGA, decided a change was in the cards. He promptly fired Harlow as tournament manager and Smith as chairman of the tournament committee, and brought in Corcoran, a round-faced Irishman with a sense of press agentry and remarkable gifts as a raconteur. Up until 1936 Corcoran had been employed by the Massachusetts Golf Association to perform a number of duties. He did them so well that in November of that year Richard Tufts, President of Pinehurst, Inc., in North Carolina, asked him to come down for a couple of weeks to help with the press and run the scoreboard at the PGA Championship, which Pinehurst was hosting. Corcoran jumped at the invitation because he liked to be where the action was.

There was plenty of action in Pinehurst that autumn. Denny Shute won the first of two consecutive titles, defeating Horton Smith, 3 and 2, Bill Mehlhorn, one up, and Jimmy Thomson, 3 and 2, in his last three matches. Corcoran was offered Harlow's job in a scene that might have been taken from a Neil Simon farce. While Jacobus huddled with Corcoran on a locker room bench, there was Harlow, peering from around the corner of a row of lockers, trying to spell out the direction negotiations were taking. They moved quickly. Corcoran was offered $5,000 a year salary and $5 per day expense money. After clearing the move by telephone with his employer, the Massachusetts Golf Association, Corcoran accepted.

Harlow and Smith, however, proved most reluctant to step aside. When he returned home to Boston, Corcoran received a rather peculiar letter in which Harlow offered Corcoran a job on the tournament bureau staff as his assistant for a salary of $75 a week and $5 a day expense money. "Bob Harlow has no authority to offer you anything," Jacobus told Corcoran. "We have already terminated his services."

Then when Corcoran arrived at the Los Angeles Open in January of 1937 to assume his duties, Smith cornered him in the restaurant at Griffith Park, where the Open was being held. He challenged Corcoran's background and his ability to do the job. He hinted darkly that there were ways of riding him out should that be necessary. Several of the equipment managers, the Boston Irishman was advised, helped finance the pro tour through an annual contribution of $25,000. Smith claimed to have much influence with the men who put up this money and could therefore hasten Corcoran's departure.

"Forget Smith," Jacobus said. "He's not even on the tournament committee any longer and so doesn't have a thing to say about how it's operated." Jacobus also told Corcoran that the PGA was now in very sound financial shape and could even refuse backing from the equipment people should they prove arrogant and domineering.

Many of the touring pros still maintained strong feelings of loyalty for Harlow, and a petition was circulated calling for his reinstatement as tournament manager. In the end it was the equipment manufacturers who came to the new man's rescue. Fearful that politicking, bickering, and internal dissension might splatter mud all over the beautiful showcase for their wares, they finally ordered their contract players to cease and desist. The petition was quashed, Harlow remained out and Corcoran in.

Corcoran was a lively, bumptious, energetic salesman who had little difficulty imparting his enthusiasm for the golf tour as a fine, profitable promotion to chambers of commerce and other civic groups. He also pointed out that when some 75 to 100 golf pros came to town they would probably spend on food, lodging, and so on about twice what they took away in prize money. A nice fringe benefit for sponsors.

Corcoran was also a master at handling the press, which he had to be, considering the drab, colorless group that were playing the tour when he moved into the job as its manager. He was an inexhaustable source of statistics, quotes, and anecdotes about the players. Newspaper coverage improved, the crowds grew in size, the sponsors were happy and upped the purses. In 1936 the purse total for 22 tournaments amounted to $100,000. By 1938 Corcoran had that figure up to $160,000. Total prize money leveled out after that, until it jumped up again directly after the war, but the tour became a very sound financial proposition. When he first became tournament manager, Corcoran traveled with a check made out by the PGA for $3,000 to help guarantee the prize money at each stop. Within a few weeks he was able to send the check back to PGA headquarters in Chicago because the sponsors, noting the steady rise in the size of their galleries and their national press coverage, were now happy to assume this hardly risky burden themselves.

But perhaps the most notable single event so far as exciting national interest in the pro tour is concerned was the arrival of a drawling, athletically gifted, twenty-four-year-old native of the Virginia mountains, Sam Snead. He brought with him one of the most beautiful golf swings of all time and a colorful, likable personality, and he certainly made Corcoran's job a great deal easier. Snead had been a high school football, basketball, and baseball star in Hot Springs who took up golf in his senior year because he thought it would help speed the recovery of a left hand injured in a football game. Soon golf dominated young Snead's life. After graduation in 1933 he worked as a general handyman and assistant pro at a couple of courses in his home town and then was lured away by the Greenbrier resort hotel in White Sulphur Springs, West Virginia. As a player, Snead had a smooth, fluid, rhythmic swing that could propel a golf ball immense distances, an aesthetic delight. In 1936 he won both the West Virginia Open and the West Virginia PGA titles and was thus encouraged to take a fling at one of the events on the big-time pro tour. He chose the Hershey Open.

Snead's debut among the touring pros was a notable one. He showed up for his first practice round at the Hershey Country Club wearing a long-sleeved white shirt and a pair of baggy trousers and with only eight cheap golf clubs carried in a scuffed, antique golf bag. On the first tee lounged four nattily attired pros who, after a look at Snead, must have figured he was either a refugee from a nearby chocolate warehouse or a seasoned golf hustler in disguise. One of them, George Fazio, invited Snead to make it a fivesome. The young man accepted and then sliced his first two drives into a chocolate factory off the course to the right and topped his third into a pond right in front of the green. At that point Snead would have been happy to crawl back into the clubhouse on his hands and knees, but after his four playing partners hit their drives well down the middle, Fazio told Snead to forget the first three, relax, and hit another. Snead did relax and did hit another drive—right onto the middle of the green 345 yards away.

That gigantic drive set the stage. He was on the back edge of the 600-yard 3rd hole in two shots, went on to score a 67 (discounting the first three disastrous tee shots) for his practice round, and in the tournament proper finished sixth. It was a strong enough omen to convince the Dunlop Company to sign Snead up to play their clubs and balls—which meant free equipment and a check for $500—and for the Greenbrier to chip in with additional financial help to enable their golf shop assistant to take a full swing at the pro circuit. After mediocre showings in the Miami-Biltmore and Nassau Opens in Florida, Snead headed for California and the 1937 tour opener at Los Angeles in January.

In those days it was a common practice for players who customarily maintained only a narrow margin between money coming in from winnings and money going out for expenses to team up with buddies in the same economic situation. The routine was to share expenses and share all earnings. Snead teamed with Johnny Bulla, a big twenty-two-year-old tour rookie from Newell, West Virginia, and the two drove to Los Angeles in Bulla's car. A sixth-place finish by Snead in the Los Angeles Open was nice, but it barely cleared expenses for the two rookies. Then on the way to the Oakland Open the car, with Bulla at the wheel, was involved in a three-way smash-up. The subsequent repair bill took $140 out of their diminishing kitty, and it looked as if at least one of the two would have to do something brilliant in the Oakland Open, where first prize was $1,200, or incur financial disaster for the pair. The result was brilliant, not just for Sam Snead but the pro tour as well.

Bulla was never in contention, but Snead—so little known at the time that on the scoreboard his name had been spelled S-n-e-e-d—started out with rounds of 69 and 65. What few spectators Snead attracted were vividly impressed by the long, soaring tee shots propelled with such graceful ease. Another Bobby Jones, but longer. He shot 69 during the third round and tied for the 54-hole lead with Johnny Revolta and Ralph Guldahl, but it wasn't until the 16th hole of the final round that Snead began suddenly to attract the kind of awed attention he would inspire for the rest of his golfing career. At that point Snead needed just three pars to finish with a 67, a tournament total of 270, and apparent victory. The word had spread that an unknown rookie from the hills of Virginia was out on the course with a chance to beat the established pros, and, as Snead recalls, thousands of people swarmed over to the 16th hole to watch him finish. Rattled by the jostling mobs, he bogeyed the 16th. Recovering his composure, Snead parred the 17th, a tough par 3, and then finished up with a flourish, birdying the par-5 18th hole to beat Ralph Guldahl by two shots. The effect on the tour was electrifying. Tournament sponsors began phoning Corcoran before he could even get out of town, clamoring for guarantees that the exciting newcomer, this long-hitting hillbilly with the fluid swing, would be present for their event. The story and Snead's picture appeared in newspapers all over the country. Corcoran showed Snead a copy of the *New York Times*, which reported Snead's victory at Oakland and provided a picture of the winner.

"How come they've got my picture in New York?" Snead asked, puzzled, or so the story goes. "I ain't ever been to New York."

When Snead was approached by Walter Hagen's old touring partner, Joe Kirkwood, about arranging an exhibition swing, Corcoran, alarmed, was once again on the phone to Jacobus, explaining that it seemed the tour might be losing its biggest box office magnet. "Sign yourself up as his business manager," said Jacobus. Corcoran did, drafting an agreement which named Corcoran as Snead's sole representative for the arrangement of exhibitions and other matters.

Staying on the tour full time proved to be a successful venture for both Snead and the tour. He won the Bing Crosby Pro-Am, shortened by rain to only 18 holes; won the St. Paul Open; won the Miami and Nassau Opens, in which he had played so poorly the year before; finished second by 2 shots to Ralph Guldahl in the U.S. Open; earned a place on the Ryder Cup team for the biennial matches with the pros from Great Britain; and finished out the year as third leading money-winner behind Harry Cooper with a total of $10,244. Snead's dramatic entry was a major step in making professional tournament golf a financial success. The emergence of other great golfers and intriguing personalities—Ben Hogan, Byron Nelson, and Jimmy Demaret, that cheerful Texan clotheshorse—solidified that successful position.

Coincidentally, the same Oakland tournament that vaulted Snead, and indirectly the pro tour itself, into national prominence was also responsible a year later for putting Ben Hogan in business as a tournament player. With financial help from Marvin Leonard, a millionaire Fort Worth department store owner, Hogan had first tackled the winter tour in 1935. He had started on the West Coast, but ran out of money by the time the tour had made it across the country to New Orleans. He quit, returned home to Fort Worth, and once again took up steady employment as a club pro. He also got married. Having saved $1,400, Hogan and his new wife, Valerie, tried the tour again, starting out late in 1937. The money went fast —for a car, for traveling expenses, for food and lodging for two—and by the time the Hogans reached Oakland in January, 1938, they were down to $86. To add to their woes, the Hogans came out of the Leamington Hotel in Oakland one morning to retrieve their car from the parking lot across the street and found that all four tires had been deftly removed by thieves.

What kept Hogan on the tour after that, and paved the way for his great career as a golfer, was a psychological boost from Henry Picard. For some years a regular winner on the tour, Picard had a lean, leathery face and a soft heart. He had helped many young players with advice, and with financial help or assurances of it. At Oakland he told Hogan not to worry, that if he needed a loan it would be forthcoming from Picard. It never was needed. Playing under considerably less pressure now, Hogan earned a check for $386. He played steadily enough for the rest of the year to emerge as the tour's 15th leading money-winner with $4,150, enough to keep a thrifty golfer and his wife going. In 1939 he moved up to seventh money-winner at $5,600.

In 1940 Hogan won his first tournament, plus three others, and on earnings of $10,655 became the tour's top money-winner. Hogan did not win his first major championship, the PGA, until 1946, but week to week he dominated the winner's circle. He was the leading money-winner again in 1941 and '42, amassing 11 more tournament titles during that span. Service as a lieutenant in the U.S. Army kept Hogan's clubs in the closet during 1943 and most of '44, and Byron Nelson's incredible string of victories shut the door on virtually everyone in 1945. Hogan's season of 1946, however, was very close to being just as remarkable as Nelson's of '45. He won 13 tournaments and led all money-earners with $42,556. It is astonishing to consider how much Hogan accomplished before winning his first major championship. By mid-1946 he had won 29 tournament titles, and had shared the tour's top billing with only Snead and Nelson. Yet his greatest years, the era in which he won the British Open, two PGA's, two Masters, and a record-tying four U.S. Opens, still lay ahead.

Despite the fact that they were both born in the same year, 1912, and both entered golf at the same time and in the same way, as caddies at the Glen Garden club in Fort Worth, the careers of Byron Nelson and Ben Hogan present one of the strangest contrasts in the history of sport. Nelson had won all five of his major championships, the Masters in 1937 and '42, the U.S. Open in 1939, the PGA in 1940 and '45, before Hogan had even won his first. By the time Hogan was ready to move into his glorious prime as a golfer, Nelson had had enough. At the conclusion of the 1946 campaign Nelson, at the age of thirty-five, retired to his cattle ranch in Texas.

Nelson was an extremely solid and accurate if not overlong or flamboyant golfer who first appeared on the tour in 1935. His first tournament victory, in the Metropolitan Open, came in 1936. In 1937 he won the Masters, as well as two other events, and from then on was always a leading figure in both the major championships and on the tour. There can be no greater proof of his deadly consistency than the fact that through the years of his prime he finished in the money at 113 consecutive tournaments, a mark that never has been and never will be approached.

The tour was a wartime casualty during 1943, only four genuine events being held, but it was back in full stride, with 22 tournaments, the following season. The lineups were relatively weak, however, with top players like Snead in the Navy and Hogan in the Army. Nelson, who had been exempted from military service because of hemophilia, had a field day. He won six of the year's 22 events and collected a pot of $37,968 in war bonds, which were being used in lieu of hard cash in those days. So far as the sheer amassing of victories is concerned, no golfer is ever likely to repeat the record Nelson compiled the next year, 1945, winning (or tying for first place) in 16 tournaments, including the Phoenix Open with a 10-under-par 274; the PGA, where he was 37 under par for 204 holes, and the Atlanta with a 13-under-par 263. He was second or tied for second in seven other tournaments. That was 16 first-place finishes and 7 seconds out of 28 tournaments in which he competed.

Nelson's task was made considerably easier by the fact that Hogan was finishing up his Army service and was not able to join the tour until late August. How Hogan, never a particularly close friend of Nelson's, must have steamed to remain in uniform while his chief rival reaped all that easy wartime wealth and glory! Hogan returned to full-time action with something of a vengeance, however, winning five of the last 16 tournaments on the tour and getting up to third on the money list with over $26,000 in war bond winnings. In addition, Snead broke an arm, missed six mid-summer tournaments, and never did really settle back into the groove that had seen him win five events prior to the accident. But even considering the slightly below-standard quality of the opposition, Nelson's record in 1945 is extraordinary: $63,336 in war bonds won, victory in 16 out of 28 tournaments, a streak of 11 wins in a row, a season's scoring average of 68.33 per round, approximately 320 strokes under par. Compare this with Hogan's per-round stroke average of 69.91 and Snead's of 70.41.

With results like that it seems that Nelson couldn't have been suffering from anything much, but he was: bad nerves.

"Putting became a nightmare for me," he says. "I would actually get nauseated over a 3-foot putt."

Nelson and his nerves stuck it out for one more year—a good one in which he won five tournaments—and then he retired, leaving the field to Snead and Hogan.

Until Nelson's great year of 1945, the tour had been digging in as a solid fixture on the year's sporting calendar, but its phenomenal growth did not really begin until after the war. Through 1944 the schedule contained usually no more than about 20 or so official events, with an annual purse that never topped $170,000. There were a few exceptions, but in 1944, for instance, most events paid a purse of between $5,000 and $10,000. The prize-money breakdown for a $5,000 tournament would start at $1,000 for first, $750 for second, $550 for third, and so on down to $20 for 20th place. A $10,000 event would generally pay about $2,400 to the winner, fall off to $1,600 for the runner-up, and on down to $50 for 20th place. Obviously there was no strict percentage formula. Comparisons with today's prize-money breakdown would reveal not much more than the fact that the average payoff is about 10 to 20 times as much. Generally the winner gets about 15 percent of the purse and the runner-up 8 percent.

As it did for sport in general, the coming of World War II put a temporary check on the tour's growth. But until the rubber for golf balls, the steel for shafts, and the athletic young men who could swing one to hit the other became scarce, tour manager Corcoran was able to keep building. With the presence of Snead, and subsequently Hogan and Nelson, to provide the excitement, Freddie the Cork had plenty of leverage with which to increase the number of tournaments on the tour and increase the prize money as well. Exhibitions drained off less of his talent because most of the big names had lucrative contracts with equipment companies and the equipment companies wanted their boys participating. Tournament victories were what sold balls and clubs, while lengthy exhibition tours netted money for the individual player, but hardly did much for the greater glory of, say, the Wilson Sporting Goods Company.

In the years just before and during World War II, sponsors started to come from outside the circle of civic groups, resort promoters, and chambers of commerce. The Goodall Round-Robin, sponsored by the Palm Beach Clothing Company of New York was one that joined the schedule. The Round-Robin was also a fresh diversion from the steady, grinding diet of 72-hole stroke-play affairs. Several minor changes were made through the years, but the Round-Robin format ultimately evolved into a 90-hole tournament requiring a limited field of 16 invitees. The players were sent out in foursomes that were rearranged for each round so that eventually every player had competed in a foursome with every other player. The winner was determined, not by who scored lowest for 90 holes, but by the total of his superiority each round over the other members of his foursome. The Round-Robin eventually became a victim of the pro tour's booming success in the postwar era. Sponsors were standing in line to get on the schedule, and so the feeling among the bulk of the touring pros, those who would not be included in any select list of 16, was negative to the idea of sitting around on their hands while the stars enjoyed a payoff. It was easy to get a sponsor to *replace* the Round-Robin, not so easy to get one who'd put on a satellite tournament the same week as the Round-Robin. Things were good, but not yet that good. The Round-Robin dropped off the tour after the 1957 season.

The same fate was also suffered by a number of other limited-field invitational specials, such as the Miami and Inverness Four-Ball tournaments.

In 1945, official prize money jumped from the $140,000 that had been available in '44 to $435,000, an average it was to maintain for ten seasons. The big reason was George S. May, an eccentric, imaginative millionaire from Chicago who had made his fortune in the management consulting business and who owned the Tam O'Shanter golf club in suburban Niles. He was to become the P. T. Barnum of golfing showmanship. As Corcoran stood behind the 18th green at Winged Foot, outside New York, during the 1940 U.S. Amateur championship, a May employee sidled up to him and said, "My boss will put up more money for one tournament than you play for on the whole circuit."

"Talk like that could always hold my attention," Corcoran said, and that evening he met with May in a room at the Commodore Hotel in mid-town New York to get May's boast down on paper. May's Tam O'Shanter Open went on the schedule the following year, and though the coming of the war postponed the really gigantic purses, by 1941 the total payoff reached $30,100. This was at a time when the next-richest tournament, the Philadelphia Inquirer Open, was paying $17,500. Byron Nelson (who else?) won the first really rich first-place purse, collecting war bonds worth $13,462. In 1945 May upped his purse to a phenomenal $60,000 and again Nelson won, beating Hogan by 11 shots and earning $13,600 in war bonds. Over the next few years May performed some interesting experiments. He held his 72-hole stroke-play tournament as usual, but in 1946, '47, and '48 sponsored 36- and 54-hole spectaculars in which a field limited to four or eight professionals competed on a winner-take-all basis for a jackpot that ranged from $5,000 to $10,000. The nonwinners would collect a very generous check for expenses.

By the Fifties May had developed a two-week golfing circus. For the first time a player could be identified through a number worn by his caddy. The pros refused to tee off when it was suggested *they* wear the numbers. Music blared from the clubhouse. The prize money was unreal and the crowds swarmed in. During the first week, usually in the heat of mid-August, the All-American Open was held at Tam O'Shanter. This event started with a total purse of $15,000 and rose to $25,000 in 1952. Not only pros played in the tournament, but men and women amateurs as well.

The second week was filled by the World Championship of Golf, again a 72-hole stroke-play event, but with an enormous purse and a field of international talent. It started as a $35,000 tournament with a first prize of $10,000 in 1949, the year Johnny Palmer won, defeating Jimmy Demaret, 68 to 70, in an 18-hole playoff. In 1950 the World, as it came to be known, put up a purse of $50,000, with $11,000 to the winner (Henry Ransom), and in 1952 paid a total purse of $75,000, with a first prize of $25,000 going to winner Julius Boros. Boros was also offered a contract to play a promotional tour of 25 exhibitions for May at $1,000 per exhibition.

The 1953 World provided golf's first television spectacular. The final round was televised nationally, and so millions of viewers saw Chandler Harper finish with a 279 and apparently win the $25,000 first prize and the lucrative exhibition contract. The only player with even a slight chance to catch him was Lew Worsham, still out on the course. On the final hole, a long par 4, Worsham's drive left him 100 yards from the flagstick, and he needed to get down in two shots just to tie. Worsham then hit the wedge heard virtually around the world. It flew onto the green and bounced right into the hole before a nation of popeyed viewers. The shot sank Harper to second-place money of $10,000 and in an instant had taken $40,000 out of his pocket and put it into Lew's. If this was golf, the millions of viewers must have thought, let's see more of it.

Given this impetus, May shoved the World's prize money up to $100,000 in 1954, giving the winner $50,000 and the runner-up $15,000. The exhibition contract for the winner was increased to $50,000. With this kind of payoff, the World winners—Boros in '52, Worsham in '53, Bob Toski in '54 (the first player to hit the $50,000 jackpot), Boros again in '55, Ted Kroll in '56, and finally Dick Mayer in '57—always finished the year as the leading money-winner as well, usually by a very substantial margin.

May was the forerunner of the big-money sponsors, but he also brought to the U.S. tour its first real savoring of golf at the highest international level. Thanks to May's tournaments, American galleries, as they toiled along the fairways at Tam O'Shanter in the midsummer heat, were able to get an early look at such renowned internationalists as Bobby Locke, Harold Henning, and Gary Player of South Africa; Norman Von Nida, Peter Thomson, Kel Nagle, and Bruce Crampton of Australia; Roberto de Vicenzo (the Latin Snead), Antonio Cerda, and Leopoldo Ruiz of Argentina; Mario Gonzales of Brazil; Stan Leonard and Al Balding of Canada; Pete Nakamura of Japan; Ugo Grappasonni and Alfonso Angelini of Italy; Flory Van Donck, the suave Belgian; Eric Brown, Dai Rees, Max Faulkner, and Dave Thomas of Great Britain; Angel Miguel of Spain, as well as lesser-known players from Europe, South America, and Asia. Considering his contributions to the pro tour, both economic and international, it was not exactly a stirring testimony to the shrewdness of the PGA Tournament Committee that after his 1957 extravaganza May became embroiled in a quarrel with the PGA over dates, purse division, and administrative jurisdiction, and his two tournaments were taken off the tour.

Of the foreign players who appeared in the May tournaments in those days, the most successful and most intriguing was South Africa's Locke. He had two brilliant years in 1947 and 1948 and, until his countryman, Gary Player, who joined the U.S. tour in 1957, started to win consistently in 1961, no foreigner did so well on U.S. soil as the golfer who later gained fame by winning four British Opens. Locke was a plump-faced, bandy-legged man who played in knee socks, plus fours, and a snap-brim wool cap. He hit the ball with a high, sharp-breaking hook that looked almost like the flight of a boomerang and he was a devastating putter. Locke would take the blade of his putter back well inside the line to the hole and then rap the ball at the target with a great deal of initial counterclockwise spin. It was said that he hooked his putts almost as sharply as he did the rest of his shots. Locke was not exactly a popular figure among his fellow tourists. They disliked him for winning so many U.S. dollars, thus taking them out of the pockets of the needy homebred. They disliked him, perhaps even more intensely, for being such a marvelous putter.

Locke first joined the U.S. tour in the spring of 1947, finishing 14th at the Masters. At the very next tournament, a month later in Houston, Locke was the winner by 5 shots over Ellsworth Vines, the old tennis star, and Johnny Palmer. In the following three weeks he tied for third at the Colonial in Fort Worth, and then won the Philadelphia Inquirer Open, and the Goodall Round-Robin in New York. Soon after, he tied for third, behind Lew Worsham and Sam Snead, at the U.S. Open in St. Louis, and three weeks later won the $7,000 first prize at May's All-American, beating Porky Oliver in a playoff. Locke finished out his first year on the U.S. tour by winning the Canadian Open and the Columbus Invitational, posting high finishes at the Western Open in Salt Lake City, the Denver Open, and the Reading, Pennsylvania, Open. When prize money for the year was added up, Locke was second on the list with a sizable total of $24,326 behind only leader Jimmy Demaret's $27,937.

Locke was back again in 1948 and had another good year. He was fourth on the money list with a total of $20,010, won the Phoenix Open, and finished second four times, but saved his most humiliating blow to the pride of the American pro tourists for the Chicago Victory Open. Locke started out with a 65, which put him in first by 2 shots over Dick Metz. Another 65 the following day and Locke then led at the halfway mark by 9 shots over Clayton Heafner. On the third day Locke "blew" to a 70, but nonetheless increased his lead, over Skip Alexander, Johnny Bulla, and Lloyd Mangrum, bunched in second place, to 13 shots. Locke finished up with a zippy 66 for a tournament total of 266.

The battle for a distant second wound up in the hands of Ellsworth Vines, who had also finished with a 66, for a four-round total of 282. It was as if Locke was playing an entirely different golf course. His winning margin of 16 shots was a record for the pro tour that still stands. Locke played the U.S. tour again in 1949 and won the Goodall Round-Robin for the second time, but entered only a few other events and placed well down on the money list. He was back just long enough in 1950 to win his second All-American at Tam O'Shanter, but in the following years found it easier and just as profitable to play elsewhere and made only rare appearances in the U.S. His absence was lamented, perhaps, by the American galleries, but hardly by the touring pros.

So far as dramatic events and personalities were concerned, the years immediately after the cessation of Locke's visits were relatively dull ones on the tour, marked only by Ben Hogan's courageous return to action at the 1950 Los Angeles Open. The previous January, after tying for first at the Phoenix Open and then losing a playoff to Jimmy Demaret, Hogan had been badly smashed up in the collision of his car with an oncoming bus. The immediate question as he lay in the hospital was whether Hogan would just stay alive, and then whether Hogan would be able to walk again. Whether or not he could ever play golf again was hardly of serious concern. Yet there he was teeing up at Los Angeles after months of what for

Hogan had always provided the most effective spiritual and physical therapy, the practice tee.

The course was the Riviera Country Club, venue for Hogan's first U.S. Open triumph in 1948, and the occasion therefore reeked of drama and nostalgia. Hogan opened with a 73, considered excellent under the circumstances, but still 5 shots behind leader Ed Furgol. From then on Hogan played Riviera as he had in 1948 when he had set an Open scoring record of 276. Now in 1950 he finished with three 69s and thus tied Sam Snead for first. The immediate comeback story did not have a fairy-tale ending: Snead shot 72 to Hogan's 76 and won. The real fairy-tale finish came later. Hogan's career as a touring regular, however, had come to an end in that automobile accident. Continually stiff and in pain from his injuries, Hogan appeared only at the Open and the Masters and very rarely at a tour event.

After 1950, when he was the tour's leading money-winner, Snead, too, seldom showed up on the tour. He made too much money giving private playing lessons at the Greenbrier. So the leading players of the day, at least on a week-to-week basis, were relatively unexciting. They were thoroughly proficient, but they lacked glamour. The best were golfers like Lloyd Mangrum, who wore a croupier's thin mustache, the leading money-winner of 1951; Jim Ferrier, a lean, stoop-shouldered transplant from Australia, who won three straight tournaments in 1951; Dr. Cary Middlecoff, once a Memphis dentist, so intense he stood over the ball for agonizing minutes before he hit it as if he were trying to extract a molar, but who won the U.S. Open in 1949 and was to win it again in 1956; Jack Burke, the ruddy-faced son of a Texas pro of an earlier era, a pleasant, boyish-looking, if not exciting, competitor; Julius Boros, the 1952 Open Champion, a golfer so relaxed he appeared to be half asleep while playing; Doug Ford, the swarthy New Yorker, who specialized in the wedge and putter and played so quickly he seemed as much concerned about getting around in the fewest possible minutes as in the fewest possible strokes; Ted Kroll, a tough, stocky ex–Army sergeant; Lew Worsham, who had won the U.S. Open in 1947 and whose famous wedge shot had won the Tam O'Shanter World six years later; Bob Toski and Jerry Barber, the tiny Paul Runyans of their time; and, finally, Marty Furgol and Chandler Harper, two players who performed with all the zest and gusto of an undertaker at work in his funeral parlor.

For spectators, the major championships were where you found the colorful personalities, that was where the action was. The tour was almost faceless, and, despite the boom that was taking place in sport after the end of the war, its purses showed that it was marking time. In the nine years that followed the big jump from $140,000 to $435,000 in annual prize money that had occurred in 1945, total purses rose comparatively little. In 1954 the amount for the year reached only $600,000, and of this $125,000 was the transfusion injected by George May at his two-week August extravaganza. Fortunately, an exciting era was about to unroll.

Among the new leading figures were Arnold Palmer, twenty-five, the muscular U.S. Amateur champion of the year before, now making his debut as a touring professional; Mike Souchak, twenty-eight, a burly, long-hitting Pennsylvanian who had played end on the Duke football team and been its placekicker as well, who had joined the tour in 1953 and in 1955 had entered the tour record books with a 27 for nine holes, a 60 for 18, a 257 for 72, all made while winning the Texas Open; Gene Littler, twenty-four, the 1953 Amateur champion from San Diego, whose swing seemed an effortless marvel of fluidity, who had turned pro just after winning the 1954 San Diego Open and was now winning tournaments after a spell in which he had finished second a few too many times. With Dow Finsterwald, Billy Casper, and, eventually, Ken Venturi, these were the best of the new breed, the young, intelligent, agreeable, talented golfers who might have been selling cars or stocks and bonds, and playing customer's golf if the pro tour had not seemed to possess such growing potential for a lucrative, interesting career.

Finsterwald, twenty-two years old when he first joined the tour in 1951, was a graduate of Ohio University. Somewhat of a protégé of Doug Ford's, he played sound, percentage golf, never gambling for birdies. He had the swing to make his philosophy effective. It was compact, efficient, and very commercial. Before he was to retire from full-time tour involvement and take up a plush job at the Broadmoor in Colorado Springs, Finsty's play-it-safe method won 13 tournaments, including the first stroke-play PGA Championship in 1958, and it put him 14th on the money list in '55, second in '56, third in '57, fourth in '58, third in '59, and third again in '60. During these years Mr. Safety also put together a string of 72 consecutive in-the-money finishes, a mark that goes into the record books as second only to the streak of 113 compiled by Byron Nelson.

When Billy Casper joined the tour in midsummer of 1955 he was twenty-four, had just been mustered out of the Navy, and looked very much like the archetypical carefree, jolly fat man. The last adjective is the only one that fit him. He was neither carefree nor jolly. Like Littler, Casper was raised in San Diego. He was an intense competitor who concentrated so hard on his business that during a round he could look directly at his wife, Shirley, from a distance of 10 feet and not recognize her.

Casper was also one of the first of the touring pros to be backed on the tour by a sponsorship syndicate, two businessmen from Chula Vista, California. The syndicate provided Casper with an allowance of approximately $1,000 a month while he played the tour. Out of his winnings he reimbursed the syndicate for his monthly advance and then added 30 percent of any winnings over that amount. This arrangement provided a working model for sponsorships that has been used by tour rookies ever since, with very good and with very bad results.

The fact that Casper became a winner on the tour so quickly was something of a puzzle back in the Fifties because he then took such a wild slash at the ball. What he had, however, was fine hand action, a very sound golfing temperament, and probably one of the finest putting touches and methods that the tour had seen since the days of Locke or Horton Smith. Later, when his swing began to develop real tempo and rhythm, Casper was able to become the great and formidable competitor he is today, a Masters and two-time U.S. Open champion.

Ken Venturi's career had been one of the most dramatic in golf, featuring both luminous success and tragic failure. But in the mid-Fifties he was by far the most promising of all the Young Guardsmen—more so than Palmer, Souchak, Littler, Casper, Finsterwald, anyone. He had learned the fundamentals of the game from a master technician, Nelson. On a golf course he sent off sparks of confidence, with good cause. Venturi's stance as he addressed the ball was in perfect balance. And so was his swing. It was upright, compact, rhythmic. He possessed the footwork of a dancer. Perhaps his temperament was not ideal. He was not pugnaciously competitive like Palmer, nor intently concentrated like Casper, nor placid like Littler. Venturi tended to overdramatize himself, but then he often found himself in dramatic situations, like his spectacular Masters blow-up of 1956. Venturi turned pro and joined the tour in 1957, abandoning a modest career selling cars for Eddie Lowry, a San Francisco Ford dealer and Venturi's financial godfather. Despite a PGA rule in effect at that time specifying that novice pros must go through a six-month probationary period before being eligible to earn official money, Venturi finished his first year as the tour's 10th leading money-winner. He won back-to-back events at St. Paul and Milwaukee in August with eight consecutive rounds of 68 or better. It was an impressive beginning, and Ken made a spectacular addition to the Young Guard of Palmer, Souchak, Littler, Casper, and Finsterwald.

The Old and Middle Guard (Hogan, Mangrum, Snead in the former; Harbert, Boros, Middlecoff, and Bolt in the latter, as characterized by golf historian Herbert Warren Wind, in *Sports Illustrated*) were still important factors at the major championships, but from week to week on the tour the Young Guard dominated. They became known as the Young Turks. Until Palmer burst out ahead of the pack, and was subsequently joined by Gary Player and Jack Nicklaus to form what became known as the Big Three, the Young Turks won just about everything. From 1956 through 1960 Palmer won a total of 20 tournaments, Casper 14, Littler 13, Souchak, Finsterwald, and Venturi 10 each. This represented a grand total of 77 victories over a span of just five seasons. There wasn't much left for the rest of the touring crowd except money. Only veterans Doug Ford and Sam Snead, with eight apiece, came close in total victories over that same half decade.

The excitement generated by the Young Turks was proving beneficial to all. The first big prize-money breakthrough occurred in 1955. The total jumped from $600,000 the year before to $782,000. Purses went over $1 million in 1958, and from then on began jumping upward like a bullish stock market gone berserk. How profitable a career the pro tour became when the Young Turks took over is indicated in the contrasting ages at which the Middle Guard had taken up the tour full-time and at what age the Young Turks had taken the same step. Middle Guarder Tommy Bolt held off until he was thirty-one, Ted Kroll and Julius Boros until they were thirty, Doug Ford and Ed Furgol until they were twenty-eight, Art Wall, Cary Middlecoff, and Chick Harbert until they were not exactly brash youngsters of twenty-six.

By contrast, Young Turk Palmer started on the tour at age twenty-four, as did Gene Littler. Souchak and Venturi were twenty-five, Casper twenty-three, and Finsterwald only twenty-two. In the late Forties and early Fifties most of the beginners had served long apprenticeships as caddies and laborers in the pro shop, occasionally getting a crack at the winter tour when their home club was closed. There simply wasn't enough money around to make it financially feasible. Nowadays the tour rookies are even younger than were the Young Turks. A college hotshot can walk straight off the campus following graduation and start picking up $1,000 a week just by holding his clubs.

Today there are about 250 regulars on the tour, many of whom travel by plane. Back in 1955 there were only about 60 regulars, and the tour seemed to be a friendlier, cozier phenomenon than it is today. Overall expenses ran close to $200 a week and, despite the jump in prize money that had just then occurred, it was still necessary to finish in the top 10 of the year's money list to bank really important money, and probably in the top 20 just to break even. The winter tour was a succession of steady, short hops that began in California, traced a path through Arizona, Texas, Louisiana, Florida, North Carolina, and finally to Augusta, Georgia, for the Masters, and so it was possible to save on expenses by using the family car as transportation. Gene and Shirley Littler, Arnold and Winnie Palmer, Dick and Doris Mayer, as well as several other couples, hooked up trailers to their cars and thus saved on bed and board. In the summer the hops were much longer and air travel became an essential convenience, but in the winter months only Cary Middlecoff traveled regularly by air. The result was that the players and their wives saw a good deal of each other socially from week to week and many regulars formed something like a large, happy family.

Nor did the golf courses on the tour of the mid-Fifties present a particularly unfriendly challenge week to week. For the most part they were short, flat, and wide open. Those who performed best with the driver, wedge, and putter usually scored best and won the money. To the others this brand of drive, pitch, and putt golf could be an enormous frustration.

The El Rio Country Club, site of the Tucson Open, was as flat as an airport runway, possessed unappetizing tan Bermuda fairways, flat greens, and black-brown earth, interspersed with tamarack and cottonwood trees, bordering the fairways in place of more conventional rough. Marty Furgol walked the first four holes of the course when he arrived for his practice rounds in 1955 and said, "This isn't my kind of track at all," climbed into his car, and headed for the next stop at San Antonio. Shades of Clayton Heafner a few years earlier. Heafner had made the entire winter swing, but he hated the golf courses with such intensity that he stayed around only long enough to play in one-fourth of the tournaments.

Not that San Antonio, where Furgol had headed in such a hurry, was much of an improvement over the El Rio. San Antonio was the site of the Texas Open, and for years the tournament was played at Brackenridge Park, a well-worn public course where Souchak was to blast out his scoring records. The tees had been so torn up by the course's regular clients, in fact, that the pros drove off rubber mats. Imagine the uproar should something like that ever occur on the modern tour!

Despite its poor condition, Brackenridge Park, until the Texas Open was shifted to other, more demanding courses after 1959, could always be counted on to provide the tour with its most eye-popping scores. Souchak's records were all set there. Three players, including Souchak, have shot the PGA tour's record of 60 at Brackenridge. Al Brosch, not exactly a name that lives in the history of golf's great performers, did it in 1951. Ted Kroll carved out a 60 there in 1954. Two of the six players who have tied the tour's record of 126 for 36 holes did it at Brackenridge, and Chandler Harper finished up with three successive 63s to win the 1954 Texas Open, a record of 189 for 54 holes, which would seem to be immune from assault by even today's horde of highly talented tourists.

The five-year span from 1956 to 1960, dominated by Palmer and the Young Turks, was also notable for a number of interesting developments. Perhaps one of the most important was the regular appearance of television cameras on golf courses.

In 1956 only the U.S. Open and George May's World Championship were visible live on network television. In 1957 the Masters was added, providing fine coverage of everyone but the winner. Doug Ford, who won the tournament that year with a final round 66, had gone into the clubhouse by the time the show went on the air. In 1958 the Tournament of Champions in Las Vegas was projected live for the first time into the nation's bars and living rooms, and so was the PGA Championship, making its debut at stroke play. In 1957 another intriguing entry also joined the lists of television programming. This was a weekly filmed show called *All Star Golf*, which pitted two name pros against each other at stroke play over 18 holes. The winner survived to meet a challenger the following week. The show received a tremendous boost from Sam Snead, who came on at midseason and then won 13 consecutive matches.

All Star Golf's ratings were sufficiently high to inspire a number of other shows, such as Shell's *Wonderful World of Golf; Big Three Golf* starring Palmer, Player, and Nicklaus; *Challenge Golf*, with Palmer and Player taking on all comers; and the CBS *Classic*, which survives today. The most successful of the tournaments televised live during the late Fifties and early Sixties was the Bing Crosby Pro-Am, which was first covered in 1959. Its combination of golfing stars and show business celebrities, plus the fact that it came along in January when most of the nation was housebound, gave it ratings that at first surpassed the Masters and the Open.

Not for long. As a televised show, the Masters made its great breakthrough in 1960. From year to year its two biggest advantages have been that it is held annually on the same course and that it has been so imaginatively covered by CBS. In 1960 Palmer took a hand. Visible to millions of viewers, he finished with birdies on the final two holes to beat Ken Venturi by a single shot. It was one of televised sport's most dramatic moments, and soon networks, sponsors, and even routine weekly tournaments were clamoring to appear on the tube. Today approximately 20 golf tournaments can be viewed live at home. They primarily feature the men pros, but the Ladies' PGA tour and even the U.S. Amateur have also become regulars.

Rather than bring golf to a state of saturation, as it did with boxing, television has been one of the reasons the popularity of the game has grown so tremendously. A golf fan didn't just have to read about Palmer finishing birdie, birdie to defeat Venturi at the Masters, he could live the moment with him as it was happening. So he watches on his television set each week until the tour comes to his town. Raised to a fever pitch by all this electronic spectating, he is out there on the course to see championship golf in the flesh. Rather than declining as the televising of tournaments became more and more frequent, the galleries have grown. After days in which 30 or 40 thousand people stormed around their course, the Masters finally, in 1965, limited the sale of tickets. The Open as well has been limiting its sale in recent years.

Meanwhile, during the year of the Young Turks, another fascinating figure strode the fairways of the pro tour. He was a golfer who at one time showed signs of being more gifted than any of them. This was Frank Stranahan of Toledo, who so far as keeping fit was concerned foreshadowed Gary Player. Stranahan, heir to the Champion Spark Plug fortune, was a wealthy young man who could have easily written his own destiny. He had won the British Amateur in 1948 and 1950 and played on three U.S. Walker Cup teams. Prior to these achievements, he had made regular appearances on the pro tour, and, playing as an amateur, had won the 1945 Durham Open and the 1946 Kansas City and Fort Worth invitationals. He was then only twenty-four. Two years later, still playing as an amateur, he won the Miami Open. Through 1954 Stranahan retained his amateur status, but played the pro tour almost as often as the fellows who needed the money, not winning again but frequently finishing up high enough to receive a big check had he been eligible to accept it.

At the end of the 1954 season Stranahan, thirty-two years old and the heir to millions, turned professional. Frank took the same route as any touring neophyte would have taken. The wonder is that he didn't try to work out a sponsorship syndicate *à la* Billy Casper. Stranahan signed up with a real estate promotion in Crystal River, Florida, to play as one of their touring pros, registering out of Crystal River. His fee? One plot of land worth approximately $7,000. He also signed to play as a member of the MacGregor golf company staff. Fee? All the free balls and clubs he could use plus a few thousand dollars a year. In winning four pro circuit events while only an amateur, Stranahan no doubt promulgated much embarrassed muttering in the professional ranks. Possibly he felt uneasy among the pros for this reason.

"To remain an amateur and play as much competitive golf as I do isn't really fair to other amateurs," was Frank's explanation, "and I still want to test my game on a full-time basis against the world's best players."

As a pro, Stranahan did not achieve the success he had attained as an amateur. In his first professional season he won the Eastern Open, but did not win another tournament until the Los Angeles Open of 1958. Win or not, Stranahan was a fascinating conversation piece. He took up weight-lifting, very much like Gary Player has done, in order to increase his distance off the tee. The result was a tremendous chest and pair of shoulders and several regional weight-lifting titles, but very little extra yardage on his drives.

Stranahan also introduced the touring valet, a servant who drove his car and tended an immense wardrobe that would have done credit to one of the world's ten best dressed men. One of the stories about Stranahan relates the time his car, a sleek, black Cadillac, was stolen from a golf club parking lot while he was playing in a tournament. A few hours later the local sheriff was able to phone Stranahan at the club and report that the car had been located, abandoned at the side of the road, and that it was still in mint condition.

"Never mind the car," Stranahan is reported to have said to the astounded constable, "how about my clothes?"

Despite his wealth and his life style, Stranahan worked with great dedication at his profession. Just after dawn on the morning immediately following his triumph at Los Angeles, the late Tony Lema recalled seeing Frank on the Pebble Beach golf course, 400 miles from Los Angeles, out on the course hitting practice shots in preparation for the Bing Crosby. Unfortunately, dedication never seemed to be a magic solution for Stranahan. He missed the cut at the Crosby that week. In fact, the Los Angeles Open of 1958 proved to be the high-water mark of his career as a pro. He never won another tournament, seldom even finished close to winning, and eventually drifted off the tour entirely. He attended Harvard Business School and then went into the investment business. The fact that Stranahan could succeed so brilliantly on the tour as an amateur and so modestly as a pro makes him one of the foremost enigmas in a sport that is loaded with them.

The tour continued to grow and flourish through the late Fifties and into the early Sixties. Its face matured too, and became sleeker; it was losing its baby fat. The giant and rich Calcutta, held each year prior to the Tournament of Champions in Las Vegas and as much of a spectacle as any act on the Strip, was dropped like a hissing snake after 1959 when the total pool reached a record $380,000, eight times what the Tournament itself offered in prize money. Bad for golf's image of integrity, purity, and clean living, it was generally agreed, and so *pfft!*

The pro-am became an incredibly popular part of weekly life on the tour. This is an affair, usually of one day's duration, in which a pro teams with an amateur partner on a best-ball basis. The pro plays his gross score, the amateur with the advantage of his club handicap. It became a weekly must as an event played the day before the start of each tournament. Bing Crosby, who for years has hosted his very special sort of pro-am played each January on courses around the Monterey Peninsula south of San Francisco, became swamped with applications from amateurs all over the country.

In 1960 the first super pro-am took place, the Palm Springs Desert Classic, played on several courses in and around the California desert resort. It was a 90-hole event, but for each of the first four days each pro played with a different group of amateurs.

The pro-am as a method of bringing big business into golf has been unbelievably successful. A decision-making corporation executive fifty or sixty years old cannot, however much he may want to, play football with Joe Namath. He can, however, play golf with Arnold Palmer. He can even do this in a tournament, teamed with Palmer and helping the team through the use of his handicap. For this corporation executive the experience provides enormous social prestige. It has become one of the great status symbols of U.S. industry.

Some companies have even gone so far as to hire name players on some vague public relations pretext, so that the company president will be invited by that player to compete with him in the major pro-ams. This close, personal connection between big business and golf has had a profound effect on the changing sponsorship of golf tournaments, from chambers of commerce and minimal prizes to corporate giants and purses at the six-figure level.

Then there was the question of purse splitting—a custom that had been in vogue since the tour first began. The act of purse splitting constituted an agreement made between two or more players prior to the start of a season, or a specific tournament, or a playoff, to evenly divide all prize money won. In the early days of the tour when tournament purses were thin, it was a neat way for a group of pros to provide a nominal degree of financial security. It was what Snead and Bulla did, for instance, on their first visit to the tour in 1937. Later, when financing was easier to arrange, an agreement to split the purse was a gamble, a hedge against possible loss.

The practice first surfaced publicly in 1957 when Dick Mayer won May's World and the $50,000 first prize. It turned out that $5,000 of that check was given to a golfer who had finished in an eight-way tie for 21st, Al Besselink, who would have done the same for Mayer had their positions been reversed.

Prize splitting was in the news three years later during the first Palm Springs Desert Classic in 1960. A bonus of $50,000 was offered to any pro who shot a hole in one during the tournament. A chubby, blond pro from Knoxville, Tennessee, Joe Campbell, performed this feat during the tournament, but the real winner was Buddy Sullivan of Yuba City, California. He had made a deal with Campbell in which the two would split the $50,000 if either of them won it, so Sullivan earned $25,000. Campbell did not fare nearly so well. He was under contract to split all winnings with a sponsorship syndicate back home and so emerged with only $12,500 of the original $50,000.

The ethics of purse splitting was given a thorough public airing in September, 1962, during the first World Series of Golf. This was the televised show from Akron in which the year's major championship winners played off over 36 holes for a first prize of $50,000, a second prize of $15,000, and a third of $7,500. That year the major champions were Palmer (Masters, British Open), Nicklaus (U.S. Open), and Player (PGA), all friends and all clients of the same business manager (Mark McCormack). A rumor rampant at the time had it that they were merely going to throw the entire purse into a pot, split it three ways, and play for nothing but the title, such as it was.

The truth, be assured, was that in this particular case they were not splitting the purse. It would have destroyed the entire appeal of the spectacle. But this kind of thing had happened, in slightly altered circumstances, such as in sudden-death or 18-hole playoffs for other tournament titles, many times before. A few weeks later *Sports Illustrated* published a story revealing that purse splitting not only occurred in approximately 50 percent of all playoffs, but that a vast majority of the players could see nothing whatsoever wrong with the practice. The title was what mattered most, not the prize money. PGA officials had always known of the practice and tacitly condoned it.

Public reaction was predictable. Playing for titles alone had no meaning outside the trade. These were not amateurs, therefore it was the check that should count. The public was being cheated every time pros involved in a sudden-death playoff agreed to split the difference. The PGA, not usually given to introspection, finally did a little soul searching and agreed the public might be right. The practice of purse splitting was banned the following year.

Meanwhile, the Young Turks continued to cut a wide swath through the tour, winning tournaments in eye-popping fashion. In 1958 Palmer, Casper, Venturi, and Finsterwald finished one-two-three-four on the money list. Souchak was 12th. Littler, about to emerge from a two-year slump, was back down in 27th place. Even with no contribution from Littler the Turks won 13 tournaments, including the Masters (Palmer) and the PGA (Finsterwald).

Venturi opened up the 1959 season by shooting a final-round 63 at the Los Angeles Open to overcome an 8-shot deficit and thrust a rather stunned Art Wall back into second place. Three weeks later, Palmer carved out a final-round 62 to win the Thunderbird by 3 shots over veteran Jimmy Demaret. Some of the Turk thunder was stolen back by Wall, who birdied five of the last six holes to win the Masters; by Ben Hogan, who, at the age of forty-seven, won the tough and prestigious Colonial Invitational in Fort Worth, defeating Fred Hawkins in an 18-hole playoff; by Sam Snead, who shot a near-miracle 59 en route to winning the aptly named Sam Snead Festival, an event regarded as "unofficial" by the PGA, at White Sulphur Springs. Wall, thanks to a fast start on the Winter Tour and his Master's victory, was 1959's leading money-winner, but Littler, Finsterwald, Casper, Palmer, and Souchak finished right behind him, in that order. Venturi was 10th.

Then came 1960 and the beginning of the Age of Arnie's Army. In the history of the pro tour 1960 is a landmark even more momentous than the coming of Snead in 1937 or the arrival of the Young Turks in 1955 and '56. Palmer personalized tournament golf to the millions who read of his deeds or watched them on television or in person. Principally because of Palmer, the pro tour ceased being just a showcase for the sport of golf, it became a gigantically successful entity of its own, with an important change in character that was to cause some bitter political battles in the late Sixties.

The first great year for Palmer began modestly enough with un-inspiring results in the first four California events: 25th at Los Angeles, 12th at Yorba Linda, 15th at the Crosby, 7th at San Diego. Then the sleeping giant shook himself awake. Palmer played the last three rounds of the Palm Springs Desert Classic in 67, 66, and 65 to win by 3 shots. Three weeks later he began another surge, this one lasting through three tournaments. In consecutive weeks he won the Texas, Baton Rouge, and Pensacola Opens. It was soon after this streak that his birdie, birdie finish edged luckless Ken Venturi at the Masters. In June at Denver his final-round 65 won the U.S. Open. In July he journeyed to Britain and just narrowly

An early Billy Casper

missed winning the British Open, losing to Kel Nagle by a single stroke. He returned in time to lead the PGA Championship at Akron with a first-round 67, but then surrendered to the fatigues and pressures of the summer and faded to 7th.

Two weeks later, obviously refreshed, Palmer closed with two 66s to tie for first at the Insurance City Open in Hartford and won a sudden-death playoff with Bill Collins and Jack Fleck on the 3rd hole. Near the end of the year at the Mobile Sertoma Open, he shot a 65 in the last round, came from 4 shots back of the leaders, and won the tournament by 2 shots. For the year Palmer won $81,000, to lead his fellow Turks, Venturi, Finsterwald, and Casper, by $30,000 to $40,000. In 1960 Palmer had won eight tournaments on the highly competitive pro tour and was a source of amazement and wonder to fans and touring pros alike. In his biography Tony Lema described some of the wonderment that his fellow pros felt about Palmer's seemingly impossible accomplishments. It took place just after the Mobile Open. Palmer and Lema were in New Orleans, bunked together in a double-decker on a friend's yacht. They talked for awhile just before dropping off to sleep and finally Lema felt called upon to ask the question he knew had been in the mind of every player on the tour.

"Do you realize what you have really done this year?" asked Lema, still two years away from accomplishing some marvels of his own.

"What do you mean, 'What I've really done'?" was Palmer's reply.

"Well, winning what you have the way you have," Lema continued. "Finishing birdie, birdie to win the Masters. Shooting a 65 on the last round to win the Open. It seems fantastic, so superhuman to have done these things in that way."

Palmer's answer provides some insights into his own character, the innate modesty of the man and his relentless determination. "I've never thought of it in those terms," Palmer responded to Lema's expression of awe and amazement. "I just kind of see what it is I have to do, and I just make up my mind that I'm going to do it. If I have a long putt to make I just think about making that putt. I shut from my mind the thought of missing it or all the other stuff that would come from my missing it."

Palmer's sweep through the 1960 season marked the end of the now-not-so-young-Turks' dominance of the tour. In that year the six players had finished in the top eight of the money list, Souchak finishing sixth behind Jay Hebert and Littler eighth, just behind Doug Ford. Palmer, of course, had his many tournaments, but the others didn't do too badly in 1960 either, winning 11 among them. But the following year the slide was on. Littler won the 1961 U.S. Open, but no other tournament, and ranked ninth on the money list. Casper finished fourth, but Venturi slipped to 14th, Souchak to 28th, and Finsterwald all the way to 33rd. Whereas Casper, Finsterwald, Littler, Souchak, and Venturi had compiled almost a dozen tournament triumphs in 1960, in '61 they could win but three.

Tony Lema celebrates his 31st birthday, 1965

Part of this lack of success can be explained by the emergence of Gary Player and Doug Sanders as genuine stars. South Africa's Player became the most successful foreign visitor to the tour since Bobby Locke and even far surpassed his fellow countryman's performance of a decade earlier. Player won the Masters and two other tournaments, and ranked first on the money list, with winnings of $68,377, over $3,000 more than Palmer had won. Sanders, of the colorful shoe-shirt-and-slacks ensembles, the exceedingly short backswing, and the playboy life style, won five tournaments and over $60,000.

But as much as the success of others, the dissolution of the Young turk group was marked by the inexplicable collapses of Souchak and Venturi as effective golfers. Both players had possessed beautifully solid golf swings. In his prime Souchak was the tour's most accurate long hitter, a player of enormous potential. In fact, the 1960 U.S. Open had been Souchak's Open until Palmer took it away with his historic finish. Souchak had started the final round the leader by 2 strokes, but shot a score for the final 18 holes that was 10 strokes higher than Arnold's. Perhaps it was the frustration of attempting to compete week after week with Palmer, then Palmer and Player, then Palmer, Player, and Nicklaus that ultimately sapped Big Mike's spirit and dulled his competitive edge. Perhaps it was the frustration of spending long weeks out on the tour when he would have preferred being home in North Carolina with his wife and children. Perhaps Souchak decided that he simply could not make the often brutal sacrifices in time and practice that are usually so essential to success as a professional on the searingly competitive golf tour. At any rate, he went winless on the tour in 1962 and '63, finishing a poor 53rd on the money list in that latter year.

Souchak made something of a comeback in 1964, winning two events, but dropped out of sight again in 1965. By 1967 his playing record was not even carried in the tour's press guide. Now Souchak is retired from the regular competitive grind.

Venturi's fall from the top was far more rapid, more emphatic, more dramatic than Souchak's. As mentioned earlier, when Venturi joined the tour his swing was sounder, his golfing sense more acute than anyone he had to play against. He was also a dedicated visitor to the practice tee. His amateur record had not been as impressive as Palmer's, but he had played well enough to make a Walker Cup team and his run at winning the 1956 Masters had created an exciting week all sports fans will remember.

When Venturi won back-to-back tournaments in midsummer of 1957, his first year on the tour, it became quite plain that his exceptional promise was about to mature, that he was simply waiting in the wings to be called out on stage and declared one of golf's greatest players. This he seemed to have achieved as he sat in Cliff Robert's cottage at Augusta in April of 1960 watching on television as Palmer faced the challenge of birdying the last two holes to beat him. The fact that Palmer did it was admittedly a traumatic experience for Venturi, who had always possessed a volatile, high-strung temperament. Since his bitter loss in 1956 the Masters had assumed the role of Moby Dick to Venturi's Captain Ahab. To have it snatched away again was unbearable.

Later that year and in the three years to follow Venturi suffered a series of illnesses and injuries, pneumonia, allergic reactions to medicine, back-muscle spasms, and tendonitis in the left wrist, but he himself attributes his loss of form more to shock, to a lack of desire, to a depression stemming from his Masters defeat, than to anything else. His beautiful swing went entirely. It became an erratic, wristy, jerky snap at the ball, not the rhythmic ballet it had once been. In 1961 Venturi won $25,000, a good year for a tour spear-carrier but hardly for a leading actor, and won not a single tournament. In 1962 his official earnings were down to $7,000, he ranked 66th on the money list, and he was no longer even exempt from having to prequalify for the weekly show. Thus in 1963 he would have had to join the rabbits in the Monday qualifying sessions, which for reasons of pride he was not about to do, or obtain one of the special invitations that each sponsor is privileged to dole out.

Not surprisingly, 1963 proved to be an even more disastrous year than '62. Venturi plummeted to 94th on the money list, winning not quite $4,000. His morale was as shot as his swing. There seemed no way to climb out of the pit a few bad breaks and a bad attitude had tumbled him into. His comeback in 1964, therefore, is one of sport's most heartening sagas. Somehow Venturi was able to give himself a heart-to-heart talk, to self-induce at least one more big try. Once again he spent long hours on the practice tee, going over old notes from the practice sessions with Byron Nelson years earlier. Little by little he rebuilt his swing along the old, beautiful lines. Little by little he regained much of the old ebullient confidence. An attitude that had turned sour began to sweeten. Venturi made some encouraging finishes early in the season, and two weeks before the U.S. Open came in third in the rich Thunderbird and won a check for $6,250. After years of poor earnings the check came in handy, but it was the third-place finish that really meant so much. Venturi's fairy-tale triumph seemed to have been achieved in his winning the U.S. Open that summer in the midst of a Washington, D.C., heat wave, but another tragic chapter was about to be written.

The severe dehydration that Venturi suffered during that long final day in Washington may have sown the seeds of the circulatory ailment that ultimately put him back again in a golfing limbo. In the fall of 1964 the skin on his hands began to flake and peel and he experienced a strange feeling of numbness. It became virtually impossible for him to hold or swing a club with any effective result. Operations, injections, a wide variety of therapeutic treatments helped somewhat, and, after being sidelined for almost the entire 1965 season—except for a surprisingly successful appearance in the Ryder Cup matches—Venturi made a dramatic return to the victory circle in his hometown of San Francisco by winning the 1966 Lucky International. But that was it. The ailment remained and his golf deteriorated once again. Now Venturi still plays the tour on occasion, but appears more often up in a tower as a golf tournament television commentator than he does down below on the fairway.

The old heroes had faded away, but a new one emerged. This, of course, was Jack Nicklaus. The coming of Jack Nicklaus to the pro tour in 1962 put into full swing the prosperity boom set in motion by Palmer. For a while, in fact, Nicklaus simply served as a pudgy, blond villain against whom Palmer could test his heroism. With Nicklaus in the picture, and Player, we now had what legitimately became known as the Big Three of Golf. This triumvirate opened up sources of income vastly more lucrative than mere prize money. The main reason was that all three had the same business manager. If the three had had three different managers the leverage of unity would have been lost. Entrepreneurs could have gone from one to the other where exhibitions, clothing, or equipment were concerned and shopped for the lowest price. These were the three biggest names in golf, but all business arrangements had to be made through a single manager, who was able to advise amateur Jack Nicklaus that professional Jack Nicklaus could expect to make at least $60,000 during his first year as a pro over and above prize money. It was a wide, wide underestimate.

Tournament money also began to increase dramatically after 1960, due primarily to the entrance on the scene of giant corporations that could afford to offer giant purses. The motive was promotion rather than profit, and the sky was the limit. Sponsors were eager to participate in the tour, and to break in, they bid high. The Carling Brewery had sponsored a tournament for years, usually in an area where they were opening up or already owned a brewery, but the race began in earnest with the first Thunderbird Classic, held in New Jersey in 1962.

Area Ford dealers sponsored the T-bird Classic and offered a total purse of $100,000. The Thunderbird thus joined with the Masters in providing the tour's only six-figure pots, the first since the days of far-sighted George May. In 1963 the Masters was again around $100,000, Thunderbird was back, and these two were joined by the $110,000 Cleveland Open and the $125,000 Whitemarsh Open. These four purses ran considerably higher than either the U.S. Open of that year or the PGA Championship, still paying more modest sums of $70,000 and $80,000 respectively to their competitors. That year of 1963 was also the first in which the money leaders hit six figures. Palmer earned a record-breaking $128,200, and Nicklaus just barely made it over the line by finishing fifth in the last tournament of the year, the Cajun Classic at Lafayette, Louisiana. He earned an official total of $100,040.

The Cajun was also to play a vital role for Nicklaus the following year in his race to win the money title for the first time. If you think that this is a meaningless distinction for golfing stars who have won everything, you should have been at the Cajun Classic that cold week in November. The Cajun paid a total purse of $25,000. During the months that preceded it, no less than five events had paid a total purse of over $100,000, and one of these, Carling's new expanded World Tournament, paid $200,000. It was rainy, it was icy. Few spectators were there to watch them play, but business and social commitments notwithstanding, there were Nicklaus and Palmer. The rub, it seemed, was that these two members of the Big Three were only $318 apart, Palmer leading, in their race for the money title. The Cajun was the last chance for each and no one was going to let go without a fight. Their struggle at Lafayette was strangely epic. *Sports Illustrated* made it the lead article of the week and entitled the story "A Matter of Pride at Endsville," which didn't exactly unloose warm feelings in the good people of Lafayette. It was a close battle all the way. Nicklaus squeezed out a tie for second in the tournament and thus won the money title by $82, a total of $113,285 to $113,203, when Palmer could do no better than fourth.

"It was the only time I've ever been happy with a second-place finish," said Jack when the ordeal was over.

The finish to the year of 1964 was exciting but so had been the entire season. After all, this was the year of Ken Venturi's dramatic if brief comeback. It was also the great year of another brilliant golfer whose career was to have a tragic finale. He was Tony Lema, an exuberant, personable, handsome Californian whose origins were in the Oakland slums, who started out in golf at the very bottom, but who had emerged after years of an uphill-downhill struggle on the pro tour to be a big winner and a British Open champion. A long, accurate driver, a wedge player of superbly delicate accuracy, a fine putter, Lema had become known as "Champagne Tony" from his habit of serving champagne in the press room after tournament victories and of denying himself few of life's pleasures.

In 1964 Lema was able to serve the bubbly at the Crosby in January. In June he did so again in consecutive weeks at the Thunderbird and Buick Opens. He won again the week after the U.S. Open, this time in Cleveland, finished high up at Whitemarsh, and then flew over to Scotland in time for one practice round on the Old Course at St. Andrews and a victory in his first shot in one of the world's most prestigious championships. In 1965 Lema reached the $100,000 plateau on the official money list, finishing second to Nicklaus, but his flame had not long to burn. The following summer, flying out of Akron at the close of the PGA Championship, on his way to fulfill an exhibition commitment, Lema and his wife Betty lost their lives in a chartered plane that crashed, ironically on a golf course, and burst into flames.

The season of 1964 also marked a mass breakthrough by foreign talent. Player had been notably successful on the tour since 1958, the year he won his first title. Australia's Bruce Crampton had been a leading player since 1962. In 1964 these two were joined among the leading money earners by Bruce Devlin and the veteran Kel Nagle of Australia and Bob Charles of New Zealand, the first lefthander ever to win a tour event, the 1963 Houston Classic, or a major championship, the 1963 British Open. With the addition of England's Tony Jacklin as a regular tourist and tournament winner in 1968, the trend continued to build momentum. There are now approximately 20 foreign-born players on the U.S. tour. In 1972 three of them, Player, Devlin, and Crampton, won in excess of $100,000 each.

Another major breakthrough: For the first time a black player, Pete Brown, won a PGA tournament. It was the Waco Turner Open in Burneyville, a forerunner of the current satellites, held for all tourists who had not qualified for the limited-field Tournament of Champions in Las Vegas. From its very beginning, the PGA tour had seen few black players, mainly because the PGA had legislated against them. Up until late 1961 its constitution had stated that membership in the association was limited to Caucasians. This discriminatory restriction was finally challenged by the Attorney General of California, who cited it as a violation of state law. He threatened to close down all the PGA's California tournaments, at least those played on public courses, if the constitution was not altered. Faced with defending the indefensible or altering its constitution, the PGA sensibly chose to alter its constitution, and the Caucasian clause was stricken at the PGA's national convention in November, 1961. Prior to that time, two black golfers, Charlie Sifford and Ted Rhodes, had made irregular appearances on the tour, but they did so only by special dispensation of the PGA and they were not welcomed in the South. But now, at least, even if blacks were not about to arrive on the tour en masse, the door had been opened.

Today there are about eight black golfers who make the swing from end to end. They are Sifford and Brown, who have won official PGA events; Lee Elder, a consistent money winner; Charlie Owens, George Johnson, and James Dent, who have taken satellite events; Charlie's cousin, Curtis Sifford, and Chuck Thorpe, who have shown steady improvement and flashes of genuine talent.

The success of Palmer and the Big Three and the attendant publicity and television coverage were accelerating the other changes taking place on the face of the tour: big business sponsorships and youthful, college-educated rookies. The civic sponsors were dwindling before the onslaught of what seemed to be the unlimited budgets of large corporations. In 1964, Lucky Lager sponsored a tournament in San Francisco and put up a purse of $50,000. The Doral Hotel and Country Club was paying a purse of $50,000 for its tournament in Florida. Thunderbird was in its third year of paying out $100,000. The purse at the Buick Open was $66,000. Firestone Tire & Rubber Company in Akron sponsored the American Golf Classic at the company-owned Firestone Country Club, and its purse was $50,000. The Sahara Hotel in Las Vegas advertised the purse at its tournament as being $77,777.77, a lucky figure so far as the pro tour was concerned. And what civic group, however earnest or well-heeled, could match the $201,600 that Carling offered for an international extravaganza it sponsored on the Oakland Hills course outside Detroit?

These were the beginnings of what has become today a tour with a minimum purse of $100,000, and, with this kind of money available, golf has become an attractive profession to athletes who might otherwise have stuck to baseball, basketball, football, or what have you. In its beginnings and right through until the late Fifties the tour was still staffed primarily by golfers who thought in terms of club jobs. They either sprang from club jobs or intended to retire to them when their competitive skills dulled. Now a horde of fine young golfers, mostly straight off college campuses and not concerned by the fact that they could not wrap club grips, stock merchandise, or cure a middle-aged slice on the practice tee, were thronging the tour. By 1965 the demand for Approved Player Cards had grown so great that the PGA decided it was time to put these players to a controlled test, rather than simply following the recommendation of regional PGA officers. In the fall of 1965 they introduced the first of what are now annual qualifying sessions. These are tournaments attended by about 75 hopefuls, survivors of regional eliminations, who must play a 108-hole marathon. The low-scoring dozen or so (it varies each session) earn an Approved Player Card, which they retain as long as their performances on the tour meet a reasonable standard. What they have earned, really, is no more than the right to compete in those Monday prequalifying horrors.

Now, finally, the tour was a career in itself. It had nothing to do with the country clubs back home or the professionals who staffed those clubs, yet the tour was still controlled by those club professionals through the PGA. The PGA's national membership consists of approximately 6,000 teaching professionals and about 300 touring professionals. In fact, a tour pro is not eligible for PGA membership until he has held his Approved Player Card for four years. With the vote ratio set up this way, it is hardly surprising that the PGA's officers—its president, vice-presidents, treasurer, and secretary—have been through the years almost entirely teaching pros. Out on the tour the players were represented by a PGA Tournament Committee, but on the PGA's Executive Board the players had only one vote. This proved a vital lack of power, since up until 1968 the PGA Executive Board had a right of veto over anything done by the Tournament Committee. It was seldom used but the power lay there ominously, like a sword in a sheath. Having the power thus placed seemed about as logical to the players as having the college football coaches of this country control the destinies of the National Football League.

Obviously this arrangement could not last for much longer. The clash between the PGA Executive Board and its Tournament Committee first started simmering in 1966, when the Board, employing its right of veto, canceled the $200,000 Frank Sinatra Open in Palm Springs, a tournament already arranged for by the Tournament Committee. The Board's argument was that the area already had the well-established Bob Hope Desert Classic and couldn't reasonably support two tournaments. Whatever the possible merits of this decision, the players on the tour took a rather lively exception to a bunch of club pros canceling their lovely $200,000 payoff. There were whisperings that the players would boycott the PGA Championship.

The pot kept simmering and then finally boiled over in 1968, when the PGA drew up a standard tournament entry form which virtually demanded that players give up numerous peripheral rights to the PGA, as well as the right to control their own playing schedule. The players decided that they wanted a tournament committee not subject to veto by the PGA Executive Board. The Board stubbornly insisted that they had started the tour, it was their baby, and by gosh, they would retain that right of veto. The quarreling went on all summer. The players hired Samuel Gates, a highly respected New York lawyer, to argue for their side. The PGA hired William Rogers as their attorney. Progress was nil and the result predictable. On August 23, the players, led by Gardner Dickinson, Nicklaus, Doug Ford, and Frank Beard, announced the formation of the American Professional Golfers, the APG. Sam Snead chose to stay with the PGA. Palmer remained a neutral, hoping to effect a compromise. By December 1, Dickinson, the APG's first president, was able to announce an independent APG tour of 28 tournaments for 1969, offering total purses worth $3.5 million. Tentatively, there were also an additional 13 events. This was not the first revolt from within the ranks. In 1949 George Schneiter, a touring pro and also the Tournament Bureau manager who had succeeded Fred Corcoran, broke away and attempted to set up a rival tour. Schneiter was summarily barred for life from the PGA and his tour failed.

This time the revolt succeeded. Deciding that it obviously could not conduct a tournament circuit featuring only Sam Snead and a retinue of teaching pros, the PGA gave in. A tournament policy board was set up within the PGA. It consisted of four touring pros, three PGA officers, and three independent and respected businessmen. Shortly thereafter Joseph C. Dey, the Executive Director of the U.S. Golf Association, was hired as tour czar. Dey, who had run the USGA with well ordered precision for many years, also supervised children's classes at his church on Sundays. He brought the kind of credibility, integrity, and efficiency to the operation of the pro tour that had not been there before. He was the Good Housekeeping Seal of Approval on something that had previously been badly organized, and full of conflict and inconsistent practices. Sponsors were no longer forced to deal with a changing set of officers from year to year. They knew they could plan ahead. The players knew the rulings concerning them would be based on fairness and integrity instead of personal bias.

It seems impossible that the tour can expand beyond the peak it has reached these last two years, but the signs are still bullish. The galleries are getting larger and larger. The prize money continues to increase and may go over $8 million in 1973. In 1971 Nicklaus, Lee Trevino, and Palmer became embroiled in a battle for the money title that carried all three over the $200,000 mark. Nicklaus won it with $244,490 to Trevino's $231,202 and Palmer's $209,603, but Lee carried off just about every other honor, including that of being the tour's most colorful personality. He won the U.S., Canadian, and British Opens within the span of a month, was named Golfer of the Year by the PGA, Male Athlete of the Year by the Associated Press, and Sportsman of the Year by *Sports Illustrated*. In 1972 it was Nicklaus's turn, almost a Grand Slam until edged by Trevino in the British Open and a record overall prize-money total, $320,542, more than twice what the entire tour paid all its players 28 years earlier.

The Big Three—Palmer, Player, and Nicklaus—are still very much at the top, but Trevino, Casper, a survivor from Young Turk days, England's Tony Jacklin, and Doug Sanders all have proved to be tremendous attractions too. Any sponsor who has a few of these in his field, especially Palmer, Player, Nicklaus, or Trevino, is virtually guaranteed a successful tournament from almost any point of view. Trevino has proved to be an indefatigable competitor. Despite being sidelined for several weeks following an appendectomy, he played in 32 events during 1971. In 1972 he was sidelined briefly by pneumonia, several times by sheer fatigue, but still managed more than 30 tournament appearances. In addition to long surges of remarkable golf, Trevino's steady parade of pranks and gags has provided the tour with a refreshing irreverence, a sweet change to galleries too often exposed to a series of stone faces.

It is remarkable to note that 1963 was the first year in which any player—in this case, both Nicklaus and Palmer—topped $100,000 in earnings. In 1972 Nicklaus led by a wide margin, but no less than 14 other players reached six figures in prize-money totals. As an evidence of how earnings have risen, in 1972 the 61st leading money-winner's total figure (not even enough to exempt him prequalifying in 1973) would make him the leading money-winner in 1958, the year Arnold Palmer first won that honor.

Whether the tour can continue to grow and prosper depends on a number of things. The tournament committee and sponsors must start reaching beyond the smug assumption that a 72-hole stroke-play event is the only viable way to conduct a tour every single week of the year. This

The Palmer swing

format tends to pall and grow dull. Needed is a more varied diet, more competitions such as the Team Championship, or a bona fide Match Play Championship, or round-robin events to sharpen fans' palates for the 72-hole stuff. It might be competitively, as well as aesthetically, refreshing to introduce a limited-field winner-take-all event for a purse of $100,000. Naturally, the tournament committee has a responsibility to provide work for its task force of 300 players as best it can, but the satellite event has proved a successful way of accomplishing this aim.

A second point for the PGA and the tour sponsors to consider is the need for more care in how they handle their events. Some abominable mistakes have been made. Dow Jones put up $300,000 in prize money two years ago, plus an additional $300,000 in expenses, and took a bath financially. Once was enough for them. Alcan, the Canadian aluminum company, spent almost $1 million a year for four years to put on and promote a big international event, most commendable to be sure. Their qualifying format, however, depended on several relatively minor events on the tour (no major championships), and so they almost always wound up with very much less than a top-grade field of players despite their enormous expense.

Both Dow Jones and Alcan dug themselves deep holes, and while it was all done to promote their corporate image, it made them look foolish rather than otherwise. Sponsorship is not a bottomless pit. If enough sponsors get burned, others might not be so eager to approach the fire.

Finally, what those directing the destinies of tournament golf in the U.S. must soon realize is that the tour has become a global affair. As of now, players in the U.S. must obtain permission from a U.S. tournament sponsor to be able to play in another event that same week somewhere else in the world. If a player agrees to play in at least 20 tour events during the course of a year, then he should be permitted to do whatever he pleases with the other 32 weeks, including travel abroad. If this very reasonable freedom does not become a reality soon, there could be another political explosion in golf as serious as what occurred in 1968. You cannot trap a professional golfer in the U.S. while big money is being offered overseas. The Pacific Masters in Japan is offering a purse of $300,000. The John Player Classic in Britain pays $150,000. The latter, in fact, had to indemnify the Quad-City Classic in Iowa to the tune of $25,000 just to gain a release from them for the American players they have invited.

There will be other big international events in other parts of the world, in Europe, in Asia, in Australia, and perhaps in New Zealand. In the not too distant future something very close to a world tour will be a reality. It would be a good thing for golf, of course, and not such a bad idea for the world as well.

⌈8⌋

SPECIAL EVENTS—TV MEANS DOLLARS

T HE SIGHT OF Alan Shepard hitting a six iron on the moon was regarded by Norman Mailer as the ultimate obscenity: as the poverty-stricken masses gazed heavenward, they saw the most profligate expenditure of public money capped by a gesture of contempt from the privileged classes. Even in heaven the golfing society has the upper hand. One can offer no balm for Mailer's tortured (and highly paid) social conscience. The more secular response was that golf and television had finally made it to the outermost reaches of man's experience. The zoom lens and the six iron were confirmed as "essentials" of life.

There is no way of measuring the effect which TV has had on golf. Obviously it has played a large part in popularizing the game, one factor, admittedly a major one, in the bandwagon process of golf's expansion since World War II. It also made, and still makes, a significant contribution to the commercial structuring of tournament golf. Certainly television was what made golfers like Arnold Palmer into familiar faces and living personalities. The effect of such exposure everywhere was to create a demand for Palmer and the other giants of golf and at the same time to breed a dissatisfaction for anything less than the best. In one way, Palmer is a bad example. No top-flight golfer responds more keenly to this feeling of being wanted. He has always felt an obligation to the world's golf fans and nobody has traveled farther to honor what he regards as a debt to golf.

Most players take a more prosaic view. The big stars naturally compete where the rewards are highest, on the U.S. tour, and they have to be tempted overseas. It is no good simply mounting a tournament with the

Tony Jacklin drives across the Thames

Palmer and "friend"

richest first prize in the history of golf and expecting that all the golfers will instantly abandon their domestic circuit and book a plane ticket. The player will ask, "What is the worst I can get out of it?" and a promoter has to ensure some pretty fancy last-place money to tempt a golfer in these circumstances to pass up a $200,000 tournament at home.

Some day there may be a proper global circuit, but at the moment the only methods by which the golf fan in Paris and Stockholm, Melbourne and Osaka can see the world's best is via the TV screen or at live tournaments with fields so limited that every competitor is guaranteed a good payday.

Television first got into this corner of golf in the mid-Fifties through the enterprise of Walter Schwimmer, a producer and impressario, who was looking around for a little variety in the sporting diet of boxing, football, baseball, bowling, and wrestling. An aide suggested golf. Schwimmer was skeptical. How could the camera follow the ball? And if the viewer couldn't see where the ball went, he could hardly be expected to be engrossed in pictures of men simply swinging the club. Anyway, they experimented with different camera angles and techniques and eventually learned enough about photographing golf to become thoroughly sold on the concept. They were sufficiently enthusiastic to set up the first match, Sam Snead against Cary Middlecoff, at Chicago's Cog Hill course. The golfers were paid $2,000 each, fat pickings for 1956, and after two days of shooting—with each hole taking an hour to complete—the first TV match was in the can, Snead's 67 making him a cliff-hanging winner by a single stroke. When the 20,000 feet of film was edited down to an hour-long program of 2,000 feet, its merit was quickly recognized by ABC-TV, which decided to run a series called *All Star Golf*.

The first show went on in late 1957 and was an immediate success. Rival networks paid the series the ultimate compliment of copying the format, and a spate of programs followed—*Celebrity Golf*, *Championship Golf*, Shell's *Wonderful World of Golf*, *Challenge Golf*, the CBS *Golf Classic*, and others. The genre of golf played specially for TV, with all the advantages to be obtained in heightening the excitement by skillful editing, was firmly established.

Innovators do not always remain leaders in the field. All too often someone comes along and, by watching the pioneer and avoiding his mistakes, makes an even greater success. So far as TV golf was concerned, the front-runner stayed out in front, thanks to another flash of inspiration. Schwimmer had the idea of matching the winners of the four classic events in a contest to decide the champion of champions. The United States PGA gave its blessing, and after months of work a network and a sponsor were found for the World Series of Golf. The Firestone Country Club of Akron, Ohio, offered to stage the match, and in due course all that remained was to sign up the winners of the Masters, U.S. Open, British Open, and PGA championships.

No one had given any thought to the question of alternates and in 1962, it will be remembered, Arnold Palmer won the Masters and the British Open and he tied for the U.S. Open. All he had to do was win the playoff and complete a Grand Slam at the PGA and Schwimmer would find himself putting up $75,000 for a one-man exhibition match. In any event, Jack Nicklaus won the playoff for the Open and Gary Player took the PGA Championship, so Schwimmer had the undisputed best three players of the day for his inaugural tournament.

Or so he thought. The PGA has strict rules about the number of exhibition matches a golfer may play every year. The World Series was then technically an exhibition—it is now official—and it had to be pointed out that they had all used up their quotas. The PGA is naturally concerned about avoiding any suspicion that it operates one law for the rich and one for the poor, and this problem caused a fair amount of soul searching. Eventually, the PGA agreed to relax the point and let the players compete.

Another embarrassment arose in the form of a protest by the sponsors of the Denver Open, which was being played on the date of the telecast. They were afraid that everybody would stay at home and watch the Big Three fighting it out for the $50,000 first prize, the biggest payout in the history of the game at the time. Again the PGA found itself in the middle. After more troubled conferences it was finally agreed that the World Series sponsors would advertise in the Denver papers urging the fans to watch the Denver Open and then enjoy the World Series, taped, in the evening. This meant blacking out the Denver area for live TV coverage.

There were other crises, including a threatened rainstorm which just held off long enough for play to be completed, but the show was a huge success. It hardly could fail to be, with the world's three finest golfers competing on one of America's great courses. Jack Nicklaus won that inaugural match and since then has been the most dominant golfer in the series, with four victories and total earnings far in excess of $200,000. The World Series has come to be accepted as an established tradition of the golfing calendar. That acceptance has not been won without opposition. Television seems to have generated hostility that is hard to define. Some people feel threatened by the sheer power of the medium. Golfing purists are suspicious of any form of golf which is "set up" for the cameras, and are affronted by the thought of golfers having to wait between shots (sometimes for half an hour or more) while camera positions are changed. There is a widespread attitude that it is in some way immoral to make money out of sport (except, that is, among the sportsmen themselves), and, of course, the World Series is immensely successful commercially. For all that, TV golf makes more friends than enemies and has been a potent force in the popularization of the game.

The British Broadcasting Corporation had achieved only moderate audience response from live coverage of the general run of British tournaments. Two film series were suggested—one, a nine-match series entitled *The U.S. versus the Rest of the World*, and the other, a film series of the Big Three in Britain, with Palmer, Player, and Nicklaus playing 54 holes over three of Scotland's outstanding courses, St. Andrews, Gleneagles, and Carnoustie. It was a fairly big decision for the BBC to make, because, although the money involved—over 100,000 pounds—was not excessive by normal program standards, it was expensive for a specialized and minority sports show. Special considerations, such as the need to make an important inauguration of color television in Britain, and the hope, to be realized later, of a sale to an American network, swung the day.

Two questions frequently asked about TV golf are: "Is it fixed?" and "Don't you worry that one of the golfers might have an off day and you'll get a dull, one-sided match?" To the first question, categorical assurance can be given that none of the BBC golf films was fixed in any way. On some golf shows made by other companies it may be that, on occasion, golfers have been allowed to play a bad shot over again, but the BBC has always played the game straight. The only concession made to dramatic interest is that the matches are not always screened in the order of shooting. Thus, in the *United States versus the World* series, the showing sequence was arranged to keep the outcome undecided for as long as possible. As to bad shots, they have always stayed in and have added to the quality of the series. Obviously, in editing 18 holes of golf down to an hour-long program, something has to end up on the cutting room floor, but the BBC normally discards these holes where players make conventional, unexciting halves in par figures.

The second question, about the risk of walk-away victories, does provoke twinges of anxiety, of course. However, if the chemistry is right—meaning that top-class golfers play really good courses—the chance of such lopsided matches is reduced to the point where the producer can discard his phenobarbital and sleep easily. The greater the player, the greater the assurance that he will do his utmost to put on a fine show of golfing skill—especially on television before millions of viewers.

That certainly proved the case with the first venture in 1966 with the Big Three in Britain. In fact, the outcome was *too* close because, believe it or not, Palmer, Nicklaus, and Player finished in a three-way tie. It posed a bit of problem, which was resolved when NBC (which had taken the series) commissioned a playoff, subsequently held in Puerto Rico!

The success of the Big Three show spawned further series—Arnold Palmer and Tony Jacklin playing the best 18 holes in Britain and more of the *United States versus the World* series. The quality of a golf hole is entirely subjective and a matter of personal opinion and many golfers would feel that the 18 "best" holes filmed would not be their personal choices. Certainly, though, they were all famous (or infamous) holes, rich in the history of the game and the scene of many notable events. Anyway, a certain amount of controversy over the choice did the series no harm at all.

When you get right down to it, everything hinges on the availability of players. It is one thing to sit down in isolation and pick a world team and a United States team. It is quite another to arrange for these players to be at a certain course at a certain time for the convenience of cameras.

It is difficult enough to plot one golf star's movements. The task becomes Herculean when you have to arrange for 26 international golfers, the cast for a *United States versus the World* series, to be at specific places on specific days, and for the production company to deploy a batallion of some 50 technicians, eight cameras, and a convoy of vehicles, and you have to complete the entire operation in the few days the stars are available. For evidence of the complexity of the operation, look at this hectic schedule . . .

The *Best 18 Holes* series was filmed concurrently with one of the U.S. vs. world series and in one four-day period the intrepid producer had to fit in the following:

First, Harold Henning versus Phil Rodgers at Royal Birkdale. Next morning they filmed two holes with Palmer and Jacklin at Birkdale, moved the entire operation the 50-odd miles to Hoylake, and filmed two more holes before lunch. Then they drove up to Royal Lytham, some 70 miles, filmed one hole of Palmer and Jacklin, drove to Blackpool, and caught a chartered plane to Prestwick in Scotland and took the caravan out to Turnberry. The following day they filmed five "best hole" matches on three different courses, Pretwick, Troon, and Turnberry. Then the next day they had a *United States versus the World* match at Turnberry. By the rather leisurely standards of other TV golf series, which devote two days to 18 holes, this sort of schedule was unprecedented. And the producer's task was not made any easier on that occasion since it was not possible to tell him who would be representing the United States as Henning's opponent until the day before the match.

To make matters even worse, the weather was so bad, with lashing rain and a gale strong enough to blow down two trees on Southport promenade, that golf was barely possible. The players were ready to quit because it was so embarrassing for them. Henning's first shot, for instance, was blown out of bounds and never seen again. Despite all the hitches, such as Miller Barber's clubs being lost and Art Wall having to play braille golf with rain smearing his glasses, some special Providence saw to it that every match was completed somehow and, in their edited forms, the films were impressively dramatic. For many young American professionals, their first impression of golf in Britain was gained from watching those films of flagsticks bowing so that the flags almost touched the green under the fury of the wind.

The aim behind all these series was simultaneously to satisfy the demands of the addict viewer and to interest those people who were not basically interested in the game at all. The viewing figures, which bore no relation to the audience for the earlier live golf coverage, confirmed the success of this policy, and market research showed that a large proportion of housewives and children became enslaved by the weekly golf programs.

From a purely chronological point of view, this account has slipped slightly out of synchronization. For although the BBC filmed golf was something unique in Britain, this type of program was already well established in the United States. At about the same time as Walter Schwimmer introduced the *World Series of Golf*, the Shell Oil Company began its program of international golf films.

Shell's *Wonderful World of Golf* ran for nine consecutive years, from 1962 through 1970. During that period some 92 matches were filmed in 50 different countries. In the process, an estimated 200 miles of film was exposed and Shell's golf budget was in the region of $20 million. With an involvement of such proportions in time, money, and effort, the average man in the locker room is entitled to ask what an oil company was getting out of golf. The company publicity department put it this way: "The program was designed to create a favorable image of Shell by describing significant contributions made by the company to the cultural, social, and economic life of the countries in which the golf matches were filmed. The objectives of the commercial messages were to portray Shell as part of a worldwide organization with a concern for progress and human welfare . . . and to leave an impression of the benefits which the company brings to consumers in the United States as a result of its international association. Golf was chosen as the theme because the sport was growing rapidly, with millions participating, and tens of thousands of new players joining the ranks every year, thus creating a growing audience. Golfers as a group are above average in income and influence, and include influential individuals who not only consume petroleum products themselves but influence their companies' purchases of these products. . . ."

Cynics sitting in traffic-jammed motor cars and coughing at the pollution from exhausts may choke even more at the oil company's "concern for progress and human welfare." But you have to admire the skill of the TV series. If crude oil (and crude business) smells, what better way could you find of sweetening the tainted air than by the application of that popular deodorant, golf, the international favorite? Anyway, the golfing aerosol worked wonders for Shell and, what is more, Shell worked wonders for golf. The series was immensely popular, and unquestionably contributed greatly to the expansion of the game. Every one of those 92 films were watched by some 15 million people and the 16-millimeter motion pictures which were later made from the telecasts for noncommercial showing in golf clubs and community groups are still in popular demand.

Another commercial promotion which was designed, like the Shell TV series, to influence people with influence was the Alcan series of tournaments. It aimed at international stature but did not comply with the original precept that the only way to give the best to the most is either by TV/film or in strictly limited-field events. It failed as a tournament and was perhaps the most ill-conceived approach to spending $500,000 a year in golf that has ever been devised.

In late 1964, two men were driving from Canada to New York for the Thunderbird tournament when they ran into a landslide. Their car hit a chunk of rock which ripped off the oil pan and there was nothing for it but to wait at a motel while repairs were made.

They talked golf for hours over drinks and as dawn broke over the Adirondacks, they believed they had devised the perfect golf tournament.

The two men were Hilles Pickens, a publisher, and Doug Smith, sports commentator. They abandoned all thoughts of getting to the Thunderbird. Instead they retraced their steps to Montreal in order to develop their scheme. In essence, the plan was a series of tournaments, played in different parts of the world, on a wide variety of courses and in disparate climates, culminating in a grand final to find the Golfer of the Year.

From a promotional point of view, the idea had one great advantage. The qualifying stages would cost little since they would be tied to regular scheduled tournaments which, with the cooperation of the sponsors, would be nominated as Golfer of the Year preliminaries. Thus whoever picked up the scheme could expect to enjoy accumulating publicity during the qualifying stages at virtually little expense.

Smith and Pickens found a taker in Alcan, the Canadian aluminum giant, and devoted themselves full time to promoting what now became the Alcan Golfer of the Year championships. They incorporated themselves under the sweetly scented title of Heather and Pine. By the beginning of 1967 the details were all arranged.

In the United States the four leader events (Alcan deliberately avoided the use of the word "qualifying" since this might be thought to denigrate the tournaments to the status of mere preliminary rounds for another tournament) were: Colonial National Invitation, at Fort Worth, Texas; Cleveland Open; Western Open, at Chicago; and the Philadelphia Classic. The continued existence of these tournaments was in doubt, and, in an effort to appease the sponsors, the PGA forced Alcan to nominate them as Alcan preliminaries. The idea, of course, was to entice Gary Player, Arnold Palmer, Jack Nicklaus, and Billy Casper into them, so they might have a crack at the Golfer of the Year title. The plan backfired. Many of the games' stars resented the thought of being pressured into appearing at tournaments they didn't want to play in just for a chance to prove what their records had already amply proved.

The way the plan operated was this:

Players selected their best three 72-hole scores from these four tournaments and the 12 with the lowest aggregates qualified for the Golfer of the

Year Championship at St. Andrews, Scotland, the following October.

In Britain the four leader events were: Agfa-Gevaert Tournament at Stoke Poges, the Martini International at Fulford, the Carrolls International at Dublin, and the Dunlop Masters at Sandwich. The leading five players, and ties, qualified on the same best three-scores-out-of-four basis. As a desperate afterthought, the three leaders of the American official money list were invited (if not otherwise qualified) plus the first two in the British PGA Order of Merit table. In theory, the system seemed straightforward enough. In practice, there was very little public interest in the qualifying stages because, although everyone knew that the ultimate championship was to be played for the (then) richest first prize in the history of golf, over $50,000, no one could keep track of the qualifying system without the benefit of a private computer. Since the players were able to discard their worst scores, it was impossible at any time during the preliminaries to state that any one golfer was leading the race.

This weakness in the system, however, did not appear to distress the sponsor unduly. Alcan was in a different position from most commercial promoters of sporting events. As sellers of a prime material, rather than a retailed product, Alcan was not essentially interested in making its name a household word. The target was the aluminum market. They wanted to make an impression on the companies which bought aluminum in bulk. Instead of a broadcast shot aimed at the millions, Alcan was focusing on a market which could be counted in the hundreds: the handful of international businessmen who controlled the purchasing policies of their companies. They might be American, French, Japanese, or German. The *lingua franca* of big business, the one activity which unites nearly every company president no matter where he comes from, is golf. Alcan's total golfing budget during the period of the tournament, which ran into several million dollars, was not to earn friends but to win customers.

And golf, as the most amateurish of the psychologists of the game recognizes, is the tycoon's most vulnerable spot. He may have the most acute mind in his business, but get him on the golf course and, like anyone else, he becomes a slave to the game. Arrange for him to play with an Arnold Palmer and you are his friend for life. And that is exactly what Alcan tried to do.

What Alcan did was take up a proportion of the spots in the pro-ams which preceded the leader tournaments and nominate their favored customers. They also had special Alcan hospitality facilities and dinner parties, and generally immersed their business friends in the exciting world of the professional golf tour.

In due course, the leader tournaments produced the field of qualifiers. From America came George Archer, Miller Barber, Homero Blancas, Julius Boros, Gay Brewer, Billy Casper, Bob Charles, Gardner Dickinson, Bobby Nichols, Mason Rudolph, Doug Sanders, Dan Sikes, Dave Stockton, and Bert Weaver. The British qualifiers were: Peter Alliss, Brian Barnes, Peter Butler, Malcolm Gregson, Tommy Horton, Christy O'Connor, and Dave Thomas.

Reading through that list, one cannot escape the feeling that something was missing. Did these 21 players really represent the cream of world golf in 1967, one of whose number would become the undisputed Golfer of the Year? What of Jack Nicklaus, who topped the money list of 1967, or Arnold Palmer, who was second? Both had decided quite independently that they had nothing to prove. Their records had firmly established them as the golfers of that or any of the preceeding ten years. With Gary Player, they had dominated world golf to an extent which made the thought of a complex eliminating system laughable.

A practical point completely overrides any personal feelings which the players may have held about the tournament: Anyone who reaches the stature of a Palmer or a Player cannot leave a blank week in his diary on the chance of playing a tournament. Their time is far too valuable for that kind of haphazard scheduling. Nor would they be happy about the idea of having to compete in four arbitrarily chosen tour events which might or might not fit into their playing schedules. Although they are sportsmen, they are also businessmen and have to apply business methods to their schedules. They had contractual engagements in Japan the week chosen for the Alcan final, so all discussion was pointless.

So no Palmer, Player, or Nicklaus. Even without the Prince of Denmark and the Queen, the golfing *Hamlet* was mounted with fanfare. A special Act of Parliament was passed to enable the sponsors to charge gate money at the Old Course on Sunday, St. Andrews being a public links and technically common land on which the people of the city have rights of recreation. The vast Gleneagles Hotel was taken over in its entirety to house the guests of Alcan. And an ancient ritual was revived, with the golfers and their caddies marching, rather self-consciously, through the ancient burgh behind a pipe band. As a gesture to the host PGA, Alcan simultaneously sponsored the Alcan International Championship, with a purse of £11,785 for the British players who had not been fortunate enough to make the field for the "Big Alcan."

In the Golfer of the Year Championship, Gay Brewer and Billy Casper tied with four-round totals of 283, and Brewer subsequently won the playoff with a 68 to Casper's 72. By an embarrassing coincidence, the "Little Alcan" was won by Peter Thomson of Australia with a total of 281. Since both tournaments were played simultaneously, and on the same course, conditions were obviously identical except for a few odd face-saving yards on certain tees. Also, one or two of the holes were shortened to suggest that the two fields were playing different courses and thus make comparisons of the score invalid. No one was fooled.

The fact was it was the same for everybody, and the winner of the consolation event had beaten the score of the mighty Golfer of the Year, which, of course, made the title even more of a farce. At the prize presentation Thomson dryly suggested that perhaps he could call himself the golfer of the week. Brewer wasn't complaining. As a good professional with no fancy pretensions to greatness, golf to him was a business, and with that fat check in his pocket he could count this as a highly successful week's work.

The following year the same formula was repeated, with minor variations. But the result was the same, for Gay Brewer won again. Fortunately, Bill Large and Irishman Christy O'Connor were able to give the subsidiary Alcan International something of a fresh look by sharing victory, sparing everyone's blushes by scoring 288 over the links of Royal Birkdale—this time 5 shots more than Brewer.

The 1969 Golfer of the Year Championship was played at the Portland Golf Club, Oregon, and the qualifying net had been spread wider to include the continent of Europe, bringing in Jean Garaialde of France. Palmer, Nicklaus, and Player were still not disposed to support the event. Although the field included some strong golfers in Casper, Trevino, and Beard from the United States, Christy O'Connor and Maurice Bembridge from Britain, Graham Henning from South Africa, and Kel Nagle and David Graham from Australia, it was again a weak one.

For the first time the event was attended by high drama on the course, plus an incident of black comedy: Nagle's marker accidentally entered his first nine-hole total in the space for the 9th-hole score. Under the rules of golf this had to stand once Nagle had signed his card and so, instead of scoring in the 70s, he was posted with a total of over a hundred. The rules leave the committee with no freedom of action in such cases. (The golfer himself must always be responsible for the details of his card, but it does seem unduly hard that obvious mistakes—and by other people, at that— cannot be rectified later. Remember the tragedy of Roberto de Vicenzo's wrongly marked card at the Masters? Some well-run tournaments these days have "scrutineers" who check cards with the players for such slips of the pen before the cards are officially handed in. If that is permissible, it seems entirely justified for the committee to refuse to accept a card bearing a blatant error, until the player has been given an opportunity to adjust it.)

The drama was something else. It involved Trevino, seemingly coasting home with an unassailable lead, and Casper, playing just in front of him. A barrage of six birdies in the final round, followed by an eagle at the 15th, gave Trevino a 7-stroke lead, and Casper was working hard for that second-place check. He rolled in birdie putts on the last four greens and came in content enough with the prospect of picking up $15,000. True, it was not $55,000, but that was clearly earmarked for Trevino. Or was it? The Mexican had dropped a shot to par at the 16th, and as Casper putted out the last green, Trevino hit a nine iron into the short 17th. It was never enough club and the ball was bunkered. It stayed that way after the first recovery attempt, and then Trevino just dug it out—but 35 feet from the flag. He three-putted. While Casper had picked up 4 shots against par, Trevino had lost that many in just two holes. Now he needed a birdie to tie. His 15-footer slipped by, and with it $40,000.

In the press room there was bedlam. The British golf writers, fighting against an eight-hour time difference, had mostly written their stories and were waiting for events to confirm their accounts. One had actually handed in his cable to Western Union and, with an Anglo-Saxon oath, had to snatch the copy back from the startled teleprinter operator and start again.

The last of the tragic Alcans was held in 1970 in Ireland, at Portmarnock. After the annual statistical review of the leader tournament results, the field as usual was a mixture of some good players and others who could hardly be described as world-class contenders, even by the most wide-eyed of fans. Ireland greeted them with half a gale, which does not sound like much when put like that, but which represented a wind force totally outside the experience of some of the Americans. Dave Hill trailed the field after a first-round 83 and began talking in terms of the next plane home. More spirited challenges were mounted to Bruce Devlin's lead by Peter Oosterhuis, Lee Trevino, Neil Coles, and Bob Rosburg, who completed his second round with only 22 putts—and using a borrowed putter at that. But this was Devlin's week. He did everything well and in the end walked home with a clear margin of 7 strokes—the kind of finish any sponsor or promoter must dread. Meanwhile, in the subsidiary Alcan International, victory had gone to Paddy Skerritt from nearby St. Anne's. Skerritt was carried shoulder high by excited well-wishers, and at one point Devlin had to wait while the victory procession was shooed off the fairway. Legend has it that the celebrations continued until dawn and that subsequently the St. Anne's clubhouse had to be totally rebuilt.

World Cup

There is an enormous appeal in the idea of friendly rivalry on the field of sport, and the golf tournament that introduces an international element starts off with a considerable advantage. The spectator has not been born who can watch a match between a fellow countryman and a foreigner without a heightened sense of involvement.

John Jay Hopkins, a Canadian industrialist, was that strange mixture of hard-headed businessman and visionary. He believed with a missionary's zeal that golf could be an agent of international friendship, and he had the ability to turn his ideas into reality.

In 1952 he founded the International Association for the express purpose of promoting a tournament among the nations of the world. The inaugural event, for what was then called the Canada Cup, was played at Montreal in 1953 with seven two-man teams—Canada, the United States, Argentina, Australia, Germany, Mexico, and a combined team from England and South Africa.

Everyone thought that the outcome would be a formality for the American pair, U.S. National Open champion Julius Boros and the PGA champion Jim Turnesa. Indeed the general feeling was that America would take the trophy every time it was put up for competition. No matter—as Hopkins put it:

"Golf is a game for good neighbors. It has the spice of competition while imposing the highest moral restraints. It offers a contest but demands in return the last full measure of discipline. In short, it is a civilized and a civilizing game. It is my earnest belief that it could contribute, in even a substantial way, to the preservation of civilization itself."

Heady stuff, indeed. As for the spice of competition which Hopkins had introduced almost as an incidental aim of the tournament, it began to loom rather larger when the first cup was won for Argentina by Antonio Cerda and Roberto de Vicenzo. The vaunted American pair finished third from last. As well as a good-will exercise, Hopkins had a valid golf competition on his hands.

Although America has subsequently dominated the series, it has not been an exclusively American preserve. Japan, Spain, Ireland, Australia, South Africa, and Canada have all had their triumphs in what has now become the World Cup contest. Whether or not the competition has fulfilled the high hopes of its founder, it has certainly done a good propaganda job for golf, and the rise of the game in Japan particularly must be largely attributed to the 1957 competition at Kasumigaseki near Tokyo. At least 40 nations now compete regularly for the Cup.

In other respects the track record of the World Cup has been less impressive, even tragic. A wonderful basic idea has been dissipated by inept organization. Since the death of Hopkins, his tournament has become the preserve of four or five very big companies promoting their commercial enterprises under the guise of international good will. The pro-am fields are padded by corporate executives and favored customers, while the prize money has been maintained at a ridiculous level. Players are conned into playing the World Cup for peanuts, since to refuse is to risk the stigma of being called unpatriotic. The corporations that wrap their commercial dealings in national flags should be forced to raise the prize money to an appropriate level, or the competition should be taken over by a genuine international golfing federation. It could be that a good commercial sponsor could make something of the World Cup. The founder may have set his sights impossibly high, but it is sad that the fulfillment has fallen so woefully short of that original shining vision.

Ryder Cup

In marked contrast, and despite a lamentable one-sidedness that would surely have throttled any other sports promotion to death, the Ryder Cup Series of biennial matches between the United States and Britain has done considerable good for the image of professional golf. For more reasons than its seniority in years (it officially started in 1927), it has gained the international respect that the World Cup so desperately needs and seeks, but cannot possibly hope to achieve with all its present shortcomings.

The spirit of nationalism lit by each Ryder Cup confrontation is both real and deep; particularly so in Britain where, with Tony Jacklin as the material symbol of what has become a David-versus-Goliath fairway feud, hope springs eternal.

The British, in 19 attempts to beat the Americans, succeeded three times, the last in 1957, and tied just once. Those three and a half moments of glory all happened in front of British galleries. The chances of an American team losing at home are no more likely than Boston apologizing for the Tea Party.

The record of the series does not add up to a marathon bore, however. On the contrary, the Ryder Cup has provoked some of the most stimulating and memorable moments in the history of the game, and it will continue to do so for a long time to come. For the players, money doesn't come into it. They are motivated by pride alone. As Arnold Palmer has said:

"It doesn't matter how many open championships or titles you may have won. When you stand on the tee at a Ryder Cup Match to play for your country, your stomach rumbles like that of a kid turning up for his first tournament."

Not surprisingly, the Ryder Cup Series has had its problems—all, in one way and another, having to do with the unequal battle. But the contribution of the Ryder Cup goes beyond deciding who wins every two years.

How it all began is a question that has been given more than one answer. It was said by the late George Sargent, who was President of the United States PGA during the 1920s, that Sylvanus Jermain of the Inverness Country Club in Toledo first had the idea in 1921, immediately following the U.S. Open on his home course. The late Bob Harlow, who once managed Walter Hagen, thought the matches were first proposed, in 1921, by James Harnett.

According to Harlow, the idea of pitting a team of Americans against the British at that time was greeted by Andrew Kirkaldy, the St. Andrews professional, with the remark, "I dinna regard it as a level match."

Whatever the arguments about the origins, the fact is that at Gleneagles in Scotland in 1921 a match between teams of American and British professionals was played. It was staged on the eve of the match-play championship and proved a disaster for the Americans, who lost by 9 points to 3, Emmett French, Freddie McLeod, and Wilfrid Reid alone being successful for the United States. Kirkaldy was right—it wasn't a level match at all.

Five years later in 1926 at Wentworth—where the world match-play championship is now sponsored by the Piccadilly Cigarette Company—another team of Americans took up the challenge of trying to beat the British at their own game. If the 1921 result was a disaster, then this was nothing short of a massacre. The U.S. professionals were thrashed by 13½ to 1½ points. But there was a happy ending, for in the gallery was a man destined to figure in the golfing ambitions of two nations.

Samuel Ryder, in the 1880s, was a young man living in the North of England. He moved to St. Albans near London after his father had disagreed with him over his idea of how to make a fortune. Sam wanted to sell seeds—"Everything from mustard and cress to orchids"—in penny packets. His father thought it would be a failure but Sam persisted and did indeed make a fortune. He was fifty before he took up golf, but in 12 months reduced his handicap to single figures. The main reason for this was that he became an extraordinarily good chipper and putter. Also, he was rich enough to be able to afford Abe Mitchell as his private professional.

When a good many of the best American players were in Britain for the 1926 open championship at Lytham and St. Anne's, Ryder suggested that they should form a team to meet the British at Wentworth.

The idea was acted upon, and on the 4th and 5th of June America put out a formidable-looking team that included Jim Barnes, Walter Hagen, Tommy Armour, Joe Kirkwood, Al Watrous, and Freddie McLeod. They won only one of the singles and none of the foursomes, the partnership of Barnes and Hagen taking a 9-and-8 hiding from Abe Mitchell and George Duncan. After the match it was Duncan who suggested to Samuel Ryder that the contest should become official. Ryder liked the idea and presented a solid gold trophy, and so the biennial competition began. Ryder helped enormously with the expenses of the British teams, and was rewarded for his generosity with two British wins in 1929 and 1933 before he died in 1936 at the age of seventy-seven. The first formal match was held in 1927; the trend was set at Worcester, with the Americans winning comfortably by 9½ points to 2½. A change in the rules limited the Americans to native-born professionals, and, as a result, only Bill Mehlhorn, Al Watrous, and Walter Hagen survived from the 1926 squad.

The British proved no match for the Americans, whose work around the greens, brilliant chipping and putting, was to set a pattern that marked America's golf for the years to come. A change came to the British, however, at Moortown in 1929, with the Americans suffering a 7 points to 5 defeat. Walter Hagen and George Duncan, as team captains, agreed that it was only right and proper that they should play one another. It was a decision that Hagen had cause to rue; Duncan gave him a 10 and 8 thrashing.

In the sweltering June heat of the 1931 match at Columbus, which America won by 9 points to 3, Hagen had his revenge. He partnered Denny Shute and hammered, by a 10 and 8 margin, Duncan and Arthur Havers in the foursomes.

Some 15,000 spectators including the then Prince of Wales were visible evidence of the growing interest in the Ryder Cup Series when the next match was staged at Southport in 1933. And with that kind of support, it was not surprising that Britain won by 6½ points to 5½. The British tried a new move by having a nonplaying captain, J. H. Taylor. He proved a stern taskmaster, even compelling his team to undertake roadwork and gymnastics in order to be fit. But the match came perilously close to developing into an international fiasco. Walter Hagen twice failed to produce his order of play at the appointed time, and, finally, Taylor, his patience gone, delivered an ultimatum. If Hagen didn't produce on the spot, he said, then the match would be called off. Hagen, fortunately for the series, came running.

There was drama too on the course. Olin Dutra, the United States PGA champion, reached a turn in level 4s, stayed 5 down at lunch, and was buried by 9 and 8. In those days the format of the match comprised four 36-hole foursomes and eight 36-hole singles. The scoring system then was for the winner to receive one point, with half a point for a tie—all points being accumulated on a team basis.

Eventually the 1933 match rested on a classic duel between Denny Shute and Syd Easterbrook, who were all square on the final tee, the American needing a point to earn his team a tie. But poor Shute took a 6 on the par-4 finishing hole and saw Easterbrook make a putt of 3 feet to win.

It was a result that cheered Sam Ryder, but it was the last Ryder Cup Match that he was to witness.

Serious administrative problems erupted over the next match at Ridgewood, New Jersey, in 1935. The British, not surprisingly, were unhappy at risking another exposure to the kind of heat they had suffered at Columbus in midsummer. There were moments when it seemed as though the series might be suspended, but eventually a member of the Ridgewood Club, James Black, who was on a business trip to England, worked out a peace plan with the British PGA secretary, Commander R. C. Roe. It was, simply, that the match should be put back to the cooler climate of September.

The British dispatched a team that included several newcomers: Alf Perry, Jack Busson, Dick Burton, and Bill Cox. They appeared to have little chance against such experienced U.S. players as Hagen, Sarazen, Revolta, Runyan, and Dutra. But, as wide as the margin was eventually to prove, the Americans had to fight for their win. Cox, for example, came back from 5 down to snatch a tie; and for the same result the U.S. Open champion, Sam Parks, had to hole from 20 feet on the last green against Perry.

Sam Snead for America and Dai Rees for Britain, each destined to compile outstanding records, made their Ryder Cup debuts at Southport in 1937. It was to be the final Ryder Cup match before World War II, and the Americans broke the pattern of home teams winning by taking it 8 points to 4. Snead, in the singles, overcame Dick Burton by 5 and 4, while Rees got his Ryder Cup career off to a great start by handing Byron Nelson a 3-and-1 hiding.

Ben Hogan, still recovering from his near-fatal car crash, captained the American team which won by 7 points to 5 at Ganton in 1949. Still hobbling painfully, he tongue-lashed his team into a storming recovery after they had lost 3 of the 4 foursomes matches. In the singles, a landslide was highlighted by Dutch Harrison beating Max Faulkner by 8 and 7; Sam Snead overcoming Charlie Ward 6 and 5; and Jimmy Demaret whipping Arthur Lees 7 and 6.

The result aside, it was one of the unhappiest of Ryder Cup matches. The British, in the first place, were not amused by the Americans bringing with them vast supplies of food to overcome the shortages imposed by rationing. Hamper baskets loaded with such luxuries as steaks and chops were viewed as displays of vulgar American wealth by some observers, and they became a source of embarrassment. Then on the eve of the match, Hogan, ever a stickler for the rule, suddenly demanded an inspection of the clubs to be used by the British professionals. As a result, the grooves on one set had to be filed to meet his requirements and those of the rules of golf. Just as the match was finishing, the British government devalued the pound, and it was to prove expensive for those Americans whose pockets were crammed with newly shrunken notes. As the U.S. team hurried to the boat Demaret was quoted as saying, "All we want of England right now is 'out.' "

Hogan, by now fit, was the playing captain for America when they won the 1951 match at Pinehurst by 9½ points to 2½. He contributed two wins: beating Ward 3 and 2 in the singles and joining Demaret to beat the partnership of Fred Daly and Ken Bousfield in the foursomes by 5 and 4.

By now the British were ready to admit that they were knocking their heads against a wall. The gap between them and the Americans was widening. The United States had a whole list of advantages: a great many more golfers to draw from; a 12-month tournament circuit on which to sharpen their competitive experience. The suggestion was made then, and a great many times since, that the British should admit that their island was too small to take on the might of America, and the most sensible thing to do would be to form a Commonwealth team. If the British were short on skill,

Snead and Hogan at 1953 Open at Oakmont

they were certainly full to the brim with pride, and this idea hurt. The attitude was one of "Our day will come," and it very nearly did at Wentworth in 1953 when America was fortunate to win by 6½ points to 5½.

Henry Cotton was appointed captain and it was a job to which he brought new methods: housing the team together at Wentworth and calling them to nightly,meetings for brainwashing. Drawing on the respect he had earned as a three-time British Open champion, Henry told his men: "Americans can be beaten and you will beat them this week." They very nearly did.

The Americans got off to a fast start and took the foursomes 3 to 1 on the first day. But in the singles, the British came back, Eric Brown knocking out Lloyd Mangrum, and Harry Weetman, the victim later of a tragic car crash, beat Sam Snead for a remarkable upset.

Snead was waltzing away to a comfortable win when his game fell apart, and Weetman, a muscle man who would chop down trees for light exercise, took the last five holes to win one up. And so, unfortunately, all rested for Britain on two young newcomers, Peter Alliss and Bernard Hunt. They both halved matches they might easily have won and so America scraped home. In fairness, Alliss and Hunt have made more than ample amends with their Ryder Cup records.

It was the same old story at Palm Springs, California, in 1955 with America winning by 8 points to 4. But in the way that all good things are supposed to come to an end eventually, so America's stranglehold on the Ryder Cup Series was broken at Lindrick in 1957 with Dai Rees leading a British team to a victory of 7½ points to 4½. The Americans, captained by Jack Burke, went into a 3-to-1 foursomes lead to suggest that it was going to be the same old story, but on the second day in the singles they collapsed in the most amazing manner. In the top match Eric Brown gave the volatile Tommy Bolt a 4-and-3 drubbing. Bolt fumed, protested about the partisanship of the galleries (which reached 20,000 and sounded like 100,000 as the British putts dropped) but it did him no good.

Peter Alliss was beaten by Fred Hawkins to give the U.S. their only point in the singles and, with six British wins, the result was a first defeat for the U.S. since 1933.

The British walked on air for two years and then came back to earth with a defeat by 8½ points to 3½ at Palm Desert in 1959. Veterans Sam Snead and Cary Middlecoff came back on the U.S. team for new strength; Julius Boros made his Ryder Cup debut at the age of thirty-nine, and "situation normal" was restored for the British side.

But they were thankful to be able to play golf at all, for, enroute from Los Angeles to Palm Desert in a chartered plane, they ran into a violent electrical storm over the San Jacinto Mountains. After suddenly plunging from 13,000 to 9,000 feet in a matter of seconds, the plane finally turned back to Los Angeles, and the whole party completed the journey by bus the next day. Harry Weetman was seen to kiss the ground on walking off the plane. He was not alone in his sentiments.

In 1961 at Lytham and St. Anne's, the matches were played over 18 holes instead of the traditional 36 with morning and afternoon rounds. So the total point score was doubled.

There was nothing new about the outcome, however, with the United States winning by 14½ to 9½ points. Once again the Americans proved themselves unbeatable on and around the greens. If they failed to get down with a chip and single putt from 30 yards, it was almost a surprise.

In beating Ralph Moffitt by a 5 and 4 margin, Mike Souchak single-putted eight greens.

Accounting for 4½ points between them, Arnold Palmer and Billy Casper began their Ryder Cup careers in this match. They were foursome partners, beating Dai Rees and Ken Bousfield in the morning, then John Panton and Bernard Hunt in the afternoon.

Casper gave Bousfield a 5 and 3 lesson in the singles, while Palmer, after a halved match with Peter Alliss, overcame Tom Haliburton for a 2 and 1 success.

Arnold Palmer was appointed captain of the American team, which defeated the British by 23 points to 9 at the East Lake Country Club, home of Bobby Jones, in 1963. He was to prove an outstanding leader. On the eve of the match, with British captain John Fallon listening, Arnie handed out what must have been one of the shrewdest psychological blows ever in the series. When asked to predict the outcome, he declined, saying that he couldn't possibly have any idea how well the British would play. "I'll only say what I have just told my boys in the locker room," he said. "And that is that I don't think there are 10 players in the world who could beat us."

The American players went around openly declaring that they couldn't dare lose—"not with Palmer as captain"—and they justified this measure of their esteem comfortably. But the British found a hero in Peter Alliss: having halved with Palmer in 1961, he now beat him one up after a tremendous match; and then he went on to finish all square against the late Tony Lema.

Eight more points were added to the score total in the 1963 matches with the introduction of four-ball duels, a format more familiar to the Americans than the British; a fact that led to the U.S. squad picking up 6 of the 8 possible points.

The Ryder Cup will always have a greater interest for British galleries than those in America, and at Southport in 1965 vast crowds went home hoarse after a first day which saw the two teams level in the foursomes. America emerged from the four-ball sessions the second day with a lead of only 2 points; not at all a bad position in British eyes. But the strength in depth of the Americans was seen yet again in the singles, and despite Alliss beating Billy Casper and Ken Venturi, it was the U.S. that took 10 points to Britain's 5 for an overall victory of 19½ to 12½.

The 1967 match at the Champions Golf Club, Houston, Texas, was not so notable for what happened on the course—America running away to a win of 23½ points to 8½—as to what happened afterward. What sense was there in continuing the match? many were to ask in the furor that followed. The position was perhaps best explained by Max Elbin, then President of the United States Professional Golfers Association, who declared:

"Another meeting of the American and British PGA Ryder Cup Teams has gone into the record books and again it was an overwhelming victory for the United States. Invariably this almost inevitable outcome is followed by an outbreak of critical evaluation. Various proposals are advanced for closing the scoring gap and restoring a genuine competitive flavor. And, of course, there are always a handful of Jeremiahs who question the wisdom of continuing such one-sided contests. Such an extreme proposal is out of the question. Anyone who has attended a Ryder Cup meeting will recognize instantly that this is more than a golf match. It is a great international sporting event, rich in tradition and color. It is golf without dollar signs, a precious link with the past when the game reflected a leisurely and amiable way of life. The world and especially the United States needs the Ryder Cup matches as a reminder that in our rush to destroy and rebuild there are certain things that should be preserved because they are part of our heritage. Perhaps the format of the matches can be revised or modified to make them matches in fact as well as name. Certainly both the PGA of America and the British PGA are open minded on this subject."

That the matches in America would prove a rout was predictable enough; but, as opposed to affairs on the other side of the Atlantic where the Ryder Cup made money, it was becoming a serious financial worry. It was hard to interest television, and at Houston the galleries were pitifully small.

The most carefully considered constructive criticism of all, possibly, came via the Houston Golf Association, which naturally had been deeply involved with the promotion of the Ryder Cup match at Champions.

In a lengthy "paper" to the United States PGA, spokesman Bob Rule, "with great respect for these traditions and with a sincere desire to see a great event become even greater," said: "Like any other event conceived 40 years ago, the Ryder Cup matches may have fallen victim of the times and perhaps could be improved with certain changes . . . necessary if the event is to attain stature in the United States equal to that enjoyed in Great Britain. . . . the Ryder Cup format is out of harmony with the wishes of the golf viewing public in the United States. Our golf fans are accustomed to seeing from 100 to 150 players in action over a four-day period. They like to pick out a favorite and, as they say at the race tracks, root him home.

The team competition in the Ryder Cup is fine and certainly should be continued as the method of determining the winner each year, but it appears that individual competition very easily could be incorporated into the format, making the matches salable for TV and doubly enjoyable to viewers."

Rule suggested: "(1) Substitute medal play for match play but retain the 'man-to-man' competition in the singles and foursomes; (2) increase the playing schedule to four days; (3) play only 18 holes daily instead of 36; (4) increase the number of players on each team to 16; and (5) expand the British team to include the Commonwealth."

The British returned home and promptly appointed a committee to investigate their Ryder Cup disaster. The decisions they reached included a new system of selecting future teams. More important it was agreed "That with a view of making every effort to improve the standard of British golf, all PGA events and section events should be played with the 1.68-inch ball for a period of not less than 3 years."

The PGA announced: "It was not felt that this in itself would ensure a Ryder Cup victory in 1969 or in 1971, but it was thought that this was a step in the right direction and should in time have the desired effect." British golf has indeed prospered since then, but how much improvement is due to having switched to the American-size big ball is a matter of some controversy.

What leaves no room for doubt, however, is that the 1969 Ryder Cup matches over the Royal Birkdale Course at Southport produced three days of golf as tense as any in the whole series. It ended in a tie, and, for that, Jack Nicklaus had to hole from 5 feet on the last green in the last singles match on the last day.

The British team looked good on paper and proved itself to be so on the course, with Tony Jacklin and Peter Townsend, hardened by their experiences on the U.S. tour, and Peter Alliss, Christy O'Connor, and Bernard Hunt all playing against the Americans for the eighth time. The British set off with a rush. Of the first four foursomes matches they won three, Jacklin and Townsend providing the highlight when they beat Dave Hill and Tommy Aaron with an eagle 3 at the 17th hole. In the afternoon foursomes Jacklin and Townsend birdied the 17th to overcome Billy Casper and Frank Beard, but at the end of the first day the British were only one point ahead.

There was a similar pattern the following day when the four-ball matches produced two wins for Britain, three for America, and three matches halved. The outstanding match of the day was unquestionably that in which Jacklin partnered Neil Coles to a better-ball score of 65—8 under par for the 7,140-yard course—to beat Jack Nicklaus and Dan Sikes by one hole.

The unhappiest clash of the day—clash in every sense—involved the meeting of young Bernard Gallacher, a Scot, and his Welsh partner, Brian Huggett, with the American partnership of Dave Hill and Ken Still. It still leaves many British golf fans with a bad taste. What happened was that on the 7th green Hill ran his approach putt to within 3 feet, stepped up, and knocked it into the hole. Whereupon Still, unable to improve on his partner's score, picked up. Huggett pointed out to the referee that Hill had played out of turn and, as he did so, the Americans walked off the green.

There will never be complete agreement on what subsequently happened. Still declared later that the referee had announced "loss of hole" though the rule specifies that the opponent may require the offending player to replay the shot in the correct order, without penalty. International good will was stretched to the breaking point; Still gave vent to his feelings loudly and was promptly booed by an irate gallery. And Hill, not renowned for remaining silent when feeling aggrieved, also had a lot to say.

In the morning singles of the final day, British hopes of a long-awaited victory soared with the Americans taking only 3 of the 8 points at stake. The most valuable of those gained by the British team was delivered by Jacklin, beating Nicklaus 4 and 3. Jacklin went to the turn in 34 and exerted sufficient pressure to cause Nicklaus to miss seven holable putts of between 7 feet and 18 inches during the match.

Fate threw them together again in the afternoon, for the last singles of the 1969 match, and, as it developed, everything rested upon it. With only two matches still out on the course, Britain and America were level. Brian Huggett was locked in a tremendous battle with Billy Casper. The American was ahead going into 16, and tossed away his lead by going into a bunker. On the same hole, Nicklaus edged one up on Jacklin.

Huggett manfully holed from a shade under 5 feet to stay level with Casper on the 17th green; and as he was lining up a putt at the last from just about the same range, a tremendous roar erupted from the 17th.

The Welshman believed that Jacklin had won his match and that therefore what would be Britain's first Ryder Cup victory since 1957 and only the fourth since 1927 rested upon him. He had a putt of 4 feet, and thousands in the gallery couldn't bear to watch. They hid their eyes as he stood over the ball and dared to look only when the enormous cheers of those braver souls revealed that he had made it. Drained to the last ounce, poor Huggett staggered to the edge of the green, fell into the arms of British captain Eric Brown, and unashamedly wept. Only then was Brown able to tell him that the match was still alive—everything now rested on Jacklin. That roar from the 17th had been to greet the putt of 55 feet by Tony to square the match. And with an eagle at that! Both Jacklin and Nicklaus were on the last green in 2. The British star rolled his approach putt up 2 feet short of the hole, while the American charged his 30-footer all of 4 feet past. It was a case of "win or lose" the Ryder Cup for Nicklaus with the return, but after what seemed an age of preparation, he safely made it. And then he picked up Jacklin's marker, an act of sportsmanship the British galleries will never forget, saying that he wouldn't want him to hole that with the Ryder Cup at stake. They walked off the green arm in arm, symbolizing what the Ryder Cup is all about—good will among British and American professionals and golfers in general. America's team captain Sam Snead puffed nervously as he said, "The greatest golf match I have ever seen. This morning I didn't think we were going to take the Cup back." Said Brown, "I'll tell you one thing—the next British team that goes to America will be one hell of a team."

It didn't quite live up to that extravagant billing but in losing by 11 points to 16 at St. Louis in 1971 the British squad put up the finest performance of any in America. There were many good omens for the future: like newcomer Peter Oosterhuis, in only his third season as a professional after leaving the Walker Cup ranks, defeating both Arnold Palmer and Gene Littler in the singles. The British won the foursomes 4 to 3; narrowly lost the singles 6 to 7; but were swamped 6 to 1 in the four-ball series. It's doubtful the British will ever be able to match the Americans in four-ball golf. It is not a part of the game for them.

Following the match, there was renewed talk about removing this feature from future matches. It would be better for a Ryder Cup Series as a whole if this were done; it could make for closer matches.

But certainly it is a series that must continue. Any time you have an event with nationalism involved it is a good idea. The Ryder Cup is an exceptional promotion, a limited-field event with the added incentive of nationalism. In the coming years, there will be more such events.

Miki Gold Cup

Although the Miki Gold Cup competition (now called the U.S. versus Japan Team Matches) is not in the same league as that for the Ryder Cup, it does have the same general form and aspirations: an international team match, with events that bring the best golf to a wide overseas audience. As to the scale of the tournament, who can tell from the acorn what size oak tree will grow?

It is an unusual, even unique, competition in many ways, not least because the original sponsor of the event was a religious community, the Church of Perfect Liberty, a relatively young order which has a growing following in the United States but is mainly based in Japan. In 1924 a Zen Buddhist priest founded a religious sect known as *Hito no Michi* (the Way of Man) which found a considerable number of adherents until it was suppressed by the Japanese government in 1937, on the grounds that it offered an affront to the Emperor. The priest died, but after World War II his son, Tokuchika Miki, with some of the leaders of the old sect founded the Church of Perfect Liberty.

The teachings of the church are based on the gentle precepts of Buddhism and its main tenet is that Life is Art, that even the most mundane activity—like washing dirty dishes—can be accomplished as an artistic act.

An example from the golf match itself best illustrates this. Usually at tournaments the golfers practice by hitting balls to their caddies, who collect them as they fall. Here, there were no caddies. So very quickly the practice area took on the appearance of a field sprouting a very fine crop of mushrooms. When the supply of practice balls had been expended, a whistle was blown and a group of doll-like girls, all in smart uniforms, "fell in" in three ranks by the tee at about company strength. Each one carried a plastic bucket. At another whistle, they turned into a column of threes and double-timed down the fairway. Again the whistle blew and they halted, broke ranks, and ran over the practice ground. Within a minute they had gathered every ball, re-formed, and double-timed back to the tee. The simple act of shagging golf balls had become transformed into a ritual which would not have disgraced a corps de ballet. What's more, this delightful display was a very efficient method of retrieving the balls.

Some two million people in ten different countries are members of Perfect Liberty, and the headquarters at Osaka is a complex of temples, apartment blocks, schools—and a country club. Recreation is an essential part of life and should be just as much an artistic creation as anything else. Hence it was entirely logical for Perfect Liberty to sponsor a competition which would demonstrate golf at its most artistic and effective level. In fact, for the inaugural event in late 1971, the exhibition aspect of the match was stressed to the point where the competitive element was almost totally submerged. Nine-man teams were selected by invitation, and each golfer played three rounds. At the end, the seven best individual scores from each team were added up and the United States proved to be the winner by a narrow margin.

Perhaps the sponsors felt that with such players as Billy Casper, Doug Sanders, Dave Stockton, Charles Coody, and Homero Blancas in the field, the Japanese professionals would be overwhelmed in a straight contest. Maybe. But in fact the Japanese are very difficult to beat on their own ground and are improving every year, thanks to a tournament program now second only to the U.S. tour in size and scope. If Japan is not quite ready to take on the U.S. head to head with any realistic hope of victory, the day may not be too far off when that standard is achieved.

In any event, Patriarch Miki made his point with the contest. Japanese television gave the matches good coverage (the Japanese viewer is the most avid golf fan in the world), and golf of the highest quality was given a good airing. International matches do not invariably equate with international good will—it sometimes seems that certain sporting fixtures stir up the most murky nationalistic fervor rather than spreading peace and good will among nations. But in this case, the American golfers to a man proved to be excellent ambassadors and made a telling impression on their hosts.

Piccadilly

Match play is the way the game began and it is the form of golf that the average player adopts when he goes out with his friends on the weekend. The last semblance of match play in America, however, ended when the PGA Championship turned to stroke play in 1958. There seemed to be a great void in the world in terms of a major match-play championship; there was, it is true, the then News of the World PGA Match Play Championship in Britain. But this didn't have an international field and certainly lacked the greats of the world of golf.

In the spring of 1963, the idea of having knockout matches with a limited field of players competing over 36 holes was presented to Philip Wilson of the Carreras Company.

Limiting the field meant the last-place finishers in the event could come out with good money and enjoy other incentives. Match play—knockout—was considered preferable to round robin, which, while it may be popular, good promotion, and attractive for television, is not pure golf. And the matches were to be 36 holes, because anybody can beat anybody over 18 holes, while in 36 the better player is bound to win.

It was stressed that it was absolutely essential for the invitation system to be flexible, since there would be times when a Palmer or Player—or whoever should be in the field because he is one of the top eight players in the world—could not qualify because he had not won a championship in a firmly established system. So it was imperative to avoid any kind of automatic system.

It was ultimately decided to invite the British Open and U.S. Open champions and the U.S. Masters winner and subsequently, of course, the defending champion of the new undertaking. And that was the beginning of the Piccadilly World Match Play Golf Championship.

In the initial stages other ideas were resisted. For instance, the British PGA put pressure on the sponsors to have the top player in its Order of Merit included. But it was felt there was no reason a British player should be included in the field if he did not warrant selection as a player of world class.

Nicklaus at the Piccadilly

Neil Coles was selected early on. He probably shouldn't have been, but it was interesting for the British public. There was one year when no British player was asked, and this created a great many problems. But there wasn't one who deserved to be selected, and staging a golf tournament in Britain without a British player was a necessary gamble. Nevertheless, in the last few years, the organizers have been conceding things to the British PGA—such as agreeing, in 1972, that the leader in the Order of Merit should indeed take part in the tournament. This may be a little premature, somewhat naive, but it seems clear that an eight-man tournament, mostly comprising overseas players, can have little appeal to the British PGA and it is probably inevitable that certain things must be done to appease them. What really matters is that, since its inception in 1964, the Piccadilly World Match Play Championship has gained a prestige that is unique. A quick rundown of the winners tells much: 1964 and 1967, Arnold Palmer; 1965, 1966, 1968, and 1971, Gary Player; 1969, Bob Charles; 1970, Jack Nicklaus.

The event has been variously described as a "small miracle" and by Gary Player, "the fifth most important golf tournament in the world." With the famed Wentworth Club and its "Burma Road" West Course as a permanent home, the Championship has become the climax to each British season. It brings to the South of England, which never sees the Open, the greatest players in the world: apart from the winners, there have been Tony Jacklin, Billy Casper, Lee Trevino, Roberto de Vicenzo, Gay Brewer, Peter Thomson, Bruce Devlin, Gene Littler, Tommy Aaron, and others. Gary Player has described match play as the "raw blood and guts of golf" and so it has proved at Wentworth each October.

To bring together eight world-class golfers is one thing, but to ensure that the golf they produce is world class is another. The Piccadilly event has been exceptionally fortunate in this respect: there has never yet been a dull week. In eight years the championship has created a proud history: In 1964, the first year, Arnold Palmer arrived at Wentworth as the U.S. Masters champion for the fourth time. Ken Venturi, so long in the golfing wilderness, had emerged with the U.S. Open title; and there was Tony Lema, winner of the British Open. Gary Player, Australian Open champion, Bruce Devlin, New Zealand title holder, and Jack Nicklaus, individual winner in the Canada Cup, completed the invasion force, while Neil Coles, the British match-play champion, and Peter Butler represented the home hopes.

The action began with Palmer facing Butler, and a great start it was to prove for a championship. Palmer set off in a hurry, took two of the first three holes, but at the halfway point, 18 holes played, they went to lunch all square.

With only 11 holes to play, Butler, in front of the biggest galleries any tournament outside of the Ryder Cup and Canada Cup had ever produced at Wentworth, commanded a lead of 3 up. Arnold Palmer snatched one back and then showed the British what was meant by a Palmer charge. He was 2 up with three to play but Butler earned a medal for courage by taking the match to the home green.

In other first-round matches, Neil Coles beat Tony Lema, who had suddenly become unwell; Gary Player took care of Ken Venturi; and Bruce Devlin sent Jack Nicklaus home with a £1,000 consolation prize.

Then in the semifinals Palmer turned ruthless against Player and was 5 under par for the morning round. He set out again by going eagle, par, birdie, birdie, birdie, birdie. The home favorite, Coles, put Devlin out at the 35th, and so the final was how anybody would have wanted it—America versus Britain, Palmer, the Masters champion, the legendary idol, against Coles, the British match-play champion, the Wentworth expert.

It proved a tremendous battle: Palmer reached the turn for the first time with a lead of two holes, but it was Coles who went to lunch 2 up. Palmer really wanted that title, he wanted to be known as the world's match-play champion. And he showed it with an outward half of 32 in the afternoon, and finally victory was his with a birdie at the 35th hole.

Next year it was Gary Player, beating Peter Thomson 3 and 2, who won the final and the title. But it wasn't the final that really mattered. It was Player's match with the late Tony Lema in the semifinals that made golf history.

It was an astonishing match—hard to believe for those who didn't actually see it—and maybe the most thrilling match of all time. Player muscled the long 4th hole down to an eagle with a drive and four iron that stopped 5 yards from the flagstick, Lema remained one down at the turn, and then the short 10th was to prove vital. He hit the trees with his tee shot and scrambled a half in 3 by eventually holing his single putt of 20 feet. After that Player missed from only 8 feet for a win.

And then the South African lost seven holes in a row. A couple were of his own doing, but Lema was in fantastic form. He had six birdies in those seven holes, and with a second half of 32 completed a round of 67. Gary, with an approximate one-under-par 73 was 6 down.

The gap widened when they set out again for Lema to birdie the 19th —7 up with 17 to play. Surely it was all over—for anyone other than Gary Player. Gary, the reigning U.S. Open champion, birdied three holes and turned 5 down with 9 to play. He won the 10th, birdied the 11th and 13th, and won the 16th when Lema, beginning to feel the pressure, hooked into the trees.

They both birdied the long 17th, and at the long 18th Player hit what he was to call one of the best shots of his whole life, a powerfully struck three wood, controlled with immaculate draw, which finished 10 feet from the hole, and, with a birdie, the match was square. And yet another birdie at the 1st again—or the 37th if you will—put Player through to the final.

In the gathering darkness of the evening, Lema stood a distraught figure on the green.

Gary successfully defended his title the following year (1966) in a final against Jack Nicklaus, who became involved in a controversy that is still debated in golf.

Wentworth is not the ideal course for spectators, with its tree-lined fairways, but there were thousands there that damp misty October morning as two of the recognized "Big Three" of world golf set out to decide who was to be hailed as the world match-play champion. Gary edged in front at the 4th when Nicklaus found a bunker, but they were level when the South African's putter failed him on the next green. It was a very temporary lapse; at the 6th Gary holed from 15 feet to go one up, and that was still the margin when they stepped onto the 9th tee. And then it happened.

Along the left side of the hole 460 yards runs a railway line. Jack hooked his drive and the ball landed in a ditch close to the out-of-bounds fence. He dropped out under penalty, still in rough. It was then that he spied, at a distance of some 50 yards ahead, an advertising sign, not unnaturally for Piccadilly Cigarettes, and he asked the referee of the match, Colonel Tony Duncan, to be granted a further drop without penalty. Jack maintained that the sign was in his line of flight to the hole and that it was a temporary obstruction. But the Colonel ruled that this was not so and denied Nicklaus a free drop.

Visibly upset, Jack asked for a copy of the local rules and, after examining them, still felt he was entitled to a free drop. But the Colonel was adamant. He told Jack to play on and walked away. After one more blow with his wedge, failing to escape from the rough, Nicklaus conceded the hole to Player. Jack's demeanor on the next tee prompted Duncan to ask whether he would like another referee to take over the match. Nicklaus sharply retorted that he would like to have one who was fully conversant with the rules. Up stepped Gerald Micklem, and the game continued in happier vein.

To this day, both Nicklaus and Duncan, a former captain of Britain's Walker Cup Team, each believes that he was right. The whole unhappy affair is perhaps best written off as an unfortunate clash of personalities (and maybe demonstrates why Nicklaus, whose tact often leaves something to be desired, has never been received as warmly by the galleries in the U.S. and throughout the world as has his archrival, Arnold Palmer). Player wisely kept well clear of the fracas, machined his way to a 7-under-par 67, and went to lunch 4 up. Setting out again in the afternoon, they both went to the turn in 33 but it was all too late for Nicklaus. Gary ran out the most convincing 6 and 4 winner, and there was nothing to be said after Nicklaus declared, "I don't think anybody living could have played better golf than he played today."

In the earlier rounds Player had beaten Neil Coles on his home ground by one hole and then Arnold Palmer by 2 and 1. Quite a week by any standards. Even for Gary Player.

The 1967 final between Arnold Palmer, who was to win the title for the second time, and Peter Thomson again proved a classic. The Australian, defending a reputation as the best small-ball player in the world, had 30 putts for a first-round score of 70 in the morning. Palmer matched his 70, and they were all square, having answered birdie with birdie.

Arnie put his putter to work again at the 23rd, holed from 30 feet for a birdie. Thomson squared at the next; they were both out in 35, and level.

Something had to give; someone had to make a break. And Palmer it was: birdie, par, eagle, birdie from the 28th—3 up! Thomson retaliated: birdie, eagle, birdie. But Palmer, with a putt of 15 feet, matched his birdie at the 34th and so stayed one up with two to play. They halved the long 17th. Thomson conceded the 18th, or the 36th, and Palmer, winner by 2 holes, was the champion again.

Those British patriots who have been incensed by the failure to include a home player in 1967 had nothing to complain about the following year: Tony Jacklin and Brian Huggett were named among the eight for battle. But Huggett met Palmer in the first round and went out. In the semifinals Player faced Jacklin. And what a story that yielded.

Player had annihilated Thomson 8 and 7 while Jacklin had delivered Lee Trevino a 4 and 3 beating; and now they were ready for one another. In the most appalling weather conditions, amounting almost to a monsoon, and with parts of the course flooded, they finished the scheduled 36 holes all square. After 18, Jacklin was one down, but, by winning the 20th and the next, he went ahead for the first time.

Player would have been quite willing to quit in the conditions—later he said that they should never have started in the afternoon because the course was unplayable. The referee, however, allowed them to improve their lies in the fairways and they carried on as best they could. British galleries need no teaching in partisanship, and their actions began to unsettle Player. A good many of those watching sat on their hands when he holed a putt, cheered when he found trouble. Despite the atmosphere, Gary went 2 up with four to play. Both birdied the 15th; Jacklin holed from 12 feet to win the 16th and then squared the match at the 17th (35th), trimming this 555-yard monster to a par-busting 4 with a pitch to 7 feet.

On the 36th Jacklin cut his second shot into the trees while Player hit a three wood just short of the green—"The longest and best fairway wood I have ever hit in my life," he was to claim. Jacklin came out of the woods, but a long way short of the pin. The green was a mass of puddles, almost a lake of casual water. Gary declared afterward, "That last green was beyond any doubt unplayable, unputtable. I did seriously think of refusing to putt it but I was scared that the crowd would lynch me."

Jacklin splashed his first putt some 7 feet short, but he made the next one. Gary approached 4 feet short. And he missed the next. The crowd roared its approval. It applauded Gary for missing. Some said it was the crowd's reaction to such a great golfer as Player missing from such short range; but there seems to be no question that it was the action of a partisan gallery. In the fast-fading light, Jacklin was ready, even eager, to carry on. But Gary had other thoughts. The referee settled the question. He ruled that they would leave it there, sleep on it, play the 37th the next morning, and let Bob Charles wait to see which of them he would face in the final.

Said Gary: "There was no skill in today's round." He was, of course, exaggerating. The day had been well spiced with tremendous golf. At the last nine holes they had shared nine birdies, three to Player and six to Jacklin.

The next morning, Saturday, Wentworth was without question un-playable following all-night storms. So all had to be settled on Sunday. Jacklin and Player stepped on the tee at 9 A.M. and 10 minutes later were in a controversy that was to last for weeks. As always in this kind of thing, there are any number of versions as to what actually happened.

Tony started the sudden-death duel with a one-iron second shot to the left front of the green. The gallery, several hundred strong even at that time of the morning, sensed that their man was about to win, and their man, of course, was Jacklin. But Gary, never better than when coming out of a tight corner, wedged up perfectly and left himself a putt of some 9 feet. Jacklin could have made it seem like 90 feet had he rolled his approach putt tight, but he didn't. He left it short by 4 feet.

Gary, agitated by gallery and photographers, took a long time over his putt. He holed it. Then came the explosion as he moved to the edge of the green and rebuked the crowd. "I know you are pulling against me but at least give me a chance, give me the courtesy of putting. I don't call that very sporting," he snarled. Gary, still smarting from the fans' partisanship suffered over the regulation 36 holes, was certain that he had heard someone whispering, "Miss it, miss it!" as he prepared for his putt. Some claimed that his hearing had misled him and what he had heard was a woman whispering, "He's missed it!" as the ball was on its way to the hole.

Whether the scene upset Jacklin's concentration is debatable, but he certainly missed the putt to lose the match, and so Player marched back to the first tee and Bob Charles, to begin the final. A lot of people thought Gary should have kept quiet until Tony had dealt with his putt. There was even a boo or two as he left the green. Jacklin himself tried to keep a diplo-matic silence. He dodged the questions of golf writers. "I don't want to say anything," he pleaded. But later he did say that it was a difficult putt, and that although what happened didn't help him, he should have had the common sense to compose himself, walk away from the ball, and then start lining it up afresh.

Gary played the 36-hole final in 4 under par and took the title for the third time with a one-up victory. His three successes earned him outright possession of the trophy, a replica of the Eros statue in London's Piccadilly Circus.

But Charles was to have his turn; he won the 1969 final, beating smooth-swinging Gene Littler at the 37th hole. On his day, Bob Charles was the greatest putter in the world. And this was certainly his day. After 18 holes the position was all square and then it began to happen. At the 8th in the afternoon he hit a poor two iron, and then a four iron into a bunker, and his recovery only just made the green. But from 35 feet he holed out. On the next green Bob made a putt of 30 feet; he added to this with another of 45 feet on the next green. All this put the New Zealander 2 up, but a poor drive cost him the 13th, and then Littler, playing better golf from tee to green, birdied the 16th, or 34th, to square.

High drama enveloped the 36th: Littler was just on the fringe of the green in 2; Charles had hooked his second shot into the trees. From a range of just over 100 yards he pitched through a gap to leave himself a putt of 27 feet, and to everyone's amazement but his own he holed it.

So to the 37th they went and it was there that Charles hit a four-iron second shot that finished within 2 feet of the flagstick. He was the new world match-play champion.

The manner of Littler's defeat was cruel, but he won new friends with his sportsmanlike remarks. "I have to congratulate Bob on his win," he declared. "He holed more yardage of putts today than anyone else has done in the history of golf. He must be the best putter in the world, including Casper or anyone you care to mention. On the 36th green I just didn't believe he could go on doing it—but he did."

The eight players who answered the call to action in 1970 were the strongest field in the history of the championship. In the lineup: Bob Charles, defending champion; Billy Casper, U.S. Masters champion; Tony Jacklin, U.S. Open champion; Jack Nicklaus, British Open champion; Gary Player, Australian Open champion; Dave Stockton, U.S. PGA champion; Gene Littler, finalist in 1969 and Masters runner-up after a playoff; and Lee Trevino, the leading U.S. money-winner at the time of selection.

Despite such great players, the golf took a while to get off the ground but it did eventually and led to another excellent final in which Nicklaus beat Trevino 2 and 1.

Jack set about Lee with a morning 66 to go 3 up. The afternoon golf by both was brilliant. Trevino eagled the 1st, birdied the 4th and 9th. Nicklaus birdied the 1st, 4th, 7th, and 9th. All this left Lee 5 down—and nine to play. Was it all over? Hardly. Nicklaus made a hash of the short 10th, Trevino holed a monster putt at the 11th, and he was back in the ball game.

From this point, as Nicklaus said later, "Trevino began knocking the flags out." When Trevino hit a three iron to within inches of the par-3 14th, he reduced Nicklaus's lead to only one hole.

Big Jack birdied the 15th, Trevino came right back with a birdie on the 16th, and so, with just one hole between them, they stepped onto the 17th tee. Millions of TV viewers saw what happened. Trevino hooked his drive out of bounds. It was all over.

Jack Nicklaus reached the final the next year, but he didn't win: it was Gary Player's turn—his fourth, to be exact. The field lacked U.S. and British champion Lee Trevino, but by now the Championship had become bigger than any one man. The last day was a repeat of the 1966 final, which Player had won by a 6 and 4 margin. But this time Nicklaus was the heavy favorite. Troubled by a hook, the little South African had practiced until darkness the night before, while Jack looked his best all week.

Nicklaus scored a 7-under-par 67 in the first round of the final, but with a magnificent display of guts, troubled Player stayed with him, scoring 68, to be only one down. It was Nicklaus, however, who was in serious trouble. On the 15th green he had missed a putt of 2 feet to lose his second successive hole. Nicklaus had won the 12th and 13th with birdies, the first 11 holes having been halved. Shaken by his failure at the 15th, Nicklaus adjusted his putting stance. He stood further behind the ball at the address, held his hands higher. It was to be his undoing.

In the first four holes of the afternoon he missed three more short putts. Gary Player, never one to waste opportunities, moved ahead, went from one down to 4 up as they turned for home for the last time. As every professional will say, "If you can't putt, you can't win," and this day Nicklaus couldn't putt. Player, the 5 and 4 winner, said, "I still hooked the ball but thankfully I putted as well as I can possibly putt, and Jack as badly as he can. He could have been 'round in 64 in the morning and I was fortunate to be only one down. But I missed only two greens in the afternoon. Can you blame me for calling Wentworth my favorite course?"

The Piccadilly World Match Play Championship has gone from strength to strength in only eight years. It has a prestige that attracts the best golfers in the world. It is not money: the £25,000 total prize money isn't exactly a compelling magnet in these days of purses that reach the £100,000 mark, but match play takes the modern game back to its origins; it is a challenge that the game in its normal way fails to offer. For that reason, the Piccadilly World Match Play Championship will hold its place in international golf.

Tournament of Champions

The success of the Piccadilly event certainly influenced the founding of the Tournament of Champions for the Trophee Lancome, conceived and put together for the first time in 1970.

Early Ben Hogan

Again the idea was to bring together eight of the best players in the world, only this time shooting 54 holes of golf, using the stroke-play format, over exclusive Saint-Nom-la-Breteche, near Paris.

To get it off the ground, the players recruited were Palmer, Player, Jacklin, Raymond Floyd, Bob Charles, Ramon Sota, Roberto Bernardini, and Jean Garaialde.

Golf is still a rich man's sport in France, but thousands of spectators turned up to see the action—and what action it proved to be! Arnold Palmer mounted one of those vintage charges, and after three rounds walked into the clubhouse 9 under par for the tournament, looking every bit the winner. But still out there, battling, were the final pair, Sota and Jacklin.

When Jacklin missed the green at the short 16th and bogeyed, he needed two birdies to tie Palmer. Possible, but unlikely. On the 17th, a challenging par 5, he put everything into a mammoth drive. It went all of 350 yards—"50 yards further than I have ever driven a ball," said Jacklin afterward. He drilled a four iron to the green, holed the putt for an eagle, and there was Palmer, sweating it out, knowing that Jacklin now needed only a par to tie.

But it wasn't a par that the young British pro had in mind; it was a birdie. He drove at the 18th, wedged to 8 feet; and down it went—a birdie indeed! Victory with an eagle and a birdie at the last two holes. How about that for the launching of a new tournament?

Later Hogan

Next year, 1971, Palmer had his revenge. He set a record score of 65 for the Saint-Nom-la-Breteche course, and kept Gary Player in second place. The aim of popularizing the game of golf in France is succeeding. The country undoubtedly has room for a vast development of the sport. But what it essentially needs is to find its own national heroes. If enthusiasm is to be sustained in France, and throughout the Continent for that matter, then they must produce their own Arnold Palmer, Gary Player, and Tony Jacklin.

[9]

THE COURSES—
PUTTING NATURE
TO WORK

GOLF COURSE architecture and design have come a long way
since the mysterious origins of the game, whether it was first played
in Scotland or elsewhere in Europe. Let's presume that golf was first played
in Scotland, where there is documentary evidence that the Scottish parliament, during the period 1457 to 1491, prohibited the playing of the game
because it was becoming so popular, and interfering with the more serious
practice of archery essential to national defense in the wars intermittently
waged against England. Golf is known to have been a popular pastime
when St. Andrews University was founded in 1411, and documentary evidence of the laws of the land indicate that it had become a national sport in
Scotland during the reign of James II.

The game was officially introduced to the United States in 1888, although historians record that the officers from Scottish ships trading in
Canada introduced the game there much earlier. The club now known as
the Royal Montreal Golf Club was formed in 1873. It is probable that
officers of Scottish regiments played golf in the United States during the
eighteenth century, but it is to John Reid, a native Scotsman, that the credit
goes officially for introducing the game to the United States. Reid commissioned another Scot, Robert Lockhart, who was about to visit his native
land, to bring back golf clubs and balls to supplement the meager supply
of six clubs that Reid already possessed. Lockhart duly purchased the
merchandise at the St. Andrews shop of Old Tom Morris, and a course of

three holes was laid out in a cow pasture at Yonkers, New York, in 1888, the holes being cut with the heads of the iron clubs. Here the first six golfers ever to indulge in such sport played the first team match ever recorded in the United States.

Formed November 14, 1888, the first golf club in the United States, the St. Andrew's Club of Yonkers, had an original membership of six, but the game increased so rapidly in popularity, thanks almost entirely to the influence of expatriate Scottish professionals, amateurs, greenskeepers, and architects, that in 1894 a national body had to be formed to oversee the game. At first it was known as the American Amateur Golf Association, but later this name was changed to the United States Golf Association. A portrait of Reid now hangs in the new headquarters of the USGA in Far Hills, New Jersey, while in the clubhouse of the American St. Andrew's Club a bronze tablet contains this fond epitaph to the father of American golf:

> Scotsman–American. The Founder of St. Andrew's Golf Club and its First President. Born in 1840 at Dunfermline, Scotland. Died in 1916 at Yonkers-on-Hudson, New York. A lover of men, of books, of sports; a loyal friend, a rare interpreter of the songs of his Native Land.

Reid could hardly have known what he was starting, since there are well over 10,000 golf courses in the United States today. The rapid spread of the popularity of the game accounts for the extreme mediocrity of so many golf courses, since—incredibly—anyone can set up in business as a golf architect. There are no minimal qualifications, no demands for degrees in surveying, achitecture, agronomy, or whatever. One of the strangest facets of the Royal and Ancient game, this has resulted in much money earned on false pretenses by singularly unqualified architects.

Obviously, the greatest factors to influence golf course design through the ages have been the development and growing sophistication of the materials used to fashion both clubs and golf balls. Until 1848 the ball was constructed by steaming a mess of feathers into a hard, heavy core packed inside a leather exterior skin. This ball was known as the "feathery." In the middle of the nineteenth century golf balls began to be made from a single, solid lump of gutta-percha, which was found in greatest quantities in Malaya and throughout the Far East. Consequent wars have forced golf ball manufacturers to develop a synthetic version of this material, since it is now in very short supply in its original form, the natural variety. The gutta-percha, molded into shape when warm and then painted white, as had been the "feathery," became known as the "guttie."

In 1899 one of the most dramatic and important developments in the history of the game occurred, one that exerted the most profound influence on golf course design. An American named Coburn Haskell invented the rubber-cored golf ball, which is in use today, although in a very much more sophisticated, durable, and long-flying form. Basically, the "Haskell," as it was then known, consisted of a tightly wound core of fine rubber thread covered with a hard plastic or vulcanized material devised by the golf ball manufacturers as a substitute for gutta-percha.

Today such things as liquid centers to maintain perfect balance and polyurethane paint of incredible whiteness, hardness, and durability have made the early golf courses, most particularly their bunkers, obsolete. New tees, even farther back, have had to be built to keep pace with the development of balls and clubs, bunkers have had to be re-sited, fairways narrowed incredibly for major championships. As surely as the "guttie" flew much farther than the "feathery," so the modern version of the "Haskell" has caused a drive of 300 yards to become almost commonplace, whereas less than 50 years ago one of 200 yards would have been considered a notable hit.

Likewise, the replacement of the hickory shaft in golf clubs in the 1920s by ever-improving steel shafts has caused the modern golf club to become a shiny, largely mass-produced weapon of unbelievable sophistication.

Golf course design, architecture, and construction have progressed easily as far as the implements of the game, but the same question marks linger in the minds of many concerning the march of progress toward sophistication. Whereas golf course construction was once made possible only by the cheapness of the labor involved—almost entirely manual—and the tools of the trade were largely crude and hand-held, there was a healthy respect among early architects for the original nature of the terrain, which was left mostly unspoiled. The development of the bulldozer and similar giants among today's earth-moving machinery has caused many architects to veer toward the artificial and contrived. Man-made lakes are commonplace, and many of them add considerably to the beauty of the golf courses on which they appear. But the ability of the architect to mold the terrain to his every whim with huge machines has caused the humps and hollows that are the dominating characteristic of the great British links courses in particular to become a thing of the past.

Most especially in America, where courses are springing up faster than anywhere else in the world, modern architects—with several notable exceptions—are placing an absurd premium on sheer length. Often, their thinking is influenced by the backers who are paying their fees. The usually vain hope expressed by these astute businessmen is that their course, at least, will never be cut to pieces by the "damned professionals." And so courses have grown ever longer as owners and developers strive to outdo each other, greens grow ever bigger in area, tees ever longer, and much of the subtlety and the demands on the golfer's intelligence, shotmaking ability, and skill for improvisation are lost. A premium is placed on brute strength, though not necessarily on ignorance, since perhaps the longest hitter among the top echelon of the world's professionals, Jack Nicklaus, could never be accused of a lack of respect for the game's traditions. An indication of this lies in the highly regarded Hilton Head course at Harbour Town, South Carolina, where Nicklaus and his partner, Pete Dye, have created a course of great popularity. Its greens are small, and there are holes on which railway sleepers or ties are used to bolster the front faces of bunkers in the style of some of the old British courses, notably Old Prestwick.

British Courses

The links is almost the exclusive property of Britain, an accident of nature. Trees have no part to play on true links courses, and many great golfers maintain that they have no part to play in golf at all—an unfair hazard. The giant sandhills are untouched by modern earth-moving equipment.

Bunkers are constructed by digging a hole in the turf, which reveals that the natural sand—incredibly soft and fluffy in texture—is superior in quality and character to the sand that is introduced to bunkers when they are cut into the earth almost anywhere else in the world. The bunkers are entirely natural. The turf has a fine quality unapproached elsewhere, although its completely natural superiority is fast being ruined and coarsened by automatic watering systems which have had to be introduced because the traffic over the great links courses of Britain has become so heavy.

To play on a links course is to feel immediately that this is golf as it was intended. Artificial lakes, bunkers, plantations of trees are absent. The battle is waged against the elements and the natural contours of the ground that can punish a good drive, and allow an inferior hit to prosper. On many occasions the pitch and run is the only shot to greens that are small and glassy and hard, over a bewildering series of humps and hollows that can throw the ball off its intended line with ruthless severity unless the shot is perfectly conceived and executed. Links courses may be an anachronism to visiting American golfers brought up to play at a lush, country club-type layout where there are no blind holes and fairways are perfectly flat in the driving area, where bunkers are no more than sandscrapes out of which it is possible to hit with a wood. But because the sponsoring body, the Royal and Ancient Golf Club of St. Andrews, has never taken the Open Championship inland, the visiting American professionals have been forced to adapt themselves to a "new" type of golf, and have done so with incredibly successful results since the legendary Walter Hagen became the first invader to win the trophy at Royal St. Georges in 1922 with the moderate score—by modern standards—of 300 shots for 72 holes.

Prestwick, on the west coast of Scotland in the county of Ayrshire, the scene of the first 12 Open Championships, is true links country in the original sense of the word. Being only 6,571 yards long, Prestwick is no longer considered suitable for Open Championship golf. It has blind holes, little space for car parking, and not enough room between the holes for the huge crowds now associated with perhaps the best-organized event in the world. But Prestwick is possibly the best example remaining in the world of the original conception of golf course architecture. If a hill was there, then the golfer was asked to hit his ball over it, and likewise burns or streams, brick walls, and sandhills sometimes fortified with railway sleepers or ties.

Although Prestwick long ago disappeared off the championship rota—the British name for those courses at which the British Open rotates from year to year—its third hole, the "Cardinal," is still one of the best holes in British links golf. The second shot here has to be played over a cavernous expanse of sand, the "Cardinal" bunker, whose face on the landing side is a dark, forbidding array of railway sleepers. But this huge bunker has ruined many a score or championship aspiration when the drive has not been quite long enough or well enough positioned. The pitch to the green is over a bewildering selection of humps and hollows to a tiny green. While Prestwick may have been left behind by the march of progress on the score of length, it is still one of the finest examples of all that is best in the traditional Scottish method of golf course design. Its subtleties make it a neglected gem comprising an experience which can only enhance the golfer's knowledge of the early history and attitudes of the game.

North of the border in Scotland, the true home of the game, the Old Course at St. Andrews must take pride of place, mainly on the score of tradition. From the point of view of design, the Old Course is in many ways slightly surprising, since several bunkers are hidden hazards. It is, in a way, a hooker's paradise because the shot that goes left will always do so to the middle of the course, while the slice is almost always cruelly punished. What many people feel makes the old course at St. Andrews so great is that, despite this, the ideal way to play the course is to hit the ball along all the out-of-bounds fences and other hazards on the right-hand side, which puts a premium on playing as close as possible to the dangers that threaten on the right.

The Old Course is one of the few in the world where huge, double greens are in use and a 60-yard putt can be commonplace if the stroke to the green lands on the wrong one. There is also an atmosphere about the course and the old, gray town always visible beyond it that reeks of tradition, which, happily, has been preserved almost unaltered.

The sad passing of the railway has robbed the great 17th, or "Road Hole," of much of its character. Long gone are the black engine sheds that had to be negotiated from the tee, and against which many drives intended to cut the corner crashed. Replacing them is netting roughly conforming to their shape to protect the new hotel that has arisen in their place.

The 17th hole is a long par 4 swinging right around the hotel, but it used to be that the second shot was even more crucial than it is today. It was and is played with anything from a medium to a long iron or wood, according to the conditions, to a plateau green that is very wide, but also exceedingly narrow from front to back. Beyond lurks the dreaded road off which the ball must be 'played, while a single, deep pot bunker cuts into the middle of the green at its sloping entrance, forcing the player to the right from the flag, which is ideally set directly behind the bunker. It is almost impossible to approach the green and stay on it to the left of the bunker. The recovery shot from the sand itself is a fearsome prospect still, although the advent of automatic watering has made the hole at least half a shot easier.

Many championship contenders have gone to a watery grave in the Swilcan Burn that runs to the right of the first fairway and then across it in front of the huge green. Likewise, the deep hollow known as the "Valley of Sin" has trapped many simple-looking pitch shots to the equally large last green. What the Old Course lacks in apparent design quality it more than makes up for in sheer tradition and hidden subtlety. It is rarely mastered by the casual invader, although the late Tony Lema put to rest the locally held theory that it could never be so dominated when he breezed to a win in the 1964 British Open on his first effort.

While St. Andrews is located on the south bank of the estuary of the River Eden, the other championship links on the east coast of Scotland are also similarly sited at the mouths of far more significant rivers. To the north of St. Andrews across the River Tay is Carnoustie, regarded as the most difficult course on the championship rota, and certainly the longest and most exposed to the vagaries of the British climate. To the south across the Firth of Forth is Muirfield, generally agreed to be the fairest of all the championship tests, since its hazards are all clearly visible, the bunkers are eminently fair, if very deep, and the whole layout perhaps the most perfect shape to provide the widest possible variety of wind directions on a given single day.

Muirfield is set out most ingeniously in two loops of nine holes, the outward half running around the outside in a clockwise direction. The bunkers are remarkable for the intricate turfing of their front walls, layer upon layer, which makes it virtually impossible for a ball to plug in the face. The floors of the bunkers are flat, and, although they are deep enough to command the utmost respect, they can all be seen as dark, ominous shadows menacing the drive or second shots. The home of the Honourable

Company of Edinburgh Golfers, whose fascinating history dates back to the year 1744, Muirfield is almost always remarkable for its beautiful condition. Those who have won Open Championships there: Harry Vardon in 1896, Walter Hagen in 1929, Henry Cotton in 1948, Jack Nicklaus in 1966, and Lee Trevino in 1972.

A pleasing feature of most of the traditional links type of courses in Britain is the naming of every hole, usually in Scottish dialect. But at Carnoustie one hole stands out for its unusual nature and the strange name, the 10th, known as "South America." Here the green is set on an island surrounded by the infamous Barry Burn, which meanders through the course to set up one of the finest finishes to a championship links in the world. The green of South America is laid out on ground of a completely inland character, and as if to emphasize that fact—the green once formed part of a garden—a solitary tree has been left behind to menace the approach to the green over the water.

The last three holes at Carnoustie are as good as any in the world. The 16th is a par 3 of roughly 235 yards where the world's best are quite often short with a driver; but it is the 17th hole, rightly known as "Island," which is so outstanding. Here the Barry Burn winds through a huge loop that demands that the drive be hit to an island over the first stretch of water, which also runs all the way up the left-hand side to trap the shot played with draw. The second shot is again played off the island over the water to a green which gives the impression of sloping away from the player, and is really difficult to hold.

Again at the last hole the Barry Burn has to be crossed twice. For the good player there is no danger in the water, since it runs across the hole some 170 yards from the tee. But the drive must be long enough if the second shot is to carry the Burn as it flows right across the front of the green on its way to Carnoustie Bay.

Another outstanding hole on the course is the long 6th, where Nicklaus virtually forfeited his chance of winning the 1968 Open when he hooked his drive out of bounds over the government fence that bounds the firing ranges. The good player is asked to hit an extra long drive here to carry the cross bunkers, if he is to have any chance of getting up in two shots at a hole measuring 521 yards. Needless to say, even the best in the world betray themselves by hooking the ball over the fence that runs down the entire length of the hole.

Most good judges rate Carnoustie the toughest championship test in the whole of Britain and Ireland, if not the world.

Turnberry, in Ayrshire on the west coast of Scotland, may well be the most beautiful and enjoyable of Scottish links courses. There are two courses here, the Ailsa and the Arran, that are built on the very edge of the Firth of Clyde 50 miles down the coast from Glasgow. During World War II the courses were plowed up and converted into an airfield.

There are many who regard Old Troon as inferior to both its neighbors, Prestwick and Turnberry, because it is much flatter. Here once again the course is built to wind out along the beach, and then back again on the inland side from the 10th tee. But there is little doubt that Troon's "Postage Stamp" 8th hole, around 150 yards, is one of the finest and most difficult short holes in the world. The tee shot is hit from an elevated tee with anything between a two iron and a nine iron, according to the weather, and the green is a fearsomely small target, set into the right-hand side of a huge sandhill that towers above it to its left. The narrow green is surrounded by bunkers that are small and deep, and the ground falls away very sharply beyond those on the right. The prevailing wind blows roughly from left to right, which stresses the difficulties of this great hole.

Another links course that must be mentioned is the little-known gem at the northeast tip of Scotland—Royal Dornoch. But for its location it surely would have its place alongside its more illustrious southern counterparts.

In addition to Prestwick, other great links courses have also failed to survive the march of progress and disappeared off the championship rota (which presently consists of St. Andrews, Carnoustie, Muirfield, Troon, Lytham, and Birkdale).

Britain's links courses tend to be grouped around the coast in tight little knots, those of Kent being a good example, since they virtually adjoin each other along the single shore. Lancashire, with its western coastline fronting the Irish Sea, is another richly endowed strip of golfing country, with sandy beaches separating the courses from the receding sea. Formby, Southport and Ainsdale, Hillside, Royal Birkdale, and Royal Lytham and St. Anne's are the pick of the riches, the last two certain of their places on the championship rota under prevalent modern conditions.

The latter is unique in that, unlike most links courses, it is set inland of the seaside resort of Lytham and St. Anne's. The sea is never visible, and because the course is virtually surrounded by dwellings, it is least affected by the rough weather that can so often make the British Open a physical ordeal, even in high summer. But Royal Lytham retains its place among the championship courses because of its excellent layout. The first three holes are set close to the railway line that is a dominating influence on most of the courses within the area, with the notable exception of Royal Birkdale. Even more crucial are the drive and second shot to a high plateau green closer than ever to the trains at the 8th hole. The outward half at Royal Lytham goes all the way out the far end of the course, as it does at St. Andrews, a similarly narrow strip of golfing excellence—or purgatory, according to your viewpoint.

Royal Lytham boasts many fine holes on the way home, but perhaps the greatest of all is the famed 17th, a long par 4 doglegging to the left, where the second shot must be hit into the full force of the prevailing wind, with a wilderness to the left, together with a myriad collection of pot bunkers that make cutting the corner totally unrewarding. Here it is, in a pot bunker, that a brass plaque was placed to commemorate the brilliant second shot with a hickory-shafted four iron from the sand to the heart of the well-bunkered green that won the 1926 Open Championship for Bobby Jones. Jones's partner and only rival in the last round of the championship, professional Al Watrous, was so unnerved by the great amateur's unbelievable stroke of genius that he promptly three-putted. Nicklaus lost the 1963 championship by a single shot, throwing away the title, at the same hole by failing to estimate the increased flow of adrenalin through his system in the event's closing stages. He went through the green by over-clubbing—club selection for the second shot being one of the great problems, since it is struck on to a flat green, with no obvious backdrop—and failed to get up and down in two shots.

In many ways Royal Birkdale is the most rugged looking of all the great links courses in Britain—terrain pitted with humps and hollows that prompted Lee Trevino to tag it "Moon Country" after he won the championship there in 1971. But in effect the holes that are cut-down valleys between the monster sandhills and dunes at least offer some protection from the elements, and tend to draw in shots struck to their greens. Judgment of distance when there is a green background is also much easier than on the flat expanses of Hoylake, for instance. A serious design fault at Royal Birkdale was still in evidence when the course came on the championship rota for the first time, and Australia's Peter Thomson won the first of his five British Open titles there in 1954. All four short holes, the 4th, 7th, 14th, and 17th, were played from elevated tees to greens set well below them.

The championships that have been staged at Royal Birkdale have been completely under the influence of the elements. When Arnold Palmer won his first British Open there in 1961, the weather was so foul that the entire tented village collapsed like a house of cards, and play was postponed for a day. Palmer won with sheer strength, allied to the skill required to wrestle the course to submission. His unbelievable stroke from the vicious rough to the right of the then 15th, now 16th, fairway, which somehow propelled the ball through the gale to the plateau green, has also been commemorated by a plaque near the spot where it was made.

By contrast, when Thomson won at Royal Birkdale for the second time, in 1965, the wind never rose above a gentle zephyr, the course was dried up and fast running, and the difficulty was to stay on the burned-up fairways at the elbows of the many doglegged holes. Thomson solved this problem, where Nicklaus and Palmer failed, by the skillful use of his three wood to the almost total exclusion of his driver. Skills like these are seldom called upon on watered American courses, despite efforts to ape British conditions.

Perhaps the outstanding of all the great holes at Royal Birkdale is the

468-yard 6th hole, a par 4 of heroic dimensions. The tee is placed in such a way at this marvelous hole, with its dogleg to the right, that the player can either gamble on carrying the huge cross bunker—set in a ridge that bisects the fairway at the angle, or play short of it; if the carry is successfully negotiated, the second shot is a comparatively simple one to a plateau green set in another horseshoe of sandhills, with two deep bunkers to the right, and a little pot bunker left of the green. A drive short of the ridge leaves a horrible second shot, particularly with the wind howling. A water-filled ditch runs all the way up the left-hand side of the hole. To the right beyond the angle of the dogleg runs a huge sandhill shaped like a hog's back. Both this and the deep bunkers to the right of the green have to be carried—a tall order. The hole's problems, alternatives, and distinct reward for the brave and talented player seem to constitute perfect design qualities for championship contenders, while it is still something of a triumph for a handicap golfer to complete the hole in 5 strokes by playing it as a par 5.

In Ireland there are many great courses, but of the links Portmarnock and Ballybunnion in the south and Portrush and Newcastle's Royal County Down in the north are outstanding. Portmarnock is long and flat, a great test of golf in a wind with magnificent greens. Ballybunnion is perhaps the most underrated links of all, set as it is on the River Shannon estuary 40 miles west of Limerick in the southwest on high cliffs. Ballybunnion becomes ever better known, as well it should be. It twists and turns through the big sandhills, with hardly an interruption from the noises of civilization. Portrush affords splendid views of the White Rocks, tall limestone cliffs that lead to Dunluce Castle and the Giant's Causeway. But possibly most beautiful of all is Royal County Down, in the sandhills close to the water under the shadow of Slieve Donard, the tallest of the Mountains of Mourne.

Of the numerous riches inland in the British Isles is the Old Course at Sunningdale. It is one of the many glorious courses clustered together in a belt of great golfing country in Surrey and Berkshire.

The chief characteristics of these courses are their heather and gorse, the profusion of mature trees, notably pines and silver birches, and the high quality of the turf. The course at Woking, Surrey, is a masterpiece in the economical use of telling bunkers, a distinct contrast to Fairhaven near Lytham and St. Anne's, which claims 365 bunkers, one for every day of the year.

The Old and New courses at Walton Heath, laid out by Herbert Fowler, are an example of much that is good in golf course design, as is Willie Park's above-mentioned beautiful Old Course at Sunningdale. These two architects have learned perfectly the lessons taught them by the British links courses—which were discovered rather than designed.

Swinley Forest is another Surrey course of staggering simplicity and merit, while further afield Ganton, near Scarborough, deserves a special mention, as does Woodhall Spa, a heathery and tree-lined oasis in the flat plains of Lincolnshire. The appeal of the latter is rather as a whole than because of any particular hole. It is the kind of magnificent golf course that never allows the player to relax for a second. There is no such thing as a simple par 4 where you can luck a birdie, for instance, nor is there ever a dull moment.

Perhaps the best-known inland course is the West at Wentworth, site of the Piccadilly World Match Play Championship, better known rather sarcastically as "the Burma Road" for its extreme length when wet and playing long. There are six par 5s, three of them in the last four holes, a merciless finish. But when the course is fast running, the realistic par drops rather alarmingly from 74 to 68 because the par 5s become accessible in two shots. Since both the courses at Wentworth are tree-lined, it would really be impractical to stage an Open there, but the course is liked by Americans, who see it as something akin to their own type of golf course.

American Courses

The small band of architects, mostly Scottish, who originally took golf course design to America copied much of what they had seen, or themselves designed back home. But it is surprising how many of the great golf courses of America have been designed by amateurs. The foremost of these was Charles Blair Macdonald, who studied at St. Andrews University in Scotland, learned the game there, and became the first amateur champion of the United States in 1895. A native of Chicago, Macdonald designed and laid out the course of the Chicago Golf Club in 1892, the first 18-hole layout in the country, and did so in such a manner that the holes followed each other in a clockwise direction around the perimeter of the plot. Thus out of bounds was invented, because the hookers of the golf ball were constantly driving out of the golf course. Not surprisingly, Macdonald played every shot with fade, or, more realistically, a chronic slice, so he became virtually unbeatable in his own back yard.

Macdonald resolved to introduce his countrymen to links golf by designing the National Golf Links at Southampton, Long Island, which he laid out between 1907 and 1911 to resemble a typical British links. He took the "Road Hole" from St. Andrews and the "Redan" from North Berwick. But his genius was such that many of the holes were his own creation, and he was immediately inundated with offers to build more courses.

Macdonald set a pattern for golf course architecture that has been followed almost to the present day. Many of the great courses are the brain-

Memorable moments at Merion

children of comparative strangers to golf course architecture, men who built their courses with loving care, always concentrating on one at a time, whereas the professional architects so often try to do too many at the same time, and succeed only in creating sadly mediocre layouts.

Perhaps the closest resemblance to an English Surrey course can be found at Clementon, New Jersey, in Pine Valley, one of the truly outstanding courses and perhaps the best known in America, built by a Philadelphia hotelier, George Crump. All 18 holes here were cut from virgin pine forest on natural sand. The carries from the tees are fearsome, in that they involve traversing unraked sand, scrub, and unkempt rough as is seldom seen in America. Any ball hit into the trees is lost rather than unplayable, but Pine Valley's challenge to every newcomer—that he does not break 90 at the first attempt—tends to get the course a name as a monster rather than one of the best courses in the world.

Merion, built in the suburbs of Philadelphia, was the marvelous creation of Hugh Wilson, a local insurance broker. Although it measures less than 6,600 yards in total, Merion contrived to throw together the two best golfers in the world for a playoff over 18 holes for the 1971 Open, Lee Trevino and Jack Nicklaus, and these two were the only players in the field who equaled par for their first four rounds. Merion remained unconquered not because it was tricked up by the United States Golf Association, but because it has been laid out in such a way that drives must be hit to the correct segment of the fairway to set up the second shot, and the latter must be just as exactly placed to avoid the difficult putts on incredibly slick, undulating greens. The challenge of Merion is mental rather than physical.

The 18 holes on every golf course should be long enough and tough enough to test the best, but should not make a round of golf a misery for the average golfer. The ideal course will force a good golfer to use virtually every club in the bag, be a perfect blend of par 3s, 4s, and 5s, and set out in two loops—or even more—to bring the player back to the clubhouse after each nine holes. Automatic watering systems are a tremendous boon, more so in America than in Britain, but they can be, and are, pitifully abused. When too much water is used, the greens become spongy, every footstep makes them bumpier, and the grass gradually coarsens and loses its health until it turns black.

In Australia, greenskeepers of great skill take up one green at least every winter, scrape up the acids and waste matter that has soaked through the turf, and replace the turves on clean soil. Britain has still to learn such a technique, and Peter Thomson opines that British greens will improve only when the same scouring system is undertaken at some of the great courses. There is little doubt that many courses in Britain need the treatment to revitalize their greens.

It was at Merion that one of the most famous types of grass was discovered by the late Joe Valentine, one of the great greenkeepers of all time, whose discovery is now known as Merion Kentucky bluegrass, or by its code name, B-27. Have there ever been greens of such a magnificent texture, smoothness, and dependable roll and uniform speed as were Merion's for the 1971 Open?

It is difficult to single out any one hole of Merion's eighteen on the East course, because each has its own individual character and challenge. But the deceptive-looking short 13th, 129 yards long, caused as much trouble as any during that championship, although it had been previously regarded as a hole where the competitors took a breather, and grabbed an easy par or even a birdie with a wedge or nine-iron shot to an island green entirely surrounded by bunkers. This green is small enough to pose problems, however, particularly to those who hit their tee shots into one of the traps. Most troublesome of these traps were those set behind the green. The recovery shot played from the downslope of the bunker to a green growing slicker by the hour was one of incredible difficulty.

Perhaps the outstanding product of an amateur architect in the whole of America is Augusta National Golf Club, lovingly fashioned by the late Bobby Jones when he prematurely retired from championship golf in the early 1930s. Jones enlisted the help of the great Scottish architect, Dr. Alister MacKenzie, to lay out a course of unbelievable beauty on the site of what had been formerly a 300-acre shrub nursery. The basic ingredient at Augusta is the giant pines through which the course meanders, but each

The Royal and Ancient Golf Club of St. Andrews, St. Andrews, Scotland

The infamous Rae's Creek (12th hole), Augusta National, Augusta, Georgia

The 13th hole at Dune's Golf and Beach Club, Myrtle Beach, South Carolina

The 18th hole at Pebble Beach Golf Links, Pebble Beach, California

The 11th hole at the Merion Golf Club, Ardmore, Pennsylvania

Cypress Point and Spyglass Hill, Pebble Beach, California

"The Church Pews," Oakmont Country Club, Oakmont, Pennsylvania

Hazeltine National Golf Club, Chaska, Michigan

The 6th hole at the Seminole Country Club, Palm Beach, Florida

The 7th hole at Pebble Beach Golf Links, Pebble Beach, California

The 1st Hole at the Merion Golf Club, Ardmore, Pennsylvania.

Muirfield Golf Links, East Lothian, Scotland

year more azalea bushes, red and white dogwood, and magnolia appear on the course for the U.S. Masters tournament played there in April. The front nine holes at Augusta are somewhat overshadowed by the back nine, chiefly because the water comes into play at the 11th, 12th, 13th, 15th, and 16th holes, but perhaps the waterless holes are more difficult to play.

The greens at Augusta are huge and fast. They undulate considerably, and pose virtually insurmountable problems to those who do not hit their approach shots close enough to the holes. The fairways are almost all very wide—the notable exception being the drive-and-pitch 7th hole—and the bunkering is sparse but mightily effective. Each year one of the many committees at Augusta National, which strive to make the Masters tournament such a showpiece, brings in fresh innovations to further the enjoyment of the spectators. So mounds around the greens will mysteriously appear from year to year, and contribute to make Augusta National perhaps the best course in the world for watching golf.

Without doubt the most difficult hole on the course is the short 12th, played across Rae's Creek into the very corner of the golf course, where the breezes swirl skittishly to make nonsense of what often appears to have been a perfectly struck iron shot. The green has little depth from front to back, being set on the diagonal, and the two bunkers behind it and single trap in front add the extra dimension to a wonderful golf hole of startling simplicity. And it is but 155 yards long.

Not far away in North Carolina is Pinehurst, with its five courses and the atmosphere of a bygone, more dignified age, laid out by another great Scottish architect, Donald Ross. Once again, as the name implies, the chief ingredient is pine trees, but there is also a profusion of silver birches and dazzling white sand. The number two course is generally regarded as the most difficult and challenging, but there is something in one or other of the courses for everyone from rabbit to scratch man. Not for nothing do those new owners of the estate boast of their resort as "the golfing capital of the world."

The Country Club of North Carolina is every bit as beautiful as any of the other Pinehurst courses, and it has the priceless advantage of a lake over a mile wide, whose inlets and lagoons interfere, or intervene to terrorize victims in the closing stages of their rounds. Those who believe that water is the best hazard of all, the ultimate penalty, will love this course.

But perhaps the best example of the use of water in the entire United States is to be found on the Monterey Peninsula in California, two or three hours by car down the coast from San Francisco. Pebble Beach is yet another product of amateur architects that has required only minor alterations since Jack Neville and Douglas Grant, both of whom were state amateur champions, designed it in the second decade of this century. The course is ranged along the picturesque cliffs of Carmel Bay, and the Pacific Ocean comes into play at Pebble Beach on no less than eight holes. In contrast to the British links courses, where the sea is hardly ever seen, let alone comes into play, the ocean is the commanding feature of Pebble Beach. Some say that the ten inland holes are inferior, but that's debatable. Some say that the 18th, par 5, 530 yards long, is the best finishing golf hole in the world. Here the ocean roars against the rocks and the new sea wall, built to stop it eroding away the hole completely. The hole swings left along the shore, with gardens, bunkers, and pine trees along the right-hand side of the hole pushing the player even closer to the water. The green, narrow from side to side, is heavily trapped on the right with two huge bunkers, while another to the left is almost a godsend, since it catches many hooked shots otherwise earmarked for the Pacific.

Just down the road—the scenic 17-mile Drive—is Cypress Point, reckoned by most to be superior scenically even to Pebble Beach. One of the most exclusive clubs in America, it has only 100 or so members, and so to play there is unusual for outsiders. The *pièce de resistance* at Cypress Point is without doubt the often-photographed par-3 16th, a devastatingly simple hole—just a huge carry from cliff top to cliff top over the little inlet below where the Pacific thunders against the rocks. Of course there is the coward's way out—a fairway to the left that is the target area for those who don't think they can make the carry. The feat of doing so is made all the more difficult by the strong and sometimes swirling winds that always seem to arise suddenly just as your shot across the bay is on its way. Such a hole is really a perfect example of all that is good in golf architecture, but such a setting is not easily found.

In the same remote area of California, Spyglass Hill was built by the most famous American course architect of the twentieth century, Robert Trent Jones. Almost to a man, the touring professionals cried out in horror when they were first asked to play this fairly new course. They found the sadistic undulations on the greens quite beyond them in the traditionally stormy weather that buffets competitors in the Bing Crosby tournament almost every January.

Jones has set a pattern for golf course design that has—some say, unfortunately—been copied by many of his inferior competitors. He goes for big greens, some of them eccentrically shaped—and similarly sculpted bunkers, many of which are superfluous but good-looking. Too often Jones seems to put a premium on length. Too often he appears not to have made the best use of the terrain, a case in point being the Hazeltine National Golf Club in Chaska, Minnesota, where Tony Jacklin won the U.S. Open of 1970 by seven shots amid a veritable torrent of abuse aimed at the golf course by runner-up Dave Hill and others, notably Nicklaus. Trent Jones produced a course on a huge plot of Minnesota farmland that had almost unlimited space, yet he chose to make it a vast collection of dogleg holes.

The fact remains that when he does build a good course, and this is often, Robert Jones does so in a grand manner. His courses are exemplary of a new era in golf during which much of the early subtlety of the game has become almost obsolete. Arnold Palmer and Gary Player (now enthusiastic architects), along with others, try manfully to build courses on traditional Scottish lines, but all architects are really in the hands of the men who put up the money and who seem determined that those "so-and-so professionals won't be able to carve up our course!"

Also worthy of note among the vast collection of golf courses in California is the Olympic Club in San Francisco, where the greens are really small and the course is all the better for it, and the Riviera Club in Los Angeles, scene of Ben Hogan's Open victory in 1948, which is a long-driving course not far from the ocean.

In Texas, the Champions' Club in Houston, owned by Jack Burke, Jr., and Jimmy Demaret, boasts 36 holes, two very different courses known as Cypress Creek, the original, laid out by Ralph Plummer (with interruptions from the owners), and the more modern Jackrabbit, the brainchild of George Fazio and Jay Riviere. The two courses could hardly be more different, since Plummer went for huge greens and immense length, while Fazio and Riviere preferred to build a course on American eastern lines with narrow fairways and small greens tightly bunkered and elevated. It has been referred to as a sort of Pine Valley with water replacing sand as the major hazard. The only characteristic in common to the two courses is the type of grass—the popular Tifton 328.

If one can generalize about golf in America, the greens in the east of the country, where the game began, are smaller and the bunkers deeper, built more on British lines. But it is the bunkers, which used to be raked in such a way that the sand was cruelly furrowed, that are the dominant feature of the Oakmont Country Club in Pittsburgh. Again this magnificent and challenging course was designed and laid out by an amateur, William C. Fownes, Jr., in 1903. Fownes, son of a steel baron, felt that any golfer who hit a shot into a bunker should be properly penalized—thus the heavy rake to furrow them. He made enormous greens of incredible pace to torture his victims further. Fownes also created what are now known as church-pew bunkers, huge seas of sand punctuated by grass mounds or ridges planted at intervals in the middle of them. No trees come into play at all, and there is no water—just a myriad collection of almost invisible drainage ditches.

When Fownes originally built the course it had as many as 350 bunkers, but this has now been cut to 184—still an average of ten per hole —and in recent years they have been properly raked smooth. There is a strong argument that Oakmont is the most difficult course in America.

Also vying for that title must be Oakland Hills, Birmingham, Michigan, and the South Course—there is a more modern North—at Firestone Country Club in Akron, Ohio, both par-70 layouts with tremendously long par-4 holes to stretch their total yardages over 7,000. Both courses boast magnificent 16th holes, that at Oakland Hills being another Jones product when he rebuilt the course for the 1951 Open won by Ben Hogan.

Here the drive has to be accurately placed in the center of the fairway to set up a second shot with a medium iron over a lake to a narrow green into the front of which the water eats most insidiously. Thick rough and trees to the right make it virtually impossible for a player to go for the green over the water, although Gary Player won the 1972 PGA title by doing this to such good effect he induced the ball to stop about a yard from the hole for a birdie. Just as surely, a hooked drive sets up a frightening second shot along the full length of the lake. From whatever spot the second shot is hit, there are problems in persuading the ball to remain on the two-tiered green, for behind it are four bunkers, out of which it is very frightening to play back toward the water.

There are many photogenic 16th holes in America—the quarry hole at Merion, the ocean hole at Cypress point—but few are better than the long par 5 down the hill to the 16th green at Firestone South, with its perfectly placed pond in front of the green challenging the big hitter to have a go for the green with his second shot. Even those who lay up have been known to fall victim to the pond because the pitch is actually a lot longer than it looks.

Southern Hills Country Club, Tulsa, Oklahoma, has several claims to fame as a championship course, one of them being its 12th hole, which Ben Hogan nominated as the best par 4 in America. This 456-yard hole swings gently left, the ground sloping down from the right, through the trees. The drive uphill must be perfectly placed at the elbow of the dogleg in a very narrow fairway to allow the golfer a chance to catch the green with his second shot, since there is a long water hazard short and left of the green, and another on the right to trap anything but the perfect hit. The green slopes down from the right to a row of three bunkers to make a really challenging hole—another example of perfection in architecture— since it rewards the brave and the talented, while giving the ordinary golfer a chance to excel himself, or sensibly lay up short of the water and hope to get down in two more shots.

There are far too many good courses in the Midwest to describe them all, but one that easily comes to mind is the Scioto Country Club, Columbus, Ohio, where Jack Nicklaus was first introduced to the game by his late father, Charlie, and he was groomed for stardom by the then professional Jack Grout. Another great Scottish architect, Donald Ross, was responsible for the creation of Scioto in 1915, and it bears his inimitable trademark, extreme length and small greens. Although simply a parkland course, Scioto is a marvelous test of accurate shotmaking, and never better than at the 2nd hole, 436 yards, par 4. The drive is hit here over a ravine from an elevated tee to a fairway sloping upward quite steeply toward the green, and awfully difficult to hold because of a hog's back down the center that can throw the ball either way—into a creek hidden among the trees on the left, or into one of two bunkers on the right. A really bad cut from the tee can send the ball bouncing up the road into gardens the other side of it. A giant maple tree is also well placed to catch drives hit in this direction. The green slopes up toward its rear end and is tightly bunkered left and right —a superb hole.

Golf courses are springing up all over Florida, but too often they have the stamp of mediocrity. This could never be said of Seminole, however, another Donald Ross creation built in 1929, or of the wonderful Bay Hill Club, built by the late Dick Wilson and now owned by Arnold Palmer. Seminole and Bay Hill are undoubtedly the two finest tests of golf in Florida. Seminole is situated right on the Atlantic Ocean, and at times the spray can be seen lashing across the course. It seldom affects the fantastic condition of the golf course because the grass is Ormond Bermuda, lush, salt-resistant, and remarkably true on the greens. This very exclusive course undulates more than most in the States, and is remarkable for its immense bunkers. The late Tommy Armour called Seminole's 388-yard, par-4 6th the greatest single hole in the United States. Hogan, too, waxed eloquent about it when practicing there for the Masters at Augusta, which he used to do regularly for about six weeks early every Spring. The hole is notable because it encompasses a vast sea of sand contained in no fewer than 11 large bunkers. The drive must be hit over the three bunkers to the left and faded down into the fairway. If the tee shot is hit over a daunting expanse of sand, then the second is even more frightening, since it has to be struck over a mass of bunkers that stretch all the way to the green, where the flag looks from the point of aim as if it has been placed in one of them.

Bay Hill, near Orlando, is a more rolling course than is generally found in Florida and has no parallel fairways which typify so many Florida courses. Its par-3 17th, a long iron even for Palmer, over menacing water is probably its best hole if not one of the best par 3s in the United States.

Further up the east coast, Robert Trent Jones has laid out a fine course, also hard by the ocean at Myrtle Beach, South Carolina, the Dunes Golf and Beach Club, famed because of the eccentricity of its huge 560-yard 13th hole. This monster is actually shaped like a horseshoe, and laid out around an alligator-infested lake. The drive is hit, believe it or not, *away* from the hole down to the very edge of the water. The second must be hit with everything the golfer can manage in the way of strength with probably a three wood to carry a large corner of Singleton Lake. According to how much of the water you have dared to bite off, you will be hitting a three iron or perhaps a seven for your third shot, to a green set on two levels, high on the left and low on the right, the two halves separated by a steep ridge running from back to front of the putting surface. One can call the 13th at the Dunes either fascinating or damnably stupid, but it is certainly different.

Two of New York's commuter courses, Baltusrol in Springfield, New

Jersey, and Winged Foot in Westchester County, are very much traditional designs, both created by Arthur Tillinghast. Baltusrol has since been modernized by Jones, and a legend exists about the alterations he made to the par-3 4th hole. The members complained that he had made this hole, with a lake between tee and green, too difficult for them. Jones went out with professional Johnny Farrell and two committee members to explain that the complaints were unfounded, and proved his point perfectly when, playing the fourth, he holed his tee shot!

Courses Elsewhere

Golf courses throughout the rest of the world are not without their pearls.

The Bahamas has been a happy designing ground for Dick Wilson and his assistant, Joe Lee. Great Harbour Cay (Lee) and Treasure Cay, Great Abaco (Wilson) are both heavily bunkered, particularly in front of the greens, requiring shots to be flown into them.

It would be hard to imagine a more beautiful scenic course than Mid-Ocean in Bermuda, with its outstanding finish along the high cliffs. Mount Irvine Bay in Tobago, designed by the British architect John Harris, is also a scenic gem.

Only Europe has been largely left behind. In Britain there is hardly room for expansion except in the remoter areas, and this will have to be the pattern there and in Japan, where there is perhaps more feverish activity in golf course design than anywhere on earth. The boom in Scandinavia has been astonishing, since Sweden's many new courses emerge from snow and darkness for only about four months of the year.

Land prices in Switzerland make the cost of building golf courses too prohibitive to hope for any major breakthrough, but Robert Trent Jones is building a hugely luxurious new course in Geneva, and has recently completed a gorgeous layout in the rocky hills close to the Mediterranean on the Aga Khan's spectacular Costa Smeralda tourist development on the island of Sardinia. Known as Pevero, this Sardinian course may be the best thing Jones has done in Europe and Africa. Pevero affords breathtaking views at practically every hole of bays and mountains, and the quality of the Penncross bent grass leaves nothing to be desired.

Spain is better set up than any of the other continental countries besides Sweden. Madrid has two fine layouts, Puerto di Hierro and Club de Campo, while the El Prat club in Barcelona, laid out by the Arana brothers, both international amateur golfers, is an outstanding 27-hole complex. The

La Galea club in Bilbao was considered good enough to host an international fixture, Britain versus Europe. At La Manga on the Costa Blanca not far from Alicante, a luxurious 36-hole development has recently opened which may well put all other Spanish courses and developments to shame. It will be the home of the Spanish Open for at least the next five years, and in late 1972 hosted the biggest pro-amateur event in the world. Designed by the Californian architect Robert Dean Putman, La Manga has the appearance of the desert courses of California and Nevada, since hundreds of palm trees were imported and planted all over the South and North courses.

Dr. Bernard von Limburger was responsible for the Atalaya Park course, also at Marbella, noteworthy for the scarcity of bunkers, particularly in the drive area. Von Limburger believes that the rough is a sufficient punishment for a wayward drive, and uses strategically placed, but few, traps to catch the second shot.

The older Guadalmina and Rio Real or Los Monteros courses make Marbella a fascinating golfing center, with yet another course at nearby Torremolinos for good measure.

The golf boom has also come to Portugal in a big way, particularly on the southerly Algarve coast, where Henry Cotton has built two courses, at Penina and Vale do Lobo near Faro—Vale do Lobo being by far better, more picturesque, and more interesting of the two. Another English architect, Frank Pennink, has created a fine course among the umbrella pines at nearby Vilamoura.

In Europe, golf is still very much the preserve of the aristocratic and wealthy, but there are signs of progress in the southwest of France. The Paris area is already well served, considering how few play the game, with courses at Saint-Cloud, a beautiful parkland layout, the new club of Saint-Nom-la-Breteche, which is gradually settling down and bidding to be considered as outstanding, and of course Chantilly.

Italy has several splendid courses, notably Olgiata in Rome and the course at Como.

Perhaps the best course in Sweden is that at Falsterbo, carved out of virgin pine forests near Malmo, while Denmark has two vividly contrasting courses in Copenhagen: the Rungsted club is typical of a Surrey, England, course while the Copenhagen club's course, set in the royal deer park, is open and heathlike in quality.

Belgium and Holland both badly need to produce a world-class golfer to help persuade businessmen to invest in golfing development, and much the same could be said for Germany, although one of the most outstanding courses in Europe is situated just outside Hamburg at Falkenstein, where the European Team Championship was held three years ago. Falkenstein is like a very much tightened and narrower version of Sunningdale, high praise indeed.

Dr. von Limburger built a difficult but fair course at Bremen in his native country and the outstanding course was the setting for the German Open won by Neil Coles in 1971, and praised by all who competed.

South Africa's Royal Johannesburg club has a course that must be high on any list of the world's 50 best, a parkland layout in the suburbs where the ball flies seemingly forever, but where low scores are a rarity. The course is superbly laid out in two loops of nine holes, none of which allow the golfer to relax, since many are narrow and tree-lined, and water also comes into play.

Durban Country Club has the reputation for having the best clubhouse in South Africa, and many consider the course even better than Royal Johannesburg. Perhaps its most difficult and challenging hole is the par-3 12th, perched on a plateau, the green of postage-stamp size. Although the tee shot is only of nine-iron length, the ground falls away sharply on both sides, and the pitch up the steep slopes can be very difficult to keep on the green. The hole is named "Prince of Wales" after the late golfing Duke of Windsor, who once played backward and forward here and ran up the score of 11. Mowbray is Capetown's best and its majestic 15th, a long par 4 with a breathtaking backdrop of mountains, can lay claim to being South Africa's best hole, if not one of the best in the world.

In Australia there is an outstanding strip of golfing country on what is known as the sand belt just outside Melbourne. Here there are no fewer than 12 courses similar to those of Surrey, England, in character, the outstanding ones being Royal Melbourne, with its East and West courses, and Victoria. For important events like the Eisenhower Trophy and World Cup, both of which have been played there, a composite layout of 18 holes is taken from the two Royal Melbourne courses to avoid crossing a busy local road. Sydney's best are Royal Sydney, the Lakes, and the Australian, while Adelaide has Kooyonga and distant Perth has perhaps Australia's prettiest and most interesting courses in Lake Karrimyup.

APPENDIX

Introduction

RECORDS-KEEPING in professional golf has been mediocre at best, particularly outside the United States. Efforts to be as complete and expansive as I would have liked ran into snags at virtually every turn except in America, where we have always thrived on statistics. While their records and statistics are dwarfed by those available on professional baseball and football and other major sports, the PGA of America and its Tournament Players Division nonetheless have maintained quite adequate details of the U.S. tournament tour through the years. Most of the material on American golf in this appendix has been drawn from these records. Within the book's framework, it is complete.

Unfortunately, this is not true for the statistics in this book on professional golf in other countries of the world. But, half a loaf is better than none and what is collected and included here does flesh out well the statistical picture of world professional golf in a fashion never before presented in a history of the game.

The Top 100 Money-Winners of the Quarter-Century

Since the end of World War II and the return to normal competition, some $75,000,000 in prize money has gone into the pockets of golf professionals from the purses of tournaments and special events of national and international scope throughout the world. But, how much into whose pockets?

This unique compilation shows how more than half of it—$46,000,000 —was collected by 100 men who are, therefore, the most successful golfers financially in the last quarter-century of the professional game.

Five—Jack Nicklaus, Arnold Palmer, Bill Casper, Gary Player, and

Gene Littler—are in the million-dollar class. Eighty-nine are Americans, not surprisingly since the U.S. Tour carried four-fifths of the total prize money of the period. This and the way the prize money has grown in recent years is clearly reflected toward the end of the list. The earlier American greats—Ben Hogan, Cary Middlecoff, Lloyd Mangrum, and others—are there. Mike Hill, the 100th man, didn't join the Tour until 1968. Such long-time British standouts as Neil Coles, Bernard Hunt, Peter Alliss, and Christy O'Connor, who competed almost exclusively in Britain and Europe, did not earn enough to "make" the Top 100.

A long and concerted attempt was made to base this master money list on all national and international competition from the start of the 1947 season through the August, 1972, week of the U.S. PGA Championship, the last of the four major events of the year. These resultant rankings have clear-cut validity.

However, it should be noted that, particularly in the cases of those who played the tours prior to the first publication of the annual book, *The World of Professional Golf*, on the 1966 season and its World Money Lists each year, financial figures simply were never recorded or have been lost in countries around the world, other than in America.

Even in the United States, the records systems of the PGA of America have changed from time to time, making it impossible to include, as the PGA now does, tour earnings in "unofficial" tournaments and pro-amateurs prior to 1966. With this inclusion, the totals for most of the players would be somewhat higher, especially those of the leading men, particularly Palmer, but the $200,000 or so that Arnold won that is not reflected in the PGA records used for this compilation would not push him past Nicklaus, who won a third of his $2 million in the 1970s.

1	Jack Nicklaus	$2,010,694	35	Mason Rudolph	$456,631	69	Tom Shaw	$274,169
2	Arnold Palmer	1,740,518	36	George Knudson	446,162	70	Bobby Mitchell	269,815
3	Bill Casper	1,549,010	37	Tony Jacklin	438,213	71	Jacky Cupit	267,852
4	Gary Player	1,327,210	38	Homero Blancas	433,694	72	Dick Lotz	264,275
5	Gene Littler	1,001,974	39	Doug Ford	426,419	73	Jack Burke	262,959
6	Julius Boros	957,253	40	Phil Rodgers	424,882	74	Ted Kroll	258,997
7	Lee Trevino	909,794	41	Johnny Pott	421,030	75	Hale Irwin	258,324
8	Bruce Crampton	860,900	42	Tony Lema	416,720	76	Tommy Jacobs	252,992
9	George Archer	852,888	43	Billy Maxwell	414,750	77	Johnny Miller	248,631
10	Frank Beard	847,413	44	Dow Finsterwald	412,526	78	Grier Jones	242,020
11	Doug Sanders	816,560	45	Dale Douglass	402,940	79	Labron Harris	237,464
12	Miller Barber	765,701	46	Lionel Hebert	389,767	80	Fred Marti	233,194
13	Gay Brewer	725,041	47	Tommy Bolt	389,298	81	Don Massengale	228,452
14	Bobby Nichols	723,711	48	Dave Marr	381,874	82	Jim Colbert	227,840
15	Tom Weiskopf	723,259	49	Ken Still	377,705	83	Bill Collins	211,403
16	Dave Hill	689,494	50	R. H. Sikes	366,847	84	J. C. Snead	210,375
17	Tommy Aaron	683,129	51	Paul Harney	361,924	85	Richard Crawford	210,287
18	Dan Sikes	659,012	52	Kermit Zarley	360,715	86	Terry Dill	209,936
19	Bruce Devlin	658,546	53	Lou Graham	347,378	87	Ben Hogan	207,376
20	Don January	627,074	54	Peter Thomson	334,151	88	Chuck Courtney	206,749
21	Sam Snead	624,319	55	Howie Johnson	333,781	89	Fred Hawkins	205,711
22	Dave Stockton	623,721	56	Kel Nagle	318,572	90	Lee Elder	204,164
23	Bert Yancey	617,768	57	Charles Sifford	314,125	91	Lloyd Mangrum	203,216
24	Bob Goalby	595,714	58	Rod Funseth	312,869	92	Dick Mayer	202,380
25	Bob Charles	594,086	59	Jerry Heard	310,363	93	Jack McGowan	199,204
26	Gardner Dickinson	589,667	60	Jay Hebert	307,051	94	Dutch Harrison	197,673
27	Al Geiberger	583,498	61	Deane Beman	306,887	95	Dave Eichelberger	194,500
28	Charles Coody	568,400	62	Mike Souchak	304,690	96	Al Balding	194,010
29	Art Wall	549,727	63	Roberto de Vicenzo	303,401	97	Joe Campbell	193,343
30	Raymond Floyd	506,064	64	Cary Middlecoff	296,443	98	Bert Weaver	193,339
31	Chi Chi Rodriguez	497,828	65	Ken Venturi	294,250	99	George Bayer	188,577
32	Bob Rosburg	464,192	66	Harold Henning	290,231	100	Mike Hill	187,406
33	Bob Lunn	463,040	67	Larry Hinson	286,888			
34	Bob Murphy	461,004	68	Orville Moody	276,635			

The Top 25 in the Major Championships

This four-section chart consolidates the performances of the leading 25 money-winners in the post–World War II period of professional golf in the four major championships. It summarizes their year-by-year finishes in the top 25 of each of those tournaments since 1946.

For the U.S. Open and Masters, we have listed beside the names the first full year each man played on the U.S. Tour, so that the reader will have some idea of the number of tournaments each played in to compile the record. For the PGA Championship, we carry only the stroke-play tournaments and indicate the first year in which each of the 25 men were eligible for (but did not necessarily qualify for and/or play in) the tournament as a stroke-play event.

The chart not only clearly shows that the greats of the era have performed consistently well in the big tournaments during their careers but also displays some interesting patterns and unusual facts. For instance, it illustrates the fact that, although Sam Snead has never won the U.S. Open nor Arnold Palmer the PGA Championship, each has frequently done very well in those tournaments. It shows just how strongly Jack Nicklaus has played in all of the major tournaments over the years. It points up the remarkable short-term record of Lee Trevino in the two Opens, yet his lack of success in the Masters and PGA. It reveals that, although winners of more than $600,000 each in careers spanning more than a decade, Tommy Aaron and Dan Sikes have never done well in the U.S. Open, Aaron never having finished as high as 25th place.

The italic figures on the charts of the U.S. Open and Masters indicate that the players (Nicklaus and Aaron) were amateurs at the time.

U.S. OPEN CHAMPIONSHIP

Player	*	1946	47	48	49	50	51	52	53	54	55	56	57	58	59	60	61	62	63	64	65	66	67	68	69	70	71	72	WINS	SECONDS	TOP 5	TOP 10	TOP 25
Jack Nicklaus	1962															2	4	1		23		3	1	2	25		2	1	3	3	8	8	10
Arnold Palmer	1955										21	7			5	1	14	2	2	5		2	2	6	6		25	3	1	4	8	10	14
Bill Casper	1955											14		13	1	12	17	6	8	4	17	1	4	9		8		11	2	0	4	6	12
Gary Player	1957													2	15	19	9	6	8	23	1	15	12	16			15	15	1	1	2	5	12
Gene Littler	1954									2	15			4	11		1	8	21	11	8				12	12			1	1	3	5	10
Julius Boros	1950					9	4	1	17	23	5	2				3			1		4	17		16	13	12			2	1	9	10	16
Lee Trevino	1967																						5	1		8	1	4	2	0	4	5	5
Bruce Crampton	1957													19			22		5	14		17			6			2	0	1	2	3	6
George Archer	1964																					17	10	16			5		0	0	1	2	4
Frank Beard	1963																				3	17				22			0	0	1	1	3
Doug Sanders	1957																2	11	21		11	8							0	1	0	2	5
Miller Barber	1958																	22					18	24	6	6			0	0	2	5	5
Gay Brewer	1956																		5	5	16		9	9		7	9		0	0	2	4	6
Bobby Nichols	1960																	3	14	14		7	23	4			9	11	0	0	2	4	8
Tom Weiskopf	1965																						15	24	22			8	0	0	0	1	4
Dave Hill	1959																					22	18	16	13	2			0	1	1	1	5
Tommy Aaron	1961																		10					15					0	0	0	0	2
Dan Sikes	1961																				6		23	9	10				0	0	0	1	2
Bruce Devlin	1962																					6	23	9	10	8			0	0	0	4	5
Don January	1956													7	19				11	11			3	24				11	0	0	1	2	8
Sam Snead	1937	19	2	5	2	12	10	10	2	11	3	24	8	8	19	17					25			9	25				0	3	5	10	17
Dave Stockton	1964																							9	9	22			0	0	0	1	2
Bert Yancey	1964																					22	6	3	22	22	9	11	0	0	1	2	5
Bob Goalby	1957															19		14				22				19			0	0	0	1	5
Bob Charles	1963																		19	3				7		3	13		0	0	2	3	5

* First year full-time player on U.S. Tour

PGA CHAMPIONSHIP

This chart includes only the stroke-play PGA Championships, beginning in 1958.

	*	1958	59	60	61	62	63	64	65	66	67	68	69	70	71	72	WINS	SECONDS	TOP 5	TOP 10	TOP 25
Jack Nicklaus	1962					3	1	2	2	22	3		11	6	1	13	2	2	6	7	10
Arnold Palmer	1958		14	7	5	17		2		6	14	2		2	18	16	0	3	4	6	11
Bill Casper	1958	2	17	24	15			9	2	3	19	6		18	2	4	0	3	5	7	12
Gary Player	1958					1	8	13		3			2	12	4	1	2	1	5	6	8
Gene Littler	1958		10	18	5	23				3	7			4			0	0	3	5	7
Julius Boros	1958	5		24		11	13	21	17	6	5	1	25				1	0	3	4	10
Lee Trevino	1967											23			13	11	0	0	0	0	3
Bruce Crampton	1958					17	3		20			23	15	6		25	0	0	1	2	7
George Archer	1964											4					0	0	1	1	1
Frank Beard	1963									11	7	6	10		13		0	0	0	3	5
Doug Sanders	1958		3	3	3	15	22		20	6						7	0	0	3	5	8
Miller Barber	1958											8	5		4	16	0	0	2	3	4
Gay Brewer	1958							8				20	25			7	0	0	0	2	4
Bobby Nichols	1960				6	23	1			14							1	0	1	2	4
Tom Weiskopf	1965													22			0	0	0	0	1
Dave Hill	1959						17			11	17	15		6			0	0	0	1	5
Tommy Aaron	1961							21	8	22	20				2		0	1	1	2	5
Dan Sikes	1961										3	8	25	18		13	0	0	1	2	5
Bruce Devlin	1962								6					18	13		0	0	0	1	3
Don January	1958			5	2					12	1		15	12			1	1	3	3	6
Sam Snead	1958	3	8	3		17			6	6			12		4		0	0	3	6	8
Dave Stockton	1964											17		1			1	0	1	1	2
Bert Yancey	1964											23	22	22			0	0	0	0	2
Bob Goalby	1958		5		15	2	17				7	8					0	1	2	4	6
Bob Charles	1963						13	19				2		13			0	1	1	1	4

* First year eligible to play in stroke-play PGA Championship

MASTERS CHAMPIONSHIP

Player	*	46	47	48	49	50	51	52	53	54	55	56	57	58	59	60	61	62	63	64	65	66	67	68	69	70	71	72	WINS	SECONDS	TOP 5	TOP 10	TOP 25
Jack Nicklaus	1962															*73*	7	15	1	2	1	1		5	24	8	2	1	4	2		9	12
Arnold Palmer	1955										10	21	7	1	3	1	2	1	9	1	2	4	4			18			4	2		12	14
Bill Casper	1955												16	20		4	7	15	11	5		10	24	16	2	1	13	17	1	1		6	14
Gary Player	1957												24		8	6	1	2	5	5			6	7		3	6	10	1	2		12	13
Gene Littler	1954									22	22	12			8		15	4	24	13	6			8	2		4		0	1		6	12
Julius Boros	1950					17	7	10	16		4	24			8	5		11	3			5	16		8	2	25			0	0		7	13
Lee Trevino	1967																						19						0	0		0	1
Bruce Crampton	1957												21			16			11	21	11	17		13			18	2	0	1		1	9
George Archer	1964																					16	22	1				12	1	0		1	4
Frank Beard	1963																				8	22		5	19	9	9		0	0		4	6
Doug Sanders	1957																11				11	4	16	12					0	0		1	5
Miller Barber	1958																							12	7	21			0	0		1	3
Gay Brewer	1956																	11		25		2	1						1	1		2	4
Bobby Nichols	1960																		24	25	25	2							0	1		1	4
Tom Weiskopf	1965																					16		2	25	6	2		0	2		2	5
Dave Hill	1959																							24	5				0	0		1	2
Tommy Aaron	1961															25				11	13		8	7	8	5	22		0	1		4	8
Dan Sikes	1961																		15	13	5			12					0	0		1	4
Bruce Devlin	1962																			4	15	10		4	19	13	5		0	0		4	7
Don January	1956															20	4	20	9	18		6	14	5	12	4			0	0		5	10
Sam Snead	1937	7	22	16	1	3	8	2	16	1	3	4	2	13	22	11	15	15	3			10			25				2	2		11	20
Dave Stockton	1964																						10		18	5	9	10	0	0		3	4
Bert Yancey	1964																						3	3	13	4		12	0	0		3	5
Bob Goalby	1957																	25						1				17	1	0		1	3
Bob Charles	1963																	25	15					19	17		22		0	0		0	5

* First year full-time player on U.S. Tour

BRITISH OPEN CHAMPIONSHIP

Player	1946	47	48	49	50	51	52	53	54	55	56	57	58	59	60	61	62	63	64	65	66	67	68	69	70	71	72	WON	2ND	TOP 5	TOP 10	TOP 25
Jack Nicklaus																		3	2	12	1	2	2	6	1	5	2	2	4	8	9	**10**
Arnold Palmer															2	1	1			16	8		10	12	17			2	1	3	5	**8**
Bill Casper																							4	23		7		0	0	1	2	3
Gary Player											4	25	7	1	7			7	8		4	3	1					2	0	5	11	13
Gene Littler																												0	0	0	0	0
Julius Boros																					15							0	0	0	0	1
Lee Trevino																									3	1	1	2	0	3	3	3
Bruce Crampton											13																	0	0	0	0	1
George Archer																												0	0	0	0	0
Frank Beard																											19	0	0	0	0	1
Doug Sanders																			11		2	18			2	9		0	2	3	4	6
Miller Barber																								10				0	0	0	1	1
Gay Brewer																							6	15				0	0	0	1	2
Bobby Nichols																												0	0	0	0	0
Tom Weiskopf																									22		7	0	0	0	1	2
Dave Hill																												0	0	0	0	0
Tommy Aaron																												0	0	0	0	0
Dan Sikes																												0	0	0	0	0
Bruce Devlin																			5	8	4	8	10	16	25			0	0	2	5	7
Don January																												0	0	0	0	0
Sam Snead	1																6											1	0	1	2	2
Dave Stockton																										11		0	0	0	0	1
Bert Yancey																								16	13	11	19	0	0	0	0	4
Bob Goalby																												0	0	0	0	0
Bob Charles																	5	1	17				2	2	13	18	15	1	2	4	4	8

The "Grand Slam" Championships

Professional golf revolves around its four major championships. The Professional "Grand Slam" is the rabbit that every tournament player of ambition pursues each season, that never-yet-attained sweep of the U.S. and British Opens, the Masters, and the American PGA Championships in a single season. These are the prestige events of the game and a player's record in these events is the best measure of his ability. Here is a compilation of the results of each of these four championships, showing the top 5 finishers in each from 1946 through 1972, along with a listing of the winners in the earlier formative years of today's large-scale tournament golf.

U.S. OPEN CHAMPIONSHIP

1972—Pebble Beach Golf Links, Pebble Beach, California
CHAMPION—Jack Nicklaus

	SCORES	TOTAL	MONEY		SCORES	TOTAL	MONEY
Jack Nicklaus	71 73 72 74	290	$30,000	Lee Trevino	74 72 71 78	295	$7,500
Bruce Crampton	74 70 73 76	293	15,000	Homero Blancas	74 70 76 75	295	7,500
Arnold Palmer	77 68 73 76	294	10,000				

1971—Merion Golf Club (East Course), Ardmore, Pennsylvania
CHAMPION—Lee Trevino

(Playoff: Trevino 68; Nicklaus 71)

	SCORES	TOTAL	MONEY		SCORES	TOTAL	MONEY
Lee Trevino	70 72 69 69	280	$30,000	Jim Colbert	69 69 73 71	282	$9,000
Jack Nicklaus	69 72 68 71	280	15,000	* Jim Simons	71 71 65 76	283	
Bob Rosburg	71 72 70 69	282	9,000				

* Amateur

1970—Hazeltine National Golf Club, Chaska, Minnesota
CHAMPION—Tony Jacklin

	SCORES	TOTAL	MONEY		SCORES	TOTAL	MONEY
Tony Jacklin	71 70 70 70	281	$30,000	Bob Charles	76 71 75 67	289	$9,000
Dave Hill	75 69 71 73	288	15,000	Ken Still	78 71 71 71	291	7,000
Bob Lunn	77 72 70 70	289	9,000				

1969—Champions Golf Club (Cypress Creek Course), Houston, Texas
CHAMPION—Orville Moody

	SCORES	TOTAL	MONEY		SCORES	TOTAL	MONEY
Orville Moody	71 70 68 72	281	$30,000	Bob Rosburg	70 69 72 71	282	$11,000
Deane Beman	68 69 73 72	282	11,000	Bob Murphy	66 72 74 71	283	7,000
Al Geiberger	68 72 72 70	282	11,000				

1968—Oak Hill Country Club (East Course), Rochester, New York
CHAMPION—Lee Trevino

	SCORES	TOTAL	MONEY		SCORES	TOTAL	MONEY
Lee Trevino	69 68 69 69	275	$30,000	Bobby Nichols	74 71 68 69	282	$7,500
Jack Nicklaus	72 70 70 67	279	15,000	Don Bies	70 70 75 69	284	5,500
Bert Yancey	67 68 70 76	281	10,000				

1967—Baltusrol Golf Club (Lower Course), Springfield, New Jersey
CHAMPION—Jack Nicklaus

	SCORES	TOTAL	MONEY		SCORES	TOTAL	MONEY
Jack Nicklaus	71 67 72 65	275	$30,000	Bill Casper	69 70 71 72	282	$7,500
Arnold Palmer	69 68 73 69	279	15,000	Lee Trevino	72 70 71 70	283	6,000
Don January	69 72 70 70	281	10,000				

1966—Olympic Country Club, San Francisco, California
CHAMPION—Bill Casper

(Playoff: Casper 69; Palmer 73)

	SCORES	TOTAL	MONEY		SCORES	TOTAL	MONEY
Bill Casper	69 68 73 68	278	$26,500	Tony Lema	71 74 70 71	286	$6,500
Arnold Palmer	71 66 70 71	278	14,000	Dave Marr	71 74 68 73	286	6,500
Jack Nicklaus	71 71 69 74	285	9,000				

1965—Bellerive Country Club, St. Louis, Missouri
CHAMPION—Gary Player

(Playoff: Player 71; Nagle 74)

	SCORES	TOTAL	MONEY		SCORES	TOTAL	MONEY
Gary Player	70 70 71 71	282	$26,000	Julius Boros	72 75 70 70	287	$6,500
Kel Nagle	68 73 72 69	282	13,500	Al Geiberger	70 76 70 71	287	6,500
Frank Beard	74 69 70 71	284	9,000				

1964—Congressional Country Club, Washington, D.C.
CHAMPION—Ken Venturi

	SCORES	TOTAL	MONEY		SCORES	TOTAL	MONEY
Ken Venturi	72 70 66 70	278	$17,000	Bill Casper	71 74 69 71	285	$5,000
Tommy Jacobs	72 64 70 76	282	8,500	Gay Brewer	76 69 73 68	286	3,750
Bob Charles	72 72 71 68	283	6,000				

1963—The Country Club, Brookline, Massachusetts
CHAMPION—Julius Boros

(Playoff: Boros 70; Cupit 73; Palmer 76)

	SCORES	TOTAL	MONEY		SCORES	TOTAL	MONEY
Julius Boros	71 74 76 72	293	$17,500	Paul Harney	78 70 73 73	294	$5,000
Jacky Cupit	70 72 76 75	293	8,500	Billy Maxwell	73 73 75 74	295	3,166.66
Arnold Palmer	73 69 77 74	293	8,500				

1962—Oakmont Country Club, Oakmont, Pennsylvania
CHAMPION—Jack Nicklaus

(Playoff: Nicklaus 71; Palmer 74)

	SCORES	TOTAL	MONEY		SCORES	TOTAL	MONEY
Jack Nicklaus	72 70 72 69	283	$17,500	Bobby Nichols	70 72 70 73	285	$5,500
Arnold Palmer	71 68 73 71	283	10,500	Gay Brewer	73 72 73 69	287	4,000
Phil Rodgers	74 70 69 72	285	5,500				

1961—Oakland Hills Country Club, Birmingham, Michigan
CHAMPION—Gene Littler

	SCORES	TOTAL	MONEY		SCORES	TOTAL	MONEY
Gene Littler	73 68 72 68	281	$14,000	Mike Souchak	73 70 68 73	284	$4,000
Bob Goalby	70 72 69 71	282	6,000	* Jack Nicklaus	75 69 70 70	284	
Doug Sanders	72 67 71 72	282	6,000				

* Amateur

1960—*Cherry Hills Country Club, Englewood, Colorado*
CHAMPION—*Arnold Palmer*

	SCORES	TOTAL	MONEY		SCORES	TOTAL	MONEY
Arnold Palmer	72 71 72 65	280	$14,400	Julius Boros	73 69 68 73	283	$3,950
* Jack Nicklaus	71 71 69 71	282		Mike Souchak	68 67 73 75	283	3,950
Dutch Harrison	74 70 70 69	283	3,950				

1959—*Winged Foot Golf Club, Mamaroneck, New York*
CHAMPION—*Bill Casper*

	SCORES	TOTAL	MONEY		SCORES	TOTAL	MONEY
Bill Casper	71 68 69 74	282	$12,000	Mike Souchak	71 70 72 71	284	$3,600
Bob Rosburg	75 70 67 71	283	6,600	Doug Ford	72 69 72 73	286	2,100
Claude Harmon	72 71 70 71	284	3,600				

1958—*Southern Hills Country Club, Tulsa, Oklahoma*
CHAMPION—*Tommy Bolt*

	SCORES	TOTAL	MONEY		SCORES	TOTAL	MONEY
Tommy Bolt	71 71 69 72	283	$8,000	Gene Littler	74 73 67 76	290	$2,000
Gary Player	75 68 73 71	287	5,000	Walter Burkemo	75 74 70 72	291	1,625
Julius Boros	71 75 72 71	289	3,000				

1957—*Inverness Club, Toledo, Ohio*
CHAMPION—*Dick Mayer*

(Playoff: Mayer 72; Middlecoff 79)

	SCORES	TOTAL	MONEY		SCORES	TOTAL	MONEY
Dick Mayer	70 68 74 70	282	$7,200	Julius Boros	69 75 70 70	284	$1,380
Cary Middlecoff	71 75 68 68	282	4,200	Walter Burkemo	74 73 72 65	284	1,380
Jimmy Demaret	68 73 70 72	283	2,160				

1956—*Oak Hill Country Club (East Course), Rochester, New York*
CHAMPION—*Cary Middlecoff*

	SCORES	TOTAL	MONEY		SCORES	TOTAL	MONEY
Cary Middlecoff	71 70 70 70	281	$6,000	Ed Furgol	71 70 73 71	285	$1,033.34
Julius Boros	71 71 71 69	282	2,650	Peter Thomson	70 69 75 71	285	1,033.33
Ben Hogan	72 68 72 70	282	2,650				

* Amateur

1955—Olympic Country Club (Lake Course), San Francisco, California
CHAMPION—Jack Fleck

(Playoff: Fleck 69; Hogan 72)

	SCORES	TOTAL	MONEY		SCORES	TOTAL	MONEY
Jack Fleck	76 69 75 67	287	$6,000	Tommy Bolt	67 77 75 73	292	$1,500
Ben Hogan	72 73 72 70	287	4,000	Julius Boros	76 69 73 77	295	870
Sam Snead	79 69 70 74	292	1,500				

1954—Baltusrol Golf Club (Lower Course), Springfield, New Jersey
CHAMPION—Ed Furgol

	SCORES	TOTAL	MONEY		SCORES	TOTAL	MONEY
Ed Furgol	71 70 71 72	284	$6,000	Lloyd Mangrum	72 71 72 71	286	$1,500
Gene Littler	70 69 76 70	285	3,600	Bobby Locke	74 70 74 70	288	960
Dick Mayer	72 71 70 73	286	1,500				

1953—Oakmont Country Club, Oakmont, Pennsylvania
CHAMPION—Ben Hogan

	SCORES	TOTAL	MONEY		SCORES	TOTAL	MONEY
Ben Hogan	67 72 73 71	283	$5,000	Pete Cooper	78 75 71 70	294	$816.67
Sam Snead	72 69 72 76	289	3,000	George Fazio	70 71 77 76	294	816.67
Lloyd Mangrum	73 70 74 75	292	1,500				

1952—Northwood Club, Dallas, Texas
CHAMPION—Julius Boros

	SCORES	TOTAL	MONEY		SCORES	TOTAL	MONEY
Julius Boros	71 71 68 71	281	$4,000	Johnny Bulla	73 68 73 73	287	$800
Porky Oliver	71 72 70 72	285	2,500	George Fazio	71 69 75 75	290	600
Ben Hogan	69 69 74 74	286	1,000				

1951—Oakland Hills Country Club, Birmingham, Michigan
CHAMPION—Ben Hogan

	SCORES	TOTAL	MONEY		SCORES	TOTAL	MONEY
Ben Hogan	76 73 71 67	287	$4,000	Lloyd Mangrum	75 74 74 70	293	$700
Clayton Heafner	72 75 73 69	289	2,000	Julius Boros	74 74 71 74	293	700
Bobby Locke	73 71 74 73	291	1,500				

1950—Merion Golf Club (East Course), Ardmore, Pennsylvania
CHAMPION—Ben Hogan

(Playoff: Hogan 69; Mangrum 73; Fazio 75)

	SCORES	TOTAL	MONEY		SCORES	TOTAL	MONEY
Ben Hogan	72 69 72 74	287	$4,000	Dutch Harrison	72 67 73 76	288	$800
Lloyd Mangrum	72 70 69 76	287	2,500	Joe Kirkwood	71 74 74 70	289	500
George Fazio	73 72 72 70	287	1,000				

1949—Medinah Country Club (No. 3 Course), Medinah, Illinois
CHAMPION—Cary Middlecoff

	SCORES	TOTAL	MONEY		SCORES	TOTAL	MONEY
Cary Middlecoff	75 67 69 75	286	$2,000	Jim Turnesa	78 69 70 72	289	$700
Clayton Heafner	72 71 71 73	287	1,250	Bobby Locke	74 71 73 71	289	700
Sam Snead	73 73 71 70	287	1,250				

1948—Riviera Country Club, Los Angeles, California
CHAMPION—Ben Hogan

	SCORES	TOTAL	MONEY		SCORES	TOTAL	MONEY
Ben Hogan	67 72 68 69	276	$2,000	Bobby Locke	70 69 73 70	282	$800
Jimmy Demaret	71 70 68 69	278	1,500	Sam Snead	69 69 73 72	283	600
Jim Turnesa	71 69 70 70	280	1,000				

1947—St. Louis Country Club, Clayton, Missouri
CHAMPION—Lew Worsham

(Playoff: Worsham 69; Snead 70)

	SCORES	TOTAL	MONEY		SCORES	TOTAL	MONEY
Lew Worsham	70 70 71 71	282	$2,000	Porky Oliver	73 70 71 71	285	$900
Sam Snead	72 70 70 70	282	1,500	* Bud Ward	69 72 73 73	287	
Bobby Locke	68 74 70 73	285	900				

1946—Canterbury Golf Club, Cleveland, Ohio
CHAMPION—Lloyd Mangrum

(Playoff: Mangrum 72, 72—144; Nelson 72, 73—145; Ghezzi 72, 73—145)

	SCORES	TOTAL	MONEY		SCORES	TOTAL	MONEY
Lloyd Mangrum	74 70 68 72	284	$1,500	Herman Barron	72 72 72 69	285	$550
Byron Nelson	71 71 69 73	284	875	Ben Hogan	72 68 73 72	285	550
Vic Ghezzi	71 69 72 72	284	875				

* Amateur

		TOTAL SCORE	COURSE
1941	Craig Wood	284	Colonial CC
1940	† Lawson Little	287	Canterbury GC
1939	† Byron Nelson	284	Philadelphia CC
1938	Ralph Guldahl	284	Cherry Hills CC
1937	Ralph Guldahl	281	Oakland Hills CC
1936	Tony Manero	282	Baltusrol GC
1935	Sam Parks	299	Oakmont CC
1934	Olin Dutra	293	Merion CC
1933	* Johnny Goodman	287	North Shore GC
1932	Gene Sarazen	286	Fresh Meadow CC
1931	† Billy Burke	292	Inverness Club
1930'	* Bob Jones	287	Interlachen CC
1929	†* Bob Jones	294	Winged Foot GC
1928	† Johnny Farrell	294	Olympia Fields CC
1927	† Tommy Armour	301	Oakmont CC
1926	* Bob Jones	293	Scioto CC
1925	† Willie Macfarlane	291	Worcester CC
1924	Cyril Walker	297	Oakland Hills CC
1923	†* Bob Jones	296	Inwood CC
1922	Gene Sarazen	288	Skokie CC
1921	Jim Barnes	289	Columbia CC
1920	Ted Ray	295	Inverness Club
1919	† Walter Hagen	301	Brae Burn CC
1916	* Chick Evans	286	Minikahda CC
1915	* Jerry Travers	297	Baltusrol GC
1914	Walter Hagen	290	Midlothian CC
1913	†* Francis Ouimet	304	The CC, Brookline
1912	John McDermott	294	CC of Buffalo
1911	† John McDermott	307	Chicago GC
1910	† Alex Smith	298	Phila. Cricket Club
1909	George Sargent	290	Englewood GC
1908	† Fred McLeod	322	Myopia Hunt Club
1907	Aleck Ross	302	Phila. Cricket Club
1906	Alex Smith	295	Onwentsia Club
1905	Willie Anderson	314	Myopia Hunt Club
1904	Willie Anderson	303	Glen View Club
1903	† Willie Anderson	307	Baltusrol GC
1902	Laurie Auchterlonie	307	Garden City GC
1901	† Willie Anderson	331	Myopia Hunt Club
1900	Harry Vardon	313	Chicago GC
1899	Willie Smith	315	Baltimore CC
1898	Fred Herd	328	Myopia Hunt Club
1897	Joe Lloyd	162	Chicago GC
1896	James Foulis	152	Shinnecock Hills GC
1895	Horace Rawlins	173	Newport GC

* Amateur

(† PLAYOFFS. Results: 1940: Little 70; Sarazen 73. 1939: Nelson 68, 70—138; Wood 68, 73—141; Shute 76, out. 1931: Burke 73, 76—149, 77, 71—148; Von Elm 75, 74—149, 76, 73—149. 1929: Jones 72, 69—141; Espinosa 84, 80—164. 1928: Farrell 70, 73—143; Jones 73, 71—144. 1927: Armour 76; Cooper 79. 1925: Macfarlane 75, 72—147; Jones 75, 73—148. 1923: Jones 76, Cruickshank 78. 1919: Hagen 77; Brady 78. 1913: Ouimet 72; Vardon 77; Ray 78. 1911: McDermott 80; Brady 82; Simpson 85. 1910: A. Smith 71; McDermott 75; M. Smith 77. 1908: McLeod 77; W. Smith 83. 1903: Anderson 82; Brown 84. 1901: Anderson 85; A. Smith 86.

BRITISH OPEN CHAMPIONSHIP

1972—Muirfield Golf Links, East Lothian, Scotland
CHAMPION—Lee Trevino

	SCORES	TOTAL	MONEY		SCORES	TOTAL	MONEY
Lee Trevino	71 70 66 71	278	£5,500	Doug Sanders	71 71 69 70	281	£2,750
Jack Nicklaus	70 72 71 66	279	4,000	Brian Barnes	71 72 69 71	283	2,450
Tony Jacklin	69 72 67 72	280	3,250				

1971—Royal Birkdale Golf Club, Southport, England
CHAMPION—Lee Trevino

	SCORES	TOTAL	MONEY		SCORES	TOTAL	MONEY
Lee Trevino	69 70 69 70	278	£5,500	Craig DeFoy	72 72 68 69	281	£2,750
Lu Liang Huan	70 70 69 70	279	4,000	Charles Coody	74 71 70 68	283	2,300
Tony Jacklin	69 70 70 71	280	3,250				

1970—St. Andrews (Old Course), St. Andrews, Scotland
CHAMPION—Jack Nicklaus

(Playoff: Nicklaus 72; Sanders 73)

	SCORES	TOTAL	MONEY		SCORES	TOTAL	MONEY
Jack Nicklaus	68 69 73 73	283	£5,250	Harold Henning	67 72 73 73	285	£2,750
Doug Sanders	68 71 71 73	283	3,750	Tony Jacklin	67 70 73 76	286	2,200
Lee Trevino	68 68 72 77	285	2,750				

1969—Royal Lytham & St. Anne's Golf Club, St. Anne's-on-Sea, Lancashire
CHAMPION—Tony Jacklin

	SCORES	TOTAL	MONEY		SCORES	TOTAL	MONEY
Tony Jacklin	68 70 70 72	280	£4,250	Roberto de			
Bob Charles	66 69 75 72	282	3,000	Vicenzo	72 73 75 72	283	£2,125
Peter Thomson	71 70 70 72	283	2,125	Christy O'Connor	71 65 74 74	284	1,750

1968—Carnoustie Golf Club, Angus, Scotland
CHAMPION—Gary Player

	SCORES	TOTAL	MONEY		SCORES	TOTAL	MONEY
Gary Player	74 71 71 73	289	£3,000	Bill Casper	72 68 74 78	292	£1,225
Bob Charles	72 72 71 76	291	1,738	Maurice			
Jack Nicklaus	76 69 73 73	291	1,738	Bembridge	71 75 73 74	293	1,000

1967—Royal Liverpool Golf Club, Hoylake, Cheshire
CHAMPION—Roberto de Vicenzo

	SCORES	TOTAL	MONEY		SCORES	TOTAL	MONEY
Roberto de				Gary Player	72 71 67 74	284	£1,125
Vicenzo	70 71 67 70	278	£2,100	Clive Clark	70 73 69 72	284	1,125
Jack Nicklaus	71 69 71 69	280	1,500	Tony Jacklin	73 69 73 70	285	775

1966—Muirfield Golf Links, East Lothian, Scotland
CHAMPION—Jack Nicklaus

	SCORES	TOTAL	MONEY		SCORES	TOTAL	MONEY
Jack Nicklaus	70 67 75 70	282	£2,100	Gary Player	72 74 71 69	286	£705
Dave Thomas	72 73 69 69	283	1,350	Bruce Devlin	73 69 74 70	286	705
Doug Sanders	71 70 72 70	283	1,350				

1965—Royal Birkdale Golf Club, Southport, England
CHAMPION—Peter Thomson

	SCORES	TOTAL	MONEY		SCORES	TOTAL	MONEY
Peter Thomson	74 68 72 71	285	£1,750	Roberto de			
Christy				Vicenzo	74 69 73 72	288	£750
O'Connor	69 73 74 71	287	1,125	Kel Nagle	74 70 73 72	289	475
Brian Huggett	73 68 76 70	287	1,125				

1964—St. Andrews (Old Course), St. Andrews, Scotland
CHAMPION—Tony Lema

	SCORES	TOTAL	MONEY		SCORES	TOTAL	MONEY
Tony Lema	73 68 68 70	279	£1,500	Bernard Hunt	73 74 70 70	287	£650
Jack Nicklaus	76 74 66 68	284	1,000	Bruce Devlin	72 72 73 73	290	500
Roberto de							
Vicenzo	76 72 70 67	285	800				

1963—Royal Lytham & St. Anne's Golf Club, St. Anne's-on-Sea, Lancashire
CHAMPION—Bob Charles

(Playoff: Charles 69, 71—140; Rodgers 72, 76—148)

	SCORES	TOTAL	MONEY		SCORES	TOTAL	MONEY
Bob Charles	68 72 66 71	277	£1,500	Kel Nagle	69 70 73 71	283	£650
Phil Rodgers	67 68 73 69	277	1,000	Peter Thomson	67 69 71 78	285	500
Jack Nicklaus	71 67 70 70	278	800				

1962—Troon Golf Club, Troon, Scotland
CHAMPION—Arnold Palmer

	SCORES	TOTAL	MONEY		SCORES	TOTAL	MONEY
Arnold Palmer	71 69 67 69	276	£1,500	Phil Rodgers	75 70 72 72	289	£750
Kel Nagle	71 71 70 70	282	1,000	Bob Charles	75 70 70 75	290	500
Brian Huggett	75 71 74 69	289	750				

1961—Royal Birkdale Golf Club, Southport, England
CHAMPION—Arnold Palmer

	SCORES	TOTAL	MONEY		SCORES	TOTAL	MONEY
Arnold Palmer	70 73 69 72	284	£1,400	Neil Coles	70 77 69 72	288	£710
Dai Rees	68 74 71 72	285	1,000	Eric Brown	73 76 70 70	289	400
Christy O'Connor	71 77 67 73	288	710				

1960—St. Andrews (Old Course), St. Andrews, Scotland
CHAMPION—Kel Nagle

	SCORES	TOTAL	MONEY		SCORES	TOTAL	MONEY
Kel Nagle	69 67 71 71	278	£1,250	Harold Henning	72 72 69 69	282	£533
Arnold Palmer	70 71 70 68	279	900	Roberto de Vicenzo	67 67 75 73	282	533
Bernard Hunt	72 73 71 66	282	533				

1959—Muirfield Golf Club, East Lothian, Scotland
CHAMPION—Gary Player

	SCORES	TOTAL	MONEY		SCORES	TOTAL	MONEY
Gary Player	75 71 70 68	284	£1,000	Syd Scott	73 70 73 71	287	£400
Flory Van Donck	70 70 73 73	286	612.10	Christy O'Connor	73 74 72 69	288	231.5
Fred Bullock	68 70 74 74	286	612.10				

1958—Royal Lytham & St. Anne's Golf Club, St. Anne's-on-Sea, Lancashire
CHAMPION—Peter Thomson

(Playoff: Thomson 68, 71—139; Thomas 69, 74—143)

	SCORES	TOTAL	MONEY		SCORES	TOTAL	MONEY
Peter Thomson	66 72 67 73	278	£1,075	Christy			
Dave Thomas	70 68 69 71	278	650	O'Connor	67 68 73 71	279	£450
Eric Brown	73 70 65 71	279	450	Flory Van Donck	70 70 67 74	281	275

1957—St. Andrews Golf Club (Old Course), St. Andrews, Scotland
CHAMPION—Bobby Locke

	SCORES	TOTAL	MONEY		SCORES	TOTAL	MONEY
Bobby Locke	69 72 68 70	279	£1,000	Angel Miguel	72 72 69 72	285	
Peter Thomson	73 69 70 70	282	500	Dave Thomas	72 74 70 70	286	
Eric Brown	67 72 73 71	283	350				

1956—Royal Liverpool Golf Club, Hoylake, Cheshire
CHAMPION—Peter Thomson

	SCORES	TOTAL	MONEY		SCORES	TOTAL	MONEY
Peter Thomson	70 70 72 74	286	£1,000	Gary Player	71 76 73 71	291	
Flory Van Donck	71 74 70 74	289	500	John Panton	74 76 72 70	292	
Roberto de Vicenzo	71 70 79 70	290	350				

1955—St. Andrews Golf Club (Old Course), St. Andrews, Scotland
CHAMPION—Peter Thomson

	SCORES	TOTAL	MONEY		SCORES	TOTAL	MONEY
Peter Thomson	71 68 70 72	281	£1,000	Bobby Locke	74 69 70 72	285	£200
Johnny Fallon	73 67 73 70	283	525	Antonio Cerda	73 71 71 71	286	90
Frank Jowle	70 71 69 74	284	400				

1954—Royal Birkdale Golf Club, Southport, England
CHAMPION—Peter Thomson

	SCORES	TOTAL	MONEY		SCORES	TOTAL	MONEY
Peter Thomson	72 71 69 71	283	£753.10	Bobby Locke	74 71 69 70	284	£353.10
Syd Scott	76 67 69 72	284	353.10	James Adams	73 75 69 69	286	108
Dai Rees	72 71 69 72	284	353.10				

1953—Carnoustie Golf Club, Angus, Scotland
CHAMPION—Ben Hogan

	SCORES	TOTAL	MONEY		SCORES	TOTAL	MONEY
Ben Hogan	73 71 70 68	282	£515	Antonio Cerda	75 71 69 71	286	£168.15
Dai Rees	72 70 73 71	286	168.15	Frank Stranahan	70 74 73 69	286	168.15
Peter Thomson	72 72 71 71	286	168.15				

1952—Royal Lytham & St. Anne's Golf Club, St. Anne's-on-Sea, Lancashire
CHAMPION—Bobby Locke

	SCORES	TOTAL	MONEY		SCORES	TOTAL	MONEY
Bobby Locke	69 71 74 73	287	£500	Henry Cotton	75 74 74 71	294	£100
Peter Thomson	68 73 77 70	288	300	Antonio Cerda	73 73 76 73	295	50
Fred Daly	67 69 77 76	289	200				

1951—Royal Portrush Golf Club, Northern Ireland
CHAMPION—Max Faulkner

	SCORES	TOTAL	MONEY		SCORES	TOTAL	MONEY
Max Faulkner	71 70 70 74	285	£320	James Adams	68 77 75 72	292	£67.10
Antonio Cerda	74 72 71 70	287	215	Fred Daly	74 70 75 73	292	67.10
Charles Ward	76 72 74 68	290	115				

1950—Troon Golf Club, Troon, Scotland
CHAMPION—Bobby Locke

	SCORES	TOTAL	MONEY		SCORES	TOTAL	MONEY
Bobby Locke	69 72 70 68	279	£300	Dai Rees	71 68 72 71	282	£96
Roberto de				Fred Daly	75 72 69 66	282	96
Vicenzo	72 71 68 70	281	205	Max Faulkner	72 70 70 71	283	35

1949—Royal St. Georges Golf Club, Sandwich, Kent
CHAMPION—Bobby Locke

(Playoff: Locke 135; Bradshaw 147)

	SCORES	TOTAL	MONEY		SCORES	TOTAL	MONEY
Bobby Locke	69 76 68 70	283	£300	Sam King	71 69 74 72	286	£62.10
Harry Bradshaw	68 77 68 70	283	200	Charles Ward	73 71 70 72	286	62.10
Roberto de							
Vicenzo	68 75 73 69	285	100				

1948—Muirfield Golf Links, East Lothian, Scotland
CHAMPION—Henry Cotton

	SCORES	TOTAL	MONEY		SCORES	TOTAL	MONEY
Henry Cotton	71 66 75 72	284	£150	Roberto de			
Fred Daly	72 71 73 73	289		Vicenzo	70 73 72 75	290	
Norman Von				Jack Hargreaves	76 68 73 73	290	
Nida	71 72 76 71	290					

1947—Royal Liverpool Golf Club, Hoylake, Cheshire
CHAMPION—Fred Daly

	SCORES	TOTAL	MONEY		SCORES	TOTAL	MONEY
Fred Daly	73 70 78 72	293	£150	Bill Shankland	76 74 75 70	295	
Reginald Horne	77 74 72 71	294		Richard Burton	77 71 77 71	296	
* Frank Stranahan	71 79 72 72	294					

* Amateur

1892–1939

		TOTAL SCORE	COURSE
1939	Richard Burton	290	St. Andrews
1938	Reginald Whitcombe	295	Sandwich
1937	Henry Cotton	290	Carnoustie
1936	Alfred Padgham	287	Hoylake
1935	Alfred Perry	283	Muirfield
1934	Henry Cotton	283	Sandwich
1933	† Denny Shute	292	St. Andrews
1932	Gene Sarazen	283	Sandwich, Prince's
1931	Tommy Armour	296	Carnoustie
1930	* Bob Jones	291	Hoylake
1929	Walter Hagen	292	Muirfield
1928	Walter Hagen	292	Sandwich
1927	* Bob Jones	285	St. Andrews
1926	* Bob Jones	291	Royal Lytham
1925	James Barnes	300	Prestwick
1924	Walter Hagen	301	Hoylake
1923	A. G. Havers	295	Troon
1922	Walter Hagen	300	Sandwich
1921	Jock Hutchison	296	St. Andrews
1920	George Duncan	303	Deal
1914	Harry Vardon	306	Prestwick
1913	J. H. Taylor	304	Hoylake
1912	Ted Ray	295	Muirfield
1911	† Harry Vardon	303	Sandwich
1910	James Braid	299	St. Andrews
1909	J. H. Taylor	295	Deal
1908	James Braid	291	Prestwick
1907	Arnaud Massy	312	Hoylake
1906	James Braid	300	Muirfield
1905	James Braid	318	St. Andrews
1904	Jack White	296	Sandwich
1903	Harry Vardon	300	Prestwick
1902	Alex Herd	307	Hoylake
1901	James Braid	309	Muirfield
1900	J. H. Taylor	309	St. Andrews
1899	Harry Vardon	310	Sandwich
1898	Harry Vardon	307	Prestwick
1897	* Harold Hilton	314	Hoylake
1896	† Harry Vardon	316	Muirfield
1895	J. H. Taylor	322	St. Andrews
1894	J. H. Taylor	326	Sandwich
1893	Willie Auchterlonie	322	Prestwick
1892	* Harold Hilton	305	Muirfield

CHAMPIONSHIPS PRIOR TO 1892 WERE PLAYED AT 36
HOLES . . . 1860–1891.
   * Amateur
   († PLAYOFFS. Results: 1933: Shute 149; Craig Wood 154. 1921:
Hutchison 150; * R. H. Wethered 159. 1911: Vardon defeated Arnaud
Massy, 35 holes. 1896: Vardon 157; J. H. Taylor 161.)

MASTERS CHAMPIONSHIP

All played at Augusta National Golf Club, Augusta, Georgia

1972—CHAMPION—*Jack Nicklaus*

	SCORES	TOTAL	MONEY		SCORES	TOTAL	MONEY
Jack Nicklaus	68 71 73 74	286	$25,000	Tom Weiskopf	74 71 70 74	289	$15,833
Bruce Crampton	72 75 69 73	289	15,833	Homero Blancas	76 71 69 74	290	6,200
Bobby Mitchell	73 72 71 73	289	15,833				

1971—CHAMPION—*Charles Coody*

	SCORES	TOTAL	MONEY		SCORES	TOTAL	MONEY
Charles Coody	66 73 70 70	279	$25,000	Don January	69 69 73 72	283	$9,050
John Miller	72 73 68 68	281	17,500	Gene Littler	72 69 73 69	283	9,050
Jack Nicklaus	70 71 68 72	281	17,500				

1970—CHAMPION—*Bill Casper*

(Playoff: Casper 69; Littler 74)

	SCORES	TOTAL	MONEY		SCORES	TOTAL	MONEY
Bill Casper	72 68 68 71	279	$25,000	Bert Yancey	69 70 72 70	281	$10,000
Gene Littler	69 70 70 70	279	17,500	Tommy Aaron	68 74 69 72	283	6,667
Gary Player	74 68 68 70	280	14,000				

1969—CHAMPION—*George Archer*

	SCORES	TOTAL	MONEY		SCORES	TOTAL	MONEY
George Archer	67 73 69 72	281	$20,000	Tom Weiskopf	71 71 69 71	282	$12,333
Billy Casper	66 71 71 74	282	12,333	Charles Coody	74 68 69 72	283	6,750
George Knudson	70 73 69 70	282	12,333				

1968—CHAMPION—*Bob Goalby*

	SCORES	TOTAL	MONEY		SCORES	TOTAL	MONEY
Bob Goalby	70 70 71 66	277	$20,000	Bert Yancey	71 71 72 65	279	$10,000
Roberto de Vicenzo	69 73 70 66	278	15,000	Bruce Devlin	69 73 69 69	280	7,500
				Frank Beard	75 65 71 70	281	5,500

1967—CHAMPION—*Gay Brewer*

	SCORES	TOTAL	MONEY		SCORES	TOTAL	MONEY
Gay Brewer	73 68 72 67	280	$20,000	Arnold Palmer	73 73 70 69	285	$6,600
Bobby Nichols	72 69 70 70	281	14,000	Julius Boros	71 70 70 75	286	5,500
Bert Yancey	67 73 71 73	284	9,000				

1966—CHAMPION—*Jack Nicklaus*

(Playoff: Nicklaus 70; Jacobs 72; Brewer 78)

	SCORES	TOTAL	MONEY		SCORES	TOTAL	MONEY
Jack Nicklaus	68 76 72 72	288	$20,000	Arnold Palmer	74 70 74 72	290	$5,700
Tommy Jacobs	75 71 70 72	288	12,300	Doug Sanders	74 70 75 71	290	5,700
Gay Brewer	74 72 72 70	288	8,300				

1965—CHAMPION—*Jack Nicklaus*

	SCORES	TOTAL	MONEY		SCORES	TOTAL	MONEY
Jack Nicklaus	67 71 64 69	271	$20,000	Mason Rudolph	70 75 66 72	283	$6,200
Arnold Palmer	70 68 72 70	280	10,200	Dan Sikes	67 72 71 75	285	5,000
Gary Player	65 73 69 73	280	10,200				

1964—CHAMPION—*Arnold Palmer*

	SCORES	TOTAL	MONEY		SCORES	TOTAL	MONEY
Arnold Palmer	69 68 69 70	276	$20,000	Bruce Devlin	72 72 67 73	284	$6,100
Dave Marr	70 73 69 70	282	10,100	Bill Casper	76 72 69 69	286	3,700
Jack Nicklaus	71 73 71 67	282	10,100				

1963—CHAMPION—*Jack Nicklaus*

	SCORES	TOTAL	MONEY		SCORES	TOTAL	MONEY
Jack Nicklaus	74 66 74 72	286	$20,000	Sam Snead	70 73 74 71	288	$7,000
Tony Lema	74 69 74 70	287	12,000	Dow Finsterwald	74 73 73 69	289	4,000
Julius Boros	76 69 71 72	288	7,000				

1962—CHAMPION—*Arnold Palmer*

(Playoff: Palmer 68; Player 71; Finsterwald 77)

	SCORES	TOTAL	MONEY		SCORES	TOTAL	MONEY
Arnold Palmer	70 66 69 75	280	$20,000	Gene Littler	71 68 71 72	282	$6,000
Gary Player	67 71 71 71	280	12,000	Mike Souchak	70 72 74 71	287	3,600
Dow Finsterwald	74 68 65 73	280	8,000				

1961—Champion—Gary Player

	SCORES	TOTAL	MONEY		SCORES	TOTAL	MONEY
Gary Player	69 68 69 74	280	$20,000	Tommy Bolt	72 71 74 68	285	$7,000
* Charles Coe	72 71 69 69	281		Don January	74 68 72 71	285	7,000
Arnold Palmer	68 69 73 71	281	12,000				

1960—Champion—Arnold Palmer

	SCORES	TOTAL	MONEY		SCORES	TOTAL	MONEY
Arnold Palmer	67 73 72 70	282	$17,500	Bill Casper	71 71 71 74	287	$5,250
Ken Venturi	73 69 71 70	283	10,500	Julius Boros	72 71 70 75	288	4,200
Dow Finsterwald	71 70 72 71	284	7,000				

1959—Champion—Art Wall

	SCORES	TOTAL	MONEY		SCORES	TOTAL	MONEY
Art Wall	73 74 71 66	284	$15,000	Dick Mayer	73 75 71 68	287	$2,625
Cary Middlecoff	74 71 68 72	285	7,500	Stan Leonard	69 74 69 75	287	2,625
Arnold Palmer	71 70 71 74	286	4,500				

1958—Champion—Arnold Palmer

	SCORES	TOTAL	MONEY		SCORES	TOTAL	MONEY
Arnold Palmer	70 73 68 73	284	$11,250	Stan Leonard	72 70 73 71	286	$1,968.75
Doug Ford	74 71 70 70	285	4,500	Ken Venturi	68 72 74 72	286	1,968.75
Fred Hawkins	71 75 68 71	285	4,500				

1957—Champion—Doug Ford

	SCORES	TOTAL	MONEY		SCORES	TOTAL	MONEY
Doug Ford	72 73 72 66	283	$8,750	* Harvie Ward	73 71 71 73	288	
Sam Snead	72 68 74 72	286	4,375	Peter Thomson	72 73 73 71	289	$1,750
Jimmy Demaret	72 70 75 70	287	2,625				

1956—Champion—Jack Burke

	SCORES	TOTAL	MONEY		SCORES	TOTAL	MONEY
Jack Burke	72 71 75 71	289	$6,000	Lloyd Mangrum	72 74 72 74	292	$2,325
* Ken Venturi	66 69 75 80	290		Sam Snead	73 76 72 71	292	2,325
Cary Middlecoff	67 72 75 77	291	3,750				

* Amateur

1955—CHAMPION—*Cary Middlecoff*

	SCORES	TOTAL	MONEY		SCORES	TOTAL	MONEY
Cary Middlecoff	72 65 72 70	279	$5,000	Bob Rosburg	72 72 72 73	289	$1,333.33
Ben Hogan	73 68 72 73	286	3,125	Mike Souchak	71 74 72 72	289	1,333.33
Sam Snead	72 71 74 70	287	2,125				

1954—CHAMPION—*Sam Snead*

(Playoff: Snead 70; Hogan 71)

	SCORES	TOTAL	MONEY		SCORES	TOTAL	MONEY
Sam Snead	74 73 70 72	289	$5,000	Dutch Harrison	70 79 74 68	291	$1,937.50
Ben Hogan	72 73 69 75	289	3,125	Lloyd Mangrum	71 75 76 69	291	1,937.50
* Billy Joe Patton	70 74 75 71	290					

1953—CHAMPION—*Ben Hogan*

	SCORES	TOTAL	MONEY		SCORES	TOTAL	MONEY
Ben Hogan	70 69 66 69	274	$4,000	Bob Hamilton	71 69 70 73	283	$1,400
Porky Oliver	69 73 67 70	279	2,500	Tommy Bolt	71 75 68 71	285	900
Lloyd Mangrum	74 68 71 69	282	1,700				

1952—CHAMPION—*Sam Snead*

	SCORES	TOTAL	MONEY		SCORES	TOTAL	MONEY
Sam Snead	70 67 77 72	286	$4,000	Al Besselink	70 76 71 74	291	$1,366.66
Jack Burke	76 67 78 69	290	2,500	Tommy Bolt	71 71 75 74	291	1,366.66
Jim Ferrier	72 70 77 72	291	1,366.68				

1951—CHAMPION—*Ben Hogan*

	SCORES	TOTAL	MONEY		SCORES	TOTAL	MONEY
Ben Hogan	70 72 70 68	280	$3,000	Lew Worsham	71 71 72 72	286	$1,162.50
Skee Riegel	73 68 70 71	282	1,875	Dave Douglas	74 69 72 73	288	750
Lloyd Mangrum	69 74 70 73	286	1,162.50				

1950—CHAMPION—*Jimmy Demaret*

	SCORES	TOTAL	MONEY		SCORES	TOTAL	MONEY
Jimmy Demaret	70 72 72 69	283	$2,400	Ben Hogan	73 68 71 76	288	$720
Jim Ferrier	70 67 73 75	285	1,500	Byron Nelson	75 70 69 74	288	720
Sam Snead	71 74 70 72	287	1,020				

* Amateur

1949—CHAMPION—*Sam Snead*

	SCORES	TOTAL	MONEY		SCORES	TOTAL	MONEY
Sam Snead	73 75 67 67	282	$2,750	Johnny Palmer	73 71 70 72	286	$440
Johnny Bulla	74 73 69 69	285	1,100	Jim Turnesa	73 72 71 70	286	440
Lloyd Mangrum	69 74 72 70	285	1,100				

1948—CHAMPION—*Claude Harmon*

	SCORES	TOTAL	MONEY		SCORES	TOTAL	MONEY
Claude Harmon	70 70 69 70	279	$2,500	Jim Ferrier	71 71 75 71	288	$750
Cary Middlecoff	74 71 69 70	284	1,500	Lloyd Mangrum	69 73 75 71	288	750
Chick Harbert	71 70 70 76	287	1,000				

1947—CHAMPION—*Jimmy Demaret*

	SCORES	TOTAL	MONEY		SCORES	TOTAL	MONEY
Jimmy Demaret	69 71 70 71	281	$2,500	Ben Hogan	75 68 71 70	284	$900
Byron Nelson	69 72 72 70	283	1,500	Jug McSpaden	74 69 70 71	284	900
* Frank Stranahan	73 72 70 68	283					

1946—CHAMPION—*Herman Keiser*

	SCORES	TOTAL	MONEY		SCORES	TOTAL	MONEY
Herman Keiser	69 68 71 74	282	$2,500	Ky Laffoon	74 73 70 72	289	$683.33
Ben Hogan	74 70 69 70	283	1,500	Jimmy Demaret	75 70 71 73	289	683.33
Bob Hamilton	75 69 71 72	287	1,000				

* Amateur

1934–1942

	Champion	Total Score	Runnersup	Total Score
1942	† Byron Nelson	280	Ben Hogan	280
1941	Craig Wood	280	Byron Nelson	283
1940	Jimmy Demaret	280	Lloyd Mangrum	284
1939	Ralph Guldahl	279	Sam Snead	280
1938	Henry Picard	285	Ralph Guldahl	287
			Harry Cooper	287
1937	Byron Nelson	283	Ralph Guldahl	285
1936	Horton Smith	285	Harry Cooper	286
1935	† Gene Sarazen	282	Craig Wood	282
1934	Horton Smith	284	Craig Wood	285

(† PLAYOFF. Results: 1942: Nelson 69; Hogan 70. 1935: Sarazen 144; Wood 149)

PGA CHAMPIONSHIP

1972—Oakland Hills Country Club, Birmingham, Michigan
CHAMPION—Gary Player

	SCORES	TOTAL	MONEY		SCORES	TOTAL	MONEY
Gary Player	71 71 67 72	281	$45,000	Sam Snead	70 74 71 69	284	$9,275
Jim Jamieson	69 72 72 70	283	20,850	Ray Floyd	69 71 74 70	284	9,275
Tommy Aaron	71 71 70 71	283	20,850				

1971—PGA National Golf Club, Palm Beach Gardens, Florida
CHAMPION—Jack Nicklaus

	SCORES	TOTAL	MONEY		SCORES	TOTAL	MONEY
Jack Nicklaus	69 69 70 73	281	$40,000	Miller Barber	72 68 75 70	285	$8,800
Bill Casper	71 73 71 68	283	22,800	Gary Player	71 73 68 73	285	8,800
Tommy Bolt	72 74 69 69	284	14,200				

1970—Southern Hills Country Club, Tulsa, Oklahoma
CHAMPION—Dave Stockton

	SCORES	TOTAL	MONEY		SCORES	TOTAL	MONEY
Dave Stockton	70 70 66 73	279	$40,000	Larry Hinson	69 71 74 68	282	$8,800
Bob Murphy	71 73 71 66	281	18,500	Gene Littler	72 71 69 70	282	8,800
Arnold Palmer	70 72 69 70	281	18,500				

1969—NCR Golf Course, Dayton, Ohio
CHAMPION—Raymond Floyd

	SCORES	TOTAL	MONEY		SCORES	TOTAL	MONEY
Raymond Floyd	69 66 67 74	276	$35,000	Jimmy Wright	71 68 69 71	279	$8,300
Gary Player	71 65 71 70	277	20,000	Larry Ziegler	69 71 70 70	280	6,725
Bert Greene	71 68 68 71	278	12,400				

1968—Pecan Valley Country Club, San Antonio, Texas
CHAMPION—Julius Boros

	SCORES	TOTAL	MONEY		SCORES	TOTAL	MONEY
Julius Boros	71 71 70 69	281	$25,000	George Archer	71 69 74 69	283	$7,500
Bob Charles	72 70 70 70	282	12,500	Marty Fleckman	66 72 72 73	283	7,500
Arnold Palmer	71 69 72 70	282	12,500				

1967—Columbine Country Club, Denver, Colorado
CHAMPION—Don January

(Playoff: January 69; Massengale 71)

	SCORES	TOTAL	MONEY		SCORES	TOTAL	MONEY
Don January	71 72 70 68	281	$25,000	Dan Sikes	69 70 70 73	282	$9,000
Don Massengale	70 75 70 66	281	15,000	Julius Boros	69 76 70 68	283	6,500
Jack Nicklaus	67 75 69 71	282	9,000				

1966—Firestone Country Club, Akron, Ohio
CHAMPION—Al Geiberger

	SCORES	TOTAL	MONEY		SCORES	TOTAL	MONEY
Al Geiberger	68 72 68 72	280	$25,000	Gene Littler	75 71 71 69	286	$8,333.33
Dudley Wysong	74 72 66 62	284	15,000	Gary Player	73 70 70 73	286	8,333.33
Bill Casper	73 73 70 70	286	8,333.34				

1965—Laurel Valley Golf Club, Ligonier, Pennsylvania
CHAMPION—Dave Marr

	SCORES	TOTAL	MONEY		SCORES	TOTAL	MONEY
Dave Marr	70 69 70 71	280	$25,000	Bo Wininger	73 72 72 66	283	$8,000
Bill Casper	70 70 71 71	282	12,500	Gardner Dickinson	67 74 69 74	284	7,000
Jack Nicklaus	69 70 72 71	282	12,500				

1964—Columbus Country Club, Columbus, Ohio
CHAMPION—Bobby Nichols

	SCORES	TOTAL	MONEY		SCORES	TOTAL	MONEY
Bobby Nichols	64 71 69 67	271	$18,000	Mason Rudolph	73 66 68 69	276	$5,000
Arnold Palmer	68 68 69 69	274	9,000	Ken Venturi	72 65 73 69	279	3,850
Jack Nicklaus	67 73 70 64	274	9,000				

1963—Dallas AC Country Club, Dallas, Texas
CHAMPION—Jack Nicklaus

	SCORES	TOTAL	MONEY		SCORES	TOTAL	MONEY
Jack Nicklaus	69 73 69 68	279	$13,000	Bruce Crampton	70 73 65 74	282	$3,750
Dave Ragan	75 70 67 69	281	7,000	Al Geiberger	72 73 69 70	284	3,125
Dow Finsterwald	72 72 66 72	282	3,750				

1962—Aronimink Golf Club, Newtown Square, Pennsylvania
CHAMPION—Gary Player

	SCORES	TOTAL	MONEY		SCORES	TOTAL	MONEY
Gary Player	72 67 69 70	278	$13,000	George Bayer	69 70 71 71	281	$3,450
Bob Goalby	69 72 71 67	279	6,700	Doug Ford	69 69 73 71	282	2,900
Jack Nicklaus	71 74 69 67	281	3,450				

1961—Olympia Fields Country Club, Olympia Fields, Illinois
CHAMPION—Jerry Barber

(Playoff: Barber 67; January 68)

	SCORES	TOTAL	MONEY		SCORES	TOTAL	MONEY
Jerry Barber	69 67 71 70	277	$11,000	Ted Kroll	72 68 70 71	281	$3,100
Don January	72 66 67 72	277	5,500	Arnold Palmer	73 72 69 68	282	2,208.34
Doug Sanders	70 68 74 68	280	3,600				

1960—Firestone Country Club, Akron, Ohio
CHAMPION—Jay Hebert

	SCORES	TOTAL	MONEY		SCORES	TOTAL	MONEY
Jay Hebert	72 67 72 70	281	$11,000	Doug Sanders	70 71 69 73	283	$3,350
Jim Ferrier	71 74 66 71	282	5,500	Don January	70 70 72 72	284	2,800
Sam Snead	68 73 70 72	283	3,350				

1959—Minneapolis Golf Club, Minneapolis, Minnesota
CHAMPION—Bob Rosburg

	SCORES	TOTAL	MONEY		SCORES	TOTAL	MONEY
Bob Rosburg	71 72 68 66	277	$8,250	Dow Finsterwald	71 68 71 70	280	$2,500
Jerry Barber	69 65 71 73	278	3,562.50	Mike Souchak	69 67 71 74	281	2,000
Doug Sanders	72 66 68 72	278	3,562.50				

1958—Llanerch Country Club, Havertown, Pennsylvania
CHAMPION—Dow Finsterwald

	SCORES	TOTAL	MONEY		SCORES	TOTAL	MONEY
Dow Finsterwald	67 72 70 67	276	$5,500	Jack Burke	70 72 69 70	281	$2,000
Bill Casper	73 67 68 70	278	3,500	Julius Boros	72 68 73 72	285	1,600
Sam Snead	73 67 67 73	280	2,400				

1957—*Miami Valley Golf Club, Dayton, Ohio*
CHAMPION—*Lionel Hebert*

Round of 16

Lionel Hebert defeated Souchak, 2 and 1.
Harmon defeated Bolt, 1 up.
Burkemo defeated Ransom, 5 and 4.
Jay Hebert defeated Ford, 3 and 2.
Whitt defeated Marusic, 2 and 1.
Mayer defeated Kroll, 1 up.
Sheppard defeated Smith, 4 and 3.
Finsterwald defeated Snead, 2 and 1.

Quarter-Finals

Lionel Hebert defeated Harmon, 2 and 1.
Burkemo defeated Jay Hebert, 2 and 1.
Whitt defeated Mayer, 2 and 1.
Finsterwald defeated Sheppard, 2 up.

Semi-Finals

Lionel Hebert defeated Burkemo, 3 and 1.
Finsterwald defeated Whitt, 2 up.

Finals

Lionel Hebert defeated Finsterwald, 2 and 1.

(Hebert defeated Max Evans, 2 up, in first round; Marty Furgol, 3 and 1, in second round.)

(Prize money: Lionel Hebert $8,000; Finsterwald $5,000; Burkemo $3,500; Whitt $3,000; Mayer $2,500; Harmon $2,000; Jay Hebert $1,500; Sheppard $1,000; round of 16 losers $500.)

1956—*Blue Hill Golf and Country Club, Canton, Massachusetts*
CHAMPION—*Jack Burke*

Round of 16

Burke defeated Harper, 3 and 2.
Hawkins defeated Hebert, 4 and 3.
Johnson defeated Lyons, 1 up, 19 holes.
Furgol defeated Kay, 4 and 3.
Johnston defeated Burkemo, 1 up.
Ransom defeated Worsham, 2 up.
Snead defeated Sarazen, 5 and 4.
Kroll defeated Turnesa, 1 up.

Quarter-Finals

Burke defeated Hawkins, 4 and 2.
Furgol defeated Johnson, 1 up.
Johnston defeated Ransom, 3 and 2.
Kroll defeated Snead, 2 and 1.

Semi-Finals

Burke defeated Furgol, 1 up, 37 holes.
Kroll defeated Johnston, 10 and 8.

Finals

Burke defeated Kroll, 3 and 2.

(Burke defeated Leon Pounders, 2 and 1, in first round; Bill Collins, 5 and 3, in second round.)

(Prize money, 1953 through 1956: Champion $5,000; runnerup $3,000; semi-finalists $750; quarter-finalists $500; round of 16 losers $350.)

1955—Meadowbrook Country Club, Northville, Michigan
CHAMPION—Doug Ford

Round of 16

Fairfield defeated Charter, 2 and 1.
Mayfield defeated Harmon, 1 up.
Hawkins defeated Ed Furgol, 6 and 5.
Ford defeated Ulrich, 12 and 10.
Worsham defeated Palmer, 6 and 5.
Bolt defeated Fleck, 3 and 1.
Middlecoff defeated Pavella, 8 and 6.
Burke defeated Marty Furgol, 2 and 1.

Quarter-Finals

Mayfield defeated Fairfield, 3 and 2.
Ford defeated Hawkins, 5 and 4.
Bolt defeated Worsham, 8 and 7.
Middlecoff defeated Burke, 1 up, 40 holes.

Semi-Finals

Ford defeated Mayfield, 4 and 3.
Middlecoff defeated Bolt, 4 and 3.

Finals

Ford defeated Middlecoff, 4 and 3.

(Ford defeated George Fazio, 2 and 1, in first round, won qualifying medal with 135 score.)

1954—Keller Golf Course, St. Paul, Minnesota
CHAMPION—·Chick Harbert

Round of 16

Bolt defeated Browning, 2 and 1.
Snead defeated Harrison, 7 and 6.
Barber defeated Bassler, 1 up, 38 holes.
Harbert defeated Oliver, 3 and 1.
Burkemo defeated Revolta, 4 and 3.
de Vicenzo defeated Marti, 7 and 6.
Middlecoff defeated Kroll, 5 and 4.
Mayfield defeated Smith, 3 and 2.

Quarter-Finals

Bolt defeated Snead, 1 up, 39 holes.
Harbert defeated Barber, 1 up.
Burkemo defeated de Vicenzo, 5 and 4.
Middlecoff defeated Mayfield, 3 and 1.

Semi-Finals

Harbert defeated Bolt, 1 up.
Burkemo defeated Middlecoff, 1 up.

Finals

Harbert defeated Burkemo, 4 and 3.

(Harbert qualified with 143 score, defeated Mike Krak, 5 and 3, in first round.)

1953—Birmingham Country Club, Birmingham, Michigan
CHAMPION—*Walter Burkemo*

Round of 16

Torza defeated Ulrich, 1 up, 38 holes.
Clark defeated Williams, 4 and 3.
Isaacs defeated Harris, 5 and 4.
Ransom defeated Smith, 1 up.
Douglas defeated Bradley, 1 up, 37 holes.
Burkemo defeated Cooper, 3 and 2.
Nary defeated Browning, 6 and 5.
Harmon defeated Furgol, 5 and 3.

Quarter-Finals

Torza defeated Clark, 1 up.
Isaacs defeated Ransom, 1 up.
Burkemo defeated Douglas, 2 up.
Harmon defeated Nary, 6 and 5.

Semi-Finals

Torza defeated Isaacs, 1 up, 39 holes.
Burkemo defeated Harmon, 1 up.

Finals

Burkemo defeated Torza, 2 and 1.

(Burkemo qualified with 142 score, defeated Lou Barbaro, 7 and 5, in first round.)

1952—Big Spring Country Club, Louisville, Kentucky
CHAMPION—Jim Turnesa

Round of 16

Kroll defeated Honsberger, 2 and 1.
Middlecoff defeated Smith, 4 and 2.
Turnesa defeated de Vicenzo, 5 and 4.
Doser defeated Isaacs, 1 up.
Haas defeated Marusic, 1 up, 38 holes.
Harbert defeated Williams, 6 and 5.
Champ defeated Burkemo, 3 and 1.
Hamilton defeated Ghezzi, 9 and 8.

Quarter-Finals

Kroll defeated Middlecoff, 1 up, 38 holes.
Turnesa defeated Doser, 2 and 1.
Harbert defeated Haas, 2 and 1.
Hamilton defeated Champ, 2 and 1.

Semi-Finals

Turnesa defeated Kroll, 2 and 1.
Harbert defeated Hamilton, 1 up.

Finals

Turnesa defeated Harbert, 1 up.

(Turnesa defeated Bob Toski, 4 and 2, in first round.)

(Prize money, 1946 through 1952: Champion $3,500; runnerup $1,500; semi-finalists $750; quarter-finalists $500; round of 16 losers $350.)

1951—Oakmont Country Club, Oakmont, Pennsylvania
CHAMPION—Sam Snead

Round of 16

Bassler defeated Bolesta, 1 up, 37 holes.
Brosch defeated Harden, 6 and 5.

Snead defeated Mangrum, 3 and 2.
Burke defeated Kunes, 4 and 3.
Burkemo defeated Shoemaker, 2 and 1.
Myles defeated Ghezzi, 1 up.
Vines defeated Bradley, 2 and 1.
Bulla defeated Ferrier, 9 and 8.

Quarter-Finals

Bassler defeated Brosch, 1 up.
Snead defeated Burke, 2 and 1.
Burkemo defeated Myles, 1 up.
Vines defeated Bulla, 1 up.

Semi-Finals

Snead defeated Bassler, 9 and 8.
Burkemo defeated Vines, 1 up, 37 holes.

Finals

Snead defeated Burkemo, 7 and 6.

(Snead qualified with 145 score, defeated Fred Haas, 1 up, in first round.)

1950—Scioto Country Club, Columbus, Ohio
CHAMPION—*Chandler Harper*

Round of 16

Gafford defeated Burke, 4 and 3.
Demaret defeated Shute, 4 and 3.
Mangrum defeated Harbert, 6 and 5.
Harper defeated Toski, 2 and 1.
Williams defeated Harmon, 1 up, 38 holes.
Douglas defeated Reed, 3 and 2.
Picard defeated Bradley, 1 up.
Palmer defeated Kroll, 1 up.

Quarter-Finals

Demaret defeated Gafford, 5 and 4.
Harper defeated Mangrum, 1 up.
Williams defeated Douglas, 1 up.
Picard defeated Palmer, 10 and 8.

Semi-Finals

Harper defeated Demaret, 2 and 1.
Williams defeated Picard, 1 up, 38 holes.

Finals

Harper defeated Williams, 4 and 3.

(Harper qualified with 148 score, defeated Fred Annon, 5 and 3, in first round.)

1949—Hermitage Country Club, Richmond, Virginia
CHAMPION—*Sam Snead*

Round of 16

Hill defeated Romans, 5 and 4.
Mangrum defeated Barron, 4 and 3.
Palmer defeated Worsham, 2 and 1.
Williams defeated Brosch, 7 and 6.
Snead defeated Douglas, 1 up.
Demaret defeated Turnesa, 5 and 3.
Heafner defeated Patroni, 5 and 4.
Ferrier defeated Furgol, 8 and 6.

Quarter-Finals

Mangrum defeated Hill, 7 and 6.
Palmer defeated Williams, 7 and 6.
Snead defeated Demaret, 4 and 3.
Ferrier defeated Heafner, 3 and 2.

Semi-Finals

Palmer defeated Mangrum, 6 and 5.
Snead defeated Ferrier, 3 and 2.

Finals

Snead defeated Palmer, 3 and 2.

(Snead qualified with 137 score, defeated Jack Burke, 3 and 2, in first round.)

1948—Norwood Hills Country Club, St. Louis, Missouri
CHAMPION—*Ben Hogan*

Round of 16

Harmon defeated Ransom, 2 and 1.
Snead defeated Gibson, 5 and 3.
Bulla defeated Laffoon, 6 and 5.
Turnesa defeated Smith, 3 and 2.
Harbert defeated Alexander, 11 and 10.
Hogan defeated Sarazen, 2 up.
Demaret defeated Worsham, 3 and 2.
Fazio defeated Oliver, 1 up.

Quarter-Finals

Harmon defeated Snead, 1 up, 42 holes.
Turnesa defeated Bulla, 6 and 5.
Hogan defeated Harbert, 2 and 1.
Demaret defeated Fazio, 5 and 4.

Semi-Finals

Turnesa defeated Harmon, 1 up, 37 holes.
Hogan defeated Demaret, 2 and 1.

Finals

Hogan defeated Turnesa, 7 and 6.

(Hogan qualified with 138 score, defeated Jock Hutchison, Jr., 1 up, 23 holes, in first round.)

1947—*Plum Hollow Country Club, Detroit, Michigan*
CHAMPION—*Jim Ferrier*

Round of 16

Laffoon defeated Sarazen, 4 and 3.
Bell defeated Metz, 1 up, 37 holes.
Ferrier defeated Harmon, 1 up, 37 holes.
Mangrum defeated Mike Turnesa, 1 up.
Ghezzi defeated Jim Turnesa, 4 and 3.
Worsham defeated Myles, 7 and 6.
Harbert defeated Oliver, 3 and 2.
Gibson defeated Joseph, 1 up, 37 holes.

Quarter-Finals

Bell defeated Laffoon, 2 up.
Ferrier defeated Mangrum, 4 and 3.
Ghezzi defeated Worsham, 3 and 2.
Harbert defeated Gibson, 2 up.

Semi-Finals

Ferrier defeated Bell, 10 and 9.
Harbert defeated Ghezzi, 6 and 5.

Finals

Ferrier defeated Harbert, 2 and 1.

(Ferrier qualified with 142 score, defeated Willie Goggin, 1 up, 19 holes, in first round.)

1946—*Portland Golf Club, Portland, Oregon*
CHAMPION—*Ben Hogan*

Round of 16

Nelson defeated Barron, 3 and 2.
Oliver defeated Harper, 5 and 4.
McSpaden defeated Harrison, 4 and 3.
Congdon defeated Schneiter, 2 and 1.

Demaret defeated Ferrier, 3 and 2.
Turnesa defeated Shoemaker, 5 and 4.
Hogan defeated Bell, 5 and 4.
Moore defeated Bassler, 4 and 3.

Quarter-Finals

Oliver defeated Nelson, 1 up.
McSpaden defeated Congdon, 5 and 3.
Demaret defeated Turnesa, 6 and 5.
Hogan defeated Moore, 5 and 4.

Semi-Finals

Oliver defeated McSpaden, 6 and 5.
Hogan defeated Demaret, 10 and 9.

Finals

Hogan defeated Oliver, 6 and 4.

(Hogan qualified with 137 score, defeated Charles Weisner, 2 and 1, in first round.)

1916–1945

	CHAMPION	SCORE	RUNNERUP	CLUB SITE
1945	Byron Nelson	4 and 3	Sam Byrd	Morraine CC
1944	Bob Hamilton	1 up	Byron Nelson	Manito G&CC
1942	Sam Snead	2 and 1	Jim Turnesa	Seaview CC
1941	Vic Ghezzi	1 up, 38	Byron Nelson	Cherry Hills CC
1940	Byron Nelson	1 up	Sam Snead	Hershey CC
1939	Henry Picard	1 up, 37	Byron Nelson	Pomonok CC
1938	Paul Runyan	8 and 7	Sam Snead	Shawnee CC
1937	Denny Shute	1 up, 37	Jug McSpaden	Pittsburgh FC
1936	Denny Shute	3 and 2	Jimmy Thomson	Pinehurst CC
1935	Johnny Revolta	5 and 4	Tommy Armour	Twin Hills CC
1934	Paul Runyan	1 up, 38	Craig Wood	Park CC
1933	Gene Sarazen	5 and 4	Willie Goggin	Blue Mound CC
1932	Olin Dutra	4 and 3	Frank Walsh	Keller GC
1931	Tom Creavy	2 and 1	Denny Shute	Wannamoisett CC
1930	Tommy Armour	1 up	Gene Sarazen	Fresh Meadow CC
1929	Leo Diegel	6 and 4	Johnny Farrell	Hillcrest CC
1928	Leo Diegel	6 and 5	Al Espinosa	Five Farms CC
1927	Walter Hagen	1 up	Joe Turnesa	Cedar Crest CC
1926	Walter Hagen	5 and 3	Leo Diegel	Salisbury GC
1925	Walter Hagen	6 and 5	Bill Mehlhorn	Olympia Fields CC
1924	Walter Hagen	2 up	Jim Barnes	French Lick CC
1923	Gene Sarazen	1 up, 28	Walter Hagen	Pelham CC
1922	Gene Sarazen	4 and 3	Emmet French	Oakmont CC
1921	Walter Hagen	3 and 2	Jim Barnes	Inwood CC
1920	Jock Hutchison	1 up	Douglas Edgar	Flossmoor CC
1919	Jim Barnes	6 and 5	Fred McLeod	Engineers CC
1916	Jim Barnes	1 up	Jock Hutchison	Siwanoy CC

Performance Cross–Section of U.S. Tour

This chart pulls together the performances of the 25 leading money-winners of the post–World War II era in the 13 established tournaments on the U.S. Tour which were chosen for this Appendix primarily on the bases of importance, strength of field, and longevity. It does not include the three major U.S. championships, which are treated separately.

It backs up what is rather obvious: The big money-winners are so because they finished 1-2-3 so often—359 times among the total of 877 finishes in the top 10 of these tournaments by this high-bracket group.

It should be noted that two of today's top stars do not stand high on this chart for good reason. Gary Player competes on only a portion of the American circuit each season and Lee Trevino did not join the tour until mid-1967. On the other hand, Sam Snead would rank higher if we included his finishes prior to 1946 in the six tournaments among those charted which were in existence during the early strongest years of his career.

Keep in mind that this is merely a cross-section of the U.S. Tour. Arnold Palmer, for instance, had 60 victories overall in American tournaments at the time this chart was prepared following the 1972 PGA Championship; Bill Casper had 48, Jack Nicklaus 41. Snead is credited with 84 victories in the official PGA records.

	First Year on Tour	Number of Finishes by Position										Total Finishes in Top 10
		1st	2nd	3rd	4th	5th	6th	7th	8th	9th	10th	
Arnold Palmer	1955	24	13	8	5	7	8	6	2	8	5	86
Bill Casper	1955	17	11	8	7	4	4	5	4	7	5	72
Gene Littler	1954	12	10	7	8	7	4	7	4	5	3	67
Julius Boros	1950	4	8	11	6	4	3	7	5	8	5	61
Jack Nicklaus	1962	11	10	9	10	5	2	2	4	2	1	56
Sam Snead	1937	15	8	9	7	3	1	3	1	4	4	55
Doug Sanders	1957	10	10	4	7	2	1	3	5	7	2	51
Gary Player	1957	3	11	3	3	5	2	4	2	4	3	40
Tommy Aaron	1961	1	5	6	3	5	1	3	2	2	5	33
Don January	1956	1	3	5	5	3	2	5	2	2	4	32
Bruce Crampton	1957	4	1	3	4	4	2	3	2	2	6	31
Bobby Nichols	1960	0	5	2	3	5	3	4	2	1	5	30
George Archer	1964	5	2	2	2	6	5	3	0	1	0	26
Gay Brewer	1956	3	4	1	2	2	1	2	1	4	5	25
Dave Hill	1959	1	3	2	4	1	2	5	3	0	3	24
Miller Barber	1958	1	5	4	3	2	1	1	1	1	4	23
Frank Beard	1963	4	1	1	2	3	0	3	2	2	4	22
Bob Goalby	1957	2	3	2	3	1	1	2	2	4	2	22
Dan Sikes	1961	1	2	1	0	0	3	3	5	2	2	19
Bob Charles	1963	1	2	1	3	4	2	2	1	1	2	19
Tom Weiskopf	1965	0	3	2	4	1	2	1	1	2	2	18
Bruce Devlin	1962	2	4	2	0	1	1	1	3	2	2	18
Lee Trevino	1967	1	3	4	1	1	1	0	2	0	3	16
Bert Yancey	1964	1	2	3	2	1	2	0	1	1	3	16
Dave Stockton	1964	1	2	3	2	0	0	2	0	2	3	15
Totals at Position		125	131	103	96	77	54	77	57	74	83	

American Golf Classic

All played at Firestone CC, South Course

	WINNER	TOTAL SCORE	MONEY
1972	Bert Yancey	276	$30,000
1971	Jerry Heard	275	$30,000
1970	Frank Beard	276	$30,000
1969	Ray Floyd	268	$25,000
1968	Jack Nicklaus	280	$25,000
1967	Arnold Palmer	276	$20,000
1965	Al Geiberger	280	$20,000
1964	Ken Venturi	275	$ 7,500
1963	Johnny Pott	276	$ 9,000
1962	Arnold Palmer	276	$ 9,000
1961	Jay Hebert	278	$ 9,000

* 1966—No tournament. PGA played at Firestone.

Colonial National Invitation

All played at Colonial Country Club

	WINNER	TOTAL SCORE	MONEY
1972	Jerry Heard	275	$25,100
1971	Gene Littler	283	$25,000
1970	Homero Blancas	273	$25,000
1969	Gardner Dickinson	278	$25,000
1968	Bill Casper	275	$25,000
1967	Dave Stockton	278	$23,000
1966	Bruce Devlin	280	$22,000
1965	Bruce Crampton	276	$20,000
1964	Bill Casper	279	$14,000
1963	Julius Boros	279	$12,000
1962	Arnold Palmer	281	$ 7,000
1961	Doug Sanders	281	$ 7,000
1960	Julius Boros	280	$ 5,000
1959	Ben Hogan	285	$ 5,000
1958	Tommy Bolt	282	$ 5,000
1957	Roberto de Vicenzo	284	$ 5,000
1956	Mike Souchak	280	$ 5,000
1955	Chandler Harper	276	$ 5,000
1954	Johnny Palmer	280	$ 5,000
1953	Ben Hogan	282	$ 5,000
1952	Ben Hogan	279	$ 4,000
1951	Cary Middlecoff	282	$ 3,000

1950	Sam Snead	277	$ 3,000
1948	Clayton Heafner	272	$ 3,000
1947	Ben Hogan	279	$ 3,000
1946	Ben Hogan	279	$ 3,000

* 1949—Tournament cancelled. Flood damage to course.

Bing Crosby National Pro-Am

1967–1972—Pebble Beach, Cypress Point, Spyglass Hill
1948–1966—Pebble Beach, Cypress Point, Monterey Peninsula
1947—Pebble Beach

	WINNER	TOTAL SCORE	MONEY
1972	Jack Nicklaus	284	$28,000
1971	Tom Shaw	278	$27,000
1970	Bert Yancey	278	$25,000
1969	George Archer	283	$25,000
1968	Johnny Pott	285	$16,000
1967	Jack Nicklaus	284	$16,000
1966	Don Massengale	283	$11,000
1965	Bruce Crampton	284	$ 7,500
1964	Tony Lema	284	$ 5,800
1963	Bill Casper	285	$ 5,300
1962	Doug Ford	286	$ 5,300
1961	Bob Rosburg	282	$ 5,300
1960	Ken Venturi	286	$ 4,000
1959	Art Wall	279	$ 4,000
1958	Bill Casper	277	$ 4,000
1957	Jay Hebert	213	$ 2,500
1956	Cary Middlecoff	202	$ 2,500
1955	Cary Middlecoff	209	$ 2,500
1954	E. J. Harrison	210	$ 2,000
1953	Lloyd Mangrum	204	$ 2,000
1952	Jimmy Demaret	145	$ 2,000
1951	Byron Nelson	209	$ 2,000
1950	Jack Burke	214	$ 1,237.50
	Dave Douglas	214	$ 1,237.50
	Sam Snead	214	$ 1,237.50
	Smiley Quick	214	$ 1,237.50
1949	Ben Hogan	208	$ 2,000
1948	Lloyd Mangrum	205	$ 2,000
1947	George Fazio	213	$ 1,625
	Ed Furgol	213	$ 1,625

Doral Eastern Open

All played at Doral CC, Blue Course

	WINNER	TOTAL SCORE	MONEY
1972	Jack Nicklaus	276	$30,000
1971	J. C. Snead	275	$30,000
1970	Mike Hill	279	$30,000
1969	Tom Shaw	276	$30,000
1968	Gardner Dickinson	275	$20,000
1967	Doug Sanders	275	$20,000
1966	Phil Rodgers	278	$20,000
1965	Doug Sanders	274	$11,000
1964	Bill Casper	277	$ 7,500
1963	Dan Sikes	283	$ 9,000
1962	Bill Casper	283	$ 9,000

Greater Greensboro Open

	WINNER	LOCATION	TOTAL SCORE	MONEY
1972	George Archer	Sedgefield	272	$40,000
1971	Brian Allin	Sedgefield	275	$38,000
1970	Gary Player	Sedgefield	271	$36,000
1969	Gene Littler	Sedgefield	274	$32,000
1968	Bill Casper	Sedgefield	267	$27,500
1967	George Archer	Sedgefield	267	$25,000
1966	Doug Sanders	Sedgefield	276	$20,000
1965	Sam Snead	Sedgefield	273	$11,000
1964	Julius Boros	Sedgefield	277	$ 6,600
1963	Doug Sanders	Sedgefield	270	$ 5,500
1962	Bill Casper	Sedgefield	275	$ 5,300
1961	Mike Souchak	Sedgefield	276	$ 3,200
1960	Sam Snead	Starmount Forest	270	$ 2,800
1959	Dow Finsterwald	Starmount Forest	278	$ 2,000
1958	Bob Goalby	Starmount Forest	275	$ 2,000
1957	Stan Leonard	Sedgefield	276	$ 2,000
1956	Sam Snead	Starmount Forest	279	$ 2,200
1955	Sam Snead	Sedgefield	273	$ 2,200
1954	Doug Ford	Starmount Forest	283	$ 2,000
1953	Earl Stewart	Sedgefield	275	$ 2,000
1952	Dave Douglas	Starmount Forest	277	$ 2,000
1951	Art Doering	Starmount Forest	279	$ 2,000
1950	Sam Snead	Sedgefield	269	$ 2,000
1949	Sam Snead	Starmount Forest	276	$ 2,000
1948	Lloyd Mangrum	Sedgefield	278	$ 2,000
1947	Vic Ghezzi	Starmount Forest	286	$ 2,000
1946	Sam Snead	Sedgefield	270	$ 1,500

Bob Hope Desert Classic

*Played at Indian Wells, La Quinta, Bermuda Dunes, Eldorado,
Tamarisk, Thunderbird*

	WINNER	TOTAL SCORE	MONEY
1972	Bob Rosburg	344	$29,000
1971	Arnold Palmer	342	$28,000
1970	Bruce Devlin	339	$25,000
1969	Bill Casper	345	$20,000
1968	Arnold Palmer	348	$20,000
1967	Tom Nieporte	349	$17,600
1966	Doug Sanders	349	$15,000
1965	Bill Casper	348	$15,000
1964	Tommy Jacobs	353	$ 7,500
1963	Jack Nicklaus	345	$ 9,000
1962	Arnold Palmer	342	$ 5,300
1961	Billy Maxwell	345	$ 5,300
1960	Arnold Palmer	338	$12,000

Los Angeles Open

	WINNER	LOCATION	TOTAL SCORE	MONEY
1972	George Archer	Rancho Park	270	$25,000
1971	Bob Lunn	Rancho Park	274	$22,000
1970	Bill Casper	Rancho Park	276	$20,000
1969	Charles Sifford	Rancho Park	276	$20,000
1968	Bill Casper	Brookside	274	$20,000
1967	Arnold Palmer	Rancho Park	269	$20,000
1966	Arnold Palmer	Rancho Park	273	$11,000
1965	Paul Harney	Rancho Park	276	$12,000
1964	Paul Harney	Rancho Park	280	$ 7,500
1963	Arnold Palmer	Rancho Park	274	$ 9,000
1962	Phil Rodgers	Rancho Park	268	$ 7,500
1961	Bob Goalby	Rancho Park	275	$ 7,500
1960	Dow Finsterwald	Rancho Park	280	$ 5,500
1959	Ken Venturi	Rancho Park	278	$ 5,300
1958	Frank Stranahan	Rancho Park	275	$ 7,000
1957	Doug Ford	Rancho Park	280	$ 7,000
1956	Lloyd Mangrum	Rancho Park	272	$ 6,000
1955	Gene Littler	Inglewood	276	$ 5,000
1954	Fred Wampler	Fox Hills	281	$ 4,000
1953	Lloyd Mangrum	Riviera	280	$ 2,750
1952	Tommy Bolt	Riviera	289	$ 4,000
1951	Lloyd Mangrum	Riviera	280	$ 2,600
1950	Sam Snead	Riviera	280	$ 2,600

1949	Lloyd Mangrum	Riviera	284	$ 2,600
1948	Ben Hogan	Riviera	275	$ 2,000
1947	Ben Hogan	Riviera	280	$ 2,000
1946	Byron Nelson	Riviera	284	$ 2,666.67

Pensacola (Monsanto) Open

All played at Pensacola Country Club

	WINNER	TOTAL SCORE	MONEY
1972	Dave Hill	271	$30,000
1971	Gene Littler	276	$30,000
1970	Dick Lotz	275	$30,000
1969	Jim Colbert	267	$20,000
1968	George Archer	268	$16,000
1967	Gay Brewer	262	$15,000
1966	Gay Brewer	272	$10,000
1965	Doug Sanders	277	$10,000
1964	Gary Player	274	$ 4,000
1963	Arnold Palmer	273	$ 3,500
1962	Doug Sanders	270	$ 2,800
1961	Tommy Bolt	275	$ 2,800
1960	Arnold Palmer	273	$ 2,000
1959	Paul Harney	269	$ 2,000
1958	Doug Ford	278	$ 2,000
1957	Art Wall	273	$ 2,000
1956	Don Fairfield	275	$ 2,200

Phoenix Open

	WINNER	LOCATION	TOTAL SCORE	MONEY
1972	Homero Blancas	Phoenix	273	$25,000
1971	Miller Barber	Arizona	261	$25,000
1970	Dale Douglass	Phoenix	271	$20,000
1969	Gene Littler	Arizona	263	$20,000
1968	George Knudson	Phoenix	272	$20,000
1967	Julius Boros	Arizona	272	$14,000
1966	Dudley Wysong	Phoenix	278	$ 9,000
1965	Rod Funseth	Arizona	274	$10,500
1964	Jack Nicklaus	Phoenix	271	$ 7,500
1963	Arnold Palmer	Arizona	273	$ 5,300
1962	Arnold Palmer	Phoenix	269	$ 5,300
1961	Arnold Palmer	Arizona	270	$ 4,300
1960	Jack Fleck	Phoenix	273	$ 3,150
1959	Gene Littler	Arizona	268	$ 2,400
1958	Ken Venturi	Phoenix	274	$ 2,000

1957	Bill Casper	Arizona	271	$ 2,000
1956	Cary Middlecoff	Phoenix	276	$ 2,400
1955	Gene Littler	Arizona	275	$ 2,400
1954	Ed Furgol	Phoenix	272	$ 2,000
1953	Lloyd Mangrum	Phoenix	272	$ 2,000
1952	Lloyd Mangrum	Phoenix	274	$ 2,000
1951	Lew Worsham	Phoenix	272	$ 2,000
1950	Jimmy Demaret	Phoenix	269	$ 2,000
1949	Jimmy Demaret	Phoenix	278	$ 2,000
1948	Bobby Locke	Phoenix	268	$ 2,000
1947	Ben Hogan	Phoenix	270	$ 2,000
1946	Ben Hogan	Phoenix	273	$ 1,500

Texas Open

	WINNER	LOCATION	TOTAL SCORE	MONEY
1972	Mike Hill	Pecan Valley	273	$20,000
* 1971				
1970	Ron Cerrudo	Pecan Valley	273	$20,000
1969	Deane Beman	Pecan Valley	274	$20,000
* 1968				
1967	Chi Chi Rodriguez	Pecan Valley	277	$20,000
1966	Harold Henning	Oak Hills	272	$13,000
1965	Frank Beard	Oak Hills	270	$ 7,500
1964	Bruce Crampton	Oak Hills	273	$ 5,800
1963	Phil Rodgers	Oak Hills	268	$ 4,300
1962	Arnold Palmer	Oak Hills	273	$ 4,300
1961	Arnold Palmer	Oak Hills	270	$ 4,300
1960	Arnold Palmer	Fort Sam Houston	276	$ 2,800
1959	Wes Ellis	Brackenridge Park	276	$ 2,800
1958	Bill Johnston	Brackenridge Park	274	$ 2,000
1957	Jay Hebert	Brackenridge Park	271	$ 2,800
1956	Gene Littler	Fort Sam Houston	276	$ 3,750
1955	Mike Souchak	Brackenridge Park	257	$ 2,200
1954	Chandler Harper	Brackenridge Park	259	$ 2,200
1953	Tony Holguin	Brackenridge Park	264	$ 2,000
1952	Jack Burke	Brackenridge Park	260	$ 2,000
1951	E. J. Harrison	Brackenridge Park Fort Sam Houston	265	$ 2,000
1950	Sam Snead	Brackenridge Park Fort Sam Houston	265	$ 2,000
1949	Dave Douglas	Brackenridge Park	268	$ 2,000
1948	Sam Snead	Brackenridge Park	264	$ 2,000
1947	Ed Oliver	Brackenridge Park	265	$ 2,000
1946	Ben Hogan	Brackenridge Park	264	$ 1,500

* No tournament played

Tournament of Champions

	WINNER	LOCATION	TOTAL SCORE	MONEY
1972	Bobby Mitchell	La Costa	280	$33,000
1971	Jack Nicklaus	La Costa	279	$33,000
1970	Frank Beard	La Costa	273	$30,000
1969	Gary Player	La Costa	284	$30,000
1968	Don January	Stardust	276	$30,000
1967	Frank Beard	Stardust	278	$20,000
1966	Arnold Palmer	Desert Inn	283	$20,000
1965	Arnold Palmer	Desert Inn	277	$14,000
1964	Jack Nicklaus	Desert Inn	279	$12,000
1963	Jack Nicklaus	Desert Inn	273	$13,000
1962	Arnold Palmer	Desert Inn	276	$11,000
1961	Sam Snead	Desert Inn	273	$10,000
1960	Jerry Barber	Desert Inn	268	$10,000
1959	Mike Souchak	Desert Inn	281	$10,000
1958	Stan Leonard	Desert Inn	275	$10,000
1957	Gene Littler	Desert Inn	285	$10,000
1956	Gene Littler	Desert Inn	281	$10,000
1955	Gene Littler	Desert Inn	280	$10,000
1954	Art Wall	Desert Inn	278	$10,000
1953	Al Besselink	Desert Inn	280	$10,000

Western Open

	WINNER	LOCATION	TOTAL SCORE	MONEY
1972	Jim Jamieson	Sunset Ridge	271	$30,000
1971	Bruce Crampton	Olympia Fields	279	$30,000
1970	Hugh Royer	Beverly	273	$26,000
1969	Bill Casper	Midlothian	276	$26,000
1968	Jack Nicklaus	Olympia Fields	273	$26,000
1967	Jack Nicklaus	Beverly	274	$20,000
1966	Bill Casper	Medinah	283	$20,000
1965	Bill Casper	Tam O'Shanter	270	$11,000
1964	Chi Chi Rodriguez	Tam O'Shanter	268	$11,000
1963	Arnold Palmer	Beverly	280	$11,000
1962	Jacky Cupit	Medinah	281	$11,000
1961	Arnold Palmer	Blythefield	271	$ 5,000
1960	Stan Leonard	Western	278	$ 5,000
1959	Mike Souchak	Pittsburgh Field Club	272	$ 5,000
1958	Doug Sanders	Red Run	275	$ 5,000
1957	Doug Ford	Plum Hollow	279	$ 5,000
1956	Mike Fetchick	Presidio	284	$ 5,000
1955	Cary Middlecoff	Portland	272	$ 2,400
1954	Lloyd Mangrum	Kenwood	277	$ 2,400
1953	E. J. Harrison	Bellerive	278	$ 2,400

1952	Lloyd Mangrum	Westwood	274	$ 2,400
1951	Marty Furgol	Davenport	270	$ 2,250
1950	Sam Snead	Brentwood	282	$ 2,600
1949	Sam Snead	Keller	268	$ 2,600
1948	Ben Hogan	Brookfield	281	$ 2,500
1947	Johnny Palmer	Salt Lake City	270	$ 2,200
1946	Ben Hogan	Sunset	271	$ 2,000

Australian Open

	WINNER	LOCATION	TOTAL SCORE
1972	Peter Thomson	Kooyonga	281
1971	Jack Nicklaus	Royal Hobart	269
1970	Gary Player	Kingston Heath	280
1969	Gary Player	Royal Sydney	288
1968	Jack Nicklaus	Lake Karrinyup	270
1967	Peter Thomson	Commonwealth	281
1966	Arnold Palmer	Royal Queensland	276
1965	Gary Player	Kooyonga	264
1964	Jack Nicklaus	The Lakes	287
1963	Gary Player	Royal Melbourne	278
1962	Gary Player	Royal Adelaide	281
1961	Frank Phillips	Victoria	275
1960	* Bruce Devlin	Lake Karrinyup	282
1959	Kel Nagle	The Australian	284
1958	Gary Player	Kooyonga	271
1957	Frank Phillips	Kingston Heath	287
1956	Bruce Crampton	Royal Sydney	289
1955	Bobby Locke	Mount Gailes	290
1954	Ossie Pickworth	Kooyonga	280
1953	Norman Von Nida	Royal Melbourne	278
1952	Norman Von Nida	Lake Karrinyup	278
1951	Peter Thomson	Metropolitan	283
1950	Norman Von Nida	Kooyonga	286
1949	Eric Cremin	The Australian	287
1948	Ossie Pickworth	Kingston Heath	289
1947	Ossie Pickworth	Royal Queensland	285
1946	Ossie Pickworth	Royal Sydney	289

* Amateur

Canadian Open

	WINNER	LOCATION	TOTAL SCORE	MONEY
1972	Gay Brewer	Cherry Hill	275	$30,000
1971	Lee Trevino	Richelieu Valley	275	$30,000
1970	Kermit Zarley	London Hunt	279	$25,000
1969	Tommy Aaron	Pinegrove	275	$25,000
1968	Bob Charles	St. George's	274	$23,225

1967	Bill Casper	Municipal	279	$27,840
1966	Don Massengale	Shaughnessy	280	$20,000
1965	Gene Littler	Mississaugua	273	$20,000
1964	Kel Nagle	Pine Grove	277	$ 7,500
1963	Doug Ford	Scarboro	280	$ 9,000
1962	Ted Kroll	Laval-sur-le-Lac	278	$ 4,300
1961	Jacky Cupit	Niakwa	270	$ 4,300
1960	Art Wall	St. George's	269	$ 3,500
1959	Doug Ford	Ilsemere	276	$ 3,500
1958	Wes Ellis	Mayfair	267	$ 3,500
1957	George Bayer	Westmount	271	$ 3,500
1956	* Doug Sanders	Beaconsfield	273	—
1955	Arnold Palmer	Weston	265	$ 2,400
1954	Pat Fletcher	Point Grey	280	$ 3,000
1953	Dave Douglas	Scarboro	273	$ 3,000
1952	Johnny Palmer	St. Charles	263	$ 3,000
1951	Jim Ferrier	Mississaugua	273	$ 2,250
1950	Jim Ferrier	Royal Montreal	271	$ 2,000
1949	E. J. Harrison	St. George's	271	$ 2,000
1948	Chuck Congdon	Shaughnessy	280	$ 1,200
1947	Bobby Locke	Scarboro	268	$ 2,000
1946	George Fazio	Beaconsfield	278	$ 2,000

* Amateur

Daks Tournament

	WINNER	LOCATION	TOTAL SCORE
* 1972			
** 1971	Brian Huggett	South Herts	284
	Neil Coles		284
1970	Neil Coles	Wentworth	281
1969	Brian Huggett	Wentworth	289
1968	Malcolm Gregson	Wentworth	284
1967	Malcolm Gregson	Wentworth	279
1966	Hugh Boyle	Wentworth	286
1965	Peter Thomas	Wentworth	275
1964	Neil Coles	Wentworth	282
1963	Neil Coles	Wentworth	280
1962	Dai Rees	Wentworth	278
1961	Bernard Hunt	Wentworth	279
1960	Peter Thomson	Wentworth	278
1959	Christy O'Connor	Wentworth	274
** 1958	Peter Thomas	Wentworth	275
	Harold Henning		275
1957	Bobby Locke	Wentworth	281
1956	Trevor Wilkes	Wentworth	276
1955	John Pritchett	Sunningdale	275

  * No tournament played
** No playoff

1954	Peter Allis	Little Aston	277
1953	Dai Rees	Wentworth	280
1952	Fred Daly	Wentworth	280
1951	John Panton	Sunningdale	282
1950	Norman Sutton	Royal Mid-Surrey	272

Dunlop Masters

	WINNER	LOCATION	TOTAL SCORE
1950	Dai Rees	Hoylake	281
1949	Charles Ward	St. Andrews	290
1948	Norman Von Nida	Sunningdale	272
1947	Arthur Lees	Little Aston	286
* 1946	Bobby Locke	Stoneham	286
	Jimmy Adams		286

* No playoff

Dutch Open

	WINNER	LOCATION	TOTAL SCORE
1972	Jack Newton	den Haag	277
1971	Ramon Sota	Kennemer	277
1970	Vicente Fernandez	Eindhoven	279
1969	Guy Wolstenholme	de Pan	277
1968	John Cockin	Hilversum	292
1967	Peter Townsend	den Haag	282
1966	Ramon Sota	Kennemer	276
1965	Angel Miguel	Toxandria	278
1964	Sewsunker Sewgolum	Eindhoven	275
1963	Retief Waltman	den Haag	279
1962	Brian Huggett	Hilversum	274
1961	Brian Wilkes	Kennemer	279
1960	Sewsunker Sewgolum	Eindhoven	280
1959	Sewsunker Sewgolum	den Haag	283
1958	Dave Thomas	Kennemer	277
1957	John Jacobs	Hilversum	284
1956	Antonio Cerda	Eindhover	277
1955	Alfonso Angelini	Kennemer	280
1954	Ugo Grappasonni	den Haag	295
1953	Flory Van Donck	Eindhoven	286
1952	C. S. Denny	Hilversum	284
1951	Flory Van Donck	Kennemer	281
1950	Roberto de Vicenzo	Toxandria	269
1949	Jimmy Adams	den Haag	294
1948	C. S. Denny	Hilversum	290
1947	J. Ruhl	Eindhoven	279
1946	Flory Van Donck	Hilversum	290

French Open

	WINNER	LOCATION	TOTAL SCORE
1972	Barry Jaeckel	Biarritz & La Nivelle	265
1971	Lu Liang Huan	Biarritz & La Nivelle	262
1970	David Graham	Biarritz & Chantaco	268
1969	Jean Garaialde	St-Nom-La-Breteche	277
1968	Peter Butler	Saint-Cloud	272
1967	Bernard Hunt	Saint Germain	271
1966	Denis Hutchinson	Le Racing–La Boulie	274
1965	Ramon Sota	St-Nom-La-Breteche	268
1964	Roberto de Vicenzo	Chantilly	272
1963	Bruce Devlin	Saint-Cloud	273
1962	Alan Murray	Saint Germain	274
1961	Kel Nagle	Le Racing–La Boulie	271
1960	Roberto de Vicenzo	Saint-Cloud	275
1959	Dave Thomas	Le Racing–La Boulie	276
1958	Flory Van Donck	Saint Germain	276
1957	Flory Van Donck	Saint-Cloud	266
1956	Angel Miguel	Deauville	277
1955	Byron Nelson	Le Racing–La Boulie	271
1954	Flory Van Donck	Saint-Cloud	275
1953	Bobby Locke	Le Racing–La Boulie	276
1952	Bobby Locke	Saint Germain	268
1951	Hassan Hassaneim	Saint-Cloud	273
1950	Roberto de Vicenzo	Chantilly	279
1949	Ugo Grappasonni	Saint Germain	275
1948	Fifi Cavalo	Saint-Cloud	287
1947	Henry Cotton	Chantilly	285
1946	Henry Cotton	Saint-Cloud	273

German Open

	WINNER	LOCATION	TOTAL SCORE
1972	Graham Marsh	Frankfurt	271
1971	Neil Coles	Zur Vahr, Gartstedt	279
1970	Jean Garaialde	Krefeld	276
1969	Jean Garaialde	Frankfurt	272
1968	Barry Franklin	Köln Refrath	285
1967	Donald Swaelens	Krefeld	273
1966	Bob Stanton	Frankfurt-Niederrad	274
1965	Harold Henning	Hamburg-Falkenstein	274
1964	Roberto de Vicenzo	Krefeld	275
1963	Brian Huggett	Cologne	278
1962	Bob Verwey	Hamburg-Falkenstein	276
1961	Bernard Hunt	Krefeld	272

1960	Peter Thomson	Cologne	281
1959	Ken Bousfield	Hamburg	271
1958	Fidel DeLuca	Krefeld	275
1957	Harry Weetman	Cologne	279
1956	Flory Van Donck	Frankfurt	277
1955	Ken Bousfield	Hamburg-Falkenstein	279
1954	Bobby Locke	Krefeld	279
1953	Flory Van Donck	Frankfurt	271
1952	Antonio Cerda	Hamburg	283
1951	Antonio Cerda	Hamburg	286

New Zealand Open

	WINNER	LOCATION	TOTAL SCORE
1972	Bill Dunk	Paraparaumu	279
1971	Peter Thomson	Balmacewan	276
1970	Bob Charles	The Grange	271
1969	Kel Nagle	Wanganui	273
1968	Kel Nagle	Shirley	272
1967	Kel Nagle	St. Andrews	275
1966	Bob Charles	Paraparaumu	273
1965	Peter Thomson	Auckland	278
1964	Kel Nagle	Christchurch	266
1963	Bruce Devlin	Wauganui	273
1962	Kel Nagle	Titirangi	281
1961	Peter Thomson	New Plymouth	267
1960	Peter Thomson	Invercargill	281
1959	Peter Thomson	Paraparaumu	287
1958	Kel Nagle	Hamilton	278
1957	Kel Nagle	Wellington	294

Portuguese Open

All played at Estoril

	WINNER	TOTAL SCORE
1972	German Gerrido	196
1971	Lionel Platts	277
1970	Ramon Sota	274
1969	Ramon Sota	270
1968	Max Faulkner	273
1967	Angel Gallardo	214
1966	Alfonso Angelini	273

* 1965		
1964	Angel Miguel	275
1963	Ramon Sota	204
1962	Alfonso Angelini	269
1961	Ken Bousfield	263
1960	Ken Bousfield	268
1959	Sebastian Miguel	265
1958	Peter Alliss	264
* 1957		
1956	Angel Miguel	268
1955	Flory Van Donck	267
1954	Angel Miguel	263
1953	Eric Brown	260

* No tournament played

South African Open

	WINNER	LOCATION	TOTAL SCORE
1972	Gary Player	Royal Johannesburg	274
1971	Simon Hobday	Mowbray	276
1970	Tommy Horton	Royal Durban	285
1969	Gary Player	Durban	273
1968	Gary Player	Houghton	274
1967	Gary Player	East London	279
1966	Gary Player	Houghton	278
1965	Gary Player	Royal Cape	273
1964	Allan Henning	Bloemfontein	278
1963	Retief Waltman	Durban	281
1962	Harold Henning	Houghton	285
1961	Retief Waltman	East London	289
1960	Gary Player	Mowbray	280
1959	Denis Hutchinson	Royal Johannesburg	282
1958	* A. A. Stewart	Bloemfontein	281
1957	Harold Henning	Humewood	289
1956	Gary Player	Durban	286
1955	Bobby Locke	Zwartkop	283
1954	* R. C. Taylor	East London	289
1953	* J. R. Boyd	Royal Cape	302
1952	Syd Brews	Humewood	305
1951	Bobby Locke	Houghton	277
1950	Bobby Locke	Durban	280
1949	Syd Brews	Maccauvlei	291
1948	M. Janks	East London	298
1947	R. W. Glennie	Mowbray	293
1946	Bobby Locke	Royal Johannesburg	285

* Amateur

Spanish Open

	WINNER	LOCATION	TOTAL SCORE
1972	Antonio Garrido	Pals	293
1971	Dale Hayes	El Prat	275
1970	Angel Gallardo	Nueva Andalucia	284
1969	Jean Garaialde	Real Automovil	283
1968	Bob Shaw	La Galea	286
1967	Sebastian Miguel	San Cugat	265
1966	Roberto de Vicenzo	Sotogrande	278
* 1965			
1964	Angel Miguel	Tenerife	272
1963	Ramon Sota	El Prat	287
* 1962			
1961	Angel Miguel	Puerta de Hierro	267
1960	Sebastian Miguel	Club de Campo	286
1959	Peter Thomson	El Prat	286
1958	Peter Alliss	Puerta de Hierro	268
1957	Max Faulkner	Club de Campo	283
1956	Peter Alliss	El Prat	285
1955	** Henri de Lamaze	Puerta de Hierro	271
1954	Sebastian Miguel	Puerta de Hierro	268
1953	Max Faulkner	Puerta de Hierro	271
1952	Max Faulkner	Puerta de Hierro	275
1951	Mariano Provencio	Puerto de Hierro	281
1950	Antonio Cerda	Cerdana	280
1949	Marcelino Morcillo	Puerta de Hierro	280
1948	Marcelino Morcillo	Neguri	268
1947	** Mario Gonzalez	Puerto de Hierro	272
1946	Mercelino Morcillo	Pedrena	281

* No tournament played
** Amateur

Swiss Open

All played at Crans-sur-Sierre

	WINNER	TOTAL SCORE
1972	Graham Marsh	270
1971	Peter Townsend	270
1970	Graham Marsh	274
1969	Roberto Bernardini	277
1968	Roberto Bernardini	272
1967	Randall Vines	272
1966	Alfonso Angelini	271
1965	Harold Henning	208
1964	Harold Henning	276

1963	Dai Rees	278
1962	Bob Charles	272
1961	Kel Nagle	268
1960	Harold Henning	270
1959	Dai Rees	274
1958	Ken Bousfield	272
1957	Alfonso Angelini	270
1956	Dai Rees	278
1955	Flory Van Donck	277
1954	Bobby Locke	276
1953	Flory Van Donck	267
1952	Ugo Grappasonni	267
1951	Eric Brown	267
1950	Aldo Casera	276
1949	M. Dallemagne	270
1948	Ugo Grappasonni	285

Ryder Cup Matches

Standings through 1971: United States, 15 victories; Great Britain, 3 victories; one match tied

	LOCATION	RESULTS
1971	Old Warson, St. Louis, Mo.	U.S. – 18½; G.B. – 13½
1969	Royal Birkdale, Southport, England	U.S. – 16; G.B. – 16
1967	Champions, Houston, Texas	U.S. – 23; G.B. – 8½
1965	Royal Birkdale, Southport, England	U.S. – 19½; G.B. – 12½
1963	East Lake, Atlanta, Georgia	U.S. – 23; G.B. – 9
1961	Royal Lytham and St. Anne's England	U.S. – 14½; G.B. – 9½
1959	Eldorado, Palm Springs, Calif.	U.S. – 8½; G.B. – 3½
1957	Lindrick, England	G.B. – 7½; U.S. – 4½
1955	Thunderbird, Palm Springs, Calif.	U.S. – 8; G.B. – 4
1953	Wentworth, England	U.S. – 6½; G.B. – 5½
1951	Pinehurst, North Carolina	U.S. – 9½; G.B. – 2½
1949	Ganton, England	U.S. – 7; G.B. – 5
1947	Portland, Oregon	U.S. – 11; G.B. – 1

World Series of Golf

All played at Firestone CC, Akron, Ohio

1971	SCORES	TOTAL	MONEY
Charles Coody	68 73	141	$50,000
Jack Nicklaus	71 71	142	15,000
Bruce Crampton	73 70	143	7,500
Lee Trevino	72 74	146	5,000
1970			
Jack Nicklaus	66 70	136	$50,000
Bill Casper	71 68	139	11,250
Dave Stockton	69 70	139	11,250
Tony Jacklin	71 70	141	5,000
1969			
Orville Moody	74 67	141	$50,000
George Archer	74 69	143	15,000

Raymond Floyd	72 73	145	6,250
Tony Jacklin	73 72	145	6,250

1968—Playoff: Player defeated Goalby, fourth hole.

Gary Player	71 72	143	$50,000
Bob Goalby	72 71	143	15,000
Julius Boros	72 72	144	7,500
Lee Trevino	79 74	153	5,000

1967

Jack Nicklaus	74 70	144	$50,000
Gay Brewer	71 74	145	15,000
Roberto de Vicenzo	70 76	146	7,500
Don January	73 78	151	5,000

1966—Playoff: Littler defeated Geiberger, Nicklaus, first hole.

Gene Littler	71 72	143	$50,000
Al Geiberger	71 72	143	11,250
Jack Nicklaus	70 73	143	11,250
Bill Casper	70 74	144	5,000

1965

Gary Player	70 69	139	$50,000
Jack Nicklaus	71 71	142	15,000
Peter Thomson	73 71	144	7,500
Dave Marr	74 77	151	5,000

1964

Tony Lema	70 68	138	$50,000
Ken Venturi	69 74	143	15,000
Bobby Nichols	77 70	147	5,000
Arnold Palmer	74 74	148	5,000

1963

Jack Nicklaus	70 70	140	$50,000
Julius Boros	72 69	141	15,000
Arnold Palmer	71 72	143	5,000
Bob Charles	70 77	147	5,000

1962

Jack Nicklaus	66 69	135	$50,000
Arnold Palmer	65 74	139	12,500
Gary Player	69 70	139	12,500

World Cup

1972—Royal Melbourne Golf Club, Melbourne, Australia

Second round cancelled because of rain

Nationalist China	438	England	449
Japan	440	Korea	452
South Africa	444	Belgium	452
Australia	445	Argentina	453
United States	445	Italy	456

International Trophy

Hsieh Min Nan	217	Jim Jamieson	222
Takaaki Kono	219	Sukree Onsham	222
Tienie Britz	220	Donald Swaelens	222
Bruce Crampton	221	Guy Hunt	223
Lu Liang Huan	221	Walter Godfrey	223
Takashi Murakami	221	Tom Weiskopf	223

1971—PGA National, United States

Team

United States	555	Philippines	582
South Africa	567	England	582
New Zealand	569	Canada	583
Argentina	575	Wales	585
Korea	581	Nationalist China	586

International Trophy

Jack Nicklaus	271	Brian Huggett	285
Gary Player	278	Bob Charles	287
Roberto de Vicenzo	281	David Graham	287
John Lister	282	Harold Henning	289
Lee Trevino	284	Ronnie Shade	289
Lu Liang Huan	285	Takaaki Kono	289

1970—Jockey Club, Argentina

Team

Australia	544	Spain	575
Argentina	554	England	575
South Africa	563	Scotland	576
United States	565	France	578
Wales	572	Japan	578
Italy	572		

International Trophy

Roberto de Vicenzo	269	Ettore Della Torre	283
David Graham	270	Haruo Yasuda	284
Bruce Devlin	274	Francisco Cerda	284
Dave Stockton	279	Harold Henning	284
Allan Henning	279	Peter Butler	284
Jean Garaialde	282		

1969—Singapore Island, Singapore

Team

United States	552	Philippines	564
Japan	560	Spain	568
Argentina	561	Belgium	573
Thailand	562	Australia	574
Nationalist China	562	Colombia	575

International Trophy

Lee Trevino	275	Ben Arda	278
Roberto de Vicenzo	276	Takaaki Kono	279
Hsieh Yung Yo	277	Haruo Yasuda	281
Sukree Onsham	277	Martin Roesink	283
Orville Moody	277	Ramon Sota	283

1968—Olgiata, Italy

Team

Canada	569	New Zealand	585
United States	571	Wales	586
Italy	573	Argentina	587
Nationalist China	576	England	588
Spain	580	Ireland	588
South Africa	584	Japan	588

International Trophy

Al Balding	274	Eric Brown	286
Roberto Bernardini	279	Lu Liang Huan	286
Lee Trevino	283	Ramon Sota	287
Gary Player	285	Julius Boros	288
Brian Huggett	285	Bill Dunk	288

1967—Club de Golf, Mexico

Team

United States	557	Nationalist China	582
New Zealand	570	Canada	583
Mexico	574	Puerto Rico	584
South Africa	579	Ireland	588
Argentina	281	Australia	588
Hawaii	581		

International Trophy

Arnold Palmer	276	Roberto Bernardini	288
Jack Nicklaus	281	Walter Godfrey	289
Bob Charles	281	Gary Player	289
Antonio Cerda	284	David Jimenez	289
Ted Makalena	285	Hsieh Yung Yo	289
Fidel DeLuca	287	Bruce Crampton	289
Malcolm Gregson	287		

1966—Yomiuri, Japan

Team

United States	548	Canada	563
South Africa	553	Argentina	565
Nationalist China	554	Belgium	571
Australia	556	Spain	572
Japan	561	England	574

International Trophy

Playoff: Knudson defeated Sugimoto, second hole

George Knudson	272	Harold Henning	276
Hideyo Sugimoto	272	Gary Player	277
Jack Nicklaus	273	Bob Charles	277
Lu Liang Huan	273	Bruce Devlin	277
Arnold Palmer	275	Roberto de Vicenzo	278

1965—Club de Campo, Spain

Team

South Africa	571	Colombia	590
Spain	579	Puerto Rico	593
United States	582	Nationalist China	594
Canada	585	Argentina	595
England	585	Scotland	595

International Trophy

Gary Player	281	Harold Henning	290
Jack Nicklaus	284	Eric Brown	291
Ramon Sota	285	George Knudson	291
Chi Chi Rodriguez	286	Kel Nagle	291
Miguel Sala	286	Roberto de Vicenzo	291

1964—Royal Kaanapali, Hawaii

Team

United States	554	Hawaii	579
Argentina	565	Canada	584
South Africa	568	Japan	585
Spain	572	Brazil	587
England	578	Belgium	588

International Trophy

Jack Nicklaus	276	Angel Miguel	285
Arnold Palmer	278	Flory Van Donck	287
Gary Player	279	Ramon Sota	287
Ted Makalena	279	Denis Hutchinson	289
Roberto de Vicenzo	281	Bernard Hunt	289
Leopoldo Ruiz	284	Peter Alliss	289

1963—St-Nom-La-Breteche, France

Shortened because of weather to 63 holes

Team

United States	482	Belgium	508
Spain	485	Italy	509
South Africa	492	England	512
Canada	495	Japan	512
Australia	497	Wales	512

International Trophy

Jack Nicklaus	237	Arnold Palmer	245
Sebastian Miguel	242	Bruce Crampton	245
Gary Player	242	Chi Chi Rodriguez	248
Ramon Sota	243	Tomoo Ishii	249
Al Balding	245	Jean Garaialde	249

1962—Jockey Club, Argentina

Team

United States	557	Uruguay	586
Argentina	559	Belgium	588
Australia	569	Wales	588
England	572	Nationalist China	589
France	585	Japan	589
Brazil	586		

International Trophy

Roberto de Vicenzo	276	Fidel DeLuca	283
Peter Alliss	278	Kel Nagle	283
Arnold Palmer	278	Mario Gonzalez	284
Sam Snead	279	Gary Player	285
Alfonso Angelini	281	Peter Thomson	286

1961—Dorado Beach, Puerto Rico

Team

United States	560	Puerto Rico	589
Australia	572	South Africa	591
Canada	579	Argentina	593
Ireland	582	Nationalist China	594
Philippines	585	Belgium	594
Wales	587		

International Trophy

Sam Snead	272	Peter Alliss	288
Peter Thomson	280	Jimmy Demaret	288
Christy O'Connor	282	Chi Chi Rodriguez	290
Al Balding	283	Dave Thomas	292
Ben Arda	286	Kel Nagle	292

1960—Portmarnock, Ireland

Team

United States	565	Scotland	580
England	573	Belgium	582
Australia	574	Wales	584
Ireland	575	Argentina	587
South Africa	578	Spain	587

International Trophy

Flory Van Donck	279	Christy O'Connor	286
Sam Snead	281	Roberto de Vicenzo	287
Arnold Palmer	284	Kel Nagle	288
Harry Weetman	284	Mario Gonzalez	288
Peter Thomson	286	Gerald de Wit	288
Eric Brown	286		

1959—Royal Melbourne, Australia

Team

Australia	563	Wales	590
United States	573	Scotland	595
Canada	574	Nationalist China	597
South Africa	580	Argentina	601
England	588	Spain	601

International Trophy

Playoff: Leonard defeated Thomson, first hole

Stan Leonard	275	Eric Brown	292
Peter Thomson	275	Cary Middlecoff	292
Sam Snead	281	Chen Ching Po	292
Gary Player	284	Flory Van Donck	292
Kel Nagle	288	Peter Alliss	293

1958—Club de Golf, Mexico

Team

Ireland	579	Argentina	594
Spain	582	Wales	595
South Africa	584	Venezuela	601
Australia	588	Belgium	603
Scotland	588	Colombia	603
England	593		

International Trophy

Playoff: Miguel defeated Bradshaw, third hole

Angel Miguel	286	Gary Player	291
Harry Bradshaw	286	Ben Hogan	291
Flory Van Donck	287	Leopoldo Ruiz	292
Miguel Sala	288	Chen Ching Po	293
Eric Brown	289	Harold Henning	293
Frank Phillips	289	Christy O'Connor	293

1957—Kasumigaseki, Japan

Team

Japan	557	Canada	576
United States	566	England	579
South Africa	569	Brazil	581
Australia	572	Argentina	586
Wales	573	Scotland	587

International Trophy

Torakichi Nakamura	274	Bruce Crampton	285
Gary Player	281	Jimmy Demaret	285
Sam Snead	281	Peter Thomson	287
Dave Thomas	281	Peter Alliss	288
Stan Leonard	283	Antonio Cerda	288
Koichi Ono	283	Harold Henning	288

1956—Wentworth, England

Team

United States	567	Scotland	589
South Africa	581	Belgium	595
Canada	583	Mexico	598
England	586	Australia	601
Japan	586	Ireland	601
Wales	587	Spain	601

International Trophy

Ben Hogan	277	Stan Leonard	286
Roberto de Vicenzo	282	Michio Ishii	289
Flory Van Donck	283	Sam Snead	290
Dai Rees	284	Ken Bousfield	291
Bobby Locke	285	Eric Brown	293

1955—Columbia, Chevy Chase

Team

United States	560	England	575
Australia	569	Ireland	580
Scotland	571	Italy	583
Argentina	573	Canada	584
Belgium	573	Colombia	584
Germany	575		

International Trophy

Playoff: Furgol defeated Van Donck, second hole; Thomson, third hole

Ed Furgol	279	Antonio Cerda	286
Peter Thomson	279	John Panton	286
Flory Van Donck	279	Roberto de Vicenzo	287
Chick Harbert	281	Friedl Schmaderer	287
Harry Bradshaw	284	Norman Sutton	287
Eric Brown	285	Celestino Tugot	287
Mario Gonzalez	285		

1954—Laval-sur-le-Lac, Canada

Team

Australia	556	France	573
Argentina	560	England	574
United States	565	Brazil	575
Canada	570	Belgium	578
Scotland	571	South Africa	578

International Trophy

Stan Leonard	275	Flory Van Donck	282
Antonio Cerda	277	Roberto de Vicenzo	283
Peter Thomson	277	Jean Garaialde	284
Jimmy Demaret	278	Bobby Locke	284
Kel Nagle	279	Harry Weetman	284
Dai Rees	282		

1953—Beaconsfield, Canada

Team

Argentina	287	United States	304
Canada	297	Germany	312
Australia	298	Mexico	321
England–South Africa	299		

International Trophy

Antonio Cerda	140	Bobby Locke	150
Stan Leonard	144	Julius Boros	150
Roberto de Vicenzo	147	Peter Thomson	151
Ossie Pickworth	147	George Bessner	151
Harry Weetman	149	Al Escalante	152

Palm Beach Round Robin

1957—Wykagyl CC, New Rochelle, New York

Sam Snead	Plus 41	$3,000
Doug Ford	Plus 33	2,000
Ben Hogan	Plus 14	1,375
Tommy Bolt	Plus 14	1,375
Fred Hawkins	Plus 13	1,000
Mike Souchak	Plus 6	900
Ken Venturi	Plus 4	800
Dow Finsterwald	Minus 6	700
Peter Thomson	Minus 7	650
Gene Littler	Minus 9	600
Bill Casper	Minus 10	525
Cary Middlecoff	Minus 10	525
Dick Mayer	Minus 14	400
Ed Furgol	Minus 17	400
Mike Fetchick	Minus 18	400
Jack Burke	Minus 34	400

Inverness Round Robin

1952—Inverness CC, Toledo, Ohio

Sam Snead-Jim Ferrier	62 plus 13 points	$5,000
Doug Ford-Porky Oliver	64 plus 1 point	3,000
Lloyd Mangrum-Cary Middlecoff	69 minus 1 point	2,500
Jimmy Demaret-Jack Burke	62 minus 2 points	2,000
Byron Nelson-Skee Riegel	67 minus 3 points	1,600
Clayton Heafner-Ed Furgol	68 minus 8 points	1,400

Goodall Round Robin

1949—Wykagyl CC, New Rochelle, New York

Bobby Locke	Plus 66	$3,000
Herman Barron	Plus 33	2,000
Sam Snead	Plus 30	1,500
Byron Nelson	Plus 29	1,250
Cary Middlecoff	Plus 27	1,000
Johnny Palmer	Plus 18	900
Clayton Heafner	Plus 7	800
Jimmy Demaret	Minus 3	675
Jim Turnesa	Minus 3	675
Dutch Harrison	Minus 9	600
Lloyd Mangrum	Minus 12	550
Fred Haas	Minus 15	500
Chick Harbert	Minus 24	450
Skip Alexander	Minus 27	400
Vic Ghezzi	Minus 58	350
Bob Hamilton	Minus 59	350

Miami Four-Ball Championship

1947—Miami Country Club, Miami, Florida

Semi-Finals

Ben Hogan and Jimmy Demaret defeated Dick Metz and Chick Harbert, 1 up.
Lloyd Mangrum and Lawson Little defeated Sam Byrd and Johnny Revolta, 2 up.

Finals

Hogan and Demaret defeated Mangrum and Little, 3 and 2, winning $1,250 each.

All American Open

All played at Tam O'Shanter, Chicago

	WINNER	TOTAL SCORE	MONEY
1957	Roberto de Vicenzo	273	$3,500
1956	Dutch Harrison	278	$3,420
1955	Doug Ford	277	$3,420
1954	Jerry Barber	277	$3,420
1953	Lloyd Mangrum	275	$3,420
1952	Sam Snead	271	$3,420
1951	Cary Middlecoff	274	$2,250
1950	Bobby Locke	282	$2,500
1949	Lloyd Mangrum	276	$3,333
1948	Lloyd Mangrum	277	$5,000

World Championship of Golf

All played at Tam O'Shanter, Chicago

	WINNER	TOTAL SCORE	MONEY
1957	Dick Mayer	279	$50,000
1956	Ted Kroll	273	$50,000
1955	Julius Boros	281	$50,000
1954	Bob Toski	272	$50,000
1953	Lew Worsham	278	$25,000
1952	Julius Boros	276	$25,000
1951	Ben Hogan	273	$12,500
1950	Henry Ransom	281	$11,000
1949	Johnny Palmer	275	$10,000
1948	Lloyd Mangrum	135	$10,000

EARNINGS, SCORING, YEAR-BY-YEAR

These earnings figures combine income from all world tournament competition included in this Appendix, along with major television tournaments and all nontour competition for which accurate totals could be obtained and in which four or more professionals competed for prize money provided by somebody other than the competitors themselves. When the first World Money List was compiled on the 1966 season, the 200th player had $3,326. The 200th player on this list earned $10,885.

World Money List Leaders

1972		1971		1970	
1 Jack Nicklaus	$341,792	1 Jack Nicklaus	$285,897	1 Jack Nicklaus	$222,583
2 Lee Trevino	256,056	2 Lee Trevino	252,861	2 Bruce Devlin	183,699
3 Gary Player	219,599	3 Arnold Palmer	233,820	3 Lee Trevino	183,360
4 Gay Brewer	179,548	4 Gary Player	167,035	4 Bill Casper	171,600
5 Jerry Heard	178,247	5 George Archer	165,269	5 Bruce Crampton	148,849
6 Tom Weiskopf	162,903	6 Charles Coody	160,701	6 Tony Jacklin	144,106
7 George Archer	151,812	7 Miller Barber	153,288	7 Frank Beard	143,865
8 Lanny Wadkins	151,617	8 Bill Casper	136,757	8 Larry Hinson	141,187
9 Grier Jones	147,928	9 Gene Littler	134,648	9 Dave Stockton	138,538
10 Tommy Aaron	142,825	10 Bruce Crampton	128,387	10 Arnold Palmer	137,932
11 Doug Sanders	130,718	11 Jerry Heard	125,689	11 Tom Weiskopf	130,966
12 Bruce Devlin	126,905	12 Frank Beard	117,338	12 Bert Yancey	127,866
13 Bobby Mitchell	123,279	13 Tom Weiskopf	111,946	13 Dick Lotz	127,039
14 Bruce Crampton	120,789	14 Dave Eichelberger	110,812	14 Bob Murphy	126,139
15 Chi Chi Rodriguez	118,504	15 J. C. Snead	108,068	15 Dave Hill	125,415
16 Hale Irwin	117,539	16 Hale Irwin	104,473	16 Gary Player	119,645
17 Johnny Miller	115,724	17 John Miller	104,264	17 Bobby Nichols	114,262
18 Jim Jamieson	112,133	18 Tom Shaw	98,721	18 Miller Barber	110,681
19 Tony Jacklin	111,847	19 Dave Stockton	96,287	19 Homero Blancas	105,994
20 Homero Blancas	105,730	20 Bert Yancey	96,127	20 Bob Lunn	105,060
21 Jim Colbert	103,802	21 Bobby Nichols	92,255	21 Tommy Aaron	102,356
22 Dave Hill	103,089	22 Bob Lunn	86,953	22 Bob Charles	94,681
23 Lou Graham	101,578	23 Deane Beman	85,248	23 Christy O'Connor	85,530
24 David Graham	100,807	24 Lou Graham	85,075	24 Gene Littler	84,191
25 Arnold Palmer	95,539	25 Dale Douglass	81,520	25 Dan Sikes	82,156

1969

1	Frank Beard	$186,994
2	Bill Casper	170,501
3	Dave Hill	163,323
4	Gene Littler	160,092
5	Orville Moody	151,683
6	Jack Nicklaus	143,640
7	Gary Player	140,384
8	Lee Trevino	139,511
9	George Archer	127,945
10	Bruce Crampton	124,156
11	Tommy Aaron	122,732
12	Raymond Floyd	122,631
13	Miller Barber	112,951
14	Dan Sikes	109,854
15	Ken Still	107,514
16	Arnold Palmer	105,128
17	Bruce Devlin	97,379
18	Dale Douglass	96,738
19	Bob Lunn	92,706
20	Bert Yancey	92,156
21	Bob Charles	89,298
22	Tom Shaw	88,332
23	Tom Weiskopf	87,094
24	Deane Beman	86,397
25	Bert Greene	84,781

1967

1	Jack Nicklaus	$267,167
2	Arnold Palmer	210,464
3	Bill Casper	167,249
4	Gay Brewer	156,588
5	Julius Boros	135,613
6	Doug Sanders	133,648
7	Frank Beard	117,325
8	Dan Sikes	115,775
9	George Archer	105,804
10	Dave Stockton	96,160
11	Bob Charles	95,332
12	Al Geiberger	93,237
13	Bob Goalby	91,364
14	Charles Coody	80,319
15	Art Wall	78,818
16	Gardner Dickinson	78,229
17	Miller Barber	76,588
18	Bert Yancey	74,506
19	Don January	73,004
20	Harold Henning	71,073
21	Gary Player	69,056
22	Roberto de Vicenzo	62,504
23	Bobby Nichols	61,073
24	George Knudson	60,670
25	Dave Hill	60,279

1968

1	Bill Casper	$222,437
2	Tom Weiskopf	172,405
3	George Archer	170,173
4	Jack Nicklaus	163,932
5	Julius Boros	161,935
6	Lee Trevino	145,170
7	Dave Stockton	135,432
8	Gary Player	130,013
9	Arnold Palmer	122,930
10	Bob Lunn	120,371
11	Bob Murphy	117,110
12	Dan Sikes	114,230
13	Bruce Crampton	112,346
14	Miller Barber	110,949
15	Frank Beard	110,057
16	Al Geiberger	99,932
17	Bob Charles	94,960
18	Gay Brewer	91,214
19	Gardner Dickinson	83,794
20	Tommy Aaron	81,035
21	Bob Goalby	79,671
22	George Knudson	77,968
23	Tony Jacklin	76,958
24	Bobby Nichols	72,546
25	Bert Yancey	71,875

1966

1	Jack Nicklaus	$168,089
2	Arnold Palmer	165,128
3	Bill Casper	156,873
4	Gene Littler	131,918
5	Doug Sanders	121,451
6	Bruce Devlin	90,058
7	Gay Brewer	88,280
8	Al Geiberger	86,694
9	Gardner Dickinson	86,629
10	Phil Rodgers	85,888
11	R. H. Sikes	75,635
12	Frank Beard	72,237
13	Don January	70,485
14	Bobby Nichols	70,145
15	Bob Goalby	64,734
16	Mason Rudolph	60,990
17	Julius Boros	60,292
18	Jacky Cupit	59,610
19	Johnny Pott	58,810
20	George Archer	56,333
21	Bert Yancey	56,008
22	Lionel Hebert	55,715
23	Dudley Wysong	54,705
24	Miller Barber	54,039
25	Don Massengale	53,397

World Stroke Average Leaders

A comparison of stroke averages is one of the more reliable ways of ranking the abilities and performances of tournament players. Its only weakness is that it does not take into account the degrees of difficulty of the various courses on which the tournaments are played. The world stroke averages that follow include the results from the U.S., British/European, South African, Australian, New Zealand, and Asian tours and two major international events. We have established 60 rounds as the minimum number for inclusion in these rankings. Without this minimum, this list would have been disproportionately dominated by South African players who played little or no tournament golf outside their country, where relatively easy courses lead generally to low scoring.

1972		ROUNDS	STROKES	AVERAGE		1970		ROUNDS	STROKES	AVERAGE
1	Jack Nicklaus	79	5,550	70.3		1	Billy Dunk	62	4,348	70.1
2	Peter Oosterhuis	120	8,483	70.7		2	Jack Nicklaus	83	5,865	70.7
3	Gary Player	104	7,378	70.9		3	Gene Littler	76	5,380	70.8
	Lee Trevino	116	8,222	70.9			Lee Trevino	136	9,631	70.8
5	Grier Jones	123	8,762	71.2		5	Bruce Devlin	103	7,299	70.9
6	George Archer	104	7,415	71.3			Tom Weiskopf	95	6,732	70.9
	Bruce Crampton	120	8,553	71.3			Bill Casper	90	6,380	70.9
	Chi Chi Rodriguez	119	8,486	71.3		8	Arnold Palmer	98	6,954	71.0
9	Billy Dunk	78	5,571	71.4			Bob Charles	135	9,581	71.0
	Graham Marsh	88	6,284	71.4			Dave Hill	104	7,381	71.0
							Larry Hinson	127	9,014	71.0
1971							Homero Blancas	116	8,234	71.0
1	Jack Nicklaus	83	5,793	69.8						
2	Roberto de Vicenzo	76	5,321	70.1		1969				
3	Gary Player	101	7,098	70.3		1	Dave Hill	104	7,324	70.4
4	Lee Trevino	117	8,236	70.4		2	Gary Player	89	6,274	70.5
5	Peter Oosterhuis	137	9,662	70.5		3	Frank Beard	126	8,897	70.6
	Arnold Palmer	96	6,764	70.5			Trevor Wilkes	40	2,825	70.6
7	Bill Casper	82	5,792	70.6		5	Bob Charles	125	8,833	70.7
	Peter Thomson	99	6,991	70.6			Tommy Aaron	119	8,417	70.7
9	Cobic Legrange	44	3,112	70.7		7	Gene Littler	77	5,449	70.8
10	Bobby Nichols	96	6,796	70.8		8	Bruce Devlin	98	6,946	70.9
							Bruce Crampton	110	7,801	70.9
							Lee Trevino	137	9,720	70.9

1968		ROUNDS	STROKES	AVERAGE	1966			ROUNDS	STROKES	AVERAGE
1	Jack Nicklaus	92	6,450	70.1	1	Jack Nicklaus		82	5,793	70.6
2	Bill Casper	101	7,085	70.2	2	Arnold Palmer		99	7,000	70.7
	Gary Player	96	6,738	70.2		Bill Casper		110	7,778	70.7
4	George Archer	112	7,894	70.5	4	Wes Ellis		61	4,320	70.8
5	Julius Boros	89	6,288	70.7	5	Roberto de Vicenzo		68	4,823	70.9
	Dan Sikes	92	6,508	70.7	6	Peter Alliss		53	3,764	71.0
7	Billy Dunk	38	2,691	70.8		Christy O'Connor		53	3,764	71.0
	Al Geiberger	90	6,375	70.8	8	Ramon Sota		44	3,128	71.1
9	Tommy Aaron	115	8,148	70.9		Harold Henning		98	6,969	71.1
	Miller Barber	133	9,433	70.9	10	Julius Boros		91	6,482	71.2

1967		ROUNDS	STROKES	AVERAGE
1	Jack Nicklaus	97	6,822	70.3
2	Arnold Palmer	98	6,895	70.4
3	Gary Player	72	5,075	70.5
4	Dan Sikes	81	5,742	70.9
5	Julius Boros	104	7,384	71.0
	Bill Casper	109	7,743	71.0
7	Bob Charles	131	9,326	71.2
	Roberto de Vicenzo	48	3,419	71.2
9	Gay Brewer	99	7,055	71.3
	Brian Huggett	60	4,276	71.3

Leading Money Winners—U.S. Tour

1972			1969			1966		
1	Jack Nicklaus	$320,542	1	Frank Beard	$175,224	1	Arnold Palmer	$154,692
2	Lee Trevino	214,806	2	Dave Hill	156,423	2	Bill Casper	145,723
3	George Archer	145,027	3	Jack Nicklaus	140,167	3	Jack Nicklaus	141,259
4	Grier Jones	140,178	4	Gary Player	123,898	4	Doug Sanders	115,671
5	Jerry Heard	137,198	5	Bruce Crampton	118,956	5	Bruce Devlin	84,792
1971			1968			1965		
1	Jack Nicklaus	$244,491	1	Bill Casper	$205,169	1	Jack Nicklaus	$154,347
2	Lee Trevino	231,203	2	Jack Nicklaus	155,286	2	Bill Casper	127,363
3	Arnold Palmer	209,604	3	Tom Weiskopf	152,947	3	Tony Lema	108,870
4	George Archer	147,769	4	George Archer	150,973	4	Doug Sanders	83,692
5	Gary Player	120,917	5	Julius Boros	148,310	5	Arnold Palmer	82,990
1970			1967			1964		
1	Lee Trevino	$157,037	1	Jack Nicklaus	$211,567	1	Arnold Palmer	$116,418
2	Bill Casper	147,372	2	Arnold Palmer	193,964	2	Jack Nicklaus	116,079
3	Bruce Crampton	142,609	3	Bill Casper	145,944	3	Bill Casper	99,541
4	Jack Nicklaus	142,149	4	Julius Boros	129,563	4	Tony Lema	85,290
5	Arnold Palmer	128,853	5	Doug Sanders	125,563	5	Bobby Nichols	78,098

1963

1	Arnold Palmer	$130,835
2	Jack Nicklaus	102,904
3	Julius Boros	84,525
4	Tony Lema	69,670
5	Gary Player	60,220

1962

1	Arnold Palmer	$82,456
2	Gene Littler	67,969
3	Bill Casper	67,103
4	Jack Nicklaus	62,934
5	Gary Player	48,116

1961

1	Gary Player	$68,337
2	Arnold Palmer	65,002
3	Doug Sanders	61,027
4	Bill Casper	42,322
5	Jay Hebert	39,879

1960

1	Arnold Palmer	$80,968
2	Ken Venturi	46,411
3	Dow Finsterwald	43,942
4	Bill Casper	38,108
5	Jay Hebert	36,840

1959

1	Art Wall	$63,209
2	Mike Souchak	47,407
3	Gene Littler	44,875
4	Dow Finsterwald	42,579
5	Arnold Palmer	39,878

1958

1	Arnold Palmer	$42,608
2	Bill Casper	41,324
3	Ken Venturi	36,268
4	Dow Finsterwald	35,393
5	Art Wall	29,841

1957

1	Dick Mayer	$65,835
2	Doug Ford	45,379
3	Dow Finsterwald	32,872
4	Sam Snead	28,261
5	Arnold Palmer	27,803

1956

1	Ted Kroll	$72,836
2	Dow Finsterwald	29,514
3	Cary Middlecoff	27,352
4	Fred Hawkins	24,805
5	Jack Burke	24,085

1955

1	Julius Boros	$63,122
2	Cary Middlecoff	39,567
3	Doug Ford	33,504
4	Mike Souchak	29,462
5	Gene Littler	28,974

1954

1	Bob Toski	$65,820
2	Jack Burke	20,214
3	Marty Furgol	19,838
4	Jerry Barber	18,885
5	Cary Middlecoff	17,594

1953

1	Lew Worsham	$34,002
2	Doug Ford	26,816
3	Lloyd Mangrum	20,637
4	Chandler Harper	19,938
5	Cary Middlecoff	19,447

1952

1	Julius Boros	$37,033
2	Cary Middlecoff	30,885
3	Jack Burke	21,003
4	Sam Snead	19,908
5	Ted Kroll	17,500

1951

1	Lloyd Mangrum	$26,089
2	Cary Middlecoff	24,076
3	Jim Ferrier	22,891
4	Ben Hogan	20,400
5	Jack Burke	18,033

1950

1	Sam Snead	$35,759
2	Jim Ferrier	27,157
3	Lloyd Mangrum	22,468
4	Henry Ransom	18,885
5	Jack Burke	18,292

1949

1	Sam Snead	$31,594
2	Cary Middlecoff	24,605
3	Johnny Palmer	24,512
4	Lloyd Mangrum	22,249
5	Jimmy Demaret	17,367

1948

1	Ben Hogan	$32,112
2	Lloyd Mangrum	31,290
3	Jimmy Demaret	23,700
4	Bobby Locke	20,010
5	Skip Alexander	18,173

1947

1	Jimmy Demaret	$27,937
2	Bobby Locke	24,328
3	Ben Hogan	23,310
4	Porky Oliver	17,941
5	Jim Ferrier	16,974

1946

1	Ben Hogan	$42,556
2	Herman Barron	23,003
3	Byron Nelson	22,270
4	Jimmy Demaret	19,407
5	Herman Keiser	18,934

Vardon Trophy Leaders—U.S. Tour

1972	ROUNDS	STROKES	AVERAGE	1965	ROUNDS	STROKES	AVERAGE
1 Lee Trevino	101	7,160	70.891	1 Bill Casper	111	7,835	70.586
2 Bruce Crampton	96	6,819	71.031	2 Tony Lema	80	5,674	70.925
3 Doug Sanders	84	5,988	71.286	3 Al Geiberger	96	6,813	70.969
4 Chi Chi Rodriguez	114	8,130	71.316	4 Dave Marr	99	7,028	70.990
5 Lou Graham	126	9,005	71.468	5 Gene Littler	90	6,399	71.100

1971				1964			
1 Lee Trevino	102	7,168	70.275	1 Arnold Palmer	96	6,721	70.010
2 Arnold Palmer	84	5,940	70.714	2 Bill Casper	117	8,232	70.359
3 Frank Beard	109	7,723	70.853	3 Ken Venturi	104	7,378	70.942
4 Bobby Nichols	83	5,881	70.855	4 Chi Chi Rodriguez	83	5,899	71.072
5 Lou Graham	124	8,819	71.121	5 Gene Littler	106	7,542	71.151

1970				1963			
1 Lee Trevino	109	7,700	70.642	1 Bill Casper	80	5,647	70.588
2 Dave Hill	91	6,444	70.813	2 Julius Boros	98	6,932	70.735
3 Frank Beard	110	7,804	70.945	3 Tony Lema	103	7,302	70.893
4 Bruce Crampton	110	7,805	70.954	4 Dow Finsterwald	123	8,763	71.244
5 Homero Blancas	112	7,953	71.008	5 Don January	99	7,063	71.343

1969				1962			
1 Dave Hill	90	6,331	70.344	1 Arnold Palmer	85	5,973	70.271
2 Frank Beard	112	7,899	70.527	2 Bill Casper	98	6,929	70.704
3 Tommy Aaron	112	7,921	70.723	3 Gene Littler	108	7,656	70.889
4 Don January	83	5,883	70.880	4 Dave Ragan	146	10,374	71.054
5 Dan Sikes	98	6,951	70.929	5 Tony Lema	120	8,527	71.058

1968				1961			
1 Bill Casper	84	5,865	69.821	1 Arnold Palmer	99	6,916	69.859
2 Frank Beard	107	7,561	70.664	2 Bill Casper	99	6,932	70.020
3 Al Geiberger	86	6,081	70.709	3 Art Wall	99	6,999	70.697
4 Dan Sikes	92	6,508	70.739	4 Jay Hebert	124	8,772	70.742
5 Miller Barber	120	8,492	70.767	5 Ted Kroll	78	5,525	70.833

1967				1960			
1 Arnold Palmer	85	5,966	70.188	1 Bill Casper	60	4,197	69.950
2 Julius Boros	95	6,777	70.789	2 Dow Finsterwald	93	6,540	70.322
3 Dan Sikes	81	5,742	70.889	3 Art Wall	88	6,189	70.329
4 Gay Brewer	82	5,813	70.890	4 Gene Littler	97	6,878	70.907
5 Bill Casper	92	6,526	70.935	5 Ted Kroll	66	4,688	71.030

1966				1959			
1 Bill Casper	87	6,114	70.276	1 Art Wall	119	8,372	70.35
2 Gay Brewer	100	7,111	71.110	2 Mike Souchak	91	6,429	70.64
3 Gene Littler	94	6,692	71.191	3 Jay Hebert	140	9,891	70.65
Johnny Pott	89	6,336	71.191	4 Doug Ford	142	10,046	70.74
5 Julius Boros	82	5,839	71.207	5 Bob Rosburg	95	6,727	70.81

1958		ROUNDS	STROKES	AVERAGE	1952		ROUNDS	STROKES	AVERAGE
1	Bob Rosburg	61	4,277	70.11	1	Jack Burke	78	5,502	70.54
2	Dow Finsterwald	131	9,194	70.18	2	Ted Kroll	104	7,359	70.74
3	Art Wall	132	9,307	70.50	3	Jim Ferrier	104	7,370	70.87
4	Jack Burke	60	4,251	70.85	4	Johnny Palmer	102	7,258	71.16
5	Julius Boros	114	8,090	70.96	5	Dave Douglas	99	7,069	71.40

1957					1951				
1	Dow Finsterwald	108	7,592	70.30	1	Lloyd Mangrum	104	7,285	70.05
2	Doug Ford	120	8,454	70.45	2	Jim Ferrier	108	7,591	70.29
3	Art Wall	117	8,299	70.93	3	Dutch Harrison	76	5,387	70.88
4	Mike Souchak	70	4,972	71.03	4	Lew Worsham	63	4,479	71.10
5	Jay Hebert	101	7,176	71.05	5	Jimmy Demaret	61	4,338	71.11

1956					1950				
1	Cary Middlecoff	66	4,643	70.35	1	Sam Snead	96	6,646	69.23
2	Ed Furgol	82	5,775	70.43	2	Jim Ferrier	119	8,362	70.27
3	Ted Kroll	75	5,294	70.59	3	Jack Burke	96	6,764	70.46
4	Doug Ford	126	8,923	70.82	4	Lloyd Mangrum	72	5,078	70.53
5	Jack Burke	69	4,889	70.86	5	Henry Ransom	97	6,888	71.01

1955					1949				
1	Sam Snead	63	4,401	69.86	1	Sam Snead	73	5,064	69.37
2	Doug Ford	128	8,975	70.12	2	Johnny Palmer	84	5,858	69.74
3	Cary Middlecoff	76	5,332	70.16	3	Lloyd Mangrum	80	5,584	69.80
4	Jay Hebert	63	4,431	70.33	4	Jimmy Demaret	65	4,562	70.18
5	Ted Kroll	104	7,318	70.36	5	Jim Ferrier	94	6,636	70.60

1954					1948				
1	Dutch Harrison	67	4,718	70.41	1	Ben Hogan	76	5,267	69.30
2	Jack Burke	89	6,297	70.75	2	Clayton Heafner	88	6,198	70.43
3	Marty Furgol	98	6,936	70.77	3	Johnny Palmer	104	7,336	70.54
4	Fred Haas	77	5,451	70.79	4	Skip Alexander	116	8,195	70.65
5	Lloyd Mangrum	68	4,815	70.80					

1953					1947				
1	Lloyd Mangrum	64	4,494	70.22	1	Jimmy Demaret	92	6,422	69.80
2	Dutch Harrison	100	7,042	70.42	2	Ben Hogan	76	5,308	69.84
3	Ted Kroll	92	6,499	70.64	3	Porky Oliver	80	5,627	70.34
4	Fred Haas	81	5,745	70.92	4	Johnny Palmer	100	7,048	70.48
5	Marty Furgol	111	7,886	71.04	5	Ed Furgol	104	7,350	70.67
						Herman Keiser	88	6,219	70.67

British PGA Order of Merit Winners

		STROKE AVERAGE
1972	Peter Oosterhuis	70.66
1971	Peter Oosterhuis	70.50
1970	Neil Coles	70.88
1969	Bernard Gallacher	71.96
1968	Brian Huggett	71.65
1967	Malcolm Gregson	71.11
1966	Peter Alliss	70.51
1965	Bernard Hunt	71.40
1964	Peter Allis	72.48
1963	Neil Coles	71.73
1962	Christy O'Connor	71.25
1961	Christy O'Connor	70.66
1960	Bernard Hunt	70.25
1959	Dai Rees	70.80
1958	Bernard Hunt	
1957	Eric Brown	
1956	Harry Weetman	
1955	Dai Rees	
1954	Bobby Locke	
1953	Flory Van Donck	
1952	Harry Weetman	
1951	John Panton	
1950	Bobby Locke	
1949	Charles Ward	
1948	Charles Ward	
1947	Norman Von Nida	
1946	Bobby Locke	

Complete statistics not available for tournaments previous to 1959.

INDEX

Aaron, Tommy, 218, 222, 226–27, 334, 350
    PGA championship, 263–65, 277–78
ABC-TV, 325
Agfa-Gevaert Tournament, 331
Alcan, 322
    Golfer of the Year, 329–34; International, 332–34
Alexander, Skip, 298
All-American Open, 5, 296
Allin, Brian (Bud), 277
Alliss, Peter, 332, 341–44
All Star Golf (TV show), 303–4, 325
Amateur Championship, 58, 65
amateur golf and golfers, 232–33; see also names
American Amateur Golf Association, 361
American Golf Classic, 317
American Professional Golfers, 235, 318
American Slam, 255, 260
Americas Cup, 202–3
Anderson, "Tip," 167
Anderson, Tom, 60
Anderson, Willie, 59, 93
Angeli, Alfonso, 297
Annon, Fred, 247
Arana brothers, 378
Archer, George, 227, 266–69, 331
Armour, Tommy, 34, 153, 158, 285–86, 337, 377
    PGA championship, 239–40, 258; U.S. Open, 70–71, 83
Associated Press, 319
Auchterlonie, Laurie, 59
Auchterlonie, Willie, 150

Augusta National Golf Club, 28, 181–85
course, 183–4, 205, 372–73; cut introduced, 205–6; PGA championship won same year as, 253; purse, 5, 104, 314; television, 303–4; tournaments (Masters) (*see also* names), 57, 185–230
Australia, courses, 372, 380

Bahamas, courses, 378
Balding, Al, 162, 297
Ball, John, Jr., 150–51
balls, 13–14, 25, 151, 287, 361–62
Ballybunnion course, 369
Baltusrol course, 377–78
Barbaro, Lou, 250
Barber, Jerry, 299
    PGA Championship, 251, 255, 257; U.S. Open, 101, 105–8
Barber, Miller, 134–35, 226, 328, 331
    PGA Championship, 266–69, 275–76
Barnes, Brian, 179, 332
Barnes, James M. (Jim; Long Jim), 22, 67, 95, 284–86, 337
    PGA Championship, 236–8, 240
Barnum, John, 258
Bassler, Charley, 248
Bayer, George, 218, 258
Bay Hill course, 377
Beard, Frank, 6, 178, 318, 333, 344
    Augusta National (Masters), 218, 222, 226; PGA Championship, 266–69
Belgium, 15, 379
Bell, Art, 244

Beman, Deane, 208, 221, 275
  U.S. Open, 130–31, 134, 137
Bembridge, Maurice, 175, 333
Ben Hogan Open, 86
Bermuda, courses, 378
Bernardini, Roberto, 358
Bertil, Prince, 7
Besselink, Al, 307
Best 18 Holes series (TV), 327–28
Bies, Don, 266, 271
"Big Three," 258, 272, 301, 314, 319;
  see also names
Bing Crosby Pro-Am, 142, 234, 292,
  304, 306
Black, James, 338
Black, John, 67
black players, 11, 316
Blancas, Homero, 143, 331, 347
Bob Hope Desert Classic, 234, 318
Bolt, Tommy, 301–2
  Augusta National (Masters), 202–3,
    212, 217–18, 222; PGA champion-
    ship, 251–52, 275–76; Ryder Cup,
    341; U.S. Open, 96, 103–4, 108,
    257
Bonallack, Michael, 164
Boros, Julius, 34, 299, 301–2, 331, 335,
  341
  Augusta National (Masters), 202,
    208–9, 211, 226; PGA Champion-
    ship, 34, 254, 260, 266–69, 275;
    U.S. Open, 34, 51, 87, 92–94, 96,
    98–101, 103, 108, 110, 117–18,
    136; World Championship, 296–97
Bourne, Alfred, 183
Bousfield, Ken, 339, 342
Brackenridge Park Course, 303
Bradshaw, Harry, 156
Brady, Mike, 60, 65–66, 69
Braid, James, 18–19, 151
Branch, Bill, 158–59
Brewer, Gay, 5, 224, 226, 277–78, 350
  Golfer of the Year Championship,
    331–33
British Broadcasting Corp., 326–29
British Open, 4, 15, 56, 148–79, 232
  American domination, 151; ball, 25,
    151; Commonwealth domination,
    156; courses, 363–70; cycle, 150,
    157; foreign winner, first, 151; for-
    mat, 150; left-handed winner, 316;
    purse, 149, 153; "unplayable" rule,
    157; U.S. Open won same year, 178
Brosch, Al, 85, 303
Brown, Eric, 159, 163, 297, 341, 345–
  46
Brown, Peter, 316
Brae, Bobby, 111
Buick Open, 317
Bulla, Johnny, 46, 87, 153–54, 193,
  291, 298, 307

Bullock, Fred, 164
Burke, Billie, 73
Burke, Jack, Sr., 238
Burke, Jack, Jr., 341, 375
  Augusta National (Masters), 202–5,
    252–53; PGA Championship, 247–
    49, 252–53; U.S. Open, 100, 299
Burke, Jimmy, 266
Burkemo, Walter, 94, 117, 209
  PGA Championship, 248–53
Burton, Dick, 153, 338–39
Busson, Jack, 338
Butler, Peter, 170, 332, 350–51
Byrd, Sam, 189, 241–43

Cajun Classic, 314–15
Calcutta, 306
Campbell, Glen, 279
Campbell, Joe, 307
Canada, 360
Canada Cup, 335
Canadian Open, 236
Cantrell, Warren, 266
Carling Brewery, 314–15, 317
Carling World Open, 277
Carmichael, Marty, 234
Carnoustie course, 365–66
Carrolls International, 331
Casper, Billy, 27, 31, 47–49, 173–74,
  300–2, 310, 319, 347
  American Open, 47–49; Augusta Na-
    tional (Masters), 49, 208–12,
    227–28; British Open, 49; earn-
    ings, 300, 308, 310; Golfer of
    the Year Championship, 330–34;
    PGA Championship, 254, 261,
    264, 273, 275–76, 278; Piccadilly
    World Match Play, 350, 355; Ry-
    der Cup, 342, 344–45; U.S. Open,
    49, 51, 104–5, 109, 127–31
Cavanaugh, Gil, 100
CBS-TV, 304, 325
Celebrity Golf (TV show), 325
Cerda, Antonio (Tony), 40, 158–59,
  162, 297, 335
Challenge Golf (TV show), 304, 325
Champions' Club courses, 375
Charles, Bob, 35, 316, 331, 358
  British Open, 166, 173–75; PGA
    Championship, 261, 269, 275; Pic-
    cadilly World Match Play, 350,
    354–55
Cherry, Don, 108–9
Chicago Victory Open, 298
Church of Perfect Liberty, 346–48
Clark, Clive, 172
Clark, Jimmy, 250
Cleveland Open, 314, 330
clubs (equipment), 13–15, 193, 286–
  87, 361–62
  grip, 27–28; irons, roughing of, 154;

clubs (*continued*)
  clubs (organizations), *see* Courses;
    names
Coe, Charlie, 208, 212–16
Colbert, Jim, 138
Coles, Neil, 175–76, 334, 344, 380
  Piccadilly World Match Play, 350–53
Colonial National Invitation, 330
Collins, Bill, 119, 252, 310
Columbine Country Club course, 265
Columbus Country Club course, 260
Compston, Archie, 152, 157
Coody, Charles, 132, 227–30, 270, 272,
    347
Cooper, Harry, 71, 72, 75, 187–88, 238,
    286
Cooper, Pete, 203, 250
Corcoran, Fred (Freddie the Cork),
    288–92, 295–96, 318
Cotton, Henry, 29–30, 34, 50, 52, 341,
    379
  British Open, 29–30, 153–55, 157–
    58, 163, 366; U.S. Open, 100
Country Club course, 116
courses, 360–63, 378–80
  American, 302–3, 370–78; British,
    363–70, 372, 378; *see also* names,
    events
Cox, Bill, 338–39
Cox, Wiffy, 75
Crampton, Bruce, 162, 297
  earnings, 316; PGA Championship,
    260; U.S. Open, 142–44, 147
Crawley, Leonard, 133
Creavy, Tom, 239, 251
Crosby, Bing, 279, 306
Cruikshank, Bobby, 68, 74–75, 236–7,
    285
Crump, George, 371
Cupit, Jacky, 51, 117–18
cut rule, 205–6
Cypress Creek course, 375
Cypress Point course, 374

Daly, Fred, 154–55, 339
Darwin, Bernard, 160
Defoy, Craig, 177–78
Demaret, Jimmy, 80, 83, 292, 296, 308,
    375
  Augusta National (Masters), 86,
    188–94, 218; earnings, 298; PGA
    Championship, 241, 243–47; Phoe-
    nix Open (Ben Hogan Open), 86,
    298; Ryder Cup, 339; U.S. Open,
    31, 84, 92, 100, 102
Denmark, courses, 379
Dent, James, 310
Denver Open, 326
de Vicenzo, Roberto, 132, 250, 297, 335,
    350
  Augusta National (Masters), 226–27;

de Vicenzo, Roberto (*continued*)
  British Open, 155–59, 162, 164–
    65, 172–75, 177
Devlin, Bruce, 125, 167, 172, 218, 226,
    275, 316, 334, 350–51
Dey, Joseph C., 90, 121, 198, 318–19
Dickinson, Gardner, 263–64, 318, 331
Diegel, Leo, 22, 69, 152–53, 285
  PGA Championship, 238–40
Doral Hotel and Country Club, 316
Doser, Clarence, 250
Douglas, Dave, 92–93, 111, 247, 250
Dow Jones, 322
Dow Jones Open, 56
Dudley, Ed, 184, 241, 286, 288
Duncan, George, 22, 152, 337–38
Duncan, Tony, 352
Dunes Golf and Beach Club course, 377
Dunlop Co., 291
Dunlop Masters, 331
Dunn, Willie, 58
Dutra, Olin, 74–75, 239, 251, 338–39
Dye, Pete, 363

earnings, *see* tours, purses and earnings;
    names; events
Easterbrook, Syd, 338
Eastern Airlines, 279
Edgar, J. Douglas, 236
Education of a Golfer, The (Snead),
    241
Eisenhower, Dwight D. and Mamie, 7
Eisenhower Trophy, 28, 380
Elbin, Max, 235, 343
Elder, Lee, 11, 316
Ellis, Wesley, 101, 218, 256
El Rio Country Club course, 303
endorsements, 13–15
equipment, 25, 151, 154, 193, 286–87,
    294–95, 361–62
  endorsements, 13–15
Erath, Paul, 263
Erickson, Bob, 138
Espinosa, Al, 71, 238–9
Europe, courses, 378–80; *see also* coun-
    tries; names
Evans, Chick, 64, 65, 74, 75, 84
Evans, Max, 253

Fallon, John, 161, 342
Farlow, Charley, 253
Farrell, John, 69, 71, 152, 239, 285,
    288, 378
Faulkner, Max, 156–57, 159, 174, 297,
    339
Fazio, George, 252, 375
  U.S. Open, 40, 87–88, 90–91, 94
Ferrier, Jim, 87, 193–94, 299
  PGA Championship, 244, 247, 251,
    256, 271

Finsterwald, Dow, 108, 117, 300–2, 310
    Augusta National (Masters), 53, 202, 208–11, 216–17; earnings, 300, 308, 310; PGA Championship, 253–54, 260, 300, 308
Firestone Country Club, 256, 264, 325, 375–76
Firestone Tire & Rubber Co., 280, 317
First Flight Co., 14–15
Fitzjohn, Val, 60
Fleck, Jack, 200, 310
    U.S. Open, 39, 49, 96–98, 108–10, 125, 129
Fleckman, Marty, 130–31, 266–69
Florida Citrus Growers Association, 279
Florida leagues, professional, 285
Floyd, Raymond, 218, 222, 358
    PGA Championship, 270–73, 277–78
Ford, Doug, 111, 299–302
    APG, 318; Augusta National (Masters), 202–4, 206–7, 212; PGA Championship, 249, 251–52, 258, 303; U.S. Open, 100–1
Ford dealers, 314
Fort Worth *Star-Telegram*, 259
Foulis, Jim, 59
Fowler, Herbert, 369
Fownes, William C., Jr., 375
France, 356–59, 379
Frank Sinatra Open, 318
Fraser, Leo, 235
French, Emmett, 236–7, 337
Furgol, Ed, 101, 252, 299, 302
    U.S. Open, 95–96, 113, 131
Furgol, Marty, 248, 253, 299, 303

Gallacher, Bernard, 49, 345
galleries
    behavior, 114, 237, 244, 246, 270, 341, 354; growth, 5, 304, 319
Garaialde, Jean, 167, 333, 358
Gates, Samuel, 318
Geiberger, Al, 134–35, 264–65, 270
George VI of England, 155
George, Dow, 285
Germany, 379–80
Ghezzi, Vic, 82, 239, 241, 244
Gilbert, Gibby, 275–76
Gleason, Jackie, 279
Goalby, Bob, 113, 137, 226–27
    PGA Championship, 258–59, 275
Goggin, Willie, 239, 241–4
Golden Age of Sport, 4, 30, 279, 286; *see also* names
Golden, John, 238
Golf Classic (TV show), 304, 325
Golfer of the Year Championship, 330–34
Gonzales, Mario, 297
Goodall Round-Robin, 295
Goodman, John, 74

Graham, David, 333
Grand Slam
    amateur, 28; professional, 27, 231, 255; *see also* names
Grand Slam Golf (Player), 258
Grant, Douglas, 373
Grappasonni, Ugo, 297
Great Britain, 8, 15, 322, 326–29
    courses, 363–70, 372, 378; *see also* names; events
Greene, Bert, 271
Gregson, Malcolm, 332
Grout, Jack, 241, 376
Guldahl, Ralph, 241, 286, 291–92
    Augusta National (Masters), 187–88, 191–92; U.S. Open, 46, 74, 77

Haas, Fred, 248, 250, 252
Hackney, Clarence, 236
Hagen, W., 5, 18, 22–27, 29, 52, 159, 193, 284–86, 288, 337
    American Open, 22; Augusta National (Masters), 186; British Open, 22–25, 67, 151–52, 364, 366; PGA Championship, 22, 233, 236–40, 249, 251; Ryder Cup, 338; U.S. Open, 62, 64–67, 69, 73
Hale America National Open, 80
Haliburton, Tom, 342
Hamilton, Bob, 243, 250
Hancock, Roland, 71
Harbert, Chick, 192, 301–2
    PGA Championship, 244–46, 248, 250–52
Hardin, Hord, 121
Harkins, Jack, 14–15
Harlow, Robert, 285–86, 288–89, 336
Harmon, Claude, 104, 192, 209
    PGA Championship, 250–51, 253
Harnett, James, 336
Harney, Paul, 212–13
Harper, Chandler, 299
    PGA Championship, 243, 247–50, 252; Texas Open, 303; World Championship, 296
Harris, Bob, 111
Harris, John, 378
Harris, Labron, 137
Harrison, Dutch, 87–88, 109, 197, 241, 339
Hart, Dick, 259–60
Haskell, Coburn, 361–62
Hassan, King of Morocco, 7, 15
Havers, Arthur, 152, 338
Hawkins, Fred, 207, 252, 308, 341
Hazeltine National Golf Club course, 374
Heafner, Clayton, 85–86, 92–93, 111, 298, 303
Heard, Jerry, 5, 277–78

Hebert, Jay, 254, 256–57, 310
Hebert, Lionel, 253–54, 256 57
Henning, Harold, 170, 175, 297, 328
Henning, Graham, 333
Henry, Bunky, 270–71
Herd, Alexander (Sandy), 18, 151
Herd, Fred, 59
Hershey Open, 290–91
Hill, Dave, 136–37, 265, 334, 344–45, 374
Hill, Mike, 273
Hilton, Harold, 150–51
Hilton Head course, 363
Hines, Jimmy, 185, 240, 286
Hinson, Larry, 272–73
Hitchcock, Jimmy, 170
Holland, 379
Hogan, Ben, 5, 31, 35–41, 47, 49–51, 53, 80, 84, 243, 258, 292–96, 301, 376–77
    accident, 36–39, 40, 85–86, 246, 298–9; Augusta National (Masters), 36, 39–40, 46, 86, 94, 188–200, 202–3, 206, 208–9, 211, 216, 218, 221, 223, 243, 377; Ben Hogan Open, 86; British Open, 19, 39–41, 94, 156, 158–60, 164, 178, 196; Colonial Invitation, 308; earnings, 5, 292–3; Grand Slam, 27; Los Angeles Open, 40, 83, 86, 298–99; North and South, 80, 83; Oakland Open, 292; PGA Championship, 36, 39, 82, 83, 236–37, 241, 243–46, 249, 261–62, 293; Phoenix Open, 298; Texas Open, 83; Ryder Cup, 339; U.S. Open, 31, 36, 39–40, 77, 80–85, 87–101, 104–11, 125–29, 133, 178, 196, 236–37, 243, 299, 375–76; Vardon Trophy, 36, 83; Western Open, 83
Hogan, Valerie, 85
Homans, Gene, 182
Honorable Company of Edinburgh Golfers, 149–51, 365–66
Hope, Bob, 279
Hopkins, John Jay, 334–35
Horne, Reginald, 154–55
Horton, Tommy, 175, 332
Houston Classic, 316
Houston Golf Association, 343–44
Huggett, Brian, 345
Hunt, Bernard, 165, 169, 341–42, 344
Hutchison, Jock, 22, 284
    British Open, 151, 181; PGA Championship, 236–7; U.S. Open, 59–60, 65, 68
Hutchison, Jock, Jr., 244–46

Inman, Walter, 100
International Association, 334–35

Inverness Four-Ball Tournament, 295
Ireland, 157, 334–35, 369; *see also* names; events
Ironman, Caddy, 210
Irwin, Hale, 273, 277
Isaacs, Jack, 250
Italy, courses, 379
IVB, 280

Jack, Reid, 164
Jacklin, Tony, 8, 15, 50, 232, 319, 327–28
    British Open, 49–50, 55, 174–79; Dunlop Masters, 50; PGA Championship, 275; Piccadilly World Match Play, 350, 353–55; Ryder Cup, 336, 344 46; Tournament of Champions, 358; U.S. Open, 50, 56, 134, 136–37, 374
Jackrabbit course, 375
Jacobs, Tommy, 119–22, 224
Jacobus, George, 288–89, 292
Jamieson, Jay, 277–78
January, Don, 226
    PGA Championship, 257, 261, 265–66
Japan, 5, 9, 322, 335, 346–48, 378
Jermain, Sylvanus, 336
John Player Classic, 322
Johnson, George, 316
Johnston, Bill, 253
Jones, Bobby, 4, 18, 19, 25, 28–29, 50–51, 64, 166, 178, 189, 191, 198, 203, 223, 286
    Augusta National (Masters), 28, 57, 182–85, 196, 222, 226; British Amateur, 71–72; British Open, 28, 66–67, 70–72, 151–53, 233, 368; Grand Slam, 4, 28, 71–73, 182, 233; U.S. Open, 28, 67–73, 77, 93, 233; U.S. Amateur, 71–73, 233; Walker Cup, 72
Jones, Robert Trent, 92, 122, 256, 374–78

Kaiser Aluminum, 280
Keeler, O. B., 182
Keiser, Herman, 5, 36, 191, 193, 243, 271
Kemper Insurance, 280
Kerrigan, Tommy, 285
Kirkaldy, Andrew, 336–37
Kirkwood, Joe, Sr., 90
Kirkwood, Joe, Jr., 90, 285, 288, 292, 337
Knudson, George, 227
Kocsis, Emerick, 241
Krak, Mike, 251
Kroll, Ted, 101, 297, 299, 302
    PGA Championship, 249–50, 252–

Kroll, Ted (*continued*)
    53, 303; U.S. Open, 98, 100–1,
    109
Kunes, Gene, 240

Ladies Home Journal, 7
Ladies PGA, 304
Laffoon, Ky, 240, 244, 286
Laidley, J. E., 19, 150
Large, Bill, 333
Laurel Valley course, 262–63
league, professional, 285
Lee, Joe, 378
Lees, Arthur, 155, 339
Lema, Betty, 315
Lema, Tony, 47, 117, 260, 265, 305,
    310, 315, 342
    Augusta National (Masters), 217–18,
    222; British Open, 40, 47, 167–69,
    365; Piccadilly World Match Play,
    53, 350–52
Leonard, Marvin, 292
Leonard, Stan, 297
Liggett and Myers Tobacco, 280
Lincoln-Mercury, 10
Little, Lawson, 36, 78, 153–54
Littler, Gene, 300–2, 308, 310, 346
    Augusta National (Masters), 202,
    212, 227–28; Piccadilly World
    Match Play, 350, 355; U.S. Open,
    95–96, 103, 113, 125, 136, 310
Littler, Shirley, 302
Lloyd, Joe, 59
Locke, Arthur D'Arcy (Bobby), 30–34,
    297–98, 312
    accident, 31; All-American, 298; Brit-
    ish Open, 27, 30–31, 46, 153–54,
    156–61, 163; earnings, 298; Good-
    all Round-Robin, 298; PGA Cham-
    pionship, 244; U.S. Open, 31, 92
Lockhart, Robert, 360–61
Loos, Eddie, 285
Los Angeles Opens, 285, 289, 291
Lotz, Dick, 273
Low, George, 60, 211
Lowery, Ed, 202–3, 301
Lu, Liang Huan, 177
Lucky Lager, 316
Lunn, Bob, 270
Lyons, Toby, 248

MacArthur, John P., 274
Macdonald, Charles Blair, 58, 370–71
Macfarlane, Willie, 69
MacGregor, 14, 305
MacKenzie, Alister, 183–84, 372
Mackey, Lee, 87, 119
Mahan, Tom, 237
Maiden, Stewart, 68
Mailer, Norman, 323
Manero, Tony, 75, 77, 240

Mangrum, Lloyd, 31, 80, 103, 241, 286,
    298–99, 301, 341
    Augusta National (Masters), 188–
    89, 193, 204, 223; PGA Champion-
    ship, 240, 244, 247–48; U.S. Open,
    5, 31, 40, 82, 87–88, 90–91
Marr, Dave, 178, 218, 263–64
Marshall, Walton H., 182
Martin, Dean, 279
Martini International, 331
Massachusetts Golf Association, 288–89
Massengale, Don, 125, 266
Massey, Arnaud, 151
Masters, *see* Atlanta National Golf Club;
    names of players
match play, 18, 253, 348
May, George S., 295–97, 299–300
Mayer, Dick, 96, 101–3, 131, 297, 302,
    307
Mayer, Doris, 302
Mayfield, Shelley, 202, 260
McBee, Rives, 127
McCallister, Bob, 258
McCormack, Mark, 307
McDermott, Johnny, 59–60, 62, 64, 77
McGee, Jerry, 138
McLean, George, 237
McLeod, Fred, 69, 181, 236, 285, 337
    U.S. Open, 59–60, 67
McNamara, Tom, 59–60, 62, 65, 284
McSpaden, Jug, 80, 240–44, 286
Melhorn, Wild Bill, 22, 70, 238, 240,
    285, 288, 337
Mengert, Al, 125, 127
Merion course, 371–72
Metropolitan Open, 284
Metz, Dick, 77, 103, 188, 286, 298
    PGA Championship, 239–41, 243,
    247
Miami Four-Ball tournament, 295
Middlecoff, Gary, 31, 34, 39, 162–63,
    299, 302, 341
    Augusta National (Masters), 101,
    191–92, 199, 200, 202–7; PGA
    Championship, 249, 251–52, 258;
    television, 325; U.S. Open, 85–88,
    98–103, 299; Walker Cup, 85
Middle Guard, 301–2; *see also* names
Miguel, Angel, 297
Miki Gold Cup, 346–48
Miki, Tokuchika, 347–48
Miller, John, 134, 144, 178, 288, 272–
    73
Mitchell, Abe, 22, 46, 337
Mitchell, Bobby, 275
Moffitt, Ralph, 342
Monsanto Chemical, 280
Moody, Orville, 134–35, 142, 271
Morocco, 7, 15
Morris, Tom, 3–4, 17–18, 148–49, 360
Morris, Young Tom, 149–50

Mowrey, Larry, 270
Muirfield course, 365–66
Murphy, Bob, 134, 273–74

Nabholtz, Larry, 238
Nagle, Kel, 123, 164, 297, 316
    British Open, 51, 164–66, 170, 310;
        Golfer of the Year Championship,
        333; PGA Championship, 255
Nakamura, Peter, 297
Nary, Bill, 252
National Airlines, 279–80
National Golf Links, 370
National Team Championship, 275
NBC, 327
NCR Country Club, 270
Nelson, Byron, 31, 34–36, 196, 203,
    246, 286, 292–94, 301, 313, 339
    American Open, 34; British Open, 34;
        Augusta National (Masters), 34,
        36, 187, 189–93, 198, 202, 293–
        94; earnings, 34, 293–94, 296,
        300; illness, 80; Metropolitan Open,
        293; PGA Championship, 34, 82,
        241–43, 251, 293–94; Phoenix
        Open, 294; U.S. Open, 46, 78, 80–
        82, 293
Neville, Jock, 373
News of the World PGA Match Play
    Championship, 232, 348
Newsweek, 7
New York Times, 184–85, 291–92
Nicholls, Gil, 60
Nichols, Bobby, 115, 138, 226, 331
    Carling World Open, 277; Dow Jones
        Open, 56; PGA Championship,
        260–62, 272
Nicklaus, Barbara, 223
Nicklaus, Jack, 7, 12–14, 18, 19, 50–
    55, 137, 158, 241, 272, 275, 301,
    312, 314–15, 363, 376
    American Slam, 260; APG, 318; Au-
        gusta National (Masters), 5, 18,
        54–55, 217–26, 228, 230, 253;
        British Open, 22, 52, 54–55, 166–
        76, 178–79, 259, 366, 368; Cajun
        Classic, 315; earnings, 5, 284,
        314–15, 319, 326; Eisenhower
        Trophy, 54; Golfer of the Year
        Championship, 330, 332–33; Grand
        Slam, 27; lifestyle, 8; National
        Team Championship, 275; PGA
        Championship, 54, 253, 255, 258–
        66, 270–77; Piccadilly World
        Match Play, 53, 54, 350–52, 355–
        56; Ryder Cup, 344–46; television,
        304, 326–27; U.S. Amateur, 54,
        114; U.S. Open, 5, 49, 51, 54,
        105–10, 113–16, 123, 127, 130–
        34, 136–47, 177, 258, 371, 374;

Nicklaus, Jack (*continued*)
    Walker Cup, 54, 55, 170; World
    Series of Golf, 307, 326–27
Nieporte, Tom, 261
Nixon, Richard M., 7, 135
North and South Open, 284

Oakland Hills course, 91–92, 375–76
Oakland Open, 291–92
Oakmont Country Club course, 375
O'Connor, Christy, 163, 167, 174, 176,
    332–33, 344
O'Donnell, John, 251
Ogg, Willie, 237
Old Course (St. Andrews), 364–65
Old Guard, 301; *see also* names
Old Troon course, 367
Oliver, Porky, 78, 82, 94, 243, 251, 298
Olympic Club course, 375
Oosterhuis, Peter, 176–77, 334, 345
origins of golf, 360–61
Ouimet, Francis, 19, 62–4, 69, 116–17
Owens, Charlie, 316

Pacific Masters, 5, 322
Padgham, Alfred, 153, 155
Palm Beach Clothing Co., 295
Palmer, Arnold, 4–5, 7, 14, 15, 18, 19,
    25–27, 41, 50–55, 75, 167, 272,
    300–3, 308–14, 318, 375, 377
    American Open, 47–49; Arnie's Army,
        41, 50, 208, 222, 308; Athlete of
        the Decade, 8; Augusta National
        (Masters), 6, 51, 53, 105, 111,
        200, 202, 206–18, 222–24, 312–
        13, 230, 258, 308; British Open,
        22, 51–52, 54, 164–66, 170, 175–
        76, 258, 368; Cajun Classic, 315;
        Carling World Open, 277; earnings,
        10, 284, 308, 310, 314–15, 319;
        Golfer of the Year Championship,
        330–33; Grand Slam, 255; Insur-
        ance City Open, 105, 310; lifestyle,
        6–11, 13, 51; Mobile Sertoma
        Open, 310; National Team Cham-
        pionship, 275; Palm Springs Desert
        Classic, 308; PGA Championship,
        234, 254–56, 258, 260–75, 277,
        310; Philadelphia Classic, 263; Pic-
        cadilly World Match Play, 47,
        350–51, 353; Ryder Cup, 336,
        342, 346; television, 6, 304, 323,
        326–28; Tournament of Cham-
        pions, 358–59; U.S. Amateur, 51;
        U.S. Open, 6, 51, 54, 101, 104–21,
        123–32, 134–37, 142–47, 208,
        258, 308, 312; World Series of
        Golf, 307, 326–27
Palmer, Johnny, 87, 193, 246–47, 252,
    296, 298
Palmer, Winnie, 302

Palm Springs Desert Classic, 306–7
Panton, John, 342
Park, Willie, 148–49, 369
Parks, Sam, 75, 339
Patton, William J. (Billie Joe), 102, 196–98, 200–2, 208
Pavella, Mike, 252
Pebble Beach course, 373–74
Pecan Valley course, 266, 269
Pennink, Frank, 379
Pennsylvania Natural Gas Association, 9
Perry, Alfred, 153, 338
PGA (Professional Golf Association), 57, 231–35, 284
    Approved Player Card, 317; black players, 316; Championship, *see* PGA Championship; Executive Board, 317–18; Golfer of the Year Championship, 330; Ladies tour, 304; membership, national, 317; purse splitting, 307–8; revolt by players, 234–35, 318–19; Ryder Cup, 343–44; television, 234–35, 303; tour development and organization (*see also* Tours), 233–34, 246, 279–80, 285–86, 288–90, 317–19; tour qualification, 280, 301, 317–18; Tournament Committee, 297, 317–18; Tournament Players Division, 235; World Series of Golf, 325–26
PGA, British, 331, 348–50
PGA Championship, 57, 235–78
    American winner, first, 236; Augusta National (Masters) won same year as, 253; back-to-back winners, 240; British winner, last, 239; brothers as winners, 256–57; civil rights agitators, 270; courses, 256, 260, 262–66 *passim*, 269, 270, 272, 274, 303; extra holes, 237, 238, 239–40; format, 232, 237, 238, 252, 253, 284; oldest champion, 269; purse, 231, 314; scoring system, 277; U.S. Open won same year as, 236–37
PGA National Golf Club course, 274
Philadelphia Classic, 263, 330
Philadelphia Inquirer Open, 296
Picard, Henry, 187–88, 191, 203, 286, 292
    PGA Championship, 240–41
Piccadilly Cigarette Co., 337
Piccadilly World Match Play Championship, 348–56
Pickens, Hilles, 330
Pinehurst courses, 57–58, 373
Pine Valley course, 371
Player, Gary, 7, 8, 18, 27, 36, 50–55, 111, 272, 276–77, 297, 301, 305, 312, 316, 375

Player, Gary (*continued*)
    American Slam, 260; Augusta National (Masters), 53, 208, 211–28, 257–58, 312; British Open, 22, 49, 52, 162, 164, 166, 172–74, 177; Carling World Open, 277; Clubs, 14–15; earnings, 312, 316; Golfer of the Year Championship, 330, 332–33; Grand Slam, 27; lifestyle, 11–15; PGA Championship, 46, 53, 232, 255, 258–61, 265–66, 270–73, 275–78, 376; Piccadilly World Match Play, 53, 54, 350–56; television, 304, 326–27; tournament of Champions, 358–59; U.S. Open, 15, 52–53, 103, 109, 123–25, 130, 136, 142, 257; World Series of Golf, 307, 326–27
Player, Winnie, 222
Plummer, Ralph, 375
Portmarnock course, 369
Portugal, courses, 379
Pott, Johnny, 109, 212, 266–70
Pounders, Leon, 252
Powers, Francis, 285
Prestwick Golf Club, 148–49, 364
professional golfers, 232–33
    commercialization and status, 3–16; earnings, *see* Tours, purses and earnings; endorsements, 13–15; league, 285; *see also* Tours; events; names
Professional Golfer, The, 244–46
Professional Grand Slam, 231, 255
Pung, Jackie, 100
Putnam, Robert Dean, 379
putting, 287

Quad-City Classic, 322

racism, 11, 51, 53, 316
Radix, Harry, 88
Ragan, Dave, 260
Ralston Purina, 15
Ransom, Henry, 105, 247, 296
Rawlins, Horace, 58–59, 66
Ray, Ted, 19, 53, 62–64, 66, 118, 123
Rees, Dai, 297
    British Open, 40, 46, 51, 159–60, 165; Ryder Cup, 339–42
Refram, Dean, 117
Reid, John, 360–61
Reid, Wilfrid, 62, 337
Revolta, Johnny, 240, 286, 291, 338
Rhodes, Ted, 316
Richardson, John, 175–76
Richardson, William D., 184
Riviere, Jay, 375
Roberts, Clifford, 57, 182–84, 191, 196, 205, 214, 216, 222, 312
Rodgers, Phil, 114–15, 166, 170, 278, 328

Rodriguez, Chi Chi, 136
Roe, R. C., 338
Rogers, William, 318
Rosburg, Bob, 334
    Augusta National (Masters), 202-3, 211-12; PGA Championship, 254-55; U.S. Open, 96, 104-5, 111, 114, 135
Ross, Alex, 59-60
Ross, Donald, 57, 70, 91, 101, 373, 376-77
Round-Robin, 295
Royal and Ancient Golf Club (St. Andrews), 148ff., 363-65
Royal Birkdale course, 367-69
Royal Dornoch course, 367
Royal Lytham course, 367-68
Royal Montreal Golf Club, 360
Rudolph, Mason, 226, 331
    PGA Championship, 261-63, 266, 273; U.S. Open, 123, 136, 147
Ruiz, Leopoldo, 297
Rule, Bob, 343-44
Runyan, Paul, 92, 239-41, 249, 287-88, 338
Ryder, Samuel, 337-38
Ryder Cup, 292, 314, 336-46

Sahara Hotel, 317
St. Andrew's Club (Scotland), 148ff., 360, 363-65
St. Andrew's Club (Yonkers), 361
St. Andrews University, 360
St. Anne's course, 367
St. Paul Junior Chamber of Commerce, 285
Sanders, Clark, 176
Sanders, Doug, 218, 224, 312, 319, 331, 347
    British Open, 54, 169-72, 175, 179; earnings, 312; PGA Championship, 255-57, 269, 278; U.S. Open, 108, 111-13, 137
Sarazen, Gene, 18, 22, 27-28, 34, 40, 87, 97, 285-86, 338; Augusta National (Masters), 27, 186, 188; British Open, 27, 31, 153, 163, 178; Grand Slam, 27, 186; Grip, 27-28; PGA Championship, 27, 233, 236-41, 244, 246, 250; U.S. Open, 27, 36, 67, 69, 73-75, 78, 103, 138, 178, 236
Sardinia course, 378
Sargent, George, 59-60, 62, 330
Schenkel, Chris, 134
Schneiter, George, 318
Schwimmer, Walter, 325-26, 329
Scioto Country Club course, 376-77

scoring
    breakthrough, 286-87; errors, 100, 226-27, 333
Scotland, 148ff., 360
    courses, 363-67; *see also* names; events
Scott, Syd, 160, 164-65
Seminole course, 377
Shakespeare, Henry, 14-15
Shankland, Bill, 174
Shaw, Tom, 270
Shell Oil Co., 304, 325, 329
Shepard, Alan, 323
Shoemaker, Dick, 248
Shute, Denny, 46, 78, 153, 286
    PGA Championship, 239-40, 251; Ryder Cup, 338
Sifford, Charlie, 316
Sifford, Curtis, 316
Sikes, Dan, 218, 265-66, 277, 331, 344
Simons, Jim, 137-38
Skerritt, Paddy, 334
Smith, Alex, 59-60, 62, 284
Smith, Bob, 277
Smith, Doug, 330
Smith, Horton, 72, 80, 206, 286-89
    Augusta National (Masters), 185, 187, 191; PGA Championship, 238, 240
Smith, Macdonald, 22, 46, 77, 153
    U.S. Open, 59-60, 62, 72-73
Smith, Willie, 59, 60
Snead, Sam, 31, 34, 36, 41-47, 80, 85-86, 243, 288, 290-95, 301, 318
    Augusta National (Masters), 46, 188-200, 203, 206, 208, 217, 218, 230, 248, 253; Bing Crosby Pro-Am, 292; British Open, 46, 153-54, 164, 248; earnings, 5, 299, 307, 325; Hershey Open, 290-91; Los Angeles Open, 86, 291, 299; Miami and Nassau Open, 292; Oakland Open, 291-92; PGA Championship, 46, 240-41, 243-44, 246-51, 253-54, 256, 265, 275; Ryder Cup, 46, 292, 339, 341, 346; St. Paul Open, 292; Sam Snead Festival, 308; television, 303-4, 325; U.S. Open, 46, 77-78, 82-84, 86, 92, 94-97, 108-9, 292, 298
Sota, Ramon, 358
Souchak, Frank, 94
Souchak, Mike, 300-3, 308-12
    Augusta National (Masters), 204-5, 208; PGA Championship, 253, 261, 303; Ryder Cup, 342; Texas Open, 300; U.S. Open, 104-8, 113, 312
South Africa, 8, 11-13, 51, 380; *see also* names
South African Marine Shipping Corp., 13

Southern Hills Country Club course, 272, 376

Spain, 13, 378–79

Sports Illustrated, 6, 301, 307, 315, 319

Sprogell, Frank, 237

Spyglass Hill course, 374

Still, Ken, 345

Stockton, Dave, 272–74, 331, 347, 355

Stranahan, Frank, 40, 155, 158–59, 163, 191, 304–6

Strath, Andrew, 149

Sullivan, Buddy, 307

Sweden, 7, 378–79

Swiss Open, 232

Switzerland, courses, 378

Tam O'Shanter Open, 5, 296

Taylor, John Henry, 18–19, 59, 62, 150–51, 165, 338

television, 6, 15, 57, 82, 234–5, 296–97, 303–4, 316, 323–30

Texas Open, 285, 303

Thirsk, Stan, 277

Thirty Years of Championship Golf (Sarazen), 236

Thomas, Danny, 279

Thomas, David, 163, 169–72, 297, 332

Thomson, Jimmy, 240, 286–88

Thomson, Peter, 101, 297, 372
    Alcan International, 332–33; British Open, 40, 47, 156–63, 166, 169, 174–75, 368; Piccadilly World Match Play, 47, 350–51, 353

Thorpe, Chuck, 316

Thunderbird Classic, 314, 316–17

Tillinghast, Arthur, 378

Time, 9–10

Tolley, Cyril, 156

Torza, Felice, 250

Toski, Bob, 247, 249, 297, 299

Tournament of Champions, 234, 303, 356–59

tours, 233–34, 246, 279–322
    black players, 11, 316; circuits, 284–85; courses, 57, 302–3; equipment, 25, 151, 154, 286–87; events, major and satellite, 280; expenses, 280–84, 302; field, 280; foreign-born players, 316; format, 5, 284, 295, 319–22; international, 322–59; league, professional, 285; match play, 18, 253, 348; pro-am, 306; promotion and management, 285–86, 288–90, 295–97, 317–22; purses and earnings (*see also* names; events), 5, 10, 56, 82, 280, 284–91 *passim*, 294–302 *passim*, 306–8, 314–17, 319, 322; purse splitting, 306–8; putting, 287; qualifying requirements, 280; scoring breakthrough, 286–87; scoring er-

tours (*continued*)
    rors, 100, 226–27, 333; special events, 323–59; sponsors, 5, 279–80, 285, 289–90, 295–97, 306, 314, 316–17, 319–20; sponsors, for rookies, 300; television, 6, 15, 57, 82, 234–35, 296–97, 303–4, 316, 323–30; *see also* events; names

Townsend, Peter, 344

Travers, Jerry, 63–65

Trent Jones, Robert, 92, 122, 256, 374–78

Trevino, Lee, 14, 31, 39, 49–50, 319
    Canadian Open, 50; earnings, 8, 284, 319; British Open, 22, 40, 49–50, 55, 175–79, 366, 368; Golfer of the Year Championship, 333–34; PGA Championship, 266–69, 275, 277; Piccadilly World Match Play, 54, 350, 355–56; Ryder Cup, 49; Sportsman of the Year, 50; U.S. Open, 49–50, 132–34, 137–44, 147, 371

Trinkle, Jim, 259

Triumvirate, 18–19; *see also* names

Trophee Lancome, 356

Tucson Open, 303

Tufts, Richard, 288

Tupling, Peter, 178

Turnberry course, 366

Turnesa, Jim, 241, 246, 249–51, 253, 335

Turnesa, Joe, 22, 70, 84, 238, 249

Turnesa, Mike, 243, 246–47, 249–50

Ulrich, Wally, 250

United Airlines, 9, 280

United States versus the World (TV show), 327–28

U.S. Amateur, 232, 233, 304

U.S. Golf Association, 57, 58, 232, 286, 318, 361, 371

U.S. Golf Association Championship, *see* U.S. Open

U.S. Open, 18, 56–147, 231–33, 284–85
    attendance growth, 5; British domination, 58–60; British Open won same year, 178; courses (*see also* names), 57–58, 371–78 *passim*; format, 39; four-time winners, 93, 95; PGA Championship won same year as, 236–37; playoff, first double-round, 69; purse, 70, 77, 82, 98, 104, 122, 314; television, 303–4

U.S. versus Japan Team Matches, 346–48

Valentine, Joe, 372

Van Donck, Flory, 162–64, 297

Vardon, Harry, 18–19, 34, 47, 116–17, 150–51, 156, 366
  U.S. Open, 59, 62–64, 66
Vardon, Tom, 150
Vardon Trophy, 36, 83
Venturi, Ken, 101, 202–3, 300–2, 304, 308–15, 342, 350–51
  Augusta National (Masters), 200–12, 252, 301, 308, 312–13; earnings, 301, 308, 310, 313; illness, 313–14; Lucky International, 314; PGA Championship, 261; Ryder Cup, 314; Thunderbird, 313; Walker Cup team, 312; U.S. Open, 101, 119–23, 313
Vines, Ellsworth, 248–49, 298
Von Elm, George, 73
von Limburger, Dr., 379–80
Von Nida, Norman, 153–55, 158, 297

Waco Turner Open, 316
Wadkins, Lanny, 137, 277
Walker, Cyril, 69, 285
Walker Cup, 203, 304, 312, 346
Wall, Art, 177, 257, 302, 308, 328
  Augusta National (Masters), 207, 224, 226
Wallace, Fielding, 183
Walsh, Frank, 239
Walt Disney World, 280
Walton Heath courses, 369
Wanamaker, Rodman, 232
Wanamaker Trophy, 238; *see also* PGA Championships
Ward, Charlie, 339
Ward, Harvey (Harvie), 96, 203
Watrous, Al, 152, 238, 337, 368
Watson, Robert C., 62
Way, Bertie, 60
Weaver, Bert, 332
Weetman, Harry, 167, 341–42
Weiskopf, Tom, 137, 174, 227

Wentworth course, 370
Western Open, 57, 284, 330; *see also* names
Western Golf Association, 57
Wethered, Roger, 151
Whitcombe, Reg, 153
Whitemarsh Open, 314
Williams, Andy, 279
Williams, Henry, Jr., 247–48
Wilson, Dick, 262, 270, 377–78
Wilson, Hugh, 371
Wilson, Philip, 348
Wilson Sporting Goods Co., 295
Wind, Herbert Warren, 22, 301
Windsor, Duke of, 7
Wininger, Bo, 261
Woking course, 369
Wolstenholme, Guy, 164
Wonderful World of Golf (TV show), 304, 325, 329
Wood, Craig, 46, 78, 153, 240, 286
  Augusta National (Masters), 185–86, 189, 191, 202
Woodhall Spa course, 369–70
World Championship of Golf, 296–97, 303, 307
World Cup, 334–35, 380
World Series of Golf, 307, 325–29
World Tournament, 315
Worsham, Lew, 46, 82–84, 247, 298, 299
  World Championship, 296–97
Wysong, Dudley, 265

Yancey, Bert, 132–33, 174, 226–28
Young, Turks, 301–4, 308–14; *see also* names
Young Guardsmen, 301; *see also* names

Zarley, Kermit, 144
Ziegler, Larry, 270

Mark H. McCormack

MARK H. McCORMACK is, in his own words, a "manager of people and concepts." The people include not only his sports' celebrity client list—Arnold Palmer, Jackie Stewart, Jean-Claude Killy, Rod Laver, Gary Player, Doug Sanders, Frank Robinson, Larry Osonka, John Havlicek, Dick Butkus, Willie Shoemaker, Pele announcer Chris Schenkel—but even such unsporty celebrities as models Jean Shrimpton and Veruschka, hair stylist Vidal Sassoon, and cartoonist Hank Ketcham.

McCormack presides over International Management, Inc., whose six management, investment, and merchandising divisions provide more than 200 clients with coordinated advice, consultation, and guidance in the development of their careers and activities.

McCormack, born in Chicago, came east to Yale Law School, spent two years in the Army teaching military law and then joined a prestigious old Cleveland law firm. An excellent golfer in his own right, he has qualified for four U.S. Amateur Championships, three British Amateurs, and one U.S. Open. In the process, he rubbed elbows with a lot of fine golfers. As a sideline he began signing up pros for exhibitions. They were soon asking him to take a look at their endorsements as an attorney. One of the first to come around was a promising, thirty-year-old golf pro with earnest, all-American good looks named Arnold Palmer. That is where it all started. In 1971 NBC purchased Arnold Palmer Enterprises for a reported $15 million.

McCormack, wife Nancy, sons Brett and Todd, and daughter Leslie reside in Pepper Pike, Ohio, a suburb of Cleveland.